D0398831

Other inscriptions also tell of the services of Nieh Ling to the royal house as a feudal lord (see pp. 403–405). For illustrations of this vessel, and discussion of it, see The Freer Chinese Bronzes, *vol. I, Catalogue, by John Alexander Pope, Rutherford John Gettens, James Cahill, and Noel Barnard (Washington, 1967), pp. 212–221.*

The Origins of Statecraft in China

WITHDRAWN
UTSA LIBRARIES

HERRLEE G. CREEL

The Origins of Statecraft in China

VOLUME ONE

The Western Chou Empire

THE UNIVERSITY OF CHICAGO PRESS
CHICAGO AND LONDON

International Standard Book Number: 0–226–12043–0
Library of Congress Catalog Card Number: 73–110072
The University of Chicago Press, Chicago 60637
The University of Chicago Press, Ltd., London
© *1970 by Herrlee G. Creel*
All rights reserved
Published 1970
Printed in the United States of America

CONTENTS

MAPS

Preface

THE novelist who complains that his characters have "taken over" his book, and have compelled him to write it in a way that he did not intend, has always left me feeling slightly skeptical. I find myself, however, in the embarrassing position of having to say something very similar, for I certainly had no intention, at any time, of writing a book, or a volume, on Western Chou.

For some sixteen years I have been studying the origins of administrative techniques in China, and their influence on other countries. Four years ago I started to write a book on the subject, which I thought would be of moderate proportions. The first two chapters went according to plan and were completed in a few weeks. The third chapter was to deal with Western Chou. It would be, I thought, a small chapter, since the material was limited. But the Western Chou period figures so importantly in Chinese traditions concerning government that I could not neglect it completely. I knew that there had been important discoveries and research since I had last worked seriously on the period, and I felt that I ought to look into them. This took longer and yielded more data than I had expected, but after a slight delay I began writing my chapter on Western Chou. When it had reached 150 pages of manuscript, I decided it would have to be two chapters; at 300 pages, I began to think it might make a small volume by itself. I finally managed to finish it within the confines of a single volume.

I HAVE tried to make clear, as fully as possible, the evidence for the positions I have taken in this book. I have referred, insofar as I could, to works and editions most likely to be available to readers. In general I have cited not only Chinese texts but also translations of them. For the *Tso-chuan* I have cited the translation of Legge, and for the *Shu-ching* and the *Shih-ching*, those of Karlgren; these works include the Chinese texts along with the translation, and I have pointed out variations from these in other texts. It should be noted, however, that my references are primarily intended to indicate the Chinese text, not the translation. Where I have followed a published translation, I have done so because I believe it to be correct; where I feel another rendering to be preferable, I have used it.

All works referred to in this volume are listed alphabetically under "Works Cited" (pp. 507–545), with full bibliographical information.

For the romanization of the pronunciations of Chinese characters, I have used the modification of the Wade system that is employed in *A Pocket Dictionary (Chinese-English) and Pekingese Syllabary*, by Chauncey Goodrich. This seems to me best to represent the Peking pronunciation. I have, however, made two modifications. Instead of *szu*, I use the commonly employed *ssu*, which seems to me preferable. I have also, following the increasingly prevalent practice, eliminated all superfluous diacritical marks, which leaves only the umlaut over the u—as in *yü*—where this is necessary. This results in forms such as *le*, *he*, and *e*, which will no doubt be found objectionable by some. There is a general tendency instead to use such forms as *lo*, *ho*, and *o*. But these do not, I think, correctly represent the Peking pronunciation, and they introduce confusion into the system of romanization.

When one writes about China, identical romanizations are a major annoyance. Examples are the states of Wei 衛 and Wei 魏 , and the two Western Chou rulers, King I 懿 (934–910 B.C.) and King I 夷 (894–880 B.C.). Usually, though not always, such characters are pronounced in different tones. To differentiate them I use the diacritical marks often employed to represent the four tones: ˉ, ΄, ˇ, and ˋ. Thus the state of 衛 is represented as Wèi, while 魏 is written as Wei (even though it happens to have the same tone). The name of King 夷 is written as Î to differentiate it. It should be noted, however, that this is a wholly arbitrary device. Thus the frequently encountered name of the barbarians called I 夷 is written without any diacritical mark. All romanizations with which diacritical marks are employed are listed in the index, with the characters and the meanings that they represent.

In double surnames I use initial capitals for each character, writing Ssu-Ma Ch'ien rather than the usual Ssu-ma Ch'ien. In these days, when many Chinese follow the Western practice of writing their surnames last, this seems to be the most feasible way of making the presence of a double surname unmistakable.

THE central theme of this volume is the proposition that the Western Chou Kings ruled an empire, rather than a loose confederation of vassal states. In very recent years a few scholars, influenced by the evidence of new discoveries and research, have voiced the opinion that the power of the Western Chou rulers was greater than has been supposed; but insofar as I am aware, none has gone so far as I in attributing to Western Chou a rather tightly controlled, relatively centralized government. To the extent that this idea is original, it was not originated by me.

Twenty years ago my wife, Dr. Lorraine Creel, at a time when she was working intensively on bronze inscriptions, told me that some data seemed inexplicable on the basis of the current theory that the activities of the King's officials were limited to a small "royal domain," beyond which they were without authority. And she suggested, as a hypothesis, that the royal government might have been considerably more effective, and wielded greater control over the whole country, than was generally assumed. At the time I was working on other things and neither accepted nor rejected this; in fact, there may not then have been enough evidence available to prove it. But years later, when I was seeking a way through the confused mass of data on Western Chou, this hypothesis proved to be the key.

This is by no means the only contribution that my wife has made to this volume. She has read and criticized each chapter as it has been completed, and there is much that is hers. I have tried to persuade her to accept the role of full collaborator, but in vain. I am still hopeful that she may do so with future volumes.

Acknowledgment of one's full indebtedness to those who have made a book like this one possible would have to begin with scholars and historians of thousands of years of ago; the references in my footnotes will best make clear my obligations. Among the works of contemporary Western scholars, those from which I have benefited most are the translations of and "Glosses" on the *Shu-ching* and the *Shih-ching*, by Bernhard Karlgren. These are monumental accomplishments, which were almost prerequisite for understanding the Western Chou period. I have inevitably differed with Karlgren on occasional points, but these are few indeed in comparison with those on which I have gratefully accepted his enlightenment.

The Chinese scholars for whose personal kindness I am obligated are so many, beginning with my "old teacher" Mei Kuang-ti, that to name all would be impossible and to name a few would be invidious. In the text and the footnotes of this volume I have made some particular acknowledgments. It will be evident, I think, to anyone who reads this volume, that it is based in overwhelming measure on the work of Chinese scholars.

The allegation of "conflict" between research and teaching has always seemed to me to be in large measure nonsense. Teaching— as opposed to mere indoctrination—must, I think, have the goal of enabling students to find their own truth for themselves. And I do not believe that a teacher can do this unless he is himself more or less constantly engaged in the pursuit of truth—that is, in research. Certainly a researcher does not have to teach, but if he does not he is deprived of the best possible source of criticism for his old ideas and stimulus to new ones. Constantly recurring waves of fresh minds are the true intellectual fountain of youth. I have been fortunate in having, over the years, a large number of keen, critical students; and I have certainly learned from them, collectively, far more than any one of them has learned from me. Among them I can only name a small number of students, past and present, who have especially contributed with ideas and with criticism to the production of this volume. They include Mr. Chao Lin, Mr. Y. T. Ch'ien, Professor Cho-yun Hsu, Professor Sydney Rosen, and Professor T'ao T'ien-yi. Mr. T'ao and Mr. Chao have also acted as research assistants, aiding greatly in the complex task of dealing with the materials. Mr. Ch'ien prepared a part of the index.

Miss June Work, my principal research assistant for more than thirty years, has played an important part in this research. By screening periodicals in several languages, she made it possible for me to cover a wide range of secondary materials. She checked and rechecked facts and references, saving me from numerous blunders, and put this difficult manuscript into its final form. She delayed her departure on a trip around the world in order to complete this task. I am, of course, deeply grateful. Mrs. Margaret L. Severns has been helpful in many ways, and Mrs. Julie Auer has assisted with the difficult problem of arranging the index.

In the long course of this research I have sought and received advice from many friends and colleagues; their help is acknowledged at various points in the volume. In three crucial areas I have been fortunate in being able to consult colleagues who are outstanding authorities. On problems of bibliography and on other matters, Professor T. H. Tsien has assisted me on innumerable occasions; I am indebted to him and to his entire staff in the Far Eastern Library of the University of Chicago for many courtesies. Concerning Chinese government, Professor Edward A. Kracke, Jr., has patiently and unfailingly answered all my questions. And Professor Muhsin Mahdi has generously given me the benefit of his unusual understanding of the philosophy of government, in many long discussions. He has also kindly read and criticized this entire manuscript.

Professor Napier Wilt and Professor Robert E. Streeter have taken a gratifying personal interest in this research. Successively occupying the office of Dean of the Division of the Humanities, they have encouraged and supported it in various ways. Professor Edwin Mc-Clellan, the chairman of my department, has made it possible for me to devote a considerable part of my time to the preparation of this volume. Support for this research has been made available by the Division of the Humanities, the Committee on Far Eastern Studies, and the Department of Far Eastern Languages and Civilizations, of the University of Chicago.

I am most grateful that Mrs. T. H. Tsien, a master of the vanishing art of Chinese calligraphy, has been willing to write the characters appearing in this volume. Archaic forms, copied from inscriptions on bone and bronze, have been written by the author.

In my experience publishers are always cooperative, but in the production of this volume the staff of the University of Chicago Press has been unusually so.

CHRONOLOGY

Western Chou	1122–771 B.C.[1]
King Wu	1122–1116 B.C.
King Ch'eng	1115–1079 B.C.
King K'ang	1078–1053 B.C.
King Chao	1052–1002 B.C.
King Mu	1001–947 B.C.
King Kung	946–935 B.C.
King I	934–910 B.C.
King Hsiao	909–895 B.C.
King Í	894–879 B.C.
King Li	878–828 B.C.
King Hsüan	827–782 B.C.
King Yu	781–771 B.C.
Eastern Chou	770–256 B.C.
Spring and Autumn period	770–464 B.C.[2]
Warring States period	463–222 B.C.[3]
Ch'in dynasty	221–207 B.C.
Former Han dynasty	206 B.C.–A.D. 8
Latter Han dynasty	A.D. 25–220

1. Concerning the date of the Chou conquest, see pp. 487–491.
2. See p.47, note 18.
3. See p. 47, note 19.

CHAPTER
1
The Problem

THE purpose of this investigation is to trace the origin and development of political ideas and governmental institutions in China, from the earliest times of which we have knowledge down to approximately the beginning of the Christian Era. The latter date is determined by the fact that in Han times there came to full stature the type of imperial government that would continue to the twentieth century. During the two thousand years of its persistence, this governmental pattern underwent further development and modification of great interest and importance, but these are not our concern. Our problem is: how did it come to be?

Although we shall probe for the earliest clues, we shall quickly find that in the present state of knowledge it is possible to speak, in any but the most general and tentative terms, only of the development of political ideas and institutions during the first millennium B.C. Within this thousand years the attempt will be made, insofar as is feasible, to utilize and analyze all of the available evidence.

This is, as everyone who knows the field will recognize, a formidable undertaking. To the best of my knowledge no investigation of comparable scope has ever been made of the development of government in China (or indeed in any other country) during the first millennium B.C. Is it worth the effort? It is, for three reasons.

First, the Chinese pattern has governed more people, over a larger area, for a greater length of time, than any other. By the first century B.C. the Chinese Empire ruled an area larger than that of the Roman Empire at its greatest extent, and at many periods it has been much larger.[1] No other system of government has maintained its sway

1. The eighteen provinces composing "China proper" have an area of some one and a half million square miles, and by the first century B.C. the Empire was considerably larger than this. Gibbon, *Roman Empire*, I, 21, said that the Roman

1

over a state of anything approaching comparable size for two thousand years in almost uninterrupted succession.[2] It has been the most viable government yet developed by man.

The mere size and persistence of the Chinese state might not, however, make it of much real interest to us if it had been only, as it has sometimes been represented, a type of "Oriental despotism" with little relevance for or analogy with governmental phenomena in the Western world.[3] But—and this is the second factor that gives point to our research—it is highly relevant. From antiquity to modern times, there are many developments in the theory and practice of government in the Occident to which Chinese history provides parallels. The problems are often analogous; the solutions are sometimes similar and sometimes very different. But the Chinese setting is so isolated and divergent from that of the West as to provide almost a "laboratory" situation. If, for instance, we compare Western political phenomena of any period with those of ancient Greece or Rome, there is always the difficulty of distinguishing between analogy and direct influence, to a far greater degree than if our comparison is with ancient China.

Such comparison is often illuminating. For example, both the Chinese and the Roman Empires had great armies and carried out far-flung conquests even before the beginning of the Christian Era. In Rome the control of the army constituted a serious problem from an early date. As early as A.D. 69 there was the famous "year of the four Emperors," set up chiefly through the agency of various military groups, and the ascendancy of a turbulent soldiery was certainly one of the factors that fatally weakened the Western Roman Empire. This

---

Empire "was supposed to contain above sixteen hundred thousand square miles." J. B. Bury, editing Gibbon, criticized his estimate of the population (ibid., 33) but did not comment on this figure.

[All books and articles cited in this volume, and all abbreviated titles, are listed alphabetically in "Works Cited," pp. 507–545.]

2. The only interruptions that could be alleged are those resulting from conquest, and even most of the conquerors have in some degree employed the Chinese administrative pattern.

3. Among terms that have achieved a certain currency, "Oriental despotism," or as Montesquieu (*Grandeur des Romains*, 65) called it, "despotisme asiatique," is surely one of the strangest. "Oriental" is commonly applied to countries all the way from Egypt to Japan; when we take into account time as well as place, the varieties of governmental systems that have existed in this area (or in Asia alone) total a number that staggers the imagination. No doubt many of them, like many governments elsewhere, may properly be called "despotic," but to suppose that they conform to a common pattern that can usefully be called "Oriental despotism" is to generalize beyond all reason.

is a perennial dilemma of governments. Every regime must be able to resort to force if necessary, and the army is the ultimate instrument of force; how then can the government keep the army responsive to its will, and prevent its leaders from usurping power? This problem has not been solved in all states to this day. The Chinese have not been nearly so pacifistic as has sometimes been supposed, and the founders of Chinese dynasties have usually been successful generals. But many dynasties have been long; and once a dynasty has been firmly established, military men as such have normally held little power and posed little threat to the government. How was this brought about? An answer to this question, even a partial one, will help toward an understanding of some very basic factors in the functioning of government in China and will throw light on the nature of the process of government in general.

Medieval Europe was dominated by an institution that has come to be known as feudalism. Whether this term may properly be used to refer to analogous phenomena in early China has been hotly debated; in my opinion, for reasons that will be detailed in a later chapter, it is quite correct to speak of Chinese feudalism. But whether one uses the term or not, the resemblances between a whole complex of ideas and practices found on the one hand in medieval Europe and on the other in early China are in some respects so close as to be almost startling. At the same time the disparity between the Chinese and medieval settings is so great that, when the institutions are compared, many accidental and confusing factors are at once eliminated. It is easier to understand either Chinese or medieval feudalism after studying both than after a searching investigation of either by itself.

The most surprising and perhaps the most illuminating similarities appear when comparison is made between China's government as it existed two thousand years ago and the highly centralized bureaucratic administration of modern states. Although such comparison is still in its infancy, a few perceptive observers have noted the resemblances. Max Weber, the father of modern studies of bureaucracy, pointed out similarities with regard to "administrative rationalization" between modern Europe and the China of the Warring States period (463–222 B.C.).[4] O. B. van der Sprenkel says that "almost to the end of the eighteenth century the Chinese were far in advance of the rest of the world in matters of administrative organization. . . . It is certainly difficult for a European to realize how long-established in

---

4. Weber, *Religion of China*, 61–62. He considered the scope of such rationalization more limited in early China, but found the phenomena comparable.

China were practices that in the West we associate mainly with the modern age."[5]

It is quite generally supposed, however, that the kind of highly centralized, highly professional bureaucratic government that we have today—what is called "modern bureaucracy"—is a unique phenomenon that has occurred only in the modern West.[6] Without modern science, modern technology, and the Industrial Revolution, it is argued, no such administrative system could have been devised. "The civil service," Herman Finer writes, "is as much of the product of the spiritual and mechanical factors of western civilization as are all other political institutions."[7] As evidence for this view some scholars cite the fact that bureaucratic organizations are called "administrative machines," and that "in the literature of administration there is considerable mechanical metaphor." Among the reasons for this, Dwight Waldo cites "a cultural orientation toward the machine." Modern man, he says, is "culturally deeply affected by day-to-day living in intimate association with actual machinery."[8]

This is quite convincing on the basis of exclusively Western experience, in which highly complex governments have made their appearance at about the same time as, or perhaps a little later than, highly complicated machinery. *Post hoc, ergo propter hoc.* But Chinese history throws a different light on this situation.

In China there was developed, even before the beginning of the Christian Era, a centralized bureaucratic government of very considerable complexity. No one would argue that that government was produced by a "machine age." And yet in discussion of the technique of administration, in ancient China as in the contemporary West, there is "considerable mechanical metaphor." Figures of speech based on mechanism are especially abundant in the aphorisms of Shen Pu-hai, the statesman-philosopher of the fourth century B.C. who was the first major theorist in the field of administration.[9] "The ruler,"

---

5. Van der Sprenkel, "Max Weber on China," 357.

6. See, for instance, Rosenberg, *Bureaucracy, Aristocracy, and Autocracy,* 2.

7. Finer, *Modern Government,* 712. See also White, *Public Administration,* 8.

8. White, *Public Administration,* 16, 50–51. Waldo, *Perspectives on Administration,* 30–32.

9. Shen Pu-hai 申不害 is little known even to Sinologists. He was chief minister of the small state of Hán 韓 , in north China, for some eighteen years until his death in 337 B.C. His doctrines enjoyed considerable vogue and played an important role in shaping the administrative pattern of the short-lived Ch'in dynasty (221–206 B.C.), which in turn was largely taken over by the Han dynasty and was thus the basic model for the imperial government of later times. Many of the ideas of Shen Pu-hai were incorporated into what came to be known as "orthodox Han

Shen said, "must have discriminating methods and correct and definite principles, just as one suspends a weight and balance to weigh
lightness and heaviness, in order to unify and organize his ministers."
He did not, naturally, speak of large and complex machines, but he
made frequent use of similes of a mechanical sort, comparing the
ruler's ministers to the spokes of a wheel, and the ruler himself to a
scale, a mirror, a foundation, and the pivot of a gate.[10]

This suggests that it may be to some degree accidental that the high
development of bureaucracy in the West has coincided in time with
the high development of machinery. Bureaucracy itself tends to cause
those who theorize about it to speak in mechanical figures, for the
simple reason that a bureaucracy necessarily operates in a manner
very like that of a machine. A machine is an assemblage of parts
arranged to function so as to achieve a preconceived purpose. A
bureaucratic organization is an assemblage of people arranged to
function so as to achieve a preconceived purpose. It is widely assumed
that our complex administrative organizations owe their inspiration
to our complex machinery, but it is arguable that the sequence was in
fact the reverse. The use of manpower preceded that of energy derived
from water, steam, and electricity, and elaborate organizations of
men performing specialized roles in cooperation preceded machines
invented to perform many of the same tasks. From one point of view
the history of machinery is that of the progressive reduction of the

---

Confucianism," while at the same time the Confucians anathematized him; this is
undoubtedly an important part of the reason why the man and his ideas were almost
completely forgotten. See: Creel, "The Meaning of Hsing-ming." Idem, "The
Fa-chia." Idem, "On the Origin of Wu-wei."

10. A book bearing the name of Shen Pu-hai, which probably incorporated
some extraneous material along with his ideas, circulated widely in Han times and
was studied by statesmen and Emperors. It was still in existence at the end of the
seventeenth century, but now seems to be lost. However, passages from it, in some
cases lengthy, are quoted in various works. I have collected, collated, and translated all such quotations that I have been able to locate. This material is extremely
difficult to understand because Shen's aphorisms are very cryptic and in some
cases have been corrupted in transmission. It is sometimes necessary to compare
as many as three different versions of the same statement to arrive at a satisfactory
text, and then to interpret it in the light of the whole context of Shen's philosophy,
insofar as that context is available. The detailed evidence for my interpretations
will be presented at the proper point in this study.

For the sources in which the statements here referred to are found, see: I-wen
Lei-chü, 19.2b, 54.1b. T'ai-p'ing Yü-lan, 390.6a, 638.4b. Liu-ch'en-chu Wen-hsüan,
20.30a, 39.5a. Ch'ün-shu, 36.25b–27a. Ch'ang-tuan Ching, 3.67. T'ang-Sung Pai-
k'ung Liu-t'ieh, 13.27a. Ku-hsiang-chai Chien-shang Hsiu-chen Ch'u-hsüeh-chi,
25.17b. I-lin, 2.10b.

necessity for human participation in such complex operations.[11] It would seem probable that cooperative organizations of human beings have had quite as much influence on the invention of machinery as machinery has had on the organization of human cooperation.

The inherent similarity between bureaucratic organizations and machines was recognized by Max Weber, who said that the professional bureaucrat is usually "only a single cog in an ever-moving mechanism which prescribes to him an essentially fixed route of march. The official is entrusted with specialized tasks and normally the mechanism cannot be put into motion or arrested by him, but only from the very top. The individual bureaucrat is thus forged to the community of all the functionaries who are integrated into the mechanism."[12] Such characteristics as "routinization" and resistance to change, for which bureaucratic government was criticized in early China as it is in modern Europe and America, tend to develop spontaneously as a result of its quasi-mechanical nature.

That bureaucracy is a problem, no one seems to doubt. It is almost universally damned by persons of all shades of opinion, from champions of capitalism to socialists and communists. Yet almost no one seems to question that all governments are destined to become more and more bureaucratic, and those who decry the ills of bureaucracy seldom suggest remedies or express any real hope for its amelioration. The prevalent attitude is one of tacit despair. It seems to be felt that, since our world is inevitably given over to accelerating mechanization, it must increasingly be plagued by a necessary consequence: bureaucratic government that becomes more and more complex and less and less concerned with human beings, all of whom are destined to become either its cogs or its pawns.

The Chinese analogy suggests that the analysis may be faulty. If early China, wholly lacking in machinery of our modern sort, could develop a bureaucratic government having important similarities to our own, it cannot be argued that our mechanization is beyond all question the cause of our bureaucratization, or that it is necessarily impossible to modify our bureaucratic government significantly without abolishing our machines.

In seeking a more objective view of the bureaucratic process as

11. See Singer et al., *History of Technology*, II, 638–639, 643, 650. There is the familiar story of the improvement of the steam engine by an arrangement whereby it opened and closed its own valves, eliminating the necessity that this be done by an attendant. Our own time has seen substitution of the automatic transmission, in automobiles, for the manual shifting of gears.

12. Weber, *Essays in Sociology*, 228.

such, which may be of use in analyzing the problems of government in our own day, it is instructive to examine the development of bureaucratic institutions in ancient China, at a place and time so remote from our own as to insure the highest degree of objectivity.

Certainly it is true that "modern bureaucracy" is in some respects unique, but the government of China very early resembled governments of our own day to a degree that is little appreciated. In the first century B.c., when it was already one of the largest states that the world has known, China had a centralized administration staffed by a professional bureaucracy drawn from all strata of the society. Of the men who held the highest office, that of Imperial Chancellor, during the second and first centuries B.c., at least twenty-two percent came from poor or humble families.[13] In comparison, it has been calculated that only eighteen percent of the men who held the highest offices in the United States between 1789 and 1953 came from lower class families.[14] China had a general pension system for higher civil servants beginning in A.D. 1; general pension systems for the British and American civil services date from 1810 and 1920 respectively.[15]

Already in the first century B.c. the Chinese bureaucracy was selected and promoted, in considerable degree, on the basis of such objective techniques as civil service examination and merit rating. In the West the first written civil service examination was apparently given in Berlin in 1693,[16] and the systematic practice of the annual merit rating of officials was started in Britain after World War I.[17] Max Weber wrote that the Chinese "introduced, for the first time in the world, the use of qualifying examinations and certification of the conduct of officials. . . . From the point of view of formal structure, this carried bureaucratic objectivity to the highest degree possible."[18]

Control by elaborate written rules is a characteristic of modern bureaucracy that is generally emphasized. Such control was an outstanding feature of Chinese administration from a very early time. Karl Bünger points out that whereas in the Roman Empire there was

13. Wang, "Han Government," 179–180. This is the percentage of those for whom biographical data are given. But it must be noted that the family background of less than half of the chancellors is known, and of these almost one-half are of humble origin. Since illustrious family background is more likely to be recorded, it seems probable that those of humble origin were in fact more numerous than twenty-two percent.

14. Mills, *Power Elite*, 400–401.

15. *Hsi-Han Hui-yao*, 434–435. White, *Public Administration*, 341–343.

16. See below, p. 26.

17. Gladden, *Public Administration*, 82.

18. Weber, *Wirtschaft und Gesellschaft*, II, 708.

little development of law regulating the administration of the government, China very early had a body of such law "of astonishing completeness" such as did not appear in Europe until a late date.[19] "Red tape" is an ancient institution in China.

We also think of bureaucratic government, with reason, as being increasingly involved with the amassing of statistics and reports. By the first century B.C. the gathering of statistics had grown into a major enterprise of the Chinese government. A whole army of officials, from the local to the national level, was engaged in collecting, recording, and checking figures of many sorts. We still have detailed data from the census of the Empire taken in A.D. 2. Roman census procedures were haphazard compared with those of China; in the West the systematic enumeration of the population of whole nations did not begin until modern times. Hans Bielenstein writes that in China "statistical material has been kept from incomparably earlier times than in any other country."[20]

The Imperial Chancellor sat at the center of this information network. In his office he had figures on land and population, maps of the Empire, and reports on harvests, banditry, and finances from the provinces. He prepared the budget and was required to keep the various departments within their allotted sums. The Roman Empire, on the other hand, operated without a budget until the end of the third century A.D., while the earliest budget in England is said to date from the thirteenth century.[21]

The pure theory of administration, abstracted from its application in any specific context, has been little developed in most parts of the world before our own time. If we examine texts on statecraft from ancient Egypt, Babylonia, Assyria, India, Greece, and Rome, from tenth-century Byzantium and the court of the Seljūk Turks, or the works of Machiavelli and Guicciardini, it is only rarely that we encounter principles that are wholly divorced from the setting in which they were produced.[22] They occur most frequently, perhaps, in the

19. Bünger, "Die Rechtsidee," 211.

20. Bielenstein, "The Census of China." Jones, Later Roman Empire, I, 62–65, 453–455; II, 798, 1040.

21. Wang, "Han Government," 145–146. Han-shu, 84.9a. Rostovtzeff, Roman Empire, I, 515. Jones, Later Roman Empire, I, 66. Course of the Exchequer, xlvii.

22. This statement is based on examination of, among others, the following works: "The Vizier of Egypt." "Egyptian Instructions." "Advice to a Prince." "The Words of Ahiqar." Kautilya's Arthásastra. Das Arthaçastra des Kautilya. Plato, The Republic. Plato, Laws. Aristotle, Politics. Cicero, De Re Publica, De Legibus. Constantine Porphyrogenitus, De Administrando Imperio. Nizām al-Mulk, The Book of Government. Machiavelli, The Prince and the Discourses. Guicciardini, Maxims and Reflections.

writings of Plato and Aristotle, but even their dicta would commonly require some modification to make them wholly applicable to our modern world.

Here again the most notable exception is to be found in early China. Consider, for instance, this statement made in the fourth century B.C. by Shen Pu-hai: "The reason why a ruler is honored is because of his power to command. But if his commands are not carried out, there is in fact no ruler. For this reason the intelligent ruler is very careful about giving commands."[23] This advice addresses itself, usefully, to problems faced by an Egyptian Pharaoh, a Byzantine Emperor, the dictator of a modern totalitarian state, the president of a corporation, or the leader of a gang of boys. Exactly the same principle was stated in different language by a prominent American authority on the theory of administration in 1938. It was considered so novel and controversial that it became a focus of discussion in the literature of social science for many years.[24]

While such close correspondence is unusual, anyone familiar with the early Chinese works on government cannot fail, in reading the literature of our own day on the theory of administration, to be struck by the frequent similarity of approach, and the not infrequent resemblance between the conclusions arrived at.[25] It seems improbable that, before our time, the problems of government were anywhere else envisioned so exclusively in terms of sheer administrative technique and applied psychology.

THE third consideration that gives China's governmental institutions special interest for us is the fact that, to an extent that is little

23. *Pei-t'ang Shu-ch'ao*, 45.9b. *I-wen Lei-chü*, 54.3a. The latter text has *tzu* 子 as its second character; it seems obvious that this is an erroneous addition.

24. Chester I. Barnard, in *Functions of the Executive*, 161–184, defined "authority" in such manner that, as he wrote, "under this definition the decision as to whether an order has authority or not lies with the persons to whom it is addressed, and does not reside in 'persons of authority' or those who issue these orders." Barnard felt this to be a daring departure from accepted theory and justified it at great length. In fact, Max Weber had made essentially the same point, in a form less likely to attract attention, earlier; see Weber, *Theory of Organization*, 152. Concerning the discussion of this theory in social science literature, see *Essays on the Scientific Study of Politics*, 132–142.

25. Such similarities are to be found, for instance, in the following works: Weber, *Essays in Sociology*. Idem, *Gesammelte Aufsätze*. Idem, *Theory of Organization*. Idem, *The Religion of China*. Idem, *Wirtschaft und Gesellschaft*. Simon, *Administrative Behavior*. Barnard, *Functions of the Executive*. Parsons, *The Structure of Social Action*. Idem, *Structure and Process in Modern Societies*. Blau, *The Dynamics of Bureaucracy*. Idem, *Bureaucracy in Modern Society*. *Reader in Bureaucracy. Essays on the Scientific Study of Politics*.

realized, they have influenced our own. It is evident that administrative techniques so highly developed at such an early date could not fail to impress those who came into contact with them. In fact their imprint can be found not only in Japan, Korea, and southeast Asia, but also deep into Central Asia. It is commonly supposed, however, that the formidable deserts and mountains and the treacherously stormy seas that made intercourse between China and Europe difficult served almost to prohibit important cultural interchange up until the time of the Mongol conquests of the thirteenth century.

This is in large measure true, but the exceptions are very important. Where obstacles exist, there are often men who surmount them. Herodotus related that in his day (the fifth century B.C.) Greeks regularly traveled eastward as far as the western border of what is now Sinkiang province, and that at least one Greek had traveled to an area that has been identified as being only some twelve hundred miles from the Chinese capital.[26] There was certainly trade. Glass beads made in Egypt found their way to China, apparently in some quantity, as early as the third century B.C.;[27] and Chinese silk was one of the five principal commodities that comprised the foreign trade of the Roman Empire.[28] But even extensive trade does not always bring about the interchange of ideas.

More significant for that purpose were China's contacts with the Islamic world. A Muslim embassy arrived at the Chinese court as early as A.D. 651, and by the eighth century Muslim ambassadors were at times received almost yearly, while Chinese representatives also went to Baghdad.[29] In 760 "several thousand Arab and Persian traders" lost their lives in a single disturbance in a seaport on the Yangtze River, and by the ninth century resident Muslims in Canton were so numerous that the Chinese government appointed one of their number to direct their religious affairs and settle their disputes according to

26. *Herodotus*, 209–214 [Book IV]. Herodotus does not, of course, mention Sinkiang province (which not only did not exist but was not then Chinese) or China by name. The identification of the places to which he refers has been much debated, but seems reasonably secure. See: Hudson, *Europe and China*, 27–52. Minns, *Scythians and Greeks*, 101–114. Needham, *Science and Civilisation in China*, I, 170–172.

27. That they must have been fairly common may be deduced from the fact that they were not only imported to China but also imitated there. See: Seligman and Beck, "Far Eastern Glass." Sarton, "Chinese Glass." White, *Tombs of Old Loyang*, 50, 147–148. Needham, *Science and Civilisation in China*, IV:1, 101–103.

28. Schoff, *The Periplus*, 264–265. Wheeler, *Rome Beyond the Frontiers*, 208–209.

29. Drake, "Mohammedans in the T'ang Dynasty," 7. Gibb, "Chinese Records of the Arabs in Central Asia," 619–622.

Islamic law.[30] The literature gives us only rare glimpses of any activities of foreigners in China, but these are revealing. Many Muslims took Chinese wives, one of them a lady from the imperial family. A Chinese author recorded that in 847 an Arab not only passed the court examination for the doctorate, given to candidates for the civil service, but did so with highest honors, surpassing all the Chinese with whom he was in competition.[31] This means that he had not merely mastered the Chinese classics, but had become thoroughly familiar with the entire context of Chinese culture. Under such circumstances, the opportunity for cultural interchange was clearly present.

The volume of trade was very great. Records show that the single port of Canton received frankincense, the costly resin exported from southern Arabia and Somaliland, to the amount of almost one-half million pounds in the year 1097 alone.[32] Excavations in Islamic Egypt and eastern Africa have discovered Chinese porcelains, coins, and other objects dating from the eighth century onward, giving tangible testimony to the extensive commerce.[33] Sir Mortimer Wheeler writes that "for the Middle Ages we have along the East Coast of Africa a possible source of information which has scarcely been tapped. I have never in my life seen so much broken china . . . literally fragments of Chinese porcelain by the shovelful. . . . In fact I think it is fair to say that as far as the Middle Ages are concerned, from the 10th century onwards, the buried history of Tanganyika is written in Chinese porcelain."[34]

Chinese porcelains were not merely imported to Egypt; they were extensively imitated there. Such imitation began at least as early as the beginning of the eleventh century.[35] Even more significant as indicating the possibility of intellectual influence is the fact, evidenced by excavated documents, that texts in Arabic were printed in Egypt by

30. Reischauer, "Notes on T'ang Dynasty Sea Routes," 143–144. *Relation de la Chine et de l'Inde*, 7.

31. Kuwabara, "On P'u Shou-keng," I, 35, 60–61.

32. Ibid., I, 18–19. Concerning the provenance of frankincense, see Schafer, *Golden Peaches of Samarkand*, 170. Writing of the T'ang period Schafer says (ibid., 158) that Canton was "one of the great incense markets of the world. . . . The quantities imported must have been tremendous, in view of the extravagant uses of the aristocracy, which extended even to aromatic architecture."

33. Wainwright, "Early Foreign Trade in East Africa," 146–147. Bahgat and Massoul, *La Céramique Musulmane de l'Égypte*. Ashton, "China and Egypt," 63–64.

34. Wheeler, "Archaeology in East Africa," 45–46.

35. Ashton, "China and Egypt." Bahgat and Massoul, *La Céramique Musulmane de l'Égypte*. Lane, *Early Islamic Pottery*.

the Chinese method from the tenth to the fourteenth century.[36]

The Islamic world was not culturally "Europe" however, even where it included most of Spain, and the barriers to the passage of ideas were considerable. These were significantly breached in Sicily under the Norman King Roger II (1093–1154). His realm, which came to include southern Italy and some of the north coast of Africa, has been called "the richest and most civilised state in Europe" in his day.[37] In his army and in his government, Roger had Muslims among his most trusted officials and retainers. At his court in Palermo, official documents were promulgated in French, Greek, Latin, and Arabic.[38]

Roger II invited to his court al-Idrīsī, the most eminent Muslim geographer of the day, and proposed that he undertake to compile a description of the entire world. Fifteen years were spent in interviewing "well-informed travellers" and checking information from various sources, an undertaking in which Roger himself participated; the resulting book was published in 1154.[39] It devotes far more space to the government of China than to that of any other state. China's fiscal system is lauded, and the policies of the Chinese ruler are praised repeatedly.[40]

King Roger was a bold innovator, gathering ideas from many sources and using them with vigor. He seems to have been the first ruler to strike a coin dated in Arabic numerals,[41] and one of his deeds appears to be the earliest extant document from Europe written on paper (papermaking had come, through the Islamic world, from China).[42]

36. *Papyrus Erzherzog Rainer* (Arabische Abteilung, by J. Karabacek), 247. Jacob, "Oriental Elements of Culture in the Occident," 526–527. Carter, *The Invention of Printing in China*, 176–182.

37. *Cambridge Medieval History*, VI, 131.

38. Caspar, *Roger II*. Curtis, *Roger of Sicily*. *Cambridge Medieval History*, V, 167–207. De Stefano, *La cultura in Sicilia nel periodo Normanno*.

39. al-Idrīsī, *Nuzhat*. The Arabic text of this work, of which there are numerous manuscripts, has never been printed in full. The only complete printed version is a French translation: *Géographie d'Édrisi*, translated by P. Amédée Jaubert (Paris, 1836–1840). My references are to this translation, but my colleague Professor Muhsin Mahdi has checked its passages that relate to China against several manuscripts of the text. I am deeply indebted to Professor Mahdi for his collaboration in connection with my research as it concerns the Islamic world.

Concerning al-Idrīsī, see also: C. F. Seybold, "al-Idrīsī," in *The Encyclopaedia of Islam*, II (1927), 451–452. *Description de l'Afrique et de l'Espagne par Edrîsî*, Introduction, ii–lv. De Stefano, *La cultura in Sicilia nel periodo Normanno*, 19–25.

40. al-Idrīsī, *Nuzhat*, I, 90–91, 100–101, 190, 194–195.

41. Sarton, *History of Science*, II, 191. Smith and Karpinski, *The Hindu-Arabic Numerals*, 139.

42. Carter, *The Invention of Printing in China*, 133–136. Sarton, *History of Science*, II, 191.

It was probably coincidental, however, that Roger set up a government which, in its gross features, had considerable resemblance to the Chinese pattern. His general policy was undoubtedly a further development of that tendency for organization and centralization that appeared in the Norman administrations in France and in England. In some respects, however, Roger seems to have departed from European precedent. While he did not abolish the feudal order, he made firm his own control by means of an elaborate centralized bureaucracy with many organs of specialized function at the capital and with local officials who were appointed by and responsive to the central government. In general he excluded the nobles from the highest offices, ruling rather through men who were chosen for their ability.[43] The administration founded by Roger II was elaborated by his grandson, the Holy Roman Emperor Frederick II (1194–1250).[44] Jacob Burckhardt said that Frederick "centralized, in a manner hitherto unknown in the West, the whole judicial and political administration."[45] Ernst Kantorowicz refers to Frederick's statutes promulgated at Melfi in 1231 as "the birth certificate of modern bureaucracy."[46]

One of his contemporaries wrote of Roger II that "with the utmost diligence he caused inquiries to be made into the practices of other Kings and peoples, in order that he might adopt those that were seen to be admirable or useful."[47] The Byzantine influence on the administration of Norman Sicily is clear and well known,[48] but the possibility of Chinese influence seems to have been almost entirely overlooked. It is not illusory. Since China had long had a government that achieved many of the goals at which Roger was aiming, and China's government was mentioned at length and with admiration in a work

---

43. *Cambridge Medieval History*, V, 184–207.

44. The authorship of his administration has often been credited to Frederick II alone. For a more just appraisal of the role of Roger II see: Giunta, *Bizantini e Bizantinismo nella Sicilia Normanna*, 143–144. Hofmann, *Die Stellung des Königs von Sizilien*, 174. *Cambridge Medieval History*, VI, 148.

45. Burckhardt, *Renaissance in Italy*, 2.

46. Kantorowicz, *Kaiser Friedrich der Zweite*, 207.

47. *Cronisti e Scrittori Sincroni della Dominazione Normanna nel Regno di Puglia e Sicilia*, I, 287.

48. See for instance Giunta, *Bizantini e Bizantinismo nella Sicilia Normanna*. A further question is involved here, of course: that of influence moving between China and Byzantium. It is important and interesting, and almost unexplored. Literary references, excavated coins, and other archeological materials make it clear that there was contact with China as early as there was a Byzantine Empire. Both had highly developed governmental systems, and some mutual influence seems inherently likely. There are some resemblances in governmental institutions that seem too close to be accidental. But the problems are difficult and complex and to explore them here would take us too far afield.

prepared at Roger's direction and with his collaboration, it is reasonable to suppose that he may have sought to adopt some Chinese administrative practices. The scarcity of records and the lapse of eight centuries make it difficult to determine to what extent he actually did so. But some interesting pieces of evidence remain.

One such is the title of the officer in charge of the salt monopoly under Frederick II: "Master of the Salt and Iron Office." "Salt and Iron Office" is the name by which the government department in charge of the salt monopoly had been known in China since the Han dynasty. However, since there had been salt monopolies in the West since ancient times, this correspondence in title might be dismissed as mere coincidence. But Robert M. Hartwell has shown that the Sicilian salt monopoly, introduced by Roger II, employed methods which not only differed from those previously employed in Europe, but were "exactly the same" as those that had been used in China since A.D. 762. On the basis of careful study of the relevant data, he also points out that "the establishment in Europe of general sales taxes, the development of national customs administrations, and the organization of state monopolies, all show marked similarity to comparable Chinese institutions." Hartwell concludes that "the introduction of Chinese methods of fiscal administration" exercised an "important influence on the economic structure of European states during the Later Middle Ages."[49]

The necessity of efficient fiscal administration for effective centralized government is evident. A great Chinese historian writing in the first century A.D., named wealth as the basic tool of the ruler.[50] In Europe the role of finance was crucial in the development of the modern bureaucratic state. In France, James W. Fesler points out, "finance was a phase of nearly every significant administrative, judicial, and military activity." As a result, in the fourteenth century, the Chamber of Accounts was, except for the Great Council, by far the most important organ of the French monarchy.[51] Joseph R. Strayer

49. Hartwell, "Iron and Early Industrialism in Eleventh-century China," 10–19. My research on this point was blocked until Professor Hartwell offered his collaboration. It seemed to me entirely possible that there was Chinese influence on the Sicilian salt monopoly, but to prove the hypothesis true—or false—required a knowledge of economic history that I do not possess. I consulted several economic historians without result; I suspect that some of them may have thought me a little mad. Hartwell, who is most unusually grounded in both Chinese and European economic history, dug into the problem and produced results far beyond my expectations.

50. *Han-shu*, 24A.2a; Swann, *Food and Money*, 113–114.

51. Fesler, "French Field Administration," 101.

says that in twelfth-century Europe "the first bureaucrats were primarily estate-managers. Their first duty was to see that their lord received the maximum amount of income from his land-holdings and his political rights. . . . It is significant that the first government bureau which kept careful records and developed a group of technical experts was the English Exchequer." The Exchequer was primarily an accounting office.[52]

"The Norman state in England," according to Max Weber, "to a large extent . . . received its unity and its push through the bureaucratization of the royal exchequer, which, in comparison to other political structures of the feudal period, was extremely strict." This bureaucratization was accomplished largely in the reign of Henry II (1154–1189). And it is an interesting fact that one of the most influential officers of Henry's Exchequer was Thomas Brown, who had previously served as a high official in the court of Roger II in Sicily.[53]

If Chinese techniques did in fact influence the development of fiscal administration in Europe, this was a contribution of no small significance toward the modern bureaucratic state.

ANOTHER technique that is almost essential to the effective functioning of a large, centralized, bureaucratic administration is what may be called "the institution of examination."[54] This was developed in China earlier than anywhere else, and it appears to have been diffused to Europe in two waves, first in the twelfth century and again at the end of the seventeenth century.

A large administration may be organized according to either of two general patterns. It may be decentralized, with much delegation of au-

52. Strayer, "Medieval Bureaucracy," 1.
53. Weber, *Essays in Sociology*, 210. *Cambridge Medieval History*, V, 573–579. *Course of the Exchequer*, xxxiv, 18, 35–36.
54. Our word "examination" is used in a wide variety of ways to denote everything from the tests given to candidates for civil service appointments and academic degrees to the diagnostic scrutiny that a physician makes of a patient, or the search of luggage made by a customs officer. Yet the kind of "examinations" given in schools, and those used in government or industry to measure qualifications (which have much in common), utilize a very specific technique for which there seems to be no specific name. To designate this technique as it may be present in (or absent from) a specific culture, I use the term "the institution of examination." I define it as follows: The institution of examination is the recurrent and systematic practice of asking questions that are identical, or are conceived to be of equivalent difficulty, of individuals who are supposed to be comparable in their advancement in learning, and the grading of the answers in such manner that the grades assigned are conceived to denote the degree of attainment of those examined.

thority to individuals in charge of relatively small segments of the whole. While sacrificing the advantages of total coordination, such an organization possesses great flexibility for meeting crises, such as the loss of key personnel. Or the administration may be highly centralized. In the latter case, a large and complex administration will be most effective if it is staffed by functionaries having a wide variety of professional qualifications, who are associated together in a manner carefully calculated to achieve the purposes for which the organization was set up.

Such a centralized bureaucracy shares with machinery the problem of the replacement of parts. When a gear in a machine, or a member of a bureaucratic administration, ceases to function for any reason, there is not time to prepare a replacement. A gear, or a person, having precisely the necessary qualifications to fill the vacant place, must be substituted at once. To determine that a gear meets the specifications, there are various methods of testing and measuring it. In a large and complex administration, which is constantly in need of replacements, such determination is made chiefly on the basis of examination.

It is true of course that specific examinations are not always administered to fill vacant positions. But in our world there is always a pool of approximately qualified persons who have been preselected by a whole series of examinations: those passed at the various levels of schooling, and in acquiring academic degrees and various certificates of proficiency. In addition, both governments and businesses make extensive use of special examinations to determine the qualifications of candidates for particular posts. We take this veritable network of examinations for granted and seldom ask ourselves how it would be possible to keep our highly complex organizations of every sort running without them. Still less do most of us realize that such examinations of whatever sort, whether academic or other, were unknown in our Western world until less than a thousand years ago.[55]

55. For a number of years I have been devoting a great deal of time to the study of the history of examination as an institution. Here it is impossible even to summarize this investigation, except to say that I have found no evidence that it existed anywhere but in China at an early date. And everywhere else that it does appear, the possibility that it derived from Chinese influence appears good. The earliest possible reference to examination outside of China that I have encountered is in the account by the Chinese Buddhist pilgrim Hsüan-tsang, who visited India in the seventh century A.D. Concerning the Buddhist University of Nalanda, in northeastern India, he wrote (Hsüan-tsang, *Buddhist Records of the Western World*, II, 170–171): "If men of other quarters desire to enter and take part in discussions, the keeper of the gate proposes some hard questions; many are unable to answer, and retire." Keay (*Indian Education*, 94–95) and Sankalia (*The University of Nālandā*,

In China an objective technique for measuring the abilities of a candidate for service in the government, against the requirements of the particular post, was devised as early as the fourth century B.C., and this led directly to the invention of the technique of examination. Examinations may have been given as early as the third century B.C., but this is uncertain. The earliest formal written examination of which we have an unimpeachable record, anywhere in the world, was given at the Chinese court in 165 B.C.[56] The use of examinations in China, both in schools and in connection with the civil service, became very common within a very short time. But the spread of the institution to other countries was long deferred.

The oldest and the most clearly traceable instance of the diffusion of examination to Europe seems to be in the field of medicine. Under the T'ang dynasty (618–906) China had an extensive state medical establishment, in which examinations were given not only to students of medicine, but also (beginning in 796) to physicians all over the Empire, in order to select those qualified for government service.[57] Such medical education and examination continued in later times. Chinese medicine was known in the Islamic world, and it is even recorded that around the beginning of the tenth century a Chinese scholar studied for a year, probably in Baghdad, with al-Rāzī, perhaps the greatest of all Muslim physicians.[58] In 931, not long after the death of al-Rāzī, the Caliph—reportedly perturbed because one of his subjects had died as a result of an error by a physician—decreed that all physicians in the region of Baghdad (unless of well-established reputation) must pass

---

66–67) have called this a kind of entrance examination; the point is debatable, and there seem to be no other references to examination in India until much later. In any case, the date is long after intercourse between China and India had become fairly common, especially in Buddhist circles, so that the possibility of Chinese inspiration is fully open.

56. Creel, "The Meaning of *Hsing-ming.*" Idem, "The *Fa-chia.*"

57. Rotours, *Traité des examens*, 233. Idem, *Traité des fonctionnaires*, I, 339–343. *T'ung-tien*, 13a. It seems impossible to determine how old the state medical establishment in China may be. An elaborate system of state medicine, dealing with several branches including veterinary, is described in a work that has traditionally been supposed to describe the government of the Western Chou period (1122–771 B.C.); see: *Chou-li*, 1.10b–11a, 5.1a–9a; Biot, *Tcheou-li*, I, 8–9, 92–99. But if there was any such establishment at that early date, no evidence of it seems to have survived. Nevertheless, this influential work undoubtedly did help to mold the practice of later times, in this as in other respects. My colleague Professor T. H. Tsien kindly brought the edict of 796 to my attention.

58. *Relation de la Chine et de l'Inde*, 20–21, 26. al-Nadīm, *Kitāb al-Fihrist*, 16–17. For the latter reference I am indebted to Professor Mahdi.

an examination by the chief physician and be licensed to practice.[59] A number of detailed circumstances make it appear almost certain that this examination in Baghdad was inspired by the Chinese example.[60]

In 1140 King Roger II of Sicily decreed that, "in order that no subjects in our realm may be endangered through the inexperience of those practicing healing," all who aspired to practice medicine must first present themselves at his court for examination.[61] This regulation is so similar to that promulgated two centuries earlier in Baghdad, and King Roger's connection with the world of Arabic learning was so close, that there can be little doubt that it provided the model.[62] Roger's grandson, Emperor Frederick II, promulgated a similar but more elab-

---

59. Professor Mahdi has kindly checked the accounts of this event in a number of Arabic works, and collaborated with me in comparing the details with those of Chinese practice. See: al-Qifṭī, Tarikh al-ḥukamā, 191–192. Abi Uṣayi 'a, 'Uyūn al-anbā' fi ṭabaqāt al-aṭibbā', I, 222. Leclerc, Histoire de la médecine arabe, I, 364–367. Browne, Arabian Medicine, 40–41. Khairallah, Outline of Arabic Contributions to Medicine, 67–68.

60. (1) My colleagues Professor Nabia Abbott and Professor Muhsin Mahdi assure me that the institution of examination was not generally employed in the Islamic world until much later (verbal communications of May 26 and February 17, 1960). Yet it is recorded that medical examination still took place in Baghdad as late as around 1100. It seems probable that if the institution of examination had been invented independently within the Islamic world, it would also have been used for purposes other than medical.

(2) The Arabic word used to stand for medical examination is very rare in this sense. The usual practice in the Islamic world was for an instructor to give a license (ijāza) to a student who had read a text under his supervision. But the term used for medical "examination" is imtiḥān, which commonly has the meanings of "to test" and "to try out," meanings that it shares with the Chinese character shih 試 which is commonly used to mean "examination." And this imtiḥān, like the Chinese examinations, was a test required by public authority which in turn recognized its outcome.

(3) In Baghdad physicians were not licensed to practice medicine in general but only to use those specific healing arts in which they were found to be proficient; this is reminiscent of the fact that in China students of medicine seem regularly to have specialized in and been examined in one or another specific branch of medicine. (Most of the information in this note is based upon verbal communications from Muhsin Mahdi, chiefly during 1960.)

61. Huillard-Bréholles, Historia Diplomatica Frederici Secundi, Tomus IV, Pars I, 149. (I am indebted to the late Professor Helena M. Gamer for her assistance with this rather difficult passage of Medieval Latin.)

62. Constantinus Africanus (c. 1020–1087), whose translations from Arabic are credited with introducing Arabic medicine to Europe, had been a secretary to Roger's uncle, the Duke of Apulia; see Sarton, History of Science, I, 769, II, 66–67, and Campbell, Arabian Medicine, I, 122–124. The Arabic scholars at Roger's court must have been aware of the practice of medical examination at Baghdad. Campbell (ibid., I, 119) suggested that Roger's establishment of medical examination was inspired by Arabic practice.

orate regulation a century later, and medical examination supervised by public authority appeared elsewhere in Italy soon after.[63]

There is little room for serious doubt that the practice of examining physicians was diffused from China, via the Islamic world, arriving in Europe early in the twelfth century.[64] Examination of any other kind seems to have been unknown in Europe until around the beginning of the thirteenth century, when it was practiced in universities.[65] The examinations given in Europe and in China in the thirteenth century were not in all respects the same, and it seems impossible to find any intermediate stage (except in the case of medical examination) to demonstrate diffusion from China. Nevertheless, the institution of examination as it existed in the two areas in the thirteenth century had a number of characteristics in common. At least four may be distinguished, as follows:

1. Insofar as our evidence indicates, examination in thirteenth-century Europe was not, as it is today, practiced widely and casually. As in China at that time, it was a process principally used in connection with higher education, and the attainment through examination of a degree gave its holder very special status. It is well known that

---

63. Huillard-Bréholles, *Historia Diplomatica Frederici Secundi*, Tomus IV, Pars I, 235–237. Sarton, *History of Science*, II, 576. Baas, *Grundriss der Geschichte der Medicin*, 221–222; Professor Ilza Veith kindly brought this passage to my attention. Ciasca, *L'Arte dei Medici e Speciali nella Storia e nel Comercio Fiorentino*, 268; I am indebted to Professor Sylvia L. Thrupp for informing me of this work and for giving me information based on her study of the early history of the medical profession.

64. For a number of years I have been engaged, with the help of several colleagues, in seeking to trace the movement of medical examination from China to Europe. In the course of this investigation I visited Sicily in 1961. A brief synopsis of my findings up to 1960, citing medical examinations in China, the Baghdad decree as the connecting link, and the statute of Roger II in 1140, and concluding that Chinese influence on the latter was probable, was published in *The University of Chicago Reports*, XI, no. 3 (1960), 2–4. A similar conclusion was stated by Gwei-djen Lu and Joseph Needham in "China and the Origin of Examinations in Medicine," in *Proceedings of the Royal Society of Medicine*, LVI (1963), 63–70. In this paper Lu and Needham give a very valuable resumé of data on the state medical establishment, medical education, and the examination of physicians in China, and they mention the establishment of medical examination in Baghdad and in Sicily, but they devote relatively little attention to the circumstances and the detailed resemblances that make it almost certain that the Baghdad examinations were inspired by those of China. There is, in fact, much more of such evidence than it has been possible for me to present here.

65. Teng, "Chinese Influence on the Western Examination System," 268–272. Malden, *On the Origin of Universities and Academical Degrees*, 15–19. Rashdall, *The Universities of Europe in the Middle Ages*, I, 16–18, 220–230, 241–249, 309–310, 339–341, 373–397, 435–488; III, 140–161, 437–438.

those having degrees in China composed an elite, enjoying the highest prestige. In Europe, Hastings Rashdall wrote, "the doctorate became an order of nobility, with as distinct and definite a place in the hierarchical system of medieval Christendom as the priesthood or the knighthood."[66]

2. In both China and Europe degrees were conferred by public authority, and they carried not merely prestige but privilege. In China degrees were conferred by the Emperor, and those who won them enjoyed special status and privilege.[67] In Europe degrees were normally bestowed either by the Pope or by a temporal ruler and carried special advantages; Rashdall says that "the degree was not a mere certificate of having passed an examination but the admission to an official position."[68]

3. Men holding degrees were considered especially eligible for appointment to positions in the government, in both Europe and China. The Chinese Imperial University was set up, in 124 B.C., for the express purpose of training men for government service, and this continued to be the prime purpose of schools in later China, whether public or private.[69] The Chinese civil service examinations were established in order to provide a roster of men qualified for appointment to office. When the Emperor Frederick II founded the University of Naples in 1224, he stated in its charter that its purpose was to prepare men for the imperial service.[70] And in Europe generally men holding degrees were, from the very beginning, a principal source from which civil servants were drawn.

66. Rashdall, *The Universities of Europe in the Middle Ages*, I, 223, 287.

67. On the basis of his extensive knowledge of the relevant documents, Professor Edward A. Kracke, Jr., assures me that in the period around 1200, as at many other times in Chinese history, men who had passed the highest examination and been given a degree enjoyed special legal status and privileges, even when they had not been appointed to office (verbal communication of October 28, 1966). See also Ch'ü, *Law and Society*, 177–182.

68. Rashdall, *The Universities of Europe in the Middle Ages*, I, 8–15, 204–205, 221–224, 228, 285–287, 290–291, 308–315, 337–343, 429–431, 470; II, 75–80. Schachner, *The Medieval Universities*, 289–290.

69. *Han-shu*, 88.4b–6a.

70. Students in the University who were considered especially promising were given posts at the court to finish their training and fit them for careers; this corresponded closely with the Chinese practice. See Kantorowicz, *Kaiser Friedrich der Zweite*, 124–126, 277. This in itself may not have been the result of Chinese influence—at any rate, not directly—for such practices had existed, at times at least, in connection with the Byzantine universities. But some of the Byzantine practice in this regard is so similar to procedures that had started centuries earlier in China that the possibility of Chinese influence cannot be ruled out. I believe, however, that we have no evidence of the use of examinations or degrees in the Byzantine universities.

4. The most striking similarity was in the nature of the process of attaining a degree. In the thirteenth century, in both China and Europe, this was a tripartite process. Success in passing the first examination did not confer a degree; it merely made the candidate eligible to study for the second examination, which was taken after a lapse of some time. The same was true of the second examination, which gave eligibility to prepare for and take the third. Only success in the third and final examination was originally thought of as making the candidate eligible for a degree. It was only at a later date, in both China and Europe, that the first and second examinations were considered formally to bring degrees.[71]

These correspondences are too close and too numerous to be wholly accidental. In China it required many centuries, after the first appearance of the technique of examination, for this elaborately structured and politically significant institution to be developed. To suppose that in Europe an examination system so similar in its structure and in its political role could have been developed spontaneously, within mere decades of the first appearance of examination of any kind, is to invoke coincidence beyond the point of credibility. Although we cannot trace the transmission, it is preponderantly probable that the academic examinations of medieval Europe, like the medical examinations, owed much to Chinese inspiration.

In one respect examination in medieval Europe was quite different from that in China. Ever since the second century B.C., examination in China had been almost—though not quite—exclusively written. In medieval Europe, however, examinations seem to have been exclusively oral.[72] But this does not rule out the possibility of Chinese influence. The elaborate procedure of the Chinese civil service examinations was so foreign to the experience of Europeans that they had

---

71. Rashdall, *The Universities of Europe in the Middle Ages*, I, 462–464.

72. The earliest date for written examinations in Europe has commonly been given as 1702. See: Teng, "Chinese Influence on the Western Examination System," 272–274. *Essays on Examinations*, 33. Ball, *A History of the Study of Mathematics at Cambridge*, 193. In fact, however, this date is almost a decade too late; see below, p. 26. The 1702 date is given in the article "Examinations" in the eleventh edition of the *Encyclopaedia Britannica*. But a new article under the same heading, introduced beginning with the 1955 edition, stated: "Written examinations were introduced by the Jesuits into the academies they founded upon the institution of their society in 1540." It appears, however, that the author of this new article has mistaken written exercises in composition for written examination. Hughes, *Loyola and the Educational System of the Jesuits*, 259, writes: "All examinations, as projected by the *Ratio Studiorum*, are conducted by word of mouth. Writing enters the examination, only when the written word itself is the subject of investigation. . . . In the higher courses, where style is no longer a matter of study, writing never appears in examinations."

difficulty in understanding it. Even missionaries and travelers who visited China and described these examinations as late as the sixteenth century sometimes gave the impression that they supposed them to be administered orally.

When, in the thirteenth century, the Mongols conquered territories stretching from the Pacific to Hungary, the movement of individuals between China and Europe was greatly facilitated. But this did not bring about the movement of ideas, in either direction, that might have been expected. Some of the reasons are clear. The Mongols' conquest of China was accompanied by great slaughter, and in their rather harsh rule they made extensive use, as officials, of foreigners, of whom Marco Polo is the most famous example. Before this the Chinese had on the whole been hospitable to foreigners and had treated them at times with great consideration. When the Mongols invaded, they received aid from some of these resident foreigners.[73] From that time onward the Chinese have tended to be indifferent if not hostile toward foreigners. Furthermore, many of the Europeans who visited China had little understanding or appreciation of China's culture.[74]

Such understanding and appreciation, however, were outstandingly characteristic of the Jesuit missionaries who gained access to China toward the beginning of the seventeenth century. Their learning, especially in the sciences, won them acceptance in Chinese intellectual circles. Some of them became officials at the Chinese court, and even the intimates of Emperors. They learned not only to read Chinese but to write it well. Becoming enthusiasts for China's thought and culture, they flooded Europe with letters and accounts of China that evoked wonder and admiration. A French authority on the eighteenth century asserts that even though this was the period of "Anglomania" in France, China "seems to have been more in favor than England itself."[75]

The new knowledge of China reached Europe at a time when it could not fail to have great impact. Those who resented the monolithic authority of Christian dogma were delighted by the alternatives provided by Chinese philosophy—with the compliments of the Jesuits!

73. Kuwabara, "On P'u Shou-keng."

74. For example, while the account by Marco Polo gives admirably accurate details on many practical matters, his silence and apparent lack of interest concerning many aspects of Chinese culture are remarkable. Thus, living in a country where books were being printed on a large scale while printing was still unknown in Europe, Polo never mentions printing—except the printing of paper money. See Carter, *The Invention of Printing in China*, 161.

75. Pinot, *La Chine et la formation de l'esprit philosophique en France*, 9. Creel, *Confucius*, 257–263::278–285.

Those who wished to evict the hereditary nobility from its place of privilege greeted the descriptions of Chinese governmental practice with cries of joy. Virgile Pinot writes that

> The admirers of China believed that they found there, and there only, a country where merit permitted one to attain to the highest dignities of the state, a country where each person was classed in the social hierarchy according to his merit ... The thing must have been rare or even non-existent in Europe, for all the missionaries, of whatever nationality they might be, celebrated in dithyrambic terms this marvelous Chinese hierarchy which was founded on nothing but merit.[76]

Adolph Reichwein writes that the philosophers of the Enlightenment, seeking to break the bonds of a metaphysical ethics and a feudal society, "discovered, to their astonishment, that more than two thousand years ago in China ... Confucius had thought the same thoughts in the same manner, and fought the same battles. . . . Confucius became the patron saint of eighteenth-century Enlightenment."[77] Voltaire asserted that "the happiest period, and the one most worthy of respect which there has ever been on this earth, was the one which followed his [Confucius'] laws."[78]

This was, of course, exaggeration and idealization. The inevitable disillusionment was precipitated by a number of factors, including the loss of favor by the Jesuits even with the Pope. By the latter part of the eighteenth century the "dream of China" was over, and adulation had been replaced by denigration.[79] The very fact that there had been this great interest in China was almost forgotten.

This could not eradicate, however, such influence as Chinese ideas —or the European conception of them—had already had on European thought and institutions. Certainly it is going too far to say, as one enthusiast has written, that "Chinese philosophy was without doubt the basic cause of the French Revolution."[80] But there can be no reasonable doubt that the new understanding of China, reaching the West in a time of sweeping and crucial change, played a role in the emergence

76. Pinot, *La Chine et la formation de l'esprit philosophique en France*, 395.

77. Reichwein, *China and Europe*, 77.

78. Voltaire, *Oeuvres complètes*, XVI, 335.

79. After being expelled from one country after another, the Society of Jesus was dissolved by a papal bull in 1773 (it was restored in 1814). The curious concatenation of circumstances that led to the change in attitude toward China in the eighteenth century is described in Creel, *Confucius*, 261–273::283–295.

80. Chu, *Chung-kuo Ssu-hsiang chih Ying-hsiang*, 295.

of new intellectual, social, and political patterns that is commonly ignored.[81]

Much of this influence was so subtle as to defy analysis, but the adoption in Europe of one Chinese institution can be traced with some confidence. Europeans seeking a more egalitarian method than inheritance for the apportionment of political power were greatly attracted by the Chinese system of competitive civil service examinations. They were described in detail by Matteo Ricci, the great pioneer of the Jesuit mission in China, in a work that by 1648 had appeared in eleven editions in five European languages.[82] From Italy to England writers commented on the system with admiration.[83]

In the twelfth and thirteenth centuries it had been the Kingdom of Sicily that had been outstanding, among European states, for its efforts to organize a highly centralized government having some similarities to the pattern that had prevailed in China for a millennium, and it is not surprising that it was in Sicily that some Chinese techniques were put into practice. In the seventeenth and eighteenth centuries the place of leadership in the development of bureaucratic government was taken over by Brandenburg-Prussia.[84] Herman Finer says that "even in the eighteenth century only one state, Prussia, had arrived at anything like our modern perception of public administration managed by a force of people, especially and systematically trained, recruited, and paid, to the exclusion of any other occupation, to execute the commands of the state."[85] But however novel this institution may have been in Europe, it was well known that in China such an officialdom, recruited by examination, had long been in existence. It is not surprising that civil service examination first appeared, in Europe, in Brandenburg-Prussia, and there is little room for doubt that the inspiration came from China.

81. See Creel, *Confucius*, 254–278::276–301. An influence that lies outside the specifically governmental scope of our inquiry, yet is highly significant, is that in the field of aesthetics. It is well known that eighteenth-century Europe was swept by a craze for *chinoiserie*, and it is sometimes supposed that Chinese art had no more lasting effect than to popularize a few such things as the willow pattern for dishes. In fact, however, Chinese aesthetic criteria played a major role in the development of modern taste. See Lovejoy, "The Chinese Origin of a Romanticism."

82. Ricci, *Journals*, xvii, 34–41.

83. See Creel, *Confucius*, 269–270::291–293.

84. The Electorate of Brandenburg was transformed, for somewhat complex reasons, into the Kingdom of Prussia in a process that started in 1701. The state, however, was essentially the same, and it is most convenient to call it Brandenburg-Prussia although in fact there was no state so called.

85. Finer, *Modern Government*, 712.

The "Great Elector," Frederick William (1620–1688), who "laid the corner stone of the Prussian bureaucratic state,"[86] took a great personal interest in China and at one point hoped to establish direct relations with that country. He purchased a very considerable number of books in Chinese and patronized scholars who studied Chinese and published on China.[87] His successor, Frederick III,[88] showed no great interest in China, but several of his advisers did. Conspicuous among them was Gottfried Wilhelm Liebniz, who was much concerned with China during all the latter part of his life. In a work published in 1697 Liebniz referred to "the mandarins' examinations, on the basis of which distinctions and magistracies are granted [in China]," so casually that he apparently assumed that his readers were familiar with them.[89]

One of the Privy Councillors of Frederick III, Samuel Pufendorf, made repeated reference to the Chinese civil service examinations in a work, first published in 1672, that was widely read and frequently reprinted.[90] Pufendorf contrasted Western methods of selecting men for office with the technique of examination used by the Chinese.[91] Elsewhere he wrote:

> Yet in some states little heed is given to birth, and every man's nobility is derived from his own virtue, and what he has done for the state in private and public capacity. . . . Martinius, *Historia Sinica*, Pref.: "This nation accords no nobility to mere family lineage. The poorest man may by learning make his way to the pinnacle of fame." . . . Now such customs may be abhorrent to ours, and yet wise men teach that nobles should not depend upon lineage alone, but much more upon virtue.[92]

86. Georg Küntzel, "Frederick William," in *Encyclopaedia of the Social Sciences*, VI, 433. See also Küntzel, *Die drei grossen Hohenzollern*, 1–76.

87. Lach, *The Preface to Leibniz' Novissima Sinica*, 43–47. Idem, "The Chinese Studies of Andreas Müller."

88. He was the Elector Frederick III of Brandenburg until 1701, when he became King Frederick I of Prussia.

89. Lach, *The Preface to Leibniz' Novissima Sinica*, 72. This entire work, including both Lach's introductory material and the text of the Preface, is an admirable exposition of Leibniz' concern with China.

90. Pufendorf, *De Jura Naturae et Gentium*, Introduction, 14a–15a, 58a–62a. This work appeared in four editions before the inauguration of written civil service examinations in 1693, as follows: Lund (Sweden), 1672; Frankfort, 1684, Amsterdam, 1688; Lund, 1692.

91. Ibid., 679.

92. Ibid., 1270.

It was in Berlin in 1693, five years after Pufendorf had joined the government there, that what appear to be the first written civil service examinations ever given in Europe were administered.[93] It would be difficult to suppose that the Chinese example had nothing to do with this event. It seems reasonably clear that here again the institution of examination had been diffused from China, this time in a form much closer to the original.

There was even, as Ssu-yü Teng has shown, a third diffusion of this institution, for it appears to have reached Britain not from the continent of Europe but directly from China. The British East India Company had an establishment in Canton which was, of course, informed concerning Chinese governmental institutions, and the Company used examinations for its personnel early in the nineteenth century. The early advocates of civil service examination in Parliament were men who had direct or indirect connections with the East India Company. Debates in Parliament in 1853 and 1854 repeatedly referred to the long Chinese experience with civil service examination; friends of the measure lauded the Chinese example, while its

93. Examinations were given in Berlin in 1692 to officials in charge of military justice, but I have seen no certain evidence that they were written. But an examination established in 1693 for legal officials included the preparation of a *Proberelation*, "test essay"; this examination is described by Friedrich Holtze, as "eine schriftliche und mündliche Prüfung." See: Holtze, *Geschichte des Kammergerichts in Brandenburg-Preussen*, 19. Goldschmidt, *Rechtsstudium und Prüfungsordnung*, 157. Schmoller, "Der preussische Beamtenstand unter Friedrich Wilhelm I.," 167.

For the above references I am indebted to my colleague Professor Donald F. Lach. Professor Lach has not only most generously made the results of his long research on this problem available to me, but has given me invaluable counsel on many aspects of the impact of Chinese influence on modern Europe. He himself has concluded: "Though the hypothesis is so far impossible to document, it may be suggested that the merit system of examination for civil service adopted by Prussia in the last decade of the seventeenth century was possibly influenced by the example of China" (Lach, *The Preface to Leibniz' Novissima Sinica*, 37).

As indicating the possibility that Pufendorf had some influence on these first civil service examinations in Berlin, it may be noted that they applied to legal officials and that Pufendorf was a jurist. In the following year (1694) Frederick III founded the University of Halle, and the leading spirit among the founders of its faculty of law was Christian Thomasius, who had been strongly influenced by Pufendorf (Irsay, *Histoire des universités*, II, 68–71). The statutes of the law faculty, dated in 1694, provided that both oral and written examinations must be passed by students seeking degrees (Goldschmidt, *Rechtsstudium und Prüfungsordnung*, 154). This is the earliest mention known to me of written academic examinations in the West. It will be noted that it came eight years before the establishment of written examinations at Cambridge, in 1702, which has commonly been supposed to be the earliest such instance.

opponents said that Britain did not want any such Chinese scheme.[94]

As recently as three decades ago, ancient Chinese practice provided the inspiration for an innovation in the activity of the government of the United States of America that has had far-reaching economic and political consequences. The Agricultural Adjustment Act enacted by the Congress in 1938 inaugurated a combined program designed to regulate the production and distribution of agricultural commodities by various means, including acreage allotments, the storage of surpluses, and "parity-payments." Its adoption was the direct result of long advocacy by the Secretary of Agriculture, Henry Agard Wallace. Wallace called his plan "the Ever-Normal Granary." This term is a literal translation of the name applied, in 54 B.C., to a plan then put into operation in China to attain similar objectives by simpler but basically similar means.[95] Wallace has himself stated that what he had read concerning the Chinese practice directly inspired him to develop this program.[96]

WITHOUT exaggeration it can be said that, among the systems of government devised by men, that of the Chinese has unusual claims upon our interest. No other system has continued in operation over so large an area embracing such a large population for so many centuries. Two thousand years ago it had already brought a very large territory and population under a complex centralized administration having many similarities to governments of our own time. Its theorists formulated, before the beginning of the Christian Era, abstract principles of administration such as are scarcely found elsewhere before the twentieth century. And some of its techniques, adopted in other

94. *Hansard's Parliamentary Debates, Third Series*, CXXVIII, 38, CXXIX, 1340–1341, CXXXI, 651–652, 661. Teng, "Chinese Influence on the Western Examination System," 292–300. Chang, "China and English Civil Service Reform."

95. *Han-shu*, 8.20b, 24A.19b. Dubs, *Han-shu*, II, 253. Swann, *Food and Money*, 195. Bodde, "Henry A. Wallace and the Ever-Normal Granary." Bodde's article includes an excellent discussion of the Chinese method and its relationship to Wallace's proposals.

96. Bodde, "Henry A. Wallace and the Ever-Normal Granary." It should be noted that Wallace's information concerning the Chinese experience with governmental measures for assisting agriculture was evidently slight. This is unfortunate, for the Chinese experienced, at various times, difficulties remarkably similar to some of those that have beset the American program. In view of the vast sums that have been expended on the latter, it might have proved useful to invest a small amount of money on research into the Chinese experience.

parts of the world, have played a significant role in the development of political institutions in other countries.

How did this rather remarkable system of government come into existence? Insofar as answers have been given, they have tended to be of two sorts.

Completely traditional Chinese scholars have supposed that the most perfect government existed in the "golden age" of certain ideal Emperors who reigned before the beginning of the traditional "three dynasties"—Hsia, Shang, and Chou. The origins of this perfect government are either not given or ascribed to the intervention of the chief deity, Heaven. During the "three dynasties" there was some deterioration of governmental practice, yet it was still admirable during most of the Western Chou period (1122–771 B.C.). During the remainder of the Chou dynasty there was progressive decay, until the Ch'in dynasty (221–207 B.C.) reunited the country under a centralized authoritarian rule. The Former Han dynasty, which succeeded, carried on many of the authoritarian measures of Ch'in but at the same time revived many of the ancient institutions as they were practiced, especially, in Western Chou times. And the Han government provided the basic pattern for later times.

Critical scholars, however, have noted that there is no valid historical evidence that the ideal early Emperors ever existed. They have traced some of China's political institutions to the Western Chou, which is, however, considered essentially a time of decentralized feudal rule. There has been a tendency to seek the origins of centralized control in the western state of Ch'in, the forerunner of the Ch'in dynasty. And in general it has been tacitly assumed that, in a way no one clearly understands, the remarkable centralized bureaucratic government that we find in the second century B.C. was evolved in a process that had its beginnings chiefly in the state of Ch'in two centuries earlier.

Others have found fault with this theory. It has been pointed out that the state of Ch'in was an unlikely place for this development, and that there are indications that some of its most important aspects should be looked for elsewhere.[97] Various scholars have done brilliant work in investigating what seem to be bits and pieces of the story, but these are difficult to understand and evaluate by themselves. What is needed is a study of all the evidence, probing as deeply as possible and going back, insofar as is feasible, to the beginnings.

97. See Creel, "Beginnings of Bureaucracy in China."

CHAPTER

2

Before Chou

ARCHEOLOGICAL excavation during the past half century has given us a great deal of information about prehistoric man in China. The finds, which may even include some of man's prehuman ancestors, cover a range from the very early paleolithic to the latest neolithic cultures. For the later periods our knowledge becomes increasingly complete and detailed.[1] Concerning government in stone age China, however, there is little basis even for speculation. We have no written records from this time, and without them it is almost impossible even to construct plausible hypotheses about political institutions.

China's traditional history begins with a series of Emperors[2] at a time alleged to be as early as the middle of the fifth millennium B.C. They are in part culture heroes, credited with the invention of writing, agriculture, and so forth, and superhuman labors such as the digging out of gorges to permit the passage of rivers. Even the names of most of these supposedly early rulers do not appear in the literature until a relatively late date. The traditions concerning them were elaborated, for the most part, in the latter half of the first millennium B.C. Philosophers and political theorists attributed to them, and to the "golden age" in which they were believed to have lived, practices that they

---

1. Cheng, *Prehistoric China*. Chang, *Archaeology of Ancient China*, 18–184.
2. The use of the titles "Emperor" and "King" in early Chinese history is rather confusing. The early mythical rulers are commonly called by the title Ti 帝 , which is translated as "Emperor." Both this title and Wang 王 , which is translated as "King," occur with reference to rulers of the Shang, the earliest historic dynasty. Chou rulers, however, are uniformly called "Wang." From the Ch'in dynasty onward the title "Emperor" is used. In my opinion the Western Chou rulers may quite properly be called Emperors, but it seems best to accord with convention and call them Kings.

conceived to be ideal. These accounts are not history, though they are valuable reflections of the ideas of the time in which they were written.

The first dynasty, according to tradition, was the Hsia, to which are assigned the dates 2205–1766 B.C. We have, in the work called the *Documents*,[3] a number of writings attributed to this period from which it might seem possible to draw valuable deductions concerning political institutions. Unfortunately, however, critical examination shows that not one of them can be accepted as having been written earlier than the Chou dynasty.[4] Great efforts have been made to identify certain excavated sites as belonging to the Hsia, but these have proved unconvincing. This does not mean, however, that the traditions concerning an early Hsia state, if not a dynasty, are necessarily false; the traditions are so pervasive that it would seem they must have some basis.[5] Nevertheless, it is not possible to begin our account of government in China with the Hsia.

Chinese history begins at some point in the Shang dynasty, traditionally dated from 1765 to 1123 B.C.[6] It is only the later centuries of this period, however, on which the light of history falls, and at best it is somewhat dim. There is good evidence that there must have been a very considerable Shang literature, and we have documents that purport to date from even the very beginning of the dynasty. But none of the supposedly Shang books or poems stands up under criticism; it seems clear that the genuine Shang literature has disappeared and that the earliest of the documents we now have were written at the beginning of Chou.[7] Nevertheless the traditions that survive to us are by no means without validity concerning the Shang period; recently excavated materials have shown, for instance, that the lists of Shang rulers embodied in the traditional histories are in general correct. But separation of the valid from the invalid among the traditions remains a problem.

Most of our knowledge of the Shang has come from the recovery during this century of a large number of inscriptions and from the

---

3. The *Shu-ching* 書經 , often called the *Book of History*. But this work is not a history; it is a collection of documents. In Chinese it is commonly called simply *Shu* 書 , "writings," for which *Documents* seems the most accurate translation.

4. See p. 448, note 14.

5. Creel, *Studies*, 97–131. Chang, *Archaeology of Ancient China*, 185–194. Cheng, *Shang China*, xxi–xxii. Erkes, "Ist die Hsia-Dynastie geschichtlich?"

6. Concerning dates in early Chinese history, which are much debated, see Appendix B.

7. Creel, *Studies*, 49–95. Cheng, *Shang China*, xxii–xxiv.

scientific excavation of a number of Shang sites. That of the city, near Anyang in northern Honan province, that was the capital during late Shang times has been the most complete and revealing, but other sites, some of which were occupied at earlier periods, have also added greatly to our information. For our present purpose, inscriptions are by far the most important source. A number of inscribed Shang bronzes are known, but unfortunately most of their inscriptions are quite brief. Far more important are the so-called "Shang oracle bones."

This is not a completely happy appellation, since many of the inscriptions are not on bone but on tortoise shell. Furthermore, not all of them are oracular, though the great bulk are. It is fortunate for us that the Shang people chose to record the questions they put to their deities, and sometimes the answers they received, on bone and shell. These materials have survived in a climate in which the rest of the literature, probably written on bamboo, wood, and perhaps silk, perished. But this accidental selection, which gives us chiefly divination inscriptions, causes the information we can derive from them to be limited and specialized.

The number of the inscriptions on bone and shell that remain to us, even after the productions of modern forgers have been eliminated, is formidable. It was estimated in 1953 that some one hundred thousand inscribed pieces were then known, of which some forty-one thousand had been published.[8] The impression that this gives can be very misleading, however. Many of these pieces are mere fragments, almost impossible to read, and most of the inscriptions are very brief. It is true that some are fairly lengthy, but one authority estimates that they average only ten characters per piece.[9] When it is remembered that a considerable proportion of the normal inscription is taken up by formulas used in dating and in describing the process of divination, it is evident that we cannot hope for much detailed information concerning the culture, much less the system of government.

The state of our knowledge of the Shang period is, in fact, exasperating. We know so much about a few things that it seems intolerable that we know so little about the culture and history as a whole. It is as if it were cut into a jigsaw puzzle, of which we have only a few scattered pieces. The individual piece may be very bright and clear, but since we can seldom find adjoining pieces, we can form no certain

8. Tung, "Chia-ku Wen Ku-chi." Hu, *Chia-ku Hsüeh Chu Mu*, 5.
9. Hu, *Chia-ku Hsüeh Chu Mu*, 7.

conception of the whole and can feel little certainty as to just where a particular piece belongs.

If the evidence provides little basis for certainty, it leaves the greatest scope for hypothesis. Thus we find a variety of descriptions of the Shang government proposed by various scholars, all having a certain degree of plausibility. It is almost equally impossible to prove them right, or wrong.

ONE problem around which much discussion has centered is that of feudalism.[10] Did it exist in Shang times, or was it an innovation of the Chou? According to the fully developed theory of feudalism in Chou times, there were five ranks: *Kung, Hou, Po, Tzu,* and *Nan.* These are conventionally translated as "Duke," "Marquis," "Earl," "Viscount," and "Baron." Tung Tso-pin pointed out that in the Shang inscriptions four of these titles—all except *Kung*—occur as the titles of individuals and are found in connection with what are evidently place names. Thus there is reference, for instance, to "Chou *Hou*," presumably the Marquis of Chou. This individual was, according to Tung, a vassal of the Shang King, enfeoffed with the territory of the people who later founded the Chou dynasty. Furthermore, individuals bearing these titles were sometimes called upon to assist the King in war. Tung deduced that these four titles denoted four ranks of enfeoffed nobility.[11]

A different system of six titles of feudal nobility is proposed by Hu Hou-hsüan. The first of these is *Fu*, a term which today means "wife." It apparently designated, however, not the principal wives of the King, but royal concubines. Hu says: "According to my research, King Wu Ting [reigned 1324–1266 B.C.][12] had at least sixty-four concubines. Including those who were favored and those who were not, they may not all have lived in the palace. Those who were not favored were enfeoffed with a piece of territory. Some were ordered to make sacrifices, and some to conduct military expeditions;

10. "Feudalism," as the term is used in this book, is defined as follows: "Feudalism is a system of government in which a ruler personally delegates limited sovereignty over portions of his territory to vassals." For discussion of this definition and its application, see below, pp. 317–324.

11. Tung, "Wu-teng Chüeh."

12. Here as in most other places I am following the traditional chronology as given in Tchang, *Synchronismes chinois.* Various dates are given for this reign, by various scholars.

they went back and forth between the court and the countryside on the King's business, like personal emissaries of the King."[13]

The second title listed by Hu is *Tzu*, which literally means "son" but as a noble rank is usually translated as "Viscount." Hu considers those known by this title in Shang times to be sons of the King, invested with fiefs. He also finds four other titles but believes that the differences between the status and duties of their holders were not great. They might be called upon to render various services, ranging from military command through the forwarding of tribute to the supervision of agriculture.[14]

Still another system of titles of individuals in charge of local areas is proposed by Ch'en Meng-chia, but in his opinion they were probably not enfeoffed.[15]

Any one of these ways of interpreting the evidence in the inscriptions *may* be correct, but there is no certainty that any one is. The evidence is too scanty and too ambiguous. Certainly it appears to be quite true that in Shang times there were subordinates of the King, functioning in local areas, known by titles that were, under the Chou, those of feudal lords. But it is a well-known fact that the same title may, at different times, be used to designate officials of very different functions. A familiar example is that of the English Sheriff, who was at one point a representative of the King so powerful that he was considered a menace to the royal authority.[16]

It is not enough to find titles that can be proved at another time to have been those of feudal nobles. We must also have evidence that the persons bearing them in Shang times were actually enfeoffed by the King, so that they stood in the personal relation of vassal to overlord and exercised limited sovereignty over their domains. But there seems to be little or no evidence on these essential points. On the basis of sheer probability, it must be admitted that it would undoubtedly have been difficult for the Shang King to have maintained close and constant supervision of areas distant from the capital, so that local officials must necessarily have had a considerable measure of discretion. But did this extend so far that they enjoyed limited sov-

---

13. Hu, "Yin Feng-chien K'ao," 4a. Not all scholars would agree with all aspects of this interpretation.

14. Hu, "Yin Feng-chien K'ao."

15. Ch'en, *Yin Tz'u Tsung-shu*, 325–332.

16. *Cambridge Medieval History*, V, 580–583. *Encyclopaedia of the Social Sciences*, XIV, 20–22.

ereignty and may properly be called vassals? We simply cannot tell.

WAS the Shang government a bureaucracy?[17] Certainly it carried on extensive functions that were performed by a considerable group of officials, at least some of whom were specialized in their duties. One group very important for us was the diviners, since their labors produced the oracle bones. A number of titles of officials, such as that of the "Maker of Books," appear to be those of men who performed predominantly secretarial functions. Men bearing a number of other titles performed various duties as ordered by the King. There were also, as we have seen, men with titles that have been interpreted as those of feudal nobles; whether feudatories or not, the evidence of the inscriptions shows that, at times at least, they assisted in the business of the King. And a number of titles have been identified as those of military officers of various kinds.[18] Unfortunately, however, we have virtually no indication of the way in which these various officials were chosen, trained, or recompensed.

Thus, while it is quite certain that the Shang state had a considerable body of officials, of whom some at least performed specialized functions, our information does not permit us to judge whether it was served by professional bureaucrats. Still less can we determine whether it was so organized that it may properly be called a bureaucracy. It would certainly appear, however, that whether the realm as a whole was feudal or not, the organization of the King's government was at least "proto-bureaucratic."

WHILE the inscriptions give us little basis for a reconstruction of the Shang philosophy of government as a whole, they do indicate that one factor of cardinal importance in the later development of bureaucracy was already present, to some degree, in Shang times.

Etienne Balazs writes:

> When taking a bird's-eye view of the vast stretch of
> China's history, one is struck by the persistence and sta-
> bility of one enduring feature of Chinese society that

---

17. "Bureaucracy," as the term is used in this book, is defined as "a system of administration by means of professional functionaries, whose functions are more or less definitely prescribed."

18. Ch'en, *Yin Tz'u Tsung-shu*, 503–522.

might be called officialism, the most conspicuous sign
of which was the uninterrupted continuity of a ruling
class of scholar officials. . . . There is no area of Chinese
civilization, from its basic institutions to the remotest
other-worldly regions of its mythology, and including
its literature and art, where the influence of these
scholar-officials is not immediately discernible.

He calls them a "dominant social group, peculiar to China and unknown in other societies."[19]

The importance of the role of ministers in the Chinese governmental pattern as it has existed over the past two thousand years
is universally recognized. Much of the time the business of administration has been conducted in harmonious collaboration between
them and the ruler. At some periods the ministers ruled very much as
they pleased, with little interference from the Emperor. At other
times strong and occasionally despotic Emperors have reduced their
ministers to ineffectiveness, but the ministers have seldom accepted
such a situation complacently. They have constituted a potent coun-
terweight to the ruler's authority and have provided a real check on
imperial despotism.[20]

It is important, therefore, to inquire into the origins of these Chinese "scholar-officials" as a group. Its beginnings can be traced to a
time at least as early as Shang. While somewhat comparable groups
are to be found in other countries, the length and continuity of the
Chinese tradition of the scholar-official is undoubtedly unique. Of
equal interest is another factor: the prestige accorded to ministers
of the ruler, and the degree to which achievements of the government
are not credited to the ruler alone but to his ministers and at times
to a particular minister who is singled out for special honor. Thus it
may happen that in history and tradition a minister may enjoy far
greater prominence than the ruler under whom he served.

This would seem to be unusual, at least in the practice of early
states.[21] In ancient Mesopotamia and Egypt all achievement was con-

19. Balazs, *Chinese Civilization and Bureaucracy*, 6.
20. Kracke, "Chinese Government." Fitzgerald, *The Empress Wu*, 10–11, 178–
179. Hucker, "Confucianism and the Chinese Censorial System."
21. In some respects the situation in India did resemble that in China. Learning
was highly respected, and in theory and to some degree in fact the highest offices
were bestowed on the basis of learning. Kautilya, a prime minister (and the reputed
author of the *Arthashastra*), is given a major share of the credit for the achievements of his ruler, Chandragupta Maurya, who founded the large and well-

sidered to be that of the ruler,[22] and in the Roman Empire little credit was given to those who helped the Emperor to rule.[23] In later regimes

---

organized Maurya Empire in the wake of the conquests of Alexander the Great. See: Smith, *Oxford History of India*, 73. Banerjea, *Public Administration in Ancient India*, 8–10. *Vishnu Purana*, IV, 186–187. *Kautilya's Arthaśastra*, vii–viii.

There were important differences, however, from the Chinese situation. Kautilya was a Brahman, and high officials commonly were Brahmans. And the learning that formed a part of the basis on which office was bestowed was predominantly sacred learning, in the keeping of the hereditary group of Brahmans. Since it was said that "the Brahman is a great divinity," it was also held that kings should be "brought up by Brahmans" and that obedience to Brahmans was a "chief cause of bliss to kings." See: Smith, *Oxford History of India*, 69–70. Banerjea, *Public Administration in Ancient India*, 21. *Ordinances of Manu*, 159, 300–301. Such statements were made chiefly by Brahmans, of course, and the rulers at times opposed their claims, but it is generally agreed that the Brahmans were a very potent force from an early time. See: *Ancient India as Described by Megasthenes and Arrian*, 43. Banerjea, *Public Administration in Ancient India*, 21–22, 50, 74, 137–138. Smith, *Oxford History of India*, x, 34, 48–49, 69–70.

When Indian ministers were credited with governmental achievements, they commonly figured not only as helpers of the ruler but also as members of a priestly class, powerful in their own right. In China, on the other hand, the learning on the basis of which ministers were appointed was essentially secular, and the ruler had a relatively free hand in appointing them. Thus in India ministers were not subject to the control of the rulers to the same extent as were Chinese ministers; this undoubtedly was a factor in causing the development of government in India to take a direction significantly different from that of China.

22. Both the Babylonian and Assyrian Empires had many officials with specialized functions, and officials known as "Scribe," "Chief Scribe," and "Scribe of the King" kept voluminous records of the business of the state; see Meissner, *Babylonien und Assyrien*, I, 115–146. The late Professor Benno Landsberger informed me, however, that Sumerian and Old Babylonian scribes performing governmental functions are anonymous in the inscriptions. A change comes in Assyria around 1200 B.C., after which the King-lists include with each King the name of his counsellor. At this point the status of the scribe appears to shrink to that of a mere secretary. The King's counsellor, who was an exorcist, became quite important, and in some cases the same counsellor acted through the reigns of several Kings. But tradition credits the achievements of the reign to the King alone. (Verbal communication from Professor Benno Landsberger, October 4, 1965.)

Egypt, from around the beginning of the third millennium B.C., had—with some interruptions—a strong state with a well-developed governmental structure and a host of officials. See: Wilson, *The Culture of Ancient Egypt*. Erman, *Aegypten im Altertum*. But the Pharaoh "as a god, *was* the state. To be sure, it was necessary for him to have officials . . . but our evidence indicates that they were his officers, appointed by him, responsible to him alone, and holding office subject to his divine pleasure." (Wilson, *The Culture of Ancient Egypt*, 49.) Professor John A. Wilson tells me that the texts list achievements of ministers as being those of the King. (Verbal communication from Professor Wilson, October 4, 1965.)

23. Professor Arnaldo Momigliano confirms my impression to this effect (verbal communication of May 20, 1965).

also the tendency to distribute credit for the successes of government seems to have been rather rare. Even in our own century the men who have occupied the office of President of the United States have not always been distinguished for it; a "passion for anonymity" has been said to be the chief qualification for a Presidential Assistant.

In China the practice of paying high honor to ministers was already present in Shang times. A document written only a few years after the end of the dynasty names six ministers who, it says, assisted Shang Kings, "protecting and directing their rulers."[24] The names of five of these have been identified, at least tentatively, in the oracle inscriptions. And later Chinese works tell of these and still other famous Shang ministers, some of whom are named in the inscriptions.[25]

Shang sacrifices, insofar as they are recorded on the known oracle bones, seem in general to have been made only to deities or spirits and to deceased members of the royal family. But quite exceptionally we find that these meritorious ministers also receive sacrifices. One inscription is interpreted as recording a group sacrifice to no less than thirteen such ministers at one time.[26] These deceased ministers were considered, like the royal ancestors, to be spirits of great power, able to affect the rainfall, the harvest, and even the personal welfare of the King.[27] One inscription appears to be a question by the King asking whether the former ministers of his family are inflicting misfortune upon him.[28]

The earliest and most important of these eminent ministers of Shang Kings was I Yin, the principal adviser of the founding King, T'ang. In a document from the very beginning of Chou we find the help that I Yin gave to T'ang described as being of the highest importance.[29] In the Shang inscriptions themselves we find I Yin mentioned

24. *Shu*, 61. There is some difference of opinion as to whether six ministers or seven are named here. Ch'en Meng-chia (*Yin Tz'u Tsung-shu*, 363–364) argues that there are seven. Kuo Mo-jo (*Yin Ch'i Ts'ui-pien, K'ao-shih*, 33ab) argues persuasively that there are only six.

25. Wang, *Ku-shih Hsin-cheng*, chap. 2, sec. 8; chap. 4. Tung, "Tuan-tai Yen-chiu," 375–378. Ch'en, *Yin Tz'u Tsung-shu*, 361–366.

26. Kuo, *Pu-tz'u T'ung-tsuan, Pieh*, 1.11ab.

27. For transcriptions of a number of the relevant inscriptions, see Ch'en, *Yin Tz'u Tsung-shu*, 346–350, 362–365.

28. *Yin Ch'i Ch'ien-pien*, 4.15.4. Some details of the transcription of this inscription in Ch'en, *Yin Tz'u Tsung-shu*, 362, may be questionable, but the purport of the inscription seems clear.

29. *Shu*, 61.

very frequently.[30] We even find inscriptions in which I Yin is sacrificed to together with deceased Shang Kings; no higher posthumous honor could have been paid.[31]

Concerning the details of the career of I Yin it is difficult to be certain. Not that details are not recorded, but the records we have are relatively late, so that it is hard to be sure whether they set down valid traditions or merely the embellishments of later times. The official class made a vigorous propaganda campaign, which was ultimately rather successful, in favor of its claim to authority even greater than that of the titular rulers. For such a purpose I Yin, the chief adviser of the founder of the Shang dynasty, was an exemplar who could not be overlooked.

This campaign began very early. In a sense the laudatory reference to I Yin by the Duke of Chou (the son of King Wen, the founder of the Chou dynasty) might be considered one of its earliest manifestations.[32] We have little concrete evidence, however, that this campaign was really under way as early as Western Chou times, but by the Spring and Autumn period it was in full swing. In the *Tso-chuan*,[33] in a conversation attributed to 552 B.C., I Yin is said to have held complete control of the Shang government at one point.[34]

One of Confucius' disciples is quoted in the *Analects* as saying that T'ang, the founding King of Shang, "choosing from among the multitude raised up I Yin, and those who were not virtuous fled far away." A later Confucian, Mencius, relates that I Yin was originally a farmer. T'ang, who was not yet King, had heard of his merit and sent messengers with gifts to attract him to his service. At first I Yin was indifferent, but at length he was persuaded to become T'ang's teacher.[35] All this harmonizes so completely with the Confucian insis-

---

30. There are a number of occurrences of the name I Yin, and many more that seem to refer to the same person simply as I. A large number of inscriptions refer to Huang Yin who, there seems to be good reason to believe, is the same person. For the case for this identification see Kuo, *Yin Ch'i Ts'ui-pien, K'ao-shih*, 33ab; against it, see Ch'en, *Yin Tz'u Tsung-shu*, 363–364. For mention of I Yin in the same inscriptions in which T'ang is mentioned, see *Yin Ch'i Hou-pien, shang*, 22.1, 22.2.

31. *Yin Ch'i Hou-pien, shang*, 22.1. Ch'en, *Yin Tz'u Tsung-shu*, 363.

32. The Duke of Chou was the earliest propagandist, of whom we have definite knowledge, for the preeminent role of the minister. And he gives us our first reference to I Yin in the literature (aside from the Shang inscriptions) in *Shu*, 61.

33. This important historical work is believed to have been edited around 300 B.C., but to embody much earlier material. See pp. 475–477.

34. *Tso*, 488::491 (Hsiang 21).

35. *Analects*, 12.22.6. *Mencius*, 2(2).2.8, 5(1).7.

tence that ministers should be chosen on the basis of virtue and ability, without regard to birth or wealth, that it is difficult to know whether it rests on any historical basis.

Mencius assigns to I Yin the principal credit for the founding of the Shang dynasty. I Yin, he says, conceived the idea that the Hsia should be overthrown and replaced, and persuaded T'ang to execute it. Mencius made I Yin a principal figure in the "Confucian" tradition, and he felt it necessary to find special reasons to explain why such a meritorious person did not himself become King.[36]

The most remarkable chapter in the story of I Yin is related in the *Tso-chuan* only briefly, but Mencius recounts it in detail. He says that after the death of T'ang his immediate successors reigned for only two and four years respectively. The next King, T'ai Chia, "overturned the statutes of T'ang." At this point I Yin (who must still, as minister, have held power) banished the King. For three years T'ai Chia "listened to I Yin teaching him," whereupon he repented of his errors, and I Yin restored him to power. The *Tso-chuan* says that after this episode T'ai Chia showed no resentment.[37]

Can this story have any basis in fact? There seems to be no way to tell. A variant tradition, recorded in a work of approximately the same date as the *Mencius*, represents I Yin as a rebellious minister who banished T'ai Chia and set himself up as ruler. According to this account T'ai Chia remained in exile for seven years, after which he escaped from captivity, killed I Yin, and resumed the throne.[38] In some ways this may seem more believable than the other version, but there is a serious difficulty. If I Yin was a usurper who sought to bring the Shang dynasty to an end, how can we explain the fact that he was highly honored by later Shang Kings, as the Shang inscriptions clearly show that he was?

Whether a minister could, at the beginning of Shang times, depose his ruler, is uncertain. But there is no doubt whatever that this was believed and became an important part of the political tradition. Much later, when an Emperor was in fact deposed by his ministers, they cited the action of I Yin as precedent.[39]

Although much of the tradition concerning the position of ministers in Shang times is uncertain, it is nonetheless quite clear, even

36. *Mencius*, 2(2).2.8, 5(1).6.4–6, 5(1).7.
37. *Tso*, 488::491 (Hsiang 21). *Mencius*, 5(1).6.5, 7(1).31.
38. Wang, *Ku Chu-shu*, 4a. For the dating of this work (the genuine *Bamboo Books*) see pp. 483–485.
39. *Han-shu*, 68.5a.

from the inscriptions that remain to us, that certain ministers did enjoy high honor. This afforded an important precedent for the position that came to be accorded to the scholar-official in later China. And this Shang tradition, known and discussed at the beginning of Chou, provided an unusual climate for the later development of political ideas and institutions in China.

CHAPTER
3

The Chou Dynasty

EVERY nation worthy of the name derives its identity and its vitality from a dynamic tradition in which virtually all of its members believe, and by which they are motivated. If any large part of the people becomes apathetic toward the tradition, and ceases to be moved by it to action, the very existence of the nation is in danger.[1] Countless national traditions have flourished for a time, and then ceased to be. A relative few have persisted, and even increased their scope by annexing to themselves people lost from less vigorous traditions. Among dominant traditions two have been outstanding: those of the Roman Empire and of China.

The triumphs of the Roman tradition have been formidable. Even after the passing of the Western Roman Empire it continued to be embodied in the Byzantine and, in some sense, the Holy Roman Empire. To this day a number of nations are considered by their people to continue the Roman tradition.

Notwithstanding all this, the achievements of the Chinese tradition are still more remarkable. It is older. We have seen that some of its aspects go back to the Shang dynasty, and some of its most fundamental characteristics were firmly established by the beginning of the first millennium B.C.—a time for which the very existence of a city at Rome, not to mention a Roman tradition, cannot be demonstrated.[2] The Chinese, like the Romans, assimilated peoples of varying

---

1. Weber (*Essays in Sociology*, 176) expresses a somewhat similar idea: "a nation is a community of sentiment which would adequately manifest itself in a state of its own; hence, a nation is a community which normally tends to produce a state of its own."

2. *Cambridge Ancient History*, VII, 333–369. Heichelheim and Yeo (*The Roman People*, 48) say that "Rome has been inhabited for almost twenty-eight centuries."

backgrounds into their culture, and it appears that the Chinese assimilation may well (at least in the area known as "China proper") have
been more complete.[3] While there has been some break in the continuity of China as a political state, because of conquest, no other
national tradition has had so much continuity for so much of the time
during the last three thousand years.

The orthodox, literary tradition of China begins, as we have seen,
with certain Emperors assigned to a remote golden age of high antiquity. But there seems to be little doubt that the dynamic tradition,
the tradition that has moved men to action, begins with the Chou
dynasty. The legendary Emperors were perhaps such idealized para-
gons that it was difficult for ordinary mortals to think of emulating
them. Confucius praised three of them in the highest terms but indicated that he considered himself to be carrying on the tradition of
King Wen, the founder of the Chou dynasty. Confucius also said,
"Chou had the advantage of observing the two preceding dynasties.
How elegant is its culture! I follow Chou."[4]

The son of King Wen, the celebrated Duke of Chou, has been
credited by persistent tradition with creating, or at least recasting,
China's whole machinery of government, and originating many basic
aspects of its culture. In 196 B.C. the founding Emperor of the Han
dynasty named King Wen as the greatest of all Kings.[5] It would

3. The Romans did, of course, disseminate a remarkably homogeneous culture
over a very wide area. But it seems to be generally agreed that this culture was
chiefly confined to the cities, and to the aristocracy, having relatively little effect
upon the mass of the people. Jones (Later Roman Empire, II, 996) says that "in
large parts of the empire it was only a thin upper crust which was Latinised or
Hellenised." Furthermore, he observes (ibid., II, 1062), "the Roman Empire seems
never to have evoked any active patriotism from the vast majority of its citizens."
On the contrary, there was a good deal of evidence of anti-Roman feeling; see:
Cambridge Ancient History, X, 840–849.Rostovtzeff, Roman Empire, I, 116–118.

Obviously, Chinese culture, in any literary sense, did not extend to the masses
either, but there does not seem to be any evidence that the peasantry continued (as
happened in the Roman Empire) for a long period of time to speak another language
while the aristocrats spoke Chinese. There were of course "barbarian" peoples who
became assimilated to Chinese culture, but the indication would seem to be that
when this happened the Sinicization was not confined to the aristocracy. Chinese
were of course resentful of those above them, and sometimes of the national government, but there is little indication that many of them were anti-Chinese. Individuals and even groups did sometimes join with "barbarians," but for the most
part all Chinese, high and low, seem to have been very conscious and very proud of
being Chinese.

4. Analects, 3.14, 6.28, 8.18–21, 9.5, 12.22.6, 14.45, 15.4.

5. Han-shu, 1B.17b; Dubs, Han-shu, I, 130.

probably be generally agreed that for most practical purposes the Chinese tradition may be said to have begun with the Chou.[6]

AMONG the countless dynasties that have held sway in many lands, that of the Chou is one of the most remarkable. It is surely one of the longest. Chou Kings reigned—if they did not always rule—according to the traditional chronology, from 1122 to 256 B.C.[7] Even if we reduce this, as the most skeptical would do, by a century, the Chou continued to hold the throne far longer than any Egyptian dynasty and even exceeded the record set by the House of Hapsburg.[8] But longevity is the least of the Chou claims to fame. It is doubtful that any other nation of comparable consequence has had its basic character more deeply or more lastingly influenced under a single ruling house than did China under the Chou.

It is true of course that, since we know so little about China before Chou times, we cannot always distinguish between what the Chou contributed to China's cultural and governmental pattern and what may have been carried over from the past. But some elements of outstanding importance can clearly be traced to the Chou period.

It is well known, for instance, that the books known as the "Chinese classics" have played a dominant role. A very large part of China's huge literary production has consisted of books that comment on and discuss these works. They formed the core of the educational curriculum and the basis of the civil service examinations over a period of two thousand years. Fung Yu-lan calls the time from the second century B.C. to the twentieth century A.D. "the Period of Classical Learning." The subject matter of the classics was, in predominant measure, the history and culture of the Chou dynasty, and most of these books were written in Chou times.[9]

6. See for instance Ch'i, "Hsi-Chou Cheng-chih Ssu-hsiang," 36–40.

7. The date of the Chou conquest has been long and hotly debated. In addition to the traditional date of 1122 B.C., scholars have proposed 1111, 1050, 1027, and still others. This problem, and the reasons for which I—like some other scholars— find it best to continue to use the traditional chronology even though I am by no means sure it is correct, are discussed in Appendix B, pp. 487–492.

8. Wilson (*The Culture of Ancient Egypt*, 319–320) gives a chronological table listing 26 dynasties within a period of 2,575 years, an average of a little less than a century for each; none of these dynasties approaches the length of the Chou. The Hapsburgs ruled longest in Austria, from 1276 to 1918.

9. Fung, *A History of Chinese Philosophy*, II, 2. Portions of the classics traditionally attributed to earlier times were actually written during the Chou period; on the other hand, some materials attributed to Chou were actually written later.

The pattern of imperial government in China, as it existed for more than two thousand years up to the establishment of the Chinese Republic in 1912, has often been called "the Confucian state." The accuracy of this designation may be debated,[10] but there can be no question that China's government has been deeply influenced by Confucianism. Confucius lived, and Confucianism was given much of its form, under the Chou. Furthermore, almost every one of China's most famous philosophers lived in Chou times.

Some conceptions that are essential to the very core of the idea of the Chinese state and Chinese culture did not exist before the Chou dynasty, but have flourished from its inception to our own day. The last Chinese Emperor, dethroned in 1912, was still called "the Son of Heaven." Not only does this term not appear in the Shang inscriptions, but it is clear that Heaven, T'ien, was not a Shang but a Chou deity.[11]

The cornerstone of the ideology of the Chinese state is the conception of the Mandate of Heaven: the idea that the ruler of China holds a sacred trust from the highest deity which permits him to rule so long as he does so for the welfare of the people—but subject to the peril that if he fails in this trust, Heaven will appoint another to rebel and replace him. This was the keynote of the propaganda by which the Chou sought, ultimately with complete success, to reconcile those they had conquered to their rule; it became the basis of the constitution of the Chinese state. Each succeeding dynasty claimed to hold

10. China's traditional pattern of government was far more heavily influenced by ideologies other than Confucianism than is sometimes recognized. But most of these also had their inception in Chou times.

11. The principal Shang deity was called Ti 帝 or Shang Ti 上帝 . After the Chou conquest the Chou treated this Shang deity as being identical with their principal deity, T'ien 天 , much as the Romans identified the Greek Zeus with their Jupiter. There appears to be no certain instance of the appearance of the name T'ien in the Shang inscriptions. In Chinese history and tradition, however, it has been supposed that T'ien was revered as a deity by the Shang, and even earlier. Insofar as I am aware, the fact that T'ien apparently came into the Chinese tradition only with the Chou was first pointed out in a paper that I published in 1935 (Creel, "Shih T'ien"). This proposition is not accepted by all scholars, but I am not aware that anyone has offered any detailed proof to the contrary. Tung Tso-pin told me in 1948 that in his long experience with the Shang inscriptions he had seen no evidence that T'ien was a Shang deity, and in an article published that same year Ch'i Ssu-ho ("Hsi-Chou Cheng-chih Ssu-hsiang," 23) indicated his agreement with my conclusion. In a paper published in 1954, Ch'en Meng-chia ("Hsi-Chou Yin-jen," 93) said that "in the language of Yin 'T'ien' was called 'Ti'," which presumably means that T'ien—under that name at least—was not a Yin deity (Yin is an alternative name for Shang). This entire problem is discussed in Appendix C.

44

the Mandate of Heaven; when the last dynasty was overthrown in 1912, this was called "ending its Mandate." Homer H. Dubs writes that the doctrine of the Mandate of Heaven "has probably been responsible for the generally good character of Chinese rule. The teaching that 'Heaven's mandate is not constant' . . . was dinned into the ears of Chinese heir-apparents by their Confucian tutors and ministers, so that rulers were induced to attempt being models for the empire, for the sake of keeping themselves on the throne and of perpetuating their dynastic lines."[12] Ch'i Ssu-ho says that "the doctrine of the Mandate of Heaven is the most distinctive aspect of Chou thought, a point of fundamental difference from that of the Shang."[13]

Only during the earliest portion of the Chou dynasty—Western Chou, 1122–771 B.C.—was China relatively unified. The latter centuries of the dynasty were characterized by disunion that was at times virtually complete, a condition deplored by men of later times. The short-lived Ch'in dynasty, 221–207 B.C., united the country, but under a harsh rule that was repugnant to the Chinese spirit and has been almost universally deplored ever since.

Under the Han dynasties (206 B.C.–A.D. 220) the pattern of imperial government that would persist to our own century was given its distinctive form. Its administrative machinery was carried over almost intact from the Ch'in dynasty. This system of efficient and sometimes despotic centralized bureaucracy was the product of a long process of development that had its beginnings as far back as Western Chou if not even earlier. But in Han times its critics, who were legion, damned it as the creation of the detested Ch'in.

The Han Emperors, faced with the task of running a huge and complex empire, had to use the governmental machinery of Ch'in and a great many officials who had served under the Ch'in. But they also had to win the cooperation of their subjects and to convince them that the house of Han, despite its peasant origin, was legitimate. They were inevitably impelled to present themselves as the spiritual heirs of the Chou Kings. And they almost necessarily proclaimed their regime as a revival of the strong yet—according to tradition—benevolent rule of Western Chou times. This led, for instance, to the intense concentration on the study of the classics that began in Han times. It brought about the frequent references to early Chou rulers and practices that occur in the edicts of Han Emperors and the memorials written by their officials. As one example, the first memorial advocating the es-

12. Dubs, *Han-shu*, III, 103.
13. Ch'i, "Hsi-Chou Cheng-chih Ssu-hsiang," 23.

tablishment of the Imperial University cited chiefly, as precedent, the alleged diffusion of education in Western Chou times.[14]

This tendency reached a high point under Wang Mang, a brilliant minister who succeeded in taking over the throne from A.D. 8 to 23. He undertook to reestablish many practices of antiquity, and especially those of early Chou times. He was depicted as a latter-day Duke of Chou. Some of his institutions were directly and avowedly modeled after the work called the *Ritual of Chou*. This book, sometimes ascribed to the authorship of the Duke of Chou, has traditionally been considered a description of the governmental system of Western Chou times. The attempt by Wang Mang to found a new dynasty proved abortive; it ended with the rebellion in which he was killed.[15] Yet the practice of looking to early Chou, in matters of government, persisted. The brief span of Western Chou has probably been cited for precedents determining proper governmental practice more frequently than any other period in Chinese history.

If we are really to understand the way government developed in China, we must know what went on in the Chou dynasty. That, however, is extraordinarily difficult to do. The fact that we do not have many genuine records is only a part of the trouble. An even greater problem is the tremendous number of documents we do have that are supposed to date from various parts of the Chou period, but which in fact were fabricated much later than the date to which they are attributed. These spurious materials—unless we can succeed in weeding them out—play havoc with any attempt to get at the real situation.

The motives of those who have forged texts, or sometimes altered good texts to serve their purposes, have commonly been pious and no doubt laudable. Because of the Chinese reverence for tradition and the veneration with which the earlier portions of the Chou period in particular were regarded, the most effective way to win acceptance for a doctrine or a practice was to promulgate a document representing that it was current in Chou times. This began very early. Mencius, around

---

14. *Han-shu*, 56.9b–13b. Emperor Wu did not act on this suggestion, which was made by Tung Chung-shu, whose criticisms of his rule were very unwelcome. The memorial that immediately led to the establishment of the Imperial University was written by Kung-Sun Hung; it cites as precedent educational institutions alleged to have existed under the Hsia, Shang, and Chou dynasties. See *Shih-chi*, 121.9; Watson, *Records*, II, 399.

15. *Han-shu*, 12, 99A–C. Dubs, *Han-shu*, III, 44–474.

300 B.C., denounced a book circulating in his day as a forgery attributed to the beginning of Chou.[16] But the flood of forgeries continued to swell. Occasionally forgers were unmasked and put to death in peculiarly unpleasant ways, but to no effect. The traditional history came to be based, in very considerable measure, on documents that are rather obviously either false or considerably altered from their original form.

THE Chou dynasty is commonly, and logically, divided into three periods. The earliest, the Western Chou,[17] extends from the time of the Chou conquest in 1122 B.C. to 771 B.C. The next, from 770 to 464 B.C., is the Spring and Autumn period.[18] The last, from 463 to 222 B.C., is the Warring States period.[19]

It would be reasonable to suppose that the latest of these periods would be the one about which we have the most complete and the most reliable information, but this is by no means the case. The reason is implied by its very name: Warring States. This was a time of disunion, marked by increasing rivalry, diplomatic intrigue, and bloody warfare. Under these pressures the religion, the mores, and the politi-

---

16. *Mencius*, 7(2).3.

17. So called because during this time the principal Chou capital was located to the west, in what is the modern Shensi province. The capital was then moved east, to the region of the modern Loyang; for this reason the period from 770 to 256 B.C. is called Eastern Chou. It should be noted that Eastern Chou ends earlier than the termination (in 222 B.C.) of the Warring States period, because the line of the Chou Kings came to an end before Ch'in had completely conquered the Empire.

18. This period derives its name from the *Ch'un-ch'iu* 春秋, the *Spring and Autumn Annals*, traditionally though erroneously believed to have been edited by Confucius. This extremely bare chronicle records occurrences in the period from 722 to 481 B.C., and that, strictly speaking, is the Spring and Autumn period. But in fact our knowledge of this period comes almost completely from the work known as the *Tso-chuan*, which is in part, but only in part, a commentary on the *Ch'un-ch'iu* (on the nature of the *Tso-chuan* see pp. 475–477). And while the *Tso-chuan* also begins with entries for the year 722 B.C., it contains much information relating to previous years. Furthermore, if we begin the Spring and Autumn period with 722, we are left with a hiatus of forty-nine years between it and the end of Western Chou. I therefore arbitrarily begin the Spring and Autumn period with 770 B.C. At the other end of the period, while the *Ch'un-ch'iu* ends with 481 B.C., the latest entry in the *Tso-chuan* is for 464. I therefore, like some other scholars, arbitrarily place the end of the Spring and Autumn period in 464 B.C.

19. Various dates are given for the beginning of the Warring States period. Like some other scholars, I begin it with 463 B.C., the year following that of the last entry in the *Tso-chuan*. Its end is determined by the fact that Ch'in completed its conquest of all the states and began its dynasty in 221 B.C., making the preceding year the last of the Warring States period.

cal procedures of earlier times deteriorated and in large measure collapsed. It was also a period of important cultural, economic, and political creativity, but in later times this was almost forgotten. From the second century B.C. almost to our own day the Warring States period has commonly been dismissed as an era of great wickedness that should not even be studied. It was in contrast to this age in particular that the men of later times looked upon the Western Chou as a period of unity, peace, order, and benevolent government.

The middle portion of the Chou dynasty, the Spring and Autumn period, was deprecated as a time of violence and growing disunion, but it was not considered wholly bad. After all, Confucius lived during its closing years. It is in part, no doubt, for this reason that it has been studied intensively. And we have for this time the very remarkable historical document known as the *Tso-chuan*. It is, in the first place, voluminous: its text includes some 180,000 Chinese characters, and since literary Chinese is very terse this would have to be multiplied several times to give an equivalent in English.[20] This work provides an amazing window through which we can see, sometimes with remarkable clarity, the China of more than twenty-five centuries ago. It gives us detailed information, not only on political and military history, but also on cultural institutions, social usages, and sometimes even on the thoughts and the love life of men and women of that distant time. It cannot always be believed; certainly there are interpolations and distortions. But almost everyone who works much with this text seems to become increasingly convinced of the basic historicity of a large proportion of its content. Ch'i Ssu-ho writes that the *Tso-chuan* "is the single thread on which the significant details of the development of the Chinese people during the Ch'un-ch'iu [Spring and Autumn] period are hung. But for the existence of this important source, the whole period would have become a dark and uninteresting one."[21]

For the first segment of the Chou dynasty, Western Chou, we have, alas, no work that is in any sense comparable. Our sources that stand up under criticism as genuine are few and give us only fragmentary data. But there are, as has been said, a multiplicity of documents that prove, under test, to be either forgeries or sadly altered from what must have been their original condition. Some of them tantalize us.

20. Ch'i Ssu-ho, in "Professor Hung on the *Ch'un-ch'iu*," 52, 61, quotes a calculation that "the *Tso-chuan* including the text of the *Ch'un-ch'iu* comprises 196,845 characters," and says that "the present texts [of the *Ch'un-ch'iu*] all contain slightly more than sixteen thousand words."

21. Ibid., 53. Concerning the nature and the authenticity of the *Tso-chuan*, see pp. 475–477.

There is, for instance, the work called the *Ritual of Chou* (also, and more descriptively, called the *Offices of Chou*). As has been mentioned, it has traditionally been ascribed to the authorship of the Duke of Chou and believed to be a description of the Western Chou government. As Max Weber has said, it "portrays a very schematic state organization under the rational leadership of officials."[22] It gives us not only the organizational scheme, but also the titles of a very great number of officials with precise data as to their duties. Its size alone is almost staggering; surely few documents on government produced anywhere before modern times can compare with this one in its combination of comprehensive organizational scope and minute detail. Weber points out that its scheme is even more rational than that of the highly organized bureaucracy of Han times.[23] It is of course too good to be true. Careful analysis has shown that the *Ritual of Chou* cannot have been written, in the form in which we now have it, before the Warring States period.[24]

We do, however, have some valid materials from Western Chou time—few, but for that reason all the more precious. They are analyzed, together with other documents that prove under scrutiny to be less reliable, in Appendix A. It may be useful briefly to mention here the materials on which this volume will be based.

The first, according to the traditional Chinese order of the classics, is the original text of the *Book of Changes*.[25] It is in effect a fortune-teller's manual, which gives only a small amount of random data concerning statecraft.

The next is the *Documents*. In this work we have a few writings, chiefly from very early in Western Chou, that were preserved in the Chou archives and have come down to us. These are intermixed, however, with a large number of works written at a date later than that to which they are attributed, and with many outright forgeries. Sifting the wheat from the chaff has occupied a great many scholars over many centuries. As sources of Western Chou date, I accept only twelve of the writings in the *Documents*.[26] This eliminates some that are

22. Weber, *Religion of China*, 37.
23. Ibid., 263–264.
24. See pp. 478–480. It is quite clear, however, that the *Ritual of Chou* was in part written on the basis of actual knowledge of Western Chou government. Thus while it can never be used as a source to determine what that government was, it is sometimes very useful in providing elucidation of points that are clearly evidenced in the authentic sources.
25. The *I-ching* 易經. The original text does not, of course, include the commentaries commonly known as the "Ten Wings." On this work see pp. 444–447.
26. See pp. 447–463.

rather generally accepted even by critical scholars, but in my opinion it is preferable to base our research only on data that are, insofar as that is possible, beyond serious question. The term "the Western Chou *Documents*," as used in this volume, is to be understood to refer to these twelve writings only.

The third of the classics is the *Poetry*. The poems in this anthology range all the way from light-hearted love songs, through laments at the hardships of war and the oppression of corrupt officials, to solemn sacrificial odes used in the royal temples. More than any other book, it gives us a view of the life of the time. While there is much difference of opinion as to the date of individual poems, they are accepted as having been composed between the approximate dates of 1122 and 600 B.C.[27] Thus they are all either of Western Chou date, or from a time only a little later.

Finally there are the inscriptions on bronze vessels cast in Western Chou times. They are at once the most important, the most difficult, and the most neglected documents we have from Western Chou. Some of these inscriptions are quite long, longer than some of the writings preserved in the *Documents*.[28] They give us information on many aspects of the life of the time and on many matters important for this investigation: appointments to office, enfeoffments, wars, intrigues within the government, relations with barbarians, and so on and so on.

The inscriptions are very difficult—and at some points impossible—to read. The interpretation of the content of particular inscriptions, by different scholars, sometimes varies widely. Anyone who uses them does so at his peril, with the danger—perhaps the certainty—of making mistakes. Yet they are so important that no comprehensive study of this subject could leave them out of account. Thousands of Western Chou bronze inscriptions are known, but most of these are brief and uninformative. To use all of them would not be feasible.[29] I am using a corpus of one hundred eighty-four inscriptions; it includes, I believe,

27. See p. 463. The *Shih* 詩 or *Shih-ching* 詩經 is often called *The Book of Poetry* or *The Book of Odes*.

28. See Creel, "Bronze Inscriptions," 338. Not all of the sections of the *Documents* that I listed as examples in the right-hand column are ones that I believe (or believed when I wrote the article) to date from Western Chou times, but some of the longest are, including the "Wen Hou chih Ming" and the "Tzu Ts'ai." Many more inscriptions have been discovered since that article was written, but not a great many extremely long ones.

29. This is true, in particular, because the very brief inscriptions have commonly been studied very little or not at all, which means that in their case the danger of including forged inscriptions, and of misinterpreting the content, is much greater than if one uses the longer inscriptions on which a great deal of research has been done.

the great bulk of the published inscriptions that contain significant evidence concerning Western Chou government. Every one of these inscriptions has been carefully studied by at least one scholar—in some cases by many scholars—of high competence in the field. These scholars have studied each inscription against the background of the whole body of the known material and have accepted each as genuine. This is not an absolute guarantee that every one of these inscriptions is genuine—there can be no such guarantee, about anything. But I believe it is improbable that many forged inscriptions occur in this corpus. And by using a relatively large number of inscriptions and consulting them as a group on each question of major importance, I have tried to insure that even a false inscription or two, and a certain amount of misinterpretation in specific cases, would be averaged out so that the total result would not be invalidated.

For the sake of brevity I shall not constantly speak of "the Western Chou bronze inscriptions of my corpus." If no other qualification is made, it is to be understood that mention of "Western Chou bronze inscriptions" or even of "the inscriptions" refers, not to all of the known inscriptions, but only to this selected corpus of one hundred eighty-four.

Some of these inscriptions have been known for a thousand years; others came out of the ground very recently. Some finds have been spectacular. A single cache (possibly buried in Chou times) discovered in Shensi province in 1961 contained fifty-three Western Chou bronzes; eleven of these were inscribed, and the inscriptions have added significantly to our knowledge.[30] Not only a flood of discoveries, but a great surge of scholarly endeavor, painstaking and often inspired, has opened up our understanding of these materials in the most recent decades as never before.[31]

When the new knowledge now made possible by the bronze inscriptions is used to supplement and illuminate the literature that has been handed down to us, a new Western Chou dynasty is revealed. It differs in significant and sometimes fundamental respects both from the account of traditional Chinese history and from the conception of Western Chou that was current, even among highly critical scholars, during the first half of the twentieth century.

TRADITIONAL Chinese history takes at face value the legends concerning Western Chou: The Chou rulers were given the Mandate of

---

30. Kuo, "Ch'ang-an Ming-wen."
31. For further discussion of the bronze inscriptions see pp. 464–475.

Heaven to rescue the suffering people from the misrule of the wicked last King of Shang. Because the Chou were virtuous, the Shang armies scarcely opposed them; there was general rejoicing when the dissolute Shang were overthrown. The Chou then sent out expeditions in various directions and, for the most part, their benevolent and civilizing rule was welcomed. The Shang, in league with barbarians, did make one great final revolt a few years after the conquest. But this was overcome, and thereafter, with slight exceptions, all was peaceful until, toward the end of Western Chou, its Kings declined in virtue, with the result that there was rebellion and this phase of the dynasty was brought to a close.

The Chou Kings—according to the tradition—kept under their direct rule only a limited royal domain, while enfeoffing feudal lords to rule over the rest of the country. Many of these lords were close relatives of the King, members of the royal family. Others were rulers of local areas who had submitted and been permitted to continue to rule as vassals of the Chou. The Kings established a highly organized government, described in the *Ritual of Chou*, which exercised power over the whole country but did not interfere in the internal affairs of the feudal states. The King had six armies, while a single large feudal state might have as many as three; this would appear to mean that the feudal lords, collectively, held the preponderance of military power.[32] But the power of the King did not depend primarily on military might, but on his relationship (by blood and by marriage) with his vassals and, above all, on the prestige of his ancestry and his virtue.

In this way, according to the tradition, the Western Chou rulers established their sway, almost from the beginning of the dynasty, over a vast area extending from a point west of their original home in modern Shensi province eastward to the Yellow Sea, northward to a point above the modern Peking, and southward to a point well below the Yangtze river. Although there were occasional disturbances by unruly barbarians on the borders, the Chou Kings kept the entire country under the firm control of their benevolent rule until the time arrived when their virtue lapsed and their dynasty came, as all dynasties must eventually come, to an end.

In the twentieth century, critical scholars, both Chinese and Western, have reacted against this traditional view of history. There has been rather general agreement that the conditions of the Western Chou period must have made it impossible to maintain a government having

32. *Chou-li*, 28.2a; Biot, *Tcheou-li*, II, 142. *Tso*, 462::466 (Hsiang 14).

any considerable degree of centralization.[33] Henri Maspero went so far as to say that "in China at that time . . . the establishment of a real state was still impossible."[34] Western Chou was not, in the opinion of most critical scholars, a unified empire, but rather a group of largely independent feudal lords under the suzerainty of the King. Royal authority was slight beyond the boundaries of the royal domain, and the power of the King depended largely on his ability to retain the goodwill of the feudal lords. Nothing resembling the governmental machinery described in the *Ritual of Chou*, most critical scholars have agreed, could have existed in that early day. There were no law codes; anything that could properly be called money was either nonexistent or little used; and there was little trade. In these circumstances any considerable control by the King over a very large territory could hardly have been feasible.

Scholars never wholly agree, and of course there have been various opinions on specific points among critical scholars. Opinion has tended to the view, however, that the original conquests could not have extended so far as the tradition alleges, that the Western Chou state was always smaller than it has been represented as being, and that some of the more distant territories that it did encompass were late additions made after a gradual process of consolidation.

I MYSELF have participated, with the inevitable personal variations, in what has just been described as the critical view of Western Chou. But in the light of the new discoveries, as I look back with the wisdom of hindsight, it seems to me that there were certain flaws in both the traditional and the critical positions that we failed to note, but that ought to have been obvious.

Undoubtedly it is true that conditions for the formation of a unified empire were far from ideal. Yet by all accounts, for three and one-half centuries—or two and one-half if we shorten the period with the skeptics—the Chou did maintain a remarkable degree of authority over a very large territory. The *Poetry*, a source of considerable validity, indicates this. For thousands of years the Western Chou period has been regarded as the prime concrete example of a government that maintained firm and stable rule over its territories without undue harshness. It had this reputation not only in later times, but immediately after the end of Western Chou, and not only within the sphere of Chi-

33. I myself took this position as recently as 1949; see Creel, *Confucius*, 146::157.
34. Maspero, *La Chine antique*, 88.

nese culture, but even beyond it.[35] We have little basis on which to deny that this reputation was, to some extent at least, deserved.

How, then, did the Western Chou Kings maintain themselves? If we deny that they had any machinery of centralized control, shall we agree with the traditionalists that they did it by their virtue? Both traditional and critical scholars have tended to believe that the power of the Kings was chiefly limited to a royal domain, and that they did not have at their disposal military power that would have enabled them to quell any major revolt by their vassals. If so, we must believe that a regime that had no machinery of centralized government and no decisive military power was able, with little serious challenge, to maintain itself in authority over a very large area for a period of some three centuries. The merest glance at what happened in feudal Europe, and in later Chinese history whenever the central power was weak, tells us that this is, to say the least, improbable.

THE new knowledge that has become available to us from recently discovered inscriptions, and from the most recent study of all the bronze inscriptions, does not support the view of the most credulous traditional scholars concerning the size of the Western Chou territories. It seems to be clear that the large territories in the Yangtze valley claimed for Western Chou by tradition remained, in fact, beyond its control. But on the other hand some achievements that have seemed incredible now present themselves as solid fact. The early planting of a Chou state in the far northeast, for instance, in a territory almost surrounded by fierce barbarians, has been authenticated by the finding of a large number of inscribed bronzes in this area; and this region appears to have been held, despite all difficulties.[36]

Of the many surprising facts that emerge from study of the new materials, perhaps the most solidly evidenced is the military power of the Western Chou Kings. It was clearly paramount. Serious trouble was normally dealt with by royal armies, dispatched by and often under the personal command of the King. When barbarian dissidence or incursion reached major proportions, it was opposed, not by the local armies of feudal lords, but primarily by royal troops. This is, in fact, the picture that also emerges from careful study of the *Poetry*. But the inscriptions give us more information, and it is quite specific. The King had—contrary to what has commonly been believed—standing armies, at least fourteen of them. They were stationed in

35. For the attitude of rulers and others in the great southern state of Ch'u toward Western Chou, see pp. 220–221.

36. See pp. 358–361.

54

garrisons and dispatched to any point at the King's pleasure. There were also royal guard posts and royal troops charged with patrolling and protecting principal roads. Neither the bronze inscriptions nor the *Poetry* indicates that there was any limit to the sphere within which the King could, and on occasion did, deploy his military power. And this situation appears to have remained essentially similar from the beginning of Western Chou to a late date in that period.

The predominant military power of the Western Chou rulers is generally recognized by scholars familiar with the new materials. It carries important implications that have as yet been little explored. A very significant one is financial. The maintenance of a competent military establishment over a large territory for a long period of time requires economic resources. Far-flung garrisons could hardly— especially in a time when agricultural techniques were not greatly advanced—merely "live off the country"; especially they could not do so without engendering a degree of resentment of which there seems to be no indication in the sources. To maintain their military establishment, if nothing else, the Kings must have had a system for the collection of revenues and for the disbursement of resources more highly developed than anything that has been supposed—by critical scholars—to have existed at the time. Whether "money" was or was not widely used, some system of credit would seem to have been necessary.

Another fact emerges from the sources. While the military power of the King was great, there seems to be no indication anywhere that his authority was maintained by naked military oppression. On the contrary, all of our sources tend to indicate that it was not. We can hardly suppose that, as the tradition would have us believe, general harmony was maintained simply by the reign of virtue. It seems clear that the King and his officers must have had a degree of control over the feudal states beyond that which has generally been supposed to have existed. There must, that is, have been a royal government having some general jurisdiction—not of course the incredibly complex administrative hierarchy depicted by the *Ritual of Chou*, but a royal government having a certain degree of sophistication and effectiveness.

Another example of the many implications of the inscriptions concerns justice. In any such far-flung state as that created by Western Chou, differences of opinion must arise over obligations, taxes, conflicting individual interests, and many other problems. If dangerous resentments are not to persist, there must be a method of adjudicating such disputes in an orderly and socially satisfactory manner. There must be some kind of effective legal system.

THE remainder of this volume will be principally devoted to asking questions of the sources. Who were these Chou people, and how did they manage to establish their remarkable regime? What indication do we have of a well-organized royal government? Was there a financial system, and a legal system?

On these and a host of other questions that will be asked, our evidence is far less than could be wished. On some points it is so scanty that we must simply say that we do not know. There are, moreover, few important matters on which our evidence is so complete that utter certainty is justified.

The picture of Western Chou that is presented here could not have been arrived at without the painstaking and brilliant work of many scholars in the field. I have not, however, adopted the conclusion of any authority unless it appeared to me to square with the evidence as we have it. My interpretation of Western Chou is based primarily on many years of study of the sources.[37] Some of my conclusions on matters of fundamental importance are somewhat—and sometimes sharply—divergent from those of other scholars as they are known to me. Certainly our evidence on Western Chou is incomplete, and it is constantly being added to. Undoubtedly it will be possible, at some time in the future, to see this period much more clearly than can be done today. On some points it may never be possible to arrive at certainty. The view that is presented here must be regarded as to some degree hypothetical. But I hope that—in some respects at least—it may represent an advance in the direction of the truth.

---

37. By this I do not mean that I have paid no attention to tradition, or to accounts contained in works written later than Western Chou; that would be foolish. But I have not used these later materials in the way that some scholars, both Chinese and Western, tend to do. Even critical scholars sometimes begin by stating flatly that such works as the *Ritual of Chou* are late and unreliable. They then present a picture of Western Chou in which the framework is drawn from works like the *Ritual of Chou*, and embellish this framework with details drawn from the early sources.

I have tried to follow a different procedure. In each particular regard I have asked, first, what the situation would appear to be solely on the basis of the sources, disregarding the tradition and later works altogether. Having determined this—insofar as is possible—I have then compared the picture drawn from the sources with the traditions and the late accounts. Where the divergence is great, I have tended to disregard the later materials. But very often one finds that conceptions that grow out of the sources and differ markedly from the traditional view find surprising corroboration in later materials. This is true, for instance, of the *Ritual of Chou*, which sometimes complements the testimony of the bronze inscriptions in such manner as to indicate that the author or authors of this work must have had some valid data from the Western Chou period at their disposal.

CHAPTER

4

The Rise of the Chou

AN event so dramatic as the rise of the Chou, and so fateful in its influence upon all of China's history, inevitably attracted to itself a whole cycle of legend. This was set down, as it existed around 100 B.C., by Ssu-Ma Ch'ien in the *Historical Records*. It related, for instance, that the Earl of the West—that is, King Wen—was a paragon whose virtue aroused the suspicion and jealousy of the wicked Shang King, who imprisoned him. Wen's admirers ransomed him with rich gifts, and he continued to practice virtue in secret. After his death, his son, King Wu, attacked Shang with only fifty thousand men. The Shang King sent seven hundred thousand to oppose them, but his own troops were so revolted by his cruelties and oppression that they had no heart to fight, and only wished King Wu to triumph quickly.[1]

There is very little of this kind of absurdity in the Chou traditions as we find them recorded in the Western Chou sources. There is some supernatural element, particularly in connection with the remote ancestor of the Chou Kings, but even this is illuminating in that it indicates the character of the people who developed the legends. We are almost wholly dependent upon tradition for the history of the Chou before they conquered the Shang. There are a few references in the Shang inscriptions that are said to relate to them, but I am not aware that we have any contemporary literary works, any archeological sites, or any bronze inscriptions that can be certainly linked with the Chou before the reign of King Wu.[2]

1. *Shih-chi*, 4.2–27; *Mémoires historiques*, I, 209–237.
2. There is a tradition that King Wen had something to do with the original text of the *Book of Changes* (*Shih-chi*, 4.15; *Mémoires historiques*, I, 221). And that text does mention a few events prior to the Chou conquest, but it tells us virtually nothing of Chou history at that time. Chang Kwang-chih (*Archaeology of Ancient China*, 258–263) discusses sites that some date as Chou before the conquest of Shang.

The high ancestor of the Chou house was Hou Chi 后稷 , literally "Ruler Millet." Quite evidently he was, like some other reputed founders of prominent Chinese families, a spirit. He was conceived, the *Poetry* tells us, when his mother stepped in a footprint of the deity Ti. Many marvels are related of him and of his prowess in agriculture. He is celebrated as the giver of grain to the people, the founder of agricultural sacrifices, and himself the object of sacrifices for harvests.[3] He was at the same time a culture hero, an agricultural deity, and the legendary ancestor of the Chou house.

It is impossible to assign dates, with even relative precision, to any of the Chou ancestors before the conquest. Furthermore, the early sources hardly give us even the genealogical sequence for the more remote period, though this is supplied—with full details but doubtful accuracy—by later writers. One poem tells of Duke Liu, who is said to have been the great-grandson of Hou Chi. It is related that he laid out and built a capital for the Chou, and went so far in organizing the government as to institute a system of taxation. But this account stands alone and may well be a retrospective fabrication; it is by no means certain that the Chou had reached, at such an early time, such an advanced level of urban culture as this implies.[4]

The earliest Chou ancestor who seems entirely plausible, as a real person, is the "Ancient Duke" Tan-fu, who is also known as King T'ai.[5] The *Historical Records* lists him, with what accuracy is uncertain, as the descendant of Hou Chi in the twelfth generation.[6] The *Poetry* says that King T'ai moved his people and built for them a new city at the foot of Mount Ch'i, some eighty miles west of the modern Sian.[7] It was located on the plain of Chou, from which the Chou

3. *Shih*, 200–202, 224, 243–244, 259–260.

4. *Shih*, 207–208. This poem conflicts with another (*Shih*, 189) which says that up to the time of the "Ancient Duke" Tan-fu, clearly later than Duke Liu, the Chou people "did not yet have houses."

5. The name Ku Kung Tan-fu 古公亶父 has been the subject of some discussion. It is argued that "Ku Kung," rather than meaning "Ancient Duke," meant "Duke of Ku," a name derived from that of the Ku 古 river; see Ch'en, *Yin Tz'u Tsung-shu*, 292. Much embarrassment has been caused by the fact that the last three heads of the Chou house *before* the conquest of Shang are called *Wang* 王 , "Kings." According to orthodox Chinese scholarly doctrine, there could not properly be more than one *Wang* at a time, and the use of this title by Chou leaders before the conquest would have constituted a grave usurpation. It has sometimes been argued that these leaders were not called *Wang* while they were alive, but were posthumously honored with this title after the conquest. In fact, however, it is clear that many early rulers other than the Shang and Chou Kings were called *Wang*; see below, pp. 215–216.

6. *Shih-chi*, 4.4–6; *Mémoires historiques*, I, 211–213.

7. *Shih*, 189–190. In fact this poem does not call him King T'ai, but the

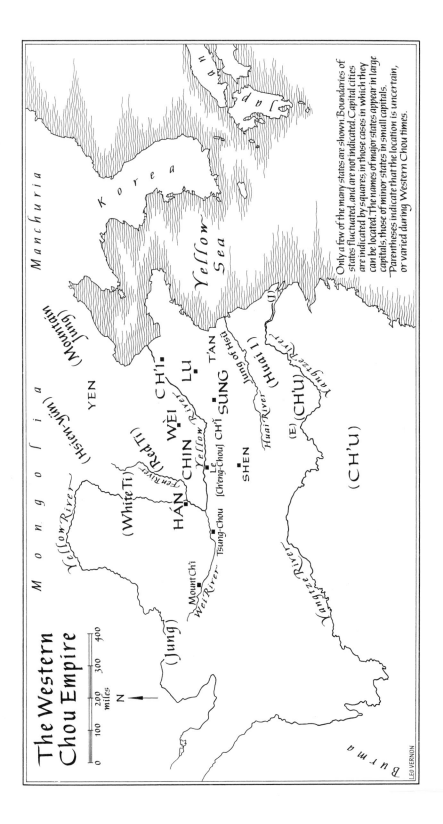

The Western Chou Empire

Manchuria

Mongolia

Korea

Yellow Sea

Japan

Burma

Yellow River

(Jung)

(White Ti)

(Hsien-yün)

(Red Ti)

YEN

Mountain (Jung)

Wei River

Mount Chi

Tsung-Chou

Fen River

HÁN

CHIN

WÈI

CH'I

Lo [Cheng-Chou]

Yellow River

CH'I

LU

TAN

SUNG

SHEN

Jung of Hsü

Huai River

(Huai I)

(I)

(E) (CH'U)

Yangtze River

Yangtze River

(CH'U)

N

0 100 200 300 400
miles

Only a few of the many states are shown. Boundaries of
states fluctuated, and are not indicated. Capital cities
are indicated by squares, in those cases in which they
can be located. The names of major states appear in large
capitals, those of minor states in small capitals.
Parentheses indicate that the location is uncertain,
or varied during Western Chou times.

LEO VERNON

people are said to have taken the name by which they would hence-forth be known.[8]

The philosopher Mencius described this removal of the Chou people as a response to the pressure of surrounding tribes. He related that King T'ai had first sought to appease them with gifts, but that when they continued to harass him, he moved away rather than subject his people to further danger.[9] This seems to be remarkably meek conduct for a people soon to carry out one of the great conquests of history. Since Mencius was the most famous Confucian after Confucius, one might conjecture that he was merely attributing to an eminent figure of early history the pacifistic sentiments that came to characterize much of Confucianism.

Since Mencius flourished around 300 b.c., we cannot attach great weight to his account, as history. Yet it is a fact that, although the Chou gained and held control of China by a series of remarkable military accomplishments, these receive very little emphasis in the early traditions. We have seen that the high ancestor, Hou Chi, was an agricultural culture hero and an agricultural deity. And while there is some mention of war in connection with later Chou ancestors, they are depicted as men chiefly concerned with such activities as building, administration, and the framing of long-range plans.

FROM ancient to modern times the Chinese attitude toward people not Chinese in culture—"barbarians"—has commonly been one of contempt, sometimes tinged with fear. It is surprising then to see the early Chou, so revered in the tradition, called barbarians. Yet even Mencius, who idealized King Wen, called him "a man of the western barbarians," and the *Bamboo Books* says that the conqueror, King Wu, "led the lords of the western barbarians to attack Yin."[10] (Yin is an alternative name for the Shang dynasty; the two are used interchangeably.)

It must be noted that, while the Chinese have disparaged bar-

---

Ancient Duke Tan-fu; nevertheless all traditions seem to identify the two. Reference to "Chou Chiang" in *Shih,* 192, may tend to support the identification, though this is not certain evidence. *Mencius,* 1(2).5.5, treats King T'ai and the Ancient Duke Tan-fu as being the same person.

8. This is the explanation of Ch'i Ssu-ho, in "Hsi-Chou Ti-li K'ao," 79. According to another theory the original place named Chou was an area in southwestern Shansi, at which the people had lived earlier and from which they derived their name; see Ch'en, *Yin Tz'u Tsung-shu,* 292.

9. *Mencius,* 1(2).15.1.

10. Ibid., 4(2).1. Wang, *Ku Chu-shu,* 6b.

barians, they have been singularly hospitable both to individuals and to groups that have adopted Chinese culture. And at times they seem to have had a certain admiration, perhaps unwilling, for the rude force of these peoples of simpler customs. Arthur Waley points out that there was even, on the part of Confucius and others, "a certain idealization of the 'noble savage.' "[11]

There are many indications that the Chou were originally one among many groups that were not culturally "Chinese," living to the west of the area that was firmly under Shang control. They were evidently related to other such groups, and probably not much different from them in culture.[12] (As to whether they were or were not different from the Shang in physical type, we seem to have no information; at any rate the early sources do not mention such differences.) A member of the Chou ruling house complained that, even after they had been conquered, the Shang still dared to look down on the Chou as being "rustic," without culture.[13]

The process of the Sinicization of the Chou, their partial assimilation to Shang culture, was apparently under way in the time of King Ta'i. In his early days, according to the *Poetry*, the Chou "did not yet have houses," but he laid out a walled city, building with the same technique of "pounded earth" by which Shang structures that have been excavated were erected.[14]

Since King T'ai was the great-grandfather of King Wu, he can hardly have flourished much more than a century before the conquest. Our evidence is hardly adequate to enable us to decide whether, in fact, the Chou did in so short a period develop from a relatively simple tribe to a people able not only to conquer the Shang territories but also to organize and administer them. But in any case their rise was rapid. It may seem incredibly so, but there is an instructive parallel in the history of the Normans.

If we did not have such complete evidence for the Norman achievement, we would probably consider it legendary. Like the Chou, the Vikings began as people with a relatively simple culture and were considered barbarians by those they attacked. They plundered and

11. Waley, *Analects*, 108, n. 1. Creel, *Confucius*, 128::138.

12. See for instance Fu, "Chiang Yüan." The *Tso-chuan* indicates that the surname of the Chou house, Chi 女乚 , occurred among the Jung barbarians and that those bearing it were considered to be of the same stock as the Chou house, so that marriage with them was incestuous; see *Tso*, 113::114 (Chuang 28), 185::187 (Hsi 23).

13. *Shu*, 37. This section of the *Documents*, the "Ta Kao," is evidently by either King Ch'eng or the Duke of Chou.

14. *Shih*, 189–190. Creel, *Studies*, 177–182.

destroyed in Europe for a century before a group of them settled down in Normandy shortly after 900. Yet by 1066 Normandy "was far better organized internally than were other parts of France, and was governed under a system which really did impose restraints, both on feudal turbulence and on ecclesiastical pretensions." After they conquered England, the Normans not only created there a feudal regime with an unusual degree of stability and centralized control, but also gave England a national unity that was rare if not unknown elsewhere in Europe.[15]

The Normans—like the Chou before them—owed much to what they learned from the political practices of their more cultivated neighbors. But it is no accident that Normans proved themselves, in Normandy, in England, and in Sicily, masters of administration superior to the heirs of Rome and Charlemagne. The Viking heritage was not only one of raiding and pillage. In their homeland the Vikings had a genius for law; our very word "law" does not come from Latin, but from Scandinavian. They were great organizers, and their history includes many Kings who reigned long and effectively. Some of their political practices still survive, in various parts of Britain, from a time even earlier than the Norman conquest.[16]

Axel Olrik mentions, among the indispensable qualities that made possible the success of the Vikings, the "courage to venture forth" and the "ability to make far-reaching plans."[17] The Chou traditions attribute these same qualities to their leaders before the conquest. King T'ai is credited with beginning the policy of aggression against the Shang, so that his great-grandson, who actually conquered Shang, is said to have "continued the work of King T'ai."[18] And of all the many virtues for which King Wen is praised, one of the most emphasized is his ability to make long-range plans.

THE solid Chou tradition, giving us something more than sporadic and doubtful references, begins with King T'ai. And there are many indications that it was in his time that there began the rise of the Chou as a people conscious that they had a special identity, and even a destiny.[19] Some traditions begin still later, with the son of King T'ai,

15. *Cambridge Medieval History*, V, 483; III, 483.
16. Ibid., III, 329, 333–338; V, 485–486. Olrik, *Viking Civilization*, 97–99, 105.
17. Olrik, *Viking Civilization*, 97.
18. *Shih*, 259.
19. *Shih*, 189, begins by saying "when the people [presumably the Chou] were first born," and the Ancient Duke Tan-fu, i.e., King T'ai, is the first leader

King Chi.[20] In the *Poetry*, however, King Chi is extolled only for his "virtue" and for his harmony with his brothers.[21] His greatest claim to fame, in Chinese history, has been the fact that he was the father of King Wen.

The history of the relations between the Shang and Chou peoples before the conquest is by no means clear.[22] Some scholars deduce from the Shang inscriptions that at the time of the Shang King Wu Ting (1324–1266 B.C.) the Chou and the Shang were enemies, but that the Chou were eventually subdued; the Chou ruler was then enfeoffed by the Shang King, who married a Chou princess.[23] In fact, however, this is far from certain.

Orthodox Chinese history represents King Wen—known as the Earl of the West—as a completely loyal vassal of the Shang King. But in the time of his son King Wu, the wickedness of the Shang ruler became so outrageous that it was no longer possible to refrain from carrying out "the punishment of Heaven": killing the King and extinguishing his dynasty.[24] This version is, of course, completely in accord with the propaganda that the Chou promulgated to justify their conquest and mollify the conquered. But it is contradicted by their own traditions as they are preserved in the *Poetry*.

The plan to conquer the Shang is attributed to an early origin in a poem written in the state of Lu, whose rulers were descended from the Duke of Chou and thus from the Chou royal house.

---

that it mentions. *Shih*, 259, describes the birth and accomplishments of Hou Chi and then says: "Hou Chi's *sun* 孫 was King T'ai." *Sun* normally means "grandson," but here it is supposed to mean merely "descendant." If we accept this reading, the passage says: "Hou Chi's descendant was King T'ai. He dwelt on the south of Mount Ch'i. He was the first to clip [presumably meaning to take territory from] the Shang."

20. *Shih*, 194, says that the deity "Ti made a state. . . . It began with Earl T'ai and King Chi." Earl T'ai was the elder brother of King Chi; according to tradition he renounced his title to the throne. The genuine *Bamboo Books* first mentions the Chou in the time of King Chi; see Wang, *Ku Chu-shu*, 6a.

21. *Shih*, 188, 194. In the current text the latter poem also attributes numerous other virtues to "King Chi," but Karlgren has shown that older texts read "King Wen" at this point and that "King Chi" is clearly a scribal error; see Karlgren, "Glosses on the Ta Ya and Sung Odes," 42. However, the genuine *Bamboo Books* depicts King Chi as a redoubtable warrior; see Wang, *Ku Chu-shu*, 6a.

22. Ch'en Meng-chia, in *Yin Tz'u Tsung-shu*, 291-293, quotes and discusses the sources and concludes that the records for the history of the Chou before the time of King Wen are scanty and uncertain.

23. This theory is developed by Hu Hou-hsüan in "Yin Feng-chien K'ao," 24b-25b.

24. *Shih-chi*, 4.10–22; *Mémoires historiques*, I, 217–228.

A descendant of Hou Chi was King T'ai
Who lived on the southern slopes of Mount Ch'i;
He began the clipping of Shang.
When it came to [Kings] Wen and Wu
They continued the work of King T'ai;
The end decreed by Heaven was effected
On the battlefield of Mu.[25]

Here we are told that the great-grandfather of the conqueror began the process of incursion against the great state, which was carried on by his descendants until it culminated in total victory.

Early relations between the Shang and the Chou peoples were evidently just what we should expect when a relatively unsophisticated but vigorous people, with aggressive intentions, expands its sphere of control alongside that of a long-established power. No doubt there was an alternation of warlike and amicable contacts, and the Chou may even, at times, have acknowledged Shang overlordship. The *Poetry*, which tells us that King T'ai was the first to make incursions against Shang, also says that his son, King Chi, took a wife who came from the Shang.[26] But the son born of this marriage, King Wen, was certainly not the paragon of long-suffering and unswerving loyalty to the Shang that he is represented to be in the orthodox tradition.[27]

25. *Shih*, 259.

26. *Shih*, 188. The genuine text of the *Bamboo Books*, which is a relatively late source, says (Wang, *Ku Chu-shu*, 6a) that "King Chi of Chou came to court" to the Shang, thus acknowledging their overlordship. It also says that King Chi was appointed to high office by the Shang ruler and was later put to death by him. It further records a Chou attack on Shang at a date that would correspond, according to the traditional chronology, with 1190 B.C.

27. The role of King Wen with regard to the Chou conquest came in later times to be a much discussed, and sometimes heatedly argued, topic. The reason is the ambivalence that has prevailed concerning the role of founders of dynasties. On the one hand they were heroes and benefactors of the people (since by definition a dynasty that lost the Mandate of Heaven was wicked); but on the other they were in most cases at best rebels and at worst regicides. King Wu is clearly depicted as the latter. But his father, King Wen, is generally credited with founding the Chou dynasty, yet he did not, according to tradition, raise his hand against his ruler. Thus Wen had the best of it both ways.

The *Historical Records* gives the tradition in very extended form (*Shih-chi*, 4.10–26, *Mémoires historiques*, I, 216–234). But while it shows King Wen as extremely long-suffering in his loyalty to the Shang, it also quotes King Wu as indicating that his attack on them was made in accord with the intention of King Wen (*Shih-chi*, 4.21; *Mémoires historiques*, I, 227).

A passage in the *Tso-chuan* says, "When King Wen led the revolting states of Yin to serve Chòu [the last Shang King], he knew what was timely" (*Tso*, 421::423 [Hsiang 4]). This would appear to mean that he was merely waiting for the oppor-

On the contrary, both the *Poetry* and the *Documents* tell us that the Mandate of Heaven to destroy the Shang was given to King Wen and that he laid the groundwork for the conquest.

CHINA has had many outstanding rulers in its long history, but none perhaps is more noteworthy than King Wen. Not the least remarkable fact about him is that, although the first Han Emperor called him the greatest of Kings (*Wang*), by official Chinese reckoning he was not a King at all, since the Chou dynasty began only with his son. There is abundant evidence, however, that at the beginning of Chou it was Wen who was considered the founder.[28] In some cases this might be ascribed to mere filial piety, since the statement is made by sons of King Wen. But we also find a son of King Wu referring to both Wen and Wu as founders.[29] And in a bronze inscription King K'ang, Wu's grandson, says that it was Wen who received the Mandate and whom he takes as his model.[30]

The *Documents* says that "Heaven grandly ordered King Wen to kill the great Yin and grandly receive its Mandate."[31] But he did not do so, and to this extent must be considered a failure (though no one ever seems to suggest this). Yet in spite of this fact, and although he was never King of the Chinese or the founder of a new dynasty, he was clearly preferred, both in Western Chou times and later, to King Wu.

One indication of this is the relative frequency with which their names occur. In all the Western Chou sources, Wen is mentioned more often than Wu; in the *Poetry* his predominance is three to one.[32] In

tune time to attack. But a passage in the *Analects* (8.20.4) says: "Possessing two-thirds of the Empire, and yet serving Yin—[at this point] the virtue of the Chou indeed reached the highest point." Commentators and scholars have argued at length as to whether this refers to the conduct of King Wen, King Wu, or both; most have considered it to refer to King Wen. See *Lun-yü Chi-shih*, I, 484–485.

28. For a few of the numerous statements that the Mandate was given to King Wen, see: *Shu*, 39, 61, 78. *Shih*, 186, 188, 198. In the Western Chou bronze inscriptions it is almost always said that both Wen and Wu received the Mandate, but this is said of Wen alone in *Chin-wen*, 33b.

29. *Shu*, 52–53.

30. *Chin-wen*, 33b–34a. This bronze is ascribed to the time of King K'ang, not only by Kuo Mo-jo, but also by Ch'en Meng-chia in "Hsi-Chou T'ung-ch'i," (3).95. If, as some scholars hold, this inscription records the words of King Ch'eng, it is still more remarkable.

31. *Shu*, 39.

32. Neither King is mentioned in the original text of the *Book of Changes*. In the bronze inscriptions Wen is named fourteen times, Wu ten. In the Western Chou *Documents*, Wen is mentioned thirty times, Wu eighteen. In the *Poetry*, the name of King Wen occurs thirty-three times, that of King Wu eleven.

many documents of later (and even much later) times, Wen is named far more frequently.[33] Whether Confucius ever refers to Wu in the *Analects* is uncertain, but he makes it clear that he considers Wen to be the founder of the tradition that he carries on.[34]

Why this strange preference for a King who was not King, a founder who did not found, a conqueror who never conquered? Part of the reason was undoubtedly historical. Undoubtedly it was Wen, more than any other single man, who prepared the downfall of the Shang. By the formation of alliances, and by victories over his enemies, he consolidated a power that, when the test ultimately came, proved invincible. As the *Poetry* says, "King Wen opened the way for his posterity; King Wu carried on the task, conquering and exterminating the Yin."[35]

It was more, however, than that. The Western Chou sources contain many characterizations of the two Kings, and there are definite differences between them. By comparing these we should be able to determine what attributes in a ruler were most highly approved at that time.[36]

Concerning the character of King Wen we have many particulars. Least clear is the meaning of repeated references to his "virtue."[37] More specific are the statements that he was pious and filial, obedient

33. The *Tso-chuan* mentions Wen thirty-nine times, Wu twenty-five. The *Mencius* names Wen thirty-four times, Wu only fifteen. In the entire text of the *Documents* as we have it today, including all the forgeries from perhaps as late as the third century A.D., Wen is named fifty-four times, Wu twenty-eight.

34. It is not certain whether Confucius is the speaker where Wu is mentioned in *Analects*, 8.20.2. The reference to both Wen and Wu in *Analects*, 19.22, is not by Confucius but by a disciple. Confucius explicitly names Wen as the source of his tradition in *Analects*, 9.5.

35. *Shih*, 248.

36. In making this comparison no account can be taken, of course, of the many references to Wen and Wu as co-founders.

37. *Shih*, 188, 193, 195, 239. *Shu*, 39, 53. The meaning of *te* 德 has been much debated. Arthur Waley (*Shih*, 346) says: "This does not mean 'virtue' in our sense of the word; for there is bad *tê* as well as good *tê*. It means 'virtue' in the sense in which we speak of the 'virtue' of a drug. The Latin word 'virtus' frequently has this sense. *Tê* means what *mana* means . . . 'magic power, prestige, influence.' In the first draft of my translation I left the word untranslated. But . . . in the end I translated it power . . . inner power (for it excludes physical strength); but sometimes virtue, in contexts where this is not misleading."

In my opinion there is too much tendency to read the idea of "magic" into *te*, at least for early texts; it is more frequently present, I think, in works of the Warring States and Han periods. Certainly *te* does not denote a colorless morality, but neither does "virtue." In early texts, unless it is specifically qualified, *te* commonly has a sense somewhat similar to that of "virtue," and often (certainly as applied to King Wen) includes something of the sense of Max Weber's much overworked term, "charisma."

both toward the deities and spirits and toward his ancestors.[38] Despite his great renown, he made no display of it.[39] He was careful, cautious, boundlessly solicitous.[40] He was accordant and accommodating to others and was able to bring those under him into harmony.[41] He cared for the people, protected them, and sought to bring about tranquillity. He did not dare to mistreat even the helpless and solitary. He was very careful about the use of punishments, and his practice in this regard was a model for his successors.[42]

King Wen was highly intelligent, and ready to accept good ideas from others.[43] His labors, in building a city at Feng and in extending the realm, left a rich heritage. His institutions and his government were a model for later times. He was an exemplar to rulers and people, of his own and later generations.[44] Above all, it is as a planner that Wen is celebrated. The intention to conquer Shang existed before his time, but he is credited with giving the project substance and direction. King Wu, and those after him who firmly established the rule of Chou, were completing the work of King Wen.[45]

The chief deity said to King Wen, "Plan with your partner states." Wen formed wide alliances and brought the various states under his leadership into harmony. He thus created order, so that the men of the western territories relied upon him, and he formed a state able to fulfill the responsibilities of the Chou.[46] This was not done, however, by peaceful means alone. One poem mentions his "martial achievements," and another describes both his defensive and offensive campaigns in some detail.[47]

When we turn to King Wu, it is much more difficult to find definite characterization in the Western Chou sources. He is most frequently

38. *Shih*, 188, 190, 192, 196, 240. *Shu*, 43. *Chin-wen*, 1a.
39. *Shih*, 196.
40. *Shih*, 188. *Shu*, 42, 62.
41. *Shih*, 195. *Shu*, 61.
42. *Shih*, 193, 198. *Shu*, 39, 42.
43. *Shih*, 193, 195. In the first of these poems (no. 240), Waley (*Shih*, 260–261), considers the subject in stanzas 2 through 5 to be King Wu. Legge and Karlgren understand the subject to be Wen. In the *Tso-chuan* a passage is quoted from the second stanza as relating to Wen, indicating that it was so understood at an early date; see *Tso*, 176::177 (Hsi 19). The second (no. 241) now has "King Chi" as the subject at the beginning of the fourth stanza, but Karlgren shows that other texts read "Wen Wang" here and that the substitution is a scribal error; see Karlgren, "Glosses on the Ta Ya and Sung Odes," 42.
44. *Shih*, 192, 195, 199, 240, 241, 253. *Chin-wen*, 34a.
45. *Shih*, 185–186, 196, 199, 248. *Shu*, 62.
46. *Shih*, 190, 195–196. *Shu*, 39, 43, 61.
47. *Shih*, 195–196, 199.

mentioned merely as one of the co-founders, "Wen-Wu." There is one reference to Wu's "virtue," and one to his "great teachings."[48] One poem refers to his building of the capital at Hao, to his labors, and to the plans that he handed down to his descendants. Another tells us that he tranquillized the myriad states and was able firmly to establish his house. One passage in the *Documents* speaks of the "planned work" of King Wu.[49] And that is about all, except for references to his martial bearing and achievements.

The latter traits, however, are emphasized: "Terrifying and strong was King Wu!" He was said to be "very martial"; there are repeated references to his "ardor." "The cohorts of Yin-Shang were massed like a forest. . . . Bright was King Wu, he killed and smote the great Shang." "King Wu conquered the Yin, he exterminated and killed them."[50]

The very names of King Wen and King Wu are symbols of their attributes. The character *wen* 文 appears to have originally had the sense of "striped" or "adorned,"[51] and it may be by extension from this that *wen* came to mean "accomplished," "accomplishments," and even "civilization": all of those adornments of life that distinguish the civilized man from the untutored barbarian.[52] In early literature *wen* is frequently used as an honorific adjective to describe ancestors and others.

Wu 武 as an epithet normally has the sense of "martial." In not a few instances we find the same individual characterized as being both *wen* and *wu*, and in one case *wu* is used to describe King Wen.[53] There is nothing remarkable in the idea that rulers and leaders should possess both qualities; even in states of our own day the supreme authority to direct activities in both peace and war is commonly vested in one man.

---

48. *Shu*, 53, 61.
49. *Shih*, 199, 252–253. *Shu*, 37.
50. *Shih*, 188, 243, 248, 252.
51. For examples of this sense see: *Shih*, 82, 120. *Shu*, 71.
52. *Wen* also means, of course, "writing" and "literature." But I do not think that we must assume, as Waley (*Shih*, 346) apparently does, that *wen* in the sense of "the arts of peace as opposed to those of war" must be either derived from the idea of "literary accomplishment," or else "another word, written with the same character." In my opinion Waley goes too far when he says that when *wen* is used as a stock epithet describing ancestors "we do not know what it means, any more than the Romans knew what 'augustus' meant." Certainty in such matters is always difficult, but we have access to a much more plausible derivation for *wen* than any that Waley cites for "augustus" in his footnote to this remark.
53. *Shih*, 121, 199, 228, 246.

Although King Wen is certainly described in the Western Chou sources as possessing martial merit, and King Wu as a competent administrator, these two names correspond very closely to the predominant aspects of their characters as they are pictured. How, then, did they get these names? Both "Wen" and "Wu" were used as names of Shang Kings, and Tung Tso-pin suggested that in Shang times they were bestowed as posthumous names on the basis of the actions, during their lifetimes, of the Kings to whom they were given.[54] Traditionally the Chou Kings also are supposed to have received these designations posthumously. Recently, however, it has been argued that these were not posthumous names; in fact, the evidence seems insufficient to make it possible to decide either way.[55] If they were not posthumous names, it is accidental that these names happened to coincide with their predominant activities. In either case it seems impossible to avoid the conclusion that in Western Chou times there was an influential preference for the ruler of outstanding administrative gifts, gaining his ends chiefly by means of negotiation and conciliation, rather than for the military hero of "terrifying" mien.

It may well be that the portrait of King Wen found in even early Western Chou sources is an idealization. To whatever extent this may be true, however, it is a portrait of the kind of ruler most admired at that time. It will not have escaped notice that this ideal ruler is in many ways very similar to what we are accustomed to call the "Confucian" ideal. But here there is no question of Confucian theories having been read backward; this is the temper, at the least, of a significant segment of Western Chou thought. This suggests that we may need to revise some of our ideas about the intellectual and political climate of Western Chou. It also tends to indicate that, while much of the orthodox Chinese tradition remains quite unbelievable, an essential point—the conviction that many of the fundamental ingredients of the Chinese attitude toward government can be traced back at least to the beginning of the Chou—must be taken more

54. Tung, "Tuan-tai Yen-chiu," 334.

55. Bronze inscriptions certainly indicate that some Western Chou Kings were known, while alive, by the names that have been supposed to be their posthumous designations; see: Wang, *Kuan-t'ang Chi-lin*, 18.5b–6b. Kuo, *Chin-wen Ts'ung-k'ao*, 89a–101b. Firm evidence does not seem to be available, however, concerning Wen and Wu specifically. Tung Tso-pin ("Tuan-tai Yen-chiu," 334) believed that posthumous names were given to some, at least, of the Shang Kings. I am not wholly convinced by Kuo's argument that posthumous names did not begin until the Warring States period. This subject merits further study.

seriously than it has been in the recent past by many critical scholars.[56]

The significance of this early prevalence of the conception of the ideal ruler as an effective administrator, rather than as a military hero, would be hard to exaggerate. In characterizing China's basic political character, Edward A. Kracke, Jr., writes: "Since force was decried and the military man suspect as a threat to political order, the civilian ideal prevailed."[57] S. N. Eisenstadt points out that in Chinese history generally (as opposed to that of Rome, Byzantium, the Caliphate, the Ottoman Empire, etc.) "the army did not constitute a permanent, semi-legitimate (or at least accepted) factor in the political process."[58] Although the military factor was by no means absent or unimportant in Western Chou times, the tendency toward a "civilian" psychology, already present, was one of the factors that would guide China's political development in a direction quite different from that of Rome.

THE victory of the Chou over the formidable and long-established Shang is commonly supposed to have been facilitated by the fact that the Shang power had been exhausted by a long campaign in the northeast. In any case, it was a considerable feat. But whatever the military difficulties of the conquest may have been, they were probably less (as is usual with conquests) than those of bringing the newly acquired territories under control. That the Chou were able to do so, in a relatively brief period, is remarkable.

The difficulties were not only military and psychological, but also geographic. To what extent forests and marshes constituted a problem has been debated,[59] but at least the mountains and rivers and the dis-

---

56. Let me make it clear that I claim no superior virtue in this regard. I have always, I think, believed that the royal government at the beginning of Western Chou was more effective than most critical scholars would credit, but I now think that I formerly underestimated the political sophistication of the early Chou rulers.

57. Kracke, "Chinese Government," 333.

58. Eisenstadt, *Political Systems*, 172.

59. Marcel Granet in his *Chinese Civilization* (originally published, in French, in 1930) wrote (p. 72): "The appearance of the ancient Chinese country is difficult enough to imagine. The regions at present treeless and entirely under cultivation, formerly contained immense marshes and important forests." In his review of this book V. K. Ting wrote: "Professor Granet asserts that Feudal China still consisted of immense marshes and forests which were only drained and cleared by the Lords of the Contending States. Now all geologists agree that in the loess there has never been any forestation. The steppe fauna that existed during the formation of the loess still survives without any change which would not be the case if forests existed after the loess had been formed. . . . The loess is not an upland formation as

tances involved must have made it difficult to move armies rapidly and to maintain the communications necessary for administrative control.[60] A further and very great hazard was the presence of many groups of hostile barbarians. For a long time many Chinese states were little more than islands of Chinese culture and military control surrounded by people who were little if at all Sinicized, and potentially if not actually dangerous.

King Wu could control such territories only by delegating some measure of power to many of his followers, to exercise control in local areas by his authority and subject to his orders. He gave fiefs to a large number of his relatives, and to others who had been associated with him in the conquest. Some rulers who had long exercised power in various localities were permitted, after submitting to the Chou, to continue to rule as their vassals. Some fiefs were given to royal officials in lieu of emolument.[61] Some fiefs planted in more remote regions were in effect garrisons, designed to maintain order and to absorb the first shock, at least, of attack from without.

The greatest danger, however, was from within the conquered territory. The Shang people had been vanquished, but they had not been crushed. Although their King was dead, his son was enfeoffed by the Chou with a state, which he ruled as their vassal. It is said that he was given this state in order that he might continue the sacrifices to the Shang Kings, and it is not impossible that such a religious motivation played a role; the favor of powerful spirits was desired, and it was

---

Prof. Granet repeatedly makes it to be, but a valley-filling deposit, hence in the loess area we have always deep miniature canyons cut in the soft material. No marsh of any kind can exist here, nor is the loess sufficiently hard to resist erosion or obstruct drainage."

Henri Maspero wrote ("La société chinoise," 346) that around the time of the Chou conquest the founder of a state was "in truth the creator of a domain, for he had to wrest it from the undergrowth, the forest, or the marsh before it could be cultivated." For Maspero's conception of the geographic situation of the time, see ibid., 336–349.

In any case, not all of the territories controlled and claimed by the Western Chou were loess plain. In the east, in particular, there were broad rivers and some marshes that must have been formidable barriers to communication. See Tsou, "Chung-kuo Wen-hua Ch'i-yüan Ti."

60. Ichisada Miyazaki points out that even as late as the Spring and Autumn period some Chinese states were isolated from each other, and communications were far from easy; see Miyazaki, "Chūgoku Jōdai wa Hōkensei wa Toshi Kokka ka," 152.

61. It is unlikely that salary played any very important role in connection with royal officials in Western Chou times, though there are some indications that it may have existed; see below, p. 150.

well to avoid their wrath.[62] But King Wu took precautions; he appointed two (or according to some accounts three) of his brothers to act as "Inspectors" over the Shang scion, living at or near his capital.

This expedient was not effective, however, beyond the lifetime of King Wu. He died not long after the conquest, and while his son succeeded as King Ch'eng, the real power was held for some time by another of Wu's brothers, the Duke of Chou. The Chou Inspectors became disaffected; perhaps they were jealous of the Duke's power; perhaps, as tradition says, they suspected him of intending to usurp the throne. Whatever the reason, the Inspectors, although uncles of the King, joined with the Shang scion and a coalition of barbarians to revolt against the Chou. The Duke of Chou reacted vigorously, marching east with an army and executing the Shang scion and the eldest of the Inspectors, his own elder brother.

These events are abundantly attested in various works of pre-Han times, but the Western Chou sources have little to say concerning most of them. It is possible to conjecture the reason. This treason on the part of brothers of the conqueror, and the fact that the Duke of Chou killed his own elder brother—a particularly deplorable event within the framework of Chinese custom—must have made this whole episode one on which men of the time had no desire to dwell. The traditions are so fully recorded in later works that there is little doubt that they happened substantially as has been described above. But a great many of the details are quite different in various versions, and it is not at all certain that we can be sure in every case which one represents the historic truth.[63]

Tradition holds that the Duke of Chou, while supporting King Ch'eng, held the governing power as regent for seven years. This is uncertain,[64] but in any case he was clearly the most powerful figure for some years after the death of King Wu. He led a military expedition to the east that may have ranged as far as the coast, extinguishing—according to one account—fifty states.[65] To replace them he enfeoffed a number of vassals; one writer tells us that he set up seventy-one states.[66] The *Historical Records* says that, after executing the rebel son

---

62. The purpose of continuing the Shang sacrifices is given in the *Historical Records* (*Shih-chi*, 3.23; *Mémoires historiques*, I, 207). It is also stated elsewhere but not, insofar as I am aware, in any source of indubitably Western Chou date.

63. The sources are very fully quoted and discussed in Ch'en, "Hsi-Chou T'ung-ch'i," (1).142–149.

64. See ibid., 149–150.

65. Ibid., 149–150, 172. *Mencius*, 3(2).9.6.

66. *Hsün-tzu*, 4.1a; Dubs, *Hsüntze*, 92.

of the last Shang King, the Duke set up a brother of the same King as ruler of the state of Sung, so that the Shang sacrifices might still be continued.[67]

The Duke of Chou also built a new capital near the modern site of Loyang. This gave the Chou a vantage point for supervision of their Empire that was much more central to their newly expanded realm than was the capital near the modern Sian. The principal Chou capital remained in the west, however, until the end of the Western Chou; the new capital was subsidiary. To it, the Duke transported a number of the remaining Shang officials, so that they could be kept under strict supervision.[68]

If King Wen has perhaps been the most famous of Chinese rulers, the Duke of Chou has beyond all doubt been the most eminent of ministers. But he was far more. It is difficult to compare his place in the tradition with that of any other individual in Chinese, or perhaps in any other, history. The closest comparison—and the two are often mentioned together—is with Confucius. Confucius is, of course, the more famous. Yet the Duke enjoyed certain advantages even over Confucius. He was for some time a ruler in fact, whether or not he held the titular power as Regent. He held much higher office than any with which even the exaggerations of tradition ever endowed Confucius. Tradition credits him with making important innovations in government and in other aspects of Chinese culture. The authorship of a number of important books has been attributed to him. As a philosopher he has often, from an early day, been considered to have founded the Confucian tradition. Ruler, statesman, cultural innovator, scholar, philosopher: for thousands of years the Duke of Chou has been regarded as one who succeeded in realizing not one but all of the highest Chinese ambitions.[69]

The Duke of Chou was held in extremely high esteem as early as the Spring and Autumn period. But when we look, in the light of his later reputation, at what is said about him in the Western Chou sources, the contrast is almost startling. What they say about him is—in view of the fact that he certainly did play an important role in establishing the Chou dynasty—almost nothing.

---

67. *Shih-chi*, 4.38, 38.22; *Mémoires historiques*, I, 245, IV, 231.

68. *Shu*, 48–56, 62–65. There has been much debate as to whether, at this time, the Chou built one city in the Loyang area or two cities close together. The evidence is not wholly clear. Kinpei Gotō reviews it in "Seishū to Ōjō."

69. *Analects*, 11.16.1, also says that the Duke of Chou was "rich."

Only a few bronze inscriptions mention the Duke of Chou at all, and in all but two the reference is quite casual. One inscription speaks of his achievement in (together with others) conquering the Shang; another tells of a military expedition in which he destroyed three states.[70]

The *Poetry* is even more surprising. We have seen that poem after poem extols the virtue and piety of King Wen, his intelligence and far-seeing plans, the institutions that he handed down, and the fact that he was a model to his own and later generations. In fact, the things that are said about King Wen in the *Poetry* are very like what was said about the Duke of Chou in later times. But in all of the three hundred five poems, the Duke is named in only two. The first of these relates that he made a military expedition to the east, correcting, transforming, and uniting the states, pitying the people and making them happy. The second is a poem that epitomizes the history of the Chou people and the state of Lu, and its mention of the Duke is minimal. It tells of the appointment of the son of the Duke of Chou as Duke of Lu, says that the Duke will give blessings to his descendants, and relates that a later ruler, by his conquests, restored "the domains of the Duke of Chou."[71]

If we had only the bronze inscriptions and the *Poetry*, we should have to think of the Duke of Chou as principally a conqueror, and a minor figure. The most voluminous and significant information we have on the Duke is found in the *Documents*, and not in what others say about him but chiefly in his own pronouncements. From the *Documents* it is evident that, whether he was called Regent or not, the Duke of Chou actually held great and perhaps controlling power in the government during the early years of the reign of King Ch'eng.

The Duke says to his nephew, the King: "Listen to my instructions . . . if you do not exert yourself in this you will not continue for long. Amply regulate your principal officers; if you follow my example in everything, they will not dare reject your orders. Go and be reverent." To this King Ch'eng replies: "You, O Duke, are a bright protector to

70. *Chin-wen*, 46a. Ch'en, "Hsi-Chou T'ung-ch'i," (1).168, (5).105–107. The Duke is mentioned casually in *Chin-wen*, 2b, 5b, 11b, 39a. Ch'en ("Hsi-Chou T'ung-ch'i," [1].161) lists nine Western Chou bronze inscriptions that name the Duke of Chou. These include the six in my corpus listed above; in the other three the reference is casual.

Noel Barnard, in "Chou China," 339–352, calls one of these inscriptions "of doubtful authenticity." This is the one published in Ch'en, "Hsi-Chou T'ung-ch'i," (1).168. Barnard comments upon the difference between the Duke's "historical status in the inscriptions" and "that given him in the traditional literature."

71. *Shih*, 103, 259–260. Commentators also say that a number of other poems refer to activities of the Duke of Chou; this may be true, but they do not name him.

me, the young man. You set forth a greatly illustrious virtue, and cause me, the little child, to extol the virtuous deeds of Wen and Wu. . . . everywhere you are an august directing arbiter . . . your achievements have aided and guided me strongly, I shall imitate them in everything. . . . May you guide and support me in the future, supervise all my officers, and greatly protect the people received by Wen and Wu, and govern and manage the Four Helpers." Karlgren explains this last as meaning that the Duke should act as "the chief among the highest dignitaries."[72]

The evidence of the *Documents*, supplemented by that from other Western Chou sources, appears to support the statement found in later works to the effect that at some time in the reign of King Ch'eng the Duke of Chou exercised general supervision over the whole of the eastern portion of the Chou territories, while similar supervision of the western part was in the hands of the Duke of Shao.[73] The Duke of Chou must have had the more difficult assignment, for the eastern regions were under less control and were more turbulent. Yet even in the *Documents* there is remarkably little praise for the Duke of Chou. In all of the twelve sections that I accept as being of Western Chou date, he is mentioned with praise in only one passage: the speech addressed to him by King Ch'eng, of which part is quoted above.[74] Since the King was apparently to some extent under the Duke's tutelage at the time, this fact and the ordinary uses of courtesy would seem to lessen its importance.

Why was the Duke of Chou so little mentioned and so seldom praised in Western Chou times? This is something of a mystery, and one can only suggest some possible reasons. Certainly one was the fact that, while he was clearly very able and important, he did not deserve the almost exclusive credit for the Chou achievements that he has been given by later tradition. The establishment of the dynasty so firmly, and with a pattern of government that would continue to be regarded as a model for three thousand years, was made possible only by the fact that at its inception the Chou had the good fortune to have not merely one but a number of outstanding men.

The exceptional ability of King Wen is beyond question, and he received full credit for it, both in his own and later times. His son, King Wu, fared less well. This may be because his military exploits were

---

72. *Shu*, 52–55.

73. *Shih-chi*, 34.2; *Mémoires historiques*, IV.133–134. The various sources for this tradition are cited, together with corroborative materials from the *Documents*, the *Poetry*, and bronze inscriptions, in Ch'en, "Hsi-Chou T'ung-ch'i," (2).98.

74. *Shu*, 52–53.

somewhat deprecated, although their results were welcomed. King Wu may have been, as tradition represents him, less able as an administrator than his father, but if so only by comparison. Two of the sections of the *Documents* that are preserved to us show his character, and it is that of a deeply conscientious ruler, concerned with conciliation, justice, organization, and orderly administration.[75] His son, King Ch'eng, was also a capable and energetic sovereign.

The Duke of Shao played a role somewhat similar to that of the Duke of Chou in pacifying and organizing the newly won territories, but we have far less information about him.[76] And there were others, of whom we know little more than the name, who made essential contributions. But tradition, in a way that tradition in many lands commonly has, in later times attributed much of the achievements of all these men to a single hero—the Duke of Chou.

Yet this does not answer the question. If his deserts were somewhat less than later tradition has allowed, they were nevertheless greater than anything that appears to be recognized in the *Poetry* and the other Western Chou sources. It is difficult not to conclude that in his own time he was a rather unpopular figure. And it is not hard to see why.

The Duke of Chou was undoubtedly an earnest and upright man, but there is little in his recorded sayings that would have been likely to make him popular. His tone was self-righteous and monitory, even when addressing the young King Ch'eng. "Listen to my instructions . . . if you do not exert yourself in this you will not continue for long . . . follow my example in everything." Such an attitude was undoubtedly resented, not only by the King, but also by others. Some accounts suggest that when King Wu died the Duke simply took over the royal power, without ceremony.[77] One passage may indicate that he was asked by the Duke of Shao to resign his office—which he declined to do.[78] It is not at all unlikely that, as later tradition insists, the Duke of Chou was widely suspected of intending to usurp the throne.[79]

75. *Shu*, 39–46. These documents do not in the least indicate that Wu was a military swashbuckler. They do show him, however, as a rather harsh disciplinarian with a certain predilection for the death penalty. This is not wholly surprising, since he had the task of organizing a newly conquered territory and a populace that was by no means wholly subdued.

76. See below, pp. 357–363.

77. *Hsün-tzu*, 4.1a, 7b; Dubs, *Hsüntze*, 91, 105–106. *Mémoires historiques*, IV, 92.

78. *Shu*, 62. On the various interpretations of this difficult passage see Karlgren, "Glosses on the Book of Documents," (2).126–127.

79. This suspicion is extensively discussed in the section of the *Documents*

From ancient to modern times modesty has been a cardinal Chinese virtue. The *Poetry* praises King Wen for the fact that, despite his great renown, he made no display of his merits.[80] The same can hardly be said for the Duke of Chou.

The most subtle form of self-praise practiced by the Duke appears in his exaltation of the role of the entire class of advisers to kings, to which he belonged. The assignment of great credit to ministers appeared, it is true, as early as Shang times and is a repeated motif in the Western Chou sources.[81] But nowhere else is such exclusive credit for the achievements of Kings given to their advisers as in the speeches of the Duke of Chou. In one of these he sets forth at length the merits of various advisers to Shang Kings, and says that the success of King Wen depended upon the guidance given to him by five able ministers. Without them, the Duke says, "King Wen would have had no virtue to bestow upon the people." In the time of King Wu four of these men were still alive to direct him. "But now," the Duke concludes, "it rests with me."[82]

His ascription of primary importance to those who were ministers and advisers to rulers was probably the chief reason for which the reputation of the Duke of Chou became so magnified in later times. In the Spring and Autumn period the power of ministers steadily encroached on that of rulers; and that time and the Warring States period saw the rise of the class of scholars who aspired, with varying success, to become powerful ministers. These scholars had a virtual monopoly on the writing of history and other literature. When ministers, and scholars aspiring to be ministers, sought to expand their power, it was natural that they should make a hero of the Duke of Chou.

The *Tso-chuan* has many references to him, which seem to make it clear that he was held in the highest esteem as early as Spring and Autumn times.[83] His military and governmental exploits are celebrated. He is credited with originating the policy of enfeoffing members of the

---

called the "Chin T'eng": *Shu*, 35–36. It is very difficult to date. Its style is not like that of early Western Chou documents, and its content may indicate that it comes from considerably later; see pp. 457–458. The tradition is set forth at length in *Shih-chi*, 33.6–8; *Mémoires historiques*, IV, 92.

80. *Shih*, 196.

81. *Shu*, 45, 73, 78–80. *Shih*, 186, 221–223, 228–230, 238–239. *Chin-wen*, 62ab, 114a, 134b–135a, 139ab, 147a. Kuo, *Wen-shih Lun-chi*, 348.

82. *Shu*, 61.

83. There is always some problem involved in drawing such conclusions from the content of the *Tso-chuan*. Since it was apparently not put into its present form until around 300 B.C., and certainly contains some admixture of ideas that became

Chou royal family so that their states might constitute a protection for the King.[84] He is also lauded as a model of virtue, and it is said that his spirit will not accept human sacrifice.[85] The power of his spirit was said to be so great (after he had been dead for six centuries) that the desire for his favor was alleged as the reason for which another state sought alliance with Lu (which was ruled by descendants of the Duke of Chou).[86]

Already in the *Tso-chuan* we find it implied that the Chou achievement was essentially that of the Duke of Chou. In 540 B.C., that work reports, an envoy of the state of Chin visited Lu, where he was shown the archives. He exclaimed: "The institutions of Chou are all preserved in Lu. Now I understand the virtue of the Duke of Chou, and why it is that the Chou became Kings."[87]

In the *Analects*, Confucius speaks of the "admirable abilities" of the Duke, and also says: "Extreme indeed is my decline. It is a long time since I dreamed that I saw the Duke of Chou."[88] This passage is commonly interpreted to mean that Confucius regarded the Duke as his model, but this is perhaps to exaggerate its significance.

Authorship was ascribed to the Duke of Chou in the *Tso-chuan*, which quotes two books, or documents, that he is said to have composed, giving maxims for conduct.[89] But it remained for the philosopher Mo-tzu, of the fifth century B.C., to depict him as a patron of scholars. Mo-tzu spent his lifetime hoping to find a ruler who would appreciate himself and his doctrines; he never seems to have succeeded. But he said, "Anciently the Duke of Chou, Tan, read one hun-

---

current only in the Warring States period, it is possible that any given passage may not in fact date from Spring and Autumn time. But there are so many statements about the Duke of Chou, and in general they are in such agreement with what we find said about him in the *Analects*, that it seems safe to suppose that they do represent the Spring and Autumn attitude.

84. *Tso*, 189::192 (Hsi 24), 750::754 (Ting 4).
85. *Tso*, 189::192 (Hsi 24), 582::583 (Chao 2), 628::629 (Chao 10), 750::754 (Ting 4).
86. *Tso*, 855::855 (Ai 24).
87. *Tso*, 582::583 (Chao 2).
88. *Analects*, 7.5, 8.11. *Tso*, 824::826 (Ai 11), quotes Confucius as referring with approval to principles that the Duke of Chou is supposed to have laid down for taxation.
89. *Tso*, 280::282 (Wen 18). The statement here that 周公制周禮 is very interesting. It appears to mean that the Duke of Chou composed a work called *Chou-li*, since it is immediately followed by a quotation from it. This passage may have contributed to the development of the tradition that the Duke created the institutions of the dynasty, and also that he wrote the book we know as the *Chou-li*. But neither of the passages supposedly quoted from these two books seems to appear in any extant work; see *Chou-li*, 20.13b.

dred chapters every morning and received seventy scholars every evening." This is clearly fantasy.[90] But it was a fantasy that was undoubtedly consoling to men like Mo-tzu, who felt themselves neglected by the rulers of their day. And such traditions, as they were elaborated, in time had great influence in heightening the prestige of scholars with rulers.

Mencius, the most famous Confucian after Confucius, was an outspoken champion of the claims, not merely of the minister, but even of the scholar who disdains to enter public service, as standing on a plane far higher than that of mere rulers. He said, "Those who counsel the great should despise them, and have no regard for their pomp and display." He asserted that a scholar whose advice was sought by a ruler should not be summoned; the ruler should go to see him. And the ruler should present his gifts in such manner that the scholar is not constantly put to the trouble of giving thanks for them.[91] It is not in the least surprising that Mencius should have seen in the Duke of Chou a man after his own heart.

Mencius praised the Duke in the highest terms and found it necessary to explain the fact that a sage of such merit did not become King. He implied that the philosophical tradition carried on by Confucius was founded by the Duke of Chou.[92] Another famous Confucian, Hsün-tzu, said that "Confucius was equal in virtue to the Duke of Chou" and called the Duke "the model for great Confucians."[93] In Han times, and later, a considerable number of Confucians held the Duke of Chou to be the author of institutions and ideas that were merely transmitted by Confucius.[94]

By the first century B.C. the Duke was pictured as having been an ideal patron of scholars after the heart of Mencius. It was said that "the Duke of Chou, bearing gifts, personally went to the humble dwellings of scholars to call upon them."[95] He had been transformed into something very much like the patron saint of scholars.

---

90. *Mo-tzu*, 12.3b; Mei, *Motse*, 226. The Duke of Chou was a very busy man, who in any case could hardly have had time for such activities. Furthermore, nothing in our sources indicates that he was a scholar to this degree, or that there were in his day numerous "scholars" of the sort that Mo-tzu was referring to.

91. *Mencius*, 5(2).6–7, 7(2).34.

92. Ibid., 3(1).4.12; 3(2).9; 4(2).20.5; 5(1).6.

93. *Hsün-tzu*, 4.2a, 15.4a; Dubs, *Hsüntze*, 93, 265.

94. *Huai-nan-tzu*, 21.6b. *Yang-tzu Fa-yen*, 1.1b. Wang, *Lun-heng*, 18.10a, 28.9a, 10a; Forke, *Lun-Hêng*, II, 23, 232, 233. Fung, *History of Chinese Philosophy*, I, 56; II, 632, 708–709. Levenson, *Confucian China*, III, 8.

95. Wang, *Lun-heng*, 7.15b; Forke, *Lun-Hêng*, I, 489–490. Wang Ch'ung brands this as exaggeration.

Not only the *Ritual of Chou* but also a large number of other works have been supposed to have been written by the Duke of Chou.[96] The more absurd aspects of his exaltation are rejected by the critical. But in our own day many eminent scholars still trace the origin of much that is essential in the political institutions of the Chou—and therefore of China—to the creative genius of the Duke of Chou.[97]

IN seeking to make a just appraisal of the role of the Duke, it is useful to distinguish two aspects: the practical and the intellectual. As a practical statesman and military leader he was clearly of outstanding importance. After the death of King Wu, at a time when the Chou fortunes hung in the balance, he stepped in and took control. He responded to the massive revolt by the Shang—participated in by his own brothers—with an extensive and effective military expedition that undoubtedly made the Chou rule of the eastern regions more firm than it had ever been before. He played a role—exactly how great we cannot tell—in further organizing the government. He appears to have been responsible for the plan to establish a subsidiary Chou capital in the east, and he executed it. When he retired from power, he certainly left the Chou house much stronger than before. It is not too much to say that without his efforts it is unlikely that the Chou rule would have survived.

His intellectual role is more difficult to appraise. To what extent were the policies that he put into effect his own? Was he in fact, as has been alleged, the author of the Chou inheritance system and of Chou feudalism? It is difficult to say; but we have no early evidence that he was, and it seems rather improbable.[98] Was he in fact a philosopher, a "Confucian before Confucius"?

We have, in the *Documents*, at least five rather lengthy writings

96. Ts'ui Shu said ("Feng Hao K'ao-hsin Lu," 5.1) that in Han times, if the authorship of an early book was unknown, it was almost automatically attributed to the Duke of Chou. Also see: Fung, *History of Chinese Philosophy*, I, 56. Forke, *Alten chinesischen Philosophie*, 9. 46, 540. Chou, *Ching Chin-ku-wen Hsüeh.*

97. See Wang, *Kuan-t'ang Chi-lin*, 10. Hu Hou-hsüan ("Yin Feng-chien K'ao," 1b–2a) denies the correctness of Wang's attribution to the Duke of the role of institutional originator, but says—with some exaggeration—that "there are no scholars who do not agree with it."

98. See the references cited in the previous note. It appears doubtful that any individual was responsible for the inheritance system; such social institutions are seldom altered by fiat. As regards feudalism, it is clear that King Wu was establishing fiefs before the Duke of Chou came to power. It is possible, of course, that the idea was suggested to him by the Duke, but we have no evidence of this.

that appear to record the words of the Duke of Chou. If we compare these with other materials, and especially with two sections of the *Documents* that come to us from King Wu, it is possible to form some opinion concerning the Duke's ideas.[99]

Two conceptions in these writings appear to have some stamp of originality. One is the emphasis, discussed above, on the importance of the minister. It is difficult to know how much of this was carried over from Shang times, but in early Chou at least no one else ascribes such weight to ministers and advisers. The second is the developed theory of the Mandate of Heaven. The Mandate itself is mentioned by King Wu, but the Duke of Chou appears to have given it a historical setting that insured its persistence as a basic and essential factor in the Chinese theory of government.[100] This may well have been his greatest theoretical contribution.

Aside from these things it is difficult to see a great deal of fundamental difference between the ideas of the Duke of Chou and those expressed by King Wu, presumably earlier. His basic conceptions and general mode of thought appear to be essentially similar to what is found in other materials of the time. The Duke was clearly an earnest and thoughtful statesman, but there is little that impels us to call him a philosopher or a scholar. Certainly there is much that reminds us of Confucius, but that is true of many writings of Western Chou time.

The Duke of Chou played an essential role in the consolidation of the Chou dynasty. After King Wen and King Wu, he probably contributed most to making the great achievement possible. But others also played their parts, and they should not be forgotten.

---

99. From the Duke of Chou we have the "Shao Kao," "Le Kao," "To Shih," "Chün Shih," and "To Fang" (the first two also contain some speeches by other persons). In addition the "Ta Kao" may be by either the Duke of Chou or King Ch'eng. From King Wu we have the "K'ang Kao" and the "Chiu Kao." For the basis of these attributions, see pp. 449–453.

100. See below, pp. 82–84.

CHAPTER

5

The Mandate of Heaven

GIBBON becomes unusually eulogistic when he discusses the policies of the early Roman Empire. "The firm edifice of Roman power," he says, "was raised and preserved by the wisdom of the ages." Specifically:

> The policy of emperors and the senate, as far as it concerned religion, was happily seconded by the reflections of the enlightened, and by the habits of the superstitious, part of their subjects. The various modes of worship which prevailed in the Roman world were all considered by the people as equally true; by the philosopher as equally false; and by the magistrate as equally useful.[1]

The Roman rulers have often been praised for their tolerance toward various religions; indifference would perhaps be a more descriptive term. Such indifference inevitably finds a responsive chord in many modern scholars, from the eighteenth century to the twentieth. But this should not blind us to the fact that the lack of a generally accepted religious basis—or even psychological basis—for the authority of the Roman Emperor was a distinct weakness. Attempts were constantly made to provide religious backing for the imperial authority, from the dignified gestures of Augustus through the grotesqueries of Caligula and Heliogabalus, but they never succeeded (until the triumph of Christianity, by which time the Empire was no longer what it had been). This was clearly a factor in the ease with which emperors were deposed and assassinated and in the ultimate lack of cohesion in the Empire.[2]

1. Gibbon, *Roman Empire*, I, 22.
2. Syme, *Roman Revolution*, 469–475. Heichelheim and Yeo, *The Roman People*, 282, 286–287, 315–316, 343, 393–394, 411–412. *Cambridge Ancient History*, XII, 704. Rostovtzeff, *Roman Empire*, I, 507–509.

The cohesion and stability of the Chinese Empire owes much to the almost universal, and seldom-questioned, acceptance of the religious basis upon which the authority of the Emperor has been founded. This acceptance persisted into the twentieth century, and it comes, in unbroken line, from the beginning of Chou. Some of its aspects certainly derive from a still earlier time, but in some respects the Chou conception of royal authority—which is essentially that of all later periods—shows characteristics that probably represent Chou innovations.

Like the Shang, the Chou called their supreme ruler *Wang*, "King," but they also called him "Son of Heaven." T'ien, "Heaven," as a deity appears to have been unknown to the Shang.[3] The Chou King was believed to derive his power, in large measure, from Heaven and from his royal ancestors. The Chou, one poem tells us, are mighty because they have "three rulers in the heavens, and the King is their counterpart in the capital."[4] The ancestors assisted their descendants if they were pleased, but could punish terribly if they were angered. It was not only necessary, therefore, to make the proper sacrifices to them, but also, by divination, to determine their wishes, and to comply with them.

Most important of all was the goodwill of Heaven. The Chou attributed their success in the conquest to the fact that Heaven, becoming displeased with the Shang, had withdrawn from them its Mandate to rule and had given it to the Chou. That they paid a great deal of attention to this point, and to securing acceptance for it, is significant. It indicates that they were not content merely to rule by force, but were deeply concerned to win acceptance as legitimate sovereigns—which shows a wisdom beyond that of some conquerors whose culture has had a longer pedigree. Yet in itself this was not very remarkable. Most people who have gone to war have argued that God, or the gods, favored them. It is the next step that was taken that makes this doctrine unusual.

We cannot tell how early the doctrine of the Mandate of Heaven was in existence,[5] but it is mentioned repeatedly in the speeches of King Wu.[6] It is of interest however that in the Western Chou sources it is only in speeches of the Duke of Chou that the Mandate of Heaven is given, as it were, the status of a historic entity, possessed first by the

3. Concerning the origin of the deity T'ien, see Appendix C, pp. 493–506.
4. *Shih*, 197.
5. Dubs ("Royal Jou Religion," 237) suggests that "it is highly likely that it was originated by King Wen," but as evidence states only that "he is stated to have received the Mandate,' " I do not see the force of this argument.
6. *Shu*, 39, 45.

Hsia dynasty, then by the Shang, and finally by the Chou.[7] In neither the *Book of Changes*, nor the bronze inscriptions, nor the *Poetry* is there any mention of the Hsia in connection with the Mandate of Heaven.[8] It may well be, then, that this conception, involving what might be called an embryonic philosophy of history, should be credited to the Duke of Chou.

The Duke of Chou says that the Mandate was possessed by the rulers of Hsia until the last of them was so evil that Heaven became alienated from him. "Heaven then sought a [new] lord for the people, and grandly sent down its bright favoring Mandate on T'ang the Successful, punishing and destroying the lord of Hsia." T'ang established the Yin dynasty, and he and all of his successors, until the last King, were virtuous. But, the Duke continues, addressing the conquered Shang people:

> Your last Shang King abandoned himself to indolence, disdained to apply himself to government, and did not bring pure sacrifices. Heaven thereupon sent down this ruin. . . . Heaven waited for five years, so that his sons and grandsons might yet become lords of the people, but he could not become wise. Heaven then sought among your numerous regions, shaking you with its terrors to stimulate those who might have regard for Heaven, but in all your many regions there was none that was able to

7. *Shu*, 49, 55, 61, 62.

8. By "the bronze inscriptions" I mean, of course, the one hundred eighty-four Western Chou inscriptions on which my notes are based. The Mandate of Heaven is mentioned in eight of these. In the *Poetry*, one passage has been interpreted by Karlgren as referring to the possession of the Mandate by a dynasty even earlier than Hsia. He translates "the lord of Yü" and explains in a note, "The dynasty prior to the Hia" (*Shih*, 186, 187). He explains this in "Glosses on the Ta Ya and Sung Odes," 10. This appears to be an original interpretation; I find it unconvincing. In another poem that speaks of the Mandate, Karlgren (*Shih*, 194) translates, "These two kingdoms (sc. of Hia and Yin), their government had failed." Legge and Waley, as well as most commentators, interpret the passage similarly. But Cheng Hsüan (A.D. 127–200) interpreted the two states in question to be Yin and Ch'ung 崇 (*Mao-shih*, 16[4].2a). This is very plausible. The third poem after this one (*Shih*, 198–199) says, "King Wen received the Mandate," and then immediately says, "He made the attack on Ch'ung." This poem does not mention Yin at all. Commentators and translators have become so thoroughly accustomed to the orthodox version of this history that they tend to overlook the fact that the conquest of Shang was only one event, though the climactic one to be sure, in the Chou rise to power. Only one poem in the *Poetry* (*Shih*, 263) says that the Mandate was received by T'ang, the founder of Yin, but this is in a section of the book that is believed to date from a time not earlier than the beginning of Western Chou; see Creel, *Studies*, 49–54.

do so. But our King of Chou treated well the multitudes of the people, was able to practice virtue, and fulfilled his duties to the spirits and to Heaven. Heaven instructed us, favored us, selected us, and gave us the Mandate of Yin, to rule over your numerous regions.[9]

In all of the early literature, this history of the transmission of the Mandate from Hsia to Yin to Chou is mentioned *only* in three discourses of the Duke of Chou, all addressed to the conquered Yin people.[10] All three are speeches made after their great revolt, when their leaders had been transported to the city near the modern Loyang where the Chou hoped to keep them harmless and transform them into submissive subjects. The Duke alternately threatens the direst punishment if they make further trouble, and promises a bright future for them and their descendants if only they will cooperate with the conquerors. "It was the relentless severity of Heaven," he tells them, "that so greatly sent down destruction on Yin. We Chou merely assisted by carrying out its Mandate. . . . It was not that our small state dared to aim at Yin's Mandate." In opposing the Chou, the Duke says, "you recklessly reject the Mandate of Heaven." Furthermore, the Chou are simply fulfilling the same historic function that the founders of the Yin dynasty performed when they accepted the divine command to destroy the last unworthy ruler of Hsia and assume his Mandate.[11]

This looks like propaganda. We cannot conclusively prove that the Yin people had no such doctrine, for we have no Yin literature.[12] The Duke of Chou said to the Yin people, "You know that the earlier men of Yin had documents and records telling how Yin took over the Mandate of Hsia," which looks very odd.[13] Why were there not extant records to which he could appeal? It is somewhat suspicious that, although we know that there must have been a Yin literature, it has vanished, while a number of Chou documents produced immediately after the conquest survive. No one can prove, at this late date, that the Shang literature was destroyed because it did not accord with the Chou version of history, but the hypothesis is tenable.[14]

If the Chou theory of Chinese history, based upon the doctrine of the Mandate of Heaven, was an innovation—as it seems almost cer-

9. *Shu*, 62–65.
10. The "Shao-kao," "To-shih," and "To-fang."
11. *Shu*, 48–51, 55–56, 62–65.
12. See Creel, *Studies*, 21–95.
13. *Shu*, 56.
14. See Creel, *Studies*, 89–93.

tainly to have been[15]—their success in winning quick and lasting acceptance for it is surprising. It is not in the least remarkable that the Chou should have promulgated such a theory, which absolved their conquest of any suspicion of being a predatory action, and represented it rather as a benevolent undertaking designed to rescue a suffering people from the oppression of a wicked ruler—an action, moreover, enjoined upon the Chou by the insistent command of the highest deity. Such justifications of conquest are so common as perhaps to represent the rule rather than the exception. But why did the conquered people accept it?

The Shang were a people who had long had a complex and sophisticated culture. Although we know almost nothing of their governmental theory, the long control they had exercised over broad territories implies that they must have had their own political ideology, settled and firmly established. The Chou were, from the Shang point of view, "rustics" if not barbarians, who stormed in from the west by force and seized the Shang lands and treasures.[16] They excused this rapine by alleging that they had come to save the Shang from the wickedness of their ruler. Their accusations against the last Shang King appear to have been, in some respects at least, demonstrably false.[17] And the Chou said that they had been commanded to kill the Shang ruler and seize his territories by Heaven—a deity apparently peculiar to the Chou and alien to the Shang. How could the Shang be expected to accept all this, which must have appeared to them to be nonsense?

At first, it is clear, they did not accept it. After the conquest, King Wu seems to have left them in considerable measure undisturbed. The son of the last Shang King was enfeoffed as a Chou vassal, ruling over a portion of the conquered people, but under the watchful eyes of Inspectors—brothers of King Wu charged with the duty of preventing defection. At the death of King Wu there was, understandably, some relaxation of cohesion among the Chou people themselves; the death of a powerful conqueror is often a critical occasion, when various of his followers see the possibility of gaining a larger share of the spoils.[18]

---

15. Ch'i Ssu-ho ("Hsi-Chou Cheng-chih Ssu-hsiang," 23) calls the doctrine of the Mandate of Heaven "the most distinctive aspect of Chou thought, a point of fundamental difference from that of the Shang."

16. *Shu*, 37.

17. Tung, "Tuan-tai Yen-chiu," 404.

18. The document called the "Ta Kao" evidently comes from this time; it appears to be either by the Duke of Chou or by King Ch'eng. It says: "There are great troubles in the western territories, and the people of the western territories are not tranquil; they are crawling about" (*Shu*, 36–37). The "western territories" are presumably the original Chou lands.

To cope with this situation the Duke of Chou, who had no obvious claim to the supreme power, took control of the government. His brothers, the Inspectors, may well have thought he intended to usurp the throne; it may also be that, living among the more sophisticated Shang, they had become converted to their ways. In any case they joined the Shang scion, and the whole east—including some barbarian tribes—rose in an attempt to restore the Shang dynasty.

The Chou reaction was, as we have seen, decisive. Its effects seem to have been almost total, not only in making further revolt impracticable, but also in eradicating any tendency toward it. For centuries, all of our sources indicate, the Chou were not again required to take any military action to enforce their authority against any of the erstwhile Shang people. Shang armies, still so called, were incorporated into the military forces under direct command of the Chou King, and they appear to have been completely obedient to him.[19] The Chou theory of the Mandate of Heaven appears to have become completely and, insofar as we can tell, almost immediately prevalent. We find it even in a poem written by a descendant of the Shang in Western Chou times.[20] Five centuries after the conquest a scion of the Shang royal house said that it would be highly dangerous to attempt to raise their line to power again, for "Heaven's rejection of the Shang is of long standing."[21]

How did the Chou bring about this remarkable and, it would seem, almost instantaneous transformation? Certainly they used force, making a prolonged and vigorous military campaign and establishing trustworthy vassals with military garrisons throughout the rebellious territories. But force alone could not have produced the psychological change that appears to have occurred, which made the conquered people agree that the Chou ruled not only by might but also by right.

One need not be credulous to agree that it must have been done, in part, by good government. We have no reason to believe that in fact the government of late Shang times was as bad as the Chou propaganda painted it, and the Chou insistence that their motivation in the conquest was to bring tranquillity and justice to the people does not, of course, merit the slightest credence. But if the Chou government had been notably bad—if the administration had been weak or corrupt, if injustice had been so rampant as to provoke prolonged and serious resentment—the Chou could hardly even have maintained

---

19. See below, pp. 308–309.

20. *Shih*, 263. On the date of this poem see Creel, *Studies*, 49–54.

21. *Tso*, 181::183 (Hsi 22). Legge, in translating this passage, appears to have overlooked the name of the speaker; see *Tso-chuan*, 15.3ab.

their power, much less won the minds and eventually the hearts of their subjects.

Nevertheless, neither military force nor good government is sufficient to explain the rapidity and the completeness with which the Chou philosophy of government and history, based on the Mandate of Heaven, won the day. Before this could happen, the patterns of thought that had characterized the Shang state must have been eliminated, insofar as they conflicted with the Chou doctrine. And the Shang people must have been rendered receptive to the new ideas, even though they came from a source that had, at the beginning, little to recommend it to them.

One factor that helped to create a psychological and cultural vacuum among the Shang people is the fact that, after their revolt was crushed, many of them were transported from their accustomed homes to new areas. This is obvious in the sources, but its full importance has not perhaps been realized.

In our modern world many of us are so accustomed to moving about that we begin to be uneasy if we live in one place for more than a few years. If we read, as in Longfellow's "Evangeline," of people who feel that their whole lives are blighted because they must leave their native soil, we are sorry for them, but it is hard for us truly to sympathize, to feel *with* them. Our pity may be less for their fate than for their curious inability to adjust themselves. To us, their stubborn sentimental attachment to a particular place may seem abnormal. It may well be, however, that it is not they but our rootless selves who are abnormal.

It has often been remarked that the most stubborn fighting in war is done by a people defending its homeland against invasion. And boundary disputes, whether between nations or neighbors, generate rancor out of all proportion to the extent or the value of the territory involved. Even if such a contest is "settled" after a war or a lawsuit, the losing side may harbor irredentist sentiments for generations. This attachment to land appears to be deeply rooted in the human species. Recent studies indicate that it is also found among men's animal relatives.

C. R. Carpenter has written that "organized groups of monkeys and apes live in, occupy, possess and defend limited ranges of space and territories."[22] Such groups, he says, "are found to be strongly

22. Carpenter, "Social Behavior of Non-human Primates," 231. In publishing this generalization in 1952 Carpenter wrote that "there are no known exceptions" to it. This must be modified on the basis of studies of the mountain gorilla published more recently. It appears that while groups of gorillas do remain within a certain range, there is seldom antagonism between groups, or conflict when two groups en-

adjusted and conditioned to their home territories. They behave differently in these territories from the way they act near their extreme boundaries and limits." Charles Southwick concluded that among certain groups of monkeys he had studied "all displayed strong traditional attachment to specific areas within their home ranges."[23]

If such a group is uprooted from its native territory, the results may be disastrous. In 1938 several hundred rhesus monkeys were moved from their habitat in India to a small island near Puerto Rico so that they might be observed more readily. An unplanned by-product of this operation was a demonstration of the effect of forced "transportation." In India these monkeys had been organized into well-regulated groups; these groups were shattered. On the voyage, mothers fought their infants away from food and in some cases killed them. After the monkeys were released in their new home under conditions of complete freedom and abundant food, a year was required before their normal social organization was reconstituted. During this transitional year approximately as many young monkeys were killed, by males and sometimes by females, as were born.[24] The society was quite literally demoralized.

It is easy to conceive that the effects of forcible mass transportation upon a human group, with its more complex and delicately balanced culture, might be still more disruptive. And many historical instances indicate that in China and elsewhere rulers have long made use of this fact to destroy the morale and the will to resist of groups showing persistent dissidence.

Mass transportation as a punishment for groups that refused to cooperate with the authorities was known in Western Chou times, but we cannot tell to what extent it was actually carried out.[25] In the Spring and Autumn period we find whole populations moved about

---

counter each other. See: Schaller and Emlen, "Social Behavior of the Mountain Gorilla." Emlen and Schaller, "In the Home of the Mountain Gorilla." Southwick, "Intergroup Behavior in Primates," 451.

23. Carpenter, "Social Behavior of Non-human Primates," 231–232. Southwick, "Intergroup Behavior in Primates," 439.

24. Altmann, "Sociobiology of Rhesus Monkeys," 344. Carpenter, "Societies of Monkeys and Apes," 199–200.

25. It is threatened by the Duke of Chou in *Shu*, 65. An early Western Chou bronze inscription (*Chin-wen*, 26a) relates that a group of men was found guilty of failing to follow the King to war. The official judging the case says that according to justice they ought to be banished (or transported), but in fact this penalty was not imposed in this case. Banishment is also mentioned as a possible punishment in *Chin-wen*, 127a.

with great frequency, and in some cases at least involuntarily.[26] In 221 b.c., after he had completed his conquest of China, the First Emperor of Ch'in "transported to Hsien-yang [his capital] all of the outstanding and wealthy persons of the empire, to the number of one hundred twenty thousand families."[27] In a similar move the founder of the Han dynasty transported more than one hundred thousand persons belonging to "powerful families" to his capital area, to prevent them from making trouble for the new regime.[28] In 127 b.c. the Han Emperor Wu moved a number of the powerful and wealthy, together with others called "disorderly" persons, to an area near his capital.[29] These are merely a few of the more conspicuous instances of the forcible transportation of large numbers of people in early Chinese history. The purpose, as memorials recommending these measures make clear, was both to put these people where they could readily be kept under surveillance and to render them harmless by uprooting them from their normal environment and associations.

A particularly interesting use of the device of transportation was made by the famous Chu-Ke Liang, in a.d. 225. The territories he administered were troubled by rebellion among tribesmen in what is now Yünnan and western Kweichow. His armies put down the rebellions, but certain Ch'iang tribesmen were such persistent troublemakers that he moved ten thousand households of them to the capital, Chengtu. "These people, taken afar to a strange land, became quite docile and were formed into a valuable and efficient military division."[30]

The Inca Empire was formed by conquests which were consolidated by mass transportation. John Howland Rowe writes:

> One of the most famous of *Inca* administrative policies was the resettlement or colonization program. The principle behind it was that by reshuffling the population older political units would be broken and it would be more difficult for the inhabitants of a province to plot revolt. When a new province was conquered, settlers were brought into it from some province which had

26. For some cases that were clearly involuntary see *Tso*, 97::97 (Chuang 18), 428::429 (Hsiang 6), 775::778 (Ting 10). In most cases it is simply stated that the people were moved; whether they liked it or not probably made little difference.

27. *Shih-chi*, 6.30; *Mémoires historiques*, II, 137.

28. *Han-shu*, 43.13b.

29. Ibid., 6.10b, 64A.19b. Dubs, *Han-shu*, II, 52.

30. Buote, "Chu-ko Liang and the Kingdom of Shu-Han," 70–71, 131–134.

been under *Inca* government long enough to know the system, and their place was filled with the most re-calcitrant elements of the new province. . . . Loyal settlers sent to colonize a newly conquered province were charged with setting an example to the original inhabitants, spreading the use of Quechua [the language used for official business], and acting as an *Inca* garrison. . . .

The scale and the effect of the *Inca* colonization program have not been fully recognized. . . . Shuffling populations on this gigantic scale made the *Inca* Empire a regular melting pot, and there is no doubt that, even if the convulsions which the Spanish Conquest brought had not speeded up the process, the old tribal divisions would have entirely lost their significance in a couple of generations, and the heterogeneous population of the Empire would have become a single nation.[31]

The Chou welded the various peoples of the territories they had conquered into a nation, and it is clear that one of the means they used was the transportation of population. After the great Shang rebellion had been crushed, when the Duke of Chou directed the building of a subordinate capital called Le near the modern site of Loyang, he had two purposes in mind. On the one hand this provided a convenient point from which the Chou could supervise their eastern territories. On the other, it provided a place in which the former officers of the fallen dynasty could be concentrated together, kept under surveillance, and indoctrinated.

The *Documents* seems to suggest that all of the labor of constructing the new city was supplied by Yin people.[32] Although the circumstances are not clear, it seems possible that large numbers of them were marched to the site for the work, and that only a portion of those who performed the labor remained to occupy the city. Its population appears to have included substantially all of the former Shang officials. One of the writings in the *Documents* begins:

In the third month the Duke of Chou first went to the new city Le, and on that occasion made an announcement to the royal officers of Shang: "The King speaks thus: 'You, the remaining many officers of Yin!' "[33]

31. Rowe, "Inca Culture at the Time of the Spanish Conquest," 269–270.
32. *Shu*, 48.
33. *Shu*, 55. Karlgren translates: "In the 3rd month Chou Kung started in the new city Lo . . ." But in bronze inscriptions 于 *yü* sometimes has the sense of "to

The Chou hoped, by bringing the Shang officials into daily contact with themselves, to remold their thinking and convert them into loyal officers of the Chou. The Duke of Chou says at one point that the King should associate the Shang officials with those of Chou so as to "discipline their minds, so that they may progress daily." Again he quotes the King as saying: "I tell you, many officers . . . I have brightly applied Heaven's punishment. I have removed you far, to associate with and serve our dignitaries with much obedience." It is clear that the Shang officials bitterly resented this removal from their homes, but the Duke tells them repeatedly that it is their own fault. If they are obedient "we lords of Chou will greatly help and reward you. We will promote and select you to be in the royal court. We will give you high office."[34]

If they remain recalcitrant however, they will, the Duke warns, be severely punished. He threatens them with death, and finally says: "I will move you far from your lands."[35] It would appear that the threat of transportation was considered even more fearful than that of death.

To what extent other Shang people were moved from their former homes is less clear, but there are indications that the amount of transportation was considerable. The *Tso-chuan* has the following account:

> Formerly King Wu conquered Shang, and King Ch'eng consolidated [the Chou dynasty]. He selected and enfeoffed those having bright virtue, to act as bulwarks and screens to Chou. . . . He gave to the Duke of Lu . . . six groups[36] of the Yin people. . . . They were com-

---

go to"; see Ch'en, "Hsi-Chou T'ung-ch'i," (2).78. This seems to make better sense here. And the "Shao Kao" (*Shu*, 48) does indicate that the Duke of Chou first visited the site after work had started in the third month. This does not of course mean that the Duke had never before been in the area, but it had not previously been a "new city."

34. *Shu*, 49, 56, 65.

35. *Shu*, 65.

36. The character that I have here translated as "group" is *tsu* 族 , which Karlgren ("Grammata Serica Recensa," 311) defines as "clan, kin, group of families." But it is very hard to be sure what this character means in Western Chou contexts, where it never seems to be linked with a surname. It does not occur in the twelve chapters of the *Documents* that I accept as Western Chou. In the *Poetry* it occurs only three times: *Shih*, 7, 69, 129. In my bronze inscriptions it is found seven times: *Chin-wen*, 10b, 18b, 20b, 88b, 133a, 135a (twice). The sense of *tsu* is often difficult to determine; in some cases it may be part of an official title (see ibid., 138b).

In the context of *Chin-wen*, 20b, *tsu* may have the sense of "army." Karlgren ("Grammata Serica Recensa," 311) says, "The graph has 'banner' and 'arrow': clan,

manded to lead their kindred, and collect their various branches, together with all those connected with them, and to take them to Chou to receive their orders, so that they might be instructed by[37] the Duke of Chou. They were then caused to take up their duties in Lu.[38]

This appears to mean that these six groups of Shang people, together with all their dependents and retainers, were first marched to the Chou capital in the west to receive instruction and then compelled to go eastward to the territory of Lu, traversing much of the breadth of north China.[39] If so, this must have left them in a chastened and receptive condition.

In a study of the origins of the state of Lu, Fu Ssu-nien concluded that its population was wholly made up of Shang people, except for a very small ruling group of Chou men. He cited various pieces of evidence to show that Shang customs and culture were carried on in the state of Lu.[40] No doubt they were. Yet Lu was also noted as the repository of the Chou archives and Chou culture, and the great pride of the state of Lu in later times was the fact that its rulers were de-

---

military unit." For other opinions that *tsu* may originally have stood for a military unit see Li, *Chia-ku Wen-tzu Chi-shih*, VII, 2231–2233. Certainly it did come to have the sense of a kinship group, but whether it did or did not have this sense in Western Chou times seems uncertain.

That *tsu* in this passage in the *Tso-chuan* did indicate kinship groups might seem to be demonstrated by the fact that these groups are listed by name, with six names each followed by *shih* 氏 . But this character too is quite rare in the Western Chou sources, and it is not clear that it ever stands in them for such a kinship group; see below, pp. 333–334. Thus its use here in the *Tso-chuan* may be anachronistic, a case of a man of Spring and Autumn times using the vocabulary of his own day rather than of Western Chou times.

37. Literally, "that they might pattern themselves after."

38. *Tso*, 750::754 (Ting 4). The characters of critical importance here are 即命於周, which I have translated "to take them to Chou to receive their orders." Legge translates "to repair with them to Chow." This is evidently the way in which the passage was understood by the commentator Tu Yü; see *Tso-chuan*, 54.15b. But in Couvreur, *Tso-chuan*, III, 502, this is translated "à suivre les ordres des souverains de la famille Tcheou." Certainly the passage is not completely unambiguous, but in my opinion the rendering I have given is justified in the context.

39. According to one opinion, the state of Lu was at first located near the Chou capital, and only later moved east, but this appears improbable; see below, p. 357. Ch'i Ssu-ho ("Chou-tai Hsi-ming-li K'ao," 216) says that the "Chou" mentioned in this passage is the subsidiary capital near the modern Loyang, but this seems quite uncertain. Ch'i says that this transportation of the Shang people was "probably to disperse them in order to prevent them from again raising rebellion, and at the same time to populate a border area."

40. Fu, "Chou Tung Feng yü Yin I-min," 286–289.

scended from the Duke of Chou.[41] In Lu, as perhaps nowhere else, we can see how completely the Chou succeeded in winning the allegiance of the conquered people.

Other evidence concerning the transportation of Shang people after the conquest is less conclusive. The *Tso-chuan* says that seven groups of Yin people were given to the first ruler of the state of Wèi, but it does not say whether they were moved to a new location.[42] A work compiled in Warring States times says that after they had revolted, the captive Yin people "were moved to nine locations." And aside from these deliberate transportations by the Chou, the civilian population must have been considerably dispersed in the course of two military campaigns, the original conquest and the suppression of the subsequent rebellion; dispersal is normal in such cases. In the *Documents* we find the Yin people referred to as "fugitive" and "scattered like chaff."[43]

CERTAINLY there was a great deal of carry-over of ideas and institutions from before the conquest—though it may never be possible to determine precisely how much. But it is also clear that, in a manner that is hardly suggested by traditional Chinese history, this was a time in which a new spirit, a new pattern of political thinking, and a new nation were forged by the heat and pressure of catastrophic events. The Shang people were battered and scattered by two great wars and by deliberate transportations thereafter. Their traditional patterns of social and political action were greatly altered if not destroyed. Their assurance of their own superiority could not be maintained in the face of the invaders who occupied almost all of the places of power and privilege.

A new concept of the state, based upon the idea of the Mandate of Heaven, came into being. No alteration of this basic concept, of anything approaching comparable scope and depth, would again occur in China before the twentieth century. The doctrine of the Mandate of Heaven became the cornerstone of the Chinese Empire.

Henceforward China was a state—and, since it ideally embraced "all under heaven," the only state—created by, and maintained under the direct supervision of, the highest deity, Heaven. Its ruler was the Son of Heaven. His office bestowed the highest glory possible to man. His officials shone in the reflection of this glory, and under weak

41. *Tso*, 582::583 (Chao 2).
42. *Tso*, 750::754 (Ting 4).
43. *Chi-chung Chou-shu*, 5.8a. *Shu*, 37, 39.

Kings the loyalty of feudal lords was often guaranteed by the fact that it was more splendid to be second to the Son of Heaven than first among rulers exercising only mundane power.

The Son of Heaven also bore the most awesome burden of responsibility. Only the continued welfare of the people could justify his continued enjoyment of his power and his title. If things went wrong, it was the duty of another to overthrow him. A successful King would become, after his death, one of the honored royal ancestors who, in the heavens, were the arbiters of destiny. But if he failed, he would join the ranks of the execrated, constantly cited as examples of infamy. The worst possibility of all was that his own end might also be that of his dynasty, making him one of the outstanding malefactors of history.

The doctrine of the Mandate of Heaven was not merely a force making for responsible conduct on the part of the monarch and cementing the loyalty of his vassals and officials; it has also been the central cohesive force binding together the entire Chinese people, even the humblest. The feeling of the Chinese that they are superior to all other peoples is undoubtedly related to the conviction that they, and they alone, have lived under a government established and supervised by Heaven. And this doctrine has given every Chinese individual a role in the unfolding drama of the Chinese state. Because it is for the people, finally, that this state has been held to exist, and no rightful government has been able to persist in the face of continued public dissatisfaction. Thus we find Confucius stating that no government can stand if it lacks the confidence of the common people, and Mencius quoting with approval the saying that it is the common people who speak for Heaven.[44]

A NUMBER of documents were produced, early in Western Chou times, discussing the Mandate of Heaven and the reasons for which it was granted and revoked. These documents have been appealed to countless times in Chinese history, by critics opposing the government and officials defending it, and even by Emperors in their edicts.[45] These documents have functioned, in a sense, as a kind of constitution, defining both the duties of rulers and the grounds upon which,

44. *Analects*, 12.7. *Mencius*, 5(1).5.8.

45. It must be noted that documents of this type that have been appealed to, in later times, have included not only those that I accept as genuine writings from the beginning of Chou, but also others that many critical scholars do not accept. At various times documents have been produced and attributed to this early period; in varying degrees they have been modeled upon and influenced by the genuinely early works.

it could be argued, they might rightfully be deposed. Both for this reason and in order to understand what conduct was approved and disapproved at the beginning of Chou, it is important to examine this literature carefully.

One somewhat curious motif need detain us only briefly, as it seems to have had little effect on later history. In the *Documents*, the *Poetry*, and at least one bronze inscription, we find it alleged that the Shang fell into evil ways because of their addiction to intoxicating liquor.[46] It appears that the Chou had been accustomed to use liquor only in sacrificial ceremonies; the association of intoxication with religious rites is not uncommon. Evidently the ways of the more sophisticated Shang appeared to them shocking, and they considered the consumption of liquor apart from sacrifice a dissolute practice. Kings Wen and Wu, living before the Chou had mingled with the eastern peoples and become familiar with their customs, appear to have been particularly exercised by the dangers of drinking. Wu was concerned to break the Shang people of this bad habit, but was willing to treat them leniently in view of their unfortunate background. But as for others, he instructed one of his brothers in sending him to his fief, "If it is reported that a group is drinking together, do not let them escape; seize them all and send them to Chou [the capital] and I will kill them."[47] There is very little indication of this kind of concern, however, after the beginning of the dynasty.[48] In the *Poetry*, while drunkenness is occasionally deplored, the pleasures of drinking are appreciated. In general, throughout Chinese history, there seems to be little puritanism as regards the use of alcohol, although moderation is usually advocated.[49]

Impiety is a charge that is leveled against both Hsia and Shang rulers who lost the Mandate. The last Shang King, it is alleged, failed to make the usual sacrifices. He "despised Heaven's command"; both he and the last Hsia ruler failed to understand, or to accept the guidance of, the supreme deity.[50] But the earlier Hsia and Shang Kings (before the last wicked ruler of each dynasty) were distinguished for their piety, and so of course were King Wen and King Wu.[51]

Concerning the last Shang King, the evidence we have seems to indicate that, very far from neglecting his religious functions, he was

46. *Shu*, 43–46. *Shih*, 215. *Chin-wen*, 33b–34a.
47. *Shu*, 43–46.
48. See, however, *Chin-wen*, 135a.
49. *Shih*, 173–174, 175, 218, 254. The permissive and even approving attitude of the *Analects* (2.8, 3.7, 6.9, 9.15, 10.8, 10.10) toward drinking, though with emphasis on moderation, is significant and has undoubtedly had great influence.
50. *Shu*, 45, 55, 62–64.
51. *Shu*, 37, 45, 49, 55, 61, 65. *Shih*, 188.

especially meticulous in discharging them.[52] Throughout Chinese history, there seem to be few cases of emperors who have failed to perform their religious duties. Even the First Emperor of Ch'in (who died in 210 B.C.) and Emperor Wu of Han (reigned 140–87 B.C.), who are condemned as tyrants, are criticized rather for their excessive addiction to religious or "superstitious" practices than for neglecting them. The official religion was the basis on which their position rested; any ruler tempted to flout it was no doubt deterred by the well-publicized fate of the last Hsia and Shang sovereigns. If later Emperors needed a lesson nearer at hand, they could find it in the career of the Han scion Liu He, who was made Emperor in 74 B.C. In his joy at this elevation he abandoned himself to conduct that violated (among other things) his religious obligations. After twenty-seven days the chief ministers adjudged him unworthy to conduct the imperial sacrifices, and dethroned him by force.[53] (Precedent for this action was found in the alleged banishment of the Shang King T'ai Chia by his minister I Yin.)[54]

A major reason for loss of the Mandate of Heaven was failure to attend earnestly to government. The last Kings of both Hsia and Shang "treated the tasks of government with contempt." The earlier Shang Kings and their ministers, on the contrary, were zealous in their administration. King Wen created a well-governed domain in the west, giving it order and harmony, and we are told by both King Wu and the Duke of Chou that it is this that attracted the attention of Heaven and led to his receiving the Mandate.[55]

The services of ministers in helping to make good government possible were recognized by King Wu, but in the earliest Chou materials it is only the Duke of Chou who declares them to be indispensable. He says that the officials of the last Hsia ruler "could not protect and benefit the people," but oppressed them. Heaven then ordered the founder of Shang "to displace the Hsia, so that men of talent might rule the land." And he and his successors had illustrious advisers who protected and directed them. Finally, when the Mandate was taken over and Chou was established by Wen and Wu, this was accomplished by the merit of their advisers—among whom the Duke is too modest to name himself.[56]

52. Tung,"Tuan-tai Yen-chiu," 404.

53. *Han-shu*, 8.3a, 63.17b–20a, 68.4b–10a. Dubs, *Han-shu*, II, 180–183, 203–204.

54. See p. 39.

55. *Shu*, 39, 45, 61, 64–65.

56. *Shu*, 45, 55, 61. A passage in the *Poetry* (*Shih*, 214–216) quotes King Wen as saying that the loss of the Mandate by Shang is impending, in part, because of

Very little that is specific is told us about the kind of government that Heaven considered bad, and the reverse. The most definite information concerns punishment. The unworthy last rulers of Hsia and Shang are criticized both for failure to punish crime and for lack of clemency. But the earlier Shang Kings put to death those guilty of many crimes, and freed the innocent. King Wen was particularly careful in the use of punishments, for which he laid down definite principles, and he did not oppress even the humblest of the people.[57]

The people, more than any other factor, are emphasized as the key to the Mandate of Heaven. More often than personal sobriety, than zeal in administration, or even than piety, the importance of treating the people well and gaining their goodwill is insisted upon. The last Hsia ruler did not protect or benefit the people, and would not even speak solicitously to them. Similarly the last Shang King did not respect the people, but mistreated them and made them miserable. Their resentment was heard on high, so that Heaven took pity on them and gave its Mandate to Chou, to put an end to the cruelties.[58]

The wise Kings of Shang, however, King Wu tells us, "feared the brightness of Heaven, and the little people." These good Shang rulers benefited and enriched their subjects. King Wen, who received the Mandate, cared for all the people and did not mistreat even the helpless and solitary.[59]

THE great impression made by the early Chou literature is that of the earnestness of the men who found themselves in very precarious control of a huge and diverse realm. Their task was indeed staggering. At its largest, the Western Chou empire was probably larger than that of the Shang.[60] The populace varied from the uncooperative to the actively and incessantly hostile. For the Chou, with no decisively superior military techniques or weapons, and relatively little political experience, the prospect of bringing such an area under real control was far from bright.

The leaders were under no illusions. Although they claimed to

---

the use of bad officials, but it is by no means certain that this poem was not written at a time later than the beginning of Chou.

57. *Shu*, 39, 45, 64–65. See also *Chin-wen*, 33b.

58. *Shu*, 37, 45, 49, 55.

59. *Shu*, 39, 45, 55, 61, 65.

60. Ch'en Meng-chia, in *Yin Tz'u Tsung-shu*, 311, estimates the Shang territories to have included the modern Shantung, Hopei, and Honan provinces, plus the northern portions of Anhui and Kiangsu. The Western Chou Empire was considerably larger; see p. 101, note 1.

have received the Mandate of Heaven, they did not suppose that this guaranteed success. The need for constant vigilance and unremitting effort is emphasized again and again, in both the *Documents* and the *Poetry*. The Duke of Chou expresses concern for the future. "If our sons and grandsons cannot be respectful above and below [toward Heaven and the people], and destroy the glory that our ancestors have brought to our house—if they do not remember that Heaven's Mandate is not easy to keep, and that Heaven is not to be relied upon, they will overturn the Mandate."[61]

The Chou claim that the last Shang ruler neglected his duties may have been a libel,[62] but they did not charge him with responsibilities that they themselves were unwilling to assume. "If there is any fault," King Wu says, "Heaven will punish and kill me, and I shall not resent it." When the Shang people revolted, it was acknowledged that a part of the fault lay with the Chou rule. The Duke of Chou said, "Now that the King has received the Mandate, it brings boundless felicity —but also boundless anxiety." The difficulty of being a ruler, and the insistence that those in high position can keep it only by unremitting application to their duties, are themes that recur again and again in the *Poetry* and the bronze inscriptions. A King is a public person; he must abide by the rules, and he cannot even afford the luxury of close friendships.[63]

"I am concerned," the Duke of Chou says, "only about heaven and the people." The people, he complains, are fickle. It is quite clear that the Chou rulers, although they talk a great deal about Heaven, have their eyes anxiously on the populace. King Wu said, "The ancients had a saying, 'Men should not mirror themselves in water, but in the people.'" On another occasion he said, "Now the people are not quiet, they have not yet settled their minds."[64] Still later the Duke of Chou refers to "the King's hostile people," and says that the King should seek good understanding with the "small people" and should "fear the danger of the people."[65]

In accord with this we find, in all the documents, repeated emphasis on the necessity of treating the people with consideration, caring for them, not oppressing them, not impoverishing them by heavy exactions, not condemning them for crimes of which they are innocent.

61. *Shu*, 43, 49, 59. *Shih*, 186, 249.
62. Tung, "Tuan tai Yen-chiu," 404, 417. Ku, "Chou E Ch'i-shih Shih."
63. *Shu*, 37, 40, 42, 48, 52, 62, 80. *Shih*, 188, 205–206, 218, 241. *Chin-wen*, 134b.
64. *Shu*, 42, 45, 62.
65. *Shu*, 49. Karlgren translates this "be apprehensive of the people's talk," and explains his translation in "Glosses on the Book of Documents," (2).68–69. I find his argument unconvincing.

In the *Documents* and the *Poetry,* and in bronze inscriptions dating from late as well as early in Western Chou, this theme is pervasive.[66] King Wu said to his officials: "Attend even to the helpless and solitary, attend even to pregnant women . . . from of old the Kings have done so."[67]

They may seem to protest too much. While we have very little knowledge of the life of the common people in Western Chou times, it is clear that it was not the idyllic existence that some of the later Confucian idealizations represented it as being. The *Poetry* makes a number of references to the oppression of the people, to excessive exactions of goods and of forced labor, and to protests on the part of the people. It also records complaints by men who must go on long military expeditions, and by their families.[68] Yet the history of any people, covering several centuries, is likely to include such things. Over against such passages we must place the poems in which the life of those who labor on the great estates is depicted as being by no means without its pleasures, and the relationships between the rulers and the ruled as characterized by a certain genuine regard.[69] Some skepticism concerning these bright pictures is undoubtedly justified, yet nothing seems to indicate that the lot of the humblest in Western Chou was often characterized by the "brutality and degradation" that were common on some of the *latifundia* of the Romans.[70]

IT is interesting and important to note that, in all of this early literature concerned with the Mandate of Heaven, attention is centered almost exclusively on the two extremes of the political scale: the King and the common people. There is some intermediation of officials and perhaps even of feudal lords; the duty of attending "even to pregnant women" could hardly be discharged by the King personally. But there is direct concern by the King for the people; and if they are neglected, it is the fault of the King, and he will be punished for it. There is scarcely any clear reference to feudal lords in this connec-

---

66. *Shu,* 39–43, 45–46, 49, 64–65, 78–80. *Shih,* 206, 208, 210–213, 218, 229. *Chin-wen,* 75b, 121a, 133a, 135a, 140b–141a.

67. *Shu,* 46. For his emendation of this passage, see Karlgren, "Glosses on the Book of Documents," (1).311. This sounds like strange language for a King. But compare (Bryce, *Holy Roman Empire,* 66) the oath by which Charlemagne bound his subjects "to do no violence nor treason toward the holy Church, or to widows, or orphans, or strangers, seeing that the lord Emperor has been appointed . . . the protector and defender of all such."

68. *Shih,* 73–74, 111–114, 125, 127, 135–137, 184–185, 212–213, 220–223.

69. *Shih,* 95–96, 97–99, 109–110, 116, 165–167, 177, 250–251.

70. *Cambridge Ancient History,* IX, 12.

tion, or any suggestion that the King delegates such functions to sub-ordinates in such manner that it is they who must assume the blame for failure.

The direct concern and responsibility of the King (in theory, at least) for the welfare of the common people that we find here is not what we should expect in a long-established feudal regime. It is typical rather of a centralized state. At the beginning of the Spring and Autumn period, when we get a clear view of a society in which feudal institutions have been functioning for centuries, we find very little evidence of concern either for the welfare or for the opinions of the common people.[71] It is probable that the reason for this is that by this time there was no longer anything that could be called "the common people" as a large group. They had become rather the subjects and retainers of a multitude of vassals and subvassals; they might, to be sure, give trouble, but they could not easily coalesce into a group large enough to become a major problem beyond a single small local-ity. But as feudalism broke down late in the Spring and Autumn period, we do find some expressions of concern for and about the people. We also find demagogues rising to power by courting popular favor.[72] This foreshadows the centralized regimes of Warring States times.

At the beginning of Western Chou, feudalism—or at least Chou feudalism—was a new institution.[73] The feudal lords were instru-ments of the King; they had not yet achieved a degree of independence that could impair the essentially centralized character of the government. The doctrine of the Mandate of Heaven, emphasizing the direct stewardship over the common people entrusted by Heaven to the King, corresponded to this situation. It was anomalous, even though it was not forgotten, in the conditions that came to prevail in the Spring and Autumn and Warring States periods.

In this respect as in many others the Western Chou period saw the rise of ideas and institutions that would not, perhaps, reach their full effectiveness until they came to be embodied, more than half a millen-nium later, in the developed pattern of China's imperial government.

71. By the beginning of the Spring and Autumn period feudalism, as a system by which the King governed China as a whole, was moribund and perhaps dead. Within individual states, however, it was—with variations—still alive. And feudal institutions and attitudes had been consolidated by development through the centuries of Western Chou.

72. A particularly famous case is that of the Ch'en family which finally suc-ceeded in taking over the throne of the state of Ch'i. See Creel, *Confucius*, 53::62–63.

73. See pp. 317–387.

CHAPTER
6

The Royal Government: Organization

THE size of the Western Chou Empire cannot be determined with precision. It appears, however, that within a few decades of the conquest the Chou King claimed, and maintained at least a network of control over, a territory considerably larger than the combined areas of France, Belgium, and the Netherlands.[1]

As is true in every state of any size and importance, the Kings maintained their control, in part, by virtue of the fact that they had well-organized military forces upon which they could call, in case of necessity, to enforce their authority. But it is a remarkable fact that, insofar as our sources indicate, they rarely did so. For a period of some two centuries, after the initial conquest and consolidation, we find almost no record of military activity against Chinese, but only against barbarians.[2]

This clearly means that there was an effective government, able

---

1. Ch'i Ssu-ho made an extensive study of the geography of the Western Chou period in his "Hsi-Chou Ti-li K'ao." Two years later he published a summary of his conclusions on the area, in Ch'i, "Hsi-Chou Cheng-chih Ssu-hsiang," 20. There he said that the Empire included all of the modern provinces of Shansi, Honan, and Shantung, and portions of Shensi, Kansu, Kiangsu, Hupei, and Hopei. His assignment of only a portion of Hopei to the Chou was presumably influenced by his opinion that the state of Yen, in the northeast, was not an early Chou fief; see Ch'i, "Yen Wu Fei Chou Feng-kuo Shuo." More recent discoveries and research have shown, however, that it was; see below, pp. 358–361.

As a basis for an estimate, I believe it is reasonable to assume that the Chou had some control over one-half of Shensi, and all of Honan, Shansi, Shantung, and Hopei. Their network of control may not have extended over all of each of these provinces, and their territories undoubtedly included additional areas, but I believe that these factors should average out for a rough estimate. The areas I have named total a little more than 282,000 square miles. The combined area of France, Belgium, and the Netherlands is approximately 237,000 square miles.

2. See below, pp. 298–300.

to rule with little use of military force. And even the maintenance and control of a far-flung military establishment implies the existence of a well-run administration with an adequate financial system and legal machinery. The question is not then—though it has often been asked—whether there was an effective central government in Western Chou times. The question is, rather, what kind of government it was, how it functioned, and how it was organized.

THE degree to which the Chou merely continued a previously existing pattern of government, or on the contrary instituted a new political system, has been hotly debated. The great prestige of the Chou, and especially the popularity of the Duke of Chou with scholars, have led many to hold that the Chou or even the Duke alone created a new system of administration that became the basis of the Chinese governmental pattern of later times. This opinion has been championed by highly critical scholars in our own time.[3] But when excavation and research in the twentieth century gave new evidence of the high de-

---

3. Wang Kuo-wei was the great and influential champion of such views among recent critical scholars; see Wang, *Kuan-t'ang Chi-lin*, 10. More recently Ch'i Ssu-ho has held that the cardinal Chinese virtues of *hsiao* 孝 and *t'i* 悌 , filial piety and regard for elder brothers, began with the Chou; see Ch'i, "Hsi-Chou Cheng-chih Ssu-hsiang," 33.

The latter point is bound up with the exceedingly complex subject of *tsung-fa* 宗法. Feng (*Chinese Kingship System*, 33–35) says: "Sib organization is called *tsung fa* in Chinese, literally, the 'law of kindred.' The *tsung fa* was bound up with the feudal system, which was swept away in the course of the third century B.C. . . . *Tsung fa* itself has been well studied, and we need here consider only those two of its characteristics which have direct influence upon the alignment of relatives, viz., patrilineal descent and exogamy. With the *tsung*, the sib, each line of descent is strictly patrilineal. . . . It is also primogenitary: the eldest brother has priority over the younger brothers." Some qualification is necessary, however. If there has in fact been "primogeniture" in China, it has not operated as it commonly has in the West, for rulers seem always to have had the legal right to designate a son other than the eldest as heir. It seems better to avoid the term, which tends to be misleading. As for "sib exogamy," Feng points out that it was by no means strictly enforced in the Chou period and has been enforced by law only since the middle of the first millennium A.D.

Some scholars have considered *tsung-fa* to be an innovation of the Chou, since in Shang times the throne was inherited (in some cases at least) by a brother of the deceased ruler rather than by his eldest son. Hu Hou-hsüan argues, however, that the institution of *tsung-fa* was fully developed during the latter part of the Shang dynasty; see Hu, "Yin Hun-yin Chia-tsu Tsung-far K'ao." This subject has attracted a great deal of debate, which in my opinion is to some degree fruitless. The evidence is obscure, and the conclusions drawn from it are sometimes more sweeping than seems wholly warranted.

gree of culture and sophistication of the Shang, a reaction against the glorification of the Chou was inevitable. As a result some have gone so far as to assert that the Chou originated very little, but merely took over the cultural and political institutions of the Shang with little change.[4] Neither of these extreme positions is tenable.

It is entirely evident that the Chou did not sweep away all Shang usages and did not have the slightest intention of doing so.[5] No people has placed a higher value on history or given more emphasis to tradition than the Chinese, and these tendencies were characteristic of the Chou from the beginning of the dynasty. "Alas!" says the *Poetry*, "our framers of plans do not take the ancients as their pattern." Disorder, another poem tells us, is caused by the fact that those in government do not sufficiently study the ways of the former Kings. Still another describes a good minister as one who "takes the ancient teachings as his model."[6] In the *Documents* King Wu appeals to authority by declaring, "The ancients had a saying . . . ," and the Duke of Chou says that the young King Ch'eng should not neglect the advice of the elders, so that he may understand "our ancient men's virtue." Similar sentiments occur in bronze inscriptions.[7]

The practical value of history is repeatedly emphasized. King Wen is quoted as saying, "The mirror for Yin is not distant, it is in the age of the lords of Hsia." (This passage directly inspired Ssu-Ma Kuang, in the eleventh century A.D., to entitle his great history *A Comprehensive Mirror for Aid in Government*.)[8] And both King Wu and the Duke of Chou say that the Chou must study the fate of their predecessors, as a mirror that reflects the fate of those who fail to measure up to the responsibilities of power.[9]

No less prominent, however, is the insistence by the Chou rulers that the good governmental practices of the Yin must be studied and utilized. We might expect that King Wu, the actual conqueror, would be contemptuous of those he had overthrown, but he is not in the least. In instructing his younger brother concerning government, he

4. Hu, "Yin Feng-chien K'ao," 1b–2a. Hsü, "Yin Chou Wen-hua."

5. This does not conflict irreconcilably with the possibility, suggested earlier, that the Chou may have had a hand in the disappearance of Shang literature that did not agree with their doctrine of the Mandate of Heaven. Those who take over traditions almost always do so selectively, consciously or unconsciously emphasizing that which suits their own purposes and ignoring or suppressing that which is inconvenient.

6. *Shih*, 142, 218, 228.

7. *Shu*, 45, 49. *Chin-wen*, 13a, 134b–135a.

8. *Shih*, 216. Ssu-Ma, *Tzu-chih T'ung-chien*, Preface, 2b.

9. *Shu*, 45, 49.

says: "Go and seek out, from the former wise Kings of Yin, that which may be used to protect and govern the people. . . . I always think of the virtue of Yin's former wise Kings, in order to tranquillize and govern the people." With regard to penal law, he tells him to "follow those laws of the Yin that have good principles. . . . Use their just punishments and just killings."[10]

When the eastern capital of the Chou, near the present Loyang, had been completed under the supervision of the Duke of Chou, he recommended to the King that the Yin officials be associated there with those of Chou. The principal purpose of this was to assimilate them to Chou usages, but there must obviously have been an exchange in both directions.[11]

The purpose of conciliation was strongly in the minds of the Chou rulers, and this was undoubtedly a part of the reason for their accommodation to Shang practices. Furthermore, if the Chou were intelligent, they must have been eager to learn from the politically far more experienced Shang—and the Chou were very intelligent. It is clear that they learned, and took over, a good deal of Shang governmental practice.

This is not the same thing, however, as taking over a system of government *in toto*. Since we know so very little about Shang government, and far less than we should like about that of Western Chou, it is not easy to compare them. But there are good reasons to think that there were significant differences.

It is doubtful that the Chou could have used the governmental system of the Shang, without major alterations, if they had wished to. They apparently thought, at first, that they could let the eastern regions govern themselves very much as before, but they were disillusioned by the great rebellion that was only crushed by a major military effort. Not only did the Chou, in all probability, lack sufficient knowledge of the Shang governmental machinery to use it effectively; they were also in a totally different position. The people of the east regarded them, however wrongly, as essentially "barbarians." The Shang, with centuries of successful rule behind them, and ties of various sorts with the different areas of their realm, could undoubtedly hold their territories with far less need for constant supervision and ever-ready force than was essential for the Chou.

So much for speculation. There are also a few pieces of evidence that, in fact, there must have been considerable differences between

10. *Shu*, 40–42.
11. *Shu*, 49.

Shang and Chou government. It has been supposed that one of those differences was feudalism, which began with the Chou. But there are also those who say that the Shang had feudalism, which was merely taken over by their successors. Since a later chapter will deal with feudalism, it is unnecessary to go into details here, except to point out that there is much reason to think that, whether the Shang had some kind of feudalism or not, feudalism as it existed under the Chou was essentially a new institution.

Our most tangible evidence concerning Shang and Chou government comes from the titles of offices. Even this is not easy to appraise; we cannot always be sure what is or is not an official title, and very often it is impossible to determine the functions that pertain to it.[12] Nevertheless, such titles do provide a guide of sorts. My notes on Western Chou bronze inscriptions list more than two and one-half times the number of official titles that was found by Ch'en Meng-chia in Shang inscriptions on bone and bronzes.[13]

We cannot necessarily conclude that the Chou government was more complex because there were more official titles. In Western Chou there seems to have been a great deal of change, so that men discharging essentially similar functions at different times bore different titles. But this in itself would appear to indicate that the Chou were experimenting, feeling their way toward a pattern of government suited to their own situation. If they did take over the Shang system, they did not follow it slavishly and permanently.

Even near the beginning of Western Chou there is clear indication that the government was by no means a complete copy of that of the Shang. Our earliest clear information on Western Chou officers comes in a section of the *Documents* that describes events at the time of the death of King Ch'eng in 1079 B.C. It lists officials who were assembled to hear the statement made by the King on the day before his death. It also contains another list, slightly different, of dignitaries

---

12. Maspero ("La société chinoise," 386–402) gives a long and detailed description of important Western Chou officials, with many references to bronze inscriptions. But he makes use, in addition to Western Chou sources, of much later material including the *Ritual of Chou* and the *Tso-chuan*. The *Tso-chuan*, despite its late date, certainly contains much valid information on Western Chou. But for the present purpose it seems better to stay with the contemporary sources.

13. Ch'en (*Yin Tz'u Tsung-shu*, 503–522) says that he has encountered "more than twenty" official titles in Shang inscriptions. As he lists these, if we include all of the minute variations, they total thirty-one. My notes from Western Chou bronzes list eight-four comparable titles, but the problems of identification are such that this can only be considered approximate. There are still other titles in the *Poetry* and the *Documents*.

gathered eight days after the death of King Ch'eng, for a ceremony in which a document containing the King's final charge was handed over to his heir.[14] It is reasonable to suppose that on one or both of these occasions virtually all of the most important officials were present.

These two lists, combined, give us eleven official titles. Five are the titles of specific officers, three are the titles of feudal lords, and three are general names for classes of officials. All of the names of classes of officials have been identified as occurring in the Shang inscriptions.[15] Two of the titles of feudal lords appear in the Shang inscriptions, but the remaining one, Duke (*Kung*), does not. (This title, which is very important in Western Chou times, was used by the

14. *Shu*, 70–74. This document occurs in the "ancient text" version of the *Documents* as two; see Legge, *Shu*, 544–568.

15. Pai yin 百 尹 , "the hundred [i.e., various] administrators," probably means in this context "all of the officers of a certain category," but what that category is one cannot be certain. *Yin* was an official title in Shang times; see Ch'en, *Yin Tz'u Tsung-shu*, 517–518. It occurs as a part of various titles in Western Chou, but not often by itself; see Ssu, "Liang-Chou Chih-kuan K'ao," 14–15. In this context Karlgren (*Shu*, 70) renders *pai yin* as "the various governors." Legge (*Shu*, 545) translates it as "the Heads of the officers"; and Couvreur (*Shu*, 345) as "les chefs des différents offices."

Yü-shih 御事 literally means "managers of affairs" and should almost certainly be understood as a general term rather than an official title. In the Western Chou sources it seems to appear exclusively in the *Documents*, except for one uncertain case in a bronze inscription; see *Chin-wen*, 66b, and Ssu, "Liang-Chou Chih-kuan K'ao," 16. In this latter case the inscription reads 御史 , which Ssu Wei-chih considers equivalent to 御事 . If this identification is correct, this title also appears in the Shang inscriptions; see Ch'en, *Yin Tz'u Tsung-shu*, 519–520.

The third of these terms that appear to be collective designations of officials is ch'ing shih 卿士 . This is a very troublesome term. It is generally believed to be, in this section of the *Documents*, a collective name for high officials of the court; see: *Shang-shu*, 18.25b–26a. *Shu*, 71. Legge, *Shu*, 557. Couvreur, *Shu*, 355. However, a poem that is traditionally dated (*Mao-shih*, 12[2].1a) to the reign of King Yu (781–771 B.C.) gives a list of royal officials with their personal names, and calls the first one Ch'ing-shih; Karlgren (*Shih*, 139) translates this as "prime minister." And in fact, by the beginning of the Spring and Autumn period this does seem to have been the title of the chief minister of the King; see *Tso*, 11::13 (Yin 3). This term is commonly held to be equivalent to 卿事 which appears on a number of bronze inscriptions and seems usually to denote a group of ministers; see: Kuo, *Chin-wen Ts'ung-k'ao*, 53a–56a. *Chin-wen*, 7a, 8b–9a. Ssu, "Liang-Chou Chih-kuan K'ao," 19–20. Ch'en, "Hsi-Chou T'ung-ch'i," (2).89. It is also considered equivalent to 卿史 , which occurs in the Shang inscriptions; see Ch'en, *Yin Tz'u Tsung-shu*, 519–520.

Two additional general terms appear in this document: hou 侯 and chün 君 . Both appear to be used as collective designations for the rulers of the feudal states. Both occur in the Shang inscriptions, but the latter is very rare.

Chou long before the conquest.)[16] Of the titles of the specific officials who played the leading roles in the government at this time, all are either lacking in the Shang inscriptions or do not figure as the titles of officers of the slightest importance in Shang times.[17]

A whole class of official titles that became very important in later history consists of those beginning with the character *ssu* 司 . It means "to have charge of," "to direct," and in titles may be translated as "director." Such titles appear in the Chou traditions relating to a time long before the conquest. The *Poetry* says that, when the Ancient Duke Tan-fu built a city on the plain of Chou, he put the task in charge of his Director of Works[18] and his Director of the Multitude.[19] One of the *Documents*, dating from the beginning of Western Chou, enumerates among the officers of a feudal state the Director of the Multitude, the Director of Horses, and the Director of Works.[20] Since all of these appear as the titles of royal officers in materials from

16. Tung, "Wu-teng Chüeh." We have seen that Chou rulers before the conquest, as far back as the "Ancient Duke" Tan-fu, were called *Kung*.

17. These five titles are *T'ai-pao* 太保, Grand Protector; *T'ai-shih* 太史, Grand Secretary; *T'ai-tsung* 太宗, Grand Master of Ceremonies; *Shih-shih* 師氏, Commandant; *Hu-ch'en* 虎臣, Tiger Retainer. Ch'en Meng-chia does not include any of these in his very comprehensive list of Shang officials in his *Yin Tz'u Tsung-shu*, 503–522. This does not mean of course that the characters composing these titles do not occur in the Shang inscriptions; some of these combinations may even occur sporadically. See for instance Ssu, "Liang-Chou Chih-kuan K'ao," 14, note 1. But they clearly did not denote officials playing any considerable role.

18. *Ssu-k'ung* 司空 . *Shih*, 190. In bronze inscriptions, the second character of this title is written as *kung* 工 . Concerning this title, see: Kuo, *Chin-wen Ts'ung-k'ao*, 65a–66a. Ssu, "Liang-Chou Chih-kuan K'ao," 13–14. Ch'en, "Hsi-Chou T'ung-ch'i," (6).121.

19. *Ssu-t'u* 司徒 . The second character of this title is written, in earlier Western Chou inscriptions, as *t'u* 土 ; Ch'en ("Hsi-Chou T'ung-ch'i," [6].121) suggests that this may denote a different office. The functions of the *Ssu-t'u*, as they appear in the bronze inscriptions, seem to have included supervision of persons engaged in farming, forestry, and herding. See: Ibid., 111–112. Kuo, *Chin-wen Ts'ung-k'ao*, 63a–65a. Ssu, "Liang-Chou Chih-kuan K'ao," 6–7.

20. *Shu*, 46. The title I have translated as "Director of Horses" is *Ssu-ma* 司馬 . This was an important title throughout much of Chinese history, and is commonly translated as "Minister of War." In this context Karlgren translates it as "the master of the horse." Legge (*Shu*, 414) renders it as "minister of War." Couvreur (*Shu*, 255) translates it as "ministre de la guerre." But although this term appears in a number of Western Chou bronze inscriptions, the contexts never make his function clear, and he never seems to be mentioned in a specifically military connection. It may be that he had to do with war or, alternatively, that his function was in fact connected with the procurement and care of horses; we simply cannot tell. For further discussion of this term, see below, p. 302.

somewhat later in Western Chou, it is entirely possible that there were such officers at the royal court from the beginning of the dynasty. The *Tso-chuan* says that one of the brothers of King Wu was Director of Crime[21] in his government,[22] and that another was Director of Works.[23]

This whole important class of officials whose titles begin with "Director" appears to have been a Chou institution, dating from before the conquest. There is no indication that it was known to the Shang. Ch'en Meng-chia concludes, at the end of his lengthy catalogue of Shang official titles, that "Director of Crime, Director of Works ... and so forth seem to be purely Chou institutions."[24]

Insofar as the testimony of official titles is valid, it is evident that the Chou government was not a copy of that of the Shang.

THE sources make it possible for us to get only a very imperfect glimpse of the way in which the government was organized. After the death of King Wu, the Duke of Chou evidently held the principal power at the court for a time, but whether he had any official title is not clear.[25] The Duke of Shao appears to have ranked next to the Duke

---

21. *Ssu-k'ou* 司寇, which I have translated literally as "Director of Crime," is common in later periods and is usually rendered as "Minister of Crime." It may well have had that sense in Western Chou times, but it is very rare. In all of the Western Chou sources that I am using, it occurs only twice, in bronze inscriptions: *Chin-wen*, 113b, 118a. Only in the latter does the context contain some reference to judicial functions, and even this is not clear. Speaking strictly on the basis of our evidence, we cannot be sure of the meaning of this term in Western Chou times. For further discussion see p. 171.

22. *Tso*, 750::754 (Ting 4). This brother, K'ang Shu (Legge's translation erroneously reads T'ang Shu), was the first ruler of Wèi. The section of the *Documents* discussing the funeral of King Ch'eng does not list the Director of Crime among the officials at the court, but it does (*Shu*, 70) mention the Marquis of Wèi. It is not certain that the first ruler of Wèi was still alive at that time, or that he still held the office of Director of Crime, but this is not wholly impossible. In any case this illustrates the point that some officials may have been present whose official titles are not mentioned, but who are designated rather by their titles as feudal lords. This exemplifies one of the great difficulties with Western Chou documents: men are often mentioned only by name, without their titles.

23. *Tso*, 750::754 (Ting 4).

24. Ch'en, *Yin Tz'u Tsung-shu*, 503–522.

25. Various titles have been attributed to him. The *Tso-chuan* says that he was *T'ai-tsai* 太宰, "Grand Intendant"; see *Tso*, 750::754 (Ting 4). It is uncertain, however, that this title was in use at the beginning of Western Chou; the *Tso-chuan* passage may have been ascribing office to him in terms of Spring and Autumn usage. See Ssu, "Liang-Chou Chih-kuan K'ao," 2–3.

of Chou in power. At one point the two Dukes are supposed to have held what amounted to viceregal power over two portions of the Empire: the Duke of Chou over the east, and the Duke of Shao over the west.[26]

At the time of the death of King Ch'eng, in 1079 B.C, the principal power in the government was held by the Grand Protector.[27] The Duke of Shao evidently held this office at this time.[28] He was named first among those called to hear the charge of the dying King, and he supervised the funeral arrangements. He also played the leading role in the ceremony of the investiture of the new King.[29] The office of Grand Protector was clearly very important; it is also mentioned in several bronze inscriptions. It is not clear, however, how many men held this office successively, and it does not seem to have continued past the early period of Western Chou.[30]

Next in order of importance, we may deduce, was the Grand Secretary.[31] This title is often translated either as "Grand Scribe" or as "Grand Historiographer."[32] In my opinion these latter renderings are dubious. Certainly there is very little to indicate to us the functions of the Grand Secretary. And it is true that, when the heir to the throne is installed, the Grand Secretary personally holds the document containing the charge of the deceased King Ch'eng and presents the charge to the new King.[33] It may be that on such great occasions the Grand Secretary wrote the necessary documents with his own hand. But it is very unlikely that this exalted official was merely the chief clerk of the royal court.

26. Ch'en, "Hsi-Chou T'ung-ch'i," (2).98. Shu, 61–62.

27. T'ai-pao 太保. The Duke of Chou was evidently dead by this time. He is not named at all in connection with the ceremonies attending the death of King Ch'eng (Shu, 70–74). And the Historical Records clearly states that he predeceased King Ch'eng. See Shih-chi, 33.15; Mémoires historiques, IV, 98–99.

28. In Shu, 70, he is called T'ai-pao Shih 太保奭. I am not sure if there is any Western Chou source that proves conclusively that he was the Duke of Shao, but it seems to be universally agreed that he was, and I know no reason to doubt it. See: Ch'en, "Hsi-Chou T'ung-ch'i," (2).94–95. Ting, "Shao Mu Kung Chuan," 90.

29. Shu, 70–74.

30. Ch'en, "Hsi-Chou T'ung-ch'i," (2).88–91, 98. Ssu, "Liang-Chou Chih-kuan K'ao," 20–21.

31. T'ai-shih 太史. Paragraph 23 of the "Ku Ming" (Shu, 71), mentions in order "the Grand Protector, the Grand Secretary, and the Grand Master of Ceremonies." It appears probable that these were the three highest dignitaries, named in hierarchical order.

32. Karlgren (Shu, 71) translates it "grand scribe." Couvreur (Shu, 355) renders it in French as "grand secrétaire," and in Latin as "summus scriba." Legge (Shu, 557) translates it as "Grand-historiographer."

33. Shu, 71.

Our word "secretary" has a wide variety of meanings in various contexts. This title is used on the one hand to denote offices of great power and responsibility, as in Secretary of State, and at the other end of the scale to describe one who is merely an amanuensis, writing what is dictated by another. We tend to think of a secretary as one who is employed in writing; yet as the word itself indicates, it originally meant one entrusted with secrets and employed on confidential missions.

The Chinese character *shih* 史 , which occurs in the title that I translate as Grand Secretary, seems to have had a somewhat similar history. It occurs as a name for officials as early as Shang times.[34] Its etymology and original sense have been the subjects of a great deal of study and speculation, which have not arrived at any wholly convincing conclusions.[35] *Shih* certainly did come to mean, among other things, "scribe" and "historiographer." But this character seems originally to have also meant "service," "officer," and "envoy."[36] It seems plausible that it originally had the sense of "functionary," one commissioned by the ruler to perform certain specific tasks. Officers called *shih* were extremely numerous in the Western Chou government.[37] They performed a wide variety of functions, some of which were no doubt scribal; but some *shih* were clearly secretaries in the sense of being entrusted with the performance of important and perhaps confidential missions. It is probable that the Grand Secretary was not

34. Ch'en, *Yin Tz'u Tsung-shu,* 519–520.

35. In a classic essay on this character, Wang Kuo-wei (*Kuan-t'ang Chi-lin,* 6.1a–5b) reviewed various theories which find it originally to have denoted the scorekeeper in archery contests (in which the King and other dignitaries often participated), or the custodian of written records, or both. See also Watson, *Ssu-ma Ch'ien,* 70–71. Wang concluded that the early sense of the character was that of an official concerned with books, and that its early use to denote a wide variety of officials attested to the early importance of written records in Chinese government. That is possible. But this character was already in wide use in the Shang inscriptions, and when a character so early gives, in its form, only slight clues to its origin, it is difficult to be certain of its original sense. It could be argued that the fact that a character, widely used for a variety of officials, came commonly to be associated with the preparation and preservation of written records, was a testimony to the importance that such records came to have in government, rather than evidence that the character originally denoted a scribe or a librarian.

36. *Shih* seems originally to have been identical in form with *shih* 事 , *li* 吏 , and *shih* 使 . See: Wang, *Kuan-t'ang Chi-lin,* 6.3b–4a. Karlgren, "Grammata Serica Recensa," 256–257, nos. 971, 975.

37. Ssu Wei-chih ("Liang-Chou Chih-kuan K'ao," 15) says that "*shih* are the officials most commonly encountered in antiquity; in bronze inscriptions those who are called '*Shih* So-and-so' are so numerous that they cannot be counted."

merely such a functionary, but rather had charge of supervising the officials of this type.[38]

The third of these principal ministers was the Grand Master of Ceremonies. This official probably had supreme charge of religious functions, but we have very little information about the office.[39]

The other officers whose specific titles we have for the year 1079 B.C. are the Commandant, who was probably the commander of the palace guard,[40] and the Tiger Retainer, who was probably the officer in command of the royal bodyguard.[41]

38. This seems to be implied by his high position. Ch'en ("Hsi-Chou T'ung-ch'i," [2].112) says that in the time of King Ch'eng the Duke of Chou, the Grand Protector, and the Grand Secretary were the highest officers of the realm (this presumably refers to the earlier part of his reign, since the Duke of Chou apparently predeceased King Ch'eng). One bronze inscription ascribed to the reign of King Ch'eng refers (ibid., 111) to "the Duke Grand Secretary," apparently indicating that this official was also a high feudal lord. Another, presumably from the same reign, refers to another Grand Secretary who was clearly a feudal lord of importance (Chin-wen, 16a). It is very difficult, however, to deduce the actual responsibilities of the Grand Secretary from the sources. See: Kuo, Chin-wen Ts'ung-k'ao, 53a–56a. Ssu, "Liang-Chou Chih-kuan K'ao," 14–16.

39. About this official, the T'ai-tsung 太宗, we are even more than usually dependent upon speculation. A literal translation of the title might perhaps be "Grand [Master of the] Ancestral Temples." Karlgren (Shu, 71) translates it as "grand master of rites." Legge (Shu, 557) renders it as "the minister of Religion." Couvreur (Shu, 355) translates it as "le grand maître des cérémonies." Karlgren ("Glosses on the Book of Documents," [2].165) discusses its meaning. This title seems to occur nowhere else in the Western Chou sources.

40. The title Shīh-shih 師氏 has been the subject of a very great deal of discussion. It has sometimes been translated as "instructor," apparently on the basis of the Ritual of Chou. See Chou-li, 14.2a–6a; Biot, Tcheou-li, I, 291–296. That work describes the Shīh-shih as having charge of instruction and also as commanding the palace guards. Bernhard Karlgren's treatment of this title is somewhat baffling. In his translation of the Poetry, first published in 1944 and 1945 (BMFEA, XVI, 236; XVII, 82) he rendered it as "commander of the guard," which seems to me correct (compare Shih, 139, 226). But in his translation of the Documents, published in 1950, he translated it in a context that is quite similar as "instructor" (Shu, 70); see also Shu, 29. In his "Glosses on the Book of Documents," (1).228, (2).156, he does not explain this change.

Kuo Mo-jo ("Ch'ang-an Ming-wen," 4) says that where the office of Shīh-shih is mentioned in bronze inscriptions it is always connected with military functions. Insofar as the contexts make its sense specific—which is as usual too seldom—this seems to be the case. Almost all scholars seem to agree that in this context in the Documents the title pertains to the commander of the palace guard. See Maspero, "La société chinoise," 390, 399. Legge, Shu, 545. Couvreur, Shu, 344. Kuo, Chin-wen Ts'ung-k'ao, 74a–75a. Ssu, "Liang-Chou Chih-kuan K'ao," 7–8.

41. Shu, 70. Legge, Shu, 545. Couvreur, Shu, 344–345. Kuo, Chin-wen Ts'ung-k'ao, 73ab. Ssu, "Liang-Chou Chih-kuan K'ao," 10.

In addition, various classes of officials are named as being among those gathered at the court on this occasion, but this does not tell us very much; the identity and functions of "the various administrators," for instance, are quite unclear. A number of feudal lords are also named as among those present, and it is wholly likely that some of these held offices that are not named. It is probable that all of the highest officials were also feudal lords, and one of the feudal lords listed may well have been Director of Crime, although this office is not mentioned.[42]

This rather random mention of certain offices that were important at the court at the end of the second reign of Western Chou is certainly interesting, but it does not go very far toward telling us how the government was organized, or how it functioned. And even if it did, the information would be of limited value, for there was evidently a rapid rate of change. We have two other lists of the chief royal officers in the *Poetry*; both of the poems in which they occur are traditionally dated to the last century of Western Chou.[43] Each of these late lists includes only one official, the Commandant, who appeared in the list we have just examined that dates from early in the dynasty; within some three centuries the transformation is almost complete. And these lists in the *Poetry*, although traditionally dated close together, differ significantly from each other. The office named first in the supposedly earlier poem has dropped to third place in the second list,[44] which is headed by an office that was not mentioned at all in the first.[45] What circumstances produced these changes, we can only conjecture.

The bronze inscriptions include a large number of official titles, from which it might seem reasonable to hope to extract a picture of

42. See above, p. 108, n. 22.

43. *Shih*, 138–140, 224–226. These poems are traditionally dated, respectively, to the reign of King Yu (781–771 B.C.) and to that of King Hsüan (827–782 B.C.); see *Mao-shih*, 12(2).1a, 18(2).12b.

44. If it occurs at all. *Mao-shih*, 12(2).6a at this point reads 家伯維宰; so does the text of Legge (*Shih*, 322). But Karlgren (*Shih*, 139) and Couvreur (*Shih*, 238) both give the text as 家伯家宰. I can find no basis for such an emendation, and where we might expect it to be discussed, in Karlgren, "Glosses on the Siao Ya Odes," 86–87, he does not mention it. Commentaries do, to be sure, say that *Tsai* is equivalent to *Chung-tsai*, but this in itself is not sufficient to justify altering the text. Perhaps there is a justification for the emendation that I have not discovered.

45. *Shih*, 139, 226.

the governmental structure. Unfortunately there are difficulties. It is only occasionally that an inscription makes quite clear what functions pertain to a particular title. There is also a great tendency for officials to be referred to only by their personal names, without their titles. Furthermore, it seems to have been common practice in Western Chou times for individuals to hold more than one office.[46] In one case the same man appears to have been entrusted with no less than five offices.[47] Although in some cases it is clear that the same man held multiple office, only one office is usually conferred at a time. And we cannot always be certain whether the official continued to hold his former office or offices, or moved from one to another.

Not only might one man hold more than one title, but men designated by particular titles were sometimes employed in ways that the title would not lead us to expect. When a certain "Secretary Mien" makes an inscription recording the fact that he followed the King on a military expedition, we cannot tell whether his duties were military or still secretarial.[48] But when we find two more inscriptions in which another Secretary figures as the leader of two different military expeditions, we must conclude that this Secretary clearly included the making of war among his functions.[49]

Still more curious is the mission entrusted to a certain Huan, whose office was Maker of Books.[50] This sounds scribal enough, and we know that men holding this office often were concerned with the making and handling of written records. But Maker of Books Huan is ordered to "pacify" or "establish"—one cannot be sure which—the Earl of I. This was apparently some sort of trip of inspection. The Earl gave Huan handsome presents, and on his return the Maker of Books cast two bronzes, bearing inscriptions that have come down to us. One is dedicated to his father, and the other expresses Huan's gratitude to the Queen, who had given him this rewarding commission.[51]

In sum, while the Western Chou sources give us many names of offices, and some information about them, these are of limited use when we seek to understand the government. Ssu Wei-chih has compiled, on the basis of both bronze inscriptions and literary sources,

46. *Chin-wen*, 80b. Ch'en, "Hsi-Chou T'ung-ch'i," (6).112.

47. *Chin-wen*, 118a. Ssu ("Liang-Chou Chih-kuan K'ao," 9, 13–14) argues that this was in fact not multiple office, but rather a situation in which colleagues worked together. But Ch'en ("Hsi-Chou T'ung-ch'i," [6].112) agrees with the interpretation of Kuo Mo-jo.

48. *Chin-wen*, 90b.

49. *Chin-wen*, 28ab. Ch'en, "Hsi-Chou T'ung-ch'i," (1).174.

50. *Tso-ts'e* 乍 冊 .

51. *Chin-wen*, 14a. Ch'en, "Hsi-Chou T'ung- ch'i," (2).117–118.

what is perhaps the most comprehensive annotated catalogue of Chou official titles yet produced. But in his conclusion he acknowledges that the Chou official system remains "difficult to verify."[52]

It is doubtful that any amount of research could produce a reliable "table of organization" for the Western Chou government, from the materials that we have or even from any that might be found in the future. The problem is not merely—though this is formidable enough —the scantiness of our sources. There is a very real question as to whether such a tidily organized system of offices existed at all—and whether, if it did, anyone paid very much attention to it.

We have already noticed the great difference that developed, over time, in the titles of the principal officers. The functions attached to the same office also varied with time. And even when we can deter-mine what the normal functions of a particular office are, this does not guarantee that the man holding the title will not do something else. Confusion is compounded by the practice of conferring more than one office on the same man.

Furthermore, the Western Chou had a tendency to use exactly the same title to cover a whole series of offices that were no doubt similar in function but were nevertheless very different in their scope and im-portance. For instance, one inscription gives the name and title of each of two officers. One of them is clearly a high royal official, while the other carries on relatively limited functions within the royal palace. Yet both of them are called Intendant, without any qualification.[53] A number of qualifying terms were available—such as "great," "mi-nor," "left and right," and so forth—that could be prefixed to official titles, and sometimes were, to show gradations between them. But much of the time there seems to have been no concern with such precision.

If we are to understand the situation at all, we must make some kind of classification of Western Chou officials. Perhaps the most feasible means is to group them by broad categories of responsibility. We may distinguish three types: administrative, functional, and military. The military will be discussed in a later chapter and need not concern us here.

---

52. Ssu, "Liang-Chou Chih-kuan K'ao," 23.

53. *Tsai* 宰 . *Chin-wen,* 102a. Kuo Mo-jo discusses the relative status of these two *Tsai* in ibid., 103b. See also Ch'en, "Hsi-Chou T'ung-ch'i," (6).122.

Administrative responsibilities are those given to officers who are charged to manage certain kinds of governmental business, or certain territorial areas, with only broad directives and with wide discretion to initiate and to apply such measures as they deem appropriate. Within their given sphere they are "policy-making" officials. In matters of local government all feudal lords might be regarded as administrative officials, but they too will be discussed in detail in a latter chapter.

At the highest level there were administrative officials of what might be called viceregal status. Whether the Duke of Chou actually held the title of "Regent" is debated, but there can be no doubt that for some years he in effect exercised almost all of the powers of the King. When, as it appears, the Duke of Chou ruled the eastern half of the Empire while the Grand Protector governed its western portion, they were probably essentially viceroys. Whether such delegation of power over portions of the Empire continued after the time of the Duke of Chou is not clear.[54] This may have been a temporary measure, prompted by the need for subduing and consolidating the Empire after the great rebellion.

To what extent there was a "prime minister" who held control over all of the other ministers, and over the government, is uncertain. Undoubtedly there was a chief minister. Early in the dynasty the Grand Protector played a leading role, and it is commonly assumed that, when lists of ministers are given, the one named first took precedence. It is hard to tell, however, whether he was more than the first among equals. In the early reigns at least, the Kings had a strong tendency to play a large personal role in the management of affairs. This was less true later on, and certainly there were some ministers who gained substantial control over the government. But this may have been more a matter of the personal force of the individuals involved than of governmental structure.

The distinction between officials who have the power to initiate policy and to administer in a meaningful sense, and those who do not,

---

54. For the evidence of this division of the Empire into two areas, see Ch'en, "Hsi-Chou T'ung-ch'i," (2).98, and *Shu*, 61–62. It is possible that the continuation of such division is indicated in the ceremonies attending the accession of the new King after the death of King Ch'eng, when it is said (*Shu*, 73) that "the Grand Protector led the feudal lords of the western regions" and "the Duke of Pi led the feudal lords of the eastern regions." Ch'en Meng-chia ("Hsi-Chou T'ung-ch'i," [2].98) links this with the actual division of the empire into regions for governmental purposes, but it might also have only ceremonial significance. There does not seem to be any indication of such division, for governmental purposes, later in the dynasty.

is not easy to draw even in a modern government. Officials of high rank and authority may lose their power through inaction, or have it taken from them; on the other hand heads of obscure bureaus may rise to positions of commanding power.[55] This line is even harder to draw in Western Chou, and there are only a few offices of which we can say that those who held them appear to have possessed discretionary administrative power within certain specific fields. One of these is the Director of the Multitude, whose duties included supervision of persons engaged in farming, forestry, and herding. The importance of this responsibility is clear, and in a poem traditionally ascribed to the eighth century B.C. we find the Director of the Multitude named second among the chief officers of the King.[56]

It is probable, as has been said, that the Grand Secretary was an administrative official and that he had charge of the large number of Secretaries, of various sorts, in the government. But these Secretaries themselves were undoubtedly functional officials, charged with the performance of specific duties or the carrying out of particular missions. Furthermore, most of the other official titles that appear seem, where the duties connected with them can be determined, to be those of functional officers.

These functional offices sometimes became transformed—no doubt because of the energies, abilities, and ambitions of men who held them —into posts of an administrative character. This happens in governments everywhere. But most of the offices in the Western Chou royal government appear, at least in their origin, to have been functional.

This is a very important fact. It indicates that, in its intent, the royal government was proto-bureaucratic in character. Bureaucracy, as the term is used in this book, is: a system of administration by means of professional functionaries, whose functions are more or less definitely prescribed.

The intent that functionaries shall do exactly what is prescribed for them is made very clear by King Wu in his charge to his younger brother (who may have held the office of Director of Crime). The King says:

> All those who are insubordinate should be greatly regulated. How much more then . . . the administrators and

---

55. A conspicuous contemporary example is that of J. Edgar Hoover, who developed the Federal Bureau of Investigation from an inconspicuous agency to one that gave him, as its head, outstanding influence.

56. *Shih*, 139. On the functions of the *Ssu-t'u* see Kuo, *Chin-wen Ts'ung-k'ao*, 63a–65a.

the various minor officers. When they depart [from the course prescribed for them] and promulgate innovations . . . you should speedily, in accord with justice, put them to death.[57]

There are many indications that King Wu and others among the Chou would have liked to set up a tightly regimented bureaucracy, of the sort that was developed in China many centuries later. To do this effectively at the beginning of Western Chou was impossible, however. China did develop many of the techniques necessary for the control of a tightly centralized bureaucracy, much earlier than this was done anywhere else. Undoubtedly the nature of Western Chou government had great influence on that development. But until the techniques were developed, a tightly centralized bureaucracy was not feasible. And there are indications that, as time went on, the regimentation of their officials by the Western Chou Kings became not more, but progressively less strict.

Even at the beginning, Western Chou was not, at the higher levels of government at least, a true bureaucracy, but only a proto-bureaucracy. For the royal officers were not professionals in the sense of getting their livings, wholly and directly, from payment for the performance of their duties. Instead, they derived their emolument chiefly or wholly from fiefs. The fiefs were given them, to be sure, to enable them to act as officers, but this did not provide the direct economic tie between office and pay that is essential to a professional bureaucracy.

The royal officials did, however, have many of the characteristics of bureaucrats. It is clear that some men at least were educated for official service and spent their whole lives in it. There is little indication that, as has often been supposed, men in Western Chou times commonly inherited offices simply because their fathers had occupied them. They were appointed, and promoted, on the basis of their personal qualities and achievements—but an illustrious ancestry was no bar to preferment, nor is it in official life in our own day.[58]

Some functional officials were of exalted status. The son of the Duke of Chou, who was the first Duke of Lu, served the court as Grand Invocator, or, as Karlgren renders the term, "prayer-master."[59] The officer in charge of divining for the King was evidently of high

---

57. *Shu*, 42. Karlgren inserts "penal" in parentheses before "innovations," but in my opinion the context gives no warrant for this.

58. For evidence on these points see pp. 396–409.

59. *Chin-wen*, 11b. Ch'en, "Hsi-Chou T'ung-ch'i," (2).73–75. Karlgren, "Grammata Serica Recensa," 267, no. 1025.

rank.[60] Such functionaries range downward to the relatively humble, like the Supervisor of Dogs.[61]

The status of some officials is not what we should expect. Even in eighteenth-century Europe, which so highly esteemed music, Mozart could be treated like a menial. In early China, however, the standing of musicians seems to have been rather high. In the Spring and Autumn period we find one music-master named among the principal officers of the state of Chin and frequently consulted on questions of state by the Duke.[62]

Musicians are not mentioned frequently in the Western Chou sources, but it is evident that some of them at least were highly regarded. One was repeatedly honored by two Kings, and given rich gifts in at least two court ceremonies. Kuo Mo-jo thinks that the bronze inscription referring to one of these ceremonies dates from the time of King Li (878–828 B.C.),[63] who is traditionally regarded as a wicked King. Kuo says that on the basis of this inscription we can see that the musician so honored "was greatly favored by King Li. It may be that his musical technique was outstanding." But this love of music is considered by Kuo to be yet another evidence that King Li was frivolous. "That the Western Chou almost came to extinction at his hand," Kuo concludes, "was not without cause."[64]

In the Western Chou sources, however, music is not condemned as blamably frivolous. It was used in sacrificial ceremonies to please the ancestors, and at feasts to entertain guests. And individuals sang and played instruments for their own pleasure, and sometimes to assuage grief.[65]

A very important part of the service performed by functional officials was the business of attending upon the King and his court. These duties ranged all the way from supervising the servants who performed the actual physical labor of keeping the royal residences and temples in order, to carrying the messages and promulgating the orders of the King. As we have seen, the title of Intendant was used for a number of officers who performed such services, both high and relatively low. A minor Intendant is ordered, in one inscription, to "take

60. *Chin-wen*, 96b. Kuo, *Chin-wen Ts'ung-k'ao*, 63b.

61. *Chin-wen*, 115ab.

62. *Tso*, 477::479 (Hsiang 19), 552::556 (Hsiang 30), 620::622 (Chao 9).

63. Since King Li was in exile after 841 B.C., his reign is sometimes considered to have ended in that year.

64. *Chin-wen*, 149a. Kuo, *Wen-shih Lun-chi*, 328–332. In the latter reference Kuo revises the interpretation that he had made of the inscription in the former reference.

65. *Shih*, 55, 70, 104–105, 163, 202, 243, 245–246, 261–262.

out and bring in the commands" of the Queen.[66] Since to "bring in commands" makes little sense, this presumably means that he is to take out her orders and to bring back information as to the way in which they are carried out. An Intendant serving the King personally presumably performed similar functions for him.[67] Another officer charged to "take out and bring in" the royal commands was the Steward.[68]

There is a general tendency for those in close attendance on a monarch to rise in power. The later rise of eunuchs in China, from being

66. I am assuming that the Chiang Shih 姜 氏 named here is the Queen.

67. *Chin-wen*, 102b. Two Intendants, of whom one is a high royal officer, are mentioned in this inscription. The *Poetry* uses much the same language concerning "taking out and bringing in commands" in reporting a charge by the King to an officer who is apparently in charge of the government, one Chung Shan-fu 仲山甫 (this name should not be confused with the title *Shan-fu* 善夫 , which is discussed in the following note). Where this bronze inscription has 出 入 , the *Poetry* (*Shih*, 228–229) has 出 納 , which in the context is virtually identical. This charge in the *Poetry* reads quite like those in the bronze inscriptions. Karlgren translates it: "The king charged Chung Shan-fu: 'Be a model to those (hundred =) many rulers, continue (the service of) your ancestors, protect the king's person, give out and bring in (reports about) the king's decrees.' "

68. *Chin-wen*, 121ab. The title *Shan-fu* 善夫 , which I translate as "Steward," is one of the most troublesome, and has been the subject of a vast amount of discussion. See Kuo, *Chin-wen Ts'ung-k'ao*, 75a–76b, and Ssu, "Liang-Chou Chih-kuan K'ao," 3–4.

A literal translation of *Shan-fu* would be "good man." This may have some analogy with the derivation of the title Baron, which derived from a Germanic word meaning "man"; a Baron was his lord's "man" (Bloch, *Feudal Society*, 333). In later literature, however, we find what may be the same title written as *Shan-fu* 膳夫. Since the first character here means "cooked food," this title has with some plausibility been supposed to be that of a cook. Whether there was such a title, or the character was altered by mistake, seems impossible to prove; see Kuo, *Chin-wen Ts'ung-k'ao*, 75a–76b, and Ssu, "Liang-Chou Chih-kuan K'ao," 3–4. This title occurs twice in the *Poetry* (*Shih*, 139, 226), both times as the title of high royal officers, and both times in the form 膳夫 . Karlgren translates these as "master of the Royal table" and "minister of the Royal table." Legge (*Shih*, 322, 533) has "chief cook." Couvreur (*Shih*, 238, 395) translates them as "grand maître d'hôtel" and "chef des cuisines." But there seems to be no contextual warrant for this, and it seems clear on the basis of the bronze inscriptions that the text of the *Poetry* here ought very probably to read 善夫 . It may be that originally it did and the later editors "corrected" the text on the basis of the currency of the other term in later literature. Unfortunately such tampering with texts is not rare. For a very clear example of it, see Creel, "On the Origin of *Wu-wei*," 131, n. 4.

There seems to be nothing, in the Western Chou sources at any rate, to connect the *Shan-fu* with the preparation or serving of food. It is evident, however, that the functions of this officer had some resemblance to those of the Intendant, and in later literature we sometimes find one title substituted for the other (see Kuo, *Chin-wen Tsung-k'ao*, 75a–76b, and Ssu, "Liang-Chou Chih-kuan K'ao," 3–4). The translation "Steward" therefore seems suitable.

palace servants to becoming, at times, the actual masters of the realm, is well known.[69] Supervision of the private apartments of the ruler has commonly led to great power, as in the case of the Lord Chamberlain of England and the *Chambellan de France*. The Mayors of the Palace of the Merovingian Kings held complete control of the government for a century before the last of them, the father of Charlemagne, was finally able to take the title of King as well.[70]

In Western Chou China royal attendants never rose quote so high, but they did very well. The office of Steward does not seem to be mentioned before the middle of the period. But in four bronze inscriptions dated to the ninth century B.C. we see a certain Steward K'e, who was highly favored by the King, given important responsibilities and rich gifts.[71] In a poem traditionally dated to the following reign we find the Steward listed fourth among the chief royal officers, and in another dated to the succeeding reign this office is still in the fourth place.[72]

The office of Intendant had a still more interesting history. Although this title is found in a few late Shang inscriptions,[73] it does not seem to appear in the Western Chou sources until well after the first century of the dynasty. Perhaps those who held this office were too unimportant, in the early years, to be mentioned. It appears likely that those called Intendants were at first little more than upper servants, or officers in direct charge of servants, at the court.[74] We see some Intendants, however, as close and trusted officers of the King. It is evident that, as has already been noted, there were Intendants of both high and relatively low status at the court, but in the bronze inscriptions they are all called "Intendant" without qualification.[75] In a poem dated to around 800 B.C., however, we find the Great Intendant named first among all the royal ministers.[76] But another, dated to the

69. Whether eunuchs were employed as palace attendants in Western Chou China, as they were later, seems impossible to determine. The evidence that has sometimes been advanced for this view seems dubious. It appears likely that, if they were, they were not a very conspicuous element.

70. *Cambridge Medieval History*, II, 575.

71. *Chin-wen*, 121ab, 123a, 123b, 124b.

72. *Shih*, 139, 226.

73. Ch'en, *Yin Tz'u Tsung-shu*, 521. Ssu, "Liang-Chou Chih-kuan K'ao," 2.

74. A poem says (*Shih*, 163) that after a sacrifice the Intendants (*chu Tsai* 諸宰) clear away the utensils. Karlgren here calls them "the attendants." Legge (*Shih*, 372) translates this as "all the servants." Waley (*Shih*, 211) has "the stewards," and Couvreur (*Shih*, 279) "tous les serviteurs."

75. *Chin-wen*, 70a, 72a, 74b, 80a, 84a, 102b, 129b, 149a. Ch'en, "Hsi-Chou T'ung-chi," (6).119.

76. *Chung-tsai* 家宰 ; *Shih*, 226.

following reign, lists the Intendant in third place—still not an inconsiderable position.[77]

Nor is this the end of the story. A bronze inscription dated to around this same time mentions the Intendant Tiao Sheng. And two other inscriptions clearly show that Tiao Sheng held preeminent power in the government. In these latter inscriptions, however, Tiao Sheng is mentioned only by name, with no official title whatever.[78] The office held seems to have counted for less than the energy and influence of the officeholder.

Whenever one office gains in prestige and power, it does so at the expense of one or more others. The post of Grand Protector, clearly first near the beginning of the dynasty, soon drops out of sight altogether. The Grand Secretary was clearly second in the early years, but while this title is still mentioned late in the dynasty those who hold it appear to belong to an order of officers below the highest level.[79] At the same time, as we have seen, offices that were humble or did not appear at all in the early years rose to high status. The rise and fall were sometimes rapid.

ALL this may sound as if the Western Chou government was in hopeless confusion and as if the Kings handed out titles and offices without thought or care. Yet no such conclusion can be correct. The early Western Chou rulers, in particular, accomplished prodigies of pacification and organization. They welded China into a nation, which would bear their impress for three thousand years. How?

Not primarily by means of an elaborate machinery of government. Shen Pu-hai of the fourth century B.C., and political scientists of our own day, agree in regarding a "table of organization" as prerequisite for effective government: a clear roster of official titles, hierarchically arranged, together with precise descriptions of their interrelations and their duties. The *Ritual of Chou* does indeed give such a scheme, which has traditionally been believed to have existed in early Chou. But

77. *Shih*, 139. Concerning the question of whether the text here should read "Intendant" or "Great Intendant," see p. 112, n. 44.

78. *Chin-wen*, 142a, 144b, 149a.

79. *Chin-wen*, 124b, 133a, 135a. The Grand Secretary is not named at all in the *Poetry*, but one list of the chief royal officers, presumably of relatively late date (*Shih*, 139), gives the Interior Secretary (*Nei-shih* 內 史) in fifth place, below both the Intendant and the Steward. And a bronze inscription of relatively late date (*Chin-wen*, 124b) names the Interior Secretary and the Grand Secretary in that order, indicating that the latter no longer occupies the first place even among Secretaries.

neither that one nor any other neat arrangement will square with the evidence.

Government in Western Chou was primarily personal. This was the Chou tradition; from the time of King T'ai most of their early rulers were men of great force. They laid careful plans, but the plans hinged upon their execution by talented leaders. There is an insistent tradition that King Wen was not in the normal line of succession, but that his grandfather, King T'ai, recognized his outstanding abilities and arranged that he should succeed. This tradition may not be without some foundation.[80]

It is evident that King T'ai, King Wen, King Wu, King Ch'eng, and the Duke of Chou and the Duke of Shao were all men of ability and decision. We have writings from King Wu and the Duke of Chou; their tone is firm and at times dictatorial. After the reign of King Ch'eng our information becomes scanty. It is clear, however, that for a long time the Kings were energetic and held their realm by means that were sometimes ingenious. They undoubtedly placed great emphasis upon choosing subordinates able to accomplish the tasks they wished performed, giving much less attention to rank or office than to the qualities of the men in question.

There was nevertheless a machinery of government. It was in fact a dual system. On the one hand local government was established in each area by handing over limited sovereignty to feudal lords, who ruled with a large measure of autonomy in local matters. The royal government, on the other hand, ideally—and, at least for a time, to a considerable extent in fact—had jurisdiction over the whole country. The King's officers carried on the functions of his court and transacted business between, and exercised jurisdiction over, the feudal lords.[81]

---

80. The tradition holds that, in order that King Wen might come to the throne, King T'ai desired his third son (Wen's father) to be his successor. This would have meant, however, passing over two older sons. These sons, knowing their father's wish, left the court and went to live among barbarians. Confucius apparently refers to this tradition in *Analects*, 8.1. There is more certain reference to it in *Tso*, 124::125 (Min 1). The elaborated tradition is given in *Shih-chi*, 4.8–9, 31.2–4; *Mémoires historiques*, I, 216–216, IV, 1–2. There seems to be little reason, however, to credit that part of the story that holds that the elder brothers of King Chi became rulers of the state of Wu on the east coast of China (see pp. 359–361). An interesting facet of this tradition is the fact that it holds that King Chi was brought to the throne, not primarily for his own qualities, but in order that his son Wen might succeed him. And Chi appears, in our materials, as the least forceful of the Chou rulers of this period.

81. Some readers may be surprised that nothing is said about the distinction that is commonly supposed to exist between feudal lords inside and outside of "the royal domain." The reason is that I, like some other scholars, find no evidence that such a "royal domain" existed in Western Chou times. See pp. 363–366.

In pure theory such a government could have worked well. The royal officials and the feudal lords acted as checks on one another. While a particular minister sometimes did achieve great power, it would not have been easy for him to usurp the throne without the acquiescence of the feudal lords. Neither could a feudal lord easily organize rebellion without the advance knowledge of the royal officials. It is evident that disaffection between these two groups might have been expected, and we have a few indications that it did exist. But such disaffection, so long as it was mild, increased the power of the King rather than undermining it.

A third force also was available to the King: the royal armies. A weak point in this whole structure, however, was the fact that the personnel of its various elements could not be wholly separated. To what extent the high officials of the King, and the commanders of his armies, were given any kind of salary is not wholly clear; in any case it appears that all of them were given fiefs. Thus they too were feudal lords. Undoubtedly there were differences between men—and there were such—who spent their whole lives as royal officials and also held fiefs, and men who were feudal lords but not royal officials. But even the King's officers were also feudal lords, subject to the divisive tendencies of feudalism, and much less subject to royal control than salaried bureaucrats would have been.

WESTERN Chou government was distinctly deficient by modern standards—and by the Chinese standards of half a millennium later—with respect to clear and carefully maintained organization. But it had another characteristic that made for stability to a high degree: an addiction to the use and preservation of written records. Wang Kuo-wei has pointed out that even at an early date a very high proportion of Chinese officials were concerned with writing.[82] We may take this as a matter of course, since government as we know it involves endless paper work—so much so that the red tape used to tie official documents has come to be a synonym for bureaucratic inefficiency, and the French speak of *paperasserie administrative*. We may not easily realize that the extensive use of written records in government was by no means universal in the world of 1000 B.C.

Arnaldo Momigliano points out that in the fifth century B.C., "when Herodotus worked on Greek history, he had very few written documents to rely upon: Greek history was as yet mainly transmitted by oral tradition."[83] Peoples other than the Chinese have maintained ar-

82. Wang, *Kuan-t'ang Chi-lin*, 6.1a–5b.
83. Momigliano, "The Place of Herodotus," 2.

chives and written history, of course, but it is doubtful that there has been, anywhere else in the world, such continuous emphasis on history from such an early time. We have seen that, at the very beginning of the Chou, history was regarded as a "mirror" from which to learn from the past lessons to be applied in the present and future.[84]

Neither is it likely that in any other country so much attention has been given to the preservation and meticulous study of archival material. Concerning Western historical practice Momigliano, writing in 1958, says that "the pre-eminence of personal observation and oral evidence lasted until historians decided to go to the Record Office. Familiarity with the Record Office, as we all know, is a recently acquired habit for the historian, hardly older than a century. It is true that the Roman and Greek antiquarians knew something about the use of documents and that the antiquarians of the Renaissance perfected this approach to the past. But this method became really effective and universally accepted only a hundred years ago."[85]

Chinese historians, by contrast, have perhaps placed almost too much emphasis on archives, although the best of them have also given due weight to oral tradition and personal observation. From the earliest times they seem to have depended very largely on the records preserved both at the royal court and at the courts of individual states.[86]

In the Western Chou sources two terms are most frequently used to stand for documents. The most common is *ts'e* 冊 , which was then written as 冊 . This is a pictograph of four vertical strips of wood or bamboo, held together by a cord knotted around each at two points, to hold them together. The form of the character was almost identical in the Shang inscriptions, and many thousands of such "books,"[87] with characters written on the strips in vertical columns, have been found from Han times in the dry climate of central Asia;

---

84. This has undoubtedly impaired objectivity at times; it is difficult to write history to teach lessons and, at the same time, to be quite objective. On the other hand, nothing is so deadly as complete objectivity. If Gibbon had been more objective, he might or might not have been a better historian, but it is unlikely that he would still be read. For an excellent comparison of the outstanding early historians of China and the West, see Teng, "Herodotus and Ssu-ma Ch'ien."

85. Momigliano, "The Place of Herodotus," 8.

86. Tsien, *Written on Bamboo and Silk*, 5–9. *Mémoires historiques*, I, CIX–CLXXI. Bielenstein, "Restoration of the Han Dynasty," 44. Beasley and Pulleyblank, *Historians of China and Japan*, 24–43.

87. It may seem unwarranted to use the word "book" for such documents. But *Webster's New International Dictionary* says that "book" is derived from an Anglo-Saxon word meaning "beech," "because the ancient Saxons and Germans in general wrote runes on pieces of beechen board."

in most of China, where it is damp, they have perished.[88] The other character that appears often is *tien* 典 . This shows such a book standing on a table. It is a book treated with special regard. This character sometimes has the sense of "canon" or "statute," and sometimes that of "archives."

No remnant of the archives of the Shang court has been preserved,[89] but it is quite certain that they existed. Decipherment of the Shang oracle bones has shown that the lists of Shang Kings preserved in the histories are so accurate that they must be based on records transmitted from Shang times. The Duke of Chou, haranguing the Yin officers, said, "You know that the earlier men of Yin had documents *(ts'e)* and records *(tien)* telling how Yin superseded the Mandate of Hsia."[90] His argument would have been pointless if the Yin officers, to whom he was speaking, had not been familiar with the practice of keeping records.

The regard for written records, and especially for those important enough to be placed in the archives, was so great that it affected the language. When King Wu says to his younger brother, "You should in everything respect the *tien*," we cannot tell whether by *tien* he means the archives containing the principles for right conduct, or simply, as Karlgren translates, "the rules." Matters were so commonly administered by committing them to writing that the Duke of Chou uses *tien* as a verb meaning "to manage."[91]

The keeping of official records is one of the important functions of government. A government that establishes, guarantees, and records the status of individuals and the ownership of property makes a solid contribution in return for the wealth it takes in taxation and the limitations it places upon freedom. Although we have only scattered pieces of evidence, they warrant the conclusion that the Western Chou government discharged this function on a very considerable scale.

We have a great many bronze inscriptions that record the bestowal by the King, upon various retainers, of offices or lands or both. Various other things were sometimes given in connection with such bestowals: retainers, regalia, cowrie shells (which were used as money),

88. Tsien, *Written on Bamboo and Silk*, 4, 90–113, and plates XV–XVIII. Loewe, *Records of Han Administration*.

89. Creel, *Studies*, 21–95.

90. *Shu*, 56. For another piece of similar evidence, see *Shih*, 216; unfortunately, however, this poem may have been written so late as to weaken the value of its testimony.

91. *Shu*, 42, 53.

metal (probably copper or bronze), horses, silk, and so forth. Such bestowals were often, perhaps always, made in a ceremony, in which a document setting forth the commission or gifts or both was sometimes and perhaps always used. It is necessary to speak with caution, for the information given in the inscriptions ranges from the complete and detailed to the very brief; in the latter cases it is probable that details are omitted for the sake of brevity.

We seem to have only one inscription that gives the longest version of this ceremony. The time, as commonly, was dawn; the place, a great hall in the capital. The various actors in this little drama took their appointed places. An officer handed the "commanding document" to the King. Obviously, this document had been prepared previously by the royal secretariat. The King then ordered a second officer to "documentarily command Sung," that is to charge the recipient by means of the document. The next words are "The King says," followed by the content of the charge. This is evidently the text of the document, read out by the officer and later copied into the inscription. After the text of the charge, the inscription continues: "Sung saluted, bowed his head, received the commanding document, suspended it from his girdle, and went out."[92]

Not only the bronzes but also the *Documents* and the *Poetry* tell of this process of giving a charge by means of a document. Even King K'ang, after the death of his father, took part in a ceremony in which the "documentary command" of his father was delivered to the new King by the chief officers of the realm. This would seem to have been an investiture of the King, analogous to that whereby Kings created feudal lords.[93]

Since the recipient of the charge or gifts received the copy of the document used in the ceremony,[94] it was necessary that a duplicate be kept at the court, if any kind of check was to be maintained. The *Ritual of Chou* says that the Interior Secretary "has charge of writing the King's orders, and makes a copy of them."[95] The Interior Secretary appears in many bronze inscriptions in which the King orders him to "documentarily charge" a recipient of favor.[96] It seems quite possible,

92. *Chin-wen*, 72ab. Ch'en, "Hsi-Chou T'ung-ch'i," (3).100–110, discusses this ceremony in great detail.

93. *Shu*, 71. See also *Shu*, 48, and *Shih*, 112.

94. This is seldom specified in the inscriptions, but it is a reasonable assumption that this was the regular practice, since the recipient of the charge often included the text of the document (perhaps in abbreviated form) in an inscription that he had cast to commemorate the event.

95. *Chou-li*, 26.25b; Biot, *Tcheou-li*, II, 118.

96. *Chin-wen*, 73b, 75b, 76b, 77a, 78b, 101b, 117a, 118a, 154b.

therefore, that in this instance (as in some others) the *Ritual of Chou* may preserve a valid tradition, and that the making of copies of such documents was among the Secretary's duties. These copies were undoubtedly kept in the royal archives. The number of such documents, filed during Western Chou times, must have run into the thousands.

We have only a little direct evidence, in the Western Chou sources, of the existence of archives. What appears to have been an office at which contracts were filed will be discussed in a later chapter.[97] Perhaps the best evidence of all is the fact that we have, in the *Documents*, a number of writings of Western Chou date that were almost certainly preserved in the royal archives.

The *Tso-chuan* says that when the state of Lu was founded, near the beginning of Western Chou, it was provided with the various essentials of a state, including Secretaries and "archival records."[98] The same work tells us, in two different passages, that records from early Western Chou times were still preserved, in the seventh century B.C., in the royal "Repository of Covenants." A covenant sworn to by various states in 632 B.C. is said to have been placed in the "Chou Repository" (Legge translates this as "royal library") and to have been available there for inspection in 506 B.C. And in 516 B.C., when a pretender to the throne was driven out of the royal capital, it is recorded that he took with him the Chou archives.[99]

Documents of various kinds were produced by the royal officials. A famous general cast a bronze inscription that tells, in language that is not at all points easy to understand, of difficulties he had in securing a document attesting his title to certain lands. He asks the officials for this document, which apparently had to be signed by the King. Apparently he got it, but only after presenting a valuable carved jade to an official—probably the Intendant.[100]

It is difficult to tell how generally deeds were used, but they were probably common. It appears that in theory all land belonged to the King; and, while parcels could be transferred, this seems to have required royal sanction.[101] An inscription believed to date from the ninth century B.C. describes a very complicated series of land transfers that

97. See pp. 183–185.

98. *Tso*, 750::754 (Ting 4).

99. *Tso*, 143::145 (Hsi 5), 197::198 (Hsi 26), 714::717 (Chao 26), 750::755 (Ting 4).

100. *Chin-wen*, 144b. For the office probably involved, see ibid., 149a.

101. *Shih*, 157. See also *Chin-wen*, 16a. In this inscription the King gives a parcel of land to the Grand Secretary, who wishes to hand it on as a fief to one of his retainers. The King permits this, but the King personally makes the presentation on behalf of the Grand Secretary to the retainer.

appears to have been supervised by three royal officials, with Steward K'e acting as a guarantor of the agreement.[102] It appears likely, though this is not stated, that a copy of this contract was filed by the government. Another inscription describes, at great length, a series of boundary lines agreed to by two parties, who swear to abide by them. Penalties for violation are stated, and a royal Secretary apparently acts as guarantor and holds a copy of the agreement.[103] In another inscription the King orders one of his officials to record in the archives lands and people belonging to Steward K'e; this presumably established his title to them.[104] We also find a high official requesting one of the royal Secretaries to make an official record of a fine that has been assessed.[105]

Written instructions and programs were drawn up for many sorts of activity. When the Chou were about to build their new capital near the present site of Loyang, the Duke of Chou gave out written orders to the chiefs of the various groups of the conquered Shang people, who were to perform the labor.[106] After the death of King Ch'eng, a written program was drawn up for the ceremonies of his funeral and the accession of the new King.[107] An army, sent by the King on a distant mission, carried written orders; and in the *Poetry* a soldier laments: "Do we not long to return? But we are in awe of the writing on those bamboo slips."[108]

Still another function that must have required a great deal of official writing was the keeping of accounts, the auditing of tax receipts, and all the financial business involved in running an extensive Empire. These will be discussed in the following chapter. Certainly there was not, in Western Chou, the veritable horde of clerical functionaries

102. *Chin-wen*, 124b.

103. *Chin-wen*, 129ab. See also Ssu, "Liang-Chou Chih-kuan K'ao," 16. Maspero ("La société chinoise," 372–375) gives a translation of this inscription with which I do not agree on some points. This inscription has been the subject of a great quantity of varying interpretation.

104. *Chin-wen*, 123a.

105. *Chin-wen*, 26a. Chou, *Chin-wen Ling-shih*, 64–69.

106. *Shu*, 48.

107. *Shu*, 70. Karlgren translates this, "order was given to make a document about the measures (sc. prescribed by the dead king)." He discusses this in "Glosses on the Book of Documents," (2).160–161. Legge (*Shu*, 551) and Couvreur (*Shu*, 349–350) also suppose this document to be one embodying the last wishes of the dead King. I think this is mistaken. The context here is speaking of the funeral activities, and to introduce the King's charge at this point is gratuitous. Karlgren's argument that tso-ts'e 作 冊 cannot be divided would seem to have no force, since when these characters are used together they normally constitute an official title. I think that what we have here is clearly ts'e tu 冊 度 , "documentary regulations," that is, written regulations.

108. *Shih*, 112.

found at the Chinese court under the Han, but their number must have been very considerable. There were a great many officials called simply "Secretary," or bearing titles including the character for "Secretary" with some qualification. As we have seen, Secretaries were charged with various functions—even military—but it is probable that such officers were most commonly involved with writing and recording. Other official titles, most notably "Maker of Books," but others also, have obvious reference to the function of creating, using, and keeping documents.[109]

No consideration of Western Chou government would be complete that did not take into account another factor—one however that is neither emphasized in the sources nor often so much as mentioned in the histories: the political role of women. At times, evidently, it was considerable.

One of the poems in the Poetry lists seven chief royal officials, and then mentions the Queen. Karlgren translates the passage thus: "the beautiful wife splendidly side by side (with the king) has her place."[110] But anyone familiar with the attitude toward women in government can feel quite sure that a derogatory interpretation was likely to be put upon this passage, and indeed it has been. The poem is attributed to the reign of King Yu (781–771 B.C.), a luckless ruler who is blamed for bringing the Western Chou dynasty, through wickedness and frivolity, to the end it met at his death.[111] He is said to have become infatuated with an evil—but of course fascinating—concubine, who hastened him on the road to destruction. Some years after the beginning of his reign he is supposed to have set aside his original Queen and elevated this concubine to her place.[112] As we might expect, commentators insist upon supposing that the "beautiful wife" mentioned in this poem is not the proper Queen but the sinister concubine, occupying the position she has usurped. Legge, following the tradition, translates the passage as "the beautiful wife blazes, now in possession of her place." Commentators interpret the listing of her with ministers as evidence that the King's infatuation was such that he forced his

---

109. For an extensive study of Western Chou secretarial officials and their activities, see Ch'en, "Hsi-Chou T'ung-ch'i," (3).98–114. See also Tsien, Written on Bamboo and Silk, 7–9.

110. Shih, 139.

111. Mao-shih, 12(2).1a.

112. Shih-chi, 4.62–65; Mémoires historiques, I, 280–285. Creel, Birth of China, 240–243.

ministers to be associated with her in the court, and thus as "describing that which disordered the royal government."[113]

The *Poetry* does, certainly, give clear evidence of a prejudice against feminine influence in government. One poem includes a sweeping denunciation:

> A wise man builds a city wall,
> A wise woman overthrows it.
> Beautiful is the wise woman,
> But she is an owl, a hooting owl.
> A woman with a long tongue
> Is a promoter of evil.
> Disorder is not sent down from Heaven,
> It is produced by women.[114]

The very vehemence of this condemnation would seem to be a clear indication that one or more women had definitely been influencing the government, and that the author did not like it.

It is entirely possible, nevertheless, that the passage in the *Poetry* in which the Queen is listed along with the chief royal officers is nothing more than a realistic recognition of the fact that she is one of those who play a role in the making of decisions, and perhaps even in the conduct of the government. We have seen that the Shang inscriptions seem to indicate that a number of the wives or concubines of a Shang King who lived around 1300 B.C. carried on many governmental functions, even including the making of war.[115] For Western Chou there is nothing so striking, but we have definite indications that the Queens were not a wholly negligible factor, even in government.

Women almost always play an important role "behind the scenes," of course, not only by influencing their husbands and others but also by performing social duties, thus making contributions that are impossible to measure and usually go unremarked. That Western Chou Queens did make such contributions is clear.[116] But in a few bronze inscriptions we see them in definite political roles. It is probable that these only suggest a great many similar occurrences of which we have no record.

The wife of King Ch'eng appears in several inscriptions. It has been suggested that she was a daughter of the first Duke of the important

---

113. *Mao-shih*, 12(2).6b. Legge, *Shih*, 322.
114. *Shih*, 237.
115. See pp. 32–33.
116. See pp. 394–395.

northeastern state of Ch'i, and this is not impossible.[117] In one inscription we see her sending Secretary Shu on some mission—what the mission was is not stated—to the Grand Protector, who rewards Shu with handsome gifts.[118] Again we find the same Queen bestowing upon the Maker of Books Nieh ten double strings of cowries, ten families of retainers, and one hundred men who are apparently slaves.[119] And two inscriptions relate that she sent Maker of Books Huan on what was apparently an inspection trip to the domain of the Earl of I, who rewarded Huan with cowries and cloth.[120] She seems clearly to have been exercising what were normally functions of the King.

There are many other passages in the bronze inscriptions that probably indicate the political activity of women, but they are ambiguous and it is better to stay with relatively solid evidence. One inscription that presents many problems of interpretation nevertheless shows quite clearly the intervention of a Queen in governmental affairs—under somewhat special circumstances, to be sure. This inscription is dated to around 800 B.C. It appears that the Queen's father was in trouble because of a shortage in his tax payments. The Queen accuses an official of being at least partly to blame for her father's delinquency. In the upshot the Queen sends a valuable gift to the official, and the official presents gifts to her emissary and also to the chief minister.[121]

A misogynist might say that this episode justifies the misgivings of those who deplore feminine meddling in government, since the Queen was involved in bribery. It should be noted, however, that two men were also involved. Furthermore, it is not always easy to be certain when gifts did, and when they did not, constitute bribes. By the Spring and Autumn period, at least, there were recognized gifts that it was considered proper to present on various occasions.[122] In our own day the heads of states exchange gifts quite publicly.

Undoubtedly there was bribery in Western Chou government, but our clear indications of it are few, and it is quite impossible to determine its extent and importance. Exactly the same can be said of almost every government, ancient or modern. Bribes are of many sorts, and those that can be expressed in terms of money are relatively rare. Favor, promotion, power, even flattery: all these can be bribes as

---

117. Ch'en, "Hsi-Chou T'ung-ch'i," (2).117.
118. Ibid., (3).65.
119. Ibid., (2).76. *Chin-wen*, 3b.
120. *Chin-wen*, 14a. Ch'en, "Hsi-Chou T'ung-ch'i," (2).117.
121. For fuller discussion of this inscription, see below, pp. 158–159.
122. *Tso*, 107::107–108 (Chuang 24).

CHAPTER

7

The Royal Government: Finance

A GOVERNMENT without wisdom is likely to find itself in trouble. A government without military force will lack protection if trouble comes. But a government without economic resources is in trouble, and if the condition is not remedied quickly it will cease to exist. If for no other reason, officials and soldiers must eat, and no amount of loyalty will enable them to perform their duties if they are starving.[1]

For a centralized government, some system of financial administration is indispensable.[2] Students of the history of government in Europe point out the close connection between the development of financial administration and the rise of the centralized bureaucratic state there.[3]

Modern critical scholars have seldom supposed that the Western Chou government involved anything sufficiently developed to be called financial administration.[4] Many have believed that such trade as

1. This might seem to conflict with *Analects*, 12.7, in which Confucius says that the prime requisite for government is the confidence of the people in the administration, which must be preserved even if it is necessary to dispense with military force and food. I do not think, however, that it really does. Confucius was certainly not counseling starvation. I believe that what he was saying was that the emphasis must be on good faith, and that the government should not attempt (as the *Fa-chia*, the so-called "Legalists," later advocated) to multiply the economic resources of the state, to make it strong, even if this meant alienating the people. Passages in the *Analects* have to be considered in the entire context of the thought of Confucius. This one should be compared with, for instance, *Analects*, 12.9, in which one of Confucius' disciples voices what would seem clearly to be a sentiment in harmony with those of Confucius.

2. It should be noted that "finance" does not necessarily, though of course it does usually, involve money. It is a French word, related to *fin*, "end." Its original sense was that of settling, that is, ending, accounts.

3. See pp. 14–15.

4. Certainly I myself, in my former publications on this period, have not; see Creel, *Birth of China*, 316–318.

was carried on at that time was conducted principally by means of barter.[5] Maspero wrote that the tribute paid to the Chou Kings by the feudal lords "was not in money since it did not exist, nor in grain which was impossible to transport; it consisted of rare and precious objects."[6]

In the past it has been assumed that Western Chou was a time of decentralization, in which financial administration by the royal government would have been relatively unnecessary. But today we know that the Western Chou Kings administered large responsibilities over a wide area. They had guard posts at many points and maintained military patrols over principal roads. They had at least fourteen standing armies which they could, and did, dispatch to enforce their will in distant places. This could not be done without economic resources. Officials require support. Armies need weapons, clothing, and above all food; and in a stable state they cannot simply seize these things from any area in which they may find themselves.

It would seem almost inevitable that, in the circumstances, the Western Chou court must have had a financial system of some kind. This need not necessarily imply the presence of money, at least as we commonly understand the term. Accounts could have been kept in terms of any of a number of commodities—grain, for instance. Let us suppose that a feudal lord whose capital is located one hundred miles from the royal capital is found to owe so many bushels of millet as tax. This could be reported to the royal court. He could then be directed to deliver so many bushels of this grain to royal troops stationed relatively near him. Such grain could also be exchanged for weapons, clothing, and so forth. It might also be used to provide support for royal officials away from the capital.

This is a purely hypothetical case. But for even such a primitive financial system there are two necessities. First, there must be some one, generally accepted, unit of value, in terms of which all accounts can be kept. And second, there must be a system by which accounts are kept and payments are credited against debts.

As we consider the activities of the royal government of Western Chou, it does not appear possible that the Kings could have had no revenues beyond gifts of rare and precious objects. And it would seem that there must have been some system, even if rudimentary, of financial administration. But of course we cannot say: there must have been, therefore there was. We must look carefully into the sources,

5. Kuo, *Shih P'i-p'an Shu*, 55. Chou, *Chin-wen Ling-shih*, 57. P'eng, *Chung-kuo Huo-pi Shih*, 5.

6. Maspero, "Le régime féodal," 142.

and address questions to them. The matter of trade is connected, if only indirectly, with finance. Our first question will then be: how much trade was there in Western Chou times? The second will be: was there money, and if so what kind? And finally we shall ask: do the sources indicate that in fact the royal government did perform functions of financial administration?

There is also a prior question we should consider. If it be assumed, for the moment, that there were trade and money and financial administration, how much could we expect the sources that we have to tell us about them? This is a very important question, which is not always asked.

For comparison let us turn again to medieval Europe. We may sometimes think that the disunity and confusion there led to financial breakdown and even to barter, and undoubtedly this did occur. But medieval Europe was the heir of the Roman Empire, in which trade, banking, and credit operations had reached a high point of development.[7] These things were not wholly forgotten. Charlemagne, around 800, took many steps to improve communications, regulate weights, measures, and coinage, and regulate and promote trade. Melvin M. Knight says that "if the Roman economic organization was somewhat more intensive (which is not entirely beyond dispute), that of the late Middle Ages exploited and knit together in its own fashion several times more territory in Europe."[8] Neither trade nor finance stopped at political borders. For example, King John of England (1199–1216) borrowed from bankers in Piacenza. Italian bankers dealt even beyond the confines of Europe. Around 1300 a single house, the Peruzzi of Florence, had regular representatives engaged in financial transactions in Naples, Avignon, Paris, Bruges, London, Cyprus, Rhodes, Tunis, and elsewhere.[9]

Keeping account of such transactions must have been a bookkeeper's nightmare. Not only did they involve numerous currencies in constant fluctuation; even the ratio between gold and silver was varied with the utmost frequency.[10] There was need of a single unit of value that could be used as an intermediary, in terms of which the value of each of the fluctuating currencies might be determined. Such a unit,

---

7. Rostovtzeff, *Roman Empire*, I, 31, 179–182.

8. *Cambridge Medieval History*, II, 657; V, 643–648. Melvin M. Knight, "Commercial Routes," in *Encyclopaedia of the Social Sciences*, IV, 21–22.

9. *Cambridge Medieval History*, VI, 485–487.

10. *Cambridge Medieval History*, VI, 488, says that "in the fourteenth century alone the official ratio of the metals was altered a hundred and fifty times by the King of France, with or without alterations in the metallic content of the coins."

almost everywhere called the "pound," was developed as a "money of account."[11] Luigi Einaudi, who has studied this phenomenon, says:

> Money of account was not created by decree but grew almost spontaneously out of men's habit of keeping accounts in monetary units, some of which corresponded in the time of Charlemagne to real coins. Later on it happened from time to time that the money of account was pegged to a real coin. . . . Such a correspondence was accidental or, if deliberate did not last long.

Because this "pound" seldom corresponded to any money in actual use, it has sometimes been called "imaginary money." Nevertheless this device performed very important functions, facilitating the keeping of accounts and financial interchange between states that had different and fluctuating moneys, and some that had no coinage of their own at all. And it did this, Einaudi says, for a thousand years, from the time of Charlemagne to the French Revolution.[12]

The historian of medieval European economic phenomena has at his disposal scores of thousands of commercial and governmental documents that embarrass him with their riches. Yet this very important monetary phenomenon, the "pound," became virtually forgotten after around 1800, when it ceased to be used. Even Europeans who wrote on monetary subjects while it was in use, from the sixteenth to the eighteenth century, were in some confusion about it, and "their strange terminology causes us," Einaudi says, "who live in another world, to wander for a while in a dark forest."[13] If so important a fact of economic life became all but unknown under the relatively favorable conditions for the study of medieval history, we should not expect too much evidence of comparable phenomena—if they existed—from our meager records from Western Chou.

There is in fact very little mention of finance and of trade even in later Chinese history, despite the fact that China has been one of the richest of countries and her people among the most energetic and accomplished traders. Etienne Balazs wrote:

> Needless to say, a society as highly civilized as China's could not have done without trade and handicrafts, least of all the bureaucrats at the top, whose way of life en-

---

11. It was called a "pound" because originally (but not for long) its value was that of a pound of silver; see Einaudi, "Imaginary Money," 230.

12. Ibid.

13. Ibid., 229–230, 235.

tirely depended on them. Trade, and usury too, was often carried on with the connivance of officials, who strove not only to gain control over it but to snatch the profits as well; yet it was never mentioned except in terms of condemnation. Thus it is only indirectly—by what can be gleaned from moralistic writings, from discussions between officials and merchants on commercial competition, from administrative measures, or from the chance mention of the role of a trader in the career of an official personage—that we are able to obtain any information about commercial activities. Hardly any private documents exist, and there are no charters of any kind . . ."[14]

In the documents that survive to us from Western Chou there is even less reason to expect to find much information about commercial and financial activity—if in fact it existed—than in Chinese literature as a whole.

REFERENCES to trade are very rare in the Western Chou sources. Yet the most interesting and suggestive one comes to us from the very beginning of the period, and in the words of King Wu, the founder, himself. He was concerned, as we have noticed, about the use by the conquered Shang people of alcoholic liquor. They should devote themselves rather, he says, to cultivating the fields and "diligently lead their carts and oxen far away to trade in commodities, in order filially to nourish their parents." This is rather striking. It has commonly been held that trade in China was confined, until a relatively late date, to traffic in small quantities of rare and quite valuable goods. But here we find reference to trade in useful commodities, and on a scale large enough to require transport in carts drawn by oxen.[15] And King Wu mentions this along with farming, as an occupation that is presumably to be engaged in by considerable numbers of people. Nothing else, I think, suggests that there was trade on such a scale at this time, yet there seems to be no reason to discredit this testimony.

In all of the Western Chou sources there seems to be only one reference to a specific individual as a trader. And he is mentioned for the

---

14. Balazs, *Chinese Civilization and Bureaucracy*, 56.

15. *Shu*, 43. This interpretation depends in part upon the punctuation of the text; see Karlgren, "Glosses on the Book of Documents," (1).298. But even if one punctuates differently, I think the conclusion holds.

reason that he was not, in fact, a trader, but only pretended to be one. In the *Poetry* a woman begins her tale thus:

A jolly man of the people,
You carried cloth to trade it for silk;[16]
But you did not come to trade for silk,
You came to lay plans for approaching me.

She goes on to tell how she at length went away with him, but in the end finds herself cast off.[17] The interesting point, for our present purpose, is the fact that a man wishing to disguise himself, in order to spy out the land for a seduction, chooses to pose as a peddler. It would seem that peddlers must have been so common that they went unnoticed—like the postman in a mystery story.

Other references to trade are random. A poem compares slanderers to those who sell goods for three times what they paid for them.[18] A bronze inscription tells of the sale of five men for one horse and one roll of silk, but only because this sale led to a dispute (which involved a royal official) that gave rise to a lawsuit.[19]

The *Poetry* has one reference to a market place. One inscription speaks of markets that were frequented, it would appear, by both Chinese and barbarians.[20] This suggests that there may have been fairs, which drew their attendance from a considerable area.

Wealthy merchants and financiers have played important roles in

---

16. The line *Pao pu mao ssu* 抱布貿絲 involves problems. Chinese commentators have ventured various opinions; see *Mao-shih*, 3(3).1b–2b. Legge (*Shih*, 97) translates it approximately as I have. Waley (*Shih*, 96) has "bringing cloth to exchange it for thread." Couvreur (*Shih*, 67–68) translates it as "il apportait une pièce de soie, et venait (disait-il) l'échanger contre du fil de soie." Karlgren (*Shih*, 40) translates: "you carried cloth to barter it for silk." But in "Glosses on the Kuo Feng Odes," 156, Karlgren introduces a different note, translating: "you came and carried cloth, i.e. money to buy silk." Apparently Karlgren is here interpreting *pu* 布 to mean "spade coins." The character certainly did come to have this sense, but whether it did so as early as Western Chou times is debated; see p. 146, n. 58. It has been argued that *pu* in this passage refers to coins, but the clear evidence against this view is well summarized in P'eng, *Chung-kuo Huo-pi Shih*, 20, and 44 n. 1.

17. *Shih*, 40–41.

18. *Shih*, 237.

19. *Chin-wen*, 96b–97a. Chou, *Chin-wen Ling-shih*, 50–51.

20. *Shih*, 88. *Chin-wen*, 143b. The character translated as "market" seems to appear only this once in the inscriptions, and the reading of a unique character is often a problem. But in addition to Kuo Mo-jo several other eminent scholars interpret this one as meaning "market"; see Jung, *Chin-wen Pien*, 5.29a. Ch'en Meng-chia appears to agree with this reading in his partial translation of this inscription in "The Greatness of Chou," 70.

the political history of many nations,[21] and China (in spite of the tendency to denigrate financial activities) was no exception. In 154 B.C., when a serious rebellion left the whole future of the Chinese state hanging in the balance, loans made by a single moneylender played an important part in making it possible for the Imperial cause to triumph.[22] And one passage in the *Tso-chuan* seems clearly to indicate that, even before the end of Western Chou, merchants had become important enough to be allied by sworn covenant with the ruler of a feudal state.

The famous statesman Tzu-ch'an, of the state of Cheng, is quoted as saying that the first ruler of that state, Duke Huan (806–771 B.C.), had sworn a covenant with certain merchants. In this covenant the Duke said:

> If you do not revolt from me, I will not interfere by force with your trade. I will neither ask for nor seize anything from you. You may have your profitable markets and precious goods, without my taking any cognizance of them.

On the basis of this covenant, Tzu-ch'an says, the rulers and the merchants "have been able to rely upon each other down to the present day," over a period of two and one-half centuries.[23]

The evidence of trade that we have from the Western Chou period is slight, but that is exactly what we ought to expect. What evidence we do have is rather striking and seems to indicate that there was probably much more trade—and that it was probably much more important—than has commonly been supposed.[24] And if we can put

21. A conspicuous example is the French merchant and financier Jacques Coeur (1395–1456). The son of a small merchant of Bourges, he came to dominate the commercial activity of France, and also became the most famous of the councillors of King Charles VII. His financial support is given a large share of the credit for making it possible for Charles to recover his kingdom. See *Cambridge Medieval History*, VIII, 265, and *Encyclopaedia of the Social Sciences*, III, 619–620.

22. *Han-shu*, 91.11b. Swann, *Food and Money*, 393–398.

23. *Tso*, 662::664 (Chao 16). Legge, and also Couvreur (*Tso-chuan*, III, 268–269), translate this passage as meaning that the original covenant was between Duke Huan and a single merchant. I find no warrant for this in the text. If the Duke swore such a covenant with a single merchant, he must have been a powerful merchant indeed!

24. Ch'i Ssu-ho ("Chinese and European Feudal Institutions," 6), writing primarily of the Spring and Autumn period, says: "The lack of a convenient means of exchange, the primitive means of communication, the hazardous nature of carrying valuables over long distances, and the self-sufficiency of the feudal community, made the commerce of the time almost negligible." In some of these respects, how-

any trust in the passage just quoted from the *Tso-chuan*, it seems clear that some merchants achieved a position of considerable consequence.

<hr />

Was there money in Western Chou?

There are a few who argue that metallic coins were in use as early as that time, but there seems to be no solid evidence either for or against this possibility.[25] There is a general tendency to suppose that, for the most part at least, Western Chou was a period of barter.[26] Ch'en Meng-chia says that during the Chou period—but he does not specify when—"the inconvenience of barter on a large scale led to the use of cowries, silks, and metal as money." But, he adds, "the actual shift to a money economy did not take place until the Chan Kuo [Warring States] era."[27]

It has been suggested that in Western Chou times pieces of metal were used in the manner of money.[28] When the sources mention "metal," they are probably referring to copper or bronze.[29] Such metal

<hr />

ever, conditions in Western Chou times may have been more favorable for commerce than those of the Spring and Autumn period. The patrolling of some roads by royal troops (see pp. 313–314) may not have been intended to facilitate trade, but it must have done so.

25. P'eng (*Chung-kuo Huo-pi Shih*, 5–6, 23, 36) thinks that there may have been coinage even in Shang times, and that there certainly was in Western Chou. Wang Yü-ch'üan (*Early Chinese Coinage*, 153) says of certain "knife coins" that they "may be as early as around 1079 B.C. and as late as the first half of the ninth century." Lien-sheng Yang (*Money and Credit in China*, 108) says that he has read the latter work in proof, but he himself says (ibid., 14): "Spade coins or *pu* and knife coins or *tao* are for the most part attributable to a period from the fifth to the third century B.C., and possibly earlier." Yang also writes (ibid., 108): "Wang Yü-ch'üan . . . considers certain prototypes of spade coins as early as the beginning of the Chou period . . . This early date of coinage . . . seems doubtful."

26. See p. 134, n. 5.

27. Ch'en, "The Greatness of Chou," 70.

28. Kuo, *Shih P'i-p'an Shu*, 55–56.

29. The character *chin* 金 in the Western Chou sources functions chiefly as an adjective. Aside from a few ambiguous cases it seldom appears in the literary sources as denoting a commodity. In the original text of the *Book of Changes* there is one occurrence of *huang chin* 黃金, "yellow metal," which both Legge (*I-ching*, 102) and Wilhelm (*I-ching*, 97) understand to mean gold; but it may be only bronze. There is also an occurrence of *chin fu* 金夫, which Wilhelm (*I-ching*, 41) translates as "ehernen Mann." This may be correct, for this work abounds in strange language, but even so "bronze man" does not seem to make much sense in the context, and Legge (*I-ching*, 65), who translates "man of wealth," may well be correct. In the chapters of the *Documents* that I accept as of Western Chou date the character does not appear. In the *Poetry*, *chin* is occasionally used as a simile, but

was valuable, for making weapons and other utensils as well as the highly prized ritual vessels. Metal is mentioned in a few bronze inscriptions as loot of war, and as gifts (usually presented by the King) in a little more than a dozen. In some cases this metal was probably given to a bronze caster as material with which to make a vessel, and may also have been used as payment for the labor involved, though this is seldom clear.[30] But aside from this possibility, the sources do not seem to mention metal as a medium of exchange. The quantity of metal is usually not specified, but one inscription does say that the King gave to the son of the Duke of Chou "one hundred *lieh*" of metal.[31] The *lieh* 寽 is believed to be a measure of weight, but the actual amount is unknown. (We shall encounter the *lieh* again.)

Another article that is widely supposed to have been used as money in Western Chou times is the shell of the cowrie. The cowrie is a small marine mollusc; its shell has been used as a medium of exchange in many parts of the world, from antiquity even into the twentieth century. This practice is responsible for the scientific name of one variety, *Cypraea moneta*. The reason for the rather amazing vogue of the cowrie, both as a decoration and as a kind of money, is rather a mystery; a number of scholars have explained it as being based on a supposed resemblance of the shell to the vulva, so that it is interpreted as a sexual symbol.[32] However that may be, cowries are mentioned in the Shang inscriptions; and not only cowries but even bronze replicas of them have been excavated from Shang sites. Much scholarly opinion holds that cowries were used by the Shang as money, but there seems to be no definite evidence of trade in terms of cowries in Shang times.[33]

---

its only appearance as denoting a commodity is in a poem (*Shih*, 257) that says that the vanquished Huai tribes "present us with southern metal."

30. The bronzes commonly record the gift and then say *yung tso* 用乍, which could be interpreted to mean that the recipient "used it to make" the vessel (*Chin-wen*, 11b, 40b, etc.). But the trouble is that this same formula may be used when the recipient has been given almost anything. In many cases this formula must mean that the recipient "therefore made" the vessel—so that its inscription could publish to the world the favor he had received. But in cases where captured metal is in question (ibid., 28b, 54a, 146a) the metal may have been used as payment. *Chin-wen*, 96b, does seem clearly to say that the recipient used the metal he had received to have the bronze cast.

31. *Chin-wen*, 11b.

32. *Encyclopaedia of the Social Sciences*, X, 602. Andersson, *Children of the Yellow Earth*, 294–312.

33. Cheng, *Shang China*, 127, 200, 204. Wang, *Early Chinese Coinage*, 54–89. Ch'en, *Yin Tz'u Tsung-shu*, 557–558. Kuo, *Pu-tz'u T'ung-tsuan*, 100b–101b. Wang, *Kuan-t'ang Chi-lin*, 3.17a–18a.

In the literary sources for Western Chou, cowries are seldom mentioned,[34] but in the bronze inscriptions they figure frequently. In those inscriptions on which my notes are based, there are fourteen instances in which the King gives cowries to subordinates, and seven cases of such gifts by lesser dignitaries. In two instances cowries are given by feudal lords to royal officials who were sent to inspect their fiefs, and two tell of the capture of cowries, in one case from "eastern barbarians." Two other bronze inscriptions mention cowries in contexts that are not clear. It is probable that in some cases the cowries were used as payment for the casting of the bronze; but as with metal, it is usually hard to be sure of this.[35] Otherwise there seems to be no direct evidence that cowries were used as a medium of exchange.

It is difficult to suppose that cowries could have been used as ordinary money, for they must have been very valuable. One inscription speaks of a gift of thirty *lieh* (the weight of unknown value) of cowries,[36] but they are usually enumerated in terms of *p'eng* or double strings. It is generally believed that one double string consisted of ten cowries.[37] Although the Duke of Chou in one case made a gift of a hundred double strings, this was quite exceptional. Gifts of ten double strings were common, and in one case we find the King presenting only one double string.[38] If only ten cowries were sufficient to constitute the entire content of a royal gift, the value of even a single cowrie must have been so great, as compared with that of ordinary commodities, that it would have been an embarrassing kind of money to use for most purposes.

34. The original text of the *Book of Changes* has a single occurrence of the character *pei* 貝 . Legge (*I-ching*, 173) translates it as "articles," while Wilhelm (*I-ching*, 190) interprets it as *Schätze*, "treasures." In the sections of the *Documents* that I accept as Western Chou, *pei* occurs only twice (*Shu*, 71), and both times it seems to denote ornamental objects. In the *Poetry* its two appearances (*Shih*, 151, 260) seem to be as ornaments. *Shih*, 120, mentions a gift of 100 *p'eng* 朋 , without mentioning cowries, but no doubt this means 100 double strings of cowries.

35. It seems likely that captured cowries were used to pay for the casting of bronzes, and one inscription may definitely say this, but it involves a problem; see *Chin-wen*, 25ab.

36. *Chin-wen*, 60b. Ch'en, "Hsi-Chou T'ung-ch'i," (5).107.

37. Ch'en, *Yin Tz'u Tsung-shu*, 557. Wang, *Early Chinese Coinage*, 83–85. Wang accepts the number of ten as "the unit of cowrie shells after they had been used as money," but believes that the *p'eng* was a single string "curved at the middle." In my opinion the form of the great majority of instances of this character in both Shang and Chou inscriptions supports the "double string" hypothesis.

38. Ch'en, "Hsi-Chou T'ung-ch'i," (2).120. This particular inscription is not included in the corpus from which my basic notes are drawn.

There is strong evidence, nonetheless, that the cowrie was in some manner intimately associated with the idea of value, and with the exchange of goods. Throughout most of Chinese history, and beginning at an early but uncertain date, money has consisted chiefly of metal—at an early time bronze coins, later supplemented by the use of gold and silver.[39] Yet examination of any Chinese dictionary will show that, while there are a great many characters that include the element meaning "metal" (*chin* 金) in their composition, very few of these have to do with money, wealth, commerce, or the transfer of goods.[40] The element that does occur in the overwhelming proportion of such characters, even today, is *pei* 貝 , "cowrie."[41] And this was also true in Western Chou. There were a large number of characters of this kind in current use at that time, having such meanings as "to sell," "to buy," "trader," "tax," "to redeem," and many others.[42]

The cowrie occurs in some surprising connections. It will be recalled that in the *Poetry* it is said that an intending seducer disguised himself as a peddler who "carried cloth to trade it for silk." The character that is here translated as "to trade" has the meanings of "to exchange, to barter," and its signific element is "cowrie."[43] What could the petty trafficking of a peddler, whose wares were so insignificant that he carried them in his arms,[44] possibly have to do with an object so valuable as a cowrie?

39. Yang, *Money and Credit in China*, 11–50. Wang, *Early Chinese Coinage*.

40. It is true of course that the common term for "money" today is *ch'ien* 錢 , which does have *chin* as its signific element. But this character does not seem to have had that sense in early Chou times. It does not seem to occur in the bronze inscriptions, and it is not present in the *Book of Changes* or the *Documents*. In the *Poetry* it occurs just once (*Shih*, 244), where it clearly denotes agricultural implements; Karlgren translates it as "spades." And a type of early bronze coin was made in the shape of a spade, and the term *ch'ien* came to be used to mean "money" (see Wang, *Early Chinese Coinage*, 90–100). But it does not appear to have been so used until after Western Chou times. Karlgren ("Grammata Serica Recensa," 61) cites as a source for the meaning of "coin, money," only the *Discourses of the States*, which cannot have reached its present form until the Warring States period.

41. Lien-sheng Yang (*Money and Credit in China*, 12) says: "To prove that cowries were used as money, scholars often point to the composition of a number of Chinese characters, or written words, which contain the element *pei*, 'the cowry,' as their 'signific' or meaningful root. . . . Obviously the relationship between cowries and wealth and commercial transactions in ancient times must have been very close."

42. The characters are: *mai* 賣 , *mai* 買 , *ku* 賈 , *fu* 賦 , and *shu* 贖 .

43. Mao 貿 .

44. This is indicated by the character *pao* 抱 (*Shih*, 40).

Perhaps monetary theory will provide a clue. T. E. Gregory writes:

> Opinion generally seems to be veering to the view that
> the difficulties of pure barter were first overcome by the
> expression of values in terms of some common prized
> object before that object or any other served as a medium
> of exchange, and that the qualities which fitted a com-
> modity to serve as a common denominator of value
> would not necessarily fit it to serve as a good medium of
> exchange. . . . Thus it is suggested by Ridgeway that the
> origin of modern metallic systems is to be found in the
> existence of an ox unit in a large part of the Eurasian
> continent. Gold, when it became the medium of ex-
> change, already had a value and the primitive weight
> units of the precious metals derive from the amount of
> gold which was equal to the ox value of gold . . .[45]

It seems probable that this points the way to the answer: that the
cowrie, though too valuable to be used as an ordinary medium of
exchange, at some time and in some way that remains unknown to
us came to be regarded as a standard of value. Traces of this fact
remain evident in the Chinese language, just as our words like
"pecuniary," "impecunious," "peculate," and others derive from the
Latin *pecus*, "cattle."

A COMMODITY that definitely was used as a medium of exchange in
Western Chou times is silk. This will surprise no one familiar with
Chinese history. Silk was employed as currency in China even long
after coinage had been in extensive use. Lien-sheng Yang writes: "In
[A.D] 221, Emperor Wen of the Wei dynasty abolished the copper
coin and ordered the people to use grain and silk as media of exchange." "In the period of disunion following the fall of the Han
empire until about [A.D.] 600, bolts of silk of a standard length
and breadth were used as the main medium of exchange in large transactions. This was also true for the first part of the T'ang period."[46]

Silk has been of primary importance in the economy of the Chinese. They may have been practicing sericulture as early as Neolithic
times, and we know that by the Shang dynasty they were weaving
silk in elaborate patterns. There is every reason to believe that in

---

45. T. E. Gregory, "Money," in *Encyclopaedia of the Social Sciences*, X, 603.
46. Yang, *Money and Credit in China*, 2, 16–17. Regarding earlier use of silk as
a medium of exchange, see: Chou, *Chin-wen Ling-shih*, 50. Wang, *Hsien Ch'in
Huo-pi Shih*, 41–44. P'eng, *Chung-kuo Huo-pi Shih*, 20–21.

Western Chou times it was relatively plentiful.[47] The Chinese had a monopoly on sericulture until well into the Christian Era, and silk was in great demand.[48] It has been suggested that Chinese silk was being traded to the Mediterranean world as early as the fifth century B.C. That is uncertain, but before the beginning of the Christian Era it was being imported in quantity to Rome, even though as late as the third century A.D. it was still, when it reached Rome, worth its weight in gold.[49] From the third century B.C. on, the Chinese sent out a huge volume of silk—by the ninth century as many as a million rolls a year—to the nomadic peoples to the north and west, and to Central Asia, to purchase cavalry horses that were vital to their defense.[50]

Silk as we commonly know it varies so widely that it may be difficult to see how it could have been sufficiently standardized to be used as money. The Chinese, however, took extraordinary pains to develop a roll of silk of standard length and breadth, and to maintain this standard without alteration.[51] How early such standard rolls were in existence is unknown, but the *Tso-chuan* attributes to 545 B.C. a conversation that includes a very interesting statement: "Wealth is like pieces of cloth or silk, made up with definite measurements which are not to be altered."[52] There is a tradition that the standard width and

47. Cheng, *Prehistoric China*, 84. Sylwan, "Silk from the Yin Dynasty." References to silk in the Western Chou literature and even in the bronzes indicate that, while it was valuable, it was far from rare.

48. Sericulture was introduced into Europe in the sixth century A.D., but before that time it may have reached areas in Central Asia. See: Needham, *Science and Civilization in China*, I, 185–186. Hudson, *Europe and China*, 103–133.

49. Schoff, The *Periplus*, 264–265. Wheeler, *Rome Beyond the Frontiers*, 208–209.

50. Creel, "The Horse in Chinese History," 665–666. Waley, *Po Chü-i*, 55. Schafer, *Golden Peaches of Samarkand*, 64–65.

51. On the basis of finds in Central Asia, Sir Aurel Stein deduced that, between the end of the first century A.D. and the beginning of the fourth century, the width of Chinese silk was maintained without alteration, despite the fact that the length of the Chinese inch had changed; see Stein, "China's Silk Trade." There has been much discussion of this question; see the notes by Paul Pelliot in ibid., 139–141. See also Sylwan, *Investigation of Silk*, 94–96, where it is pointed out that patterned silks did not usually have the standard breadth. This is not surprising, however, for variations of pattern would immediately remove such silks from standardization.

52. *Tso*, 539::542 (Hsiang 28). There is no question that such standard lengths of silk were well established by the first century B.C., when we find a high Chinese official boasting of the purchasing power of "a single length of plain silk"; see *Yen-t'ieh Lun*, 15b, and Gale, *Salt and Iron*, 14. The *Records on Ceremonial*, compiled in the same century, prescribes the length of rolls of silk to be presented in the marriage ceremony; see *Li-chi*, 43.16b; Legge, *Li-chi*, II, 172; Couvreur, *Li-chi*, II, 200.

length of the roll of silk to be used for monetary purposes was set at the very beginning of Western Chou, but since we have no record of this tradition until the first century A.D., it is impossible to determine its validity.[53]

There are a few references to rolls of silk in the Western Chou sources.[54] One of these occurs in the *Book of Changes*.[55] A bronze inscription mentions "a roll of silk cloth" among gifts presented to an emissary of a Queen. And another inscription involves the sale of five men for "one horse and one roll of silk."[56]

In the *Documents* presentations made to the King by feudal lords are repeatedly called *pi* 幣 . Translators render this as "gifts," "presents," and "offerings," but the literal sense of this character is "silk cloth."[57] It also came to mean "money," a sense that it retains to this day.[58]

One bronze inscription describes a payment made to the King,

---

53. *Han-shu*, 24B.1b; Swann, *Food and Money*, 221.

54. The character *shu* 束 , when used as a noun, is interpreted by Karlgren ("Grammata Serica Recensa," 313) as "bundle," and this is the way it is generally understood. I believe, however, that when the object in question is cloth it is reasonable to interpret it as meaning "roll," for a roll is the most convenient way of making cloth into a bundle. Legge (*I-ching*, 104), translates it as "roll." Of course we cannot always tell if the silk in question is cloth, thread, or raw silk; if either of the latter, "bundle" may be the better translation, but "roll" still remains entirely possible, because even raw silk (as it was removed from the cocoon by the Chinese method) was in long fibers which could best be kept in order by being rolled on something.

55. *I-ching*, 3.15b; Legge, *I-ching*, 104.

56. *Chin-wen*, 96b, 142a.

57. *Shu*, 48, 51, 73. Legge, *Shu*, 424, 433, 562. Only Couvreur (*Shu*, 261, 269, 359) translates *pi* as "pièces de soie."

58. For numerous cases of the early use of cloth in the manner of money, see P'eng, *Chung-kuo Huo-pi Shih*, 20–21. There is some evidence that *pu* 布 was used as a medium of exchange. *Pu* is commonly rendered simply as "cloth," without specifying what kind. Wang Yü-ch'üan (*Early Chinese Coinage*, 94) says that "this textile, a material for everyday clothing, was made from the fiber of the kê [dolichos?] plant and hemp." We have seen that the *Poetry* (*Shih*, 40) speaks of trading "cloth [*pu*] for silk." And we have two bronze inscriptions (recording the same presentation) telling of a gift of "cowries and *pu*"; see *Chin-wen*, 14a, and Ch'en, "Hsi-Chou T'ung-ch'i," (2).117. But early bronze coins, called "spade coins," are known in Chinese as *pu*, and the character occurs as the legend on certain of these coins. There are various theories to account for this. One is that the cloth called *pu* was early used as a medium of exchange, and that this character therefore was used to designate early coins; see P'eng, *Chung-kuo Huo-pi Shih*, 20–22, 44. Wang Yü-ch'üan (*Early Chinese Coinage*, 90–114) argues, however, that the character *pu* was used for these coins for purely phonetic reasons, and that spade coins may have been being made even in Shang times. The latter point, at least, seems rather improbable.

146

probably of taxes, with a character that is composed of two elements meaning "silk cloth" and "cowrie." It might be permissible, in accordance with the way in which characters are often constructed, to interpret this one as meaning "monetary silk," though this must remain conjectural since the character seems to be unknown elsewhere.[59]

Other references to silk reckon it in terms of *lieh*. One inscription says that a fine was assessed in the amount of three hundred *lieh* of a commodity that is not certainly identifiable, but is probably silk.[60] Another speaks of a payment of "three *lieh* of silk."[61] This brings us to the most interesting character of all. But before we can discuss it, we must learn more about the *lieh*.

THERE are some intriguing resemblances between the pound used in medieval Europe and the *lieh* of early China. The pound, it will be recalled, was in use for roughly a thousand years; the *lieh* seems to have been employed as a unit of value for almost as long, from the beginning of Western Chou until at least into the fourth century B.C.[62] The history of the pound is obscure and has only with difficulty been reconstructed; that of the *lieh* is still more so, and we may never understand it fully. Yet it is clear that, like the pound, the *lieh* long served as a measure of value, and that in its later history it provided a common standard against which the currencies of different states might be evaluated, just as the pound provided such a standard for the countries of Europe.

The character *lieh* occurs in the legends[63] of four different types of coins issued during the fourth century B.C. by the state of Liang.

59. *Chin-wen*, 147a.

60. *Chin-wen*, 26a. This character (see Kuo, *Chin-wen Lu-pien*, 12b) seems definitely to include the "silk" element. Chou (*Chin-wen Ling-shih*, 49–51) discusses the character, quoting various opinions, and concludes that it means silk.

61. *Chin-wen*, 97a.

62. Kuo Mo-jo (*Chin-wen*, 26b) and after him Wang Yü-ch'üan (*Early Chinese Coinage*, 207) argue that the *lieh* must have existed in Shang times, but the evidence given seems to me unconvincing. It seems clear from *Chin-wen*, 26a, however, that the *lieh* was current as a standard of value quite early in Western Chou. And it appears as a definite standard of value on coins that were evidently minted in the fourth century B.C.; see Wang, *Early Chinese Coinage*, 137–143. The *lieh* was still known as a unit of weight in Han times (*Chin-wen*, 12ab), but the date at which it ceased to be used as a unit of value seems to be unknown.

63. By "legend" I here mean all characters appearing on the coin. I avoid the numismatic term "inscription," to obviate confusion with inscriptions on bronze vessels.

One of these is translated as: "Liang money to be used as one *chin* and equal to one *lieh*." Another is translated: "Liang money to be used as five *chin* and equal to twelve *lieh*."[64]

Wang Yü-ch'üan suggests that the rulers of Liang issued these coins in order to facilitate transactions between their merchants and those of other regions. Liang was a rich and powerful state in a central location through which much of the trade of the time passed. The *chin* was a local monetary unit, while the *lieh*, Wang believes, was used over a wider area. These coins "were cast as a sort of interregional currency between the area where the *chin* was the monetary unit and the area which used the *lieh*." For this reason each coin bore on its face its value in terms of both of these monetary units.[65]

There is a further problem. On one of these coins the *chin* is said to be equal to the *lieh*, while another says that five *chin* are equal to twelve *lieh*. Since these coins are supposed to have been issued within a fairly brief period, this would seem to indicate rather rapid fluctuation in the relative value of the *chin* and the *lieh*.[66] It appears that the *lieh* was initially a unit of weight, but attempts to determine what the weight was have resulted in a variety of answers. It seems quite possible that the *lieh*, having started as a measure of weight, became transformed into a unit of monetary value, which fluctuated as currencies normally do.[67] In Europe this has been the history of the "pound." The British "pound sterling" originally had the value of a pound of silver, but today it varies quite independently of the value of silver. The medieval pound also had the value of a pound of silver

64. Wang, *Early Chinese Coinage*, 138.

65. Ibid., 142–143.

66. Concerning the date of these coins, Wang Yü-ch'üan (ibid., 142) says that Liang "achieved a sort of hegemony to be emulated by other feudatories over a period of some eighty years from 425 to 344 B.C. It was during this Old Spade period that the 'Special Old Spades of Liang' were in circulation. Indications are that Liang cast these special spades in addition to its ordinary Old Spades, after the state moved its capital to Great Liang in 362 B.C." This would seem to mean that these coins were cast in the brief period of 362–344 B.C.

67. We have seen that the *lieh* 釿 was used in Western Chou times as a measure not only of silk, but also of metal and even of cowries. It could hardly, then, refer to such measures as length and breadth. Concerning the problem of the weight it denoted, see: *Chin-wen*, 12ab. Chou, *Chin-wen Ling-shih*, 54. Wang, *Early Chinese Coinage*, 209–211. Yang, *Money and Credit in China*, 40–41.

Concerning the *chin* (written as either 釿 or 斤), Wang, *Early Chinese Coinage*, 211–217, maintains that it was a monetary unit and is not to be confused with the weight called *chin* 斤 (commonly translated as "catty") which has been in use from ancient times to the present.

around A.D. 800, but by 1690 it had depreciated to less than three percent of that value.[68]

The character *lieh* scarcely occurs in the early literature.[69] In Western Chou bronze inscriptions, however, it is not rare. We have seen that it is used in connection with metal, cowries, and silk. And eight of the inscriptions of my corpus speak of "so many *lieh* of"—what?

The character that occurs in these inscriptions has been intensively studied, but it cannot be said to have been certainly deciphered. With some others, I believe that this character probably represents silk.[70] If so, since it includes the element meaning "cowrie," it might be supposed to have the sense of "monetary silk." Most forms of this character include elements meaning "to go." We might perhaps, without being too fanciful, interpret these as meaning "circulating monetary silk," that is, "silk currency."[71]

All this is hypothetical, however, so that we shall call the undeciphered character simply "X." What "X" really stands for may be of minor importance, for it is quite possible that "five *lieh* of X" soon came to have primarily a symbolic, monetary value—just as "five pounds sterling" has a definite meaning, but one that has nothing to do (except historically) with a pound weight of sterling silver.

If we do not know what X means, we are happily able to form some idea of its value. For one inscription states the price of five men as "100 *lieh* of X."[72] Thus one *lieh* was presumably worth one-twentieth of the value of a man. This is still far from precise, since these men might have been anything from laborers to skilled artisans. Never-

---

68. Einaudi, "Imaginary Money," 230.

69. The section called "Lü Hsing," in the *Documents*, mentions fines from 100 to 1,000 *huan* 鍰 (*Shu*, 77). I agree with Kuo Mo-jo (*Chin-wen*, 12b–13a) in thinking that the text probably read *lieh* originally, but was corrupted through similarity of form. Karlgren ("Glosses on the Book of Documents," (2).188) agrees that it should possibly be read *lieh*, but on different grounds. See also Wang, *Early Chinese Coinage*, 206, and Yang, *Money and Credit in China*, 40–41. The "Lü Hsing," while traditionally ascribed to Western Chou times, contains language and ideas that clearly stamp it as much later; see p. 463.

70. For opinions favoring the interpretation of this character as meaning silk, see Chou, *Chin-wen Ling-shih*, 53–56, 83. Kuo (*Shih P'i-p'an Shu*, 49) argues that it is metal because it is measured in terms of *lieh*, but this is unconvincing since both cowries and silk are also measured in *lieh*. For other identifications, see Wang, *Early Chinese Coinage*, 208. Jung Keng, (*Chin-wen Pien, Fu-lu hsia*, 9a) leaves it undeciphered.

71. The added element is sometimes 彳 and sometimes 辵 . The simplest form of this character, occurring in Kuo, *Chin-wen Lu-pien, yu* 131a, is 寅 .

72. *Chin-wen*, 96b–97a.

theless it would seem that the value of one *lieh* of X was small enough to make it usable in many financial transactions.

The other seven inscriptions in which character X is found all involve officials. It occurs in a formula of four characters, which literally mean "take so many *lieh* of X." In the inscriptions it occurs in every case after the King has charged an official with duties, and presumably means that the official is to receive such and such recompense.[73] The number of *lieh* ranges from five (in four cases) through twenty (in one case) to one instance of thirty.

Just what this means is not at all clear. Five *lieh* of X—one-fourth the price of a man—seems rather small to figure as a royal gift if this were a single payment; it appears more likely that it is to be recurrent. Kuo Mo-jo suggests that this designates a monthly salary.[74]

BETWEEN the first and second halves of the Western Chou period, there is a dramatic shift, in the bronze inscriptions of my corpus, in the occurrence of characters that have been supposed to represent money of various kinds.[75] In a total of eighty-seven inscriptions dated to the first half, metal is mentioned twelve times. In ninety-seven inscriptions dated to the latter half, it is mentioned only three times. For cowries the shift is much greater: they appear in twenty-four inscriptions for the first half, against only three in the second half of the dynasty.

For silk the trend is reversed. Characters that have been interpreted as silk used for monetary purposes (excluding character X) appear in only one inscription during the first half of the period, but in three in the second.

Most interesting of all is the *lieh* of X. In all of the first half of Western Chou it occurs in only one inscription, and that is in the final reign of the first half. But in the second half of the dynasty we find it in seven inscriptions.

---

73. *Chin-wen*, 57a, 75b, 118a, 119b, 133a, 135a, 150b. In ibid., 75b, the second and third characters of the four-character formula are illegible, so that character X is not in fact readable here, but the formula is so regular that there seems to be no question that it should be supplied.

74. *Chin-wen*, 57b. Ch'en "Hsi-Chou T'ung-ch'i," (6).121–122, says that this formula refers to fines to be assessed in criminal cases. This is perhaps plausible in some contexts, but not by any means in all.

75. According to the traditional chronology, the Western Chou period is exactly bisected by the end of the reign of King Mu in 947 B.C. In fact, the dating before 841 B.C. is problematical, but this does not invalidate comparisons if one regards the period to the end of the reign of King Mu as the early period, and the remainder of the dynasty as the latter.

It must be noted, however, that while these figures are interesting, their meaning is by no means clear. It will be pointed out below that soon after the beginning of Western Chou the Kings started presenting to their vassals trappings for their horses and chariots, and gifts of this character became increasingly prevalent as marks of royal favor.[76] This might have influenced the disuse of the cowrie. And the *lieh* of X was not bestowed in the same way as the cowrie, so that it cannot be said, in any simple sense, to have replaced it.

Nevertheless, the increasing appearance of the *lieh* of X is an interesting phenomenon. Economists distinguish two functions of money: (1) as a medium of exchange, and (2) as "money of account." We commonly think of money as a medium of exchange, which passes from hand to hand. Yet vastly more money is simply transferred as credit, as "money of account." The administration of an empire like that of Western Chou clearly needed such a "money of account," and the *lieh* of X had characteristics that would have adapted it to this purpose.[77] We know that in later times the *lieh* (possibly a pure monetary unit, freed like the "pound" from any qualification) did become a money of account, in terms of which even the exchange between different currencies was reckoned. The growing prevalence of the *lieh* of X during the course of the Western Chou dynasty may indicate that there was an increasing tendency to simplify accounting by using this device.[78]

DID the royal government of Western Chou include financial administration among its functions?

We have seen that many critical scholars have supposed that there was little that could be dignified with description as financial administration. In support of this position they can, and sometimes do, cite testimony from a time as early as the Spring and Autumn period. The *Tso-chuan* relates that in 656 B.C. an emissary of the state of Ch'i reproached the great Yangtze valley state of Ch'u with failing to send to the royal court its proper tribute, consisting of certain rare rushes

76. See pp. 281–282.
77. For one, its relatively modest value as compared, for instance, with the cowrie. That the "*lieh* of X" may have been used as a money of account would seem to be indicated, for instance, by the fact that it is always encountered, on the bronzes, in multiples of five. The numbers actually stated are 5, 20, 30, and 100.
78. Four occurrences of X in the inscriptions, one-half of the total, occur in what is virtually the final century of Western Chou, the period from 878–782 B.C. There are no occurrences in the final reign, that of King Yu (781–771 B.C.), but this brief reign is traditionally supposed to have been a troubled one, and my corpus includes only four inscriptions from it.

used to strain liquor for the royal sacrifices. The implication is that this was the total contribution that had been expected, even in Western Chou times, from the extensive and rich state of Ch'u.[79]

This incident probably happened substantially as it is recorded, but the conclusions that are often drawn from it are quite erroneous. It is unlikely that Ch'u was a vassal state of the Western Chou at all, and still less likely that, if it had been, this would have been the sum of its financial contribution. The envoys of Ch'i and Ch'u were engaging in some elaborate diplomatic maneuvering for their own purposes, and those purposes did not include the accurate reporting of history.[80]

This account does, however, illustrate an important fact. Men of the Spring and Autumn period often tended, quite naturally, to suppose that the past had been essentially like their own time. Thus they frequently applied the terms of their own day to Western Chou situations and assumed that institutions of that period were essentially like their own. This does not mean that they do not often provide us with accurate and valuable information about earlier times; indeed they do. But always we must evaluate their testimony, like any other.

Neither can we accept testimony even in Western Chou documents, unless it squares with plausibility. The *Poetry* tells us that Duke Liu, supposed to have been the great-grandson of the mythical founder of the Chou line, "taxed the fields for the provision of grain."[81] It may be true, but the validity of such a tradition is difficult to assess.

There is some indication in the *Documents* that the Chou did not, immediately after the conquest, have a fully organized system of taxation. A member of the royal family tells the King that, if he conducts himself properly, "all the states will grandly bring offerings." And the Duke of Chou, speaking to King Ch'eng in connection with the ceremonies surrounding the establishment of an eastern capital, says: "You should carefully record which of the many rulers [i.e., vassals] bring offerings and which do not."[82] This does not sound as if there had been, at that time, a regular schedule for the taxing of vassals, and a developed system of accounting.

The *Poetry* tells us that the Marquis of Hán presented to the King

---

79. *Tso*, 139::140 (Hsi 4).
80. For fuller discussion of this incident and its background, see pp. 222–223.
81. *Shih*, 208.
82. *Shu*, 48, 52.

"skins of leopards, of red panthers, and of brown-and-white bears." The *Documents* also speaks of gifts presented by feudal lords to the King, but these are usually for special occasions. In two instances these gifts are called *pi*, the character that early meant silk cloth and today means "money."[83] Of course we do not know that, even at the beginning of the dynasty, voluntary offerings made up the entire revenue that the King received from his vassals, but in the situation immediately following the conquest they may have. The royal treasury must have been swollen with loot, so that the King may not have needed extra income. And the feudal lords, faced with the task of establishing themselves, may have had little to spare.[84]

The Chou conquerors did not, however, overlook one obvious source of revenue: the conquered people. The Duke of Chou, addressing the Shang people some years after the conquest and reproaching them for recalcitrance, said: "As to the expected contributions, and the many exactions, small and large, there are none of you who cannot follow the law."[85]

The character that is here translated as "contributions" is *fu* 賦 . Its left-hand portion is "cowrie"; that on the right means "military." As to the origin of this term we can only conjecture. It may have derived from the idea of taxes levied under threat of military force, or taxes raised for a supposedly military purpose. Whatever its origin, *fu* became a very common term meaning "tax." The *Tso-chuan* quotes Confucius as saying, in 484 B.C., that with regard to taxes (*fu*) on land "the regulations of the Duke of Chou are still in existence."[86]

We know almost nothing, however, about taxes levied on ordinary individuals during Western Chou. We do not even know, certainly, whether such taxes were levied, or whether those who lived on the lands of feudal rulers made their economic contribution in some other

---

83. *Shih*, 232. *Shu*, 48, 51, 52.

84. It is commonly said that in Western Chou the feudal lords paid to the King "tribute," *kung* 貢 . This is based, I believe, upon statements in works not earlier than the Spring and Autumn period; see: Ch'i, "Hsi-Chou Cheng-chih Ssu-hsiang," 21. *Tso*, 646::652 (Chao 14). In fact, the character *kung* does not occur once in the Western Chou sources. In the entirety of the *Documents* it is found only in the section called "Yü Kung." Although this document is traditionally ascribed to the early date of the mythical Emperor Yü, scholarly opinion holds that it cannot be as early as Western Chou; see: Ch'en, *Shang-shu T'ung-lun*, 112. Ch'ü, *Shang-shu Shih-i*, 27. Creel, *Studies*, 98–99, n. The character *kung* is not present in the bronze inscriptions, the original text of the *Book of Changes*, or the *Poetry*.

85. *Shu*, 65. This is Karlgren's translation, based upon the *chin-wen* text. See Karlgren, "Glosses on the Book of Documents," (2).142–143.

86. *Tso*, 824::826 (Ai 11).

manner.[87] It seems probable—but we can by no means be certain even of this—that taxation for the royal coffers came chiefly from vassals rather than directly from the common people.[88]

There is a gap in our information on taxes after the early years of Western Chou. But when we again encounter reference to taxation, near the end of the period, there is a good deal of it, both in the *Poetry* and in the bronze inscriptions. And it seems to imply such a well-developed system, so completely taken for granted, that it appears obvious that a machinery for bringing revenue to the royal coffers had been developing for a long time—at least, in all probability, since the early reigns of the dynasty.

A poem that is generally dated to around 800 B.C. is translated by Karlgren as saying that the ruler of a newly established state "made acres of fields . . . made divisions for the tax."[89] More literally, however, this could mean merely that he divided and registered the fields.[90] Yet registration in itself probably does imply something like taxation.

An important bronze inscription that appears also to date from

---

87. Those who write about Western Chou commonly devote a great deal of attention to the *ching-t'ien* 井 田 , or so-called "well-field" system. In it, eight families are supposed, in addition to cultivating plots for themselves, to have cooperated in cultivating a plot of which the produce went to their lord as his revenue. In all of the Western Chou sources there is only one passage, I believe, that has been held to give real basis for the "well-field" idea; it occurs in the *Poetry* (*Shih*, 166). Karlgren translates it: "It rains on our public field, and then comes to our private fields." Waley (*Shih*, 171) translates it—perhaps more plausibly in the context of the time—as "raining on our lord's fields and then on our private plots." There is nothing whatever in this that points specifically to the "well-field" system. Some scholars, while not accepting this system as a literal description of a Western Chou institution, have supposed it to be an idealization of a historic situation. See: Ch'i, "Chinese and European Feudal Institutions," 7. Maspero, "La société chinoise," 365.

Yet the "well-field" system was important—but not, insofar as we can tell, in Western Chou, but in later times. From around 300 B.C., when men at least believed that it had existed in antiquity, down to our own day, the "well-field" system *as an idea* has been very important. See: Balazs, *Chinese Civilization and Bureaucracy*, 101–102. Levenson, *Confucian China*, III, 16–43.

88. It is highly probable, of course, that the King had his own estates, from which he received revenue directly just as his vassals did from theirs. But such royal estates should not be confused with the "royal domain" that has commonly been supposed to have existed in Western Chou but for which there seems to be no evidence; see pp. 363–366.

89. *Shih*, 232. On the date of this poem, see: Karlgren, "Glosses on the Ta Ya and Sung Odes," 129. Waley, *Shih*, 147, n. 1. Legge, *Shih*, 546. Couvreur, *Shih*, 405. *Mao-shih*, 18(4).8a.

90. Waley (*Shih*, 148) translates: "He divided the land and apportioned it." But most commentators and translators agree with Karlgren in taking the passage to refer to taxation; see: *Mao-shih*, 18(4).10b. Legge, *Shih*, 551. Couvreur, *Shih*, 407.

around 800 B.C.[91] includes a charge in which the King puts the Duke of Mao in control of his government and commands him, among other things, to "establish small and great taxes (fu)."[92] The King also admonishes him not to oppress the people and—apparently—not to try to enrich himself by graft from the tax collections.[93] This would seem to indicate some experience with the institution of taxation—and with financial administration.

Another inscription from around this same time relates that the King placed a certain officer in charge of supplies in an area that included the environs of the eastern capital (near the site of the modern Loyang) and extended to the territories of the "southern Huai barbarians." The King said that these barbarians had long been his tributaries, contributing both their wealth and their service, and if they failed to do so they should be punished. This inscription has been interpreted as meaning that the King also charged this officer to levy taxes in order to maintain supplies in this area, but this point is debatable. There may also be some allusion to taxes on trade, but some passages of this text are so obscure that it is better not to draw conclusions from them.[94]

Did the royal government of Western Chou keep careful account of its finances and audit its accounts?

The *Ritual of Chou*, as we might expect, describes an elaborate establishment for the collection and reception of tribute, taxes, and gifts, the custody of the goods and wealth involved, and its proper disbursement. The numerous functionaries concerned in this are supervised by the Grand Treasurer and three other treasurers. There is also a Director of Accounts who, with his staff, checks receipts and expenditures

91. *Chin-wen*, 134b–135b. This is the famous "Mao Kung Ting" 毛公鼎 , which has been the center of much controversy regarding its date; Noel Barnard has questioned its authenticity. In my opinion the best authorities place it either in the reign of King Hsüan (827–782 B.C.) or in the opening years of the reign of his predecessor.

92. The character that precedes *fu* 賦 here has been the subject of a vast amount of discussion and proposed emendation; see *Chin-wen*, 137ab. It may also denote a kind of tax.

93. This is the interpretation that Kuo Mo-jo makes of a passage that is not easy to understand; it seems plausible. See *Chin-wen*, 138ab.

94. *Chin-wen*, 143b–144b. With regard to the official's duties concerning this area, the text has *cheng* 政 , which in this context may mean "to control." Kuo Mo-jo, however, reads it as standing for *cheng* 征 , "to tax." This interchange is not impossible; Karlgren ("Grammata Serica Recensa," 221) says that the *Chou-li* uses 政 as a loan for 征 , in the sense of "levy." Ch'en Meng-chia ("The Greatness of Chou," 70) gives a partial translation of what is obviously this inscription; his interpretation of it varies somewhat from that of Kuo.

of all kinds, using the duplicate copy of each document that is filed with his office. He makes yearly accountings, monthly accountings, and even daily accountings. He also checks on other aspects of the administration. "Thus he is completely informed concerning the administration of all of the states of the four quarters. He communicates his findings to the King and to the Great Intendant, who depose and promote accordingly."[95]

This is an extensive and in some ways a sophisticated financial administration. Critical scholars have been skeptical that it actually existed, in just this way, in Western Chou times, and their skepticism is justified. Even the principal officers that it mentions do not seem to appear in the Western Chou sources.[96] At the same time there can be no doubt that the Chinese did develop techniques for financial administration and even for the auditing of accounts at a remarkably early time.

It is related that in the state of Ch'i, around 300 B.C., a number of officials spent their whole time, "day and night," in checking the accounts of grain and other commodities received by the government.[97] And a century earlier an honest local official in the state of Wei was dismissed when he handed in his yearly financial report, because the corrupt officials at the court disliked him; while it is not so stated, it would seem that this must have been because they audited his account unfairly. He asked for an extension of one year in office, and it was granted. He then taxed the people heavily and made handsome presents to the officials. The next time he handed in his yearly account, the ruler congratulated him. He resigned in disgust.[98]

In all of the Western Chou sources, the most interesting light is thrown upon the financial operations of the royal government in connection with Earl Hu of Shao. The Earl was a descendant of the famous Duke of Shao, who had played such a great role in the early years of Western Chou;[99] he was apparently a contemporary of King Hsüan (827–782 B.C.).[100]

---

95. *Chou-li*, 6.13a–23a, 7.1a–11b; Biot, *Tcheou-li*, I, 121–141. Broman ("Studies on the Chou Li," 9–10) discusses these offices.

96. Broman, "Studies on the Chou Li," 9.

97. *Han-fei-tzu*, 14.8b–9a; Liao, *Han Fei Tzŭ*, II, 134–135. For a brief version of this incident, see *Chan-kuo Ts'e*, 8.2a.

98. *Han-fei-tzu*, 12.7b; Liao, *Han Fei Tzŭ*, II, 76–77.

99. This relationship, which we should normally expect, seems to be indicated in *Shih*, 234. The change of title from Duke to Earl does not indicate a demotion; they were used more or less interchangeably in Western Chou times.

100. Earl Hu is generally identified with Duke Mu of Shao, whose history is given in *Shih-chi*, 4.53–58; *Mémoires historiques*, I, 271–276. See also *Kuo-yü*,

The *Poetry* includes two poems, both significant in connection with taxation, that evidently involve Earl Hu of Shao.[101] One of these poems describes the establishment of the state of Shen: "The King commanded the Earl of Shao to establish the dwelling of the Earl of Shen ... The King charged the Earl of Shao to tax the soil of the Earl of Shen ... The King commanded the Earl of Shao to tax the soil and territory of the Earl of Shen, in order to furnish his provisions of grain."[102]

The second poem begins by telling of a great military expedition made to pacify the Huai barbarians. After it had been brought to a successful conclusion

> The King ordered Hu of Shao:
> Open up the regions of the four quarters,
> Tax my territories and soil,
> Without distressing, without pressing;
> Go all through the royal states,
> Go and draw boundaries, go and make divisions,
> All the way to the southern sea.[103]

The "southern sea" mentioned here was undoubtedly not the South China Sea, but the sea at the southern end of that portion of the east coast over which the Chou claimed control. This poem, like other sources we have seen, makes it clear that the Western Chou Kings sought, at least, to exercise jurisdiction going even to the point of taxation over extended territories, far beyond the limited scope of a

---

1.4b–6b. Ting Shan, in his "Shao Mu Kung Chuan," has marshaled the evidence for this identification, and Kuo Mo-jo (*Chin-wen*, 145a) seems to accept it. But I am not aware that any work earlier than Han says that Duke Mu and Earl Hu are the same, and while it is no doubt possible, I am rather skeptical of it. Kuo dates both of the inscriptions referring to Earl Hu to the reign of King Hsüan.

101. *Shih*, 232–234, speaks of "Hu of Shao," and clearly refers to Earl Hu. *Shih*, 226–228, speaks of "the Earl of Shao," and its similarities to the previous one make it plausible that it refers to Earl Hu, as Ting Shan ("Shao Mu Kung Chuan," 89) supposes. The prefatory words in *Mao-shih*, 18(3).1a, and 18(4).12b, attribute the events of both poems to the time of King Hsüan; Waley (*Shih*, 133) suggests that the King mentioned in *Shih*, 226–228, may be his successor.

102. *Shih*, 227. The character translated as "to tax," which occurs twice here, is *ch'e* 徹 . Although it occurs a number of times in the *Poetry*, it seems to have the sense of "to tax" only in this poem, in the one to be discussed next (*Shih*, 232–234), and in the one concerning Duke Liu mentioned above (*Shih*, 208). But at least in these poems concerning the Earl of Shao the sense seems unmistakable; see Karlgren, "Glosses on the Ta Ya and Sung Odes," 78–79. For later use of the character in this sense, see *Analects*, 12.9, and *Mencius*, 3(1).3.6.

103. *Shih*, 234. I have followed, with only slight alteration, the translation of Karlgren. It is in essential agreement with that of Waley (*Shih*, 131) but differs considerably from those of Legge (*Shih*, 553) and Couvreur (*Shih*, 408).

"royal domain," which has commonly been supposed to be the only territory within which they had such control.

It is evident that the Earl of Shao was charged by the King with important duties in connection with taxation; it seems probable that he held an office concerned with such duties, but if he had a title denoting this, we have no record of it. We have two bronze inscriptions in which Earl Hu of Shao is named.[104] In one of these he announces a victory to the King, who rewards him.[105] Quite clearly Earl Hu was a very important man who stood high in the royal favor. But that did not prevent his accounts from being audited.

The other inscription that concerns Earl Hu is the most interesting of all we have concerning finances. Unfortunately it is very difficult to understand at some points, but its general sense seems clear. It begins by saying that Tiao Sheng (apparently the Intendant, who controlled the government at this time)[106] had again caused Earl Hu to come to the capital "to check the matter of my contribution," that is, his payment of taxes.[107] Since he was "again" asked to come, he had apparently paid them in earlier, but the officials wanted to recheck the account; from what follows it is clear that they were charging him with a shortage.

104. *Chin-wen*, 142a, 144b–145a. Ch'en ("Hsi-Chou T'ung-ch'i," [2].94–95) cites a number of inscriptions that name an Earl of Shao or Duke of Shao, but says that only these two come from the latter part of Western Chou. Ting Shan, in "Shao Mu Kung Chuan," supposes some of the others to refer to Earl Hu, but I think he is mistaken.

105. *Chin-wen*, 144b–145a. Kuo Mo-jo (ibid., 145ab) supposes this to be the announcement of victory over the Huai tribes, and the subsequent reward to Hu of Shao, described in *Shih*, 233–234; this seems plausible.

106. Tiao Sheng 玊周生 is named in three inscriptions: *Chin-wen*, 142a, 144b–145a, and 149a. He is given the title *Tsai* only in the last of these, but the first two show that he was quite powerful and apparently in control of the government. Kuo Mo-jo (*Chin-wen*, 142b) deduces that he was the Grand Intendant of King Hsüan. The *Poetry*, in a poem traditionally dated to the reign of King Hsüan (*Shih*, 226), lists the Great Intendant first among the royal officers.

107. *Chin-wen*, 142a. The passage reads: he shih yü hsien 合事余獻. Although *he* by itself does not normally mean "to check," there seems to be no doubt that that is its sense here. *He* is commonly used to denote the action of joining the two portions of a tally to see whether they agree. Thus in *Mo-tzu*, 4.8a (Mei, *Motze*, 90), we read: "Suppose that their words and actions agree [*he*], like joined [*he*] tallies." Ting Shan ("Shao Mu Kung Chuan," 99) reads this character in this inscription as *kuei* 會 (so pronounced in the sense of "to calculate"), and the bronze forms of the two characters are similar, but there seems to be no room for doubt that this is *he*; see Kuo, *Chin-wen Lu-pien*, 133b. Nevertheless, the two characters have a number of meanings in common, and it is by no means unlikely that *he* is used here in the sense more commonly attached to *kuei*. In the *Chou-li*, 6.21b (Biot, *Tcheou-li*, I, 129), the accounting at the end of the year is called *kuei*, and the auditing of accounts is supervised by the *Ssu-kuei*, Director of Accounts.

It is hard to form a clear picture of what happened after Earl Hu was called to the capital. Apparently the Queen sent an emissary to him, saying that the Queen's father, the Duke of Chih, was deeply in default for the taxes on his lands, and that this must be because Earl Hu had been too lenient with him. The basis for this is not clear; perhaps, as the poems that have been cited suggest, Earl Hu was responsible for the collection of taxes over a wide area. The Queen appears to suggest that Hu should be responsible for a part of her father's shortage. Neither is it easy to be certain what was the outcome. The Queen's emissary presented a gift to Hu on her behalf, and he gave gifts to her emissary. Hu then made an excuse and presented a valuable gift to Tiao Sheng. And there, it would appear, the matter rested.

It is unfortunate that this inscription is not easier to understand.[108] Yet despite its difficulties it seems clearly to show that there was a systematic approach to the problems of finance, and a regular practice of auditing. It should be noted, however, that it is only a combination of circumstances (in addition to the fortuitous preservation of the bronze) that makes this information available to us. It is unlikely that the normal working of the financial system would have produced a record that would come down to us. This inscription probably owes its origin to the fact that this incident involved three important persons: Earl Hu, Tiao Sheng, and the Queen.

We have very little information concerning the way in which officials were recompensed for their services. It is generally assumed that higher officials were feudal lords and received their incomes from their fiefs. This seems to agree with such facts as we have.[109] There is also the curious practice, discussed above, which we see in seven inscriptions, whereby the King, after charging an official with duties, tells him to "take so many *lieh* of X." It appears that this is a recompense of some kind. The suggestion of Kuo Mo-jo that it represents a

108. In general I have followed the interpretation of Kuo Mo-jo in *Chin-wen*, 142a–143b; I have omitted, however, what seem to me the more speculative points. An interpretation that is very different indeed is given by Ting Shan in "Shao Mu Kung Chuan," 99; he comments that "the language of this inscription is extraordinarily difficult and obscure."

109. We have one bronze inscription (*Chin-wen*, 225a) which tells us that a retainer of the ruler of the state of Wèi was charged with certain duties and given "one hundred 'acres' of grain." The significance of this is not wholly clear; for further details see pp. 374–375. It evidently does indicate, however, that some kind of recompense in grain was given, at least to subordinates of royal vassals, as early as the beginning of Western Chou. But as to whether such bestowals were made by the royal government, we seem to have no information.

"monthly salary" does not seem to be supported by any concrete evidence, but what it is remains a puzzle.

THERE is perhaps no single official title appearing in the Western Chou sources which is obviously that of one whose duties were concerned with finance. In view of what we know of this government, that is not wholly surprising. We shall see in the next chapter that much the same is true in connection with justice, where the activities were many and unmistakable, yet where there are few officials who can be exclusively linked with them. With regard to finance, as to justice, it may well be that the functions were diffused among officers bearing various titles and performing a variety of duties.

We have seen three officials who appear to have held controlling authority with regard to taxation: the Duke of Chou, the Duke of Mao, and the Intendant Tiao Sheng. Every one of these men appears to have been the principal officer in the government of his time. There is nothing unusual in this. In the complex and extensive bureaucracy of the Former Han dynasty it was the Imperial Chancellor who prepared the budget and checked on the various departments to see that they did not exceed it.[110] In Britain the Prime Minister has usually been the First Lord of the Treasury.[111]

WITH regard to financial matters, the evidence in the Western Chou sources is particularly slight and obscure. Nevertheless, even the transmitted literary works suggest the existence of a large amount of trade, media of exchange of various kinds, and extensive financial operations by the government. When these are supplemented by the bronze inscriptions, we are able to see the outline of a systematic governmental approach to finance—not clearly, but unmistakably. The Western Chou government, it is quite evident, had a financial administration adequate to meet its very considerable economic needs.

---

110. Wang, "Han Government," 146. *Han-shu*, 84.9a.

111. Finer (*Modern Government*, 590) says that the Prime Minister's "salary is still drawn in part as First Lord of the Treasury, an office bound up with the premiership since 1721."

8

The Royal Government: Justice

In many ways the picture of Western Chou that emerges from the sources differs markedly from the conception that has been generally held. Nowhere is this contrast sharper than in the area of justice and law.

Tradition assigns to Western Chou the composition of the treatise in the *Documents* called the "Punishments of Lü."[1] This work sets forth a philosophy of law and describes the working of a legal system in some detail. It begins by ascribing the invention of the "five oppressive punishments" to certain barbarians; apparently this is to relieve the Chinese of the onus of this responsibility. And it sets forth these punishments, gives some description of the methods of trial, and prescribes a schedule of fines to be applied in exceptional cases.[2]

It is abundantly clear, however, that the whole pattern of thought that this document represents is that of the Warring States period. The concept of the "five punishments," around which it is constructed, does not appear in any Western Chou text, even where penal sanctions are discussed in some detail, nor even in the *Tso-chuan*, which concerns the Spring and Autumn period.[3] Yet eminent students of Chinese law have considered it, and other documents no more authentic, to be valid depictions of the legal procedures of Western Chou times.[4]

1. "Lü Hsing" 呂刑 , also called "Fu Hsing" 甫 刑] . For the ascription of this document to Western Chou time, see *Shang-shu*, 19.16a, which says that the author was King Mu (1001–947 B.C.). Jean Escarra (*Encyclopaedia of the Social Sciences*, IX, 251) gives it the precise date of 952 B.C. Ch'ü Wan-li (*Shang-shu Shih-i*, 3) says that it is difficult to be sure whether the "Punishments of Lü" was or was not written in Western Chou times.

2. *Shu*, 74–78.

3. For the dating of the "Punishments of Lü," see p. 463.

4. As has been mentioned, Jean Escarra dated the "Punishments of Lü" to 952

A great many critical scholars go to the opposite extreme and say that there was no legal code until a very late date. Maspero wrote that the earliest code was that of Ch'in, dating only from the third century B.C. Before that time, he stated, there was no code, and custom alone reigned.[5] Others cite a passage in the *Tso-chuan*, for the year 536 B.C., which relates that in that year the state of Cheng cast its laws in bronze, and that this provoked criticism; from this it is deduced that before this time there were no written laws, or at least no laws that were generally promulgated. But in fact this same passage says, as an argument against promulgating laws, that when the government had fallen into disorder under each of three dynasties, the Hsia, Shang, and Chou, law codes *were* set up. Certainly this passage is not sufficient evidence that the three codes mentioned actually did exist in antiquity, but neither can it be used as proof that the promulgation of written codes began only in 536 B.C.[6]

T'ung-tsu Ch'ü writes: "When the people were kept from knowing the law, the ruling class could manipulate it as it saw fit. Its words were the law—and a law that the people could neither doubt nor question. . . . Not until the sixth century B.C. were the laws of the various states revealed to the general public."[7] It may be that in some states during Spring and Autumn times the law was not made public, but the Western Chou sources seem to give no evidence of secrecy in this regard.[8]

B.C. In his *Le droit chinois*, 10, he also refers to two other sections of the *Documents*, the "Yao Tien" and the "Kao Yao Mo." The late date of the latter two documents is clear and recognized; see: *Wei-shu T'ung-k'ao*, 120–125. Creel, *Studies*, 97–98, n. 2.

5. Maspero, "Le régime féodal," 139.

6. *Tso*, 607::609 (Chao 6). Ch'ü, *Law and Society*, 171. Bünger, "Die Rechtsidee," 194, 197. A. F. P. Hulsewé (*Han Law*, 5–6, 331, 366–367) does notice the latter part of this passage as well as its beginning, but he nevertheless seems to regard it as evidence that written codes were first established around the seventh and sixth centuries B.C. V. A. Rubin ("Tzu-ch'an and the City-state," 23–25) interprets this as the publication of a code that already existed.

7. Ch'ü, *Law and Society*, 170.

8. There is also very little to indicate this even in the literature of the Spring and Autumn period—almost nothing, in fact, except the two passages to which Ch'ü refers: *Tso*, 607::609–610 (Chao 6), and 729::732 (Chao 29). Both of these philosophical disquisitions look as if they could be scholarly additions to the text, such as certainly are present in the *Tso-chuan*. The two are remarkably similar. The latter one is put into the mouth of Confucius, where it is wholly out of place; it is completely at variance with the whole tenor of everything that we have reason to believe to be his philosophy. I have shown the dubious character of these two passages in detail, in a paper entitled "Legal Institutions and Procedures During the Chou Dynasty," to be published shortly.

There are indications, in fact, to the contrary. King Wu admonishes his younger brother—who may have been the principal legal officer in his government[9]—to set forth, that is, to display, to make public, the items of the law. He also prescribes different treatment for offenses that are intentional violations of the law and those that are unintentional, which would seem to imply that the people were supposed to know what was unlawful. Again, when a feudal lord exhorts his soldiers before an expedition, he warns them that if they are guilty of each of a number of specified crimes they will incur "the regular punishment" for it. And his hearers, men so humble that they are expected to provide fodder, posts, and so forth, are assumed to know what the regular punishment is for each of the crimes that he names.[10] There is little basis for believing that, in Western Chou times at least, the law was kept secret.

JEAN Escarra, whose pioneering work on Chinese law is justly respected, begins his discussion of the conceptions underlying Chinese law with these words: "One of the most ancient guiding principles of the Chinese spirit is the belief in the existence of an order of nature and in the efficacy of an accord between it and the social order." In describing this "order of nature," he discusses such conceptions as the positive and negative principles, *yin* and *yang*; the so-called "five elements" and the way in which phenomena are catalogued in many different series of fives (five metals, five virtues, five punishments, etc., etc.) and other numerological arrangements; and the manner in which man and nature are conceived to interact (so that, for instance, injustice by the ruler produces excessive rain).[11]

It is quite commonly said that Chinese law has been based upon the Chinese conception of the natural order, and that is certainly true. The same thing could be said of the Greeks of the Age of Pericles, and of us today.[12] And Chinese law has been based, for more than two thousand years, on a conception of the order of nature that included the characteristics mentioned in the preceding paragraph. This is considered—and quite correctly—to be the "typical Chinese" view of nature. It was formerly supposed that these ideas were present from the earliest times. But today we know that to a Chinese of Western Chou

9. See p. 171.
10. *Shu*, 40, 80.
11. Escarra, *Le droit chinois*, 7–12.
12. C. M. Bowra (*The Greek Experience*, 65) says that "the Greeks thought that the city-state was the natural and right unit for human society."

or even of early Spring and Autumn times, many aspects of this conception would have seemed almost as strange as they do to us. For not
one of the specific ideas mentioned above, from *yin* and *yang* to the
preoccupation with numbers and the detailed correlation of human
actions with the weather, was present, at the earliest, until late in the
Spring and Autumn period, and they did not begin to be pervasive
until the time of the Warring States.[13]

In such respects Western Chou is a different world, and this fact is
reflected in a different legal system. This has been discerned by Derk
Bodde, who says concerning a series of Western Chou bronze inscriptions involving legal contests:

> The give-and-take spirit apparent in these disputes dis-
> tinguishes them sharply from the vertically oriented
> court procedures of imperial times, and suggests a soci-
> ety closer in spirit to Western society than was later
> possible when Chinese government became bureaucra-
> tized.[14]

It is necessary, then, to lay aside preconceptions and see what the
Western Chou sources themselves tell us about justice and law.[15]

IT is a curious paradox that the Chinese, who have emphasized written

13. Bodde and Morris, *Law in Imperial China*, 43–44. Waley, *The Way*, 109–
110. Fung, *A History of Chinese Philosophy*, I, xxi. Ch'en, "Wu-hsing chih Ch'i-
yüan." Kuo, *Chin-wen Ts'ung-k'ao*, 32b–35b, 42a–48b. Creel, *Confucius*, 198–200,
203, 317–319::213–216, 219–220. Li, *Yin-yang Wu-hsing Hsüeh-shuo*, 47–49.

14. Bodde and Morris, *Law in Imperial China*, 48, n. 95. Part One of this book is
said (ibid., vi) to be by Bodde, and the first chapter appears to be virtually identical
with his article entitled "Basic Concepts of Chinese Law," in *Proceedings of the
American Philosophical Society*, CVII (1963), 375–398. Bodde makes this comment on the basis of the bronze inscriptions treated in Maspero's article, "Le serment dans la procédure judiciaire de la Chine antique." Bodde continues: "It
should be noted, however, that our picture is necessarily one-sided, since the disputes of which we have knowledge are all between members of the aristocracy,
i.e., between men who were more or less social equals, and do not involve any of
the common people." That is true of the inscriptions discussed by Maspero. But
Chin-wen, 26a, does involve people of definitely humble status, and there is, even
toward them, a surprising amount of the "give-and-take" that Bodde mentions.

15. Maspero's paper, "Le serment dans la procédure judiciaire de la Chine
antique," was an important pioneering study of legal procedure as embodied in
certain Western Chou bronze inscriptions. In my opinion, however, its effectiveness is somewhat reduced by the fact that he first tried to derive a picture of early
judicial procedure from such works as the *Ritual of Chou*, and then to corroborate
it by data from the inscriptions. This study also suffers from the unavoidable
handicap that it was published in 1935, when much less headway had been made
in understanding the inscriptions than has been made today.

records as have few other peoples, have placed much less stress on codes of law, and on their interpretation, than has been customary in the West.[16] No doubt this is a part of the reason why it has been widely believed that there were no codes, and not even any written law, until a late date. There is a good deal of evidence, none the less, that written law existed quite early—perhaps even before Chou times.

There are several references to the legal practice of the Yin dynasty. The Duke of Chou tells the Yin people that all their rulers, from the beginning of the dynasty up until the last wicked reign, were "careful about punishments. . . . They tried those who were arrested, put to death those guilty of many crimes . . . and set free the innocent."[17] King Wu tells his younger brother: "You should set forth the items of the law,[18] and follow those laws[19] of Yin that have good principles. . . . take for punishments and verdicts the norms of the Yin. Use their just punishments and just killings."[20] It is beyond all reason to suppose that the Chou were so thoroughly versed in Yin law that they had committed it to memory and could refer to and apply it without making use of written records. It is hardly likely that the Chou, so addicted to the use of writing in other connections, did not use it in connection with law.

One character that is used for "law" seems to indicate strongly that it was written. We have already noticed the character *tien*, originally a pictograph of a book lying on a table, used in the sense of archives, etc. At one point King Wu tells his younger brother that the death penalty must be applied even for small offenses if the offender has intentionally done that which is "not *tien*," which Karlgren translates as "unlawful."[21] That is to say, it is an offense to do that which does not accord with the written records, the statutes, the laws. On a later occasion the Duke of Chou says to the conquered Shang people: "You recklessly reject the command of Heaven. You do that which is not lawful (*tien*). . . . I will therefore make you fearful, and arrest you for trial."[22] Beyond any doubt there were laws, and written laws.

As to whether there was a "code" of laws, this is perhaps a matter of definition. The Chou were indefatigable keepers of records and seem to have been somewhat systematic about it; there seems to be no reason to suppose that they would not have given some kind of ar-

16. Escarra, *Le droit chinois*, 3–4.
17. *Shu*, 64.
18. See Karlgren, "Glosses on the Book of Documents," (1).290.
19. Literally, "punishments," but I believe that "law" is justified here. Legge (*Shu*, 390) renders it as "penal laws."
20. *Shu*, 40–42.
21. *Shu*, 40.
22. *Shu*, 65.

rangement to their laws. The "Announcement to K'ang," in the *Documents*, would seem to be the oldest extant Chinese work dealing with law. While it is relatively brief and summary, King Wu does in this document deal with various types of crimes, and problems of jurisprudence, in order. Elsewhere in the *Documents*, the mention of "regular punishments" for each of a list of offenses by soldiers would seem to imply the existence of some kind of code of military law.[23]

Quite certainly, there were bodies of law having some system well before the highly publicized code of 536 B.C. But even in the relatively abundant records of the Spring and Autumn period they are mentioned only when some exceptional circumstance brings them to attention. The *Tso-chuan* tells us, for instance, that around 621 B.C. the officer Chao Tun, in charge of the government of the state of Chin, inaugurated a reform of its administration, and that as a part of this reform he "rectified the laws concerning crime and regulated [the procedures for] trial and punishment."[24] This appears to imply that there had been a code well before this time.

THE principal source of Western Chou law was undoubtedly tradition. This is normal for any body of law; Roscoe Pound has said that "systems of law are systematizings or organizings of tradition."[25] The Chou considered themselves the heirs of the Shang dynasty; we have seen that Shang justice was mentioned with admiration, and that the use of Shang laws—selectively, and no doubt with some modification —was enjoined.[26]

Bodde writes:

> A striking feature of the early written law of several major civilizations of antiquity has been its close association with religion. . . . The contrast of the Chinese attitude to the belief in the divine origin of the law is indeed striking, for in China no one at any time has ever hinted that any kind of written law—even the best written law—could have had a divine origin.

Bodde cites the attribution of the invention of law, in the "Punish-

23. *Shu*, 39–43, 80.
24. *Tso*, 242::243–244 (Wen 6).
25. Roscoe Pound, "Common Law," in *Encyclopaedia of the Social Sciences*, IV, 51.
26. *Shu*, 40–42, 45, 64.

ments of Lü," to barbarians, which he interprets as reflecting "an abhorrence of law."[27]

No doubt this interpretation is correct. But if there was such an abhorrence of law in Western Chou times, it does not appear in our sources—though perhaps it would not in any case.[28] We have seen that (as Bodde himself indicates) the "Punishments of Lü" was undoubtedly written well after the Western Chou period,[29] and it certainly reflects a different climate of thought. It seems to be true, however, that no specific laws were assigned to divine origin, even in Western Chou.

On the other hand, since the Chou Kings believed that they ruled by virtue of the Mandate of Heaven, they also believed that Heaven was intimately concerned with the meting out of justice. There was nothing remarkable in this. Concerning the ancient Greeks, C. M. Bowra says: "Since laws were derived from ancient custom, it was only natural to assume that they had a divine sanction and represented in some sense the will of the gods. This was the Greek equivalent to the notion of natural law, and it was held by Heraclitus, who said, 'All human laws are fed by the one divine law.' "[30] Religious ideas have been an important part of the background of the whole development of the legal tradition of the West.[31]

The Duke of Chou gives, as one of the reasons for which Heaven destroyed the Hsia dynasty, the fact that its wicked last ruler and his officials punished excessively and without pardon. King Wu says that one of the faults for which the last Shang King was destroyed by Heaven was his failure to punish crime. Wu also takes upon himself the responsibility for the proper administration of justice throughout his realm, and he says, "If there is any fault, Heaven will punish and kill me, and I shall not resent it."[32]

27. Bodde and Morris, *Law in Imperial China*, 8–14.

28. Most of our meager materials on law come from persons who were in the government, who would naturally tend to favor it. It is no doubt true that in most times and places people in general, conceiving themselves more as potential victims than as beneficiaries of the law, have tended to view it with a certain latent hostility.

29. See p. 463. Bodde indicates that he believes this document to be of relatively late date, since he says (Bodde and Morris, *Law in Imperial China*, 14): "The abhorrence of law expressed in this story no doubt reflects a period in legal development (sixth or fifth·century B.C.) when written law was still a novelty and hence viewed with suspicion."

30. Bowra, *The Greek Experience*, 67.

31. Friedrich, *The Philosophy of Law in Historical Perspective*, 8–12, 27–50. Bodde and Morris, *Law in Imperial China*, 8–10.

32. *Shu*, 42, 45, 64.

With regard to specific legal injunctions, however, there seems to be no reference to Heaven or the supernatural in any connection but one. When King Wu speaks of the necessity of enforcing proper family relations by legal penalties, he mentions "the younger brother who does not think of Heaven's brightness and cannot respect his elder brother," and says that if all those who fail in their familial duties are not punished "the norms given by Heaven to our people will be greatly disordered."

King Wu says that these familial offenses should be dealt with "according to the punishments made by King Wen."[33] This seems to be the only case in which a specific individual is cited as a source of law.

⚜

FAILURE in familial duty ranks high among the offenses for which punishment is prescribed. King Wu describes the "primary evil-doers" as "robbers and thieves and villains and traitors, who kill and destroy and go for spoil, and are forceful and do not fear death." But even these, he says, are less to be deplored than "the son who does not serve his father with respect, but greatly wounds his father's heart; the father who cannot love his son, but hates him; the younger brother who does not think of Heaven's brightness, and cannot be respectful to his elder brother; the elder brother who feels no compassion for his tender younger brother, and treats him coldly." All these must be punished without pardon.[34]

We have seen that there were laws concerning the payment of taxes, and punishment for violating them. A bronze inscription from late in Western Chou speaks of the punishment of barbarians who failed to make the required payments.[35]

Mere failure to obey orders was a serious offense. It is not surprising that the conquered Shang people were threatened with death if they were not obedient, but we have seen that King Wu also prescribed speedy execution for officials who dared to promulgate innovations.[36] On the other hand, in a case that we shall consider later, men who failed to go to war—apparently in defiance of orders—seem to have been dealt with leniently.

The death penalty was decreed, at the beginning of the dynasty, for those who drank intoxicating liquor in groups—unless they were tak-

33. *Shu*, 42.
34. *Shu*, 42.
35. See p. 153. *Chin-wen*, 143b.
36. *Shu*, 42, 65.

ing part in a sacrificial ceremony.[37] But there seems to be no indication of such legal prohibition of the use of liquor after the initial period.

WHO enforced justice? Formally, the responsibility seems to have rested with the King. We have seen that King Wu, in the *Documents*, says that if there is any fault in administering justice Heaven will kill him for it. Some Kings of the Hsia and Shang dynasties are blamed for unjust administration of punishments, while others are lauded for their justice.[38] King Wu praises his father, King Wen, for his justice, and in a bronze inscription another King (probably Wu's grandson) mentions the "punishment of criminals" as one of the principal achievements of King Wu.[39]

The King was, of course, the natural arbiter over the feudal lords, who were his direct subordinates. King Wu threatened one of them not only with the loss of his fief but even with death if he did not carry out orders and rule well—even though in this case the feudatory was Wu's own brother.[40] To what extent later Kings were able to act so drastically against their vassals is uncertain. A tradition, which is found only in works of a date later than Western Chou, says that in 892 B.C. King Í "caused the feudal lords to boil Duke Ai of Ch'i in a caldron."[41]

A bronze inscription from late in the period tells of a formal appeal made to the King by a landowner, presumably a feudatory, for adjudication of a complaint concerning certain lands; the King complies with the request.[42] A slightly earlier inscription tells of a lawsuit involving a series of contracts, of which one was apparently registered at the "Royal Comparison Office." This appears to have been a royal institution concerned with contracts.[43] A number of other inscrip-

37. *Shu*, 46.

38. *Shu*, 42, 45, 64.

39. *Shu*, 39. *Chin-wen*, 33b. Ch'en ("Hsi-Chou T'ung-ch'i," [3].93) also dates this inscription to the reign of King K'ang.

40. *Shu*, 43, 46.

41. The genuine *Bamboo Books* seems to be the earliest source for this account; see Wang, *Ku Chu-shu*, 8a. See also: *Shih-chi*, 32.11; *Mémoires historiques*, IV, 41. *Kung-Yang Chuan*, 6.11a. A commentator is quoted in the latter reference as saying that this story occurs in the *Kuo-yü*, but this seems to be an error; see *Kung-Yang Chuan*, 6(*Chiao-k'an Chi*).3a. There are discrepancies in the various accounts given by commentators; see p. 430, n. 34.

42. *Chin-wen*, 127a.

43. *Chin-wen*, 96b, 98a. Concerning my translation of the name of this institution, and its function, see below, pp. 183–185.

tions show royal officers acting in one capacity or another in connection with guaranteeing or enforcing contracts.[44]

It has commonly been said that in the Western Chou period the feudal lords were completely autonomous insofar as the government of their states and the regulation of internal affairs were concerned. The bronze inscriptions show that this is not entirely true. We have very little evidence, regarding the administration of justice, to indicate whether and to what extent the feudal lords had a free hand within their fiefs. It is true that regarding one group of offenders, those who drink together, King Wu does say, "Send them to Chou and I will kill them."[45] But the early Chou rulers seem to have been somewhat fanatical on the subject of the use of intoxicating liquor, so that this is a special case. There seems to be no other instance in which the King can be interpreted as claiming the right to review criminal penalties. Even in the "Announcement to K'ang," in which King Wu gives elaborate instructions as to the manner in which justice is to be administered, he takes it for granted that the decisions are to be made by his brother, K'ang Shu.[46]

In the absence of definite evidence, it seems probable that in this area as in many others there were no hard and fast rules. It is unlikely that the King, or his officers, normally bothered to interfere with the disciplinary measures taken by a feudal lord in dealing with his humbler subjects. But there is nothing to indicate that the royal officers could not, on occasion, be concerned with the administration of justice within a fief. A bronze inscription from quite early in the dynasty relates that some of the subordinates of a man who was undoubtedly a feudal lord refused to follow the King on a military expedition. Their overlord did not punish them himself, but laid a complaint against them with a dignitary who was undoubtedly a royal officer, who then pronounced judgment against them. This is almost certainly a case in which a royal officer—on the application of a feudal lord—administered justice within the feudal lord's domain.[47]

It is not easy to determine what were the titles of the officials who managed the administration of justice in the royal government. The

44. *Chin-wen,* 124b, 127a, 129b, 144b. Chou, *Chin-wen Ling-shih,* 64–72.
45. *Shu,* 46.
46. *Shu,* 39–43. Unfortunately we cannot be certain whether K'ang Shu is being addressed here as merely a feudal lord or as the Director of Crime, the chief royal officer of justice.
47. *Chin-wen,* 26a. For other inscriptions that throw light on the status of those involved, see ibid., 25ab, 27a. Chou (*Chin-wen Ling-shih,* 38–88) has a long and detailed study of this inscription.

Ritual of Chou describes a large and complex establishment for this purpose, but most of the numerous titles of its officers do not appear in the Western Chou sources.[48] It is headed by a Grand Director of Crime. The title "Director of Crime," often translated as "Minister of Justice," is common in later times, but in all of our Western Chou sources it occurs only twice, in bronze inscriptions. And even in these the office is not unmistakably linked with the administration of justice.[49]

The *Tso-chuan*, however, states that a younger brother of King Wu, K'ang Shu, acted as Director of Crime in his government.[50] And it is an interesting fact that the treatise in the *Documents* called the "Announcement to K'ang," in which King Wu addresses K'ang Shu, is devoted almost entirely to a discussion of the administration of justice.[51] It seems possible, therefore, that this office did exist in the royal government, but if so it has left very little trace of itself.

One royal officer who appears in a bronze inscription as definitely concerned with the administration of justice is the *Ssu-shih* 司 士 . It may be that this term should be translated as something like "Director of Police," but since it occurs only twice, and only once in a context that throws any light on it, it is hard to be sure of its precise meaning.[52]

48. *Chou-li*, 34–38; Biot, *Tcheou-li*, II, 286–455. See also Broman, "Studies on the Chou Li," 47–54. Many of the officials included in this section have functions that we would not place under the heading of justice.

49. *Chin-wen*, 113b, 118a. In the latter inscription the King bestows, on the maker of the bronze, the charge of several functions, including that of *Ssu-k'ou* 司 寇, which is not the last on the list. He then gives him gifts, and only afterward is there mention of trying cases. This inscription, and the related problem of the office of Director of Crime on the bronzes, has given rise to much discussion; see: Ibid., 118ab. Kuo, *Chin-wen Ts'ung-k'ao*, 66ab. Ssu, "Liang-Chou Chih-kuan K'ao," 9. Two other inscriptions, not included in my corpus, have the title *Ssu-k'ou*, but shed no light on the function of the office; see *San-tai Chin-wen*, 12.15a, 21a.

50. *Tso*, 750::754 (Ting 4). It should be noted that Legge's translation mistakenly reads "T'ang Shu" instead of the "K'ang Shu" of the text.

51. *Shu*, 39-43.

52. *Chin-wen*, 75b–76a. Kuo, *Wen-shih Lun-chi*, 313. Since this term is so rare, there seems to be no established translation for it. Kuo suggests that it is equivalent to *Shih-shih* 士 師, which is found both in the *Analects*, 18.2 and 19.19, and in *Chou-li*, 34.1b (Biot, *Tcheou-li*, II, 287). Biot translates this as "prévôt chef de justice," and Legge as "chief criminal judge." Waley (*Analects*, 218) stays closer to the sense of the characters by rendering it as "Leader of the Knights"; however, I do not think that "knights" is a good translation for *shih* here. This character sometimes means "soldier" or "military officer," and I suspect that here it refers to the staff of armed men who actually dealt with malefactors. Thus I think that "police" may be our closest equivalent for it.

While we have a number of inscriptions that record activities concerned with justice, it is not often that these activities can definitely be linked with an official whose title is clearly that of one whose specific function has to do with justice. In one inscription that tells of the assessment of a fine, a Secretary is asked to make an official record of it, but this is presumably as a part of his duties as a recorder, rather than specifically as an officer of the law.[53] In another, when the King is asked to adjudicate a case concerning lands, he has it investigated by two officers; one of these is a Secretary, but the other, who pronounces judgment, is mentioned only by his name.[54] In most cases, even when the individual who acts as the King's agent in administering justice is specified, he is merely named, with no indication of the official title he may have held.[55]

There are at least three possible reasons for this. First, we have seen that in the inscriptions there is a tendency for men, even those who held high office, to be mentioned merely by their names without any title. Secondly, it seems to be characteristic of Western Chou to emphasize the individual rather than the office, and it may be that the King assigned specific judicial tasks to men he considered capable of discharging them, without primary regard to their office. A third reason is that the function of administering justice may have been diffused rather than specialized. This has been the case in Chinese government through much of its history. A. F. P. Hulsewé says that "characteristic for the administration of justice, not only during the Han period, but also in later times, is that this task belongs to the sphere of duties of the imperial official who governs a territory . . . The only official in Han times with purely judicial duties was the Commandant of Justice, a member of the metropolitan administration."[56] Edward A. Kracke, Jr., says that in the imperial government, as late as the tenth century A.D., "the judicial functions were in part performed by special organs and specialized personnel, but many

---

53. *Chin-wen*, 26a. Concerning the significance of the character *shih* 史 here, see Chou, *Chin-wen Ling-shih*, 64–69.

54. *Chin-wen*, 127a. Maspero ("Le serment," 300–301) gives a different explanation of the identity and relations between these officers, but I think it is clearly mistaken. He apparently followed the 1932 edition of Kuo's *Chin-wen*. Kuo made some changes in his revised edition of 1935, which was probably not available to Maspero.

55. *Chin-wen*, 26a, 34a, 96b–97b (two different cases are recorded in this inscription), 119b, 127a, 134b–135b, 140b–141a.

56. Hulsewé, *Han Law*, 10. He adds: "Beside him one should perhaps mention commandery (i.e. 'provincial') and prefectural offices, which were 'in charge of lawsuits,' but regrettably little is known of their functions."

functions were in the hands of general administrative officials." To the end of the Chinese Empire, in fact, the administrative officers in charge of each *hsien* (roughly comparable to our "county") were responsible for the whole range of governmental activities, including justice.[57] It seems reasonable to suppose that, in Western Chou times, not only did the King and the feudal lords have charge of justice in their respective spheres, but other officials also included this function among their duties.

It is probable that all three of these reasons contribute to the difficulty of determining with any precision what officials enforced the law in Western Chou. This is further indication that the government of this period did not emphasize a clearly defined and carefully maintained organization of its official hierarchy.

By what process were judicial decisions arrived at? The *Ritual of Chou* gives a description of the procedure used in trying cases that is in some respects quite detailed. It says that various witnesses are questioned, including both officials and common people. Those examined are to be judged not only on the basis of their words, but also by their appearance, their breathing, their ears, and their eyes. The Latter Han commentator Cheng Hsüan explains that when one giving testimony is dishonest, his hearing is confused and his breathing becomes irregular.[58] (This would seem to anticipate a part of the principle underlying the modern device popularly known as the "lie detector.")

We cannot, of course, assume on the basis of the *Ritual of Chou* that any of these procedures were followed in Western Chou times; we must see what the sources have to say. But before examining techniques it is important to consider objectives. Some of those who write on early Chinese law would have us suppose that those in authority pronounced judgment on the basis of nothing but their own desires, if not whims. This was undoubtedly true, at times, in the Spring and Autumn period. But the Western Chou rulers tell us, again and again and again, that their objective is justice.

In the "Announcement to K'ang," King Wu begins by saying that his father, King Wen, was "careful about punishments." He repeatedly emphasizes the necessity of proceeding with the utmost caution, to avoid miscarriages of justice. "Having tried a case, deliberate on it for five or six days, or as much as ten days or a season, before deciding.

57. Kracke, *Sung Civil Service*, 41, 46. Bodde and Morris, *Law in Imperial China*, 4–5, 113.

58. *Chou-li*, 35.2a–5a; Biot, *Tcheou-li*, II, 319–323.

... Take for punishments and verdicts the norms of the Yin. Use their just punishments and just killings. Do not use them so as to accord with your own wishes."[59] This passage includes two important terms:

When Wu speaks of "the norms of the Yin," the character translated as "norm" is *i* 彝 . This sounds as if *i* is an external, objective standard. But a little later in the same document, King Wu speaks of "the *i* given by Heaven to our people," which normally caused them to fulfill their familial duties. In the latter instance, and in a passage in the *Poetry*, *i* seems to be regarded as an innate sense of right and wrong, according to which men normally did that which was both customary and appropriate.[60] In either case, to do that which was not *i* was to offend so that one might become liable to punishment. And those administering justice must always render judgment not only in accord with the law, but also in consonance with *i*.[61]

When Wu spoke of "just punishments and just killings," the character translated as "just" is in both cases *i* 義 . It has the sense of that which is appropriate in all the circumstances, fitting, just; occasionally it is used with the sense of "justice." We find it with these meanings in the *Documents*, the *Poetry*, and an early Chou bronze inscription.[62] "Appropriateness," also, was to be taken into account in making judicial decisions.

It seems clear that, in the process of reaching a verdict, attention was supposed to be given not only to the law but also to what is sometimes called equity, in the sense of "a liberal and humane application of the law."[63] The Duke of Chou, as well as King Wu, urges caution in the matter of punishments, and the necessity of justice and even clemency. Similar concern is found in a few bronze inscriptions, even late in Western Chou.[64]

One need not be cynical to recognize that the motivation for this was not exclusively altruistic. King Wu said, "Now the people are not quiet, they have not yet settled their minds. . . . Be careful! Do not

59. *Shu*, 39–43.

60. *Shu*, 52. *Shih*, 228. This term is rare in the literature outside the *Documents*. The character does not occur in the *Book of Changes*. In the *Poetry* it appears only once, in *Shih*, 228. The character *i* is common in the bronze inscriptions, but usually as meaning "sacrificial vessel"; it appears to have the sense of "constantly" in *Chin-wen*, 20b.

61. *Shu*, 42, 43, 45, 51, 52, 61.

62. *Shu*, 37, 42, 64, 73. *Shih*, 186, 215. *Chin-wen*, 26a.

63. Walter Wheeler Cook, "Equity," in *Encyclopaedia of the Social Sciences*, IV, 51.

64. *Shu*, 39–43, 46, 51, 64. *Chin-wen*, 75b, 135a, 140b–141a.

create resentment. . . . May your verdicts be correct, and such as to inspire confidence."[65] The rulers were wise enough to know that dissatisfaction with the administration of justice could only undermine their power.

This concern of the rulers must have borne some fruit, for tradition represents Western Chou (except for certain "wicked" periods) as a time of unusual tranquility and justice. The Confucian philosopher Hsün-tzu, in the third century B.C., said:

> The Sage Kings' use of capital punishment was extremely limited. King Wen executed only four persons, and King Wu only two. The Duke of Chou completed the task [of establishing order], so that under King Ch'eng all was peaceful and there was no capital punishment.[66]

This was, certainly, a gross idealization.[67] But there are many indications that Western Chou justice, while undoubtedly harsh at times, was probably superior to that which has prevailed at some other periods in China—and in some other countries.

Although there were certainly judicial inquiries, we have no complete description of a Western Chou trial, and it is difficult to be sure of the specific procedure. On many points, however, we have a good deal of information.

That some careful consideration was given to the evidence against the accused is indicated by the term *yao ch'iu* 要 囚 . *Ch'iu* is a pictograph of a man in an enclosure; it means a jail, and also the case of one who is under arrest. *Yao*, as an extension of its sense of "important," means a précis, which summarizes important points. We find it used in the *Tso-chuan* to mean a brief, which summarizes the

---

65. *Shu*, 42–43.

66. *Hsün-tzu*, 3.14b–15a; Dubs, *Hsüntze*, 84. Wang Hsien-ch'ien (*Hsün-tzu Chi-chieh*, 3.25a) proposes an emendation of the text which Dubs has apparently followed. I prefer the partial emendation made by Liang Ch'i-hsiung (*Hsün-tzu Chien-shih*, 70).

67. It may be that these were the only instances of capital punishment under these rulers that were mentioned in the history available to Hsün-tzu, but that of course means little. To speak of King Wu alone, he recommends and threatens the death penalty on a broad scale, and even threatens his own brother with death if he does not obey him (*Shu*, 42, 46); it is hardly likely that only two persons were executed during his reign.

evidence for a contender in a lawsuit.[68] Thus *yao ch'iu* has the sense of putting in order all the points in connection with a prosecution, that is, trying the case.[69] Both King Wu and the Duke of Chou use this term. The Duke, even when he is obviously trying to frighten the conquered Shang people into submission, does not threaten them with summary execution; he says that he will *yao ch'iu*, arrest them and bring them to trial.[70]

Another term that seems to have the sense of "to bring to trial" is *hsün* 訊 . This word has a wide range of meanings, from that of simply "to inquire" to what Karlgren defines as "to interrogate, to put to the question."[71] In the bronze inscriptions it has both of these senses, but in three cases it clearly refers to judicial inquiry.[72] Unfortunately there is nothing to indicate the manner in which such inquiry was conducted. If *hsün* does mean "to put to the question," this might seem to suggest examination under torture, and in fact the *Tso-chuan* speaks of an interrogation (*hsün*) in the Spring and Autumn times under the threat of a naked sword—but this does not appear to have been a judicial proceeding.[73] Certainly it is possible that judicial examination in Western Chou was conducted under threat or under actual torture, but there seem to be no references to judicial torture in the sources. One passage in the *Documents* appears in fact to condemn torturers, along with "traitors and villains."[74]

Some prisoners of war were called *hsün*. Apparently not all prisoners were called *hsün*, but only a special group, possibly of officers.[75]

---

68. *Tso*, 445::449 (Hsiang 10).

69. See Karlgren, "Glosses on the Book of Documents," (2).142. He says that *yao* "is a technical judicial term, well attested to mean: to summarize, to sum up a charge, epitomize the essential points in a prosecution." He points out that *yao* is repeatedly used in this way in the *Ritual of Chou*. See *Chou-li*, 35.12a, 14b, 17b; Biot, *Tcheou-li*, II, 336, 339, 343. Biot translates *yao* as "fait sur eux un rapport spécial," which I think misses the particular sense of this term.

70. *Shu*, 40, 64, 65.

71. Karlgren, "Glosses on the Siao Ya Odes," 43–44.

72. This character does not occur in the *Book of Changes*, nor, curiously enough, in the *Documents*. In the *Poetry* it occurs seven times, but never in a sense unequivocally connected with the administration of justice. In three contexts, however, Karlgren (*Shih*, 113, 123, 196) translates it as "prisoners for the question," captured in war. In this latter sense it occurs in the bronze inscriptions in *Chin-wen*, 106a, 109b, 143b. In the sense of "inquire" it occurs twice in ibid., 144. The contexts make it clear that *hsün* is used in the sense of "judicial inquiry" in ibid., 75b, 118a, 119b.

73. *Tso*, 686::688 (Chao 21).

74. *Shu*, 46. See also Karlgren, "Glosses on the Book of Documents," (1).307–308.

75. *Chin-wen*, 109b, speaks of the capture of forty *hsün* and four hundred *jen* 人 , "men."

Karlgren calls them "prisoners for the question." Waley, however, says that they were captured "for trial. Enemies are criminals, and their instigators must be tried at law, like criminals."[76]

The verdicts in "war crimes trials" have a tendency to be foregone conclusions, so that it is a question whether they can properly be considered representative of judicial procedures. The summary nature of such trials is exemplified in a bronze inscription that describes a triumphal ceremony, held in a temple, celebrating a great victory over certain barbarians. Three captive chiefs of the barbarians are brought forward, and the King orders them to be interrogated as to the reasons for which they have resisted the Chou. After they have stated their reasons, they are decapitated.[77]

Another term that is used to describe legal actions is sung 訟 . It means "to sue, to litigate," and it appears to refer to cases in which one individual lays an information against another and requests judicial action.[78] The records we have of the adjudication of such cases in Western Chou are so brief that they supply almost no details. For the Spring and Autumn period we have a number of accounts that are fuller, and it appears probable that the procedure in the earlier time was substantially similar.[79] One case, tried in 563 B.C., is especially informative. It was a contest in which two royal ministers sued (sung) each other. Each was seeking preeminent power in the royal govern-

76. Shih, 113, 123, 196. Waley, Shih, 125, 331.

77. For more detailed description of this incident, see pp. 232–233. In this instance, the chiefs who are interrogated and executed are not called hsün.

78. The Shuo-wen Chieh-tzu said that the function of kung 公 in this character was merely phonetic. But the great commentator on this work, Tuan Yü-ts'ai (1735–1815), considered it to have a signific function; see Shuo-wen, 1069b. It seems probable that the meaning of the character is "yen 言 to state kung 公 publicly," that is, to bring a complaint before public authority, to make it a matter for governmental action, to make a formal complaint and seek remedy from the state.

79. In the original text of the Book of Changes the term sung occurs only in connection with the hexagram that is given that name; see: I-ching, 2.4a–7a; Legge, I-ching, 69–70; Wilhelm, I-ching, 46–48. Here it clearly denotes "contention," but whether legal or not is uncertain. In the Documents, sung does not occur in any of the chapters that I accept as of Western Chou date, nor indeed in any that has traditionally been supposed to be from that period. In the Poetry it occurs only once: Shih, 10. Here Karlgren translates it as "a litigation," and it seems clear in the context that a private individual is being urged to begin a lawsuit. In the Tso-chuan, sung is repeatedly used to mean a legal action in which a plaintiff initiates the prosecution of another; see Tso, 206::212 (Hsi 28), 265::267 (Wen 14), 354::355 (Ch'eng 4), 375::376 (Ch'eng 11), 445::448 (Hsiang 10), 476::478 (Hsiang 18), 637::640 (Chao 12). In the bronze inscriptions it occurs three times: Chin-wen, 34a, 118a, 119b. The contexts make it quite clear that sung in the inscriptions refers to legal action, but they do not give us much detail as to how it was carried out.

ment. The state of Chin (which was the real power in China at this time) sent an envoy to settle matters; the envoy heard the case in the King's court. Each minister appointed one of his retainers to be his advocate in pleading the case. Each advocate put forth arguments for his principal and against his adversary. The envoy then ordered both parties to submit briefs (yao) of the evidence for their claims. But one of the ministers was unable to produce evidence, and fled.[80]

One interesting feature of this case is the fact that the arguments are presented to the court, for the litigants, by advocates. This was a common practice in Spring and Autumn times, and we also find it mentioned in connection with two legal actions described in Western Chou bronze inscriptions.[81] There is no way to tell on what basis these advocates were selected. Neither is there any indication that a special class of advocates developed, as it did in Rome, where Cicero was no doubt the most famous of such men. This early practice never eventuated in China, as it did in the West, in the development of the professional legal advocate or "barrister," who regularly appears in court for and with the parties involved in cases. In later times such persons have normally been excluded from Chinese courts.

Bodde attributes "the nonexistence of private lawyers" in China to "the background of Legalism"—the tendency toward totalitarian subordination of all activities to the purposes of the centralized state. Escarra writes: "There have almost never been advocates (avocats). They have always been looked upon with disfavor. Above all, for all the reasons that one can deduce from the special conception that the Chinese have developed of the law. To admit that its application and interpretation could be the subject of discussion, or that the judge could be differed with, would indicate an intolerable confusion. The fact is that there is no place for an advocate in the traditional Chinese judicial organization."[82]

This attitude toward the judicial process is one aspect of the tightly organized conception of the nature of government, and of its intimate relationship with the very functioning of the universe, that developed in China in a process that began during the Warring States period. There are many indications that before that time the situation was significantly different.

That legal procedures in Western Chou were rather flexible is in-

80. Tso, 445::448–449 (Hsiang 10).

81. Tso, 206::212 (Hsi 28), 265::267 (Wen 14), 354::355 (Ch'eng 4), 375::376 (Ch'eng 11), 445::448 (Hsiang 10). Chin-wen, 26a, 96b.

82. Bodde and Morris, Law in Imperial China, 4, 28. Escarra, Le droit chinois, 255; see also ibid., 326.

dicated by a well-known inscription from early in the period.[83] This flexibility is surprising, for the case involved a breach of military discipline, which might be expected to have been strict near the beginning of the dynasty. The bronze was cast by (that is, of course, for) Commander Ch'i.[84] He relates that a group of his subordinates (probably men living on his fief) failed to follow the King—as presumably they had been ordered to do—on a certain military expedition. Ch'i therefore asked his colleague, Hung, to inform Po Mou Fu of their offense.[85] Po Mou Fu thereupon adjudged that they should pay a fine of three hundred *lieh* of silk(?).[86] However, they were unable to pay the fine. Po Mou Fu then issued an order saying: "In accord with justice

83. Kuo Mo-jo (*Chin-wen*, 26ab) dates it to the reign of King Ch'eng (1115–1079 B.C.). Ch'en ("Hsi-Chou T'ung-ch'i," [5].105) places it at the beginning of the following reign. This inscription has been studied by a number of scholars. Chou Fa-kao (*Chin-wen Ling-shih*, 38–88) refers to and quotes from previous studies and goes exhaustively into the various problems that it involves. I have in general followed Chou's interpretation on this inscription.

84. Shīh Ch'i 師旂. There seems to be no standard translation for *shīh* as the title of a military officer; I am using "commander." Kuo Mo-jo and some other scholars read this name as Lü 旅 ; Ch'i is preferred by others, including Chou Fa-kao and Ch'en Meng-chia.

85. The identity of Po Mou Fu has not been certainly established, though it has been discussed by a number of scholars; see Chou, *Chin-wen Ling-shih*, 44–49. There seems to be some reason to believe that he was the grandson of King Wen and the son of the K'ang Shu to whom the "Announcement to K'ang" in the *Documents* was addressed. He is mentioned in a number of bronze inscriptions, from which it is clear that he was an important military commander and almost certainly a feudal lord and an important officer of the King.

86. A fine of "about three hundred," according to Chou Fa-kao (*Chin-wen Ling-shih*, 49–60). If this is correct, the flexibility of this whole procedure was great indeed.

The interpretation of the several characters concerning this fine has been the subject of wide disagreement among specialists; even the number involved has been disputed. Chou summarizes various theories, with extensive quotation. One problem is the character *ku* 古 which precedes "three hundred," which I have ignored in reporting the content of the inscription. While Chou believes it is equivalent to another character meaning "about," Kuo Mo-jo (*Chin-wen*, 26b) believes that it refers to an "old," or Yin, *lieh* which was heavier than the Chou *lieh*, and that this is the reason why the fine could not be paid. Kuo also interprets the character (for which there is no exact modern equivalent) which I have rendered as "silk," as meaning "to present." But Chou Fa-kao makes a good case for the sense of "raw silk" or "floss." Certainly the "silk" element is unmistakably present in the inscription, and we know that silk was sometimes measured in terms of *lieh*; it is reasonable, therefore, to suppose that the commodity in question is silk.

Even though there is so much disagreement about details, they do not seriously affect the interpretation of the inscription for our present purpose. For it is generally agreed that this is a fine, assessed in terms of so many units of some article of value.

(*i* 義) they should be banished for failing to follow their leader to war, but if they are not banished, then they should make a payment to Commander Ch'i." Hung informed a Secretary of this and asked him to record it.[87] Ch'i (the inscription concludes) also recorded it on a sacrificial vessel.

In this case, Hung acted as advocate for Commander Ch'i throughout. He initiated the case by laying the complaint before Po Mou Fu. He probably (though this is not stated) reported back that the culprits could not pay the fine. And after the final decree had been given, he had an official record made of it.

Another litigation is recorded in an inscription that Kuo Mo-jo dates to the reign of King Li (878–842 B.C.). It opens as is usual with the date, and says that the King was in the capital, in a certain great hall. The maker of the vessel, Kuo Ts'ung, spoke to the King, accusing Yu Wei Mu. It is clear that the dispute was over certain lands, but its nature is obscure. The King ordered that the matter be investigated. A royal official, Kuo Lü, resolved the case by ordering Yu Wei Mu to swear to give satisfaction to Kuo Ts'ung or suffer banishment if he failed to do so. The latter celebrated his triumph by casting a record of the event on a bronze.[88]

One of the most interesting of all bronze inscriptions, insofar as legal procedures are concerned, is one of those cast by a very important man named Yao.[89] Living around 900 B.C., he held several offices including that of Intendant, so that he may at one time have been the most powerful man in the royal government.[90] It seems likely, how-

87. The meaning of *chung shih* 中 史 here is debated. Kuo Mo-jo, in *Chin-wen Ts'ung-k'ao*, 372a, interprets it as an official title, but in *Chin-wen*, 26ab, he treats *chung* as a proper name. Chou Fa-kao (*Chin-wen Ling-shih*, 64–72), and others incline to view it as an official title. But in any case the individual in question is clearly a Secretary.

88. *Chin-wen*, 127a. That Kuo Lü was a royal official, though his title is not given, appears very clearly from ibid., 127b.

89. In fact, this is probably not the correct reading of his name, which seems to be unknown. *Yao* 舀 , however, is the character given for it in Ch'en, "Hsi-Chou T'ung-ch'i," (6).122. Others, including Wu Ch'i-ch'ang (*Chin-wen I-nien Piao*, 57) and Wu Shih-fen (*Chün Ku-lu Chin-wen*, 3[3].46b–50b), read it as *hu* 曶 . Kuo Mo-jo (*Chin-wen*, 96b–97b) and Jung Keng (*Chin-wen Pien*, 5.9b) transcribe it as 舀 . If we compare it with the rubbing of the inscription (Kuo, *Chin-wen Lu-pien*, 83), there seems to be no doubt that the latter is the correct transcription. Unfortunately, however, neither the *Shuo-wen* nor any other dictionary seems to list this character, so that it is impossible to tell how it should be romanized. I am therefore following the transcription of Ch'en Meng-chia in order to obtain a reading and avoid referring to "X."

90. *Chin-wen*, 96b, 102b, 112ab. This name also occurs in *Chin-wen*, 100a, but Ch'en ("Hsi-Chou T'ung-ch'i," [6].116) doubts that it is the same man.

ever, that he had not yet risen so high when this particular bronze was cast, for in its inscription he complains of the misconduct of others toward him; if he had then been so powerful, they would probably have treated him with more circumspection. This one inscription consists of three independent parts, of which two are concerned with legal affairs. Unfortunately, it is extremely difficult even to read, and still more so to interpret, and it is hardly likely that anyone has been able to understand it without error. It is nevertheless highly informative.[91]

The third section of this inscription concerns a case of theft. It relates that formerly, in a year of famine, a band of twenty men, subordinates of K'uang Chi,[92] stole ten *tzu*[93] of grain belonging to Yao. Yao laid a complaint against K'uang Chi with Tung Kung.[94] (Tung Kung was almost certainly an important vassal, and a high official, of the King.)[95] Tung Kung then said to K'uang, "Control your men![96] If you cannot, you will be punished severely." K'uang then acknowledged to Yao that he was at fault, and offered him five fields and four men—whose names are given—as redress. K'uang also made a statement of which the sense is not clear, apparently minimizing his guilt. But Yao was not satisfied, and he again complained to Tung Kung against K'uang Chi, pointing out that his stolen grain had still not been restored. Tung Kung then said, "Give back to Yao ten *tzu* [of grain], and another ten *tzu*, making [a total of] twenty *tzu*. If restitution is not made by the coming year, then [your liability will be]

91. I am for the most part following the interpretation of Kuo Mo-jo (*Chin-wen*, 96b–99b). Maspero gives a translation of parts of this inscription in "Le serment," 273–280. In some respects my understanding of this inscription differs widely from his.

92. This may be the same individual as the K'uang who is mentioned in *Chin-wen*, 82b, as being favored by the King. See also Ch'en, "Hsi-Chou T'ung-ch'i," (6).105, 116.

93. Kuo (*Chin-wen*, 98b–99a) says that a *tzu* equals two hundred handfuls.

94. I have supplied "Yao" as the subject of this sentence; it is demanded by the context, and this interpretation is supported by similar language, in contexts where the subject is present, in the second section of this inscription and in two others. See *Chin-wen*, 26a, 96b, 127a.

95. This name occurs also in *Chin-wen*, 100b, 101b–102a. Ch'en Meng-chia discusses these two inscriptions in "Hsi-Chou T'ung-ch'i," (2).72, (5).112–113. He dates them as much earlier than this inscription concerned with Yao, which he dates as later than 947 B.C. For this reason he thinks that the Tung Kung mentioned in them is not the same individual. Ch'en also suggests that Tung Kung may have been, rather than a proper name, the name of a high royal office.

96. Literally, "seek out your men," which I take to be an order to bring them back from wherever they may be, to call them in, and to keep them under control.

doubled,[97] to forty *tzu*." K'uang then offered Yao two more fields and one more man. "Altogether," the inscription concludes, "Yao received seven fields and five men, and Yao gave up his claim on K'uang for thirty *tzu* [of grain]."[98]

This incident shows that in Western Chou theft was punished severely even if the man responsible (in this case K'uang) was a person of consequence. Of course, Yao was an important man also, but it is significant that the two did not settle matters by fighting between themselves (as they might have in Spring and Autumn times) but through legal action. This also shows that there was, in addition to the concept of the restitution of goods taken, that of "exemplary" or "punitive" damages, awarded because of the wrongful character of the action. It further illustrates the flexibility that characterized legal process. After judgment was given, it was not rigidly enforced by officials, but a settlement was reached between the two parties.

The second section of this same inscription is even more interesting. It begins by stating that on a certain day Ching Shu was at a place called I, performing some function—what we do not know, because of a blank in the text. (Ching Shu, as we can tell from other inscriptions, was an official closely associated with the King.)[99] Yao[100] used this opportunity to have his subordinate,[101] Yün,[102] bring suit against (*sung*) Hsien[103] before Ching Shu. The story is a tangled one. It seems that Yao had made a bargain to purchase from Hsien five men, and had

97. The identification of this character as *pei* 俖 is somewhat conjectural, but it is not impossible and the context calls for something of the kind. *Pei* is uncommon in Western Chou prose, but it does occur in this sense; see *Shih*, 237.

98. Apparently, settlement was not made until the following year, when forty *tzu* would have been due. But in consideration of the other payments, Yao agreed to be content with only the return of the ten *tzu* that had been stolen.

99. He appears in a number of other inscriptions; see Ch'en, "Hsi-Chou T'ung-ch'i," (6).106–116.

100. There is also a gap in the text here, but Kuo Mo-jo supplies the name, and this is surely correct.

101. Specifically, his *hsiao tzu* 小子. This is the name of an office, of wide occurrence in the inscriptions, but it seems impossible to be sure what functions were connected with it in this context. See: *Chin-wen*, 80b. Ssu, "Liang-Chou Chih-kuan K'ao," 11–12.

102. This is an arbitrary romanization that I am using for this very complex character, based on the element *yün* 允 that appears as its upper right-hand corner. The whole character does not seem to have been identified with any modern equivalent. Jung Keng (*Chin-wen Pien, Fu-lu, hsia*, 19a) lists it in his appendix of undeciphered characters.

103. From what follows, it appears that Hsien was an officer, in some capacity, in the service of the King.

paid over to a certain Hsiao Fu (apparently an agent of Hsien) the agreed price, namely, one horse and one roll of silk. For some reason Hsien did not fulfill the bargain, but promised that he would have Kuo[104] (apparently another agent of Hsien) return the horse, and Hsiao Fu return the silk. Then Kuo and Hsiao Fu made another promise to Yün.[105] They said that they would do something—here is another gap in the text—at the "Royal Comparison Office." Whatever they undertook to do involved a wooden tablet, and Kuo Mo-jo suggests that they agreed to write a new contract on tallies (of which more below). This new agreement was to call for the purchase of the five men for one hundred *lieh* of the currency which we have been calling "X." At this point missing and unintelligible characters make the sense quite uncertain, but apparently this new agreement did not work out either.

Ching Shu then delivered his verdict. He said that Hsien, being one of "the King's men" (presumably meaning that he was a royal official), having agreed to sell, should not fail to make delivery to Yao, and that he should not cause his subordinate, Kuo, to be involved in double-dealing. Thus Yao finally got his five men.[106]

Several points are worth noting. It appears that members of the royal government were expected to maintain a high standard of conduct, even in their private financial transactions. The verdict indicates that, whereas theft was punished by the imposition of punitive damages, mere breach of contract was—in this case at least—not punished; the judgment was merely that the contract must be carried out. Finally, this inscription gives us an example of the operation of royal justice in the realm of private financial transactions.

In this connection, special interest attaches to what I have suggested translating as the "Royal Comparison Office." This rendering is ad-

---

104. This name is also listed in Jung, *Chin-wen Pien, Fu-lu, shang*, 53b, among undeciphered characters. Kuo Mo-jo transcribes it as 𢼌 , which on the basis of the squeeze, if not certain, is possible. But this character does not seem to occur in dictionaries. It is, however, a duplication of *kuo* 𢼌 , which I am using as a conventional romanization.

105. In fact, the name used here is not Yün—still another name is introduced. But Kuo Mo-jo says that this must be a different name for Yün, and in the context this seems certainly right. This reference to the same individual by a variety of names is of course common in early Chinese texts, such as the *Tso-chuan*, and sometimes makes reading them a maddening business.

106. There is considerably more to this section of the inscription, concerning what went on after the verdict was delivered. Kuo (*Chin-wen*, 98b) gives a complete explanation of it, but I do not find it wholly satisfactory.

mittedly hypothetical, but I believe it is justified.[107] This would appear, from the context, to have been a royal institution at which contracts—in this case a private contract concerning a sale—were registered with the government, presumably so that in case of dispute the copy registered with the government could be referred to as evidence. Governments of our own day record contracts for the sale of real estate—that is, deeds—in this manner. But there seems to be no other mention of this "Royal Comparison Office," and such an institution seems very sophisticated and out of context if viewed in the light of the prevalent conceptions concerning Western Chou government. We must see, therefore, whether there is corroborative evidence that makes its existence appear probable.

We have already seen that there is a great deal of evidence, chiefly from Spring and Autumn times, that the Chou had extensive archives. And the *Tso-chuan* says, in two different places, that records from early Western Chou times were still preserved, in the seventh century B.C., in the royal "Repository of Covenants."[108] These records, however, did not concern contracts between private individuals, like the one that appears to have been registered at the "Royal Comparison Office." But here again the *Ritual of Chou* has some rather interesting information.

107. In the expression *wang ts'an men* 王參門 there is no problem, of course, with the first character, which means either "King" or "royal." The second, *ts'an*, is most commonly encountered in Western Chou texts in the sense of "three." But in the *Ritual of Chou*, the comparison of financial records by the Director of Accounts, in arriving at his accountings, is called *ts'an*; see *Chou-li*, 6.22b, and Biot, *Tcheou-li*, I, 131. The *Ritual of Chou*, however, is in its present form a late text. The earliest datable and unmistakable case of *ts'an* used in the sense of "to compare" is in *Hsün-tzu*, 15.5b (Dubs, *Hsüntze*, 268); this too is, of course, rather late. But the first poem in the *Poetry* has two occurrences of the expression 參差, which is read as *ts'en tz'u*. It means "irregular" or "uneven." In this poem it is used to describe a kind of water weed, and Karlgren (*Shih*, 2) translates it as "of varying length." In this expression I believe that the character in question refers to three objects laid out together, which as the second character indicates are seen to vary. If this is true, then in this Western Chou context it already has the sense, which becomes common later, of comparing things together.

The greatest problem comes in connection with the third character, *men*, "gate." It is not used to mean "office" in any early text that I know, but it is used to stand for what is inside the gate of an establishment. In *Tso*, 553::557 (Hsiang 30), and elsewhere, *men*, "gate," is used to mean the family that lives inside the gate. And in *Tso*, 586::589 (Chao 3), we find *cheng tsai chia men* 政在家門, meaning "government lies in the hands of the [powerful] families," with *men* standing for the establishments of the families. Thus when this inscription says "at the Royal Comparison Gate," it is reasonable to suppose that it really refers to the establishment within the gate, that is, the "Comparison Office."

108. *Tso*, 143::145 (Hsi 5), 197::198 (Hsi 26).

That work lists two staffs of officials working under a Director of Agreements and a Director of Covenants. These staffs were occupied with recording and enforcing agreements and covenants of all kinds, ranging all the way from treaties between feudal lords to agreements between private persons. Copies of each agreement, written on tallies, were held by each party, and another copy was preserved in the archives. If there were a lawsuit (*sung*) or other legal action, the officially preserved copy was brought out for comparison, and judgment was rendered in accordance with it.[109] This is certainly reminiscent of our inscription, in which the parties involved in a lawsuit over a contract take action involving a wooden tablet at the "Royal Comparison Office."

There is no other reference to the "Royal Comparison Office," so that my hypothetical translation of this title, and the existence of the institution, remain in question. But in other inscriptions we do find the King personally directing his officials to adjudicate concerning and to record agreements involving lands, and royal officials apparently acting as guarantors of contracts.[110] That there was such an office seems plausible.

Whether the wooden tablet at the "Royal Comparison Office" was or was not a tally is uncertain, but tallies were used in Western Chou. As we know the practice in later times, contracts were written in duplicate, in vertical columns on the right half and the left half of a piece of wood or bamboo. The piece was then split down the middle, producing two tallies, one of which was given to each party to the agreement. In order to prove one's title to whatever the tally called for—goods, money, service, or privilege—it was necessary to produce one's tally and match it with that kept by the other party. Such a tally constituted a proof of indebtedness or obligation that was extremely difficult to forge. The use of such split tallies, for a wide variety of purposes, continued in China for thousands of years and even persisted well into the twentieth century. Wood and bamboo decay quickly in most of China, but a number of such tallies dating from as early as Han times, preserved in the dry climate of Inner Mongolia, have been excavated.[111]

---

109. *Chou-li*, 34.3b, 36.3b–7a; Biot, *Tcheou-li*, II, 291–292, 357–361.

110. *Chin-wen*, 124b–125a, 127a, 129b–131a, 144b. Chou, *Chin-wen Ling-shih*, 64–72.

111. Lao, *Chü-yen Han-chien K'ao-shih, K'ao-cheng*, 3–6. H. F. Schurmann ("Traditional Property Concepts in China," 509–510) writes: "One of the popular tales of the Sung, called 'The Account of the Tally Document' ('Ho-t'ung wen-tzu chi'), concerns two brothers who separate because of poverty. The younger one

If this should seem a rather primitive method of recording debts and other agreements, it may be compared with a remarkably similar system employed in England far more recently. The importance of the British Exchequer, in the development of modern governmental institutions, is universally recognized; we have seen that Strayer calls it "the first government bureau which kept careful records and developed a group of technical experts."[112] In the twelfth century the Exchequer was, according to the Cambridge Medieval History, "the heart of the government."[113] The British Exchequer used a system of split wooden tallies which, while having certain differences from that of China, was essentially quite similar.[114] Hilary Jenkinson asserts

---

obtains from his elder brother a tally, one portion of which the latter also retains. The half-tally certifies the younger brother's permanent interest in the family property." The son of the younger brother later establishes his claim by means of the tally. See also Des Rotours, "Les insignes en deux parties."

112. Strayer, "Medieval Bureaucracy," 1.

113. Cambridge Medieval History, V, 574.

114. For descriptions of the British tallies, with illustrations, see Jenkinson, "Exchequer Tallies," and Jenkinson, "Medieval Tallies." The English tallies were not, like the ancient Chinese, pairs of pieces of approximately equal size. They were so cut that one piece was longer, and thicker at one end, than the other. Furthermore, the quantity of money, or other goods, involved in the transaction, which was only recorded in writing on the Chinese tallies, was represented on the British tally by notches of various kinds cut into the edges. These notches are said to have been necessitated by the fact that some of those in charge of the Exchequer were "laymen and ex officio illiterate"; see Course of the Exchequer, xxviii, xliv. In spite of these considerable differences, however, the use of split tallies to record debts seems to have been basically similar in England and in China.

Split tallies have been used for various purposes in various countries, but I am not aware that they have been used so extensively, both for private and for official government purposes, anywhere but in these two countries. One wonders, then, whether there can have been any connection between the Chinese and the English practices. The origin of the use of tallies in England seems to be obscure. Certainly they were used in the twelfth century and probably earlier. It has been argued that they came in with the Norman Conquest, but others say that they must have been in use before that time. See: Jenkinson, "Exchequer Tallies," 368. Course of the Exchequer, xxxvii. That the use of tallies as they were employed in England might have been suggested by the Chinese practice seems clear. The road between China and Europe was far more open at most periods, from a very early time, than is usually supposed. Needham's statement (Science and Civilization in China, I, 245) that "the early +12th century, before the Mongol conquests, was a most unpropitious time for the passage of any idea from China to Europe," is an exaggeration. Communication through the Muslim world was more or less continuous. As was noted earlier, the book written by the Muslim geographer al-Idrīsī at the court of King Roger II of Sicily, completed in 1154, contains a number of references to China, its government, and even its finances; see al-Idrīsī, Nuzhat, I, 90–91, 100–101, 190, 194–195. Another possible route of

that "upon this tally system most of the Exchequer administration of medieval times . . . undoubtedly hinges." In fact, he says "the more we examine financial conditions in medieval England . . . the more do we find that all development of this kind—development of the system of Public Accounts, of Exchequer Bills and their discounting, of Public Loans and Public Credit—is conditioned at every turn, to a greater or less degree, by that system of tally-cutting which was already well established in the twelfth century and which continued in action with very little alteration down to the nineteenth." The Exchequer continued to use tallies as late as 1829, and they were also used extensively in England in private business, not only for financial purposes but also to keep check on inventories.[115] It appears likely that our modern system of writing checks, and keeping a stub with the particulars in duplicate to be compared later, grew out of the tally system.[116]

Although we have very few details concerning the use of tallies in the Western Chou period, scattered references in the bronze inscriptions make it evident that they were widely employed. There is no evidence of their governmental use on a scale to compare with that of the British Exchequer, but officials of the royal court do appear as playing roles in transactions in which tallies were involved.[117] Their function,

---

transmission is through the Jewish merchants who are well known to have been numerous in China. A celebrated Muslim geographer who is believed to have held the office of Director of Posts in Iraq described, in the middle of the ninth century, routes regularly traveled by Jewish merchants trading between Europe and China, "sometimes by land, sometimes by sea" (Ibn Khorradādhbeh, *Kitāb al-masālik wa'l-mamālik*, 114–115, 153–154). A number of the English tallies bear Hebrew inscriptions, and tallies were regularly used by Jewish moneylenders in England (Jenkinson, "Medieval Tallies," 293, 313). Thus the possibility that the Chinese practice might have provided the stimulus to that in England certainly exists. But to prove that in fact it did would require, among other things, tracing the transmission through intermediate stages. And independent invention is certainly possible. The point is perhaps more curious than important.

115. *Proceedings of the Society of Antiquaries of London*, 2d ser. XXV(1912–1913), 38–39. Jenkinson, "Medieval Tallies," 290, 310–324.

116. Jenkinson, "Exchequer Tallies," 369 n. 1, suggests this, and there is much reason to believe that he is right. A seventeenth century Exchequer document refers to the portion of the tally kept in the "Chamberlain's Chest," for later matching, as "a Comptroll or Cheque" (*Proceedings of the Society of Antiquaries of London*, 2d ser., XXV[1912–1913], 34). This retained tally was known as the "foil," and the stub of a bank check is sometimes called a "counterfoil." The counterfoil or stub of a bank draft was formerly called a "cheque."

117. For an excellent study of the use of tallies in Western Chou, see Chou, *Chin-wen Ling-shih*, 64–72. For reference to tallies in bronze inscriptions, see *Chin-wen*, 26a, 40b, 81b, 124b, 129b (another possible instance is 96b). An indi-

however, is not financial, but rather that of seeing that justice is done.

This official concern, in Western Chou, with transactions and contracts between individuals is rather surprising. One might expect that it would have led, in the later development of Chinese jurisprudence, to some emphasis on what is known as "private law." But authorities are agreed that in fact nothing of the kind happened. Karl Bünger says: "In particular, the law concerning daily business, law regulating debt and commerce, developed late and only in rudimentary fashion. . . . The field was left to usage and custom."[118] Escarra writes that in China law has traditionally been little concerned with such matters as "a sale, a rental, a contract of whatever sort. This is the vast domain of custom, of usage, of private agreements, under the authority of the innumerable traditions established by those collective entities within whose orbit every individual, in China, must move: clan, family, guild, village, etc."[119]

There is risk, certainly, in attempting to deduce too much from our evidence concerning Western Chou, which is slight and difficult to evaluate. Nevertheless, the indication that we have of governmental concern with areas that were later left, in large measure, to control by "collective entities," seems to fit with the picture of the Western Chou situation that emerges in other connections. Western Chou was a period of becoming. The aristocracies, the "clans,"[120] the "collective entities" that no doubt existed before the Chou conquest, had been weakened or swept away. The "new men" who gained power under the Chou rapidly developed into an aristocracy, but the situation was initially rather fluid.[121] If such entities as guilds existed, they had not yet acquired great authority. In this situation there was both the need and the opportunity for the government to provide justice in spheres that could later be left, to a much greater degree, to self-regulation.

Further evidence of this is provided by the insistence of King Wu

---

cation that the use of tallies was very widespread at an early date is the fact that the *Tso-chuan* uses the character *ch'i* 契 , meaning "tally," to mean "evidence" in a generalized sense, where there is no question of a literal tally being involved; see: *Tso-chuan*, 31.13b. *Tso*, 445::449 (Hsiang 10).

118. Bünger, "Die Rechtsidee," 212. See also Bodde and Morris, *Law in Imperial China*, 4.

119. Escarra, *Le droit chinois*, 76.

120. I avoid the use of the term "clan" because it falls within the domain of the anthropologists, and it seems to be very difficult to use it in a way that meets with the approval of all anthropologists.

121. See pp. 331–342.

that it was the duty of the government to punish all those who were remiss in their relationships within the family. Ch'i Ssu-ho points out that this envisages governmental supervision over an area of conduct within the family far wider than that of later times.[122] Chinese law has certainly provided, and enforced, drastic penalties against such crimes as unfilial conduct. But during all of the periods we know well, conduct within the family has been left to control by the family, to a degree far beyond that which is familiar to us in the West.[123]

CONCERNING judicial penalties, we have seen that in a case of breach of contract there was no penalty; the party who had failed to carry out his part of the bargain was merely ordered to do so. When grain was stolen, however, the culprit was ordered not only to make restitution but to pay over another amount, equal to that stolen, to the injured party as punitive damages, and to pay double the total amount if payment was delayed for a year. It does not appear, however, that any fine was to accrue to the state in this action. And the exact amount of the actual settlement, which was arranged between the plaintiff and the defendant, differed somewhat from the award made by the court.[124]

Rather surprisingly, there seems to be only one reference to a fine. This occurs in the early inscription in which the verdict is pronounced that certain men who failed to follow the King on a military expedition should pay three hundred *lieh* of an undetermined commodity—probably silk. This must have been a heavy fine, for when they protested that they could not pay it the excuse was accepted. The final verdict was that they should make a payment (unspecified) to their superior.[125] This shows that the fine, as a penalty, was known, and it is likely that fines were actually assessed in other cases of which we have no record.[126] While there were evidently jails in which persons under detention were kept, there is no indication of the use of im-

---

122. *Shu*, 42. Ch'i, "Hsi-Chou Cheng-chih Ssu-hsiang," 33. Ch'i points out that whereas later Chinese practice punished sons and younger brothers for failing in their duties, penalties are here prescribed also for fathers and older brothers who behave improperly to their sons and younger brothers. See also Bodde and Morris, *Law in Imperial China*, 37–38.

123. Ch'ü, *Law and Society*, 15–90.

124. *Chin-wen*, 96b–97b.

125. *Chin-wen*, 26a.

126. The text in the *Documents* called the "Lü Hsing" has a very elaborate schedule of "redemption-fines" to be imposed in "doubtful cases" instead of the "five punishments." But although this document was traditionally ascribed to Western Chou, it can hardly have been written before the Warring States period; see p. 463.

prisonment as punishment for those who had been convicted of crime.[127]

Mutilation, cutting off the nose or cutting off the legs, as punishment, is mentioned only in the instructions of King Wu to his brother.[128] Similarly the death penalty is rarely mentioned, except in sections of the *Documents* that date from the early decades of the dynasty.[129] In them, however, it is very frequent. The threat that the Duke of Chou makes to the Shang people, that they will be put to death if they do not obey orders, may be regarded as normal treatment of the conquered. But King Wu mentions the death penalty so frequently that it appears to have been very common indeed. He threatens even his own brother with death if he does not rule his fief well. He says that he will himself have all those executed who are guilty of drinking intoxicating liquor "in companies." Death is the penalty he prescribes for officials who depart from the prescribed course and "promulgate innovations." In fact, Wu says, even small offenses, if they have been committed intentionally, must necessarily be punished with death. When the law is enforced in this way, the King says, "the people will completely abandon their errors . . . and become tranquil and orderly."[130] This is remarkably similar to a statement attributed to Shang Yang, who lived in the Warring States period, some eight centuries later: "Small faults should be punished severely; then, if small faults are inhibited, great crimes will not appear."[131]

The frequent reference to harsh punishment, and especially to the

127. The existence of jails can be deduced from the character *ch'iu* 囚 , which is a very graphic representation of a man confined within an enclosure. It occurs once in the *Poetry*, where Karlgren (*Shih*, 257) translates it as "captives," in this case prisoners of war. It also occurs repeatedly in the *Documents* (*Shu*, 40, 64, 65), where it seems to have the sense of "the case against one arrested for trial."

128. *Shu*, 40. For the emendation of the text at this point, see Karlgren, "Glosses on the Book of Documents," (1).289. There are also some references in the *Book of Changes* to "deprivation of ears," "branding the forehead," "cutting off the nose," and "cutting off the feet." See *I-ching*, 3.13a, 4.11b, 5.13b; Legge, *I-ching*, 102, 139, 163. Although the context never states specifically that these represent punishments imposed by judicial process, some of them undoubtedly do, while others may not. But the *Book of Changes* is so difficult to date precisely, and so generally vague, that it is hard to deduce much from such references.

129. The text in the *Documents* called the "Pi Shih" (*Shu*, 80) is a harangue to troops by a feudal lord, in which he threatens with the death penalty those who do not bring forward the required amount of provisions. This text is not easy to date, but some opinion places it near the beginning of Western Chou; see pp. 454–455.

130. *Shu*, 40, 42, 46, 65.

131. *Han-fei-tzu*, 9.9a; Liao, *Han Fei Tzǔ*, I, 295.

death penalty, that we find in documents from the very beginning of Western Chou, contrasts strongly with what we find in the later sources for the period. This might also tempt us to suppose that, as the *Hsün-tzu* suggests, the use of capital punishment was chiefly limited to the turbulent days of the initial establishment of the dynasty.[132] It is highly doubtful, however, that such a conclusion would be justified. Our sources are extremely uneven. The "Announcement to K'ang," is almost unique among documents we have from early China, in that it is a long discussion of the administration of justice, by a ruler, which treats the subject both generally and in some detail. We have nothing of the kind from later in Western Chou. There is little reason to expect such information in the bronze inscriptions, though in fact an incomplete inscription from late in the dynasty includes a brief statement by the reigning King that mentions the death penalty.[133]

Anyone able to have a bronze cast for himself was necessarily a man of position, and it is only very incidentally that ordinary persons are mentioned in the inscriptions. It is hardly to be expected that capital punishment, and mutilation of the body, would often have been carried out against feudal lords and men of rank. This is not merely, as is sometimes supposed, because of an *esprit de corps* that prevented aristocrats from injuring other aristocrats. In the Spring and Autumn period, for which our information is fuller, they often treated each other quite ruthlessly, when they were able to do so. The reason for dealing circumspectly with men of position was a more compelling one. Once the feudal lords had consolidated their positions in their fiefs, and once powerful families had become entrenched in the enjoyment of wealth and privilege, it was not easy for the King or his officials to impose drastic penalties on those who were backed by armies, or by potent kinsmen. To kill such persons was decidedly dangerous, leaving open the distinct possibility of revenge. (In Spring and Autumn times this danger was sometimes avoided by the expedient of extinguishing the entire group of kinsmen in a body.)[134] It is not very surprising, then, that we find in the inscriptions relatively little mention of harsh punishments and execution. It is likely —though this is speculation—that these occurred, but that the victims were for the most part persons so obscure that their fate is unrecorded.

In fairness, however, it must also be noted that the subordinates

---

132. *Hsün-tzu*, 3.14b–15a; Dubs, *Hsüntze*, 84.

133. So much is clear, but I find much of this inscription very hard to understand; see *Chin-wen*, 140b–142a.

134. See for instance *Tso*, 295::297 (Hsüan 4); 531::535 (Hsiang 27); 654::655 (Chao 14).

of Commander Ch'i who failed—presumably refused—to follow the King to war, and who were treated with what seems a considerable degree of leniency, were not men of high position. They probably were not, as some have argued, slaves, but they were definitely men of low status.[135]

It will be recalled that the official judging this case said that these men ought in accord with justice to be banished. Obviously banishment as a punishment was known. But we seem to have no record of its actual application in Western Chou times as a judicial penalty, unless the transportation of various groups of the conquered Shang people can be so considered.

IT may be useful to summarize the results of this lengthy and somewhat diffuse investigation of the administration of justice by the royal government of Western Chou.

There were certainly laws, and written laws. There may have been codes, but if so none has been preserved. There is nothing to indicate that the law was kept secret.

The principal source of Western Chou law was that of law everywhere: tradition. Some Shang law was preserved. There is one reference to laws instituted by King Wen. Religion played some role in the background of this law, but little more than it does in some legal systems today. No special relationship is discernible between Western Chou law and cosmological theories or speculations.

The offenses mentioned as meriting punishment cover a wide range. Robbery, murder, treachery, tax evasion, and breaches of military discipline are considered crimes almost everywhere, but the death penalty for group drinking and for the failure of officials to follow prescribed procedures are unusual. It is also unusual, even in comparison with later Chinese practice, that not only the unfilial son but also the unloving father are denounced as criminals.

The prime responsibility for the administration of justice was ascribed to the King. We find application made directly to him, in his court, for redress of wrong; he then directs certain officials to investigate and remedy the situation. Royal officials also adjudicated between individuals concerning private contracts, and we find at least one case in which a royal official appears to dispense justice within the fief of a vassal. There may have been one royal official who held the title of Director of Crime—sometimes called "Minister of Justice" —who had general charge of such matters, but the evidence on this

135. Chou, *Chin-wen Ling-shih*, 43–44, 72–73.

point is uncertain. If there was an organized hierarchy of officials specially charged with the administration of justice, the sources give little clue to its existence. It is probable that this function was diffused among men who also performed other duties.

In arriving at judgments, not only law but also equity was supposed to be taken into account. Those trying cases were urged to be cautious, to weigh the evidence for a long time, and to frame their verdicts in accord with propriety and justice.

Not only was evidence considered, but briefs were studied before judgment was pronounced. There were judicial interrogations, apparently actions instituted by the state, as well as lawsuits in which individuals accused other individuals and sought judgment. In two cases, parties involved were represented by advocates. There was some flexibility in the imposition of penalties, which might be adjusted after sentence had been pronounced.

In Western Chou times "private law," dealing with such matters as contracts between individuals, was an area in which the state operated to a considerable extent. It appears that contracts might be registered with the government, and royal officials seem to have played some role in guaranteeing contracts.

No penalty was imposed in a case of breach of contract of which we have record, beyond the obligation to fulfill the contract. But for theft —again a single case—the culprit was required to restore the stolen goods and to pay the victim further goods of the same value as punitive damages. There is only one sentence calling for payment of a fine, and no mention of imprisonment as punishment. Mutilation as a penalty is mentioned only at the beginning of Western Chou, and the death penalty is rarely mentioned after that time, but this may well be because of the limited nature of our evidence. Banishment, the mass transportation of a group, is mentioned, but we have no clear case of its actual imposition as a judicial penalty.

The administration of justice in Western Chou appears to have resembled governmental practice in other areas. There was clearly much thought about the principles and the objectives of the judicial process. But the machinery for attaining those objectives, the technique, the detailed procedures, seem, in so far as our sources disclose, to have been but little elaborated—at least as compared with later Chinese practice, which sometimes went to the other extreme. Justice, in Western Chou times, clearly depended in very large measure upon the energy, the intelligence, and the fairness of the individuals who administered it. But given these qualities—in the total absence of which no system can function—there would seem to be no reason why it could not have worked reasonably well.

CHAPTER

9

The Barbarians

THROUGHOUT Chinese history "the barbarians" have been a constant motif, sometimes minor, sometimes very major indeed. They figure prominently in the Shang oracle inscriptions, and the dynasty that came to an end only in 1912 was, from the Chinese point of view, barbarian. In some periods the barbarians have been no more than an intermittent rumble of off-stage thunder; in others occasional tornadoes, making incursions and disappearing as swiftly as the wind; and at some times hurricanes that devastated the whole country and left it under alien rule for centuries.

The role of barbarians in the Western Chou period was extremely important. They were the enemy, the opposition toward which almost all of the recorded military activity was directed. Many of them were also subject to the Chou and to their vassals—an uneasy subjection, punctuated by rebellion and conflict. Subject barbarians paid taxes or tribute to the Chou treasury, and thus were of economic importance. The downfall of the Western Chou dynasty is blamed on an attack in which certain barbarian troops had a considerable part. But perhaps the most important role that the barbarians played was one that is far from obvious and almost paradoxical: their opposition to the rule of the Chou Kings may have been essential to keeping it alive.

Great conquests are not unusual phenomena. Greed, poverty, boredom, the lust for excitement and loot, make it easy for one who can promise his followers success to recruit a conquering horde. First victories swell the tide, which rolls on to become irresistible. But at some point limits are reached, and it is then necessary to organize the conquered territory, which is quite another matter. Subordinate leaders must be rewarded with power and kept loyal even when the lure of new booty is no longer present. They see no reason why the lion's share of the prizes should go to one man—unless, thinks each, that one should be himself. It is only rarely that states formed by rapid conquest endure for centuries. The empire of Alexander the

Great hardly outlasted his life. Even the Islamic Empire, organized and administered with unusual skill and wisdom, remained unified only a little more than a century after the first conquests began. In both of these cases the fragmentation was caused, not by external pressure, but by internal division.

Certainly the rulers of Western Chou, and especially the early Chou Kings who laid much of the foundation of what was to become China's traditional pattern of government, were extremely able men, who achieved far more in devising a viable administration than has often been credited. But it is a serious question whether this administration could have succeeded in holding together, in subordination to the Chou house, the many feudal lords, if these vassals had not been kept occupied by the threat and sometimes the reality of barbarian dissidence and incursion. Undoubtedly many of them could not have maintained themselves without the possibility and occasionally the fact of the support of the King and his armies. This was a powerful incentive to cohesion.

That such an incentive was necessary is clear if we remember the earliest years of the dynasty. When the Shang people and others revolted, they were joined even by sons of King Wen, uncles of the reigning King. If ties of loyalty did not bind them to the new regime, it is evident that something more than sentiment was necessary to hold its far-flung vassals in continued allegiance to the Chou house. It may not be wholly fanciful, therefore, to say that the barbarians quite unwittingly fulfilled a function that was necessary to permit the fledgling state to develop.

To understand Western Chou it is necessary to understand the barbarians. It is almost impossible, however, to derive any meaningful picture of them from the Western Chou sources. They are mentioned frequently, but almost always as the adversaries in war. And without exception, what little information we get about them comes from the Chinese point of view. Since in these references the barbarians are almost always the enemy, the information they give us is no more unbiased, and no more satisfactory, than information secured from enemies ever is. In order to gain something approaching an adequate conception of these people and their role, we must first consider the much fuller information on barbarians that is available for the Chou period as a whole, and especially for Spring and Autumn times. Having done this, we can go back and examine the evidence relating purely to the Western Chou period in more useful perspective.

Who, in fact, were the barbarians? The Chinese have no single term for them. But they were all the non-Chinese, just as for the Greeks the barbarians were all the non-Greeks. The question then becomes: who were the Chinese? It is not wholly easy to answer.

We have seen that the Chinese tradition, at least as it was set forth at the beginning of Chou, spoke of two previous dynasties, the Hsia and the Shang. Descendants of the Hsia presumably had a clear title to be considered Chinese, and we find the term Hsia used to mean "Chinese."[1] The Shang also were unquestionably Chinese.

The pedigree of the Chou, on the other hand, was subject to some doubt. The people of the east regarded the Chou, even after the conquest, as uncultivated intruders.[2] As late as the end of the fourth century B.C. Mencius said that King Wen was "a man of the western I," that is, a barbarian. And the genuine *Bamboo Books* says that the army that King Wu led to conquer Shang was composed of "western I."[3] Rightly or wrongly it was believed that the Chou royal house was so closely related to the rulers of one tribe of Jung barbarians that intermarriage with them constituted incest.[4]

---

1. But neither this term nor any other seems to have been extensively used in Western Chou times to distinguish Chinese from others. Hsia 夏 in the sense of "Chinese" does not seem to occur in any Western Chou bronze inscription, nor in the original text of the *Book of Changes*. In the *Documents* it occurs only twice in the sections that I accept as Western Chou: *Shu*, 39, 61. In the *Poetry* it has this sense twice: *Shih*, 242, 244.

The character *hua* 華 , having the sense of "flower," "flowery," and "ornamented," occurs as early as the *Tso-chuan* in the sense of "Chinese" and "China." Lin (*Chung-kuo Min-tsu Shih*, I, 46–47) cites several theories as to its origin. But insofar as I can determine, this character does not occur with this meaning in the Western Chou texts.

The common term used for China today, *chung-kuo* 中國 , occurs once in the *Documents* (*Shu*, 48) and in three poems in the *Poetry* (*Shih*, 210–212, 215–216, 222). Karlgren translates it as "central kingdom," and Waley (*Shih*, 252) as "the Middle Kingdom," but I suspect that in these Western Chou contexts it might better be rendered merely as "the central states."

2. *Shu*, 37.

3. *Mencius*, 4(2).1.2. Wang, *Ku Chu-shu*, 6b. In both of these cases "western I" simply means "western barbarians," in a very general sense.

4. The rulers of the state of Chin were (or were at least believed to be) descended from the Chou royal house, and had its surname, Chi 姬 . The nineteenth ruler of Chin married a Jung woman who also had this surname, and the marriage was considered incestuous; see *Tso*, 113::114 (Chuang 28), 185::187 (Hsi 23). The Chi surname was also used by many other groups that seem to have been non-Chinese originally; in some of these cases, at least, it seems likely that their pedigrees were acquired retrospectively in the process of Sinicization. But in the case of these Jung, who lived in the same general area in which the Chou seem to have lived before the conquest, some genuine relationship is not impossible.

We may be sure, however, that once the Chou were firmly in power it was very seldom that anyone dared openly to question that they were Chinese. And all the states whose rulers descended from the Chou house shared its high position. Similarly, states that could trace their founding back to enfeoffment at the beginning of the Chou dynasty basked in reflected glory. As for the others, their status was sometimes equivocal.

The fundamental criterion of "Chinese-ness," anciently and throughout history, has been cultural. The Chinese have had a particular way of life, a particular complex of usages, sometimes characterized as *li*.[5] Groups that conformed to this way of life were, generally speaking, considered Chinese. Those that turned away from it were considered to cease to be Chinese. We find even the state whose rulers were believed to be the heirs of the ancient Hsia Kings accused of adopting barbarian customs, and thus putting this state outside the Chinese community.[6]

It was the process of acculturation, transforming barbarians into Chinese, that created the great bulk of the Chinese people. The barbarians of Western Chou times were, for the most part, future Chinese, or the ancestors of future Chinese. This is a fact of great importance. But we can hardly expect to learn this from the writings of the men of Western Chou, because of course they could not know it themselves. It is significant, however, that we almost never find any reference in the early literature to physical differences between Chinese and barbarians. Insofar as we can tell, the distinction was purely cultural.[7]

There seems to be no single Chinese character that may properly be translated as "barbarian." While various names were used for groups regarded as barbarian, four came to predominate: Jung 戎 , Ti 狄 , Man 蠻 , and I 夷 . These were probably the names of ethnic groups originally; there were specific peoples called the Huai I (the I of the region of the Huai river), the White Ti, etc. Some of these names may have been given by the Chinese as terms of contempt

5. *Li* 禮 is of course a term that was used in many ways; see pp. 335–338. For its employment as something very close to a synonym for the complex of usages that made up Chinese culture, see *Tso*, 715::718–719 (Chao 26). This passage concludes that *li* is "what the former Kings received from Heaven and Earth, in order to govern [literally, 'to form'] their people."

6. *Tso*, 181::182 (Hsi 22), 200::201 (Hsi 27), 545::549 (Hsiang 29).

7. We have remarkably little data on the ethnic character of the peoples involved. Chang (*Archeology of Ancient China*, 347) says that the Chou conquest of the Shang "cannot be called a conquest by an alien people having an alien culture."

—this is hard to determine—but it is unlikely that all of them were. *Jung* appears to have had the sense of "military" before it was used as a name for people,[8] and Jung barbarians were indeed noted for their martial valor. The Chinese gradually came to use these terms in a conventional manner, so that the *Records on Ceremonial* tells us that I is the name of non-Chinese people on the east, Man of those on the south, Jung of those on the west, and Ti of those on the north.[9] As early as Spring and Autumn times we find the compounds Jung-Ti and Man-I used as general terms for barbarians.[10] One passage in the *Tso-chuan* uses all four names, saying: "When any of the Man, I, Jung, and Ti do not obey the King's commands, and by dissoluteness and drunkenness violate morality, the King gives the order to attack them." We even find these four names reduced to an abbreviation, the "Four I."[11]

It is evident that the Chinese came to use "Jung-Ti" and "Man-I" as generalized terms denoting "non-Chinese," "foreigners," "barbarians." Such a statement as "the Jung and Ti are wolves" is very much like the assertion that many people in many lands will make today, that "no foreigner can be trusted."[12] The Chinese had at least two reasons for vilifying and depreciating the non-Chinese groups. On the one hand, many of them harassed and pillaged the Chinese, which gave them a genuine grievance. On the other, it is quite clear that the Chinese were increasingly encroaching upon the territory of these peoples, getting the better of them by trickery, and putting many of them under subjection. By vilifying them and depicting them as somewhat less than human, the Chinese could justify their conduct and still any qualms of conscience.[13]

The idea that all peoples called Jung, Ti, Man, and I were essentially similar is quite erroneous. Even some modern scholars seem to think that these peoples were much alike, all consisting of tribes that

8. The early form of the character consists of a dagger-ax and, possibly, a coat of armor.

9. Legge, *Li-chi*, I, 229.

10. *Tso*, 123::124 (Min 1), 179::180 (Hsi 21), 422::424 (Hsiang 4), 645::652 (Chao 13). "Jung-Ti" also occurs in the *Poetry* (*Shih*, 259–260), but there it is difficult to know if it is being used as a general term or to designate two specific groups.

11. *Tso*, 343::349 (Ch'eng 2), 666::668 (Chao 17).

12. *Tso*, 123::124 (Min. 1).

13. Evidence of such qualms is rare in the early literature, but it exists; see *Tso*, 422::424 (Hsiang 4), 459–460::463–464 (Hsiang 14). See also the interesting statements of Confucius in *Analects*, 9.13, 13.19, 15.5.

moved about, having no settled place of residence. But in fact there was a great deal of difference between the various peoples that were, rightly or wrongly, designated by these four names. Some of them lived in walled cities.[14] We cannot even assume that, for instance, all of the people called Ti were alike. The Chinese texts not only give us very little information about the non-Chinese people, but much of the information that they do give us may well be unreliable.

The peoples called Jung and Ti do seem to have lived, generally speaking, to the west and the north, not only beyond the borders of Chinese territory but also in numerous enclaves within it.[15] Some of them were probably ancestors of some of the nomadic people like the Hsiung-nu, who in Han times and later made so much trouble for the Chinese. It must be noted, however, that they were, culturally at least, significantly different from people like the Hsiung-nu, for they did not yet have that weapon that was to make the nomads almost invincible when they were firmly united: the cavalry horse. Although both the Chinese and their non-Chinese neighbors had had the horse from an early day, the technique of riding on horseback, and thus the mounted warrior, seem to have been unknown in China and adjacent areas until the fourth century B.C.[16]

It is sometimes supposed that the Jung and Ti were nomads who had moved to the borders of China from the steppes of Central Asia. Some of the people known by these names may have been, but it is doubtful that most of them were. They may have had some contact with Central Asian nomads, but there is reason to doubt that such contact was extensive.[17] It seems quite clear that many of those called

14. *Tso,* 657::659 (Chao 15), 691::693 (Chao 22).

15. But these designations are by no means used consistently. The genuine *Bamboo Books* speaks of the "western I" (Wang, *Ku Chu-shu,* 6b). And we find in *Shu,* 80, reference to the Hsü Jung 徐 戎. But the same passage mentions attacking them together with the Huai I 淮 夷, and the literature consistently mentions the Hsü people as being in the eastern region of the Huai river and near the state of Lu; see *Shih,* 235–236, and Fu, "I Hsia Tung Hsi Shuo," 1125. The Hsü Jung were evidently, therefore, an eastern people rather than, as "Jung" is supposed to denote, a western one.

16. Creel, "The Horse in Chinese History," 649–656. Lattimore, *Inner Asian Frontiers of China,* 341. See also pp. 262–263, note 61.

17. If peoples on the border of China had been in intimate contact with those of Central Asia, one would expect that the cavalry horse would have appeared among them much earlier. Mounted bowmen are pictured in an Assyrian relief of the ninth century B.C., and the cavalry technique spread to Central Asia early, yet it does not seem to have reached the border of China until shortly before 300 B.C. See Creel, "The Horse in Chinese History," 649–651.

Jung and Ti had long been in what we call "China," and had been displaced by the Chinese.[18]

To what extent the peoples that are called Jung and Ti were nomadic is a question. In one passage in the *Tso-chuan* a Chinese says that the Jung and Ti move about and are quite willing to sell their lands for goods.[19] And Western Chou records of booty taken from Jung and Ti peoples do include horses, cattle, and sheep.[20] No doubt some of them were nomadic herdsmen. On the other hand, another passage in the *Tso-chuan* seems to indicate that some Jung practiced agriculture.[21] Such archeological evidence as we have indicates that, in the general region in which these people were found, nomadism, farming, hunting, and fishing were all pursued.[22] It seems probable that people designated by these names included groups that found their livelihood by various means; some of them may well have had a mixed culture.

Nomadism is less likely to have been practiced, on any considerable scale, among the peoples known as Man and I, who commonly (though the usage is by no means consistent) were located to the south and east of the central area. We do, to be sure, find a bronze inscription mentioning sheep and cattle among the booty captured in an expedition against the Huai I.[23] But we know that both horses and cattle were known to, and may have been domesticated by, people living in eastern China even at a time that probably preceded the Shang period—and by people who were so settled in their habit of life that they lived in a walled city.[24] In general the southern and

18. See for instance *Tso*, 459–460::463–464 (Hsiang 14). Owen Lattimore, in *Inner Asian Frontiers of China*, 340–354, develops this theme. See also Ch'ien, *Kuo-shih Ta-kang*, 36–37.

19. *Tso*, 422::424 (Hsiang 4). There is some difference of opinion about the sense of the text here. It may either mean that they "change their residence," or that they "are dwellers on the grass," presumably meaning that they move about to find new grass for their animals.

20. *Chin-wen*, 35b. Wang, *Ku Chu-shu*, 8a.

21. *Tso*, 460::464 (Hsiang 14). A Jung chieftain says that when certain undesirable land was given to his people they "cleared it of thorns and brambles," which certainly sounds like the act of farmers rather than of nomads. Lattimore (*Inner Asian Frontiers of China*, 349) interprets this passage as indicating that they were farmers.

22. Chang, *Archaeology of Ancient China*, 351–362.

23. *Chin-wen*, 146a.

24. Creel, *Studies*, 176–194. *The Black Pottery Site at Lung-shan-chên*, 152. Chang, *Archaeology of Ancient China*, 121–160. Cheng, *New Light on Prehistoric China*, 40–42. Cheng, *Prehistoric China*, 87–95. Cheng Te-k'un says in ibid., 92, that "the Lung-shan people . . . were 100 per cent agriculturists living in perma-

eastern areas were suited to farming and hunting, and these seem to have been the chief pursuits of the people who lived there.[25]

Articles of booty taken from eastern and southern peoples differ somewhat from those from the north and west. An early Chou inscription mentions the capture of cowrie shells from the Eastern I, and the *Poetry* relates that, after the state of Lu had defeated them, the Huai I came "to present their treasures, large tortoises, elephant tusks, and a great quantity of southern metal." A bronze inscription also tells of the capture of metal from the Huai I.[26] The metal was almost certainly bronze, and archeological finds have indicated that the technique of metallurgy was known in Western Chou times, and in some places even earlier, in southern and eastern regions that appear to have been beyond the sphere of Chinese culture. It seems probable, however, that the use of metals was confined (as indeed it probably was even in the Chinese areas) to certain cultural centers.[27] The people in general may have moved about to a limited extent, tilling the soil of a particular area until its fertility was exhausted and then moving on to another; this is a usual pattern where agricultural techniques have not been highly developed.[28]

Detailed data on the cultural differences between Chinese and barbarians is very scanty. We are told that they wore their hair hanging loose,[29] and Confucius implied that it was a barbarian characteristic to button clothing to the left rather than to the right; if this was the only difference in clothing, it seems slight, though no doubt it would have appeared considerable to the people of the time.[30] In a speech in the *Tso-chuan* a Jung chieftain is quoted as saying: "The drink, the food, the clothing of us Jung are all different from those of the Flowery [i.e., Chinese, states]. We do not interchange silks and other ceremonial gifts with their courts. Our language does not permit intercommunication with them."[31]

We have some further indication that the speech of Jung—or at

nent villages. They must have supplemented their vegetable diet with meat from their domestic animals, the game on the hills, and fish and shell-fish in the river."

25. Chang, *Archaeology of Ancient China*, 351–354, 376–394.

26. *Chin-wen*, 28a, 146a. *Shih*, 257.

27. Chang, *Archaeology of Ancient China*, 386–391.

28. Cheng, *Prehistoric China*, 125. Chang, *Archaeology of Ancient China*, 92–95.

29. This characteristic is attributed to Jung in *Tso*, 181::182 (Hsi 22), and to both the Jung and the I in Legge, *Li-chi*, I, 229. *Analects* 14.18.2 implies that it is a barbarian characteristic, but without specification.

30. *Analects*, 14.18.2.

31. *Tso*, 460::464 (Hsiang 14).

least of some of those called Jung—was different from that of the Chinese.[32] Yet we cannot tell how different their speech was. Even today, many of those who speak Chinese in different parts of China cannot understand each other at all, because of dialectical differences. It is quite remarkable that we do not find more mention of difficulties of communication, and of the use of interpreters, in the early literature.[33] Undoubtedly there were some interpreters, and it is possible that they are seldom mentioned because they were taken for granted.[34] No doubt there were major differences between some of the languages that were originally spoken in what is now China. But there is much, also, that suggests that some of the various peoples concerned may have spoken what were, from a linguistic point of view, varieties of the same language.[35] If so, this undoubtedly facilitated the eventual welding of them into one people.

32. *Mémoires historiques*, II, 40–41, relates that in 626 B.C. the King of the Jung sent a certain Yu Yü to the state of Ch'in, where he negotiated with the ruler of Ch'in. It is explained that the ancestors of Yu had been refugees from Chin who had settled among the Jung, so that he could therefore speak the language of Chin. This apparently qualified him to talk with the men of Ch'in.

33. Wang Li ("Chung-kuo Yü-yen-hsüeh Shih," 242) interprets an incident recorded in *Tso*, 262::264 (Wen 13), as indicating the need for interpreters to communicate between men of the states of Ch'in and Chin. In my opinion it is uncertain, however, that the intelligibility of speech is what is in question here. Wang also cites the incident described in the preceding note. But there we see a man sent by the Jung to deal with Ch'in because he could speak the language of Chin; this would seem to indicate that the speech of the two states was not so different as to interfere with intelligibility.

34. The scant mention of interpreters is nonetheless noteworthy. The *Ritual of Chou* in two passages mentions interpreters attached to the royal court (Biot, *Tcheou-li*, II, 407, 435–436). But Broman ("Studies on the Chou Li," 52) cites only a single passage in any other early work that mentions interpreters: *Kuo-yü*, 2.7a. Here, in a conversation dated to around 600 B.C., we find interpreters who are apparently royal officers, but designated by a name different from that given in the *Ritual of Chou*.

35. See Wang, "Chung-kuo Yü-yen-hsüeh Shih," 241–245. Kuo, "Hsin-yang Mu," 5. Lattimore, *Inner Asian Frontiers of China*, 454–459. Maspero, *La Chine antique*, 14–16. The *Tso-chuan* relates that a ruler of Wèi, who was held captive in the southeastern barbarian state of Wu, when he returned to his state in 483 B.C. imitated the speech of Wu (*Tso*, 827::829 [Ai 12]). This sounds as if the speech of Wu had been very much like Chinese, and bronze inscriptions from that state of the Ch'un-ch'iu period are written in language essentially similar to that of the central states, though with some differences (*Chin-wen, yu* 153–156). Much the same thing is true of inscriptions from other comparable states. There are, however, at least two problems. First, we know that these states underwent a progressive acculturation during the Western Chou period. Second, it is quite possible that Chinese was cultivated at the courts of these states as an elegant language, so that we cannot necessarily deduce very much, from such inscriptions, about the language in general use.

Many of the statements that we find made about barbarians are in the nature of vituperation. "The Ti are covetous and greedy." "The Jung and Ti know nothing of affection or friendship, and are full of greed; the best thing to do is to attack them." "The I are light-minded; they cannot maintain the same course for long."[36] This latter accusation recurs in various forms, and the many accounts of the conduct of the non-Chinese groups, especially in war, do seem to indicate that they commonly lacked endurance of purpose. Again and again we read that barbarians lack organization and discipline in warfare, and that the Chinese defeat them by taking advantage of this fact.[37]

There seems to be no doubt that, generally speaking, the Chinese were better organized, both in peace and in war, and cooperated more effectively than did most of their non-Chinese neighbors. This was a prime factor in the ultimate victory of the Chinese way of life. It must be noted, however, that if the Chou people themselves started, as is often said, as barbarians, they did not share these failings. On the contrary, as we have already seen, they were conspicuous for their ability to plan far ahead, and for their discipline, even before their conquest of the Shang. They had two virtues that the early Romans held in high esteem: *gravitas* (gravity) and *constantia* (constancy). Yet this does not mean that the Chou were necessarily more cultured, before the conquest, than some of the other peoples called barbarian, particularly those to the east and south. This is by no means certain.

We have seen that there was a persistent tendency to regard the Chou as barbarian in origin. This cannot have helped them in their attempt to win acceptance as not only the rulers, but also the religious leaders and cultural exemplars, of the Chinese world. We have also seen that they used an intensive propaganda to convince their subjects that they were the legitimate, Heaven-appointed heirs of the Hsia and Shang rulers. The Chou insisted that they had been a part of the "Hsia" group well before the conquest.[38]

On the whole, while there are many references to groups called Jung, I, and so forth, there is relatively little emphasis in the Western Chou literature on the distinction between "Chinese" and "barbarian"—a distinction that is very sharp in the succeeding Spring and Autumn period. Even terms that mean "Chinese" as opposed to non-Chinese occur only rarely in Western Chou documents.[39] And the

36. *Tso*, 189::192 (Hsi 24), 422::424 (Hsiang 4), 830::832 (Ai 13).
37. *Tso*, 27::28 (Yin 9), 273::275 (Wen 16), 572::579 (Chao 1).
38. *Shu*, 39, 61. *Shih*, 244.
39. See p. 196, note 1.

literature of that period very seldom makes contemptuous reference to non-Chinese people, of the sort that became common later.[40]

There were undoubtedly several reasons for this. In the first place the Chou themselves were in a delicate position regarding their own pedigree. Certainly they were building their state and their culture on foundations that were derived in part from those of the Shang and others, but there was much that was distinctively Chou in the blend. And the Chinese culture that was formed was shaped, in very large measure, by the selection and the emphases that the Chou chose to make. There came a time when "Chou" was synonymous with all that was most urbane and cultivated, but it was not that in the beginning. In their early years the Chou were in no position to sneer at others as "barbarian"; this would have been too likely to attract attention to their own origins.

Secondly, it is quite clear that the Chou were wisely committed to a policy of conciliation—conciliation, at least, of all those who would accept them as sovereign. They were deliberately trying to weld together peoples of diverse cultures into a political and cultural whole. It would have been unwise for them to harp upon differences. Furthermore, it would probably have been harder to draw a clear line between "Chinese" and "non-Chinese" at the beginning of Western Chou than at its end.

Finally, it was difficult to be contemptuous of the non-Chinese because they were too powerful. If we look at the record of wars and incursions, even as fragmentary as it is from the bronze inscriptions that are known, it is clear that the unassimilated peoples were an almost constant threat, and a very grave one. People who are feared may be disliked or hated, but it is not easy to be wholly contemptuous of them.[41]

SOME of the Chou fiefs were states that had existed under the Shang, which were permitted to continue if they submitted to the Chou.

---

40. In *Shih*, 177, there is what appears to be an insinuation that Man and Mao barbarians are inconstant, but even this is indirect.

41. This argument may seem weak because barbarians were still a threat in Spring and Autumn times, when they were regarded with contempt. There are those who argue that the barbarian attacks became even more of a menace in the later period, but I think this is because the Western Chou record has not been studied carefully. In Spring and Autumn times most of the barbarians were dealt with rather easily, from a military point of view, and it was only dissension among the Chinese that gave them much opportunity to make serious trouble. I suspect that in Western Chou times the barbarian threat was greater, but it was held in check by the power of the royal armies, which was no longer present in the Spring

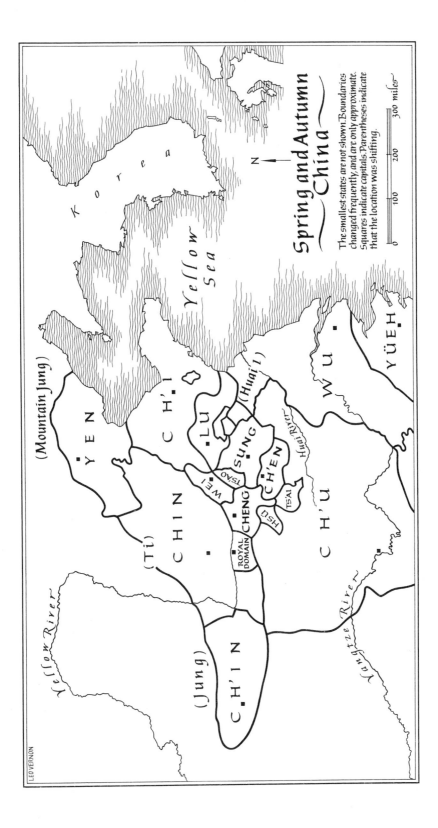

Spring and Autumn
—China—

The smallest states are not shown. Boundaries changed frequently, and are only approximate. Squares indicate capitals. Parentheses indicate that the location was shifting.

N

0   100   200   300 miles

LEO VERNON

(Mountain Jung)

Korea

Yellow Sea

Yellow River

YEN

(Ti)

CHIN

(Jung)

C H'I N

ROYAL DOMAIN

CHENG

WEI

TSAO

HSÜ

CH'I

LU

SUNG

CH'EN

TS'AI

(Huai 1)

Huai River

C H' U

W U

YÜEH

Yangtze River

But the new Chou fiefs were essentially walled cities, garrisons holding varying degrees of control over the surrounding countryside. The populations over which they ruled were in part Chinese, but undoubtedly large numbers of the people theoretically within many states were non-Chinese tribesmen. Many of these people were gradually assimilated to Chinese culture. Some of them were in a state of precarious submission. Others were quite independent, sometimes allied with the Chinese, sometimes neutral, sometimes actively and dangerously hostile.

An extremely interesting conversation is recorded in the *Tso-chuan* for the year 559 B.C. It occurred at a strategy meeting between the officers of a number of states, presided over by the representative of Chin, which then held the leadership; the subject was methods of countering the aggressive might of the great southern non-Chinese state of Ch'u. One of those present was the chief of a Jung tribe, here called a Viscount. The Chin officer accused this barbarian leader of treacherously disclosing the plans of the Chinese states and sought to bar him from the conference. The Jung Viscount replied:

> Formerly, the people of the state of Ch'in, relying on their numbers and coveting our territory, drove out us Jung. Then Duke Hui of Chin [650–637 B.C.] displayed his great kindness and, considering that we were descendants of the Four Mountains[42] and should not be cut off and abandoned, gave us some lands on his southern borders. It was a place where foxes dwelt and wolves howled, but we Jung cleared it of thorns and brambles, drove away the foxes and wolves, and became his loyal subjects, neither making incursions [on Chin] nor renouncing our allegiance to it. To this day we have never been unfaithful. . . . In the battle of Hsiao [627 B.C.] Chin met the enemy in front and we Jung withstood him in the rear. That the army of Ch'in did not return to their state was the result of our efforts.[43] As in catching a stag, Chin laid hold of the horns and we Jung

---

and Autumn period. In that time, it is true, such states as Ch'u and Wu were quite formidable, militarily. But it is to be noted that as the power of these states increased they were less and less regarded with contempt, and came in fact to be looked upon as essentially Chinese. Of course, this situation is complicated by the fact that these states did also become progressively assimilated to Chinese culture.

42. *Ssu-yüeh* 四嶽 . In *Shu*, 3, this is interpreted as an official title. It seems probable that here it denotes a mythological ancestor or ancestors.

43. The *Spring and Autumn Annals* credits this victory to the joint efforts of Chin and these Jung; see *Tso*, 221::224 (Hsi 33).

grasped the feet, and together with Chin we brought [Ch'in] to the ground. Why are we not spared [this accusation of treachery]? From that time on, in all of Chin's wars, one after another, we have followed its leaders with the same fidelity as at Hsiao. How could we dare to follow a separate course? But now when the troops of your officers have committed some errors that have alienated the feudal lords, you seek to blame us Jung. . . . Not to take part in your conference will cause me no grief.[44]

The representative of Chin apologized.

Undoubtedly the Chinese did in some cases covet the land of the barbarians; another Chin officer recommends buying land from the Jung and the Ti.[45] But the Chinese rulers were probably as much interested in gaining subjects as in gaining lands. When Western Chou bronzes tell of the taking of barbarian captives—as many as 13,084 in one eleventh-century B.C. inscription—it is unlikely that any except a few leaders were executed.[46] The others almost certainly ended up as serfs, subject to some Chinese lord.

One of the poems in the *Poetry* says that the King has given to the Marquis of Hán the tribes of Chui and Mo; whether they had already been conquered or were his to rule after he had conquered them is not clear.[47] One of the *Documents* concerns a military expedition against the Jung of Hsü, and a poem tells of an expedition dispatched by the King to subdue the state of Hsü—undoubtedly the same people. The poem concludes by saying that Hsü was defeated, so that its ruler came to court to show his submission, and Hsü was "annexed"—that is, it became a state subject to the Chou. In Spring and Autumn times Hsü appears as a state ruled by a Viscount.[48] This would seem to have been a case of assimilation in which the state as such was permitted to continue.

In many cases, however, non-Chinese groups were wiped out as political entities. This probably happened frequently in Western Chou times, though we have little record of it, but the fuller accounts of the Spring and Autumn period show many such cases. We read

44. *Tso*, 459–460::463–464 (Hsiang 14).
45. *Tso*, 422::424 (Hsiang 4).
46. Ch'en, "Hsi-Chou T'ung-ch'i," (4).85–89.
47. *Shih*, 232.
48. *Shu*, 80. *Shih*, 234–236. *Tso*, 593::597 (Chao 4). See also Fu, "I Hsia Tung Hsi Shuo," 1125. This state, Hsü 徐, should not be confused with another small state, Hsü 許.

that one militant group of the Ti fought with one Chinese state after another until its leaders were killed off, one by one, so that it finally became extinct.[49] In 594 b.c. the state of Chin "extinguished" a tribe of another group, the Red Ti. In the following year Chin extinguished three more Red Ti tribes. Another tribe—possibly the last of the Red Ti—was attacked by Chin in 588, whereupon it is said they "dispersed, because their ruler had lost the people." Presumably they had lost faith in the ability of their leader to protect them.[50]

When we read that a group or a tribe or a state "was extinguished" or "became extinct," we are commonly left in the dark as to the fate of its territory and its people. We should not suppose, however, that the people were annihilated. We may be sure that in most cases the territory was annexed and the people acquired as subjects by some ruler. The extinction was usually just the extinction of the corporate group, while the people became assimilated as Chinese—unless the extinction was by a victorious barbarian group, which also happened. In the case of one Red Ti tribe, we are told that, when it was extinguished, the state of Chin carried off its ruler, took over its people, and annexed its territory.[51]

The fate of extinction was not peculiar, of course, to barbarian groups. Some forty years ago Chinese archeologists excavated, in Shantung province, the remains of the walled city that was the capital of the small state of T'an. It appears that this state existed before the beginning of Western Chou and persisted into the Spring and Autumn period. Its rulers intermarried with the ruling family of the large and powerful state of Ch'i. But in 684 b.c. an army of Ch'i extinguished T'an; the reason given for this action was that the Viscount of T'an had been "discourteous" to the Marquis of Ch'i.[52]

To allege a reason for extinguishing a Chinese state was considered good form. But the destruction of barbarian groups was, in some cases at least, considered cause for celebration and profound moral commendation.[53] There was often reason for this, for some barbarian groups made a habit of raids and depredations that were annoying to say the least. And this was no doubt the excuse that was considered

49. *Tso*, 257::258 (Wen 11).
50. *Tso*, 325–327::327–329 (Hsüan 15), 329–330::330 (Hsüan 16), 351::353 (Cheng 3).
51. *Tso*, 325–327::327–329 (Hsüan 15).
52. *The Black Pottery Site at Lung-shan-chên*, 162–166. Cheng, *Chou China*, 18–21. *Tso*, 85::85, 87 (Chuang 10). It seems that at some later date a state by this name appeared again, but this was not unusual.
53. *Tso*, 330::330 (Hsüan 16).

justification for every sort of deceit and trickery in dealing with them.

In war between Chinese it was considered proper (though the principle was violated) not to attack an unprepared enemy,[54] but such scruples seldom appear to have applied to attacks on barbarians. Not only were barbarian armies attacked before they were deployed, but all manner of subterfuge was used to defeat and sometimes to "extinguish" barbarian groups. On one occasion Chin sent some officials, with a military escort, to make a sacrifice to the river Le. A Jung tribe in the vicinity suspected nothing until the Chin army fell upon it. The ruler fled, and the people were captured; one of the officers of the Chou King had foreseen this event and posted an army in the vicinity, so that some of the captives were secured for the King. A few years later a number of men disguised as rice buyers stopped to rest at the gate of the capital city of a tribe of the White Ti. Suddenly they reached into the bags that each man carried, brought forth their arms, and captured the city for Chin. The ruler was carried away as a captive, and the territory put in charge of a Chin official. In 590 B.C. the King entered into a sworn covenant of peace with the Jung. Immediately afterward the King's brother, thinking that this would have lulled them into a false sense of security, led his army in a sudden attack on one of the Jung tribes. In this case he had miscalculated; he was soundly defeated.[55]

The Chinese did not use military might alone to get the better of the barbarians; sometimes the balance of might was on the other side. They also used guile, sometimes working on the superstitious credulity of their adversaries.[56] Not all of the barbarians were naïve, by any means, but the Chinese were, generally speaking, more cultivated—a fact that played a very large role in the ultimate Sinicization. Thus they were sometimes able by eloquence to get the better of adversaries whom they could never have matched on the field of battle. Lu, the state of Confucius, was considered the most polished of the states, and in an incident in 482 B.C. we see a courtier of Lu—an acquaintance, though probably not an intimate, of Confucius—in debate with the ruler of Wu. Wu was a very powerful southeastern state, essentially barbarian in character and a newcomer in Chinese diplomacy, which aspired to the leading role. The representative of Lu is determined that his state shall not take the humble role that Wu wishes to assign it. By a combination of flattery and casuistry he manages to

54. *Tso*, 260::261 (Wen 12), 849::850 (Ai 17).
55. *Tso*, 336::337 (Ch'eng 1), 666::668 (Chao 17), 691::693 (Chao 22).
56. *Tso*, 127::129 (Min 2).

win his point. Later, however, when the Wu ruler realizes that he has been outwitted, he is furious and causes the officer of Lu to be imprisoned—until the officer again succeeds in talking his way to freedom.[57]

After the descendants of the Chou invaders had been in possession for so long that they believed that they were not only Chinese, but the *most* Chinese of all people, some of them became very arrogant. This is illustrated by a story in the *Tso-chuan* laid in the fifth century B.C., more than six centuries after the conquest. In some of its details, at least, this tale seems incredible, but it probably reflects attitudes more or less accurately. The Marquis of Wèi, it is said, was once looking out over the countryside from the wall of his capital and asked the name of a village that he saw. He was told that it was called "Jung-town." The Marquis said, "We here are Chi [the surname of the Chou royal house]. What are Jung doing here?" And he pillaged the place. On another occasion when the Marquis was looking out from his wall—he seems to have had remarkably sharp eyes—he noted that one of the women of this Jung settlement had very beautiful hair. He immediately had it cut off, to make a wig for his wife. Later, when there was an uprising, the Marquis took refuge in the home of this woman, and her husband killed him.[58]

The question of surname, and of relationship, became very important. The "Chi states," those whose rulers were descended—or at least claimed descent—from the Chou royal house, formed a group with ties that were considered especially close.[59] A lesser degree of affinity was felt toward states related by marriage, and all of the Chinese states came to be bound by intermarriage between their ruling houses into a great network of relationships. In 587 B.C. the Duke of Lu wanted to abandon the leadership of the Chinese state of Chin and follow the great southern barbarian state, Ch'u. But one of his ministers demurred, saying:

> The book of the historiographer I says, "If he is not of
> our kindred, he is sure to be of a different mind." Al-

---

57. *Tso*, 830–831::832 (Ai 13). The Lu spokesman here is Tzu-fu Ching-po. In *Analects*, 14.38, we see Confucius politely but definitely refusing his offer to intrigue on behalf of one of Confucius' disciples. *Analects*, 19.23, indicates that Tzu-fu Ching-po was probably more intimate with the disciple Tzu-kung than with Confucius.

58. *Tso*, 849::850–851 (Ai 17). There are various problems of translation and chronology in connection with this improbable tale, but it is not worth while to discuss them.

59. *Tso*, 204::209 (Hsi 28), 545::549 (Hsiang 29).

though Ch'u is great, it is no kindred of ours. Can it be willing to treat us with affection?[60]

Intermarriage occurred, in fact, not only among the rulers of Chinese states but also between them and barbarian rulers. But in many cases at least these marriages do not seem to have led to any great feeling of kinship. They appear to have been regarded, like the matrimonial alliances among European rulers, as having little personal significance.

If barbarians were sometimes treated rather badly, it must not be supposed that they were powerless to help themselves. Militarily, many of them were potent indeed. Various states, and the Chou King, were glad to have the help of barbarian armies.[61] Alliances with powerful barbarian groups were considered to be major assets of Chinese states. The state of Chin, once supreme in power, had lost some of its superiority by 569 B.C., but it was still a very strong state. In that year one of Chin's ministers advised strongly against alienating the Jung and Ti, and proposed cultivating friendly relations with them. Among the reasons he advanced were the following: "Our borders will not be kept in fear. . . . When the Jung and Ti serve [i.e., are allied with] Chin, our neighbors will be terrified and the feudal lords will be overawed and cherish our friendship. . . . Our armies will not be toiled and our arms will not be ruined."[62]

The victories were not all on the Chinese side. Barbarian raids were frequent, and sometimes they were very serious. In 660 B.C. Ti captured the capital of Wèi and brought that important state close to extinction. In 649 a Jung tribe invaded the royal capital and was dislodged only after some months.[63] Ch'u annexed so many of the Chinese states, eating its way northward, that there was well-grounded fear that it would end by displacing the Chou in the rule of all China.[64]

Ch'u was only one of the barbarian powers that were able to maintain their independence throughout the Spring and Autumn period. It continued as a state until 223 B.C., when it shared the common fate of being extinguished in the rise of the Ch'in dynasty. In the *Poetry*

60. *Tso*; 354::355 (Cheng 4).
61. *Tso*, 222::225 (Hsi 33), 358::360 (Ch'eng 6), 624::625 (Chao 9), 691::694 (Chao 22).
62. *Tso*, 422::424 (Hsiang 4). See also *Tso*, 720::723 (Chao 27).
63. *Tso*, 126–127::129–130 (Min 2), 158::158 (Hsi 11).
64. See p. 220, note 106.

the state of Lu boasts of having conquered the Huai I and having made them completely submissive. Yet throughout the Spring and Autumn period we find them acting independently, and at the very end of that time the willingness of the Huai I to act in concert with Lu is cited as one of Lu's assets.[65] It was not until the time of the Ch'in conquest, according to one account, that the Huai I "dispersed and became ordinary people."[66] The Hsien-yü are said to have been a branch of the White Ti; their state was known as Chung-shan. Though a small state, it was militarily formidable, on occasion even defeating Chin. It continued in existence until 299 B.C. At one point the ruler of Wei is reported to have had in his library two chests full of books devoted to plans for the conquest of Chung-shan.[67]

IF we looked only at the warfare and the expressions of contempt, we might suppose that the relationships between the Chinese and the barbarians were characterized by unmitigated hostility. But that was by no means the case.

We have seen that in Spring and Autumn times the state of Chin was in frequent conflict with Jung tribes, and extinguished many of them and absorbed their territory and their people. But two curious passages in the *Tso-chuan* seem to suggest that Chin may at an early time have been almost a dependency of the Jung.[68]

We have seen that there was a good deal of intermarriage between Chinese and barbarian rulers, and that it did not put an end to strife. It is notable, however, that the children of barbarian wives of Chinese rulers seem to have suffered no disability with regard to succession. Duke Hsien of Chin (676–652 B.C.) seems to have been fond of Jung women, for he married four of them. And each of the four had a son

---

65. *Shih*, 257. *Tso*, 720::723 (Chao 27).

66. *Hou-Han Shu*, 85.2a.

67. *Tso*, 747::748 (Ting 3). *Mémoires historiques*, II, 79. *Lü-shih Ch'un-ch'iu*, 16.11a.

68. *Tso*, 657–658::660 (Chao 15), 750::754 (Ting 4). The second of these passages says that the territories of the state of Chin were originally "laid out according to the methods of the Jung." In the former passage an officer of Chin is chided by the King, in 527 B.C., for not making valuable presents to him. In reply the dignitary from Chin says that his state is located deep in the mountains, next to the Jung and Ti, far from the benign protection of the royal house. Furthermore, he says, 拜戎不暇. Legge translates this as meaning that Chin "has hardly had time to repay its obligations to the Jung." Couvreur (*Tso-chuan*, III, 257) translates: "Tsin est sans cesse obligé de s'humilier devant les Joung." Commentators try to interpret this in a manner less embarrassing to Chinese pride, but not very convincingly.

who became ruler of Chin, though in some cases only briefly. One of these sons became Duke Wen who, though he reigned only from 635 to 628 B.C., was the most powerful man in China in his day and left a deep impress on history. During the reign of Duke Wen, half barbarian in blood, there began a drastic reform of the administration of Chin that was destined to have important consequences for the development of governmental institutions in China.[69]

Long before Wen became Duke of Chin, he had to flee from that state because of an intrigue against him, and he took refuge with the Ti, among whom he lived for twelve years. During this time both he and his follower Chao Ts'ui married Ti women and had sons by them. Chao's son, Chao Tun, grew up among the Ti, but later he went to Chin and was made his father's principal heir. Later, Chao Tun became the chief minister of Chin, and the real power in the state. Since Chin was one of the most powerful—perhaps still the most powerful —of all the states, this made him an influential man indeed, and in 613 B.C. we see this half-Ti minister adjudicating a quarrel between the King and members of the royal family. Chao Tun is credited with making important and sweeping reforms in the government of Chin. His descendants founded the state of Chao in 403 B.C.[70]

It was not in the least unusual for Chinese to flee to barbarian states, and sometimes to take up permanent residence there. Insofar as the records go, they seem to have been almost uniformly well received. The Chinese accounts say that those who took this step were fleeing from trouble; whether any may have gone because they preferred another way of life, we can only conjecture.[71] There was also movement from the non-Chinese states to the Chinese. In 547 B.C. it was said that so many of the able ministers of Ch'u had fled to Chin, and been given office there, that Ch'u was placed at a disadvantage.[72]

Chinese rulers frequently married barbarian women and gave their own daughters and sisters in marriage to barbarian chiefs. In 626 B.C. the King, who had a quarrel with the state of Cheng, secured the help of a Ti army to invade that state. Grateful for this assistance, the King decided to make the daughter of the Ti leader his Queen. One of his ministers remonstrated:

69. *Tso*, 113::114 (Chuang 28), 152–153::154–155 (Hsi 9), 188::190 (Hsi 24). Creel, "Beginnings of Bureaucracy in China," 180–182.

70. *Tso*, 143::145 (Hsi 5), 184::186 (Hsi 23), 188::191 (Hsi 24), 242::243–244 (Wen 6), 265::267 (Wen 14). *Mémoires historiques*, V, 53.

71. *Tso*, 243::245 (Wen 6), 375::376 (Ch'eng 11), 402::405 (Ch'eng 17). *Mémoires historiques*, II, 41.

72. *Tso*, 521–522::526–527 (Hsiang 26).

> It may not be done. I have heard it said that the one who
> rewards becomes tired, while the receiver is never satis-
> fied. The Ti are certainly covetous and greedy, and yet
> your Majesty encourages them. It is the nature of
> women to be limitless [in their ambition], and their
> resentment is undying. The Ti will certainly be your
> sorrow.

The King refused to listen, and married the lady. His brother had an
affair with her, she was deposed as Queen, and an army of the Ti occupied the royal capital.[73]

Such marriages were primarily political alliances. This implies that
the barbarian groups were regarded as political entities, as states, as
indeed they were. The *Spring and Autumn Annals*, the official chronicle of the state of Lu, lists a number of states that held a diplomatic
meeting in 559 B.C. In commenting on this the *Tso-chuan* reports a
long speech by a Jung Viscount, although the Jung were not among
the parties listed. James Legge remarks that this "is interesting, as
showing how the chiefs of the various ruder tribes might be present
at the meetings of the States, though there be no record of such a
thing in the text [of the *Spring and Autumn Annals*]."[74] In view of
the important role that barbarian groups played, both in war and in
peace, it seems quite probable that their representatives were present
at such meetings far more frequently than their participation is recorded. It is occasionally mentioned, however, and we find the White
Ti listed with a number of Chinese states as sending representatives
to pay a court visit to Chin in 545 B.C.[75]

We have already noticed that barbarian armies sometimes fought
beside those of Chinese states, against other Chinese states. This was
very common. We find them fighting for the King, and acting with
Chinese against the King.[76] There is nothing to indicate that these
barbarian troops were mercenaries, fighting for pay. They were the
soldiers of political entities, whose help was requested in just the
same way that Chinese states asked help from each other. Time after
time we see alliances with barbarian groups cited as important assets

---

73. *Tso*, 189–190::192–193 (Hsi 24), 326::328 (Hsüan 15), 601–602::605
(Chao 5).

74. *Tso*, 459–460::463–464 (Hsiang 14).

75. *Tso*, 536::540 (Hsiang 28), 591::595 (*Ch'un-ch'iu*, 2) (Chao 4).

76. *Tso*, 158::158 (Hsi 11), 189–190::192–193 (Hsi 24), 301::301 (*Ch'un-
ch'iu*, 6) (Hsüan 8), 368::370 (*Ch'un-ch'iu*, 11) (Ch'eng 9), 624::625 (Chao 9),
691::694 (Chao 22), 793::795 (Ai 1), 804::805 (Ai 4).

of states fortunate enough to be able to make them, and policy was sometimes shaped so as to avoid offending barbarian allies.[77]

It appears probable that transactions with barbarians—especially transactions in which they were treated as equals—were not always placed in the historical record. Certainly such interaction as we have noted must have required more consultation than we find mentioned. Yet the Chinese apparently felt that it was beneath their dignity to carry on diplomatic intercourse with barbarians. In 598 B.C. the ruler of Chin went into the territory of the Ti to make an alliance with them. His officers protested that this compromised his position; he should have summoned the Ti to his capital.[78] We are told, nevertheless, that a sworn covenant—that is, a treaty—was entered into between certain Jung and the state of Chin, and even between Jung and the King.[79] This is interesting, because such sworn covenants were guaranteed in theory by religious sanctions; this may indicate that there was a certain degree of congruence of religious belief between the Chinese and some, at least, of the barbarians.

If we look at the concrete situation, it is not always easy to see a clear functional distinction between Chinese states and barbarian groups or states. The barbarian groups not only fought beside as well as against Chinese states, and entered into treaties with them; they also shifted their support from one Chinese state to another. The Hsien-yü (the state of Chung-shan) played a role in the internal politics of the state of Chin, siding with one of the warring factions. We even find barbarian armies, on more than one occasion, playing an important part in fighting designed to determine which of two candidates shall succeed to the Chou throne.[80] The Chou royal house not only sought the military assistance of the Jung, and entered into a treaty with them, but also recognized their political identity in another way. In 568 B.C. King Ling complained of the conduct of the Jung to the state of Chin, which was apparently considered to control them, as it then theoretically held hegemony over the Chinese states.[81]

Where, in fact, did the barbarian tribes and states fit into the political system of Chou times? It is hard to answer that question from the evidence available to us today, and it might have been hard to answer for a Chou Chinese.

77. *Tso*, 422::424 (Hsiang 4), 450::453 (Hsiang 11), 460::464 (Hsiang 14), 720–723 (Chao 27), 749::753 (Ting 4), 801::802 (Ai 3).

78. *Tso*, 309::310 (Hsüan 11).

79. *Tso*, 336::337 (Ch'eng 1), 422::424 (Hsiang 4).

80. *Tso*, 158::158 (Hsi 11), 691::694 (Chao 22), 793::795 (Ai 1), 804::805 (Ai 4).

81. *Tso*, 425::426 (Hsiang 5).

In two Western Chou bronzes we find chiefs of two different groups called *Chiu* 酋 , a term that was apparently used only of non-Chinese leaders.[82] One early Chou inscription says that "the King attacked the Earl of Ch'u."[83] In the *Tso-chuan* we find various barbarian rulers called "Viscount," and one "Baron."[84]

Another phenomenon is quite surprising, if viewed from the perspective of orthodox Chinese history. We have already noted that the *Documents* speaks of the Jung of Hsü, and that a poem says that the King subdued Hsü so that it became a state subject to Chou. In the *Tso-chuan* the ruler of this state is called a Viscount. But in a number of bronze inscriptions, which Kuo Mo-jo dates to the Spring and Autumn period, the rulers of this state call themselves *Wang* 王 , "King."[85] This same title is used in bronze inscriptions by the rulers of the states of Ch'u and Wu.[86] More remarkable still, the rulers of Wu and Ch'u are frequently given the title of "King" in the *Tso-chuan*, although that work is usually most zealous in upholding the prerogatives of the Chou royal house.[87]

Mencius quoted Confucius as saying, "There are not two suns in the sky, nor two Kings (*Wang*) over the people,"[88] and the theory has been that the Chou King was the only ruler to hold the title of *Wang* after the Chou has wrested the succession from the Shang. This monopoly is supposed to have continued until, late in the fourth century b.c., a number of the rulers of states mutually agreed to call each other *Wang*.[89] But too many facts contradict the theory that, before late Chou times, *Wang* was used—or at least might properly be used—only to denote the ruler of the whole Chinese world.

We have already seen that chiefs of the Chou were apparently

82. *Chin-wen*, 35b–36b, 146a. Ch'en, "Hsi-Chou T'ung-ch'i," (4).86.

83. *Chin-wen*, 3b. Ch'en, "Hsi-Chou T'ung-ch'i," (2).76–79.

84. For a few examples, see *Tso*, 113:114 (Chuang 28), 326::328 (Hsüan 15), 422::424 (Hsiang 4), 459::463 (Hsiang 14), 691::693 (Chao 22).

85. *Chin-wen*, 159a–163a.

86. *Chin-wen*, *yu* 153a–156a, 165a–170a. Whether the ruling family of Wu was or was not of barbarian origin is debated; see pp. 224–225.

87. *Tso*, 512::517 (Hsiang 25), 707::712 (Chao 25), etc. There is also one reference to the King of Yüeh: *Tso*, 786::788 (Ting 14).

88. *Mencius*, 5(1).4.1.

89. *Mémoires historiques*, V, 159. This is a strange story, lacking in all details and probably untrue; see the commentary in *Shih-chi*, 44.23. It is true, however, that after this time the title *Wang* seems to have lost its virtue, so that in later dynasties it was not used to denote "the Son of Heaven." From the Ch'in dynasty on, rulers of all China were most commonly called *Ti* 帝 , while *Wang* 王 came to mean something like "prince" and was a title often bestowed on imperial relatives.

called *Wang* well before the conquest of the Shang.[90] And Wang Kuo-wei pointed out that in Western Chou bronze inscriptions the title *Wang* is used, of persons other than the Chou King, by individuals who quite evidently are loyal vassals of the Chou.[91] In addition we have just noted that not only in bronze inscriptions of the Spring and Autumn period, but even in the *Tso-chuan*, the rulers of some states are called *Wang*. The most probable explanation would seem to be that *Wang* was simply one of the many titles meaning "lord," "chief," or "ruler" that were in use at the time. It also appears that the Chou probably tried to discourage others from using it—with fairly considerable success. But we cannot deduce very much from the fact that certain rulers of barbarian states are called *Wang*.

We may be reasonably certain that the title of "King" was not conferred by the Chou upon any vassal. But what about barbarian rulers called Earl, Viscount, or Baron? Had they been enfeoffed by the Chou King? We have seen that it is probable that the ruler of the Hsü Jung, after being defeated, was enfeoffed as Viscount of Hsü. But in most cases we have little basis even for speculation. If the picture we can draw from our evidence today is confused, it is by no means certain that such matters were always completely understood at the time.

For one thing, who was and who was not barbarian? We have seen that the descendants of the Hsia and the Shang appear to have been, by definition, Chinese, but even the Chou were originally viewed as doubtful. That soon passed, however, and not only the Chou rulers but all the states whose rulers descended from the Chou house, and all that could claim to date from the beginning of Chou, were assured of acceptance. But beyond these there was the area of question.

There are many indications that the state of Ch'in, which was destined to conquer all of China and establish the Ch'in dynasty in the third century B.C., was Jung in origin. This state remained rather isolated, in its Western seat, and is said to have followed barbarian customs down to a rather late date. In fact, it is not unlikely that the full integration of Ch'in as a part of China—culturally speaking—came only as a result of its conquest of the whole country.[92] But this was of course a very unusual case.

An unassailably Chinese pedigree was valuable. The state of Lu

90. See p. 58.
91. Wang, *Kuan-t'ang Pieh-chi Pu-i*, 9b–10a.
92. *Mémoires historiques*, II, 10–11. *Shih-chi*, 68.15. The T'ang commentator Ssu-Ma Chen was scandalized that the Ch'in rulers should be included among Chinese sovereigns, since they were "originally western Jung": *Shih-chi*, 5.1.

was, by common consent, considered the repository of Chou culture in its purest form. During the Spring and Autumn period the prestige of the Duke of Chou was very great, and the state of Lu found the descent of its rulers from him to be a practical asset of great value, which it exploited to the full. Although Lu was relatively small and weak, its goodwill was valued by states that were far more powerful.[93] And Lu was not at all above sneering at other states—usually small and weak ones—as "barbarian," and sometimes using this allegation as a justification for taking territory away from them.[94]

Not even the state of Ch'ï 杞 ,[95] accepted even by Confucius as carrying on the line of the Hsia Kings,[96] was safe from attack by Lu. It was impossible to impugn its pedigree, but Lu accused it of abandoning Chinese culture and adopting barbarian customs. Whether this was true, or whether Ch'ï simply maintained a tradition older than that of the Chou, we cannot judge now. But this alleged lapse was considered to justify Lu in helping itself to whatever territory it wished.[97]

China was in effect a very exclusive club, of states and of rulers. Membership in it carried privileges, and exclusion from it disadvantages, both material and nonmaterial. For small and weak states, the advantages of membership and the dangers of being outside the circle were clear and tangible. For large and powerful states, too, there were certain material advantages in being Chinese, such as somewhat greater ease in making alliances and somewhat greater hope that they would last. But the chief attractions for the powerful were of a less palpable sort, yet they were nevertheless very great. Membership in the Chinese group meant, in all the known world, acceptance as being among the cultured elite. Even wealthy and potent rulers desired it, as men of great wealth and power still seek acceptance among those whom the world considers "socially" more elevated than themselves.

The most striking illustration of this is the case of the great southern state of Ch'u. Its origins are obscure and debated; there seems to be reason to believe that it first developed in the region of the

93. *Tso*, 259::261 (Wen 12), 394::399 (Ch'eng 16), 545::349 (Hsiang 29), 645–646::652 (Chao 13), 855::855 (Ai 24).
94. See for instance *Tso*, 645::651–652 (Chao 13).
95. Ch'ï 杞 should not be confused with the far larger and more important state of Ch'i 齊 .
96. *Analects*, 3.9.
97. *Tso*, 200::201 (Hsi 27), 545::549 (Hsiang 29). In the latter passage the speaker is an officer of Chin, but it is quite probable that, as is suggested in the text, he had been bribed by Lu, and the argument was probably the one advanced by that state.

Huai and lower Yangtze rivers, and later came to center in the middle Yangtze region.[98] The culture of Ch'u was probably a variant of "Chinese" culture. There are many indications that before the Chou conquest Ch'u had been in contact with the Shang and influenced by them; Cheng Te-k'un goes so far as to assert that "Ch'u was an inheritor of the Shang culture."[99] Both architecture and art were highly developed in Ch'u, and it has been suggested that Han dynasty painting may have been derived from that state.[100] Its literary culture was apparently considerable and ultimately had great influence on that of China; Ch'ü Yüan, who lived in Ch'u during the fourth century B.C., has been called "China's first known poet."[101] We know that philo-

98. A number of Chinese scholars have supposed that the Ch'u people derived from the eastern I; see: Hu, "Ch'u Min-tsu Yüan yü Tung-fang K'ao." Kuo, *Yin-Chou Ch'ing-t'ung-ch'i Ming-wen Yen-chiu*, I, 51–52. Yang, "Chung-kuo Shang-ku-shih Tao-lun," 93, 119. Wolfram Eberhard, however, supposes them to derive from the southwest. He writes, in *Lokal-kulturen im alten China, II*, 371: "Der Staat Ch'u entstandt im Gebiet der Pa-Kultur und verlagerte sich im Lauf der Chou-zeit immer weiter nach Osten." See also: Eberhard, *Kultur und Siedlung der Randvölker Chinas*, 331–332. Eberhard, *Lokalkulturen im alten China, I*, 321, 357–359, 363. But Ch'en ("Hsi-Chou T'ung-ch'i," [2].78) thinks that early Western Chou bronze inscriptions locate Ch'u in the east, in the Huai region.

99. Cheng, *Chou China*, 11–12. For links between Shang and Ch'u, see also: *Chin-wen*, Preface, 4b. Hu, "Ch'u Min-tsu Yüan yü Tung-fang K'ao," 32–38. Fu, "Hsin-huo Pu-tz'u Hsieh-pen Hou-chi Pa," 349–370. Eberhard, "Early Chinese Cultures and Their Development: A New Working-Hypothesis," 524. Concerning recent discoveries of bronzes of Shang type in eastern south China, see Cheng, *Shang China*, 160, and Chang, *Archaeology of Ancient China*, 382–394. When one considers that there were some geographical barriers between the people of Ch'u and those of north China, the differences between them as they appear in literature do not seem great. The *Tso-chuan*, which has many long and detailed passages on events in Ch'u, gives the impression of people whose culture was on the whole similar to that of the north. Waley (*An Introduction to the Study of Chinese Painting*, 21) writes that the people of Ch'u "were not wholly different from the Chinese either in speech or race; the relation may be compared with that of Rome to the Italic tribes."

100. Lawrence Sickman writes: "The recent finds of magnificently decorated lacquer at Ch'ang-sha are added evidence to support the suggestion of Arthur Waley that painting in the Han dynasty may have been derived from the State of Ch'u"; Sickman and Soper, *The Art and Architecture of China*, 31. Waley, *An Introduction to the Study of Chinese Painting*, 21–23. On archeological remains of Ch'u, see Chang, *Archaeology of Ancient China*, 394–412. On the admiration with which a Duke of Lu, in the seventh century B.C., viewed the architecture of Ch'u, see *Tso*, 559::563 (Hsiang 31). For other references to architecture in Ch'u, see: *Tso*, 612–613::616–617 (Chao 7), 674::675 (Chao 19). *Kuo-yü*, 17.5b–6a.

101. Hung Liang-chi (*Keng-sheng-chai Wen Chia-chi*, 2.11a–12b) said that insofar as literature was concerned, Ch'u was the most cultivated of the states. James R. Hightower, in his Foreword to Hawkes, *Ch'u Tz'u*, writes: "It is not too much to say that Ch'ü Yüan . . . was China's first known poet. . . . It must be granted

sophical ideas somewhat different from those of the north developed in Ch'u, and there has been a tendency to ascribe some role in the rise of Taoist philosophy to that state.[102] It must be noted, however, that we know almost nothing about the culture of Ch'u before the Spring and Autumn period, and much of our information comes from Warring States times, when there had been much mutual influence between Ch'u and the north; nevertheless, since Ch'u culture still showed so many differences, it is reasonable to deduce that it had possessed a distinctive character from an early day.

From the time when the state of Ch'u first comes into the light of history, in the eighth century B.C., its government appears to have been not inferior, but in some respects superior in its effectiveness to the governments of the Chinese states. While the latter were increasingly torn by dissension, a single ruling house maintained a remarkably centralized rule of unique longevity, throughout the Spring and Autumn and the Warring States periods, over Ch'u. Ku Tung-kao (1679–1759) made what is perhaps the most thorough study ever undertaken of the Spring and Autumn period; he concluded that "although Ch'u was a barbarian (*Man-I*) state . . . it attained the highest excellence of administrative institutions."[103] In a number of respects the government of Ch'u appears to have been not behind, but rather ahead of, the governments of the north, in the path of development that government in China was eventually to take.[104] Statesmen of the north sometimes acknowledged this superiority. We have already noted that refugees from Ch'u had no trouble in finding governmental posts in Chin, where they seem to have contributed to the strength of its government.[105] In the eventual amalgamation that produced the Chinese state and Chinese culture as they have existed for the past two thousand years, it seems likely that Ch'u contributed quite as much as it received.

---

that a couple of bare names of authors of poems have come down from the time of the *Book of Songs*, but here was the first man to achieve fame through his poetry. . . . The shortest list of 'China's greatest poets' would have to find a place for his name."

102. *Mencius*, 3(1).4, mentions several philosophers from Ch'u who went north to propagate their doctrines. Mencius did not care for this competition and called one of them a "shrike-tongued southern barbarian (Man), whose doctrines are not those of the former Kings." See also: Fung, *History of Chinese Philosophy*, I, 175–176, 220–222.

103. Ku, *Ch'un-ch'iu Ta-shih Piao*, 102.15–16a.

104. Creel, "Beginnings of Bureaucracy in China," 174–182.

105. *Tso*, 312::317 (Hsüan 12), 468::469 (Hsiang 15), 521–522::526–527 (Hsiang 26).

Furthermore, throughout most of the Spring and Autumn and Warring States periods Ch'u was larger, and perhaps richer and more powerful, than any of the northern states. It annexed the territory of many small barbarian states, and then started annexing Chinese states to the north. For a time it was almost fatalistically accepted, in the north, that Ch'u would end by taking over all China.[106] Something of a climax was reached when, in 632 B.C., a northward invasion by Ch'u was met by a coalition of northern states under the leadership of Chin. Ch'u was disastrously defeated, yet the victors did not feel able to invade Ch'u.[107] Conflict continued from time to time, with victory going sometimes to one side, sometimes to the other, but what was in effect a stalemate had been reached. Ch'u could not capture the north, but the north could not take Ch'u.

If we examine the situation as it existed in the Spring and Autumn period, there is little obvious reason why the rulers of Ch'u should have considered the culture of the states nominally subject to Chou to be superior to their own, or have desired to be accepted as Chinese. They were not looked down upon; the people of the north were often quite admiring of Ch'u, and on those rare occasions when they speak of the men of Ch'u as "southern barbarians" it is usually clear that this was only an expression of envious spite.[108] There was little to be gained by Ch'u in a material way from acceptance as Chinese; those Chinese states that felt that the balance of power made it more prudent to adhere to Ch'u did so without scruple.

The rulers of Ch'u might well have called the Chou barbarians and have sought to make not only their own rule but also their own culture supreme, but they did not. Even while they were striving to conquer the north, they were open in their admiration for Chou culture. High officers of Ch'u quoted from both the *Poetry* and the *Documents* and cited with approval the examples of Kings Wen and Wu of Chou. King Chuang of Ch'u (613–591 B.C.) quoted stanzas from the *Poetry* that he attributed to King Wu, and praised Wu's administration as the model for good government. Pronouncements and practices of the early Chou Kings were cited at the court of Ch'u as precedents and appear to have been accepted as binding there. An officer of King Ling of Ch'u (540–529 B.C.) admonished him that, if

106. *Kuo-yü,* 16.3b. *Tso,* 204::209 (Hsi 28), 292::293 (Hsüan 3). Fu, "Hsin-huo Pu-tz'u Hsieh-pen Hou-chi Pa," 351–352.

107. *Tso,* 203–205::208–210 (Hsi 28).

108. *Tso,* 714::718 (Chao 26). *Mencius,* 3(1).4.14. In *Kuo-yü,* 18.8b, an officer of Ch'u refers to it ironically as a "Man-I" state.

he hoped to realize his ambition to secure the leadership of the Chinese states, he must take the early Chou Kings as his model.[109]

It seems very clear that it was the achievement of the Western Chou rulers that constituted the attraction which caused the men of Ch'u to look to the north. The Western Chou had established, and maintained for centuries, a state that became the standard both of government and of culture. This gave their heirs, the Chinese states of the Spring and Autumn period, an enviable position, and caused even a state as large, rich, and powerful as Ch'u to wish to rank among their number. The rulers of Ch'u would certainly have liked to be the first, politically, among them, and they sought to win this position by conquest. But they also took over Chinese culture, very rapidly.

This process of acculturation was under way as early as the eighth century. King Wu of Ch'u, who reigned from 740 to 690 B.C., married a woman from a small Chinese state. She seems to have been a blue-stocking (no doubt the King had other ladies in his harem for relaxation). She lectured him on virtue and duty in strictly Chinese terms, and he seems to have taken her advice very seriously.[110] The account that we have of her in the *Tso-chuan* is probably embellished, but there is no reason to doubt that it is based on fact. Such marriages were undoubtedly important agents in the spread of Chinese culture.

King Ling of Ch'u married a daughter of the ruler of Chin. Architecture seems to have been a great interest of Ch'u rulers, and King Ling built a tower of which he was extremely proud. Apparently it was really quite splendid, and it may well have surpassed anything of the kind in the north.[111] But it was not enough for the King merely to

109. *Tso*, 146::147 (Hsi 6), 255::256 (Wen 10), 314::319 (Hsüan 12), 315::320 (Hsüan 12), 341::347 (Ch'eng 2), 342::348 (Ch'eng 2), 611–612::615–616 (Chao 7), 751::757 (Ting 4). See also *Kuo-yü*, 17.7ab, 10a, 10b; 18.1a.

It might be argued that this placing of quotations from Chou works in the mouths of Ch'u men was simply the work of Chinese scholars writing history. This is possible. The *Kuo-yü* is in my opinion a less reliable work than the *Tso-chuan*, and if it occurred only in the former I should be more suspicious. There is reason to think, however, that the compiler or compilers of the *Tso-chuan* did have available a good deal of accurate information about Ch'u. If the compilers of the *Tso-chuan* had written of Ch'u only from fancy, and from a northern point of view, there would hardly be the absence that we find of mention of the familial groups called *shih*, which were ubiquitous in the northern states; see Creel, "The Beginnings of Bureaucracy in China," 179–181, notes 118–119.

110. *Tso*, 60::61 (Huan 14), 76::77 (Chuang 4).

111. *Kuo-yü*, 17.6a, speaks of its great height and elaborate ornament. Duke Hsiang of Lu (572–542 B.C.) was so taken with the architecture of Ch'u when he

build the tower and to possess it. Quite humanly, he wanted to show it off, and to the people who mattered. He wanted the rulers of the Chinese states to attend the inauguration ceremonies. But it was not easy to persuade them to come to Ch'u; aside from any other consideration, King Ling was well known to be unreliable and violent—in fact, murderous. He determined, however, that he would at any rate secure what was, from a cultural point of view, the outstanding prize: the Duke of Lu. Ling sent a high official to Lu, to invite the Duke to attend and to say, in diplomatic but perfectly clear terms, that if he did not do so a Ch'u army would invade his state. The Duke of Lu went to the celebration.[112]

It became clear at an early date that it might be dangerous for Ch'u to be treated as "beyond the pale" of Chinese civilization. Ch'u obviously wanted to belong; to take her into the club could not make matters much worse, and might make her a less belligerent neighbor of the Chinese states. The means by which the gesture was made was most ingenious.

In the seventh century B.C., when the power of the Chou King was no longer able to control China, the state of Ch'i stepped into the breach and attempted, with some success, to fill the leading role. Ch'i was acknowldeged as leader by all but the largest states, but its position entailed the responsibility of protecting the small states adjoining Ch'u, which were increasingly menaced by its power. In 656 B.C. Ch'i, together with seven other states, made what seems to have been a surprise attack and pushed a short distance into the territory of Ch'u. Ch'u sent an emissary to ask the reason for this incursion. He said that Ch'u and Ch'i were so distant from each other that they had nothing in common—"our horses and cattle cannot interbreed"—so that it was impossible to fathom the occasion of this visit.

The Ch'i minister Kuan Chung answered for Ch'i. He said that at the beginning of Western Chou the founder of Ch'i was given the duty of punishing the guilty among the feudal lords, in order to uphold the house of Chou. And now, he said, Ch'u did not send in its proper tribute, a certain kind of rush that was necessary to strain the

---

visited that state that, on his return, he built a palace in the Ch'u style, which seems to have scandalized his subjects; *Tso*, 559::563 (Hsiang 31). No buildings of size from the state of Ch'u seem to have yet been discovered in archeological excavation, but the art from that state that is known, and the almost unbelievably beautiful carved and lacquered wood fittings that have been found in tombs in the Changsha region, make it quite clear that a Ch'u pleasure pavilion must have been something very remarkable.

112. *Tso*, 612–613::616–617 (Chao 7).

liquor for the royal sacrifices. Also, Kuan Chung declared, Ch'i had come to ask about the fate of the Chou King Chao, who had never returned from a military expedition he made to the south.

These alleged reasons for the incursion are quite absurd. The mysterious death of King Chao had occurred three and one-half centuries earlier; the spokesman for Ch'u said that they had better inquire about it in the region in which he had presumably disappeared. The tribute of rushes, as composing the entire contribution due from a vassal state so large and rich as Ch'u, is ludicrous. But the important point here was, of course, that if Ch'u owed tribute, its ruler was presumably a vassal of the Chou King, and thus a member of the Chinese circle. The emissary of Ch'u was quite happy with this. "As for the tribute not having been delivered," he said, "that is the fault of my ruler; how should we dare not to contribute it?"[113]

There seems to be no good evidence for the traditional Chinese view that the rulers of Ch'u were vassals of the Chou from early in Western Chou, and much against it. It seems probable that Ch'u was an independent state from the earliest time we know until it was finally conquered by Ch'in in 223 B.C.[114] Nevertheless, after this encounter with Ch'i we find the ruling house of Ch'u insisting that its early rulers had been loyal vassals of the Chou, and the Chinese do not seem to contradict them.[115]

The upshot of this little incursion that Ch'i made into Ch'u in 656 B.C. was that the two states swore a covenant pledging mutual friendship, and Ch'i and its allies returned home. Both states had achieved something. Ch'i had gained the prestige accruing from the fact that it had—nominally—invaded Ch'u and compelled its ruler to swear to be loyal to the Chou house. Ch'u had gained acceptance as a Chinese state. Thereafter, Ch'u went right on attacking the Chinese states on its border and trying to absorb them.

113. *Tso*, 139::140 (Hsi 4).
114. The *Historical Records* says that the ruler of Ch'u was enfeoffed in recognition of loyal service by the Chou King Ch'eng (1115–1079 B.C.) and gives the impression that his heirs were loyal vassals until the reign of Hsiung Ch'ü (887–878 B.C.) (*Shih-chi*, 40.5–11; *Mémoires historiques*, IV, 340–344). But a bronze inscription dated to the reign of King Ch'eng himself speaks of a military expedition by the King against the ruler of Ch'u; see *Chin-wen*, 3b, and Ch'en, "Hsi-Chou T'ung-ch'i," (2).76–77. And the original text of the *Bamboo Books* says that in 1037 B.C. King Chao made an expedition against Ch'u; Wang, *Ku Chu-shu*, 7a. In this work the state of Ch'u is named in fourteen passages, of which ten concern military actions and not one indicates that Ch'u was a vassal state of the Chou house, or subordinate to it (ibid., 7a, 9b, 11b, 12b, 15a, 16a, 17b–19a).
115. *Tso*, 637::641 (Chao 12).

The lower Yangtze River was held by the fierce rulers of the state of Wu, who were in some degree of subjection to Ch'u. A disaffected officer of Ch'u, who had found refuge and office in Chin, conceived the idea of training the Wu barbarians in military tactics so that they might revolt from Ch'u and neutralize its threat to the north. Around 587 B.C. he went to Wu with a group of military instructors and carried out the plan. The men of Wu learned their lessons so well that they were soon not only a match for Ch'u, but within a century had become a more serious threat to the north than Ch'u had ever been.[116]

It seems clear that Wu was initially not by any means so cultured a state as Ch'u, but it was nonetheless welcomed into the Chinese community. A pedigree was found for the rulers of Wu—where it came from seems impossible to establish—tracing their descent to a very early Chou ancestor, T'ai-po, a son of the Ancient Duke Tan-fu. T'ai-po is supposed to have renounced his title to the throne and to have gone to live among the barbarians. The fact that the rulers of Wu had lived among barbarians for so long was considered to account for the fact that in the sixth century B.C. they were, it would appear, almost completely without any vestiges of Chinese culture, even though so illustriously descended.[117]

This genealogy had one distinctly awkward aspect. Since T'ai-po was senior in the Chou line to both King Wen and King Wu, the rulers of the state of Wu as his descendants could, and did, claim precedence over all of the other rulers of states. While they did not like this, the other rulers did not dispute the claim, and although they sometimes (but not in their presence) referred to the men of Wu as barbarians, they did not challenge their pedigree. Whether they would have been so agreeable if Wu had been less dangerously powerful is doubtful.

Whether the rulers of Wu were in fact descended from a member of the Chou house is debated. On the whole it seems improbable, but the question can hardly be decided now.[118] If not, they were not en-

---

116. *Tso*, 362::364 (Ch'eng 7), 830–831::832–833 (Ai 13). The exact date of the embassy to Wu is not given. The context shows that it was not earlier than 590 B.C. and not later than 584. "Around 587" is a compromise.

117. *Tso*, 733::734 (Chao 30), 792–793::794 (Ai 1), 812::813 (Ai 7), 830::832 (Ai 13). The *Historical Records* says that T'ai-po renounced the succession because he knew that his father wished King Wen to have the throne (*Mémoires historiques*, I, 215–216). See also *Analects*, 8.1.

118. Certainly it would not have been impossible for a Chinese to go among barbarian tribesmen and be accepted as leader; such things have happened in later history. But it must be remembered that T'ai-po seems to have lived at a relatively

titled to the surname Chi, of the royal house, which they claimed.[119] The Chi surname was said to be possessed not only by certain Jung in the northwest—which is not implausible, since that is the general area from which the Chou came—and by Wu in the far southeast, but also by people in the southwest of China.[120] This seems to stretch credulity somewhat.

Genealogies appear to have figured largely in the process of merging the populace of what we now call China into a single people. It will be recalled that a Jung chieftain, complaining of the treatment the Jung had received, said that they were worthy of special consideration because they were descended from the "Four Mountains." This is probably the name of a mythical ancestor. When the lore concerning the early mythical Emperors was elaborated, beginning late in Spring and Autumn times, an individual called the "Four Mountains" was identified as a minister of Emperor Yao.[121] The successor of Yao, Emperor Shun, was said to have had as one of his ministers Hou Chi, the mythical ancestor of the Chou royal family; he was an agricultural deity and here, very appropriately, he figures as having charge of agriculture.[122] The reputed ancestors of a number of other states—Chinese, barbarian, and borderline—appear in the completed tradition of early Chinese history, each in a highly respectable place, as a minister of an early Emperor or in some cases as Emperors themselves. Thus the ruling house of Ch'u was found to be descended from a very

---

early period in the cultural rise of the Chou people. He was the son of the Ancient Duke Tan-fu, who according to the *Poetry* made for the people kiln-like huts and caves, for "as yet they had no houses" (*Shih*, 189). It is hard to know just how much more advanced, if at all, the Chou may have been at that time than were the people of the Wu area. For further discussion of this problem, see p. 361, note 159.

119. There seems to have been some question in the Spring and Autumn period as to whether the surname of the ruling house of Wu was in fact Chi, the Chou surname. A woman from that house was married to Duke Chao of Lu, and in the records her surname is given not as Chi but as Tzu 子 . This gave rise to much discussion, and it was said that this was done in order to conceal the fact that the Duke had contracted an incestuous marriage, since his surname was also Chi; see *Tso*, 827::828 (Ai 12), and *Analects*, 7.30. But it seems possible that Tzu may have been the surname used by the rulers of Wu before their relationship to the Chou house had become accepted doctrine.

120. *Tso*, 113::114 (Chuang 28), 644::650 (Chao 13).

121. *Tso*, 459::463 (Hsiang 14). *Shu*, 3. I do not mean that the "Yao Tien" dates from Spring and Autumn times, but that the elaboration of the mythical Emperor lore evidently began then. To say exactly when any particular item of it originated is often difficult.

122. *Shu*, 7.

early Emperor.[123] Some of these genealogies may be valid,[124] but it is scarcely possible that all or even most of them are.

It seems quite clear that when the fabric of early Chinese history was elaborated, beginning in late Spring and Autumn times, the reputed progenitors of a very large number of groups were worked into the tapestry. The tradition was full of inconsistencies; it was not constructed by any one person, or with conscious guile.[125] No rich tradition ever is. But in China, where tradition and family and long association have been of the highest importance, this interweaving of genealogies produced a united people with a sense of solidarity that could, perhaps, have been brought about in no other way.[126]

As more and more barbarians became converted to Chinese culture, and accepted as being Chinese, the attitude toward barbarians as such became less hostile. The people of Ch'u, as we have seen, had never been held in contempt. And while the usages of chivalry, which forbade taking advantage of an enemy in a vulnerable position, did not usually apply in warfare with barbarians, we do find such usages in warfare with Ch'u to a rather suprising degree.[127] The men of Ch'u were evidently considered, while not Chinese, worthy of full respect. It is only occasionally that we find, in the *Tso-chuan*, such an attitude toward other barbarians.[128]

The fact that the barbarians did not at once adopt Chinese culture was deplored, of course, but in time it came to be felt that they were, at any rate, human beings who were capable of becoming Chinese. Confucius was an outstanding advocate of this view. One of his disciples asked how one should conduct himself. Confucius replied, "Let

123. For Ch'u, see *Mémoires historiques*, IV, 337–338. For the reputed ancestors of other states, see: ibid., IV, 418–419. *Tso*, 665::667 (Chao 17), 742::744 (Ting 1).

124. For instance, the rulers of the far southeastern state of Yüeh were supposed to be descended from the sixth ruler of the Hsia dynasty (*Mémoires historiques*, IV, 418–419). This dynasty can hardly be called historical, since we have no solid evidence to corroborate the traditions concerning it. But we have to be cautious, for the recent discovery and decipherment of Shang inscriptions has shown that the transmitted list of the Shang Kings is remarkably accurate. As for the state of Yüeh, we know virtually nothing of its early history. Thus, while skepticism regarding this genealogy is justified, we can hardly say that it is certainly false.

125. The efforts of Ssu-Ma Ch'ien to produce order out of the sometimes chaotic mass of tradition, and the footnotes of Chavannes pointing out the difficulties, make this very clear; see *Mémoires historiques*, I, 25–96.

126. Such use of genealogy has not been confined to China, of course, but this would seem to be one of the most extensive and effective cases of its employment.

127. *Tso*, 181–182::183 (Hsi 22), 313::319 (Hsüan 12), 392::397 (Ch'eng 16).

128. *Tso*, 422::424 (Hsiang 4), 657::659 (Chao 15).

his words be sincere and faithful, and his actions earnest and respectful." One who conducts himself in this way will get along very well, he said, even in the states of the barbarians. There are other passages of similar nature in the *Analects*.[129] The *Historical Records* even includes a passage, attributed to the seventh century B.C. but certainly written much later, in which the states of the Jung and the I are idealized and said to be much better governed than the Chinese states because they are not burdened with the institutions of civilization.[130]

The *Tso-chuan* describes an interview, between Confucius and the ruler of a small state, in which Confucius asked for information about the governmental arrangements of the ruler's ancestors. Afterward Confucius commented, "I have heard the saying, 'When the administration of the Son of Heaven is in disorder, seek information among the barbarians.' It seems to be correct." The story is certainly apocryphal, but the saying may well have been current.[131] Many Chinese undoubtedly realized that there were things to be learned from the traditions of many peoples. Quite clearly it was the confluence of numerous traditions, and the opportunity that this provided for cross-fertilization and selection, that made Chinese culture great, just as the interaction of many city-states produced the glory that was classical Greece.

THIS thumbnail sketch of the status of barbarians during the Chou dynasty throws some revealing light on Western Chou. Imitation is indeed the most sincere form of flattery. If it is true as Ku Tung-kao wrote that among all the states of the Spring and Autumn period Ch'u "attained the highest excellence of administrative institutions," the fact that rulers of Ch'u repeatedly cited the Western Chou government as a model, and adopted its practices, is very significant. They had little reason to be prejudiced in its favor, for Ch'u was almost continuously in conflict with the Chinese states. The rulers of Ch'u were close to Western Chou both in time and in space; they had access to information that has not been and never will be available to later scholars. Their testimonial to the effectiveness of Western Chou

129. *Analects*, 9.13, 13.19, 15.5.

130. *Mémoires historiques*, II, 40–42. The appearance of the name of the Yellow Emperor, if nothing else, would show this passage to have been written later than the seventh century B.C. Ssu-Ma Kuang thought that it was written under Taoist influence, and this is probably correct; see *Shih-chi*, 5.33, commentary.

131. *Tso*, 665–666::667–668 (Chao 17). The whole tone of this passage is that of the Warring States period rather than of Confucius' time. This is especially true of the use of the numbers five and nine.

administration is perhaps as impressive as any that could be imagined.

It is also worthy of note that references to early Western Chou rulers, quoted by the *Tso-chuan* as being made by rulers and ministers of Ch'u, do not alone praise them for the efficiency with which they held their territories in subjection. They also praise Kings Wen and Wu for their courtesy, clemency, and conciliation, and their policy of "giving repose to the people and harmonizing the multitudes."[132] It may be argued, of course, that these are merely little Confucian homilies written by the editors of the *Tso-chuan* and made more effective by being put into the mouths of barbarians.[133] This is certainly possible, and such speeches were probably, at the least, embellished. But the Ch'u rulers wanted very strongly to get control of the whole Chinese world, and were clearly much impressed by the earlier success of the Western Chou rulers. And they apparently realized that that success had not been achieved by military might and repression alone.

While the Western Chou sources give us little information on the treatment of barbarians at that time, the picture they do give is one of frequent military chastisement and probable exploitation. Yet we have seen that in the Spring and Autumn period the relations between Chinese and barbarians were not by any means a matter of unmitigated hostility. Barbarians intermarried with Chinese and fought beside them as well as against them. And it seems clear that, however the Chinese treated them, the barbarians in general developed a good deal of admiration for Chinese culture—so much so that the great majority of them ended by becoming Chinese. Undoubtedly many of them were subjected to more or less forcible conversion, but in a number of cases this was the result of wholly voluntary acculturation.

WE have seen that in Spring and Autumn times the various barbarian groups constituted a factor of very considerable political importance. Yet in spite of the relative completeness of our information for that period, there is—except in the case of first-class powers like Ch'u and Wu—very little mention of political activity in connection with them. It is almost as if the Chinese wished to ignore the existence of the bar-

---

132. *Tso*, 147::147 (Hsi 7), 315::320 (Hsüan 12), 341::347 (Ch'eng 2).

133. I did argue this very vehemently concerning the long speech attributed to King Chuang of Ch'u (*Tso*, 315::320 [Hsüan 12]), in Creel, *Confucius*, 203–204::220–221. I think there is little doubt that this speech is embellished, and it may of course be entirely false. But in fact conquerors often do avow themselves to be dedicated to peace and conciliation, once their conquests have been secured—this is, of course, necessary to consolidate their gains.

barians. For Western Chou we have so little information that it is difficult to form a comparable judgment. But certainly it is also true that the Western Chou Chinese did have political, or at least administrative, dealings with the barbarians, and that we have very little record of them. In fact, barbarians are only rarely mentioned in the Western Chou sources, except as the enemy in war.

We have seen that the state of Lu boasts, in the *Poetry*, that the Huai I and certain other barbarian groups have been conquered by it and rendered obedient, but when we look at the record of later times it would seem that this either described a temporary phenomenon or was a sheer exercise of poetic license. Again we read that the two tribes of Chui and Mo were "given" by the King to the Marquis of Hán, and that he also was charged with supervising a number of barbarian tribes. Elsewhere the *Poetry* describes a great expedition sent out by the King against the Hsien-yün barbarians, with the result that they were "pacified."[134] But what does all this mean? How did they supervise? Did they pacify barbarians merely by defeating them in war and then keeping them in fear of punishment? Or was there some kind of regular administration over the barbarians?

Apparently there was, but our clues to it are very slight. Most of our information comes from two bronze inscriptions, both dated to the reign of King Hsüan (827–782 B.C.).[135] As so often happens with important inscriptions, they are difficult to interpret in detail. But even the broad outlines are illuminating.

One of them is made by a royal officer named Hsi Chia, who apparently is charged by the King with the responsibility of collecting taxes "from Ch'eng-Chou to the southern Huai I." The King tells Hsi Chia that "the Huai I have long been my tributary people." They have never dared, he says, not to make the required payments of goods and of labor service.[136] If they do not obey orders, they are to be punished and attacked.[137]

The second inscription begins: The King said, "Commander Huan, the Huai I have long been my tributary subjects." But now, he says,

---

134. *Shih,* 112–113, 232, 256–257, 260.

135. These inscriptions are so dated both by Kuo Mo-jo in *Chin-wen,* 143b, 146a, and by Hsü Chung-shu in "Yü Ting," 62. One of them, the "Hsi Chia P'an," is so dated by Wang Kuo-wei, *Kuan-t'ang Pieh-chi Pu-i,* 14a.

136. Kuo Mo-jo interprets this as labor service, but Hsü Chung-shu says they provided slaves; the text could be interpreted in either way.

137. *Chin-wen,* 143b. Hsü, "Yü Ting," 62. Wang, *Kuan-t'ang Pieh-chi Pu-i,* 14a–15a. The balance of this inscription is undoubtedly important, and both Kuo and Hsü give interpretations of it, but in my opinion its meaning is uncertain.

"they have rebelled against their Supervisors,[138] and do not follow after my eastern states." The King therefore orders Commander Huan to attack the Huai I and punish them.[139]

This reference to "Supervisors" is the clearest evidence we have of royal officers specifically charged with the function of overseeing barbarians. Ch'en Meng-chia says that they "seem to be officials sent by the Chou house to the various barbarians." Another inscription refers to a royal official whose title appears to be "Director of Supervisors"; whether he was in charge of such supervisors of barbarians it is difficult to say.[140]

If it is possible even to frame a hypothesis with so little evidence, it would appear that various barbarian tribes that were nominally subject to the Chou were permitted to function under their own chieftains, so long as they remained obedient. They seem to have been expected to "follow after" the neighboring Chinese states—presumably meaning that those states were expected to provide them an example, and to keep a watchful eye on them. But the King's tax collectors took tribute from them, and they were required to provide labor service. Officers called Supervisors were placed among them to see that they acted properly. When they did not, the King dispatched an army to chastise them, even if it meant sending it to the farthest corner of the realm.

Two other inscriptions refer to groups of I who apparently served at the capital and perhaps in the palace. No doubt some of them were servants, but it appears likely that some of them were guards. Kuo Mo-jo says that they were slaves. This is possible, but if they were used as guards in close proximity to the court, it is unlikely that they were treated very badly.[141]

In the *Book of Changes* barbarians are mentioned only twice, both

---

138. *Kung-li* 工 吏 is a difficult term to translate. The common sense of *kung* is "work," so that one might be tempted to translate the title as "Work Official." But in the Western Chou sections of the *Documents*, and in the *Poetry*, *kung* seems always to have some such sense as "officer"; see *Shu*, 39, 45, 46, 52, 53, and *Shih*, 162, 163, 244. Since *li* also means "officer," we might take this as a compound term merely meaning "official." In *Shih*, 162 and 163, Karlgren translates *kung chu* 工 祝 as "officiating invoker." These *Kung-li* would appear to be officers sent to superintend the barbarians; I therefore translate the title as "Supervisor." For discussion of this term, see: *Chin-wen*, 146ab. Ch'en, "Hsi-Chou T'ung-ch'i," (6).121. Ssu, "Liang-Chou Chih-kuan K'ao," 13.

139. *Chin-wen*, 146a. Hsü, "Yü Ting," 62.

140. Ch'en, "Hsi-Chou T'ung-ch'i," (6).121. *Chin-wen*, 118a.

141. *Chin-wen*, 88b. Kuo, *Wen-shih Lun-chi*, 348–350. In one of these inscriptions the "Western Gate I" are listed immediately after the Tiger Retainer, who

times as the objects of military attack. In those sections of the *Documents* that I regard as of Western Chou date, there is a single reference to them; it comes in a brief harangue addressed by a feudal lord to his troops, who are about to attack the Huai I and the Jung of Hsü.[142] Of the three hundred and five poems in the *Poetry*, fourteen mention barbarians, and eleven of these are concerned with military operations. Of the remaining three, one speaks of the necessity for military preparedness in order to keep the barbarians at a distance, one speaks of supervising the barbarians, and one uses barbarians as an example of inconstancy.[143] The bronze inscriptions have many references to barbarians, which it will be useful to review in some detail.

The reign of King Ch'eng (1115–1079 B.C.) immediately followed that of Wu, the conqueror. It saw the great revolt of the Shang and eastern peoples, which was crushed by the eastern expedition of the Duke of Chou, and the military consolidation of the Chou rule. It is natural, therefore, that we should find a good deal of reference to military activity against barbarians. One inscription may relate to the eastern expedition; it says that the Duke of Chou made a punitive attack on certain states of the eastern I, and extinguished them.[144]

Three attacks on barbarians in the east were led by the King in person. One was against the Earl of Ch'u—at this time that state is believed to have been located farther east than it was later. Another was on a Marquis, the name of whose state is in question. The third was simply on "eastern I." The King also ordered the Duke of Mao to lead a large force to attack "all the eastern states" of certain Jung.[145]

Already in this early reign we read of barbarian revolts. Presumably those who revolted had previously been, or had been believed to be, brought to subjection. One inscription records that "the Duke Grand Protector came to attack the revolting I." Whether this Grand

---

was apparently in charge of the royal bodyguard, and in the other almost immediately after him. The *Ritual of Chou* mentions *I li* 夷隸, a part of whose function is to guard the royal palace, carrying weapons; see *Chou-li*, 36.16ab, and Biot, *Tcheou-li*, II, 372–373.

142. Legge, *I-ching*, 205, 208. *Shu*, 80.

143. *Shih*, 111–112, 112–113, 120–121, 122–123, 177, 190, 218, 232, 233–234, 234–236, 256–257, 260–261, 265–266, 266.

144. Ch'en, "Hsi-Chou T'ung-chi," (1).168–169. The inscription mentions the "eastern I" and two named states. Ch'en interprets this to mean that there were three states, of which the "eastern I" was one, and that all were extinguished. This is possible, of course, but we find the eastern I mentioned so constantly thereafter that it is clear that in fact they were not extinguished. I realize, of course, that states are said to be extinguished and then reappear, but it seems to me more likely that the two states are mentioned as being states of the eastern I.

145. *Chin-wen*, 3b, 11b, 20b, 28a. Ch'en, "Hsi-Chou T'ung-ch'i," (1).174–175; (2).70–73, 73–76, 76–79.

Protector was the Duke of Shao, or the son of the Duke of Chou, is in some question, but the trouble must have been serious to demand the attention of one of the highest officers in the land. Again we read that "the King ordered Nan Kung to attack the revolting Tiger Territory." This "Tiger Territory" was mentioned in the Shang inscriptions, and was apparently in the southeast. The King ordered another officer to attack the "eastern revolting I." Another inscription begins: "The eastern I greatly rebelled. Po Mou Fu led the troops of the eight Yin garrisons[146] to make a punitive expedition against the eastern I." This was a large operation; one commander took his troops all the way to the seacoast. Since the King later rewarded the army, it is clear that the expedition was made by royal command.[147]

The genuine *Bamboo Books* says that under King Ch'eng and his successor, King K'ang (1078–1053 B.C.), "all under heaven was at peace." These words are repeated in the *Historical Records*.[148] This is probably a part of the legend of the manner in which a "great peace" enveloped the land in the wake of the Chou conquest. It may be that the latter years of Ch'eng's long reign were relatively less troubled than its turbulent beginning, but the bronze inscriptions show that the reign of K'ang was by no means uneventful. Two of them tell of warfare with barbarians. In this reign we find the first specific reference to the Huai I, who were destined to be the cause of so much difficulty. The introduction is fitting. The King says, "The Huai I have dared to attack the interior states," and directs that appropriate countermeasures be taken.[149]

One of the most interesting of all inscriptions in which barbarians are mentioned is dated to the reign of King K'ang. The people it concerns were located in the northwest. Their country is called the "Demon Territory" (*Kuei Fang* 鬼方). It is mentioned in the Shang inscriptions, and the *Book of Changes* says that a Shang King—probably Wu Ting (1324–1266 B.C.)—"attacked the Demon Territory, and conquered it after three years." There is ground for believing that these people were a division of the Ti, and scholars identify them with various barbarian groups mentioned in Western Chou and in Spring and Autumn times.[150]

---

146. Concerning the nature of the "eight Yin garrisons" see pp. 305–309.

147. *Chin-wen*, 17a, 20a, 23a–24b, 27a. Ch'en, "Hsi-Chou T'ung-ch'i," (1).170, 170–173, 173–174.

148. Wang, *Ku Chu-shu*, 7a. This passage is repeated verbatim, without citation of source, in *Shih-chi*, 4.42 (*Mémoires historiques*, I, 250).

149. *Chin-wen*, 61b. Ch'en, "Hsi-Chou T'ung-ch'i," (5).108.

150. Legge, *I-ching*, 205; see also ibid, 208. This "Demon Territory" has been much discussed, with somewhat varying conclusions, but it is generally agreed that it was located in the northwest, and that the King referred to in the *Book of*

This inscription records a great triumphal celebration of victories over the Demon Territory, which took place in the Chou ancestral temple at the capital. The account is impressive, even in this at times undecipherable language. The effect is one of great spaces, dimmed light, awe-inspiring and sometimes gruesome pageantry. It opens with the entry of the various dignitaries, and of the King. The maker of the vessel, Yü, announces that, having received the royal command to attack the Demon Territory, he did so. In two campaigns he captured many prisoners and much booty, which he enumerates for each campaign. Combining the two, the total is: Three chieftains. Five thousand and forty-nine severed left ears (or heads)[151] of the slain. More than (some of the numerals are missing) thirteen thousand and eighty-one men. More than one hundred and four horses. More than one hundred and thirty vehicles (these were probably carts rather than war chariots).[152] Three hundred and fifty-five cattle. Thirty-eight sheep.

The King then congratulates Yü. Yü brings forward the three captive chiefs, and the King orders that they be interrogated as to the reason they have resisted the Chou. The reply is in part unintelligible; Ch'en Meng-chia suggests that they say that they have been harassed by a Chou vassal, to the point where they were impelled to join in revolt with the Shang. It appears that these "Shang" were some subjects of the former dynasty who, unwilling to live under the conqueror, had fled to a peripheral area where they could hope to live in freedom. The interrogation being completed, the three chieftains are decapitated. The thousands of severed ears (or heads) are then offered as a burnt sacrifice.[153]

In the succeeding reign of King Chao (1052–1002 B.C.) the attention shifts to the south, foreshadowing the menace of the rising power of Ch'u. The genuine *Bamboo Books* and the *Historical Records* speak only of trouble with the south at this time, and bronze inscriptions attributed to this reign agree in locating its military campaigns almost

---

Changes is Wu Ting. See Ch'en, *Yin Tz'u Tsung-shu,* 274–275, and Ch'en, "Hsi-Chou T'ung-ch'i," (2).88. For a map, giving his somewhat different opinion as to where in the northwest these people were located in Shang times, see Tung Tso-pin, *Yin-li P'u, hsia,* 9.40b.

151. There is much discussion as to whether the character *kuo* 䤴 (and 䤴 which is considered to be its alternate form) refers to severed left ears or heads. See Ch'en, "Hsi-Chou T'ung-ch'i," (4).86–88. In *Tso,* 350::352 (Ch'eng 3), we find a captive officer who apparently has lost his *kuo* 䤴 yet continues to live; obviously it was not his head that was cut off. The character may have been used with more than one significance, and of course its meaning may have changed over time.

152. See p. 266.

153. *Chin-wen,* 35a–38b. Ch'en, "Hsi-Chou T'ung-ch'i," (4).85–89.

exclusively in the southern region.[154] Kuo Mo-jo assigns to this period an inscription that some would date as late as the reign of King Li (878–828 B.C.). In it, the King says that a certain southern state has dared to make incursions into his territory. He therefore attacked it, pressing as far as its capital. The upshot was that "all the southern I and eastern I, twenty-six states," came to him in submission.[155] This is a rare instance, in the Western Chou sources, of recognizing that the barbarian groups were political entities, dealt with as such.

The genuine *Bamboo Books*, as reconstructed by Wang Kuo-wei, has three entries concerning King Chao. The first says that in his sixteenth year he attacked Ch'u-Ching (Ch'u was also called Ching, or sometimes Ch'u-Ching) and crossed the Han river where he met a large rhinoceros. The second says that in his nineteenth year he lost (his) six armies[156] on the Han river. The third says that in his last year King Chao made a tour to the south and did not return. We saw previously that in the *Tso-chuan* King Chao is said to have failed to return from an expedition to the south, and that more than three centuries later Ch'u was asked to explain what had happened to him.[157]

The mystery has never been solved. But several inscriptions dated to this time (in addition to the one mentioned above) seem to attest King Chao's military activity in the southern region. One says merely that "the King made a punitive military expedition against the southern I." Another reports that "Tzu followed the King in attacking Ching," that is, Ch'u, and used his booty to cast a bronze. A third says that "the Earl of Kuo followed the King to attack rebelling Ching, and captured metal." The fact that Ching is said here to have been in rebellion might seem to indicate that it had previously been subject to the Chou; it is possible that Ch'u was one of the "twenty-six states" that were subdued. Yet the Chinese have long had a tendency to call

154. Wang, *Ku Chu-shu*, 7a. *Shih-chi*, 4.42; *Mémoires historiques*, I, 250. Such unanimity may, however, be less important than it appears, for in dating inscriptions scholars have a tendency to be influenced by the traditional history. For instance, an inscription (*Chin-wen*, 120b) that is dated by Kuo Mo-jo to the reign of King Li (878–828 B.C.) is assigned to that of King Chao by Ch'en Meng-chia, in "Hsi-Chou T'ung-ch'i," (5).117–118. This inscription says, "The King made a punitive military expedition against the southern I." Ch'en says, "If we ascribe this vessel to the time of King Chao, then it corresponds with the historical fact that King Chao made a punitive expedition to the south." Ch'en probably had additional evidence for this ascription, but he does not state any.

155. *Chin-wen*, 51a–54a.

156. Six was the regular number of the King's armies at this time. See pp. 305–308.

157. Wang, *Ku Chu-shu*, 7a. *Tso*, 139::140 (Hsi 4).

every enemy a rebel, and it seems probable that if Ch'u ever was subject to the Chou it was not for long. It should be noted also that, if in fact King Chao attacked Ch'u in the region of the Han river, that state, by this time at least, controlled an area that was almost directly south of the eastern Chou capital, so that Ch'u was already a southern power.[158]

King Mu (1001–947 B.C.) is said by the genuine *Bamboo Books* to have carried on extensive military expeditions in every direction, but it seems likely that these accounts include some traditions of dubious value. The *Historical Records* lists only one expedition against barbarians for this reign, and bronze inscriptions dated to it include none that mentions military activity.[159] Throughout the next three reigns, of Kings Kung (946–935 B.C.), I (934–910 B.C.), and Hsiao (909–895 B.C.), there is no mention of war or barbarians in the bronze inscriptions, the genuine *Bamboo Books*, or the *Historical Records*.[160] Under King Í (894–879 B.C.) there is very little mention of war with barbarians, and in what there was the Chinese appear to have held the initiative. The genuine *Bamboo Books* tells of one expedition, in which the King ordered the Duke of Kuo to attack certain Jung to the north; he did so and captured a thousand horses.[161] We have a bronze inscription, supposedly made by the ruler of Kuo, who relates that he attacked the Hsien-yün barbarians in an area that may have been very close to that named in the *Bamboo Books*. He reports to the King that he cut off five hundred heads and captured fifty prisoners for interrogation. The genuineness of this inscription seems, however, to be in some question.[162]

This long period of relative quiet may well have persuaded the Chinese that the barbarian menace had at last been brought under effec-

---

158. *Chin-wen*, 54a, 54b, 120b. Ch'en, "Hsi-Chou T'ung-ch'i," (5).117–118.

159. Wang, *Ku Chu-shu*, 7a–8b. *Shih-chi*, 4.46–47; *Mémoires historiques*, I, 258–259. Hostilities with barbarians are mentioned in *Chin-wen*, 61b, which Kuo Mo-jo dates to this reign, but this bronze is assigned to that of King K'ang in Ch'en, "Hsi-Chou T'ung-ch'i," (5).108.

160. It must be noted, however, that both the genuine *Bamboo Books* and the *Historical Records* have very little information of any sort on these reigns. *Chin-wen*, 90b, which Kuo Mo-jo dates to the reign of I, does say that a certain Secretary has cast a bronze to use "to follow the King in punitive military expeditions," but it does not say that there were any such expeditions.

161. Wang, *Ku Chu-shu*, 8a. The *Historical Records* has no information on this, and almost nothing on any other subject, for the reign of King Í. War with barbarians is mentioned in *Chin-wen*, 106a, 107ab, 108b–109a, and 109b–110a, which Kuo Mo-jo formerly dated to this reign. But he later changed the dating of all these inscriptions to the reign of King Li; see Kuo, "Yü Ting Po."

162. Concerning the genuineness of *Chin-wen*, 103b–104a, see p. 473.

tive control. If it did, they were to be disillusioned, for the storm was about to break.

The reign of King Li (878–828 B.C.) was exceedingly troubled. On that point all accounts are agreed, and even the bronze inscriptions contain bitter laments.[163] But on the exact nature of the troubles there are great differences of opinion, and their causes remain obscure. The *Historical Records* devotes a great deal of space to this period without shedding much light on it, and with no mention at all of clashes with barbarians, which undoubtedly were an essential aspect of the situation. This tendency to ignore the existence of the barbarians, which persisted into much later times, creates a serious lacuna in the historical record. An account of the "eastern I" written in the fifth century A.D. says that "King Li lacked [the Right] Way; the Huai I invaded and plundered. The King ordered Kuo Chung to attack and punish them, but he could not defeat them." Wang Kuo-wei believes that this passage is quoted from the genuine *Bamboo Books*.[164] The passage implies, in the usual moralistic manner of orthodox Chinese history, that the barbarian inroads were a consequence of the King's lack of virtue. In a sense, they may have been, but whether they were caused by Chinese mistreatment of the barbarians, or occasioned by the lack of military vigilance, or both, is not wholly clear.

Five inscriptions dated to the time of King Li tell of war with barbarians. One of them relates that, when the Hsien-yün made an invasion, the Marquis of E commanded a part of the royal armies that repulsed them. He cut off many heads and took many prisoners for interrogation, and was richly rewarded.[165]

A second reports that the "southern Huai I" made an incursion that penetrated as far as a place that Kuo Mo-jo identifies as Shang-hsien, in the southeast of the modern Shensi province. This is a long distance from the coastal region that was the normal habitat of the Huai I, and at first glance such an excursion seems improbable. Yet in 1934 and 1935 the Red Army of the Chinese Communists made a longer march, from Kiangsi province to Yenan in northern Shensi, in spite of enemies equipped with wireless communications and airplanes. The Huai I may have been equally hardy. The maker of this vessel

---

163. *Ch-ing-t'ung-ch'i T'u-shih* (preface by T'ang Lan), 2–3.

164. *Hou-Han Shu*, 85.1b. Wang, *Ku Chu-shu*, 8a. The current text of the *Bamboo Books*, which is generally considered a forgery, includes much but not all of this passage; see Wang, *Chin Chu-shu*, (2).9a.

165. *Chin-wen*, 106a. The maker is not actually identified as "Marquis of E" in this inscription, but Kuo Mo-jo makes the identification from his name, and it seems clearly correct.

says that he fulfilled the King's order to repulse them, cutting off a hundred heads, capturing forty prisoners for interrogation, and taking four hundred men prisoner.[166]

Two of these inscriptions tell of military expeditions to the south led by the King in person. One of these was specifically against the southern Huai I. On his return from the other one the King stopped to be entertained by the Marquis of E, who was mentioned above. There was a banquet and an archery contest, a form of entertainment that in feudal China filled something of the place of the tournament in feudal Europe. The King presented gifts to the Marquis, not—as was usual —through an intermediary, but in person, apparently as a mark of special favor.[167]

The Marquis of E was evidently a person of consequence. His state is said to have dated from Shang times, and his family was intermarried with the Chou royal house. The location of his fief has been much debated. The two most probable locations are either in southern Honan, or possibly even farther south and east, in Hupei province near the site of the city of Wuchang. Hsü Chung-shu suggests that the Chou depended upon him to control the southern and eastern barbarians, and this is not impossible.[168] We have seen that in one inscription a King implied that the Huai I were expected to "follow after" the neighboring Chinese states, and it is clear that the Marquis of E had great influence with the barbarians of his region.

A long inscription on a bronze unearthed in 1942 has disclosed an event, previously unknown to history, that was considered, at the time, a major disaster.[169] The inscription says: "Alas! Woe! Heaven has sent down destruction upon all the states. The Marquis of E . . . has led the southern Huai I and the eastern I in a great attack upon [our] southern states and eastern states, all the way to . . . " a place that has not been identified. Concerning the background of this inva-

---

166. *Chin-wen*, 109b–110a. As to the difference between "prisoners for interrogation," *hsün* 訊, and ordinary prisoners, *jen* 人, one can only conjecture. It seems probable that the former were important men, who might be held responsible for resisting the Chinese, or who might be able to divulge useful information.

167. *Chin-wen*, 107a–107b, 120a.

168. Hsü, "Yü Ting," 62–63. *Ch-ing-t'ung-ch'i T'u-shih*, 2–4. *Chin-wen*, 107b–108a.

169. Hsü, "Yü Ting," 53. Kuo, "Yü Ting Po." In one sense this inscription had long been known, for what seems to be the same inscription (perhaps copied from a vessel identically inscribed) has been known since Sung times in a hand-copied form. But this copy, it is now clear, included many mistakes. Thus Kuo Mo-jo acknowledges that his former explanation of this inscription was erroneous in some very crucial respects (*Chin-wen*, 108b).

sion we know nothing. It seems possible to conjecture, however, that the Marquis of E thought that if King Wu had been able, two centuries earlier, to lead the "western I" (as the *Bamboo Books* says) to conquer the Shang, he might do equally well with the eastern I. There is little doubt that the Chou rule was by this time less firm than it had been in the beginning, and it is obvious that there must have been resentments and ambitions among the barbarians that the Marquis could work upon.

It is hard to determine the actual course of the war from this inscription, and this may not be solely because of the difficulties of translation. Mortal combat is usually a confused and confusing business, and the well-known "fog of war" makes it difficult even for participants and commanders to follow the course of events with precision.

The King was enraged at the defection of his vassal. "The King then ordered the troops of the western six garrisons and the Yin eight garrisons, saying, 'Attack the Marquis of E, and do not spare either the old or the young!' " These armies, however, were for some reason unable to undertake this mission. Hsü Chung-shu says that they were afraid to attack E. But T'ang Lan interprets this part of the inscription to mean that they were so occupied with defending other areas that they could not move against E. This is plausible, for the invaders had probably attacked at various points. In any event, this task was undertaken by the troops of a certain Duke Wu, which not only attacked E but also captured the Marquis.[170]

The fate of the Marquis of E and of his state seems to be unknown. But in any case it is unlikely that the King could any longer depend upon that state to exercise surveillance over the southern and eastern barbarians. The next King, Hsüan (827–782 B.C.), appears to have established the Earl of Shen, in a state located near the southern border of the modern Honan province, for the purpose of carrying on this function.

A long poem in the *Poetry*, which is assigned to this reign both by tradition and by some modern scholars,[171] says that the state of Shen became "a support to Chou," a "fence" and a "protecting wall" to all the Chinese states.[172] "Vigorous was the Earl of Shen . . . he went

170. For various readings and interpretations of this inscription, see: *Ch'ing-t'ung-chi T'u-shih*, 2–4, 24, and plate 78. Hsü, "Yü Ting." Kuo, "Yü Ting Po." Ch'en, "Yü Ting K'ao-shih." The identity of Duke Wu is much debated, but certainty on this point seems to be impossible.

171. *Mao-shih*, 18(3).1a. Ting, "Shao Mu Kung Chuan," 97.

172. *Shih*, 226–227. The poem as a whole is devoted entirely to the establish-

and took up his residence in Hsieh, he became a model to the southern states. The King commanded the Earl of Shao to establish the dwelling of the Earl of Shen; he went to that southern state. . . . The King charged the Earl of Shen to be a model to those southern states. . . . The King sent to the Earl of Shen a state carriage and a team of four horses, [saying]: 'I have planned for your residence, the southern land is the best. . . . Go, King's uncle, to protect the southern territories.' . . . The King commanded the Earl of Shao to tax the soil and territory of the Earl of Shen, in order to furnish his provisions of grain; and so he hurried on his march. The Earl of Shen, very martial, has entered into Hsieh; his footmen and charioteers are very numerous. All of the Chou states rejoice, for warfare they have an excellent support; the greatly illustrious Earl of Shen, eldest uncle of the King, is a model in peace and in war. The virtue of the Earl of Shen is mild, kindly, and upright; he tranquilizes these myriad states, his renown spreads throughout the land."[173]

Another poem refers to the work of the Earl of Shao, who in the one just quoted was charged with establishing the Earl of Shen in his fief and taxing his territories. This poem begins by describing a great military action against the Huai I, which resulted in tranquilizing the whole realm. Then "the King ordered [Earl] Hu of Shao,[174] 'Open up the regions of the four quarters, tax my territories and soil, without distressing, without pressing; go all through the royal states, go and draw boundaries, go and make divisions, all the way to the southern sea.' "[175]

This poem is reminiscent of a bronze inscription, also dated to the reign of King Hsüan, that was mentioned earlier. In it the King orders the officer Hsi Chia to collect taxes from his territories all the way from the eastern Chou capital at Ch'eng-Chou to the southern Huai I. The King says that "the Huai I have long been my tributary people,"

---

ment of Shen, but these statements are made, in its opening stanza, about both the states of Shen and of Lü. We have good evidence that these states did in fact function as buffers between the Chinese states on the north and non-Chinese lands to the south. *Tso*, 362::363 (Ch'eng 7), records a conversation of 584 B.C., when these states have passed into the possession of Ch'u, in which they are described as a protection for that southern state against the north.

173. *Shih*, 226–228. See also: *Mao-shih*, 18(3).1a–11a. Waley, *Shih*, 133–135. Legge, *Shih*, 535–540. Waley makes the Earl of Shen the "father-in-law" of the King, but I have followed the preponderant scholarly opinion.

174. This "Hu of Shao" seems clearly to be the "Earl of Shao" of the previously quoted poem. Two bronze inscriptions that Kuo Mo-jo dates to the reign of King Hsüan (*Chin-wen*, 142a, 144b) name "Earl Hu of Shao."

175. *Shih*, 233–234.

and have never dared to fail to make the required payments of goods and labor service. If they are not obedient, they are to be punished and attacked.[176]

A second inscription, also dated to this reign (and also quoted previously), indicates that punishment became necessary. It begins: "The King said, 'Commander Huan, the Huai I have long been my tributary subjects.' " But now "they have rebelled against their Supervisors and do not follow after my eastern states." The King orders Huan to attack the Huai I and punish four chieftains, whom he names. Huan presses the attack and cuts off heads, takes prisoners for interrogation, and captures "men, women, sheep, cattle, and metal."[177]

Only one other military action against barbarians, an attack led by the King against the Hsien-yün, is mentioned in bronze inscriptions dated to this reign.[178] The *Discourses of the States* has a story (which the *Historical Records* repeats in abbreviated form) to the effect that King Hsüan neglected his ritual duties, and—presumably for this reason—his army was defeated in battle by certain Jung. The genuine *Bamboo Books* reports seven conflicts with barbarians during this reign, all with Jung.[179]

The final reign of Western Chou, that of King Yu (781–770 BC.), was brief and undoubtedly troubled. The *Tso-chuan* records an announcement made by a scion of the Chou house in 516 B.C., which includes this statement: "When [the rule] came to King Yu, Heaven did not pity Chou. The King was benighted and did not follow [a proper course], and lost his throne."[180] Only a few bronze inscriptions are dated to this reign, and they say nothing about barbarians. Yet there are such persistent traditions, occurring in a number of sources including the *Tso-chuan*, attesting to widespread troubles with barbarians in the time of King Yu, that they undoubtedly have some basis in fact.[181]

The *Discourses of the States* includes a long conversation that is supposed to have taken place between Duke Huan of Cheng, who was Director of the Multitude under King Yu, and the royal Grand Secretary. This conversation, at least in the form in which we have it,

176. *Chin-wen*, 143b.
177. *Chin-wen*, 146a.
178. *Chin-wen*, 143b.
179. *Kuo-yü*, 1.6b–8b. *Shih-chi*, 4.59; *Mémoires historiques*, I, 276–277. Wang, *Ku Chu-shu*, 8ab.
180. *Tso*, 714::717 (Chao 26).
181. *Tso*, 593::597 (Chao 4), says that "the Jung and Ti revolted" from King Yu. See also: *Kuo-yü*, 16.1a–6b. *Shih-chi*, 4.65; *Mémoires historiques*, I, 284–285. *Hou-Han Shu*, 85.2a, 87.2ab.

was certainly written at a time much later than Western Chou; nevertheless it is interesting as an analysis of the situation that was made, at all events, before Han times.[182] The Duke tells the Grand Secretary that he fears the Chou power is doomed and wishes to know where he can flee for safety. The Grand Secretary tells him that some of the strongest of the Chinese states are disaffected toward the royal house, and that there are many barbarian groups that are very formidable. And he predicts that the destruction of Western Chou will come, in part, at the hands of barbarians.

The story of the end of Western Chou, as it is told in the *Discourses of the States* and the *Historical Records*, includes supernatural elements, but it may well be based on fact. Omitting the embellishments, it is said that King Yu had incurred the deadly enmity of the ruler of Shen. It will be recalled that Shen had been established to be "a support to Chou" and "a protecting wall" for the Chinese states against the barbarians. Nevertheless, it is related, the ruler of Shen allied himself with two groups of barbarians and attacked the King and killed him. His successor was established in the eastern Chou capital, under the patronage of a group of feudal lords.[183] So ended Western Chou.

---

182. *Kuo-yü*, 16.1a–6b. This conversation has supernatural elements that are more common in literature of the Warring States period. It also makes predictions that were almost certainly made after the events had come to pass. And it makes use of the concept of the five "elements" (*wu-hsing* 五行) in a manner that is not found until the Warring States period.

183. *Shih-chi*, 4.65–66; *Mémoires historiques*, I, 284–285. *Kuo-yü*, 16.6ab. The latter work gives only part of this story, and not as history but as prediction.

CHAPTER

10

The Military

ALTHOUGH no government can maintain itself for long by force alone, every government must, if it is to survive, have effective control of the use of force within its territory. Thus continuous command of the military, while it is by no means the only essential, is one of the prime requisites for stable government. And the character of the military forces of a state, and the manner in which they are controlled, are very significant factors that have broad and deep influence not only on its administration but even on the culture of its people.

It is well known that the Chinese attitude toward the military has, in most periods of Chinese history, been rather different from that found among many other peoples. It is sometimes said that the Chinese have been "pacifistic," but this is hard to reconcile with their many bloody wars and sometimes far-flung conquests. A more judicious appraisal is that of John King Fairbank: "Disparagement of the soldier is deeply ingrained in the old Chinese system of values."[1] Even this has not always been true, but there are not many generalizations that will apply to every segment of this long and complex tradition.

If we compare the status of the military man in China with the position that he has enjoyed in many other parts of the world, a significant difference is apparent. The only other great early state that is really comparable with China is the Western Roman Empire. A look at the Roman situation in this regard helps one to appreciate the distinctive character of the Chinese attitude and its bearing upon government.

It has been said that the Romans' "main industry was war."[2] They venerated the Trojan warrior Aeneas as their ancestral hero and

---

1. Fairbank, *The United States and China*, 50.
2. *Cambridge Ancient History*, IX, 789.

ascribed the founding of their city to Romulus, the son of Mars, god of war. In Rome it was almost without exception military service and achievement that carried the highest prestige. Under the Republic the armies were commanded by the Consuls, the highest officials of the state. Candidates for public office were always in theory and commonly in fact required to be veterans, sometimes of as many as ten campaigns. When Augustus became Emperor, he made service as an army officer a prerequisite for a governmental career, and offices of importance continued to be filled, in large part, by men of military background.[3]

Rostovtzeff says that under Septimius Severus, who reigned from A.D. 193 to 211:

> The old upper classes were gradually eliminated from the commanding posts in the army and from the administrative posts in the provinces. They were replaced by a new military aristocracy. Like the emperors themselves, this aristocracy sprang from the ranks of the Roman army and, like the emperors, it was subject to perpetual change: new men constantly rose from the rank and file of the army to replace those who were advanced to equestrian offices and to a seat in the senate.[4]

Under later Emperors, as the administration became increasingly bureaucratized, many officials were not military men at all, but by a curious fiction they were commonly enrolled as soldiers and even issued military rations and uniforms. Yet there was a sharp distinction between these fictitious soldiers and real ones, and officers who commanded troops often treated civil officials, even of higher rank, as their inferiors.[5]

The title of *Rex*, "King," was abhorrent to many Romans, and Caesar's alleged intention to assume it was one of the crimes for which he was assassinated. But the Senate conferred upon his heir the title of "Emperor," *Imperator*. Literally this meant "Commander"; it was originally a title bestowed upon victorious generals, for a limited time. Its permanent retention by the ruler of the Empire symbolized his position as commander-in-chief of the armies. The "imperial purple" was the color of a military cloak, at first worn by Roman generals cele-

---

3. Boak and Sinnigen, *History of Rome*, 88. *Cambridge Ancient History*, X, 161, XI, 432.

4. Rostovtzeff, *Roman Empire*, I, 449.

5. Jones, *Later Roman Empire*, I, 376–377, 566.

brating a triumph, which became an imperial prerogative.[6] The body-guard of the Emperor, the Praetorian Guard, naturally occupied a very sensitive position. But the functions of this elite corps of troops soon became much more than military. The Prefect of the Praetorian Guard came in time to act as a virtual deputy to the Emperor, combining in himself the function of chief of staff of the armies and the highest authority in the Empire in matters of finance and even of law. Three of the most eminent of Roman jurists, Paul, Papinian, and Ulpian, held this office. The latter two, incidentally, were killed by the Praetorian Guard.[7]

In 107 B.C. the method of recruitment of the Roman armies was altered in a way that was to have far-reaching consequences. As the military activities of the Republic increased, the men of property who did all the fighting became somewhat weary of it, understandably. They made little protest, therefore, when Marius accepted volunteers without regard to any property qualification. Since service as a private soldier had far more attraction for the landless poor than for men with other concerns to occupy them, it was the former who came increasingly to fill the ranks. Roman armies came to consist, in large part, not only of the poorer class of Romans but also of provincials and, ultimately, "barbarians." Under Augustus Roman citizenship was granted to all who served in the armies. Around A.D. 200 the population of the Empire came to be divided into *honestiores*, a privileged class, and *humiliores*, the proletariat. Soldiers of all ranks were classed as *honestiores*, and as such suffered lighter penalties than ordinary citizens if convicted of the same crime.

A very curious transposition had taken place. In the early Republic, when the heads of state personally led the Roman army in battle and only landowners could serve even as common soldiers, military men were necessarily those who possessed the greatest political power, the highest social position, and the greatest wealth. These facts, together with the Roman fascination with war, combined to insure that membership in the army carried the highest possible prestige. A great deal of this prestige continued to adhere to the soldier when the army came to be composed in considerable measure of riffraff and barbarians. At last the transition was complete: all soldiers became, together with officials, members of a privileged class, while ordinary Romans,

6. Boak and Sinnigen, *History of Rome*, 448–449.

7. Gibbon, *Roman Empire*, I, 97, 121. *Cambridge Ancient History*, XII, 23. Jones, *Later Roman Empire*, I, 50.

including even some of the small landowners, were of lower status before the law.[8]

By the latter part of the third century, Rostovtzeff says:

> The new Roman army was no longer a Roman army. . . . It was not a part of the Roman population and did not represent the interests of that population. It was a special caste, maintained at the expense of the population to fight foreign enemies. This caste now furnished the administrative personnel of the Empire, the greater portion of the ruling class, and the emperors themselves. . . . it was constantly being recruited by new elements coming from foreign lands, and so it remained a foreign military caste. Its upper layers now formed the ruling aristocracy of the Roman Empire.[9]

The extraordinary attention that the Romans devoted to the art of war is undoubtedly the force that created and maintained the Roman Empire. Although we tend to think of that Empire as the great early example of orderly administration, its organization was in fact very simple (and that was undoubtedly one of its strengths) as compared with that of contemporary China.[10] In spite of their vast responsibilities, Romans in general had very little interest in the theory of government. If modern students of political theory speak of ancient writers, it is chiefly of Greeks: Plato and Aristotle. The principal Roman works on government are the *De re publica* and *De legibus* of Cicero. But these books say very little that is enlightening about either the machinery or the theory of administration; Cicero remarks complacently that "the form of government handed down to us by our an-

8. Heichelheim and Yeo, *The Roman People*, 387. Rostovtzeff, *Roman Empire*, I, 496.

9. Rostovtzeff, *Roman Empire*, I, 468. Also see Heichelheim and Yeo, *The Roman People*, 387.

10. Max Weber, who was far better informed on Rome than on China, wrote in *Essays in Sociology*, 210–211, that "the Roman Empire and the British world empire, during their most expansive periods, rested upon bureaucratic foundations only to a small extent. . . . In the domination structure of Rome, the strictly military character of the magistrate authorities—in the Roman manner unknown to any other people—made up for the lack of a bureaucratic apparatus with its technical efficiency, its precision and unity of administrative functions, especially outside the city limits. In Rome . . . the state authorities increasingly 'minimized' the scope of their functions at home. They restricted their functions to what was absolutely demanded for direct 'reasons of state.' "

cestors is by far the best of all."[11] Rome administered her Empire as a series of communities that in most respects governed themselves but were held in obedience to Rome by ties of loyalty and self-interest, to be sure, but above all by its invincible military power.

The same exaltation of the military that created Rome's Empire made it very difficult for that Empire to enjoy stable government. In the early Republic, when even common soldiers were men of property, they were anxious to get wars over and return to their own affairs. But after recruits were accepted without regard to property qualifications, the armies were made up increasingly of men who chose army life because they had little to hope for from peace. They would urge their generals on to further conquests if there was any hope of booty—and were quite capable of coercing their commanders if their wishes were thwarted. It was only twenty years after this change in recruitment policy that, in 88 B.C., a Roman army refused to obey the government and murdered a Consul, who had been sent to take charge of it, because the men preferred to keep their former general in command.[12]

Roman politics came increasingly to be dominated by generals, who were backed by their veterans. The loyalty of the veterans to their leader was insured by the hope that he would provide them, on their discharge, with lands. This hope was not disappointed if their general was successful; he gave them lands confiscated from those he charged with being his enemies. Octavian (the future Augustus) seized cities and lands in Italy to recompense 170,000 of his veterans; Horace and Virgil were among those expropriated.[13]

Such conditions clearly foreshadowed the passage of control of the government into the hands of a military commander, an "Emperor." In theory the Emperor was selected by the Senate with the consent of the army, but the Senate soon came to play little real role. In one year, A.D. 68–69, four Emperors were set up in succession by various military forces; one took his own life when his army was defeated, and two were killed by soldiers. The Emperors, of course, sought to protect themselves by preventing generals from becoming powerful and especially by strengthening their own Praetorian Guard. But the Guard itself soon proved a menace. It made Emperors, and murdered them. In 193 it put the Empire up at auction and sold it to the highest

11. Cicero, *De re publica, De legibus,* 59.
12. *Cambridge Ancient History,* IX, 210.
13. It must be noted, however, that both were young men at the time, and both prospered later; both poets were treated well by Augustus as Emperor. But few of those who suffered were so fortunate.

bidder—who was killed by a soldier two months later. The Prefect of the Praetorian Guard (or Prefects—there were often more than one) exercised great power, but this office too was dangerous, as was shown by the murder of Ulpian when he tried, as Prefect, to discipline the Praetorians.

The exaltation of the military that was characteristic of the Romans inevitably caused them to attach relatively little value to the unexciting functions of civil administration. Under the Republic and the early Empire, extensive use was made of slaves and freedmen in these tasks, which did not add to their luster. Secretarial duties were later taken over by men of rank, and a separation was made between military and civilian careers. But the miiltary continued to dominate the scene; "power passed to men whose distinction in war was their only fame; and to its lasting harm the Empire found itself in the hands of soldiers whose humble origins and warlike occupations left them strangers to the arts of civil government."[14] Under the later Empire direct intervention by the troops in the affairs of the central government was more rare, but high military officers still selected the Emperor, sometimes without consulting the civilian dignitaries. The administration became thoroughly bureaucratized, but it does not seem to have been imbued with a great amount of *esprit de corps*. A. H. M. Jones concludes, from his exceptionally thorough study of the evidence, that "as a whole the civil servants of the later Roman empire seem to have been an unambitious and unenterprising class."[15] The business of government, as compared with the business of war, could arouse little enthusiasm in Roman breasts.

When we examine the Chinese attitude toward the military in the light of the Roman, the contrast is striking. The difference had important consequences in many aspects of the culture, and especially in government.

Few if any of China's greatest heroes were accorded that status on the basis of military merit alone; many of them have had nothing whatever to do with war. The "legendary Emperors," whose reigns are ascribed to the remote past, are for the most part culture heroes, credited with the invention of such things as writing, musical instruments, the domestication of animals, agriculture, and the calendar.[16]

14. *Cambridge Ancient History*, XI, 432–433.
15. Jones, *Later Roman Empire*, I, 359–360, 601–606.
16. One of them, the Yellow Emperor, is however said to have made war on those who were "oppressing the people," and established peace (*Mémoires historiques*, I, 26–29). None of the traditions concerning these allegedly early Emperors seems to have existed much before the time of Confucius; it can be argued,

The Chou gained control of China by a long course of military aggression. It might be expected, therefore, that their traditions would emphasize martial achievement, but we have seen that they did not. Their legendary ancestor, Hou Chi, was an agricultural deity, and a culture hero who invented agriculture. And the Chou legends make far less mention of military exploits than of the capacity to lay plans, build cities, and cement alliances. Most surprising of all is the decisive preference in all of the literature both early and late for King Wen, who is described chiefly as a framer of plans and a wise administrator, over his son King Wu, the actual conqueror and founder of the dynasty, whose martial mien is celebrated.

The next dynasty after the Chou to control all of China was the Ch'in (221–207 B.C.).[17] The Ch'in rose to power through a series of very bloody conquests, but its founder does not figure in China's tradition as a hero, but as a subject of execration. In the civil war that followed the overthrow of the Ch'in there were two chief protagonists. One of them, Hsiang Yü, was a superb general; it was said that he never lost a battle that he personally commanded. But he was a ruthless and arrogant autocrat, and his followers gradually melted away so that he finally committed suicide. China's most famous historian, Ssu-Ma Ch'ien, condemned him in these words: "He boasted of his military prowess, vaunted his superior wisdom, and would not learn from history. . . . He wished to conquer the world and rule it by sheer force."[18]

His adversary, who succeeded in founding the Han dynasty, is known to history as Han Kao-tsu. He rose from peasant origins to be a bandit chief and then a revolutionary general, and his rule was established by force of arms. Yet Kao-tsu himself was not an effective field general, nor even the best of strategists. He acknowledged this publicly but dismissed it as unimportant—what he could do, he claimed quite correctly, was to engage the loyalty of those who excelled him as generals, and make effective use of them.[19] Kao-tsu has been a hero to the Chinese, though the cultivated have deplored his crudities, but he

---

therefore, that they reflect Confucian ideas. One of the legendary Emperors is called Yü, and his name does occur in the *Poetry* (*Shih*, 164, 199, 259, 264, 266). But there he figures not as an Emperor, but as a kind of mythical civil engineer, who surveyed the land and opened up watercourses.

17. The Chou did not, of course, control as large a territory as did the Ch'in, but they did control virtually all of the area that was Chinese in culture in their day —and some that was not.

18. *Shih-chi*, 7; *Mémoires historiques*, II, 247–323.

19. *Han-shu*, 1B.16b; Dubs, *Han-shu*, I, 106–107.

has been admired far less for his military exploits than for his shrewdness and his success in bringing China to a state of peace and prosperity. Founders of later dynasties have usually, though not always, been successful generals,[20] but they have had to be far more than that in order to be considered highly meritorious in China.

The establishment of the Han dynasty just before 200 B.C. was roughly contemporaneous with the beginning of the great expansion of the territory ruled by Rome. In China, from that time forward, the political role of generals has in normal times been far less conspicuous that it was in Rome or, indeed, in many other states. When dynasties —which on the average lasted far longer in China than in Rome—became notably weak, generals might dominate or even replace them. But in ordinary times two factors prevented this. First, the soldiers usually were loyal to the Emperor and feared him more than any particular general, which made insurrection difficult. Second, since military men as such were not admired in China as they were in the Roman Empire, generals did not normally command great prestige. While there certainly were instances in which Emperors were dominated and even murdered by generals, there were probably many more cases in which Emperors treated their generals quite badly.[21]

As for common soldiers in China, it is not clear that there was ever a time when they felt such pride in their position as was normal for the Roman legionary. This was made difficult by, among other things, the attitude represented by the well-known proverb: "Good iron is not used to make a nail, nor a good man to make a soldier." At many times armies have been composed in large part of men convicted of crime. There have been mutinies in China, as elsewhere, but concerted action by the common soldiery was nothing like so usual a factor in influencing the conduct of the government as it was in the Roman Empire.

All this does not mean that men holding military titles never exercised great authority in China's government. At times they did, but their titles were not always won through outstanding achievement in war. A conspicuous example is the practice whereby, in the last century of the former Han dynasty, the supreme administrative power

20. Lien-sheng Yang points out (*Chinese Institutional History*, 5) that in a significant number of cases new dynasties were founded by powerful ministers whose "influence became so overwhelming that the last ruler of the old dynasty was obliged to abdicate."

21. Perhaps the most celebrated such case was that of Li Ling. See: *Han-shu*, 54.9b–16a. Watson, *Ssu-ma Ch'ien*, 60–62. For other cases, see "Trois généraux chinois de la dynastie des Han Orientaux."

(which formally remained with the Chancellor) was actually put into the hands of a series of personal representatives of the Emperor who held military titles. But these men were seldom if ever appointed on the basis of military achievement, but rather for their services to or in connection with the Emperor. Almost all of them, in fact, were related to the Emperor either by blood or by marriage.[22]

The *Book of Lord Shang,* probably compiled in the third century B.C., says that "office and rank should be determined exclusively on the basis of military merit," but that work is far outside the main stream of Chinese thought and it is unlikely that this principle was ever put into practice.[23] Certainly the Roman requirement of long military service as a prerequisite for civil office would have seemed very strange to most Chinese. When the Duke of Chou spoke of illustrious ministers of the past who had assisted their rulers—including I Yin who helped the founder of the Shang dynasty overthrow the Hsia—he spoke of their virtues, but said nothing whatever of any military abilities they may have possessed.[24] As the Chinese bureaucracy developed, there were two careers, civil and military, and the latter was almost invariably considered inferior. Speaking of the situation in the tenth century A.D., Kracke says that while the two services were theoretically equal "the civil service was generally prized and favored above the military." It was possible to transfer from the military service into the civil, but when offices were assigned, those who had taken degrees in military subjects were in the lowest class and received the least desirable posts.[25] Even heirs to the imperial throne were selected, in Han times, in part on the basis of their scholarship and their reputations for benevolence and filial piety, while little if any attention seems to have been paid to their knowledge of military affairs.[26]

22. Wang, "Han Government," 166–169.
23. *Shang-chün Shu,* 4.5ab; Duyvendak, *Lord Shang,* 275. On the date of this work, see ibid., 141–159.
24. *Shu,* 61. However, the Duke does say of four ministers of his brother, King Wu, that together with him "they grandly wielded Heaven's majesty and killed all his enemies."
25. Kracke, *Sung Civil Service,* 56, 91.
26. The succession was not regulated, in any strict sense, by primogeniture. An Emperor could designate any of his descendants as his heir, and if he failed to do so the successor was selected by the chief ministers. Of four heirs to the Former Han throne concerning whose selection we have data, two were selected by Emperors and two by the ministers. Other considerations of course entered into these choices, but the reasons alleged are significant as indicating the qualities considered desirable in an Emperor. We are told very explicitly that the future Emperor Ai was chosen by Emperor Ch'eng as his heir in part, at least, because he demonstrated to Ch'eng his abilities as a scholar. The future Emperor Hsüan was recom-

Among the differences between the Romans and the Chinese that may be supposed to be related to, if not necessarily consequent upon, their contrasting attitudes toward military pursuits, is the esteem in which the art of civil administration was held. If Romans wrote little about government, it sometimes seems that the Chinese wrote about little else. It has been carefully estimated that "China at the close of the fifteenth century A.D. probably had produced more books than all other countries put together,"[27] and the great bulk of them were more or less directly concerned with government; those that were not even indirectly so concerned were a very small proportion. But the Chinese have not only written and thought about government; most of them have considered active participation in it to be the noblest and most desirable of occupations. Since as early as Shang times, if we may judge by the mention of eminent ministers in the inscriptions, civilian administrators have been the great heroes. Chinese civil servants have often been accused, with varying degrees of justice, of being grasping and oppressive. But they could not commonly be described as being, as Jones calls the bureaucracy of the later Roman Empire, "an unambitious and unenterprising class." In China, the concentration and fervor that the Romans devoted to war were channeled into government.

The attitude toward the military, since the beginning of the Han dynasty, has in general been that it is a necessary evil. It is necessary, as the police are necessary, because there are bad people in the world who do not behave as they should. In the case of external enemies, in addition to whatever other crimes they may have committed, they are also guilty of failing to recognize the superiority and the justice of Chinese culture and Chinese rule. It is quite true that in connection with certain periods, such as that of the "Three Kingdoms" (A.D. 221–265), there has been admiration for military heroes and "chivalrous" conduct. But such interludes of what was in effect civil war, with Chinese fighting other Chinese, are merely minor variations within the prevailing pattern.

Attitudes toward the military before Han times are less clearly

---

mended as being learned, moderate, economical, and benevolent. The claims of the candidates who became Emperor Hui and Emperor Wen were advanced on the ground that they were both widely known to be benevolent and filial. In none of these cases is there any mention of military experience or knowledge. See: *Shih-chi*, 9.35, 99.18; *Mémoires historiques*, II, 439; Watson, *Records*, I, 296. *Han-shu*, 8.3a, 11.1a, 2a; Dubs, *Han-shu* II, 204, III, 15–18.

27. Tsien, *Written on Bamboo and Silk*, 2. Although Professor Tsien states his result with modest simplicity, I know that he did a very great deal of arduous research in order to arrive at it.

discernible. The circumstances of the Spring and Autumn and War-ring States periods placed a premium on military prowess. Confucius, living at the end of the former and the beginning of the latter, was a determined champion of the civilian as opposed to the military ideal, and from his time onward there was a growing tendency, in intellec-tual circles, to disparage the warrior. From this it has been deduced, by myself among others, that the time of Confucius marked a turning point, a time before which the warrior had always been esteemed more highly than the administrator. Yet we must ask ourselves whether this is really the case, or if, in the long sweep of Chinese history, the Spring and Autumn and Warring States periods may represent an anomaly. The question is important for its bearing upon one of the great motifs underlying the development of government in China. To answer it we must ask: what was the attitude toward war, and toward the military, in Western Chou?

Kuo Mo-jo wrote, in one of his early books, that the Western Chou "in the practice of government, placed the greatest emphasis on mili-tary measures." He offered no detailed analysis of evidence for this, but said that it is evident from many passages in bronze inscriptions, some of which he cited. He also said that the highest rewards were given for military achievements.[28]

It would be difficult either to prove or to disprove these statements. But even if we assume that they are true, it is still necessary to evalu-ate them with care. The Western Chou was a period in which war, or the possibility of war, was more or less constant. The Chou acquired almost all of the territory over which they ruled by conquest, and had to keep it garrisoned. Within what they considered to be their borders there were large enclaves of people who were unassimilated or only partially assimilated to Chinese culture, and by no means wholly rec-onciled to their rule. The Chou were constantly in the process of as-similating them, but the need for military vigilance was perpetual. In addition they were surrounded by barbarians who were ready at any sign of weakness to raid, and who periodically made deep incursions into their territory; to counter this the Chou made punitive expedi-tions.

For the Chou Kings to have relaxed their attention to military af-fairs would have been to court disaster. Military exploits and military heroes are always esteemed in times of war and danger. If the West-ern Chou, in a time of almost constant danger, laid great emphasis on

28. Kuo, *Chin-wen Ts'ung-k'ao*, 19a–20a.

military measures and gave rich rewards to those who were successful in war, they could hardly have been expected to do otherwise in the circumstances.

There is little indication, however, in the traditional history, the literature, or the bronze inscriptions, that during the Western Chou period prowess in war often led to great power and high position.[29] This contrasts sharply, of course, with the situation in the Roman Empire, where officials were commonly military veterans and many of the Emperors were generals placed on the throne by the armies.

The basic question is: Did the men of Western Chou regard war as a necessary business, to be got over and done with—or did they, like the Romans, consider it a glorious and noble pursuit, to be dwelt upon and celebrated in and for itself?

Insofar as the Romans are concerned, the answer to this question is clear. The glorification of war is evident even in their archeological remains. It speaks from almost every page of their national epic, Virgil's *Aeneid*, which has been called "Rome's greatest literary legacy."[30] It begins: "Of arms . . . I sing." The founding of Rome is foretold in the words, "Then . . . shall Romulus take up the nation, build the wargod's town." Again and again the reader is assured of the felicity of those who die in battle. "Rage and wrath drive my soul headlong and I think how glorious it is to die in arms!" Even in those passages in which the *Aeneid* is not speaking of war, the motifs of violence and death are never absent for long. And they are dwelt upon in loving detail: "What god may now in song for me tell o'er the tale of horrors, diverse forms of death, and fall of chieftains?" Battle scenes are depicted with the most gruesome particulars:

> So saying, he rises high
> To his uplifted sword, and with the blade
> Full betwixt either temple, a grisly stroke,

29. Men of high rank often led armies, but there is little to indicate that it was their exploits in war that won their position. Undoubtedly this did happen at the time of the Chou conquest; military merit unquestionably did have something to do with the initial apportioning of fiefs. And lands were given as rewards to victorious commanders, but it is not clear that these vastly enhanced their power. For the traditional history, see *Shih-chi*, 4.1–65; *Mémoires historiques*, I, 209–285. The data in the bronze inscriptions is so fragmentary and so obscure that it cannot be held to prove very much, but there does not seem to be any clear case of the award of great power or high position solely on the basis of military exploits. There is, however, one inscription (*Chin-wen*, 139ab) in which we find the King giving great power over the administration to an official whom he addresses as *Shih*, "Commander." But whether it was his military achievements that caused his preferment we cannot tell.

30. Heichelheim and Yeo, *The Roman People*, 304.

Cleft him through forehead and through beardless cheeks.
A loud crash followed; earth reels with the vast weight;
Rolled in a heap, with his brain-spattered arms,
The limbs fell dying; in equal halves the head
This way and that from either shoulder hung.[31]

This passage is especially grisly, but in the *Aeneid* it is by no means unique.

When we turn to the literature of Western Chou, the contrast is striking. Certainly this was a time of war, and we can find things that remind us of the fact and are sometimes distinctly unpleasant. The preceding chapter discussed the inscription that describes a great ceremony, held in the ancestral temple, celebrating a triumph over the Demon Territory. In it captive chieftains were interrogated and decapitated, severed left ears (or heads) were offered as a burnt sacrifice, and the victorious commander was rewarded. We have a little other evidence of such ceremonies in Western Chou.[32] But celebrations of victory are a common accompaniment of war and do not necessarily prove that the men of Western Chou gloried especially in it.

The literature as a whole produces two impressions: war was common, and those who fought it seem on the whole to have derived very little pleasure from it. In all of the Western Chou literature there seems to be scarcely anything that could be called a battle scene, in the sense of a description of a battle in which the exploits of individual warriors are recounted in detail. Such descriptions abound, of course, in the *Aeneid*. They are also fairly common in the *Tso-chuan*, which is one of many reasons for believing that the attitude toward war was by no means the same thing in the Spring and Autumn period that it was in Western Chou.[33] And nowhere, I believe, in the Western Chou literature, do we find mention of the actual flowing of blood—a subject so agreeable to writers on military themes in many lands.[34]

31. These passages have been selected from two translations: Rhoades, *Virgil*, and Fairclough, *Virgil*. They translate the following lines of the *Aeneid*: I.1, 276–277; II.316–317; IX.749–755; XII.500–502.

32. *Shih*, 256–257, seems to describe a rather similar ceremony in the state of Lu. *Shih*, 196, probably refers to such a ceremony, though this is in the time of King Wen and therefore technically before the beginning of Western Chou. This practice seems to have persisted into the Spring and Autumn period. *Tso*, 206::212 (Hsi 28), seems to describe a similar ceremony held by Duke Wen of Chin in 632 B.C., to celebrate his great victory over Ch'u.

33. My notes list twenty-one such "battle scenes" in the *Tso-chuan*. For a few of the longer ones, see *Tso*, 44–45::45–46 (Huan 5), 164–165::167–168 (Hsi 15), 204–205::208–210 (Hsi 28), 313–315::319–320 (Hsüan 12).

34. In fact blood is rarely mentioned in the *Tso-chuan* either. Such reference does occur in *Tso*, 340::345 (Ch'eng 2), but this is very unusual.

Many of the bronze inscriptions record the military services of those who had them cast, and they were undoubtedly intended to preserve the memory of their deeds. Yet for the most part their accounts are very brief and unembellished, and if they record the conquest of enemies and the seizure of booty, their tone is almost statistical. A boastful tone concerning military exploits is exceedingly rare in Western Chou—in sharp contrast to the situation in the Spring and Autumn period.[35]

The place where we should expect to see warlike scenes portrayed in some detail is, of course, the *Poetry*. These expectations are not wholly disappointed.

> We bring out our chariots
> On to those outskirts.
> Here we set up the tortoise-and-snake banner,
> There we raise the ox-tail flag;
> The falcon flag and the tortoise-and-snake banner
> That flutter, flutter.

Always there is a keen eye for pageantry, and that is the one aspect of war that seems to delight the poets. They are perhaps even more lyrical, and more explicit, in describing the great hunts, which involve the same pageantry but lack the grim undertone.[36] But this poem now goes on to the characteristic note that is seldom absent from Western Chou verses on war:

> Our grieved hearts are pained;
> The grooms are distressed and exhausted.
> The King has ordered Nan-chung
> To go and build a fort on the frontier.
> The departing chariots rumble,
> The dragon banner and the tortoise-and-snake
> banner are brilliant. . . .
> Awe-inspiring is Nan-chung;
> The Hsien-yün [barbarians] are expelled.
> Long ago, when we set out,
> The millets were in flower.
> Now as we return
> Snow falls upon the mire.
> The King's service brings many hardships.

35. For an unusual inscription in which the maker does boast of his military merits, see *Chin-wen*, 103b–104a. But there appears to be some doubt of the genuineness of this inscription: see p. 473.

36. See for instance *Shih*, 81–82, 123–124.

We have no time to kneel or rest.
Do we not long to go home?
But we are in awe of the writing on those bamboo slips.[37]

Even victory over the barbarian foe does not eradicate the pain of hardship. "In one month there are three victories. . . . Long ago, when we marched, the willows were luxuriant; now when we return the falling snow is thick. We travel the road slowly, we are hungry, we are thirsty, our hearts are pained; no one understands our woe."[38] When a soldier has gone to war, his whole family laments—"may he be careful, may he return, may he not die there." What the soldiers fear is not so much the shock of battle as the loneliness, the boredom, and the arduous toil of military service. They long for home, for rest, and for civilian clothes.[39]

There are a few poems that depict warlike expeditions as a splendid show, but it is as a show that they are described, with only the pageantry and the victorious results, without the gory details. The Chou conquest of the Shang is naturally regarded as glorious, but even this is treated with remarkable brevity and restraint.[40]

In the Documents we have a number of writings from the Western Chou period, of which many were produced in the years just after the Chou conquest. The reference to warfare in them is minimal. It will be recalled that the Poetry says that King Wu was "very martial," "terrifying and strong!"[41] Two of the Documents are apparently his utterances, and a third is probably from him.[42] It would be natural to expect from this warlike conqueror some proud if not boastful reference to his exploit. In fact, he mentions it exactly once, in a statement to a younger brother. He says, "Your elder brother exerted himself, and thus you . . . are here in this eastern territory."[43]

WARFARE was regarded, in Western Chou, as a task, important and necessary but on the whole, insofar as the sources indicate, rather dis-

37. Shih, 112–113.
38. Shih, 112.
39. Shih, 46, 71, 101–102, 111–112, 125, 159–160, 184–185. Concerning the possibility that there were military uniforms at this time, see pp. 287–288.
40. Shih, 188, 198–199, 248.
41. Shih, 243, 252.
42. King Wu appears to be the author of the "K'ang Kao" and the "Chiu Kao," and probably of most of the "Tzu Ts'ai"; see pp. 450–452.
43. Shu, 39–40. This reticence in speaking of military exploits is not peculiar to King Wu. His son, King Ch'eng, described the conquest in these words (Shu, 70): "The former rulers, King Wen and King Wu, displayed their brightness one

tasteful. There is little suggestion of any thought by officers or men of failure to perform their duty, but neither is there evidence that war was thought of as an enjoyable game. There is virtually no indication of "chivalrous" ideas or conduct in connection with war in the Western Chou period. This stands in sharp contrast with the situation in Spring and Autumn times.

The term "chivalry" is quite appropriate to use in connection with the conduct of warfare in the Spring and Autumn period. It is derived, of course, from the Latin word for "horse," and related to "cavalier." In medieval Europe chivalry was the code of the mounted knights, and in Spring and Autumn China a comparable code was peculiar to aristocrats who rode in horse-drawn chariots to fight.[44] But not every man who rides a horse, or even fights from one, is necessarily a "cavalier," and not all of those who fought from chariots drawn by horses in early China did so under a code of chivalry.

In Spring and Autumn China, as in medieval Europe, the concept of chivalry came to include much more than a code of proper conduct in fighting; this we shall consider later. Our present concern is with its purely military aspect. One of the most interesting indications of the similarity between the early Chinese and medieval European concepts is a passage in the *Tso-chuan* that appears to say that in 552 B.C. Duke Chuang of Ch'i "instituted an order of bravery" to which men who had distinguished themselves for this quality were appointed. Unfortunately, however, this passage stands alone, and it is difficult to be clear as to the details.[45]

Bravery was important, but it must be shown in fighting in con-

---

after the other and set forth their refinement. In spreading their instructions they toiled, but in toiling they did not go too far. Thus they could reach to Yin and achieve the great Mandate." And the Duke of Chou not only repeatedly dismisses the conquest with similar brevity, but passes very lightly over his own very considerable achievement in putting down the great rebellion; see *Shu*, 49, 55, 56, 61.

In this review of material on war in the Western Chou sources, nothing has been said of the original text of the *Book of Changes*. It contains only some eight references to warfare; these are not very illuminating and do not contradict the picture to be drawn from the other sources.

44. As was pointed out earlier, the ridden horse and the mounted warrior seem to have been unknown in China until long after the Western Chou period; see p. 262, note 61.

45. *Tso*, 489::492 (Hsiang 21). Both Legge and Couvreur (*Tso-chuan*, II, 373) interpret the passage in this way, and so does the commentator Tu Yü of the third century A.D. The passage has been construed not to refer to an order of nobility at all; see Takezoe, *Tso-shih Hui-chien*, 16.29b. On the whole, however, this interpretation seems probable.

formity with the rules. In 632 B.C., when the armies of Chin and Ch'u were encamped near each other, the Ch'u commander sent a messenger to the Marquis of Chin with a challenge, saying, "I request a game with your men. Your lordship may lean on the cross-board of your carriage and look on, and I too will observe." The Marquis caused one of his subordinates to reply, "I will trouble you, sir, to say to your officers, 'Prepare your chariots, see reverently to your ruler's business!' Tomorrow morning I will see you."[46] This elaborate nonchalance is rather impressive, for the affair that followed was the great battle of Ch'eng-p'u, one of the most decisive engagements in early Chinese history.

One must not, of course, exaggerate. In Spring and Autumn China, as in medieval Europe, the code of chivalry was perhaps more often violated than observed. Yet it is important that in theory at least, and sometimes in fact, war was treated as a game played by gentlemen in which, while winning was important, it was even more important to abide by the rules.

This is vividly illustrated by a passage in the *Tso-chuan* concerning the year 638 B.C. An army of Ch'u had invaded the state of Sung.

> The men of Sung were all drawn up in battle array before the forces of Ch'u had finished crossing the river, and the Minister of War said to the Duke [of Sung], "They are many and we are few. I request permission to attack them before they have all crossed over." The Duke replied, "It may not be done." After they had crossed over, but not yet formed their ranks, the Minister again asked leave to attack, but the Duke replied, "Not yet." The attack was not begun until the enemy was fully deployed.
>
> The army of Sung was disastrously defeated. The Duke himself was injured in the thigh, and his guards of the palace gates were all killed. The people of the state all blamed the Duke, but he said: "The gentleman does not inflict a second wound, or take the grey-haired prisoner. When the ancients fought, they did not attack an enemy when he was in a defile. Though I am but the unworthy remnant of a fallen dynasty, I would not sound my drums to attack an enemy who had not completed the formation of his ranks."[47]

46. *Tso*, 204::209 (Hsi 28).
47. *Tso*, 181–182::183 (Hsi 22). The Dukes of Sung continued the line of the Shang Kings. This reference to "the ancients" might be supposed to indicate that

It is interesting to compare with this the medieval European ideal, as described by Carl Stephenson: "Prowess, above all else, implied valor and fidelity. No gentleman could afford to incur the merest suspicion of cowardice or treachery. Because it was braver to attack boldly, the true knight disdained all tricks in combat; he would not strike an unarmed or unprepared foe."[48]

In Spring and Autumn China chivalry was sometimes carried to extreme lengths. In one of the intrastate wars that were common in that period, a son of a later Duke of Sung found his chariot opposite, in battle, that of another warrior of Sung who was evidently more expert with the bow. Before the Duke's son could fire a single shot, the other had loosed one arrow that narrowly missed and had another ready. At this the Duke's son cried, "If you don't give me my turn to shoot, you are a base fellow!"[49] His opponent held his fire, and the Duke's son shot him dead.[50]

The Chinese code of chivalry, as variously interpreted, called for refaining from injuring a ruler, even though he were an opponent in battle; not attacking a state in mourning for the death of its ruler; and not taking advantage of internal disorders within a state to attack it. Before battle was joined, messengers should pass between the two armies, and a stipulated time and place be arranged.[51] It is possible to extract many more such injunctions from the texts, but difficult to determine to what extent each was generally recognized in theory and observed in practice.

It is a striking fact that in all of the Western Chou sources there seems to be no indication that at that time any such code of chivalrous conduct in war existed.[52] Although it seems to appear suddenly, and

---

the Duke was carrying on a tradition of chivalry from Shang times. I suspect, however, that in fact this was the code that was developed in the Spring and Autumn period, and possibly in late Western Chou times, here attributed in the usual Chinese manner to antiquity.

48. Stephenson, *Medieval Feudalism*, 51.

49. Literally, *pi* 鄙 , "rustic." As a term of opprobrium, this seems to be comparable to our "villain," which originally had the sense of a countryman or peasant.

50. *Tso*, 687::689 (Chao 21).

51. *Tso*, 44::46 (Huan 5), 204::209 (Hsi 28), 260::261 (Wen 12), 339::345 (Ch'eng 2), 392::397 (Ch'eng 16), 421::423 (Hsiang 4), 848–849::850 (Ai 17).

52. The absence of this motif from the *Poetry* has been noted by Miss Magdalene von Dewall, in *Pferd und Wagen im frühen China*, 186. She writes that in the Spring and Autumn period "eine echte ritterliche Haltung drückt sich aus . . . Diese geistige Haltung des Kriegers ist allerdings etwas ganz Neues gegenüber der, die sich in dem unkriegerischen Wagenjunkerideal der Lieder niedergeschlagen hat."

fully developed, at the beginning of the Spring and Autumn period, it must in fact have been in process of evolution during the latter part, at least, of Western Chou times. Nevertheless, the difference is a fact, and at first sight a puzzling one, which must be accounted for. It is probably the result of more causes than one.

First of all is the fact that, to all appearances, a genuine aristocratic class scarcely existed at the beginning of Western Chou. And a code of chivalry presupposes an aristocratic class. Individual warriors may be brave, magnanimous, and faithful; but for these qualities to be embodied in a definite code, generally recognized and enforced by social pressure, requires the kind of environment that can only be provided by an aristocratic class that nurtures its usages and hands them on from generation to generation. In feudal Europe it was not until long after the establishment of feudalism that a definite code of chivalry came into being. And this occurred at about the same time that knights, who originally had not been considered nobles but merely warriors, came to be considered aristocrats and, in some areas, to be a closed hereditary class.[53]

A second reason, that seems clearly to be important in accounting for the lack of any evidence of chivalrous ideas in connection with war in Western Chou, is the fact that war in that period was predominantly waged against barbarians.[54]

In the Western Chou sources that I am using, there are fifty-five references to military encounters during that period,[55] but only forty-two in which the identity of the enemy can be established with reasonable certainty.[56] Of these, thirty, almost three-quarters, are actions against barbarians alone. Of the remainder, three are against barbari-

---

53. Bloch, *Feudal Society*, 283, 312–322. Strayer, *Feudalism*, 25, 57–60.

54. This point is noted in Dewall, *Pferd und Wagen im frühen China*, 186.

55. In most cases I have made no attempt to eliminate duplication in these references, but I believe the duplications are not many. They are most likely in the case of references to action by the Duke of Chou and King Ch'eng to crush the revolt of the Shang people in the early years of the dynasty. There are five references that may concern this, but the situation is not so clear that we can say that all refer to the same military activity. Furthermore, this was a very extensive series of campaigns, lasting for several years, so that some duplication would not really falsify the picture. I have, however, counted two mentions of this action within one document (*Shu*, 37 and 39) as a single reference.

56. The distribution of these is as follows: In the bronze inscriptions, thirty-four cases, of which one does not name the adversary and one has an adversary who may be either Chinese or barbarian. In the *Poetry*, eighteen cases in ten of which no adversary is named; this is not surprising, since some of the poems are simply complaints against the hardship of military service. In the *Documents*, three cases, in one of which the adversary is unnamed. In the *Book of Changes* there are

ans and dissident Chinese acting in concert, and nine against Chinese alone.[57]

Furthermore, of the nine attacks against Chinese alone, seven occurred in the opening years of the dynasty, and two of the three attacks on Chinese and barbarians together fell in this same period. Thus three-quarters of our recorded engagements in which Chinese opposed each other came in the initial period of consolidation. Only three further actions involving Chinese on both sides are recorded, and all three fall in the last century of Western Chou.

Thus after the opening years of the dynasty there was a period of some two centuries in which, insofar as our sources indicate, Chinese armies did not fight other Chinese at all, and even in the final century of Western Chou they did so only on three occasions.[58] Thus even if a code of aristocratic conduct was growing up in Western Chou—as it surely was—it could not frequently be applied in battle. For such a code can operate in fighting only when both sides know it and abide by it.

War as it was fought in Spring and Autumn times was, ideally at least, a game played between gentlemen. And there is no doubt that much of the contempt for barbarians that we find expressed in that period derived from the fact that the barbarians did not abide by the rules, or even know them—in fact, they were not gentlemen. We read in the *Tso-chuan* that barbarians are capable of making surprise attacks, that the Jung "maintain no proper order" in battle, and that the Ti lack a sense of shame that would prevent them from turning tail

---

eight references to warfare, but most of them (as is usual in this divination manual) are hypothetical and only one (Legge, *I-ching*, 205) refers to a specific event; that one took place in the Shang period, and therefore has no relevance here.

57. This undoubtedly understates the role of barbarians. Four of these references have to do with the quelling of the rebellion of the Shang people early in the reign of King Ch'eng. There is strong tradition indicating that barbarian tribes took part in this, and it is quite probable; see Ch'en, "Hsi-Chou T'ung-ch'i," (1).146–149. But the Western Chou sources do not say so, and I have therefore counted these as attacks on Chinese.

58. It cannot be supposed, of course, that our sources are at all complete or even in their coverage; the bronze inscriptions are especially lacking in this respect. It should be noted, however, that in the *Poetry*, which might be supposed to give a more balanced picture, the predominance of warfare with barbarians is even more pronounced. Of the eight cases in which the enemy is identified, seven are engagements with barbarians alone. The eighth (*Shih*, 103) says that "the Duke of Chou made an expedition to the east" and corrected the states of the four quarters. Because we know that in his eastern expedition the Duke of Chou attacked both Chinese and barbarian states, I have counted this as an attack against the two.

whenever it seems advantageous.[59] Quite clearly they did not fight in the Chinese manner or according to the Chinese code.[60]

THE Chou period—up at least until the time of the Warring States—is dominated by the chariot. The medieval "age of chivalry," if interpreted literally, means "the age of cavalry." And most of the Chou dynasty could be called, without too much exaggeration, "the age of the chariot."

While this is beyond question, careful study of the new materials available to us indicates that the role of the chariot, in Western Chou times and even later, was not precisely that which it has long been assumed to have played. It has rather generally been supposed that the chariot was outstandingly effective on the field of battle and that, while there were some foot soldiers, they were relegated to a position of mere attendance on the chariots. Yet there is a great deal of evidence that in fact the chariot was not very effective in warfare and that the actual winning of battles may have been done, in Western Chou times and even later, at least as much by infantry as by those who fought from chariots.

This does not mean, certainly, that the chariot was unimportant. It was very important indeed, but primarily as a symbol of status. As such it profoundly influenced not only the making of war but the shaping of the culture and the evolution of political institutions. Since its importance was so crucial, and this interpretation of its role is so much at variance with the preponderant opinion, we must examine the evidence in careful detail.

Almost any discussion of war in early China lays chief emphasis on the chariot.[61] It is the chariots that almost monopolize the attention

59. *Tso*, 27::28 (Yin 9), 150::151 (Hsi 8).

60. Against this it may be objected that the men of Ch'u appear to have fought by essentially the same code as those of the north, and that chivalrous action was conspicuous in fighting with Ch'u. This is certainly the case in the *Tso-chuan;* see *Tso*, 311–315::316–321 (Hsüan 12), 390–393::395–398 (Ch'eng 16). But we have already seen that the people of Ch'u were not really regarded as barbarian in Spring and Autumn times; to what extent they were in the Western Chou period, we cannot clearly tell.

61. There is no convincing evidence that cavalry, or riding on horseback, was known or used in China until shortly before 300 B.C. Nevertheless a number of scholars, both Chinese and Western, persist in asserting or taking it for granted that these things go back to Western Chou or even to Shang times. See: Maspero, "La société chinoise," 394. Cheng, *Shang China*, 198. Yü, " 'Liu Shih' he 'Pa Shih,' " 154–155. Dubs, "The Great Fire in the State of Lu3TU in 492 B.C.," 15–16. Shih, "Yin-tai ti Kung yü Ma." But where evidence is cited, it is capable of other

of the poets when they describe Western Chou expeditions setting forth. In the *Tso-chuan* the great battles of the Spring and Autumn period are described as a series of duels between warriors dashing about in chariots. The importance of states came to be calculated in terms of the number of chariots they could supposedly muster, so that we read of "a state of a thousand chariots."[62] Cheng Te-k'un says that in Chou times "the main striking force depended on the chariots."[63] Samuel B. Griffith, describing the way in which war was carried on "until about 500 B.C.," writes:

> The illiterate and docile serfs played but a small part in the battles of the time, in which the principal role was reserved to the four-horse chariot manned by a driver, a spearman, and a noble archer. The expendable footmen, protected only by padded jackets, were grouped about the chariots. A small proportion of selected men carried shields woven of bamboo or at best more cumbrous ones of crudely tanned ox or rhinocerous hide. Their arms were daggers and short swords, bronze-tipped spears, and hooking and cutting blades tied with leather thongs to wooden shafts. The bow was the weapon of the noble.[64]

Some modern scholars have a tendency to evaluate the war chariot as an extraordinarily formidable weapon. V. Gordon Childe writes:

> Even before 3000 B.C. the wheeled vehicle was being used ... as a military engine. Chariotry was undoubtedly a decisive arm in Sumerian warfare before and after 2500 B.C. By 2000 B.C. it was playing a similar role in north Syria. Considering the relatively small total re-

---

interpretation. Erkes ("Das Pferd im alten China," 50–52) quotes a number of passages in the literature that have been supposed to prove that riding took place in China before the fourth century B.C., but shows that they do not.

The evidence against the early use of cavalry in China is overwhelming. There is no certain reference to it in the early sources. The *Sun-tzu*, said to be the earliest extant Chinese work on the art of war, is of uncertain date but is generally considered to date from the Warring States period; see *Wei-shu T'ung-k'ao*, 797–801, and Griffith, *Sun Tzu*, 1–12. This work mentions chariots but not cavalry. In his Introduction Griffith (ibid., 11) comments that "it is reasonable to assume that if cavalry had been familiar to Sun Tzu he would have mentioned it." For fuller discussion of this problem, see Creel, "The Horse in Chinese History."

62. *Tso*, 836::838 (Ai 14).
63. Cheng, *Chou China*, 295.
64. Griffith, *Sun Tzu*, 32.

sources available to early urban societies, the war chariot is fairly comparable to the tank of today; it was an engine which only a rich civilized state could produce and maintain, and against which no barbarian tribe or rebellious peasantry could compete.[65]

Professor A. Leo Oppenheim, however, considers the role of the chariot in early Mesopotamia comparable to that of an armed personnel carrier rather than that of a tank. It was used, he finds, to transport infantry who dismounted to fight. Thus chariots were useful to move troops quickly for a surprise attack, and to pursue fleeing enemies. But he has seen no evidence that chariots themselves were used for the purpose of attack.[66] In Egypt, according to Professor John A. Wilson, chariots were sometimes used in battle for shock purposes and also to move commanders about the field; but the role of the chariot in Egypt could not be compared to that of the tank, for chariots were quite vulnerable and easily overturned if they were not protected.[67] In ancient Greece, Professor Gertrude E. Smith tells me, war chariots played little role in historic times, though they are mentioned a great deal in the Homeric period. Even in the earlier time their function was only that of providing transport; warriors dismounted from their chariots to fight.[68]

More than thirty years ago I expressed the opinion that in ancient China:

> In so far as one can tell from the accounts the chariot itself was never a very formidable engine of war. It is true that there is some intimation that charges were led by a group of them. But the bow and arrow can be discharged from the ground as well as from a chariot, and with surer aim. The spear or lance carried by the chariot was no doubt formidable, but it could, after all, menace only one man at a time. The frequency with which important nobles were wounded and even killed in battle shows that chariots afforded no certain protection to their occupants. Even in Chou times their chief use was probably the fact that they gave to the commanders a mobile point of vantage from which to direct operations.

65. Singer et al., *History of Technology,* I, 209–210. See also Childe, "The First Waggons and Carts," 179, 188.
66. Verbal communication of March 28, 1967.
67. Verbal communication of March 28, 1967.
68. Verbal communication of March 31, 1967.

They did also constitute a force which could be moved quickly to any point in the field at which a special emergency might arise.[69]

Further research has only served to deepen that impression. In a study of the chariot in early China published in 1964, based on both literary evidence and the most recently discovered archeological materials, Miss Magdalene von Dewall came to some rather similar conclusions.[70]

Anyone who has bumped along in a modern, springless, two-wheeled "Peking cart," and had it overturn while moving at very low speed on a road, must wonder how Chou chariots could be maneuvered with the precision necessary for the purposes of war on terrain of the slightest roughness. They were undoubtedly beautifully made and often lavishly ornamented, but they seem to have been as completely without springs as the Peking cart.[71] On a surface as smooth as a polo field they could probably be handled very well, but on ground of any roughness they must have provided a very poor platform from which to discharge a bow with any accuracy.

There is much evidence in the *Tso-chuan* that, once they left level and solid ground, chariots were likely to be in trouble. Thus we read that the root of a tree causes a chariot to overturn, and the rider is killed by the enemy. A Marquis of Chin is warned against using horses unfamiliar with the terrain, but he disregards the warning and, even though the battle is fought on a plain, his horses turn aside into a muddy spot; the chariot is mired fast, and the Marquis is captured. A later Marquis of Chin also became stuck in mud during a battle, but his chariot was dragged out before any harm was done.[72] So long as a chariot remained on the appointed field of battle, it might do well enough; but when the defeated tried to flee in chariots, they were likely to get into trouble. It was considered chivalrous not to take advantage of a fleeing enemy who was having trouble with his chariot; an especially chivalrous adversary might even help him on his way.[73]

After the state of Chin had defeated Ch'i in battle, the victor demanded that all fields in Ch'i should be cultivated with the furrows running east and west, to facilitate the entry of Chin's chariots into its

69. Creel, *The Birth of China*, 153–154.

70. Dewall, *Pferd und Wagen im frühen China*, 161–162, 183–187.

71. See Cheng, *Chou China*, 265–273.

72. *Tso*, 164–165::167–168 (Hsi 15), 392::397 (Ch'eng 16), 498::501 (Hsiang 23).

73. *Tso*, 314::320 (Hsüan 12), 340::345 (Ch'eng 2).

territory. Before a battle, we read repeatedly, the ground was prepared by filling in wells and leveling the holes made for cooking.[74] For chariots to be used to advantage, it was necessary that the ground be as favorable as possible.

It was not difficult to avoid the dangers of an attack by chariots; a simple entrenchment around a camp would protect it against them, and it was only necessary to remain quietly behind one's defenses and ignore all challenges to come out and fight on suitable ground.[75] But of course a true gentleman of the Spring and Autumn period could not do that.

But what of those who were not, according to the Chinese code, gentlemen? How did barbarians fight?

Not, according to all of our information, in chariots. We have some mention of the capture of horses and of vehicles from barbarians, but there is no indication that these were war chariots. They were probably carts used to transport baggage.[76] Miss von Dewall says that in early Chou China the barbarians "did not possess the war chariot," and in general this seems clearly to be true.[77] The *Tso-chuan* specifically says that both Jung and Ti were foot soldiers and did not fight in chariots.[78]

There seems to be no specific information available on the way in which barbarians fought in Western Chou times, and very little for

74. *Tso*, 391::396 (Ch'eng 16), 460::464 (Hsiang 14), 522::527 (Hsiang 26).
75. *Tso*, 391::396 (Ch'eng 16).
76. If the vehicles captured from the Demon Territory had been war chariots, we might expect at least two horses for each one; but while the numbers are incomplete, it is evident that there were not nearly that many; see Ch'en, "Hsi-Chou T'ung-ch'i," (4).86. The genuine *Bamboo Books* (Wang, *Ku Chu-shu*, 8a) tells of the capture of a thousand horses from certain Jung in the ninth century, but makes no mention of vehicles; as was mentioned earlier, however, the cavalry horse was apparently unknown in the neighborhood of China at that time. We know that the nomads of Western Asia used carts from an early date; Childe says that wheeled vehicles are attested as appearing on the steppes of Central Asia not long after 2500 B.C. See: Childe, "The First Waggons and Carts," 193. Minns, *Scythians and Greeks*, 50–52. McGovern, *Central Asia*, 52–53. We have clear evidence that the tribes living on the borders of China in the second century B.C. used vehicles to transport their baggage, and there is every reason to suppose that they did so earlier. See *Shih-chi*, 110.30, 44, 52; Watson, *Records*, II, 168, 177, 182.
77. Dewall, *Pferd und Wagen im frühen China*, 186. Ch'u is, of course, a special case. In the Spring and Autumn period the men of Ch'u seem quite as adept in the use of chariots as those of the north, so that they may well have had them in Western Chou times. But as we have seen, whether or not Ch'u was barbarian is a difficult question. In 584 B.C., when instructors went from Chin to the barbarian state of Wu, they are said to have taught the men of Wu "to ride in chariots"; *Tso*, 362::364 (Ch'eng 7).
78. *Tso*, 27::28 (Yin 9), 572::579 (Chao 1).

the Spring and Autumn period. A passage in the *Tso-chuan*, dated to 714 B.C., gives us a rare glimpse. It relates that a body of northern Jung made a raid into the state of Cheng, and the Earl of Cheng, noting that his forces were based on the chariot while the Jung were infantry, was concerned as to the best method of opposing them. His son suggested:

> "Order some men who are brave, but not persistent, to pretend to attack the brigands and then quickly fall back. At the same time put men in ambuscade in three places to await them. The Jung are nimble but they have no order; they are greedy and feel no regard for each other. When they are winning no one will yield place to another, and when they are defeated they make no attempt to save each other. When their front men believe that they are gaining the victory they will think of nothing but advancing; when they move forward and fall into our ambush they will quickly flee, and those behind will not come to their rescue, so that they will have no support. This will relieve your anxiety."
>
> This plan was followed. As soon as the front men of the Jung encountered the ambuscade they fled. Chu Tan [a Cheng official] pursued them, and surrounded them so that they were attacked both in front and in the rear, and annihilated. The remainder of the Jung army fled.[79]

There is no mention here of the use of chariots, by either the Jung or the Chinese.

Even on perfectly level ground war chariots were not immune from harm. In a battle in 575 B.C. an officer of Chin was pursuing the Earl of Cheng—both were in chariots. The spearman in the Chin chariot proposed that some foot soldiers be sent ahead to intercept the Earl's chariot, thus making it possible to drag him from it as a captive. The Chin officer refused, not on the ground that it would be impossible, but that it was improper to injure the ruler of a state (and even, such was his sanctity, dangerous), even though he were an enemy.[80] There is no reason to suppose that such scruples would have deterred barbarians, or that they were not quite as fleet of foot and as able to intercept chariots as Chinese foot soldiers.

Neither, of course, is there any reason to suppose that barbarian troops would normally oppose Chinese warriors in chariots on the

79. *Tso*, 27::28 (Yin 9).
80. *Tso*, 392::397 (Ch'eng 16). See also *Tso-chuan*, 28.11b.

ground best suited to the chariots. They were raiders, adept at surprise attack. The Chinese were unfavorably impressed with the fact that they felt no shame about fleeing when they found it advantageous to do so. This is, of course, the typical attitude of "regular" soldiers, accustomed to war of position, toward guerrilla fighters. And it seems clear that that is what the barbarians, or most of them, were: guerilla warriors.

Even in our own day, regular soldiers equipped with firearms, high explosives, tanks, and airplanes, find guerrilla fighters extremely difficult to defeat; it is calculated that a given number of guerrillas can only be overcome by several times that number of regular soldiers. There is no reason to suppose that chariots would have given the Chinese an advantage even comparable to that of modern weapons. Furthermore, it is not possible to dismiss the barbarians, or all of them, as mere rabble. They probably did not have as much technique as the Chinese, but since we read that the Chinese defeated barbarians by attacking them "before they were deployed," it appears that barbarian troops sometimes did deploy for battle.[81]

We saw in the previous chapter that, in the Spring and Autumn period at least, barbarians often fought alongside Chinese troops as well as against them. Barbarians not infrequently gained the victory. Chinese were glad to have them as allies. An officer of Chin said that if that state could secure the friendship of the Jung, the neighboring states would be terrified, and Chin's armies would not be toiled and its weapons ruined.[82] The barbarians were formidable foes—and they fought on foot.

How did the Chinese manage to defeat them? It must have been done by foot soldiers. Even today tanks and airplanes, while they may help, do not serve to vanquish determined guerrillas. There is no substitute for the foot soldier who carries the fight to the enemy on the ground. This must have been at least as true in Western Chou times. Not only does it seem clear that fighters in chariots could not have defeated the barbarians; chariots must have been a definite disadvantage in fighting them.

It is quite true that, as Griffith says, "terrain suitable for chariots dictated and restricted the form of battle,"[83] but this dictation could not apply to the barbarians; they were not chivalrous warriors who fought duels on fields agreed upon with the enemy, but wily raiders

81. *Tso*, 572::579 (Chao 1). See also *Tso*, 391::396 (Ch'eng 16).
82. *Tso*, 422::424 (Hsiang 4).
83. Griffith, *Sun Tzu*, 32.

who fought where and when they chose. Miss von Dewall, who recognizes that the chariot had serious limitations, suggests that it did give the Chinese an advantage over the barbarians in battle because of its mobility, which made it possible to move both men and information quickly.[84] This is a question. That a chariot of that time, loaded with warriors, really could cover the ground faster than a barbarian fighter running seems doubtful; certainly the barbarian had greater maneuverability and could operate on more varied terrain.

We do not have to speculate as to whether Chinese of the Spring and Autumn period, using chariots to fight barbarian infantry, found themselves at a disadvantage. This is recorded fact. In 541 B.C. a Chin army was facing a group of Ti tribes. A Chin officer said: "They are foot soldiers, while we have chariots. Furthermore, we have to meet them in a narrow pass. . . . Let us all become infantry." And as we have seen, in 714 B.C., just after the end of Western Chou, when the Earl of Cheng was taking measures to counter an invasion by Jung, he said, "They are footmen, while we have chariots. I am afraid that they will make a surprise attack on us."[85]

Even more convincing than such statements concerning the defects of the chariot as a fighting machine is the almost total lack of any claim that it has virtues in this regard. Even in the *Tso-chuan*, where so much of the talk is of battles almost all featuring chariots, there is almost nothing that would lead one to suppose that the war chariot was formidable. This is even more true of the Western Chou sources. The poets never tire of telling us that the chariot is beautiful and awe-inspiring, but they are almost completely silent as to how it was used in war. Miss von Dewall notes that in the *Poetry* chariots are not depicted as taking, in the actual fighting, "any part worth mentioning," and concludes that that work lays emphasis on the chariot, not for its actual contribution to the fighting, but rather for "its role as a visible symbol of martial might and pre-eminence."[86] Cho-yun Hsu says that, as an instrument of war, chariots "were inefficient."[87] I believe that anyone who examines the evidence carefully must come to the same verdict.

FOR chivalrous fighting between Chinese gentlemen in the Spring and Autumn period, the chariot was an excellent device. But in Western

---

84. Dewall, *Pferd und Wagen im frühen China*, 186–187.
85. *Tso*, 27::28 (Yin 9), 572::579 (Chao 1).
86. Dewall, *Pferd und Wagen im frühen China*, 56, 184.
87. Hsu, *Ancient China*, 69.

Chou times, when most of the fighting was with barbarians, it is hard to avoid the conclusion that, *as a weapon*, the war chariot must have been rather worse than useless. Why then is it so persistently and so conspicuously found, not only in the poems but also in excavated tombs? It seems clear that the reason is prestige.

Childe says that some of the earliest vehicles known from Mesopotamia were "royal hearses," and that "burial with a hearse was clearly a royal prerogative. Within a few centuries of its invention the new means of transport [the wheeled vehicle] was thus firmly associated with kings, if only in death; the persistence of this association will be found to be among the most convincing arguments for its diffusion."[88] A man riding in a vehicle is conspicuously lifted above his fellows. We think of "the man on horseback" as the figure of power; in early China it was the man in the chariot.

All this does not mean that the war chariot had no usefulness. The very fact that it lifted its occupants above the field of battle made it valuable to commanders, giving them a much better view of the situation. We even read of a chariot surmounted by a "nest"—this is comparable to our "crow's-nest," the lookout platform atop the mast of a ship; from it the ruler of Ch'u was able to observe all of the movements of the opposing army.[89] And the chariot was a movable observation platform, on which the commander—who did not even have to drive himself—could be transported wherever he wished to go (and his chariot could operate) without exertion, leaving his mind and his energies free for the task of supervision. The chariot was also useful as a command post. Chariots carrying important men were surmounted by their flags, providing a symbol and a rallying point for their troops. The command chariot also seems to have carried the drum used to signal the advance and the bell (or gong) that was sounded for retreat.[90] As a "command car" the chariot was certainly valuable.

Chariots also played another important role. They were extremely impressive. Their ornamentation, both in Shang and in Chou times, far outshone the fittings of the most luxurious custom-built automobile of our day.[91] The setting forth of military expeditions as described in the *Poetry* is pure pageantry, and it was probably far more awe-

88. Childe, "The First Waggons and Carts," 179.
89. *Tso*, 391::396 (Ch'eng 16).
90. *Shih*, 123, 233. *Tso*, 85::86 (Chuang 10), 126::129 (Min 2), 339::345 (Ch'eng 2), 392::397 (Ch'eng 16), 823::825 (Ai 11).
91. See the plates in Dewall, *Pferd und Wagen im frühen China*, and Creel, *The Birth of China*, plate XIV.

inspiring than a parade of tanks. As visual symbols to impress both Chinese and barbarians with the sophistication of the ruling group, chariots were undoubtedly most effective.

Thus chariots clearly were useful for their psychological effect and as moving command posts for higher officers, even if their value as offensive weapons in battle was less than is often supposed. So long as they were comparatively few, in relation to the total military force employed, they undoubtedly made a contribution. It is only when they were conceived as the principal means of fighting that they made an army *less* effective, except in duels with another force that also fought with chariots according to the same code.

THERE is little indication that large numbers of chariots were used in warfare in Shang times.[92] It seems probable that they were used somewhat more extensively in Western Chou. The Chou undoubtedly had had the war chariot before the conquest,[93] and Miss von Dewall finds that almost immediately after that event Chou craftsmen show "a paramount artistic engagement in the design of horse trappings, which in their variety and abundance overshadow anything known from the Shang equipment for the horse." She further writes:

> Apart from practical usefulness, a certain prestige ensued from the possession of spectacular driving equipment. It did not lie so much in the owner's martial reputation, as it was deeply rooted in the whole pattern of feeling, thinking and acting of Chou society. The contemporary literary documents confirm the results suggested by the archaeological investigation and by the attempt at an aesthetic appreciation. The ideal of the

92. In two indices to the published oracle bone inscriptions, a total of only twenty-two occurrences of the character *ch'e* 車 are listed. See Sun, *Chia-ku Wen Pien*, 14.3ab, and Chin, *Hsü Chia-ku Wen Pien*, 14.5a. When the Shang raised armies, they spoke of raising so many men, but do not seem to have mentioned chariots; see Hu, *Chia-ku Hsüeh*, *Ch'u-chi*, "Yin Fei Nu-li She-hui Lun," 2b–3b. Shih Chang-ju, on the basis of excavated Shang tombs, seems to assign a principal place to the chariot in Shang armies; see: Shih, "Yin-hsü Fa-chüeh ti Kung-hsien," 22–23, and Cheng, *Shang China*, 208–209. But there is some question as to how far one is justified in generalizing from such data; see Dewall, *Pferd und Wagen im frühen China*, 150–162. Wu Tse (*Ku-tai Shih*, 415) concluded, on the basis of the Shang inscriptions, that while the Shang certainly did have the war chariot, it did not constitute the basic strength of their armies, since inscriptions dealing with war seldom mention chariots, but mention infantry frequently.
93. *Shih*, 188, 189. Dewall, "New Data on Early Chou Finds," 546.

Chou nobility was the eye-catching display of splendour and gaiety and it was pursued in driving the chariot with a stupendous array of horses, carriages, and occupants. An indulgence in ostentation and rotating movement, which also shines through the bronze ornamentation as the artisan's mental attitude, remains the prime impression of the Chou design in comparison with the very dignified yet much more stereotyped Shang models. The impression of pageantry, being a main occupation of the Chou elite, is not far-fetched. . . . The datable archaeological evidence of chariots, horse-trappings and weapons . . . goes right back into the incipient stage of the Chou period. This leaves no doubt that, after its restricted ceremonial use in Shang times, the chariot was developed in all its potentialities only by the organisatory and political ingenuity of the Chou dynasty, who depended on it to secure power and to establish the control over their new dominions.[94]

Miss von Dewall points out a very significant difference in the manufacture, in early Chou times, of horse trappings and of the dagger-ax—a very practical battlefield weapon. She finds that the design of the dagger-ax "was determined by a straight forward strife for security and efficiency, to the extent of neglecting decoration almost completely," whereas "the horse-gear was dominated by a luxurious craze for display even at the expense of practicability."[95]

It seems possible to reconstruct what happened with a good deal of probability. From the excavations and the oracle bones, we know that the Shang rulers performed elaborate sacrificial ceremonies with great frequency. We also know that they had chariots ornamented with surpassing beauty, and that they bred teams of horses matched both as to color and as to size.[96] Even if we had no other evidence, we could reasonably suppose that Shang dignitaries, like their Chou ancestors, rode in these splendid vehicles in awe-inspiring pageants. And in a poem written in the state that continued the Shang line we find it said that the Shang King Wu Ting, "with dragon banners and ten chariots, went and presented the great sacrificial grain."[97] No doubt to the Chou as well as to others the act of parading in such glorious fashion

94. Dewall, "New Data on Early Chou Finds," 546–548.
95. Ibid., 548.
96. Kuo, *Pu-tz'u T'ung-tsuan, K'ao-shih,* 155b–157a.
97. *Shih,* 263. Creel, *Studies,* 49–54.

seemed the very epitome of Chinese sophistication and power. We know how eager the Chou were to be accepted as Chinese, and as the legitimate successors to the Shang. Nothing was more natural, then, than that they should try to match and to outshine the splendor of Shang chariots. As their "luxurious craze for display" accelerated, an eye-catching equipage came to be an indispensable hallmark of the person of consequence. The *Discourses of the States* said that a man's rank was shown by "his chariot, his dress, his banners, and his insignia."[98] In the Spring and Autumn period we read of a noble of Ch'i who had a beautiful chariot that was so highly polished that "it could be used as a mirror."[99]

GENTLEMEN of the Spring and Autumn period cultivated the arts of archery and charioteering.[100] In the *Tso-chuan* and elsewhere we find the two mentioned together, as if they were an inseparable pair.[101] But in fact they had somewhat different histories.

Archery was cultivated as early as Western Chou times both as a skill of practical usefulness in war and as a polite accomplishment. Bronze inscriptions tell us of an archery school under royal patronage and of archery contests in which the King personally took part.[102] These contests seem to have been festive occasions, and the *Poetry* tells of festive archery contests.[103] The *Book of Etiquette and Ceremonial* has two long sections that describe in detail the procedures to be used in archery contests; while this work was compiled relatively late, it no doubt embodies a certain amount of valid tradition.[104] Con-

98. *Kuo-yü*, 1.14a.
99. *Tso*, 538::542 (Hsiang 28).
100. It is commonly said that "six arts," *liu i* 六 藝 , were cultivated by the Chou aristocrat. They are listed by the *Ritual of Chou* as *li* (probably here best translated as "conduct" or "ritual"), music, archery, charioteering, literature (or writing), and arithmetic (*Chou-li*, 10.24b; Biot, *Tcheou-li*, I, 214). The expression *liu i* does not seem to occur, however, in the Western Chou sources, nor even in the *Tso-chuan*, the *Analects*, the *Mo-tzu*, or the *Mencius*. It must be concluded that the expression was not current in Western Chou or even Spring and Autumn times. This certainly does not mean, however, that aristocrats of the Spring and Autumn period had no familiarity with these subjects; certainly they did, with most of them. There is a single reference to archery as an "art," *i*, in *Tso*, 392::397 (Ch'eng 16).
101. *Tso*, 362::364 (Ch'eng 7), 522::527 (Hsiang 26), 562::566 (Hsiang 31). *Shu*, 81. The two are mentioned in successive lines in *Shih*, 53.
102. *Chin-wen*, 30b, 40b, 55b, 69a, 107b. Kuo, *Chin-wen Ts'ung-k'ao*, 17b–19a. Ch'en, "Hsi-Chou T'ung-ch'i," (6).98. Ssu, "Liang-Chou Chih-kuan K'ao," 12.
103. *Shih*, 69, 173–174, 202.
104. *I-li*, 11.1a–13.20b, 16.1a–18.22b; Steele, *I-li*, I, 74–121, 150–188.

fucius, living at the end of the Spring and Autumn period, tended to repudiate the military ideals of the aristocracy, yet he shot with the bow and regarded archery with favor. The festive nature of archery contests, and the decorum prescribed for them, seem to have appealed to Confucians. And archery continued in favor with scholars, even as late as Han times.[105]

Charioteering as a skill, on the other hand, is only rarely mentioned in the Western Chou sources, and it seems clear that it did not at that time have the status of being one of the recognized accomplishments of a gentleman. Three poems speak with admiration of skill in driving, but in none of them is there any suggestion that this is employed in warfare.[106] In bronze inscriptions, even late in Western Chou, the drivers of war chariots are specifically said to be menials. It was not until Spring and Autumn times that the prestige of the chariot came to glorify even the man who held the reins.[107]

THE armor worn by knights, and the battleships commanded by admirals, were originally very practical tools of warfare. But they came to be prized as symbols of prestige, sometimes clung to stubbornly after their usefulness had passed. The chariot was valuable in war, if only as a moving command post. But the time came when every man of aristocratic status must fight from a chariot, and aristocrats felt themselves demeaned by fighting on foot, even if it were more effective. In 541 B.C., when a Chin commander ordered his chariot fighters to turn themselves into infantry in order to meet a coalition of Ti barbarians, he got down from his own chariot first to set the example. One of those with him refused to do this, and although he was an influential man, the commander had him beheaded on the spot. Stimulated by this the others dismounted, and they gained a great victory over the barbarians.[108]

In the Warring States period wars were no longer matters of chivalrous duels between gentlemen. The aristocrats of Spring and Autumn times had all but vanished, and wars were fought in earnest, to win. Armies became much larger. Chariots were still used; they had some value. But the principal reliance was placed on infantry, and the pro-

105. *Analects*, 3.7, 3.16, 7.26. Creel, *Confucius*, 82, 170–171, 312::91, 155 (n. 4), 182.

106. *Shih*, 52–53, 168. Kuo Mo-jo (*Chin-wen Ts'ung-k'ao*, 18a) says that of the "six arts . . . it is only the study of archery that appears" in the bronze inscriptions.

107. See pp. 276–280.

108. *Tso*, 572::579 (Chao 1).

portion of chariots to infantry became relatively small.[109] Yet the chariots found in tombs of this time are even more splendid than those of the Spring and Autumn period. Cheng Te-k'un says that chariot fittings of the Warring States period "are so rich that the overwhelming variety of shapes and imaginative designs is known not only in China but also in collections all over the world. . . . Some of them are . . . decorated with intricate patterns in gold and silver, inlaid with precious stones and glass, and ornamented with animals in the round."[110] No matter that the chariot was no longer important in battle; it was still a luxurious symbol of the wealth and importance of its owner, as it had always been.

WHILE there were probably more chariots in the Western Chou period than in Shang, there is little indication that they approached the numbers of the Spring and Autumn period, when the *Tso-chuan* tells us that the single state of Chin could raise 4,900 chariots.[111] This is especially true of the opening years of the dynasty.

In the *Documents* we have lengthy statements by King Wu and the Duke of Chou, both justly celebrated for their martial achievements. Yet the only mention of vehicles by either of them, which comes from King Wu the conqueror, refers to oxcarts used to carry commodities. The only other vehicles mentioned in Western Chou sections of the *Documents* are chariots used at the funeral of King Ch'eng, and there is no indication that they were numerous.[112] The *Book of Changes* includes a certain number of references to vehicles, but in each case only to a single one. These include vehicles of various sorts; in only one instance does there seem to be fairly clear indication that a war chariot is in question.[113]

While the poets were clearly fascinated with the chariot and were untiring in describing the beauty of the vehicles, the pennons and other accouterments that decked them, and the processions that they made, actual numbers of chariots are very seldom given in the *Poetry*. It seems reasonable to deduce that the numbers were in most cases not

109. Hsu, *Ancient China*, 67–71. Armies of the Warring States period are frequently enumerated simply as so many men, presumably infantry, with no mention of chariots. See *Chan-kuo Ts'e*, 15.4a, 20.1a, 21.1b, 22.4a, 22.4b, 23.5b, 24.2a, 24.2b, 26.1b.
110. Cheng, *Chou China*, 273.
111. *Tso*, 602::605 (Chao 5).
112. *Shu*, 43, 71.
113. *I-ching*, 3.26a; Legge, *I-ching*, 112.

extremely large, for if they had been the poets would probably have mentioned this impressive fact. Two poems speak of processions of a hundred vehicles escorting brides—in one case a niece of the King— to their future homes.[114] Only two specify numbers of war chariots; both are dated to the reign of King Hsüan, almost at the end of Western Chou. One tells of an expedition sent out by the King to repulse an attack by the Hsien-yün barbarians, and says that "ten great war chariots went in front, to open up the march." The other concerns an expedition against both the Hsien-yün and Ch'u; it paints a striking picture of the setting forth of the army, with sound and color and detail, and of its "three thousand chariots." Whether there were in fact this many, or the poet was merely giving an impressive figure for the sake of effect, is a question; the contrast with the ten chariots in the other poem is considerable. In any case, this poem is dated close to the Spring and Autumn period, by which time there probably were a good many chariots.[115]

Information on the number of chariots used is still more rare in the bronze inscriptions. Although thirty-four of those in my corpus mention military action, the nature of the forces employed is seldom specified, and only a single late inscription gives the number of chariots involved. This is the one that describes the rebellion in which the Marquis of E led the southern Huai I and the eastern I in an extensive invasion of Chinese territory. The King ordered the royal armies to attack the Marquis, but apparently they were too heavily engaged elsewhere to do this. A certain Duke Wu therefore moved against the Marquis; and the maker of the vessel, a subordinate of the Duke, tells us of the force that he personally commanded. It consisted of one hundred chariots and one thousand foot soldiers. This was probably only a small part of the forces employed on the Chinese side, but the number of chariots is not impressive.[116]

It seems to be unquestioned doctrine, among ancient and modern students of Chinese history, that those who fought in chariots were, at least from as early as any time we know about, aristocrats. Everyone, certainly including myself, seems to have accepted this without question. Yet if we examine parallel phenomena in medieval Europe, they

114. *Shih*, 7, 231.
115. *Shih*, 120–121, 122–123. For the traditional attributions of these poems, see *Mao-shih*, 10(2).1a, 8b.
116. *Ch'ing-t'ung-ch'i T'u-shih*, 24. T'ang Lan, in ibid., 2, minimizes the role of the maker of this vessel in winning the victory—correctly, I think.

suggest another possibility. We tend to think of any man in medieval Europe who went into battle riding a charger and wearing armor as a knight, and every knight as being an aristocrat. But Strayer points out that it was not until centuries after the beginnings of knighthood that such conditions prevailed.

> Lords who needed soldiers did not worry about their social origins, and a peasant who proved to be a good cavalryman could pass his occupation on to his son. Serfs who served as knights remained common in Eastern France and Germany clear into the thirteenth century. No one in 1100 would have thought that the knightly class as a whole was noble or aristocratic. Some knights were of noble descent, some were not, but as a class they were simply a group of specially trained and specially rewarded retainers. They could be given by one lord to another, just as any other dependents could be given. For example, an eleventh-century Norman duke gave a monastery a village with its peasants, mills, meadows, and knights.[117]

Carl Stephenson points out that the word "knight" derived from the Anglo-Saxon *cniht* (related to the German *knecht*), which meant "boy" and "might be used to designate either a slave, a free servant, or a military retainer."[118]

The Chinese character *yü* 馭 , originally having the sense of "to drive a chariot" or "charioteer,"[119] had a history that was in some ways parallel to that of the word "knight." It came to be used not only for the driver, but also for all those who rode in chariots to fight. Where it is used in this sense, it may be translated as "chariotry," as distinguished from infantry. It is not always easy to be certain, however, whether a text is referring solely to charioteers, or to chariotry.

An inscription dated to the eleventh century B.C. records a gift by

117. Strayer, *Feudalism*, 25.
118. Stephenson, *Medieval Feudalism*, 8.
119. This character is composed of the pictograph for "horse" on the left, and on the right a human hand which (in the early graph) holds something—possibly, though this is uncertain, a whip. The form *yü* 御 , of uncertain origin, is used for "charioteer" in the *Poetry* and almost uniformly in the *Tso-chuan*. Both forms occur in the bronze inscriptions, but the one that includes the ideograph for "horse" seems always to occur in contexts having to do with chariots. There appears to be no doubt, however, that these are different graphs for the same word; see: Jung, *Chin-wen Pien*, 2.26ab. *Shuo-wen*, 829b–831a. Karlgren, "Grammata Serica Recensa," 40 (no. 80).

the King of "six hundred and fifty-nine men," including an unspecified number of *yü*, either charioteers or chariotry. All of these men are designated as belonging to a class that is commonly supposed to consist of slaves.[120]

There is a rather general tendency to use the term "slave" very loosely. Even in our own society very few of us are free from obligations that legally bind us to some extent—obligations of marriage, parenthood, debt, liability for military service, and so forth. Obligations were undoubtedly heavier and more ubiquitous in early China, but it is generally agreed among objective scholars that there were relatively few who may properly be called slaves.[121] But just as in medieval Europe, where Vinogradoff speaks of "a large and varied mass of half-free people," there was a great range of gradation in social status from the highest to the lowest.[122] It is doubtful that these chariot drivers or fighters were in fact slaves, even though they might, like knights, "be given by one lord to another." They were not at the very bottom of the social scale, but neither were they aristocrats.[123]

An inscription dated to the reign of King Li (878–828 b.c.) lists *yü*, even this late in Western Chou, along with artisans and several other classes of persons of definitely inferior status.[124]

Most interesting of all is the inscription, also dated to this reign, that tells of the great revolt and invasion led by the Marquis of E. The maker of the bronze details the composition of the force under his

---

120. *Chin-wen*, 33b–34b. Ch'en, "Hsi-Chou T'ung-ch'i," (3).93–97. All these men are called *jen li* 人鬲 . On the meaning of this term see ibid., (1).167, and Kuo, *Chung-kuo Ku-tai She-hui Yen-chiu*, 296. I am not certain, however, that anyone really understands this term.

121. C. Martin Wilbur, in *Slavery in Former Han*, 237, writes: "During the Former Han period the percentage of China's population that was enslaved appears to have been greater than at any other time, and the slavery system seems to have reached its economic peak. Pre-Han data on slavery are so scarce and fragmentary, and so indecisive as to create the impression of a weak and underdeveloped system, a situation to be expected in an economy based upon serfdom." Elsewhere (ibid., 241) he says that "slaves seem to have made up not more than one percent of the total population even at the time when the institution was most fully developed." E. G. Pulleyblank ("The Origins and Nature of Chattel Slavery in China," 190) says "there is very little evidence of the buying and selling of human beings before the Warring States period (5th to 3rd centuries) and what little there is is very difficult to interpret."

122. *Cambridge Medieval History*, II, 652. A passage in the *Tso-chuan* grades men into ten classes, from the King downward: *Tso*, 611::616 (Chao 7).

123. The inscription says that these *jen li* ranged "from *yü* to *shu jen* 庶人 ." Ch'en Meng-chia says ("Hsi-Chou T'ung-ch'i," [1].167) that *shu jen* are the lowest class of slaves—which may or may not be the case.

124. *Chin-wen*, 114a.

command. It consisted of "100 chariots [with their accompanying] menials:[125] 200 *yü* and 1000 foot soldiers." The fact that two *yü* were assigned to each chariot raises an interesting question.[126] It has some-

125. Because there is so much difference of opinion concerning the reading of this inscription, the basic text must be considered to be the squeeze published in *Ch'ing-t'ung-ch'i T'u-shih*, plate 78. The character I am translating as "menials" is *ssu* 𣪠 ; the text actually reads *ssu* 斯 . This character is interpreted as 𣪠 by T'ang Lan (ibid., 2, n. 6) and by Hsü Chung-shu ("Yü Ting," 54, n. 8). The character is read quite differently by Kuo Mo-jo in "Yü Ting Po," and by Ch'en Chin-i in "Yü Ting K'ao-shih." But both of the latter works were published much earlier than those of T'ang and Hsü, who may have had better copies of the inscription at their disposal.

126. It must be noted, however, that Kuo Mo-jo, Ch'en Chin-i, and T'ang Lan read this inscription as referring, not to 200 *yü*, but to 100. As was mentioned in the preceding note, Kuo and Ch'en may have been working from an early and inferior squeeze, but T'ang was not. The reading of "200" is that of Hsü Chung-shu, in "Yü Ting," 54. In my opinion careful examination of the squeeze shows that Hsü is clearly correct.

Hsü says that in the inscription the figures "2 and 100 are written in combined form." This is a common practice, but it is not always easy to be certain of the meaning of such combined forms. What the squeeze shows is the character for "100" surmounted by a single line, that is, "1." Jung Keng interprets such combined forms in bronze inscriptions as meaning "100," while he interprets forms having two lines (the figure "2") above "100" as meaning "200"; see Jung, *Chin-wen Pien*, 4.5b. On the other hand, Ch'en Meng-chia interprets "100" surmounted by a single line, in Shang inscriptions, as "200"; compare Ch'en, *Yin Tz'u Tsung-shu*, 108, and *Yin Ch'i Ch'ien-pien*, 2.30b, 4.4a. Of course, Shang practice may not have been the same as that of Chou times. But it is seldom possible to verify such interpretations by context, and there is no way of knowing whether different individuals always followed the same convention.

Precisely this problem is discussed at great length in Chou, *Chin-wen Ling-shih*, 58–60, in connection with the inscription on the "Shih Ch'i Ting." It has the character for "100" surmounted by two strokes; see Kuo, *Chin-wen Lu-pien*, 12b. Scholars have divided rather equally between reading this as "200" and as "300." Kuo Mo-jo, who calls this vessel the "Shih Lü Ting" (*Chin-wen*, 26a), joins those who read it as "300." To be consistent with this, Kuo should read the figure on the "Yü Ting" as "200."

In such cases only internal evidence within the specific inscription can make the sense certain. In the "Yü Ting" there is very clear internal evidence. The character for "100" occurs here twice, with only three characters in between. Both are quite clear. The first "100" is not surmounted by a line, and there is not room for a line between it and the character above it. The second "100" is well below the character above it, and is surmounted by a very clear line. It seems improbable that the writer of the inscription would have written the same character twice, so close together, in such different ways, if he had not intended to distinguish between them.

T'ang Lan undoubtedly had the best rubbing of the inscription available; I suspect that his reading was based not so much on the writing of the inscription as on what he believed it must say. In a note (*Ch'ing-t'ung-ch'i T'u-shih*, 2, n. 6) he says that the inscription states that "each war chariot, in addition to warriors, had one

times been held that in Western Chou times the war chariot carried only two men;[127] if so, this inscription appears to call all those manning the chariots menials. In fact, however, it seems quite possible that at this late date in Western Chou chariots may have carried three men. In any case, this inscription seems clearly to designate as menials not only the driver but also at least one of the warriors fighting from the chariot.

All this is changed in Spring and Autumn times. The principal occupant of a war chariot was undoubtedly its owner, and an aristocrat. He was armed with a bow. The chariot of that time normally carried three men (though occasionally there were four). The two additional occupants were the driver *(yü)* and a spearman.[128] The driver of the chariot was obviously a very important man, for the success and safety of all depended in considerable measure on his performance. In the *Tso-chuan* we read repeatedly that the archer (the principal) chose a certain person, or had a certain person, as his driver *(yü)*. And from the very beginning of the Spring and Autumn period these *yü* seem to have been aristocrats. The first one mentioned, in 709 B.C., is an important aristocrat of Chin; so also is the second. The drivers of even relatively unimportant officers are named and seem clearly to be men of aristocratic status.[129] The prestige of the chariot had ennobled all who rode in it.

THE sword and armor of the European knight were at first just the tools of his trade, but in time they came to be invested with an almost mystical significance. In China the chariot became a very potent symbol of status.

Aristocrats in ancient Egypt became distinguished for their skill in charioteering, and they delighted in their spirited horses.[130] The Western Chou Chinese, too, delighted in their beautifully matched and mettlesome teams, but they were even more interested in their im-

---

yü [charioteer] and ten foot soldiers. Warriors belonged to the nobility, charioteers and foot soldiers were slaves." According to T'ang's interpretation, if each chariot had two *yü*, this would mean that a warrior was a slave, which would be contrary to his understanding of the facts.

127. Cheng, *Chou China*, 295.

128. *Tso*, 123::125 (Min 1), 127::130 (Min 2), 257::258 (Wen 11). See also Legge's discussion in ibid., 337.

129. *Tso*, 41::42 (Huan 3), 123::125 (Min. 1), 127::130 (Min 2).

130. Verbal communication from Professor John A. Wilson, March 28, 1967. See also Wilson, *The Culture of Ancient Egypt*, 196–197.

pressively embellished chariots. Miss von Dewall describes the appearance that must have been made by a chariot actually excavated from a Western Chou tomb, "with lustrous bronze mountings of all forms, dangling bosses and jingles, colourful pendants and—as we may add from literary description—with floating pennons and banners, scarlet and fur hangings and mounted lances and shields."[131] Much of their penchant for such things can certainly be explained by what Miss von Dewall has called "a luxurious craze for display," but there was evidently another motivation also.

In the bronze inscriptions we repeatedly find the King, in making gifts to his vassals, presenting them with trappings for horses or chariot. For example we find King Mu presenting an Earl with these gifts: a goblet of sacrificial spirits, a chariot ornamented with bronze fittings, four horses, decorated upturned side bars for the chariot, a decorated leaning-board for the chariot, red chest straps for his horses, a decorated canopy for the chariot, metal-ornamented reins, and four other appurtenances for the chariot. Thus of these twelve gifts, eleven pertained to the chariot.[132] This high proportion is unusual, but not unique. "Metal-ornamented reins" are among the most usual gifts, and in one inscription this is the only gift mentioned.[133]

A gift from royalty is always prized, and it is not remarkable that the recipients of these presents cast costly bronzes to celebrate them. It is reasonable to suppose, however, that their significance was greater than that merely of the physical objects themselves. It appears probable that the King gave to the recipients not only these tangible things, but also *the right to use* such distinctive trappings as he conferred. The bronze inscriptions mention presentations to their subordinates by lesser dignitaries, including gifts of horses and chariots, but none (of those in my corpus, at least) records the conferring of trappings for horse or chariot by anyone except the King. It seems likely, therefore, that the war chariot of a Western Chou officer was somewhat comparable with the military dress uniform of our day, with its ribbons showing honors that have been conferred.[134]

131. Dewall, "New Data on Early Chou Finds," 547–548.
132. *Chin-wen*, 62b.
133. Ibid., 117b.
134. There is much reason to believe that the gift consisted more in the license to use the objects than in the objects themselves. We repeatedly read of the granting of distinctive articles of clothing, and banners. It would be absurd to think that the recipients, who were certainly wealthy men, could not have afforded to have such things made for themselves, and the same is true of most of the chariot trappings. We also find the King conferring upon men the flags and trappings of their ancestors (*Chin-wen*, 34a, 65b, 141a, 154a). It is not clear whether the King actually

Presentation of gifts concerned with the chariot is rare in bronze inscriptions dated to the early years of the dynasty. But they become increasingly common, and the high point of frequency is reached in the last century of Western Chou.

LET us try to form a hypothesis concerning the employment of the war chariot in Western Chou. The Chou knew the war chariot before the conquest, but they may well have taken it over from the Shang. Certainly the beautiful bronze chariot fittings of the earliest Chou times, while they rapidly became characterized by their own style, owed much to the basic inspiration of Shang art. The Chou clearly admired the Shang chariot and sought to produce even more splendid vehicles for their own use. In Western Chou times, as it surely had been in Shang, the chariot was prized as a symbol of luxury and power, in which parading rulers might impress their subjects and the barbarians with their invincibility and sophistication.

The chariot was also useful in war. It provided transportation for higher officers, just as in modern times higher officers even of infantry have ridden on horses, and later in automobiles. It was also useful as a mobile observation post for officers, and a movable command post and rallying point. Although it could not operate on all terrain, this was not a critical limitation so long as the main reliance was on foot soldiers, who were merely directed in their movements by officers transported in chariots.

This was probably the situation at the beginning of Western Chou. We have seen that nothing indicates that there were a very large number of chariots, although the military operations of the time must have required a large number of troops. If, in the eleventh century B.C., an army sent against the Demon Territory killed 4,812 and captured 13,083 of the enemy, the army that did this must have been sizable.[135] It seems probable that the number of foot soldiers commanded by each chariot was then rather large.

---

took back these insignia when the recipient died, or merely had to confer upon his descendants the right to use them. But this again tends to indicate that such articles as chariot trappings were not merely physical gifts, but insignia of royal favor.

135. Ch'en, "Hsi-Chou T'ung-ch'i," (4).86. These are the numbers of those slain and captured only in the first campaign. I was formerly inclined to think such figures exaggerated, but it is not inconceivable that they may be at least approximately correct. As we learn more of the scope of Western Chou operations, former scepticism seems less warranted.

Important officers who rode in chariots of course had a driver, just as modern officers do for their cars. It is possible that sometimes in Western Chou—as we know was normal in Spring and Autumn times—a third man, a fighter, also rode in the chariot. In our own day those who drive cars even for generals are not normally of high rank, and we have seen that, through much of Western Chou at least, the driver of the war chariot was of low status. As late as the final century of Western Chou, chariot drivers, and some of those who rode in chariots to fight as well, were called "menials."

While the chariot was important from the beginning of Chou, gifts of horse-and-chariot trappings by the King seem to indicate that as a prestige symbol the chariot came to be increasingly prized, and that this attitude reached a high point toward the end of Western Chou. Concomitantly the men of power who were vassals of the Chou came to compose an aristocratic class, and developed a code of that class. Their power and wealth increased, and so—aided by polygamy—did their offspring. As the chariot became a preeminent symbol of aristocratic status, every man of pretensions must have his own. And not only the rulers and their relatives but, as commonly happens, their close attendants and even their servants became elevated in status. This elevation must have seemed particularly appropriate for those who were closely associated with that symbol of majesty, the chariot. Thus we find that in the Spring and Autumn period, a *yü*, a charioteer, is no longer a menial. By that time it appears that all aristocrats rode in chariots, and all those who rode in chariots were considered aristocrats.

That the numbers of chariots had increased considerably by late Western Chou times would seem to be indicated by the force opposing the Marquis of E, concerning whose composition we have details. There were 1000 men and 100 chariots, one chariot to every ten men. It seems doubtful that this was a desirable ratio from a purely military point of view, especially for fighting barbarian infantry.

THE book on warfare called *Sun-tzu* was evidently written in the Warring States period, possibly in the fourth century B.C.[136] B. H. Liddell Hart says of it:

> Sun Tzu's essays on "The Art of War" form the earliest of known treatises on the subject, but have never been surpassed in comprehensiveness and depth of under-

136. See Griffith, *Sun Tzu*, 1–12, and *Wei-shu T'ung-kao*, 797–801.

standing. They might well be termed the concentrated essence of wisdom on the conduct of war. Among all the military thinkers of the past, only Clausewitz is comparable, and even he is more "dated" than Sun Tzu, and in part antiquated, although he was writing more than two thousand years later. Sun Tzu has clearer vision, more profound insight, and eternal freshness.[137]

The armies of which the *Sun-tzu* speaks consisted chiefly of effective and well-disciplined infantry. It has commonly been supposed that such armies did not exist until a time less than two centuries before the *Sun-tzu* was written.[138] But the production of such a work, on the basis of so little prior development, would be most surprising.

The foot soldier of the Western Chou and Spring and Autumn periods is the forgotten man of Chinese history. The Chou achievement in conquering, and holding, their really huge territory is one of the great and significant military feats of history. Their opponents were (after the initial conquest) almost entirely barbarians who fought on foot, and the effective opposition to them had to be by foot soldiers. We have no indication that the Chinese had any monopoly of effective weapons—except insofar as this has been claimed for the chariot, but the sources themselves discredit this. Why, then, did the Chinese (most of the time) win? It must have been because of the greater effectiveness of their infantry.

In the *Tso-chuan* we have a certain number of criticisms of the barbarians as fighting men, and explanations of the reasons why the Chinese are able to defeat them. Their lack of chariots is *never* cited as a weakness. Four points are made or may be deduced: (1) barbarians lack discipline, (2) they do not cooperate with each other in battle, (3) they lack persistence, and (4) they do not maintain vigilance.[139] We may infer, and the sources seem to bear it out, that Chinese infantry were disciplined, cooperative, persistent, and vigilant.

Yet almost everyone, including myself, seems to have assumed that the foot soldiers of this time were farmers who were, from time to time, called from their fields to become soldiers for the occasion.[140] It is generally taken for granted that they counted for little. Granet writes: "The foot-soldiers are poorly armed. They act as trench-

137. Griffith, *Sun Tzu* (Foreword by B. H. Liddell Hart), v.
138. Griffith, *Sun Tzu*, 7, 11, 30–38.
139. *Tso*, 27::28 (Yin 9), 273::275 (Wen 16), 572::579 (Chao 1), 646::652 (Chao 13), 830::832 (Ai 13).
140. Creel, *The Birth of China*, 154.

makers and valets." Maspero seems to conceive the task of the infantry as purely that of guarding the chariots. Griffith says that "the illiterate and docile serfs played but a small part in the battles of the time" before about 500 B.C., and that "the undrilled peasant levies of the Spring and Autumn could not possibly have been capable of such maneuvres" as are discussed in the *Sun-tzu*. It seems to be taken for granted that since accounts of battles say much of the chariots but almost nothing of the foot soldiers, the infantry did almost nothing.[141]

In our own day infantrymen sometimes complain that they get all of the dirt and most of the fighting, while the air force gets the publicity and the glory. We need to remember that even in a work like the *Tso-chuan* it is only rarely that actual battlefield exploits of chariots are described, and this never happens, I believe, in the Western Chou sources.[142] There is little reason, then, to expect accounts of infantry warfare. Certainly our information concerning it is rare. Yet it is enough to establish that there were standing armies that must have included infantry, that this infantry was trained, and that even in the Spring and Autumn period when the chariot had come to usurp all the attention, infantry still played a role of importance.

Even peasants who regularly tilled their fields might receive military training, according to a famous poem. It depicts the activities of the peasant's year, and says: "In the days of the second month there is the meet, and so we keep up our prowess in warfare."[143] This "meet" is interpreted as being a great hunt which was used as training for warfare. Descriptions of hunting in the *Poetry* show strong resemblance to descriptions of military expeditions.

> The hunting chariots are splendid,
> The four stallions are very large . . .
> These gentlemen go to the hunt,
> They count the footmen noisily,
> They set up the tortoise-and-snake banner and the oxtail flag.
> We yoke those four stallions,

141. Granet, *Chinese Civilization*, 262. Maspero, "Le régime féodal," 140. Griffith, *Sun Tzu*, 32. Hsu, *Ancient China*, 69.

142. An exception to this might be alleged in *Shih*, 120–121: "ten great war chariots went in front, to open up the march." But the context does not indicate that this was a description of actual battle.

143. *Shih*, 98. Tradition dates this poem to the beginning of Western Chou (*Mao-shih*, 8[1].7a). Waley (*Shih*, 164) suggests that it was probably composed in the eighth or seventh century B.C. Hsü ("Pin-feng Shuo," 438–439) would date it as late as the Spring and Autumn period.

The four stallions are large.
There are red-adorned knee-covers and gold-adorned slippers;
The meet is grand. . . .
If footmen and charioteers are not attentive
The great kitchen will not be filled.[144]

The term here for "footmen and charioteers" is *t'u yü*, which we regularly find in connection with war in the sense of "infantry and chariotry."[145] In this poem the role of the footmen is clearly not a negligible one.

If the foot soldiers counted for nothing, and all the real fighting was done by the chariots, it is hard to understand how a hunt could have provided preparation for war. Presumably the game, or some of it, was shot by men in chariots after it had been driven into the open by footmen. But this would hardly give preparation for meeting other chariots in the shock of battle. What such a hunt could do is to facilitate coordination between foot soldiers and their superiors who, riding in chariots, directed them. In the *Tso-chuan* we read of the use of hunting as preparation for war. It is related that, after Duke Wen of Chin (635–628 B.C.) had gained power, he wished to embark on military operations but could not do so until the common people had been trained for war. He trained them by means of great hunts. "When the common people could understand their orders and obey them without confusion he used them" to carry out his military plans. Elsewhere in the *Tso-chuan* we read that a high military officer of Chin was required, at a later date, "to instruct infantry and chariotry [in the way in which they should] cooperate in carrying out their orders."[146]

That infantry were trained in the Western Chou period is also shown by a poem that says:

Fang-shu came,
His chariots were three thousand,
With a host [literally, "an army"] of well-trained guards.

The character that is here translated as "guards" literally means "shield"; by comparison with bronze inscriptions, we can tell that it refers to foot soldiers. It may be, of course, that the meaning is simply that of soldiers carrying shields. But since shields of some sort are

---

144. *Shih*, 123–124.

145. *T'u yü* 徒御. In bronze inscriptions the latter character is written as 馭.

146. *Tso*, 200::202 (Hsi 27), 407::410 (Ch'eng 18). The term for "infantry and chariotry" in the latter reference is not *t'u yü*, but *tsu ch'eng* 卒乘, which is common in the *Tso-chuan* in this sense.

rather simple and inexpensive, and the contexts make it clear that these men were an elite group of infantrymen, it seems more probable that the sense is that of men acting as a shield, that is, guards.[147]

In modern armies the uniform is considered an important element in training and discipline.[148] One poem that is dated to a late period in Western Chou has soldiers speaking of "regular clothes"—or as Karlgren translates it "regulation clothes"—and again of "war clothes." Karlgren makes a plausible case for interpreting this as reference to uniforms.[149] It is difficult to know, however, whether these uniforms were worn by infantry. There is no such ambiguity in a passage in the *Poetry* which can be dated by internal evidence to the seventh century B.C. It says:

> The Duke's chariots are a thousand . . .
> The Duke's foot soldiers are thirty thousand,
> With helmets decorated with cowries on crimson strings.
> The many footmen are a great crowd.
> He withstands the Jung and Ti
> And represses Ching [Ch'u] and Shu.[150]

Although bronze helmets were made as early as Shang times, we do

147. *Shih*, 122. Karlgren, whose translations I commonly find preferable, translates this passage as "his chariots were three thousand, for use as a host of protectors." He discusses his interpretation, and others that have been made of the passage, in Karlgren, "Glosses on the Siao Ya Odes," 51–53. The interpretation that I have followed is that of Chu Hsi, which was also adopted in Legge, *Shih*, 285, Waley, *Shih*, 128, and Couvreur, *Shih*, 203. The idea that chariots would act as "protectors" for footmen, in fighting barbarians, seems to me implausible; it is the chariots that need protection in such a situation, as the early Chinese well realized.

Evidence that the translation I have preferred is almost certainly correct comes from bronze inscriptions. One of these—Ch'en, "Hsi-Chou T'ung-ch'i," (2).70–72—tells of an attack on Jung by "infantry, charioteers, and *kan jen* 盾人 (shield men)." Ch'en also quotes here an inscription of Spring and Autumn date that uses the same character *kan* and speaks of "shield foot soldiers four thousand." This *kan* is interchangeable with the *kan* 干 of this passage in the *Poetry*. The reference here would seem to be to infantry conceived as especially able to act as a shield, i.e., guards.

148. Charles Francis Atkinson writes: "Although in ancient history we occasionally meet with uniformed soldiers, such as the white and crimson Spanish regiments of Hannibal, it was not until the beginning of large standing armies that uniforms were introduced in modern times"; see *Encyclopaedia Britannica* (11th ed.), XXVII, 582. Whether the existence of standing armies in Western Chou stimulated the development of uniforms is an interesting question.

149. *Shih*, 120. Karlgren, "Glosses on the Siao Ya Odes," 50. Karlgren's translation in *Shih*, 101, depicts soldiers weary of service as longing for civilian clothes.

150. *Shih*, 260.

not know of what material these helmets were made. An inscription records that King K'ang gave to a victorious military commander a helmet decorated with cowries. Bridles for horses decorated with many cowries have been excavated from Chou tombs. Since cowries were valuable, it may be that the helmets of these 30,000 foot soldiers were decorated with imitation cowries; these have been excavated in great numbers, made of a variety of materials.[151]

In any case it is clear that these infantrymen of Lu were garbed in quite a distinctive manner. It is obvious that they were not regarded as a negligible rabble.

It would be unusual to find a book on the art of war so sophisticated as the *Sun-tzu* that had no predecessor. In fact that work itself quotes from one, the title of which Griffith translates as *The Book of Military Administration*.[152] The *Tso-chuan* includes several quotations from a work called a *Treatise on the Army*. The quotations are general, and none is explicit enough to inform us whether this work dealt with the employment of infantry; neither, however, do they mention chariots. It seems fairly clear, nonetheless, that this work was not exclusively based upon the chivalrous code for the conduct of war that was at least theoretically in vogue during the Spring and Autumn period.[153] It may, therefore, have embodied earlier doctrine on tactics and strategy.

It may well be true that techniques for the effective deployment and maneuver of infantry became more complex after 500 b.c., but it is not the case, as is sometimes supposed, that they did not exist before that time.[154] Since the sources tell us virtually nothing about the way in which chariots were used in battle in Western Chou and Spring and Autumn times, it is not surprising that we find very little information on the use of infantry. It is only an occasional glimpse that lets us see that there clearly existed a body of practice and experience, the details of which are never given.

It will be recalled that in 714 b.c., half a century after the end of

---

151. Ch'en, "Hsi-Chou T'ung-ch'i," (4).87–89. Cheng, *Shang China*, 77, and plate XXXVIII. Cheng, *Chou China*, 93, 100, 189–190, 268.

152. *Sun-tzu*, 7.16a; Griffith, *Sun Tzu*, 106. The characters of this title, *chün cheng* 軍 政, appear twice in the *Tso-chuan: Tso*, 312::317 (Hsüan 12), 505::507 (Hsiang 24). But they do not appear in these contexts to be the name of a book.

153. *Tso*, 204::209 (Hsi 28), 314::319 (Hsüan 12), 686::689 (Chao 21). Both of the latter passages advise attacking the enemy when he is at a disadvantage.

154. Griffith, *Sun Tzu*, 7, 30–38.

Western Chou, the Earl of Cheng expressed apprehension that some marauding Jung foot soldiers might overwhelm his chariot fighters in a surprise attack. The Earl's son immediately proposed a rather complicated maneuver involving four different bodies of men, who had to coordinate their movements so as to lure, ambush, and annihilate the enemy. It was forthwith executed, successfully. It is unlikely that the Earl's son improvised this strategem on the spot, or that the Chinese who executed it were entirely unused to such operations. Yet it seems clear that this was entirely a matter of infantry warfare.[155]

Seven years later we see Chinese fighting against Chinese: this time the Earl of Cheng was resisting the King, who had invaded Cheng with the help of some other feudatories. The troops of Cheng were drawn up, we are told, in squares. There follows the description of a complicated formation. Legge translates the passage that describes it as saying that the center of the Cheng army "was drawn up in fish-scale array. There was always a force of 25 chariots, supported by 5 files of 5 men each, to maintain a close and unbroken front." Couvreur translates this passage somewhat differently: "They deployed their troops as a fisherman deploys his nets in the water to catch fish, placing rows of twenty-five war chariots in front and groups of five men behind. The groups of five men had the responsibility of filling up gaps." In fact, the text here is very terse, and everything depends upon the manner in which technical terms are interpreted—and it is not certain that we can now know how to interpret them properly.[156]

Yet two points seem clear. This was an intricate and demanding style of fighting, and it required that the foot soldiers play their part in close cooperation with the chariots. To attempt to use "undrilled peasant levies" in such an operation would have been to court disaster—but the army of Cheng achieved a great victory. These infantrymen had clearly been trained, and they had been trained in a code of rather intricate doctrine for the tactical cooperation of foot soldiers and chariots.

In the final century of the Spring and Autumn period, in 541 B.C., a Chin army (as we have seen) found itself opposing Ti barbarians in a narrow pass. The Chin commander dismounted his men from their chariots and made them fight on foot; it appears, though the

---

155. *Tso*, 27::28 (Yin 9). Legge here, and Couvreur, in *Tso-chuan*, I, 50–51, as well as Chinese commentators (*Tso-chuan*, 4.14b–15a), seem to assume that this must have been an infantry maneuver. As indeed it must. That three bodies of chariots could have been concealed in ambush is very unlikely.

156. *Tso*, 44::46 (Huan 5). Couvreur, *Tso-chuan*, I, 83. *Tso-chuan*, 6.10a.

text is not wholly clear, that he used them to supplement his infantry.[157] He then deployed his infantry as follows:

He made five dispositions, at a distance from each other: *liang* in front, *wu* in the rear, *chuan* as the right horn, *ts'an* as the left horn, and *p'ien* as the vanguard.

The meanings of these terms are unknown; they are apparently a part of a body of lore concerning infantry tactics that has been lost.[158] But it is very interesting that at this late date, when infantry were so looked down upon that one chariot fighter had to be decapitated before the others would fight on foot, the Chin commander was still familiar with this complicated infantry maneuver. And his forces were able to use it well enough to defeat the Ti.

WHEN we turn to the actual references to infantry in the Western Chou sources, there are not a great many, but they are significant.

Only one of the *Documents* of Western Chou date seems to give any information about the nature of military forces. It is called "The Harangue at Pi," and is traditionally attributed to the son of the first Duke of Chou, who was Duke of Lu. While this attribution is uncertain, there is a general tendency to ascribe it to the early years of Western Chou.[159] It includes no mention of chariots, though it does refer to horses; no doubt there were some chariots (if only to convey officers) and some baggage carts.[160]

The poets were so dazzled by the chariot that this may blind us to the fact that there are a number of references to infantry in the *Poetry*. Some of these are very clear, others more conjectural. It seems likely that a fair number of the complaints we find of the hardships of war come from men who had to go on foot.

157. The text—*Tso*, 572::579 (Chao 1)—appears to say that the Chin commander proposed that they should use ten men in place of each chariot. Legge, as well as Couvreur (*Tso-chuan*, III, 28) and Chinese commentators (*Tso-chuan*, 41.19a), agree on this interpretation. But a chariot carried only three or at most four men.

158. *Tso*, 572::579 (Chao 1). *Tso-chuan*, 41.19a. The commentator Tu Yü, of the third century A.D., said that these were "improvised names." Commenting on this, K'ung Ying-ta (A.D. 574–648) pointed out that previous attempts at understanding these terms were unconvincing, and concluded—with a candor perhaps superior to that of Tu—that their significance "is impossible to determine."

159. See pp. 454–455.

160. *Shu*, 80.

Oh, to go home, to go home,
Our hearts are grieved,
Our grieved hearts are burning.
We are hungry, we are thirsty;
Our keeping guard is not yet finished. . . .
The service to the King must not be defective,
We have no leisure to kneel down or rest. . . .
What chariot is that?
It is the chariot of the lord. . . .
The four stallions are strong;
The lord is conveyed by them
And the small men follow on foot.[161]

Following on foot was sometimes a problem. In two poems we read of men on foot who have to hurry to keep up with the speedy horses. Sometimes they complain. One poem says, "We fear that we shall not arrive at the goal," and makes a suggestion: "You should give orders to the baggage carts, and tell them to carry us."[162]

They complained, like soldiers throughout history, and went on doing their duty. We see them going, under command of a high officer dispatched by the King, to build fortifications in the east. Again, when the Earl of Shen went south, charged by the King to build a center of strength in that area, "his footmen and charioteers were many."[163] An infantryman says:

What plant is not yellow?
What day do we not march?
What man does not go
To regulate and dispose all within the four quarters?
What plant is not dark?
What man is not pitiable?
Alas for us who march—
We alone are as if we were not men.
We are not rhinoceroses, we are not tigers. . . .[164]

At least ten of the pieces in the *Poetry* seem clearly to refer to

---

161. *Shih*, 111–112.
162. *Shih*, 106, 182, 230.
163. *Shih*, 228, 230.
164. *Shih*, 184–185. What I have translated as "us who march" is *cheng fu* 征夫, which Karlgren here translates as "us men on war service." But in a note on *Shih*, 230, he explains it as: "Properly: 'The marching men.' "

infantry,[165] and there are a number of others that probably do. Four poems speak of "infantry and chariotry." This is a very common expression, found not only in the *Poetry* but also in bronze inscriptions and in the *Tso-chuan*. It is an interesting fact that wherever this expression occurs it seems always to place "infantry" first; this is true even in passages in the *Tso-chuan* that come from late in the Spring and Autumn period.[166] This does not, of course, mean that the infantry was, throughout that time, considered more important than the chariots. It seems probable that this manner of speaking initially came into vogue because, early in Western Chou, an army was conceived primarily as a certain number of foot soldiers, who were accompanied and commanded by a few officers riding in chariots. Thus "infantry and chariotry" probably meant, at that time, a body of foot soldiers with their accompanying chariots.

In the bronze inscriptions we find King Ch'eng, the second ruler of the dynasty, ordering an Earl to attack certain Jung in the east, using "infantry, chariotry, and 'shield men.' " These "shield men" were evidently an elite infantry, "guards."[167]

The only inscription that specifies the actual makeup of a Western Chou military force is the one concerning the revolt of the Marquis of E. There, as we have seen, Yü tells us that he commanded "100 war chariots [with their accompanying] menials: 200 *yü* (chariotry) and 1000 foot soldiers." If these chariots carried three men—which is uncertain—there may also have been an additional officer riding in and commanding each chariot. Here the priority is clearly given to the chariotry.

This seems to be the only instance in the Western Chou sources— and it comes from the reign of King Li in the final century of the period —of a practice that became usual in Spring and Autumn times: referring to a force as "so many chariots," and treating the accompanying foot soldiers as being appended to the chariots. A little later the author of the inscription, referring to his troops in more summary fashion, calls them "infantry and chariotry."[168] The cliché, naming infantry first, had become fixed. It is in this same reign that we find the sole

---

165. *Shih*, 98, 101, 114, 123–124, 180, 182, 184–185, 228, 230, 257.

166. *Tso*, 636::639 (Chao 12), 793::795 (Ai 1). In the *Tso-chuan* we find, instead of the *t'u yü* 徒御 of the Western Chou sources, *tsu ch'eng* 卒乘 in this sense.

167. Ch'en, "Hsi-Chou T'ung-ch'i," (2).70–72. Ch'en's reading of this inscription differs from that of Kuo Mo-jo in *Chin-wen*, 20b; examination of the inscription itself shows that Ch'en is certainly correct.

168. *Ch'ing-t'ung-ch'i T'u-shih*, 24.

instance, in the Western Chou inscriptions of my corpus, in which chariots are mentioned as being used in a military action, without any accompanying mention of infantry.[169]

There has been endless debate from ancient times to our own day, by Chinese and Western scholars, concerning *the* number of foot soldiers that accompanied each chariot in ancient China. No doubt specific armies had more or less specific ratios, but there is no reason to suppose that once a figure had been arrived at it would be preserved forever, like a magic formula. In fact, there were clearly many variations, which some scholars have found very perplexing.[170] To ask how many footmen accompanied each chariot in ancient China is like asking what has been the size of an army division in the twentieth century. To answer the latter question one must further ask: what army, what kind of division, when?

The final mention in these inscriptions of the character of troops used in a campaign comes in the reign of King Hsüan (827–782 B.C.). Commander Huan relates that he was ordered by the King to attack the rebellious Huai I. He did so, achieving a great victory. In this operation, Commander Huan tells us, he "made no error [in employing either] infantry or chariotry."[171] Even at the end of Western Chou, infantry was not considered a negligible factor in warfare.

A DETAILED analysis of the use of infantry in the Spring and Autumn period is beyond the scope of this volume. Nevertheless, the subject has a certain retrospective relevance. If foot soldiers played—as they surely did—a more significant role even in this later period than has commonly been supposed, this makes more plausible the thesis that they were quite important in Western Chou.

The authors of the accounts we find in the *Tso-chuan* were quite as fascinated by the chariot as were those of the *Poetry*. And by the Spring and Autumn period there was an aristocracy, in full flower, which at least pretended to fight according to a code of chivalry. What we find in the *Tso-chuan*, when it goes into any detail, is stories— rather factual ones in many cases, undoubtedly, but nevertheless stories, often told with wit and gusto. Attention was naturally focused on

169. *Chin-wen*, 106a.
170. For a good summary of the discussions on this point, see Hsu, *Ancient China*, 66.
171. *Chin-wen*, 146a–147a.

such epic struggles as that between Chin and Ch'u, and between the various Chinese states vying for power. These were wars led by protagonists subscribing to essentially the same code and conducting themselves as great gentlemen—or great rogues. They fought in chariots, as a matter of course. But even in these battles we seldom see more, in the *Tso-chuan*, than an occasional duel between leaders or champions. One might almost suppose that all but a few of those who went to the battlefield in chariots were mere spectators—and how much more the foot soldiers. But this is unlikely.

Yet it is occasionally mentioned that men also fought on foot, not only against barbarians but also against other Chinese. It is generally agreed that infantry did come to be important in warfare toward the end of the Spring and Autumn period.[172] But there is abundant evidence, as a few random references will demonstrate, that in fact they always played an important role.

One difficulty is that a term frequently used for "foot soldier" in Spring and Autumn times (*tsu* 卒) is also used to mean "troops" generally. But in some cases we are very definitely told that it is infantry that is in question. In 719 B.C. a group of allied states invaded the state of Cheng. "They defeated the Cheng infantry, seized its grain harvest, and withdrew." Cheng was a state of considerable power, which had for some time played a dominant role and controlled the royal house, yet here we see that when its infantry was overcome it accepted defeat and submitted to the very serious loss of its grain. More than a century later, in 590 B.C., we find the infantry of Cheng defeated by Chin, and again this seems to have decided the issue.[173]

We get a rare glimpse of infantry, along with chariots, involved in a battle between Ch'u and Chin in 597 B.C. As the army of Ch'u attacked, "the chariots dashed along and the footmen ran recklessly, and they fell on the army of Chin." The Chin soldiers, fleeing, had to take to boats to cross a river. There were not enough boats, and those who got in first hacked off the fingers of those trying to follow; "fingers could be scooped up by the double handful."[174]

In 620 B.C. the Duke of Ch'in sent a scion of the ruling house of Chin to that state, to become its ruler. He commented that a previous ruler, entering the state under similar conditions, had experienced dif-

---

172. Hsu (*Ancient China*, 68–69) gives a number of instances of the important use of infantry from 570 B.C. on. Griffith (*Sun Tzu*, 32–34) dates the importance of infantry as beginning "shortly before 500 B.C."

173. *Tso*, 15::16 (Yin 4), 412::413 (Hsiang 1). In both of these passages the infantry are called *t'u ping* 徒兵 , "foot soldiers."

174. *Tso*, 314::319 (Hsüan 12).

ficulty because he lacked guards. He therefore "gave him many foot guards." There is no mention of chariots.[175]

As we have seen, the expression "infantry and chariotry" was used throughout the Spring and Autumn period. In 722 B.C. a brother of the Duke of Chin, planning a rebellion, "prepared infantry and chariotry" for the purpose. In 597 B.C. a high official of Chin declared that the excellence of the army of Ch'u was due to, among other good qualities, the fact that "its infantry and its chariotry operate in harmony with one another." In an interval in a battle in 575 B.C. the army of Ch'u "supplied deficiencies [caused by casualties] among its infantry and chariotry," and Chin "inspected its chariotry and supplied deficiencies [caused by casualties] among its infantry."[176]

We have seen that around 587 B.C. a new element was injected into the military and political situation. An embassy from the state of Chin, seeking to stimulate a new force to neutralize Ch'u, brought the fierce men of the state of Wu on the lower Yangtze River into active participation in the struggles of the time. Up to a point this plan worked very well. Wu did indeed become a menace to Ch'u, and for a time threatened to destroy it. But Ch'u, although weakened, survived, and Wu turned its attention to the states of the north. It claimed the leadership among them, and it is not inconceivable that Wu might have conquered the north if it had not itself been destroyed in 473 B.C.

To the men of the north—or at least to the authors of the *Tso-chuan*—the great military technique that the Chinese had to impart was the use of the war chariot. Thus we are told that the instructors from Chin "taught [the men of] Wu to ride in chariots and to deploy for battle."[177] It would be easy to conclude that it was the newly acquired weapon, the war chariot, that made it possible for the men of Wu to become so formidable. But if we look at the circumstances closely, this is by no means certain. The new knowledge of the military discipline of the northern states, and of methods of deployment for war, undoubtedly did increase the fighting strength of Wu. And contact with these states revealed a new world of luxury and rich areas for conquest. All of these were important factors.

Certainly there were chariots in Wu's armies.[178] This was inevi-

---

175. *Tso*, 246::248 (Wen 7).

176. *Tso*, 2::6 (Yin 1), 312::317 (Hsüan 12), 392::398 (Ch'eng 16).

177. *Tso*, 362::364 (Ch'eng 7), 522::527 (Hsiang 26).

178. *Kuo-yü*, 19.6b, mentions horses in the Wu army, and *Tso*, 793::795 (Ai 1), indicates that it included "infantry and chariotry." Nothing is said, however, of numbers, or of the importance of chariots in fighting.

table. The rulers of Wu were very anxious to be considered Chinese, and they undoubtedly had the finest chariots obtainable. At least their highest officers, as well, must have been similarly outfitted, if only as a matter of prestige. But the crucial question is whether Wu converted its armies so as to place their chief reliance in battle on the chariot. There seems to be no indication that they did, and a good deal of evidence that they did not.

There is very little mention of chariots in connection with the battles fought by Wu, though we do find mention of fighting boats (suited to the watercourses characteristic of the Wu terrain) [179] and infantry. We read that a battle against Ch'u was begun by a Wu force of 5000 men, and again that an army of Yüeh was attacked by a Wu officer leading "'5000 infantrymen.'"[180] We also have some positive evidence that the army of Wu was not converted into a force consisting predominantly of chariot fighters. It is related that when the last ruler of Wu was planning a career of conquest in the north, one of his counselors advised against it, saying that they should instead conquer the state of Yüeh. For if Wu conquered Yüeh, he said, "we can live on their land and ride in their boats." The northern states, on the other hand, were alien, he said to the habits of the people of Wu. "We could not live on their land, or ride in their chariots."[181] And this was a century after the instructors from Chin had supposedly taught the men of Wu to ride in chariots.

In the end Wu was, it is true, conquered and destroyed. But this was not done by the Chinese states, but by the still more "barbarous" state of Yüeh, which lay to the south of Wu. And one account tells us specifically that the final defeat was administered, not by chariots, but by "three thousand good-for-nothing soldiers."[182] The adjective presumably reflects the disdain of the Chinese for infantry, who, no matter how effective they might be, were after all not gentlemen.

WHEN we seek to learn what was the organization of the military, from the Western Chou sources, we find ourselves at even more of a

179. Reference to such boats is frequent; see for instance: *Tso*, 746::746 (Ting 2), 751::756 (Ting 4), 820::821 (Ai 10). For boats that have been excavated in this area, see Chang, *Archaeology of Ancient China*, 390–391.

180. *Tso*, 751::756 (Ting 4), 830::832 (Ai 13).

181. *Kuo-yü*, 20.2a.

182. *Chan-kuo Ts'e*, 22.4a. The text reads 散卒三千, which almost certainly indicates that the force did not include chariots. This is made still more certain by the statement that immediately follows, which lists both soldiers and chariots used by King Wu: 卒三千人革車三百乘.

loss than in the case of the civilian administration. It seems to be impossible to determine which, if any, of the royal ministers had charge of military affairs. There is no clear hierarchy of military titles. We have many references to military expeditions, and in a number of cases the commanders are named. But they are almost never designated by military titles.

One might conclude from this that there was no organization of the military, and no discipline. Yet the very fact that the Western Chou maintained themselves for more than three centuries, in the face of very formidable enemies, proves that this cannot have been true. And if we look more closely we can see that, while there may not have been a great deal of organization in the purely formal sense—in fact, we simply cannot tell whether there was or not—the military was under firm and effective control. Here, even more obviously than elsewhere in the administration, government was personal.

It is evident that, whatever the formal arrangements may have been, many at least of the Western Chou Kings functioned as their own Ministers of War. In the bronze inscriptions of my corpus there are thirty-four that mention specific military actions. Of these, there are only four that do not mention the King as being in some manner concerned with this activity.

In nine cases the King personally accompanied, and presumably commanded, his armies. In six cases we are told that "the King attacked," or "the King conquered," a certain foe; here we cannot be sure whether the King was personally with his forces, but he may have been. In fourteen inscriptions it is said that "the King ordered" one of his officers to make the attack. In one case we are not told directly that the King was the instigator of the military action, but the context clearly implies that he was.[183]

The remaining four inscriptions, which tell of military actions without any mention of the Chou King, are all dated to the time of King Ch'eng. The commanders in three cases are well-known officers of the Chou court: the Duke of Chou, the Grand Protector, and Po Mou Fu. In the fourth inscription the commander is a more obscure Secretary, but he too is identified by other inscriptions as being in the royal service.[184] Thus it appears that, without much doubt, every single one of the thirty-four military actions mentioned on these bronzes was sanc-

183. In *Chin-wen*, 23a, the armies used are those of the King, and the King rewards the troops after the victory.

184. *Chin-wen*, 25a, 27a, 28b. Ch'en, "*Hsi-Chou T'ung-ch'i*," (1).168. The obscure Secretary named as commander in *Chin-wen*, 28b, is linked with the royal service by ibid., 28a and 29a.

tioned by—and in most cases they were instigated if not led by—the Chou King.

There were also, of course, adversaries. If war was waged thirty-four times by the Chou King or at his behest, there must have been those who opposed him in each case. It is not always easy to identify the opponents, but it is quite certain that in the overwhelming proportion of cases they were barbarians. There were, as we should expect, numerous campaigns against Chinese—and some who may have been Chinese—in the reign of King Ch'eng; this was the time of the great revolt of the Shang and other peoples, and of the eastern expeditions of conquest.[185] But once the country had been pacified and the rule consolidated, *internal* military activity appears—insofar as these inscriptions testify—to have been almost completely unnecessary, for two full centuries. In this period we find reference to ten campaigns; in nine of them the enemy is certainly barbarian, and in the tenth probably so.[186]

King Li (878–828 B.C.) figures in Chinese tradition as a wicked ruler, whose misdeeds provoked rebellion and caused his exile. During his reign we find two inscriptions that may record action by his troops against Chinese. One is on a recently excavated bronze that possibly speaks of an expedition by a royal army against the important state of Ch'i, which occupied much of the modern Shantung province—but the interpretation of this inscription is difficult.[187] The other is the one that describes the great revolt of the Marquis of E, leading the southern Huai I and the eastern I. The single remaining inscription that speaks of military action against Chinese is dated to the reign of Li's successor, King Hsüan. It appears to have been a mild affair, designed to remind a petty vassal to come and pay his taxes, which he does.

The picture this presents is remarkable. The Chou came in as con-

185. All of the early inscriptions that appear, with any great probability, to refer to military actions against Chinese, are dated to the reign of King Ch'eng except for *Chin-wen*, 100b. Ch'en ("Hsi-Chou T'ung-ch'i," (2).72) dates this inscription to "the opening period of Western Chou."

186. In *Chin-wen*, 26a, the expedition is against the "Yü Territory." Its identification is uncertain, but the fact that it is called "Territory" probably means that it was not considered a Chinese state.

187. Ku Mo-jo ("Ch'ang-an Ming-wen," 6–7) publishes and discusses this inscription. His reading of the crucial portion of the inscription seems to mean that a certain Commander was ordered by the King to "advance and pursue to Ch'i." But pursue whom? Barbarian invaders, or men of Ch'i? It seems impossible to tell. The context gives no help with this problem. It does indicate, however, that strong opposition is expected, for the King warns: "Take care that you are not disastrously defeated!"

querors who were initially considered culturally inferior. They established some network of control over an area much larger than France, containing many people who were initially hostile. Yet it would appear that after mere decades of consolidation they were so firmly in power that for two centuries they had no need to resort to military action—except against barbarians—to maintain themselves. And even in their final century such action was only rarely necessary.

When we consider the conditions of the time, especially communications and technology, this picture seems hardly possible. Almost certainly, it is not entirely true. There must have been a great many incidents, minor ones at least, of which we have no record. Our bronze inscriptions are at best only a very random and very small sample. But is there *any* validity to their depiction of the situation? To try to answer this, we must compare data from our other sources.

The original text of the *Book of Changes* seems to tell us nothing about wars in Western Chou times. The *Documents* includes a number of references to the Chou conquest and to the military consolidation under King Ch'eng, but little that is informative concerning any later time.[188] The other obvious place to look is in the *Poetry*, but it is not so helpful as one might hope. Not only are individual poems hard to date, but many of them contain such references to war as laments over its hardships without giving us any facts about what is going on. Nevertheless, what they do have to tell us is very interesting.

There are some ten accounts in the *Poetry* of specific military actions that seem datable, with some probability, to the Western Chou period.[189] In eight, the King is mentioned in such manner as to make it clear that he is the prime mover; three of these speak of the prosecution of the war as "the King's business." Of the remaining two, one says that "the Duke of Chou marched to the east," and the second

188. There seem to be only two of the *Documents*, of Western Chou date, that may give information about war after the initial period. "Wen Hou chih Ming," which may date from late in Western Chou, quotes the King as lamenting an invasion (*Shu*, 78). The "Pi Shih" (*Shu*, 80) is a harangue, evidently by a Duke of Lu, to his army which is about to attack the Huai I and the Jung of Hsü; it makes no mention of the King. This latter document is difficult to date, but a number of scholars would place it quite early in Western Chou.

189. This excludes, of course, the many references to the Chou conquest and earlier wars. It also excludes *Shih*, 19. This poem is difficult to interpret, it does not certainly concern warfare, and it is traditionally attributed to a time later than Western Chou. Also excluded are *Shih*, 256–257 and 259–261, both poems of Lu. The latter contains internal evidence dating it to the Spring and Autumn period, and the former is traditionally, and plausibly, so dated. The ten are: *Shih*, 86, 103, 111–112, 112–113, 114, 120–121, 122–123, 180, 232–234, 234–236.

also seems beyond much doubt to describe war under the auspices of the King, even though he is not mentioned.[190] The King personally leads his army in at least two of these poems, and probably in three.[191]

In three of these ten poems the enemy is not identified. The states in the east, which one poem tells us were "corrected" by the Duke of Chou, undoubtedly included both Chinese and barbarians; this was in the initial period of consolidation. But in each of the remaining six cases the enemy is specifically said to be barbarian. Thus the picture we derive from the *Poetry* is even more homogeneous than our deductions from the bronzes. After the early period there is no case in which the King need use military force against Chinese. And the King is completely master of the military situation.

The bronze inscriptions and the *Poetry* reinforce each other. The *Poetry* could—indeed, it may—have been edited to show Western Chou times in a manner harmonious with tradition. The bronze inscriptions could not be subject to the same control, but their testimony is scanty and random. The fact that they come so close to depicting the same situation is impressive. When later Chinese thought and wrote of the Western Chou as a time of relative order and internal peace, they appear to have had some solid basis for this conception.

This relative rarity of conflict between Western Chou Kings and their vassals contrasts sharply with the situation in medieval Europe, where, as Marc Bloch writes:

> Struggles of the great feudatories against the kings; rebellions against the former by their own vassals; derelictions of feudal duty . . . these features are to be read on every page of the history of feudalism. . . . Of all the occasions for going to war, the first that came to mind was to take up arms against one's lord.[192]

190. In *Shih*, 122–123, Fang-shu, his equipment and insignia, and his victory over the barbarians, are all typical of an officer of the King. He is traditionally supposed to have been an officer of King Hsüan.

191. In *Shih*, 120, the line *Wang yü ch'u cheng* 王 于 出 征 has been the subject of much debate; see Legge, *Shih*, 281, note, and *Mao-shih*, 10(2).4ab. Legge, Karlgren, and Waley (*Shih*, 126) all translate this in such manner as not to indicate that the King himself went on the expedition. But in bronze inscriptions this *yü* often has the sense of "to go," and Karlgren ("Grammata Serica Recensa," 44) says that it has this sense in the *Poetry*. This line is very similar to language found in inscriptions; see Ch'en, "Hsi-Chou T'ung-ch'i," (2).76–78. I believe that it can be translated, "The King goes out on a military expedition." Admittedly there are still some problems with the poem, but they are not insoluble.

192. Bloch, *Feudal Society*, 235.

While other factors were certainly involved, the relative immunity of the Western Chou Kings from attack by their vassals was undoubtedly due, in no small measure, to the fact that the royal military forces were powerful and under the firm control of the King.

The personal involvement of the King with military affairs does not seem to have changed markedly from the beginning to the end of Western Chou, insofar as the testimony of the bronzes is concerned. The greatest number of campaigns is recorded for the reign of King Ch'eng; this is not surprising, since this was still a period of conquest and consolidation. Of twelve campaigns, we are told that the King attacked (or conquered) in four cases, and in two more it is clear that he was personally present on the expedition. Under his successor, King K'ang, we have three campaigns, with the King present on one. For the next ruler, Chao, there are five references to military expeditions; in two of these we are told that the King attacked, and in each one of the other three we have evidence that the King personally accompanied his troops.[193] All five of these inscriptions relate to fighting in the south. The impression they give, that King Chao was personally preoccupied with coping with enemies on his southern borders, accords with the testimony of the genuine Bamboo Books. There we are told that he attacked Ch'u, that in another expedition he "lost [his] six armies on the Han River," and that he made an expedition to the south from which "he did not return."[194]

Perhaps King Chao's labors, and even his death, were not wholly in vain. Whatever the reason, China appears to have enjoyed a remarkable era of peace, if one may judge from these inscriptions. During all of the five reigns that followed, there is almost no mention of war, either internal or with the barbarians.[195] Under King Li (878–828 B.C.)

193. Since Chin-wen, 53b–54a, 54a, and 54b all refer to attacks on Ch'u, it is of course possible that they give us three references to the same expedition. But since the fragmentary remnants of the genuine Bamboo Books include what appear to be records of three different expeditions to the south (Wang, Ku Chu-shu, 7a) by King Chao, these may also refer to three different expeditions.

194. Wang, Ku Chu-shu, 7a.

195. The one exception is Chin-wen, 103b–104a, but serious doubt has been cast on its genuineness; see p. 473. While none of these inscriptions records military action under King I (934–910 B.C.), one dated to that reign says that "Secretary Mien" makes a sacrificial vessel designed to be taken along "in following the King on military expeditions"; this implies, at least, that such expeditions were contemplated. It should be noted that the genuine Bamboo Books does not accord with this peaceful picture of the time; under King Mu in particular it tells of many expeditions, sometimes to distant areas, but the historicity of these is uncertain. See Wang, Ku Chu-shu, 7a–8a.

we find six expeditions, with the King personally accompanying two. For his successor, Hsüan, almost at the end of the dynasty, three wars are recorded, and the King is personally present in one of these.

BELOW the King it is difficult to discern a "chain of command" in military operations. Our inscriptions are usually found on bronzes cast by men important enough to be given their charges by the King; they commonly record this fact and nothing more. In a few cases we find recorded the name of a subordinate. In the reign of King Li a high official was ordered by the King to repulse an attack by Hsien-yün barbarians; he in turn provided the Marquis of E with chariots, so that the Marquis might prosecute a part of this attack.[196] When the Marquis of E led the southern and eastern barbarians in rebellion, the King ordered the "western six armies and the Yin eight armies" to attack him. But the Marquis was actually captured by troops under a certain Duke Wu, who delegated a part of the fighting to a man named Yü, to whom he entrusted the command of a hundred chariots and a thousand infantrymen. Here we see the delegation of authority, but no individual except the King stands out as exercising overall supervision of the military.

Some titles that appear in the sources have been translated as "Minister of War." One of these is Ssu-ma 司 馬 , literally "Director of Horses."[197] It appears both as the title of a high royal officer and as the title of officials serving within feudal states. Unfortunately however there is nothing to show what the functions attached to this office may have been; such officers never seem to be mentioned in a specifically military connection.[198] In later periods of Chinese history we find this title used in a variety of ways; at times it certainly did have the sense of Minister of War.

More prominent in the Western Chou literature is another official

196. In Chin-wen, 106a, the Marquis of E is not actually designated by this title but by his name. There is little doubt, however, that this is the same man, though of course it is possible that at this time he did not yet hold the title.
197. Karlgren translates Ssu-ma as "master of the horse" in Shu, 46. Legge (Shu, 414) and Couvreur (Shu, 255) both render it as "minister of war."
198. Shu, 46. Chin-wen, 57a, 77a, 78b, 79a, 115a, 116b, 117a, 129b. Kuo, Wen-shih Lun-chi, 313. From the not very clear statements of Chin-wen, 57a, Ssu Wei-chih, in "Liang-Chou Chih-kuan K'ao," 8–9, deduces that the Ssu-ma named here, who is attached to a vassal, had the function of supervising justice and discipline within the army. From this he appears to draw the conclusion that the Ssu-ma was an official who supervised military justice; the evidence, however, appears slight. See also Kuo, Chin-wen Ts'ung-k'ao, 66b–68b.

whose title has been considered equivalent to "Minister of War": the Ts'ou-ma 趣 馬 . This might be translated literally as "Runner of Horses." In a poem traditionally dated to the last reign of Western Chou we find this official listed as sixth among the royal officers, and in one dated to the previous reign he is listed as second.[199] This title does not seem to appear in the bronze inscriptions, but the inscriptions contain another which has almost the same literal meaning and is considered its equivalent; this title also appears as that of a high officer of the King.[200]

There seems to be no definite evidence, however, to link any of these officials whose titles include the character for "horse" with specifically military functions in Western Chou times.[201] And there are some indications that they may, as their titles literally suggest, have been concerned with the care and management of horses.[202] The Ch'in, Han, and later dynasties had special bureaucratic structures to supervise governmental activities concerned with horses, and under the Han the official in charge of it ranked eighth among the highest ministers.[203] In any case, there seems to be no clear evidence that any of these, or any other Western Chou official, discharged the functions of a Minister of War.[204]

199. Shih, 139, 226. For the traditional dating of these poems, see Mao-shih, 12(2).1a, and 18(2).12b. Karlgren translates Ts'ou-ma (Shih, 139) as "director of the horse (minister of war)," and Legge (Shih, 322) as "master of the horse."

200. Tsou-ma 走 馬 . Chin-wen, 88a, 150b, 152a, 154a, 155b. Men designated by this title appear to have been both of high rank and of lower status. For discussions of this title see: Ibid., 152b. Kuo, Chin-wen Ts'ung-k'ao, 70a–73a. Ssu, "Liang-Chou Chih-kuan K'ao," 9–10.

201. In Chin-wen, 155b, we do find the title of Tsou-ma held by two men who are called Shih, Commander. But this is not sufficient to prove that it was a military title.

202. In Chin-wen, 88a, the King directs a Tsou-ma to bestow thirty-two horses on a man named Ta. And while Karlgren in the Poetry translated Ts'ou-ma (Shih, 139) as "director of the horse (minister of war)," in his "Grammata Serica Recensa," 54, he defines it as having the sense, in the Poetry, of "manager of horses." In the Ritual of Chou we find the Ts'ou-ma listed as a minor functionary who supervises the feeding and care of horses; see Chou-li, 33.6ab, Biot, Tcheou-li, II, 259. See also Yü, " 'Liu Shih' he 'Pa Shih,' " 154.

203. Sun, Ch'in Hui-yao, 214. Han-shu, 19A.12a–13a, 19B.1a. Hsieh, Chung-kuo Yang-ma Shih, 68–71.

204. Still another title has commonly been translated as "Minister of War." In Shu, 46, it appears as Ch'i-fu 圻 父 . Karlgren, in "Glosses on the Book of Documents," (1).305, says that all commentators agree that this is equivalent to Ssu-ma, "i.e., minister of war." Ch'i-fu 祈 父 , which is considered to be a variant form of the same title, appears in Shih, 127. Karlgren ("Glosses on the Siao Ya Odes," 63) states the grounds on which commentators interpret this to be equivalent to Minister of War. This same translation is used in: Legge, Shu, 411. Legge,

The *Shih-shih* 師氏 , Commandant, is frequently mentioned. In one of the early *Documents* he appears among the higher royal officers. In two lists of the King's officers that appear in the *Poetry*, dated to late in the dynasty, he appears in third and seventh place respectively—in both cases just after the *Ts'ou-ma*.[205] This title is also found with some frequency in the bronze inscriptions. Those who held it were evidently military officers of some importance.[206] In the list of officers in the *Documents* we find the Tiger Retainer (*Hu-ch'en* 虎臣) named immediately after the Commandant, and this title appears in military contexts in the *Poetry* and in bronze inscriptions. It appears likely that this term sometimes designates a fairly high official, but that elsewhere it is a name for the members of an elite corps of guards.[207]

By far the most common military title in Western Chou is *Shih* 師 , Commander. Yet it is very rarely that men in command of military actions are designated even by this title.[208] Where the context gives some clue as to function, *Shih* usually seem to be military, but whether this title was also used for civilian officers is debated and remains a question.[209]

Careful examination of the evidence fails to indicate that any single official was entrusted by the King with full powers over the military. Instead the King himself often led his armies, and when he did not he usually appointed for each specific military enterprise a selected in-

---

Shih, 298–299. Waley, *Shih*, 118–119. But these seem to be the only occurrences of this title in the Western Chou sources, and the contexts are inadequate for certainty. In the *Documents* the *Ch'i-fu* is said to "suppress transgressors," and in the *Poetry* to be "the claws and teeth of the King." This could mean that he is a military officer; it could also mean that he punishes criminals. Certainly the distinction between police and military functions was not always wholly clear in ancient China. But in the last analysis it seems impossible to say, on the basis of the evidence, precisely what was the nature of this office.

205. *Shu*, 70. *Shih*, 139, 226.

206. Concerning the nature of this office, see: *Chin-wen*, 61b–62a. Kuo, "Ch'ang-an Ming-wen," 4. Ssu, "Liang-Chou Chih-kuan K'ao," 7–8. Kuo, *Chin-wen Ts-ung-k'ao*, 74a–75a.

207. *Shu*, 70. *Shih*, 235, 256. Ssu, "Liang-Chou Chih-kuan K'ao," 10.

208. In *Shih*, 188, we find a Commander Shang-fu, who appears to have been the principal general of King Wu in the decisive battle in the conquest of the Shang. In bronze inscriptions, see: *Chin-wen*, 146a. Kuo, "Ch'ang-an Ming-wen," 6.

209. Kuo, "Ch'ang-an Ming-wen," 4. Ssu, "Liang-Chou Chih-kuan K'ao," 7–8. Whether *T'ai-shih* 大師 was ever a military office seems to be uncertain. At times men holding this office appear to have wielded the highest power in the royal government. See: *Shih*, 133, 234. *Chin-wen*, 80b. Ssu, "Liang-Chou Chih-kuan K'ao," 20–21.

dividual. Most commonly these military chieftains are identified to us only by their names; if they bear titles, they may be those of feudal lords, or Commander, or even Secretary.[210]

AMONG all the discoveries made about Western Chou in recent years, perhaps the most important in its implications is the fact that the Chou Kings maintained a number of strong standing armies.

"Six armies" are mentioned in one of the early *Documents*. At the accession of King K'ang, in 1079 B.C., two of his chief ministers are quoted as urging him to "display and make august the six armies."[211] The *Poetry* has three such references: "The Chou King marches, and the six armies go along with him." "The King charged . . . 'Put in order my six armies.' " "The lord comes . . . to raise the six armies."[212] Although this latter passage does not mention the King, commentators and translators agree in supposing that the six armies it mentions are those of the King.[213] And the genuine *Bamboo Books* says that King Chao "lost six armies on the Han River."[214]

These passages have customarily been interpreted on the basis of this statement in the *Ritual of Chou*: "The King has six armies. A large [feudal] state has three armies; a state of the next size has two; a small state has one."[215] This may have been based upon the statement in the *Tso-chuan* that "the Chou [King] maintained six armies; a great vassal might have three."[216] Since there was one King and a number of feudal states, this would clearly have left the King's forces in a very inferior position, numerically.

A new dimension has been given to this whole problem by the bronze inscriptions. In them, we often find the six armies mentioned together with another group—eight armies—which rather unac-

---

210. *Chin-wen*, 28a, 28b.

211. *Shu*, 73.

212. *Shih*, 167, 191, 234.

213. *Mao-shih*, 14(2).1b. *Shih*, 167. Waley, *Shih*, 195. Legge, *Shih*, 382–383 (see notes).

214. Wang, *Ku Chu-shu*, 7a.

215. *Chou-li*, 28.2a; Biot, *Tcheou-li*, II, 142. This work, and the *Tso-chuan* passage cited in the following note, speak of *liu chün* 六 軍 , while the *Documents*, the *Poetry*, the *Mencius*, and the bronze inscriptions to be discussed below read *liu shih* 六 師 ; it is probable, however, that this passage in the *Ritual of Chou* is based on traditions handed down from Western Chou. The passages in the *Poetry* are discussed in terms of this statement in the *Ritual of Chou* by the commentator Cheng Hsüan in *Chou-li*, 28.1a, and by Maspero in *La Chine antique*, 73–74.

216. *Tso*, 462::466 (Hsiang 14).

countably does not seem to be mentioned elsewhere.[217] Even Mencius, writing about 300 B.C., knew that the King had had six armies. He said that if a vassal failed three times to make his proper visit to the royal court "the six armies removed him."[218] But of eight armies he says nothing.

It will be useful first to quote from the inscriptions in which these armies are mentioned, according to the order in which they are dated:

The eastern I greatly rebelled. Po Mou Fu used the Yin eight armies to attack the eastern I.[219]

[Invaders from] Ch'ao made a harassing incursion. The King ordered Tung Kung to drive them back, using the six armies.[220]

The King ordered Li, saying: "Take charge of the six armies' and the eight armies' . . ."[221]

The King ordered . . . Yao, saying: "Succeed your grand-

217. I have been unable to find any such reference, and Yü Sheng-wu (" 'Liu Shih' he 'Pa Shih,' " 152) says that the Yin eight armies "only appear in Western Chou bronze inscriptions."

218. *Mencius*, 6(2).7.2.

219. *Chin-wen*, 23a. Ch'en, "Hsi-Chou T'ung-ch'i," (1).170. That Po Mou Fu here acted under orders of the King is shown by the fact that the inscription later relates that the King ordered him to reward the troops.

220. *Chin-wen*, 100b. Ch'en ("Hsi-Chou T'ung-ch'i," (2).72) dates this inscription to the first period of Western Chou.

221. This inscription occurs on a bronze dug up in 1956, and it bristles with problems. See Kuo, *Wen-shih Lun-chi*, 312–319. There is one previous mention of the six armies, before the passage quoted. The solutions that Kuo Mo-jo proposed for the problems, in his initial study of this inscription, may be correct, but I do not find all of them wholly satisfactory; I prefer, insofar as possible, to leave them to one side. In the passage quoted, "eight armies" is followed by a character that Kuo reads as being an early form of *i* 埶 . Kuo considers this to denote certain minor officials. In his reading, therefore, Li is not being given charge of the armies, but of certain officers of the armies. Yü Sheng-wu, in " 'Liu Shih' he 'Pa Shih,' " 154, agrees in reading the character as *i*, but he understands it in its literal meaning, "to plant." Thus Yü supposes that this inscription is saying that the King orders Li to take charge of planting for the six armies and the eight armies.

father and your father as Great Director of the Multitude to the Ch'eng-Chou eight armies."[222]

The Marquis of E . . . led the southern Huai I and the eastern I in a great attack upon [our] southern states and eastern states . . . The King then ordered the western six armies and the Yin eight armies, saying, "Attack the Marquis of E, and do not spare either the old or the young!"[223]

The King ordered Steward K'e to promulgate orders in Ch'eng-Chou, to rectify the eight armies.[224]

The problem of the identity and the nature of these armies has been the subject of much discussion and a number of theories.[225] It is unlikely that anyone can answer, with certainty, all of the questions that can be asked about them. But some deductions can be made that are at least reasonably safe.

Almost without exception, the contexts clearly show that these fourteen armies[226] were firmly under the control of the Chou King. And these armies were evidently in existence from near the beginning of Western Chou until close to its end. Both the six armies and the eight armies are mentioned in bronze inscriptions dated from the

222. *Chin-wen*, 100a. For the pronunciation of this name as Yao, see p. 180, n. 89.

223. *Ch'ing-t'ung-ch'i T'u-shih*, 24.

224. *Chin-wen*, 123b.

225. Yü, " 'Liu Shih' he 'Pa Shih.' " Hsü, "Yü Ting," 63–65. Ch'en, "Hsi-Chou T'ung-ch'i," (1).171. *Chin-wen*, 100a–101a. Kuo, *Chin-wen Ts'ung-k'ao*, 63b–64a, 331b. Kuo, *Wen-shih Lun-chi*, 317.

226. I assume, as most of those who study these materials seem to do, that all references to "six armies" are to the same group, and that the same is true when "eight armies" are named. But Kuo Mo-jo, in *Chin-wen*, 101a, supposes that there were *two* groups of eight armies, and that when "six armies" were mentioned, this referred to six from one or the other—which one is often uncertain—of the two groups of eight. This seems to me to introduce an unnecessary complication into a situation that is already confused enough. And it seems clear from the *Documents* and the *Poetry*, and from the bronze inscriptions that mention both "the six" and "the eight" armies, that "the six armies" were a regular institution, and not an improvised grouping as Kuo suggests.

early decades of the period to its closing century. In the literature we find the six armies mentioned in one of the early *Documents*, and in poems traditionally assigned to the last decades of the dynasty.

The six armies were evidently a Chou institution from an early date. In fact the *Discourses of the States* indicates that King Wu had six armies in the battle in which he conquered the Shang. This is not, of course, an early or an unquestionably reliable source.[227] But an inscription dated to an early time records that the six armies were used to repel an incursion, and in 1079 B.C. the newly enthroned King is exhorted to "display and make august the six armies."[228] It is reasonable to suppose that "the six armies" were a basic, and possibly the basic, element in the military power of the Chou house.

While in one poem the King speaks of "my six armies," reference is usually merely to "the six armies"; this was apparently a body so well known as to need no further identification. An exception is found in the inscription describing the action to put down the revolt of the Marquis of E; here the King orders "the western six armies and the Yin eight armies" into action. The Chou had their seat, before the conquest, in the west, in the territory of the modern Shensi province, and they kept their principal capital there throughout Western Chou, even after establishing a secondary capital in the east in the region of the modern Loyang. It is rather natural, then, that the troops of the Chou should be called "western." There seems to be no way of certainly knowing, however, whether these six armies were normally stationed in the west, in the Wei valley, or whether their base (or bases) changed during the course of the period.[229]

The "eight armies," too, are referred to without qualification, but we also find them called "the Ch'eng-Chou eight armies" and "the Yin eight armies." This latter designation is found in an inscription

227. *Kuo-yü*,3.19ab. See pp. 477–478. It is interesting to note, however, that this text calls the six armies *liu shih* 六 師 , which agrees with the Western Chou sources (and with *Mencius*), rather than *liu chün* 六 軍 as in the *Tso-chuan* and the *Ritual of Chou*.

228. *Chin-wen*, 100b. Ch'en, "Hsi-Chou T'ung-ch'i," (2).72. *Shu*, 73.

229. Kuo Mo-Jo (*Chin-wen*, 101a) supposes that the reference to the "western six armies," in the inscription concerning the rebellion of the Marquis of E, designates "six of the Ch'eng-Chou eight armies." And he supposes the Ch'eng-Chou eight armies to have been stationed in the region of the modern Loyang, while the Yin eight armies were stationed at a place called Yin, which he locates near the modern town of T'ang-yin, not far south of Anyang. Since the location of the Ch'eng-Chou eight armies was, according to his calculation, west of that of the Yin eight armies, he deduces that it was for this reason that this inscription refers to "the western six armies." Kuo is a most able commentator on this data, but on this point I am unable to follow his reasoning.

dated to the second reign of Western Chou, which says that they were used to attack the rebelling eastern I. It is generally agreed that these were armies taken over from the conquered Yin people and made a part of the military force of the Chou Kings. We know from the *Documents* that the Chou made great efforts to assimilate some of the Yin officials into their government,[230] and they would have had at least as much reason to try to take over and utilize the military forces of those they had conquered.

This attempt seems to have been quite successful; if these Yin armies ever gave the Chou trouble, we have no record of it.[231] This says a great deal for the ability of the Chou to conciliate, and inspire loyalty in, the conquered people. No doubt they did, as Yü Sheng-wu suggests, take the elementary precaution of replacing at least the higher officers with Chou appointees.[232] It is rather surprising that these eight armies, which must have made up a sizable proportion of the military force available to the King, continued to be designated by the name of "Yin," but we find them so called even in a late inscription. This was probably a part of the Chou strategy of conciliation and amalgamation, somewhat comparable to the practice whereby an heir to the British throne is called "Duke of Cornwall" and "Prince of Wales."

That these armies should be called "the Ch'eng-Chou eight armies" is not very surprising. Ch'eng-Chou was one of the names by which the Chou called their secondary capital, established near the site of the modern Loyang to exercise supervision over their eastern territories. These Yin armies were presumably kept in the east, and under supervision from Ch'eng-Chou. Whether they were also stationed at, or in the immediate vicinity of, Ch'eng-Chou seems to be impossible to determine.

Nor do we have any indication of the size, nature, or composition of any of the six or eight armies.[233] For reasons that have already been

230. *Shu*, 49, 56, 65.
231. It seems impossible to be certain whether these eight Yin armies had been taken under Chou command before the great rebellion early in the reign of King Ch'eng. It seems probable, however, that this was done after that event; it was then that Yin officials were moved to the Loyang area and put under direct Chou control, and it is reasonable to suppose that this step regarding the miiltary was taken at the same time.
232. Yü, "'Liu Shih' he 'Pa Shih,'" 152–153.
233. The *Ritual of Chou* says that each of the King's six armies consisted of 12,500 men, but there is no reason to suppose that this was the actual figure—if, indeed, these armies were all of the same size. See *Chou-li*, 28.2a; Biot, *Tcheou-li*, II, 142.

set forth, I believe that Western Chou armies relied heavily on infantry. I suspect, therefore, that these armies consisted chiefly of infantry, though undoubtedly their officers—or some of them—rode in chariots. But this is conjecture.

One important point does emerge rather clearly from the references to these armies. They can hardly have been—as royal armies in Western Chou have sometimes been supposed to be—wholly or even chiefly composed of temporary levies. They were permanent institutions. They were called upon for action in emergencies, to repel invasions. The appointment of Yao as "Great Director of the Multitude to the Ch'eng-Chou eight armies," an office in which he succeeded his grandfather and his father, evidences a continuing organizational entity. So does the commission to Steward K'e to "rectify" the eight armies. These were standing armies.

THUS far matters are relatively simple. Further problems are more complicated. On the bronze inscriptions these armies are not denoted by the character shīh 師 , having the sense of "army" (among others),[234] but by its left-hand portion, 𠂤 , which is commonly pronounced tui. It is quite normal for characters in bronze inscriptions to be thus abbreviated as compared with the modern form. Some scholars, however, believe that this character should not be read as shīh, "army," but as another character having the sense of "military camp."[235]

---

234. Shīh 師 in the Western Chou sources has a number of meanings, including "army," "Commander," "camp" or "garrison," and others.

235. Hsü Chung-shu ("Yü Ting," 63) reads it as tz'u 次 , with the sense of an encampment of guards. Kuo Mo-jo (Chin-wen, 2b–3a) interprets it as t'un 屯 , "camp." Kuo argues that 𠂤 cannot be a briefer form of shīh 師 because, for instance, in Chin-wen, 60b–61a, we have three inscriptions in which both forms appear, the former in the sense of "camp" and the latter as a title, "Commander." In my opinion this argument is not valid, for we have many cases of what is essentially the same character developing different written forms in specialized senses, and the two forms may quite readily be found in the same passage. For instance, tao 道 is simply a specialized form of tao 道 , but there is no reason why both forms may not appear in the same passage.

There is, I think, rather conclusive evidence on this point. The royal "six armies" or "six garrisons" are referred to once in the Documents (Shu, 73), three times in the Poetry (Shih, 167, 191, 234), and three times in the bronze inscriptions (Chin-wen, 100b; Kuo, Wen-shih Lun-chi, 313; Ch'ing-t'ung-ch'i T'u-shih, 24). In every case the bronze inscriptions read 𠂤 , where the Documents and Poetry have 師 . It seems clear that in this sense the two were interchangeable in Western Chou times.

Certainly this character does have the sense of "camp"; in the inscriptions we frequently read that someone is "at" a certain *shih*. It is probable that this character originally represented an enclosure of earthen walls within which an army could encamp in safety.[236] Such walls were sometimes hastily thrown up to protect an army encamped temporarily, but the *shih* referred to in the inscriptions were clearly large, permanently fortified places.[237]

Such military camps must have had a good deal in common with the Roman *castra*, built by the legions to garrison the empire. A number of British towns originated as Roman camps. The name of the city of Chester derives from *castra*, as do the endings of such names as Lancaster, Manchester, and Worcester. Chinese cities, too, must have sprung up about the sites of such garrisons; it is interesting to note that the most common Chinese term for "city," *ch'eng* 城 , literally denotes a wall made of heaped-up earth, which is very close to what was probably the original sense of *shih*.

A few years after the conquest of the Shang, when the Chou decided that they must establish a secondary capital in the east to keep watch over that area, they fixed upon the region of the Le River, in what is now northwestern Honan, as suitable. There was still the question, however, of the exact site. In the "Announcement Concerning Le" the Duke of Chou relates that he went to the region to determine, by divination, what should be the exact location. The place to which he went was, he tells us, "the Le *shih*." It is clear, then, that before the Chou had a city in this area there was a garrison, a fortified military town which the Duke could use as his headquarters in planning and supervising the building of the new city.[238]

A little later in the same document King Ch'eng speaks of "dwell-

236. A number of early works give the sense of *tui* 𠂤 as being "a small mound"; see *Shuo-wen*, 6470b–6472a, and *Chin-wen*, 3a. In the *Tso-chuan* we find the character *lei* 壘 which has the sense of an earthen wall used as a fortification, which was clearly used to surround an encamped army; see *Tso*, 340::345 (Ch'eng 2). That *shih* originally had the sense of an earth-walled encampment is hypothetical, but I believe that this is the most reasonable theory as to its origin. For some similar opinions, see Li, *Chia-ku Wen-tzu Chi-shih*, 4419–4421.

237. There is what appears to be a reference to such a *shih*, at the end of the Spring and Autumn period, in *Tso*, 860::861 (Ai 27).

238. *Shu*, 51. This passage has given translators much trouble; they take *shih* to mean "capital" and assume this to be a prospective reference. Thus Karlgren reads: "I came to (the intented [sic]) capital Lo." Legge (*Shu*, 436) says, "I came to the city of Lo," but explains in a note that the place is called *shih* "as being intended to be the capital." Couvreur (*Shu*, 270) renders the passage as "'j'arrivai à la ville de Lo, destinee a devenir la capitale de l'empire.'"

ing in the *shih*," which makes it appear that the new city itself was called a *shih*.[239] It is possible—but there is no way to be sure of this now—that the city may have been built around the camp as its nucleus. The character *shih* is often interpreted as meaning "capital city"; it is sometimes used in this sense even in modern Chinese.[240] But its early significance was that of a fortified garrison, a very real and potent center of governmental authority. We find the character *shih* as an element in the makeup of other characters having the sense of "to govern" and "government office."[241] It also appears in a character found in the inscriptions with the sense of "to repel" invading barbarians.[242] The *shih* was clearly an important institution, a seat of governmental power and a source of protection against danger.

In one sense the *shih* were places, fortified locations in which troops were stationed. In this sense they may perhaps best be called "garrisons." But this same term also denoted the troops themselves, the armies that garrisoned the area—and that might be sent wherever the King ordered them to go.

Were the six armies all located in one place? Were the eight armies, sometimes called the "Ch'eng-Chou eight armies," all stationed in the immediate vicinity of Ch'eng-Chou? We simply don't know. From a logistical point of view, it is more likely that they were somewhat spread out. Provisioning an army is a problem under any conditions, and with the relatively less developed agriculture of Western Chou times, each army may well have been stationed where it would have a considerable countryside to draw from.

In addition to the six armies and the eight armies, there is reference in the bronze inscriptions to a number of individual *shih*. Most of these are referred to as places; presumably they are garrisons. Whether any of these named *shih* were among the "six armies" or the "eight armies" we cannot tell. In the inscriptions of my corpus, seven such garrisons are named. Matching place names with specific localities in ancient China is always a difficult and dubious business; at least three of these seem to be impossible to locate. Two are located with some plausibility within the boundaries of the modern Honan province. Of the remaining two, one is believed to have been in the

---

239. *Shu*, 52. See also Karlgren, "Glosses on the Book of Documents," (2).83.

240. In the *Poetry* we find three occurrences of *ching shih* 京師 (*Shih*, 96, 207, 211). Karlgren translates this as "capital city" and as "capital."

241. The early form of *shih*, 𠂤 , occurs in *kuan* 官 and in *hsieh* 辥 , as well as in other characters. For the latter, see *Shuo-wen*, 6285a–6586a, and Karlgren, "Grammata Serica Recensa," 89 (no. 289).

242. *Chui* 追 .

center of the modern Shansi province, and the other in the south-western portion of the modern Shantung.[243]

The six and eight armies were, as we have seen, clearly under the direct command of the King. Concerning these individual garrisons the evidence is a little more complex, but hardly less conclusive. One inscription tells us merely that the King was at the Ch'eng garrison; he could have been a guest. But another says that "Po Hsi Fu marched east with the Ch'eng garrison, under orders to stand guard against the southern I."[244] This language is so typical that there can hardly be any doubt that the orders were given by the King. Again we read that the Duke Grand Protector, one of the highest royal officials, on a campaign against rebellious I, was at the Chou garrison.[245]

Three inscriptions tell us merely that Commander Yung Fu was on guard duty at the Yu garrison.[246] But a fourth makes it clear that Yung Fu was a royal official, and in this same inscription we read that the King ordered another officer, saying: "The Huai I dare to attack our inner states; you . . . go and take up guard duty at the Yu garrison."[247] This was clearly a royal establishment. In still another inscription we read: "The King personally ordered K'e to patrol the area from Chīng[248] east up to the Ching garrison."[249]

243. For references to these places, and discussions of the location of some of them, see: *Chin-wen*, 2b, 23ab, 27a, 60b–61b, 66a, 112a–113a. Ch'en, "Hsi-Chou T'ung-ch'i," (1).161, 171b, (5).109. Kuo Mo-jo (*Chin-wen*, 19b) reads one of these as E *shih* 蓋 邑 . It would be very interesting indeed if a royal garrison was located in the territory of the Marquis of E, and it may have been. But this inscription is known only from a Sung copy, and the character there does not closely correspond with the character *e* in the two inscriptions we have that concern the Marquis of E; compare Kuo, *Chin-wen Lu-pien*, 8a, 90b, and *Ch'ing-t'ung-ch'i T'u-shih*, plate 78.

244. *Chin-wen*, 66a. But see the better reading in Ch'en, "Hsi-Chou T'ung-ch'i," (5).111.

245. *Chin-wen*, 27a.

246. Ibid., 60b–61b. The name of this garrison occurs in two forms, and the proper identification of the character is a problem. Yu 盄 is the reading of Ch'en Meng-chia, "Hsi-Chou T'ung-ch'i," (5).107–109. I am not sure it is correct, and I should hesitate to follow Ch'en in all of his interpretations of these particular inscriptions, but I adopt this reading for the sake of simplicity.

247. *Chin-wen*, 61b.

248. It is difficult to be certain of the exact significance of Chīng 涇 here, although it is clearly a geographical name. It occurs as the name of more than one river. Here it may mean the river that flows in a southeasterly direction through the modern central Shensi province and empties into the Wei River a short distance east of Ch'ang-an. If K'e was given the task of patrolling the area from there eastward to Ching 京 , and Ching was as Kuo Mo-jo supposes in the center of the modern Shansi province, he had the responsibility for a considerable area. This is not, however, inconceivable.

249. *Chin-wen*, 112a–113a. The translation of "patrol," which is the interpretation of Kuo Mo-jo, is I believe justified by the context.

Similar patrolling action is described in another inscription: "Commander Yung Fu patrolled the road up to Fu."[250] The Kings not only had strategically located garrisons, but guarded the roads to keep communications open.

We read of guard duty being carried on at places where we are not specifically told that there are garrisons, shīh. If shīh were not located (as they may have been) wherever guards were stationed, there were no doubt at least fortified guard posts of some kind. Not only on the bronzes, but also in the *Poetry*, we read of this guard duty.

> She [my wife] is not with me keeping guard at Shen.
> I yearn, I yearn,
> What month shall I return home?

Successive stanzas speak of guard duty at Fu and at Hsü; all three were places on the southern border. Another poem laments the hardship of long service in standing guard against the Hsien-yün barbarians. But even as he complains the author says, "The service to the King must not be defective."[251]

This far-flung military establishment must have required the expenditure of considerable economic resources. The fact that it was formerly believed that the Chou Kings could not have disposed of such resources is one of the principal reasons for which it has been supposed that their power must have been relatively limited. Yü Sheng-wu believes that we have evidence that in fact the garrisons, shīh, were to some degree self-supporting.

We have seen that in one inscription the King orders one of his officers to succeed his grandfather and his father as "Director of the Multitude to the Ch'eng-Chou eight armies."[252] And from other inscriptions we can see that the functions of the Director of the Multitude appear to have included supervision of persons engaged in farming, forestry, and herding.[253] Yü interprets another inscription as a charge by the King to one of his officials to "take charge of planting for the six armies and the eight armies."[254]

On the basis of this and other evidence, Yü deduces that these

---

250. Ibid., 59b. For the interpretation of this inscription, and the identification of the place as Fu, see Ch'en, "Hsi-Chou T'ung-ch'i," (5).108–109. Ch'en considers Fu to have been a state on the southern border.

251. *Shih*, 46, 111.

252. *Chin-wen*, 100a.

253. Ch'en, "Hsi-Chou T'ung-ch'i," (6).111–112. Kuo, *Chin-wen Ts'ung-k'ao*, 63a–65a. Ssu, "Liang-Chou Chih-kuan K'ao," 6–7.

254. See n. 221 above.

Western Chou armies tilled the soil and raised domestic animals in the vicinity of their camps, thus providing much of their own food. Such a method was used in Han times, but it was formerly supposed that this was a Han innovation.[255] It seems probable that Yü's theory is correct; it certainly helps explain the ability of the Chou to meet the expense of their military undertakings. Yet this could still have met only a part of the cost. It is unlikely that the soldiers could even have provided all of their own food, and there was of course other heavy expense for such things as clothing and weapons.

CERTAINLY there were military forces in Western Chou that were not under the direct control of the King, but it is not often easy to be clear on this point. When the King commands a man who holds the title of a feudal vassal to make a military expedition, we cannot usually tell whether the troops he commands are his own, which he brings from his fief, or the King's—but in fact it is very rarely that we find the commanders of military actions called by feudal titles. In one inscription we find the king ordering two of his officers, successively, to join in an attack on Jung barbarians, saying in each case, "use your army."[256] In two, or possibly in three inscriptions, we find reference to what may have been kinship groups fighting in a body, but this is very uncertain.[257]

The feudal lords, and especially those on the boundaries, were established in considerable measure for the purpose of guarding the Empire against barbarians. This means that they must have had a good deal of military force, and must have used it when necessary without explicit orders from the King. There are, as we have seen, a few references in the *Poetry* to the military action of some of the feudal states against barbarians. But it is clearly not the case, as has

255. Yü, " 'Liu Shih' he 'Pa Shih.' " See also Loewe, *Records of Han Administration*, I, 56–57.

256. *Chin-wen*, 20b.

257. The character in question here is *tsu* 族, which is commonly interpreted as having the sense of "kinship group." But it was pointed out on page 91, n. 36, that this character is rare in the Western Chou sources and may in fact have stood rather for a military unit. In *Chin-wen*, 20b, we find an officer told, "use your *tsu*" to join in an attack. *Tsu* here stands in the same contextual position in which we find *shih*, "army," elsewhere in the inscription. In *Chin-wen*, 10b, the King orders a Duke to "send three *tsu* to attack the eastern states." In both of these cases, it would seem quite possible that *tsu* is the name of a military unit. Whether the second reference to *tsu* in ibid., 135a, does or does not concern military action seems impossible to determine.

sometimes been supposed, that the power and the activities of the King did not extend all the way to the borders of Chinese territory. In the bronze inscriptions we have seen the King charging Hsi Chia to collect taxes all the way from Ch'eng-Chou, the eastern capital, to the southern Huai I on the eastern coast, and saying that if they do not obey orders they are to be attacked. Another inscription, dated to the same reign, says that the Huai I have been disobedient; the King orders Commander Huan to attack them. There is no question here of any dependence by the King upon the military power of feudal lords to maintain his authority.[258]

All of the sources collaborate to give the impression that the Western Chou Kings were able to retain a control over their domain that was, in the circumstances, remarkable. Whether their military power was equal to that of all of their vassals combined we cannot tell; it may not have been. But powerful vassals on the borders were in exposed positions vis-à-vis the barbarians, which neutralized their power insofar as the royal house was concerned. And they were dependent upon the help of the King's armies. Whenever there was a great barbarian incursion, it was almost always troops under royal command, not the feudal states, that stemmed the tide.

The vassals were caught, then, between the royal power on the one hand and the barbarians on the other. Insofar as our sources indicate, it was only when vassals combined with barbarians that they could make great headway against the King.[259] It is significant that tradition attributes the fall of the Western Chou to an attack by disgruntled feudal lords in league with barbarians.

258. *Chin-wen*, 143b, 146a. Hsü, "Yü Ting," 62.
259. An exception may be provided by the revolt against King Li of which tradition tells (see pp. 431–432), but this is not attested, directly at least, by the Western Chou sources.

CHAPTER
11
Feudalism

THOSE who write about early China commonly use such terms as "fief," "vassal," and "feudalism." And authorities on European feudalism often seem to regard this as a kind of poaching on their preserves. In the opinion of many feudalism is a phenomenon that occurred once, in medieval Europe; as a concession they may grant that it may have occurred also in medieval Japan.[1]

This is a problem that may not be evaded. Phenomena that have been called feudal—either rightly or wrongly—are central to our investigation. Two questions must be asked, and answered. Can the term "feudalism" properly be employed in the study of early China? If not, we must abandon it. If it can, what in fact is "feudalism"? Neither of these is an easy question.

Popular usage is hopelessly confused. Claude Cahen points out that "some journalists and politicians denounce the 'feudalism' of syndicates or trusts." Marxists brand as "feudal" a wide variety of institutions and practices of which they disapprove. The *Wall Street Journal*, not to be outdone, asserts that "the Soviet Union is a feudal society, in the true sense of that word." John Whitney Hall writes that "in Japan today, feudalism has taken on a popular prejorative meaning which is applied to almost any aspect of contemporary life which seems old-fashioned or touched with the older social or family ethic —a term with which children criticize their parents."[2]

1. Ganshof (*La féodalité*, 13) writes: "La féodalité au sens strict, c'est-à-dire le système d'institutions féodo-vassaliques, est aussi—et plus encore que la féodalité au sens large—propre aux Etats nés du démembrement de l'Empire carolingien et aux pays influencés par ces Etats." See also: Coulborn, *Feudalism in History*, 185. "A Comparative Discussion of Feudalism," 50–51. Miyazaki, "Chūgoku Jōdai wa Hōkensei ka Toshi Kokka ka."

2. Cahen, "L'usage du mot de 'féodalité,'" 4. Vermont Royster, "Soviet's New-Style Feudalism," in *Wall Street Journal*, August 22, 1962, p. 8. Hall, "Feudalism in Japan," 19.

Scholarly usage is of course more precise, but scholars are far from having reached a consensus concerning the nature of feudalism. Hall points out that despite the fact that a great deal of effort has gone into the attempt to define it, "there has been little agreement among historians, even among those working exclusively within the field of European history, on a common set of criteria."[3] That the prospect for such agreement is far from bright was demonstrated in 1950 when the American Council of Learned Societies brought together twenty-three scholars (of whom I was one) for a two-day conference entitled "A Comparative Discussion of Feudalism." In the final session three specific definitions were proposed. One of them characterized feudalism as a "society," the second as "a system of government," and the third as "a pattern of culture values, and of social and economic life."[4] It is doubtful that a majority of the conferees would have voted for any one of these definitions.

Some students construct a "model" or an "ideal type" of feudalism, against which they measure any phenomena that may be in question in order to determine whether they constitute "true" feudalism. Such constructs may be useful for some purposes, but they have two characteristics that make them difficult to apply in comparative historical investigations. They are usually based upon the conditions of a particular time and place—most commonly, one or more countries of medieval Europe. If this is the standard, then every other situation is ruled out by definition; it cannot be true feudalism. Secondly, they are static, limited not only to a particular place but also to the complex of conditions prevailing at a particular time. Few of the characteristics often called essential to feudalism in fact prevailed, over *all* of the period that even purists call "feudal," in any country of Europe. History is a process of ceaseless change, and static yardsticks cannot measure it effectively.

A. L. Kroeber suggested "a broadly comparative method using common concepts. Feudalism," he said, "is such a concept and so are monarchy, democracy, and civilization."[5] "Democracy" is an excellent example. The word and the concept are of course Greek in origin. Yet as William Linn Westermann has pointed out, while most of the Greek states of the fifth and four centuries B.C. had democratic governments, "as judged by the standards of the inclusive adult citizen

---

3. Hall, "Feudalism in Japan," 24–25. This paper gives an excellent survey of definitions and characterizations of feudalism, not merely in Japan, but as a concept; it makes clear the very wide areas of disagreement.

4. "A Comparative Discussion of Feudalism," 76–78.

5. Ibid., 61.

privilege of modern democratic practise, the Greek city-states were actually organized as oligarchies." It has been estimated, for instance, that in Attica in 431 B.C. perhaps only one-sixth of the population could vote.[6] If the same standard were applied that some insist on for the term "feudalism," we could hardly use the word "democracy" in a modern context at all.

First of all we must answer the basic question: what is "feudalism"? Hall writes: "The Marxists are not alone in conceiving of feudalism in almost anthropomorphic fashion as a living social organism which can be described as 'taking over' a society, as 'bringing' certain institutions into being, as 'resisting' change or 'leading' to other stages of society."[7] But in fact of course "feudalism" is a term, a word. It has never had an objective existence, even to the extent that "Platonism" has. Very few persons have ever consciously practiced feudalism, for the term was not coined until the eighteenth century, when feudalism as a functioning institution had almost disappeared.[8]

Students of European feudalism feel a sense of propriety in the term with some justice, since it was coined in France as a description of certain phenomena of medieval Europe. But what, we must ask, was the term coined to denote? Marc Bloch traces the origin of the concept of feudalism to the writings of Henri, Comte de Boulainvilliers (1658–1722), and of Montesquieu (1689–1755). He says:

> To Boulainvilliers and Montesquieu, living in an age of absolute monarchy, the most striking characteristic of the Middle Ages was the parcelling out of sovereignty among a host of petty princes, or even lords of villages. It was this characteristic that they meant to denote by the term feudalism . . .[9]

Later scholars have added—with what warrant is not wholly clear —a great variety of other characteristics that are considered, by one or more of them, to be essential to genuine feudalism. But the importance of the "parcelling out of sovereignty" is still recognized. Joseph R. Strayer writes that "the most important idea which developed out of the confusion of early feudalism was the idea that all po-

6. William Linn Westermann, "Greek Culture and Thought," in *Encyclopedia of the Social Sciences*, I, 12.

7. Hall, "Feudalism in Japan," 36.

8. Bloch (*Feudal Society*, xvii) says that the word *féodalité* "goes back at least to the seventeenth century," but was at first used only in a narrowly legal sense. Its earliest use with a meaning comparable to that of our term "feudalism" occurred, according to his research, in 1727.

9. Ibid., xvii–xviii.

litical power was delegated from a higher to a lower lord. God gave the king his realm with full powers; the king then gave a county to a count with wide powers (but not independence); the count gave out baronies with lesser powers; the barons gave their knights fiefs with police-court justice."[10] Carl Stephenson says that "seignorial government originated as a delegation of power by the monarchy."[11]

This original sense of the term, that of a system of delegated sovereignty, provides the basis for a functional definition of feudalism. Such a definition has the advantage that it is dynamic rather than static, and concentrates on essentials while disregarding superficial particulars. In this work, the following definition will be used:

> Feudalism is a system of government in which a ruler personally delegates limited sovereignty over portions of his territory to vassals.[12]

There are many who will find this definition lacking because it concentrates solely on the political aspect of feudalism.[13] That it does so does not result from any disposition to ignore the very important social and economic circumstances that normally accompany feudalism. But they do accompany, or even result from it; they are not the fundamental factor. Strayer and Coulborn put it very well: "Feudalism is primarily a method of government, not an economic or a social sys-

10. Strayer, *Feudalism*, 47. He continues: "Needless to say, this concept of the delegation of political power represented neither historical experience nor actual practice." But in early Chou China, insofar as we can tell, this does to some degree describe the actual situation. This is only one respect in which feudalism in early China seems to be closer to a pure, or at least relatively uncomplicated, kind of feudalism than does that of medieval Europe.

11. Stephenson, *Medieval Feudalism*, 32.

12. This definition is one that I had developed, on the basis of my own study of feudalism, before I encountered Bloch's study indicating that the term was originally used in the sense of the delegation of sovereignty. This reinforces my feeling that this does constitute its essential characteristic.

In this definition I refer to the delegation of "limited sovereignty" because, if the ruler conferred complete sovereignty, the recipient would no longer be subordinate to the ruler. By referring to those to whom limited sovereignty is delegated as "vassals," I mean that they stand to the ruler in a special relationship of personal loyalty, and are not mere officials to whom certain powers have been delegated.

13. It is rather generally recognized, however, that the political aspect was very important. Max Weber (*Theory of Organization*, 351) writes that "the situation where an administrative staff exists which is primarily supported by fiefs, will be called 'feudalism.'" Stephenson (*Medieval Feudalism*, 14, 96) concludes that in Europe, "feudalism became the basis of a new political organization" and observes that "to regard feudalism as something apart from practical politics is utterly to misunderstand the life of the Middle Ages." See also: Bloch, *Feudal Society*, 187. Cahen, "L'usage du mot de 'féodalité,'"11–12.

tem, though it obviously modifies and is modified by the social and economic environment."[14]

There is a remarkable degree of similarity in the social and economic conditions that feudalism—the feudal pattern of government —tends to produce in quite different times and places. Bloch writes:

> A subject peasantry; widespread use of the service tenement (i.e. the fief) instead of a salary, which was out of the question; the supremacy of a class of specialized warriors; ties of obedience and protection which bind man to man and, within the warrior class, assume the distinctive form called vassalage; fragmentation of authority—leading inevitably to disorder; and, in the midst of all this, the survival of other forms of association, family and State, of which the latter, during the second feudal age, was to acquire renewed strength—such then seem to be the fundamental features of European feudalism. Like all the phenomena revealed by that science of eternal change which is history, the social structure thus characterized certainly bore the peculiar stamp of an age and an environment.[15]

Yet this would require very little change to be used as a description of feudalism in China in the Chou dynasty, beginning two millennia before feudalism in Europe. The greatest modification would need to be made, not to fit it to the Chinese situation, but to adapt it to *either* China or Europe. For one would have to say that these conditions varied in the course of the history of feudal institutions, so that at the

14. Strayer and Coulborn, "The Idea of Feudalism," 4. Even as describing a system of government, my definition does not, it is true, cover some phenomena that many would describe as feudalism. There is the practice of granting land that is called a "fief" to a retainer who is given the right to the income from it but no powers of government over it. This is sometimes called a special type of feudalism; see: Weber, *Theory of Organization*, 378–380. Mei, "Ch'un-ch'iu Cheng-chih," 166–167. But in fact this is not feudalism at all. As Strayer ("Feudalism in Western Europe," 16) says, "it is the possession of rights of government by feudal lords and the performance of most functions of government through feudal lords which clearly distinguishes feudalism from other types of organization."

Grants were sometimes made merely of income. These were called "money fiefs," and this is sometimes considered a form of feudalism. But in fact, as Bloch (*Feudal Society*, 174–175) says, this was a system whereby "under the old name of military tenure, the great baronial and princely families were able to pass imperceptibly to what was to all intents and purposes a system of cash remuneration, characteristic of a new economy founded on buying and selling." This was not feudalism, but a clever use of the honorific term "fief" to abolish feudalism.

15. Bloch, *Feudal Society*, 446.

beginning some of them were scarcely present at all, even though feudalism as a political system was in full vigor.

The resemblances between feudal Europe and feudal China go even further. The code of aristocratic honor, the practice of regarding war as a game, the value placed on reckless courage, and many other characteristics are surprisingly similar in the feudal nobility of ancient China and medieval Europe. A feudal warrior of the Spring and Autumn period would have felt great spiritual compatibility with a medieval knight. But both of them would have felt very much out of place in Han dynasty China or in modern Europe.

At the conclusion of his list of "the fundamental features of European feudalism," quoted above, Bloch adds that "it is by no means impossible that societies different from our own should have passed through a phase closely resembling that which has just been defined. If so, it is legitimate to call them feudal during that phase."[16] On this basis—and others—there is full justification for using the term "feudalism" to denote phenomena found in China during much of the Chou dynasty.

Not merely the phenomena but also the concept of feudalism, and some of the terminology associated with it, appeared far earlier in China than in Europe. The most common term meaning "to enfeoff" in Chinese is *feng-chien* 封建 . This two-character expression is found as early as the Spring and Autumn period, but does not occur in this sense in the Western Chou sources.[17] But each of these characters individually does occur with this meaning.

In the bronze inscriptions *feng* is found in the form 丰 , a pictograph of a plant (perhaps a seedling), and 邦 and 封 which show a hand or two hands holding the plant, evidently "planting" it.[18] From this it develops the sense of to establish a new state, "to enfeoff," and that of "fief." The *Poetry* says of the Chou: "There are no fiefs *(feng)* that are not your states; it is only the King who establishes them."[19]

Chien also means "to establish" and thence "to enfeoff." We even

16. Ibid., 446.

17. *Tso*, 189::192 (Hsi 24). These characters occur in *Shih*, 266, but not with the sense of "to enfeoff."

18. *San-tai Chin-wen*, 13.10b. Kuo, *Chin-wen Lu-pien*, 127a, 135a. The first of these inscriptions, consisting of only six characters, is not included in my corpus; in it, *feng* is a proper name. The character does not seem to have the sense of "to enfeoff" in any of these inscriptions. The etymology commonly given for this character, involving a mound of earth, seems to have no specific support in the early form of the character. The *Shuo-wen* (6125a–6127a) erroneously supposes it to contain *t'u* 土 , "earth."

19. *Shih*, 240. The character *feng* does not appear in the original text of the *Book of Changes*, and in the sections of the *Documents* that I believe to be of Western Chou date it occurs only as a proper name.

find it said in the *Documents* that Heaven "enfeoffed," *chien*, the Shang Kings. This is entirely logical, for according to the Chou theory it was indeed limited sovereignty that was conferred on a King by Heaven. He might do what he would, but if he flagrantly and repeatedly flouted the will of Heaven, Heaven would give its Mandate to another to replace him. In another of the *Documents* King K'ang says that Kings Wen and Wu "appointed and enfeoffed *(chien)* feudal lords in order to set up a protecting wall for us, their successors."[20] This term is used similarly in the *Book of Changes*,[21] and the *Poetry* describes the founding of the state of Lu in these words:

> The King said, "Uncle,
> I enfeoff *(chien)* your eldest son
> To be lord in Lu.
> I grandly open up for you a domain
> To be a support for the house of Chou."
> And so he appointed the Duke of Lu
> To be lord in the east,
> Giving him mountains and streams,
> Lands and fields and attached states.[22]

20. *Shu*, 55, 73–74. In the latter passage I am translating *hou* 侯 as "feudal lords," although it is commonly translated conventionally as "Marquis." But here it does not refer to men of a particular rank, but to feudatories in general. *Chu-hou* 諸侯, literally "the various *hou*," is regularly translated as "feudal lords."

21. *I-ching*, 1.28a; 2.34a; Legge, *I-ching*, 62, 91.

22. *Shih*, 259–260. "Attached states" is a conventional translation of *fu-yung* 附庸. The first of these characters means "attached" and the second has among others the meaning of "service," but whether that is its meaning in this compound is uncertain.

This is a curious term. It is very rare in, if not absent from, the Western Chou sources; this poem bears internal evidence that it is of Spring and Autumn date. Kuo Mo-jo (*Chin-wen*, 143ab) interprets two other characters in one inscription as being equivalent to *fu-yung*. *Mencius* 5(2).2, says that "[rulers whose] territories were not as large as fifty *li* could not have direct relations with the Son of Heaven; their holdings were attached to those of a feudal lord, and called 'attached states' *(fu-yung)*."

Commentators on the early literature call many states *fu-yung*. We can only conjecture concerning this institution. It seems unlikely that the Kings would have set up feudal lords with the intention that they be attached to others. It seems much more probable that such dependency came about as the result of conquest —a very frequent occurrence—in which the victor, rather than following the common course of annexing the territory, permitted the state to persist in a condition of subservience. This poem, however, says that Lu was given "attached states" when it was founded. But it should be noted that since this poem names Duke Chuang of Lu, it cannot have been written before the seventh century B.C. It is quite possible, therefore, that this language was used to gloss over the well-known fact that Lu made a practice of domineering over neighboring states weaker than itself.

Even though the delegation of limited sovereignty was clearly practiced in early China, some would insist that this was not true feudalism, because genuine feudalism, such as existed in medieval Europe, can only succeed the breakdown of a highly centralized state.[23] But to insist that feudalism can only come into being in one particular way is a good deal like saying that "real" marriage can be brought about only by one particular rite—whether that rite be purchase, or capture, or the ceremony of some particular church.

It is not merely the case that the fact of feudalism existed in China much earlier than it did in Europe. So did the theory. We have a record of a discussion of the merits of feudal rule, through the delegation of sovereignty, *versus* bureaucratic rule by means of centrally appointed and controlled functionaries, as early as 221 B.C. This debate continued in China for centuries. One much-admired essay on the subject, entitled "A Discussion of Feudalism," was written by Liu Tsung-yüan, who lived from A.D. 773 to 819.[24] In Europe, on the other hand, the earliest beginnings of the institution of feudalism are seldom if ever assigned to a time earlier than the Carolingian Empire (751–911), while the concept is traced by Bloch to an origin in the eighteenth century.[25]

WHEN we address ourselves to the problem of discovering what, specifically, was the character of Western Chou feudalism, our most difficult problem is a negative one. We must first learn what it was not. For thousands of years it has been supposed that, while some details may be regrettably lacking, we are very adequately informed concerning the general nature of the political, social, and economic circumstances attending Western Chou feudalism.

The Confucian philosopher Mencius (c.372–c.289 B.C.) seems to have been the first person to hold forth on this subject in a systematic way. The *Mencius* says:

> Pei-kung I asked, "What was the arrangement of the ranks and emoluments conferred by the house of Chou?" Mencius replied, "It is impossible to learn the

23. For a discussion of this proposition, see Coulborn, *Feudalism in History*, 236–253.

24. *Shih-chi*, 6.25–28; *Mémoires historiques*, II, 131–133. Liu, *Liu He-tung Chi*, 1.34–49. Pulleyblank, "Neo-Confucianism and Neo-Legalism in T'ang Intellectual Life, 755–805," 102–104.

25. Ganshof, *La féodalité*, 11. Strayer, *Feudalism*, 12. Strayer, "Feudalism in Western Europe," 18. Bloch, *Feudal Society*, xvii–xviii.

details. The feudal lords, because they disliked them as being injurious to themselves, have made away with the records concerning them."

Mencius' idea was, apparently, that because the feudal lords had usurped the powers of the Chou Kings in the Spring and Autumn period, they did not wish any evidence to remain concerning the system of royal government they had destroyed. On its surface this has a certain plausibility, but there are reasons for doubt.

Mencius goes on to say that, while the details cannot be known, he has heard about the general outline of these institutions.

> Son of Heaven was one rank; Duke was one rank; Marquis was one rank; Earl was one rank; Viscount and Baron, of equal status, together constituted one rank. Thus there were altogether five degrees of rank.

(It should be noted, however, that the "five degrees of rank," as they are commonly referred to, do not include the Son of Heaven, but do include the Viscount and Baron as two ranks, in that order.)[26] Mencius also tells us exactly how much land was allotted to persons of each rank.

> According to the regulations, the Son of Heaven had a square of one thousand *li* of territory.[27] The Duke and the Marquis each had squares of one hundred *li*, the Earl seventy *li*, the Viscount and baron each fifty *li*, in all making four degrees. [Rulers whose] territories were not as large as fifty *li* could not have direct relations with the Son of Heaven; their holdings were attached to those of a feudal lord, and called "attached states."[28]

In this same passage Mencius also gives many other particulars, concerning such matters as the ratios between the incomes of the ruler and the various ministers in states of various sizes, and even the

26. These English translations of the ranks are conventional, and are used only for convenience. The Chinese terms are: *kung* 公 , *hou* 侯 , *po* 伯 , *tzu* 子 , and *nan* 男 . The sources for the more traditional order are: *Chou-li,* 18.21b–22b; Biot, *Tcheou-li,* I, 431–432. *Li-chi,* 11.1a; Legge, *Li-chi,* I, 209.

27. Swann (*Food and Money,* 362) gives the length of the Chou *li* 里 as more than 1364.1 feet, English measure. Thus an area 1000 *li* square would have contained approximately 66,745 square miles. This is slightly larger than the modern Honan province.

28. *Mencius,* 5(2).2. Concerning "attached states" see p. 323, n. 22.

number of mouths that could be fed by farmers of different degrees of excellence.

All this information is so admirably detailed and so systematically presented as to cause one to wonder whether Mencius may not, after all, have possessed sources a good deal more adequate than he has represented them to be. Elsewhere he gives us particulars concerning early economic arrangements, and even mentions what appears to be a system of public schoois.[29] Unfortunately, however, when we examine the sources they provide almost no support whatever for Mencius' assertions. It is difficult not to suspect him of having a lively, not to say a creative, imagination.

Chinese scholars have for centuries been expressing some doubt that the system of feudal ranks was precisely as Mencius describes it.[30] And in our own day, on the basis of our new knowledge of ancient China, it is generally realized that not only was there not the particular tidy system that Mencius gives us for the feudal hierarchy, but that no such rationally ordered arrangement existed in Western Chou times. When one plunges into examination of the way in which feudal titles are actually used in the Western Chou sources, it is difficult not to look with regret—and even a certain admiration—on the beautiful order of the scheme set forth by Mencius. When we seek to derive anything approaching this from the sources, our troubles are many.

It is far from easy, in many cases, even to be sure what is and what is not a title denoting feudal rank.[31] Context and word order help, but there are ambiguities that sometimes leave room for serious question, and for differences of opinion between eminent authorities.[32]

Neither is the use of titles always consistent. A poem says, "The

---

29. *Mencius,* 1(1).3, 7; 3(1).3.

30. *Meng-tzu Hui-chien,* 201–203.

31. For instance, the character *po* 伯 , when used as a feudal title, is conventionally translated as "Earl." But it is also employed in the sense of "eldest of brothers" and "eldest of sisters." This usage is common in the bronzes, and was long continued. We also find this same character used as a numerative of men, as we use "head" for cattle, as in "a hundred head of cattle." But what kind of men it serves to enumerate is not agreed upon. In one inscription Ch'en Meng-chia, in "Hsi-Chou T'ung-ch'i," (1).167, interprets it as a numerative of slaves; in the same inscription Kuo Mo-jo (*Wen-shih Lun-chi,* 310) understands it to be a numerative of officials. Where the context is otherwise clear, such things may not lead to confusion, but where there are many ambiguities, like those discussed in the following note, they may.

32. Ch'en Meng-chia, in "Hsi-Chou T'ung-ch'i," (3).90, says that when *po* 伯 means "eldest," it precedes the person's name, and where it means "Earl," it follows the name of the place with which the Earl is enfeoffed. In general this is the case. Thus in *Chin-wen,* 62ab, we find a bronze made by the ruler of the small state of Lu 彔 . Here he is called, in the usual manner, Lu Po Tung, Earl Tung of

Marquis of Lu has come," and a little later, speaking of the same person, "All follow the Duke in his going."[33] Various poems appear to refer to the same individual as Duke of Shao and Earl of Shao.[34] Titles in the bronze inscriptions are not always used consistently. In virtually every case scholars have found ways of explaining these inconsistencies away. The explanations are often ingenious and in some cases certainly valid, but it seems clear that the usage was sometimes inconsistent in fact.[35] Even as late as the Spring and Autumn period we

---

the state of Lu. But in *Chin-wen*, 64b, we find what is evidently the same man called Po Tung, Earl Tung.

Again, the title Duke normally follows either the name of the fief or the personal name, but here too there are exceptions. In references to the Chou ancestors, the Ancient Duke Tan-fu and Duke Liu, the title precedes the personal name. In *Chin-wen*, 33a, we find what is evidently a personal name following "Duke." There is similar inversion in the case of the Chou ancestor *Wang* Chi, King Chi.

33. *Shih*, 256. In this passage Karlgren translates both *hou* 侯 and *kung* 公 as "prince"; elsewhere (*Shih*, 10, 96) he also translates *po* 伯 as "prince." It would appear that he considers them to be various titles between which there is no very great distinction.

34. *Shih*, 10, 234, 238. Concerning the identification of the individual referred to in the first of these poems, see *Mao-shih*, 1(4).8a.

35. For discussion of some of these problems see Kuo, *Chin-wen Ts'ung-k'ao*, 39b–42a. The way in which titled makers of bronzes refer to their ancestors is a very difficult problem. Noel Barnard ("A Bronze of Western Chou Date," 31) notes that the Marquis of Ch'ien refers to his deceased father as "Duke of Ch'ien," "illustrating thus the practice of elevating the rank of a deceased ruler by one degree." In a note he says that "the statement concerning the elevation of the rank of a deceased prince 'by one degree' is, of course, an assumption." Barnard observes that "if the general body of inscriptions is consulted a most confusing picture results—assisted, no doubt, by unscrupulous bronze-founders of recent centuries." It seems possible, however, that it could be our understanding of the ancient practice that is at fault.

Various rules have been propounded to explain the situation. Legge (*Tso*, 385) says that "the style of 'duke' is always given in mentioning the burials of princes," and (*Tso*, 755) that "towards the end of the Chow dynasty, all the nobles of the [royal] domain received the title of *Kung* [Duke] after their death." In the Western Chou inscriptions we do find cases in which Marquises refer to their fathers as "Duke"; see: *Chin-wen*, 115b–116a. Ch'en, "Hsi-Chou T'ung-ch'i," (1).165, (3).83. These might seem to illustrate "the practice of elevating the rank of a deceased ruler by one degree"—if, that is, one believes that in Western Chou times there was a definite hierarchy of feudal ranks, which I certainly do not. But we also find (*Chin-wen*, 144b) an Earl calling his grandfather "Duke," which would be an elevation of two degrees—again if one believed in the hierarchy. On the other hand we find (*Chin-wen*, 31b) a Marquis making a sacrificial vessel dedicated to one whom he titles merely "Marquis"—almost certainly an ancestor, although the relationship is unspecified. Again we find (*Chin-wen*, 147ab) a mere Earl making a vessel for his father whom he calls "King" (and this is not one of the Chou Kings). Finally we have two vessels which Kuo Mo-jo plausibly attributes to the same maker (*Chin-wen*, 61b–62a), who is an Earl; he calls both his father and his grandfather "Duke."

sometimes find the same man called by various feudal titles.[36]

Finally, there is no convincing evidence for the hierarchy of position that the tradition supposes to have existed, in which the Duke ranked above the Marquis, the Marquis above the Earl, the Earl above the Viscount, and the Viscount above the Baron.[37] The title of "Baron" occurs so rarely in the sources as to be negligible, and scholars who have studied the source materials for Western Chou carefully are in general agreement that the other four titles seem to be used without any clear distinction between them.[38] The lack of any careful gradation seems clearly indicated by the account, in the *Documents*, of the officials called together by King Ch'eng on the day before he died, to hear his final commands. One would expect that on such a solemn occasion the feudal lords present would be listed in strict order of their precedence. But they are named in this order: two Earls, a Duke, a Marquis, and another Duke.[39] It is impossible to find any hierarchical order, based on title, in this.

WHAT can we make of all this confusion? Let us look again at medieval Europe and see whether we can find any parallels.

We can indeed. Baldwin V of Flanders was a puissant ruler who became Regent of France and the father-in-law of William the Conqueror. A charter that he granted in 1038 reads, "I, Baldwin, by the grace of God Count of Flanders," and at the end, "The mark of Baldwin, the Marquis, who ordered this document to be made." A grant made by William, shortly before the conquest of England, refers to him in the body as "the Duke of the Normans, William," but is signed: "The mark of Count William." Strayer points out that William was also called "Marquis." Bloch writes:

---

36. *Chin-wen*, 12a. Kuo, *Chin-wen Ts'ung-k'ao*, 39b–42a. Bodde, "Feudalism in China," 54. James Legge (*Tso*, 3) notes inconsistencies in the usages of titles in the *Tso-chuan*.

37. This order is given in: *Chou-li*, 18.21b–22b; Biot, *Tcheou-li*, I, 431–432. *Li-chi*, 11.1a; Legge, *Li-chi*, I, 209.

38. *Chin-wen*, 12a. Kuo, *Chin-wen Ts'ung-k'ao*, 39b–42a. Fu, "Lun So-wei Wu-teng Chüeh." Hu, *Chia-ku Hsüeh*, *Ch'u-chi*, "Yin-tai Feng-chien Chih-tu K'ao," 37b. Hsu (*Ancient China*, 5) says that as late as the Spring and Autumn period "all the states enjoyed *de facto* sovereignty, and their rulers were equal in this key respect despite differences in their titles." Henri Maspero, writing before the crucial discoveries and research of the last forty years, said (*La Chine antique*, 83, n. 1) that "the hierarchy consisted only of three degrees in the Chou period, and not five." But his evidence is not at all convincing, even for this formula.

39. *Shu*, 70.

To describe those who controlled several counties, ancient usage provided no precise label. They were called and they called themselves, more or less indiscriminately, "arch-counts," "principal counts," "marquises" (that is to say, commanders of a march, by analogy with the governments of frontier regions which had provided the model for those of the interior), and finally "dukes," a borrowing from Merovingian and Roman terminology. But this last term was seldom used except where an old provincial or ethnic unity served as the basis for the new power. Force of habit slowly led to the adoption in this place or that of one or the other of these titles; or else, as at Toulouse and in Flanders, the simple title of count was retained.[40]

The title "Baron" developed from a late Latin word meaning "man." A Baron was "the man" of his overlord, to whom he had done homage. Thus this term might initially be applied to any vassal. Eventually it was necessary to distinguish those who were of the specific rank of Baron, and those who were not, but this was not easy. Strayer says: "In England, where it was legally important to draw the line between knight and baron, it is evident that there was some difficulty in doing so—a man listed as a baron in one year will be called a knight the next, and vice-versa."[41]

The time came, in medieval Europe, when orders of precedence were nicely established. But this came about principally in the later period of feudalism, when lawyers debated points of privilege and nobles quarreled about the places to which they were entitled in ceremonies. In the earlier phase, when feudal institutions were developing and feudal lords were too busy establishing themselves to worry about what they were called, it was power, not title, that mattered. And there was little of the "neat, pyramidal structure of the textbooks."[42]

In the matter of titles, Western Chou China appears to have resembled the early period of the development of feudalism in Europe. In fact, if we may fairly judge from our sources, Western Chou Chinese may have been even more indifferent about titles than the men of early feudal Europe. It seems likely that most of those able to

40. Strayer, *Feudalism*, 107–108, 111–112. Strayer, "Feudalism in Western Europe," 18. Bloch, *Feudal Society*, 395.
41. Stephenson, *Medieval Feudalism*, 60. Strayer, *Feudalism*, 60.
42. Strayer, "Feudalism in Western Europe," 18–20.

afford the considerable expense of casting a bronze had feudal titles. Among the inscriptions of my corpus there are many that mention more than one individual who probably had a title. Yet almost half of the inscriptions seem to include no titles of feudal rank.[43]

It is improbable that, to the men of early Western Chou at least, these titles had the kind of sense that we attach to "Duke," "Marquis," and so forth. These were merely various words by which a ruler of a piece of territory might be designated. This was even true of *Wang*, "King." We have seen that this term was used by many others beside the Chou King, some of them his loyal vassals, but that the Chou rulers succeeded to a large degree in establishing a monopoly for themselves in the use of this particular title.[44]

Others were employed more loosely. One of the *Documents*, describing the ceremonies at the accession of King K'ang, speaks of the attending feudatories as *chu hou* 諸侯 . Literally, if we used the conventional rendering of *hou*, this would mean "the various Marquises." But here *hou* merely means "feudal ruler," and *chu hou* is regularly and properly translated as "the feudal lords." At the end of the same document these same dignitaries are referred to as *ch'ün kung* 羣公 , literally—again if we used the conventional translation—"the assembled Dukes."[45] But it is quite evident that the terms we now translate as "Marquis" and "Duke" were here used merely as general terms for "feudal ruler." In fact, these various terms were not confined, in their application, to vassals of the Chou. We find them used of barbarian rulers also, and one inscription refers to an attack by the King on "the Earl of Ch'u" at a time when it seems quite certain that that state had never been subject to Chou.[46]

In medieval Europe there were various titles that were sometimes held by feudal lords, such for instance as *Seigneur*, which never became firmly embedded in the system of feudal titles, or else passed out of use. The same was evidently true in Western Chou China. In early Chou documents we find various titles for what seem to be territorial rulers, which appear very little later on; it is plausibly argued that these were titles that had been in use under the Shang.[47]

43. I calculate that such titles occur in 100 inscriptions out of 184. It is necessary to speak with caution, however, because of the difficulty of being sure of what is and what is not a title.

44. See p. 215.

45. *Shu*, 73–74.

46. *Chin-wen*, 3b.

47. *Shu*, 45, 46, 48, 61, 73. *Chin-wen*, 5b–7a. Ch'en, "Hsi-Chou T'ung-ch'i," (2).86–90. Fu, "Lun So-wei Wu-teng Chüeh," 110–111.

But there would be little point in going into such details of nomenclature, for they appear to have been of minor importance in the political realities of the time.

IT has generally been believed—by myself among others—that from the very beginning of the Western Chou period there was a fairly numerous and well-defined aristocratic class. Opinions have differed as to the sharpness of the cleavage that existed between aristocrats and plebeians. Henri Maspero stated the case with uncompromising emphasis:

> Chinese society, as it appeared in the Chou period, was divided into two distinct classes: below the peasant commoners, above the patrician class, the nobles, *shih* 士 . The principles of organization of each of these two classes were absolutely opposed: in the one a sort of group instinct, a life in groups, in communities in which individuals and families became lost and were of no consequence; in the other, a sort of familial individualism. . . . The difference extended even to the moral rules of life; the patricians practiced the rites, *i-li* 儀禮 , the plebeians had only customs, *su* 俗 : "The rites [*li* 禮] do not extend down to the common people."[48]

This statement contains several propositions, which must be examined carefully.

Maspero says that there was a patrician class called *shih;* in a footnote to the quoted passage he says that it was composed of persons "who belonged by birth to the aristocratic class." This is a proposition that finds much support in the traditional literature. The work called the *Book of Etiquette and Ceremonial* sets forth in great detail the intricate ceremonies that are supposed to have pertained to the class called *shih.* It has been attributed to the authorship of the Duke of Chou, but in fact there is no reason to believe that he had anything to do with it. This work was probably elaborated into its present form chiefly during the Warring States period.[49]

The character *shih* 士 occurs with some frequency in the Western Chou sources, but there is perhaps only one case in which it might

48. Maspero, *La Chine antique,* 89–90. The quotation at the end is found in *Li-chi,* 3.6a; Legge, *Li-chi,* I, 90.
49. *I-li* 儀禮. On its date, see pp. 485–486.

be used as the name of an aristocratic class—but even there it probably is not.[50] By far its most common sense is that of "official," and it forms part of various titles. Very often it is almost impossible to determine, from the context, how *shih* should be translated. In one passage in the *Poetry* Karlgren renders it as "gentleman," where both Waley and Legge translate it as "man."[51] Karlgren—perhaps under the influence of the traditional belief that *shih* was the name of an aristocratic class—has a tendency to translate it as "gentleman" even where this is clearly out of place, as in one poem where the person in question is depicted as a peddler and specifically called a "man of the people."[52] In the Western Chou sources *shih* can often be rendered as "gentleman" only if we understand the term in the contemporary American sense, in which any man is assumed to be a gentleman until proved otherwise. Very often *shih* means simply "a male (as distinguished from female) person." One poem refers to agricultural laborers as *shih*. A bronze inscription lists, among the booty captured in an expedition against the Huai barbarians, "*shih* [that is, men], women, sheep, and cattle."[53]

Careful examination of the Western Chou sources leads to the conclusion that they provide no basis for the supposition that there was, at that time, an aristocratic class known as *shih*. It is hard, indeed, to find much evidence for such a class even in the Spring and Autumn period.[54] Certainly there was a definite and flourishing aristocratic class in the later period, but whether there ever existed *a distinct aristocratic class known as "shih,"* which practiced the elaborate rituals

50. *Shih*, 236, refers to *shih min* 士 民 , seeming to name *shih* and common people as two categories. But Karlgren, Legge (*Shih*, 560), and Couvreur (*Shih*, 413) translate *shih* here as "officers." In the context this seems most probably correct, but there is hardly any way of being certain.

51. *Shih*, 74. Waley, *Shih*, 199. Legge, *Shih*, 174–175.

52. *Shih*, 40. The use of *shih* here together with *nü* 女 , "woman," makes it clear that "man" is the correct translation.

53. *Shih*, 251. *Chin-wen*, 146a. *Shih nü* in the sense of "males and females" occurs in *Shih*, 166, 204.

54. It is quite true that, as Ch'en Meng-chia points out in "Hsi-Chou Yin-jen," 101, there are four passages in the *Tso-chuan* that list *shih* as one of a number of strata into which the population is divided. But if it there denotes hereditary aristocrats, so do at least two strata above it. Legge translates *shih* in one of these passages as "scholar," and in the other three as "officer": *Tso*, 437::440 (Hsiang 9), 462::466 (Hsiang 14), 611::616 (Chao 7), 797::799 (Ai 2). Couvreur, in these passages, translates *shih* as *officier* and *simple officier* (Couvreur, *Tso-chuan*, II, 238, 309, III, 129, 607). How *shih* ought to be understood here is not wholly certain, but it is fairly clear that it does not denote *the* aristocratic class. Ch'en also argues that in Shang times *shih* denoted an aristocratic class ("Hsi-Chou Yin-jen," 90), but I do not find his case convincing.

described in the *Book of Etiquette and Ceremonial*, remains a question.[55]

But of course this matter of name is unimportant. The real question is: was there, in the Western Chou period—by whatever name, or none—an aristocratic class comparable to that of the Spring and Autumn period? In the documents from the later time, its existence is never in any doubt. The scene is dominated by aristocrats, boasting of their descent, quarreling (and sometimes fighting) over precedence and points of honor, intermarrying and cementing alliances in other ways, conforming or pretending to conform to an elaborate code of aristocratic conduct and criticizing others for failing to do so. In the Western Chou sources, on the other hand, we find very little evidence of such things.

In Spring and Autumn times the center of the stage was occupied, except for the feudal lords, by aristocratic kinship groups known as *shih* 氏 (this term should not be confused with *shih* 士). *Shih* is used as a suffix to the name of the family, much as we prefix "Mister" to surnames, and the family is also known as the *shih* of such-and-such a surname.[56] But in sharp contrast to the Spring and Autumn

55. That work opens with a long and detailed account of the rites of the "capping" ceremony, with which adolescent males belonging to the *shih* class were supposedly initiated into manhood. See *I-li*, 1–3; Steele, *I-li*, I, 1–17. I have been unable to find any mention of this ceremony, or even of the wearing of such a cap as the mark of adulthood, in the Western Chou sources. Even in the *Tso-chuan*, which gives us so many details on so many aspects of life in the Spring and Autumn period—and especially on the life of the aristocracy—this ceremony seems to be mentioned only twice, and in each case those who are "capped" are rulers of states; see *Tso*, 342::348 (Ch'eng 2); 438::441 (Hsiang 9). The *Tso-chuan* includes a number of references to *kuan* 冠 , "caps," but in many cases it is quite clear that these are headgear of various sorts, with no discernible special significance. Only in one passage is such significance evident: *Tso*, 842::843 (Ai 15). There Confucius' disciple Tzu-lu is set upon and mortally wounded. His cap falls to the ground, and he picks it up saying, "The gentleman, when he dies, does not leave off his cap." It seems clear that at some time—probably beginning before that of Confucius—there was a ceremony of "capping" young men as a mark of adulthood; see *Analects*, 11.25.7, and *Mencius*, 3(2).2.2. But when this practice began, and whether it was linked with a hereditary aristocratic class, seems to be obscure.

56. The subject of surnames in ancient China is very complex. The degree of complexity is indicated by the fact that Ssu-Ma Ch'ien, writing around 100 B.C., although he was undoubtedly the most learned historian of his time, did not understand it; see *Shih-chi*, 8.2–3, and *Mémoires historiques*, I, 3–5 (n. 3), II, 324–325. In Chou times—but beginning and ending when is uncertain—most aristocrats had two names that could be called "surnames." One of these was the *hsing* 姓 , the surname of a kinship group (the group was also called the *hsing*). This *hsing* (that of the Chou ruling house was, for instance, Chi 姬) was shared by all of

situation, the Western Chou sources seem to show no single case where *shih* is clearly the name of a kinship group.[57] Even more important is the fact that there is little reference to kinship groups under any other name.[58] If aristocratic kinship groups were an important feature of the Western Chou scene, this fact has left little trace in the sources.

There is, however, one term that is much used in the *Poetry* that does, in some cases, seem clearly to mean "aristocrat." This is *chün-tzu* 君子 , literally "ruler's son." There is reason to believe that at

---

the members of a group descended, or supposedly descended, from a common ancestor; this ancestor was often supernatural. The *hsing* was patrilineal and, in theory and usually in fact, exogamous. Collateral branches of the *hsing* were segmented into groups, known as *shih*. The *shih* had it own name, which was its *shih*; an example of a *shih* was Ssu-Ma, the surname of the great historian. Literally, *ssu-ma* 司馬 means "director of horses"; as we have seen, it was an official title of varying significance. *Shih* might derive their names from an office held by their founding ancestor, or in other ways. When a member of an aristocratic family was enfeoffed (with a fief not previously held by the family), this normally started a new *shih*, which might take its name from the name of the fief. Evidently, the subdivision of the *hsing* group into *shih* was a device that produced a kinship group that was not so large as to lose significance. Traditionally it has been said that after five generations a new *shih* was established. See *Li-chi*, 32.7b–8a; Legge, *Li-chi*, II.43. This is probably, however, only one of those many rules by which late scholars tried to bring order out of the confusion of early history. It should be noted that descendants in the direct line (normally, eldest son of eldest son of eldest son, etc.) from the founder of a *hsing* had no *shih* "surname," but only the *hsing*.

It appears that at some time before the Han dynasty, probably as a result of the dying out of the old aristocratic structure, this system of two kinds of "surnames" became obsolete and forgotten, so that by around 100 B.C. even a scholar so learned concerning antiquity as Ssu-Ma Ch'ien was unaware of it, and treated *hsing* and *shih* as interchangeable words meaning "surname."

57. In its three occurrences in the twelve chapters I am using of the *Documents*, it is always part of an official title: *Shu*, 37 (twice), 70. In four passages in the *Poetry* (*Shih*, 17, 133, 188, 235) Karlgren interprets it as being linked with a surname, but in the second and fourth cases it may be part of an official title; the other two passages refer to the same person, a woman. My notes list *shih* as occurring in nineteen bronze inscriptions, often as part of the name of an office, but at times probably linked with a surname; it is often difficult to determine precisely how it is being used.

58. The character *tsu* 族 , which Karlgren ("Grammata Serica Recensa," 311) defines as "clan, kin, group of families," does occur. But it never seems to be linked with a surname, and it is even rarer than *shih*. In the *Documents* it does not occur at all in the twelve chapters that I accept as Western Chou. In the *Poetry* it is found only three times (*Shih*, 7, 69, 128). In the bronze inscriptions of my corpus it occurs seven times (*Chin-wen*, 10b, 18b, 20b, 88b, 133a, 135a [twice]). The sense of *tsu* is not always easy to determine; in some cases it may be part of an official title (see ibid., 138b). Concerning the possibility that it sometimes denoted a military group, see p. 91, n. 36, and 315, n. 257.

the beginning of Western Chou it may have been restricted to those who were, in fact, close relatives of rulers.[59] Sometimes we get references to *chün-tzu* as distinguished from *hsiao-jen* 小 人 , "little people," who were undoubtedly the great mass of ordinary people.[60] It is probable that those called *chün-tzu* were at first in fact the sons of rulers, and that their descendants continued to be known by this honorific term.[61] Because rulers practiced polygamy, many of them had a great many sons, and the number of those who could legitimately claim descent from them multiplied rapidly. Yet no one seems to have suggested that *chün-tzu* was a name for members of a definitely circumscribed aristocratic class, and the way in which the term was used indicates that it was not.[62]

THE code of conduct that came to be formulated for the Chinese aristocrat was known as *li*. This is, perhaps, the term that most nearly occupied the place of the medieval European term *courtoisie*, from which our term "courtesy" is of course derived but which meant something different and more.[63]

The character *li* 禮 has as its left-hand element "spirit"; its right-hand component is a pictograph of a sacrificial vessel containing an offering. It appears that its earliest meaning was probably that of "a sacrifice" or "to sacrifice"; from this it developed the sense of religious

59. In all of the twelve sections of the *Documents* that I accept as Western Chou, there are only two occurrences of *chün-tzu* (*Shu*, 43, 51). Both of these are from the first years of the dynasty, and in both cases the expression clearly refers to men of high official standing. Karlgren translates it as "noble chiefs" in one case and as "grandees" in the other. It is sometimes so used in the *Poetry* (*Shih*, 140–141).

60. *Shih*, 112, 154, 176.

61. There is a close analogy in the term *Kung-sun* 公 孫 , "Duke's grandson," which in Spring and Autumn times was used not only to refer to the grandsons of Dukes but also to their somewhat remote descendants, who used it is a kind of surname (i.e., *shih*).

62. In the Spring and Autumn period and later, *chün-tzu* has been used, especially by Confucians, to mean "gentleman" (or in Legge's well-known rendering, "superior man") in a moral sense, without any other connotation. In this usage, *hsiao-jen* has the sense of "mean man." It is possible that *chün-tzu* was extended to apply to others than relatives of rulers even in Western Chou times, but the context often makes certainty impossible. In poems dealing with courtship and marriage (Waley groups together poems that he believes to belong in these categories: Waley, *shih*, 21–109) *chün-tzu* is very commonly used to refer to the beloved or the husband. While it might be argued that all of those so called were aristocrats, this is certainly a special use of the term.

63. Bloch, *Medieval Feudalism*, 305–306.

ritual. In medieval Europe the dignified and orderly conduct proper to a court became the standard of proper, or at least aristocratic, "courteous" behavior. In China the decorum observed in religious ritual became the standard for conduct in other spheres. (One might therefore deduce that ancient China was more religious, and medieval Europe more secular, but like some other conclusions that are perfectly logical, this one would not necessarily be correct.)

Li, too, became a code of aristocratic conduct, including that which Europe called "chivalrous." It continued also to denote religious ritual, and came to include the proper conduct in rituals of every sort. It prescribed the precise height at which one should hold a jade tablet in a court ceremony—neither too high nor too low.[64] And it dictated the protocol for relations between states and rulers, and the "courteous" conduct that should characterize the intercourse between all men of position. In this sense the passage that Maspero quoted from the *Records on Ceremonial* is correct: "*Li* does not extend down to the common people."[65]

The use of the term *li* was also broadened, however, to denote the course of proper conduct for all men, of whatever station. Finally it came to be used to denote nothing less than the Chinese tradition, the code by which society was—or should be—governed.[66]

Certainly both the term and the concept of *li* existed at the very beginning of Western Chou. But it is important to remember, as is not always done, that *li* meant different things at different times. What did *li* mean in the Western Chou period?

The character *li* does not seem to occur on the Shang oracle bones or in the bronze inscriptions. It is not present in the original text of the *Book of Changes*. In all of its four occurrences in the *Documents* that I date as Western Chou, it has only the sense of religious ritual.[67]

One other source remains: the *Poetry*. If *li* was common, in the sense of a code of aristocratic behavior—the Chinese equivalent of *courtoisie*—we should expect to find it here with some frequency. The character occurs ten times, in seven poems. In seven instances it refers to religious ritual.[68] One occurrence is very curious. A poem

---

64. *Tso*, 790::791 (Ting 15).

65. *Li-chi*, 3.6a; Legge, *Li-chi*, I, 90. It should be noted that there is no evidence that this passage comes from an early time; it has been suggested that it may have been written during the Han dynasty.

66. *Tso*, 715::718–719 (Chao 26).

67. *Shu*, 52 (twice), 53, 61.

68. *Shih*, 162 (twice), 163, 174 (twice), 245, 251.

variously dated to the latter years of Western Chou or even later is a lament concerning bad government, and especially the inflictions visited on the people by a particular high minister. It reads: "He tears away our walls and houses, our fields are all weed-covered; he says, 'I am not mistreating you, according to *li* it is so.' " Both Karlgren and Legge translate *li* here as "law"; Waley renders it as "ritual." However it should be interpreted, it is doubtful that it stands here for a code of aristocratic conduct.[69]

The remaining two instances occur in a single brief poem. Karlgren translates it:

> Look at the rat, it has its skin;
> A man without manners—
> A man without manners,
> Why does he not die?

> Look at the rat, it has its teeth;
> A man without demeanour—
> A man without demeanour,
> Why does he tarry to die?

> Look at the rat, it has its limbs;
> A man without [*li*] decorum—
> A man without [*li*] decorum,
> Why does he not quickly die?[70]

Here *li* is said to be as essential to a man—not to an aristocrat, but merely a man, *jen* 人 —as its limbs are to a rat. Legge here translates *li* as "rules of propriety," and Waley merely as "manners."[71] It is hardly possible to understand it as referring to a special code of conduct peculiar to aristocrats.

Certainly one cannot say categorically that *li* was never used, in

69. *Shih*, 139. Legge, *Shih*, 323. Waley, "The Eclipse Poem and Its Group," 245–246. *Mao-shih*, 12(2).1a.

70. *Shih*, 33–34.

71. Legge, *Shih*, 84–85. Waley, *Shih*, 299. In a footnote Waley adds: "But *li* includes a great deal that we should call religion; for example, sacrificing at the right time."

the Western Chou period, to denote such a code. But one can say that the term itself is quite rare in the sources, and that—in sharpest contrast to the situation in Spring and Autumn times—there is no single case in which *li* is unmistakably used as the name of an aristocratic code.

WE have seen many indications that, contrary to what has been generally believed, the aristocratic class that was such a salient feature of Spring and Autumn society was not evident in the Western Chou period—or at least in its earlier portion. There was no stable system of feudal titles. The great aristocratic families so prominent in Spring and Autumn times were not present—or at least are not visible in the sources. The aristocratic warrior, as inseparable in China from his war chariot as the medieval knight was from his war horse, became prominent only toward the end of Western Chou. The code of chivalry by which such warriors fought is not discernible in the literature of the earlier period. *Li*, in its ubiquitous later sense of a code of aristocratic conduct, cannot certainly be identified even once in the Western Chou sources.

Let us try to make a hypothetical reconstruction of the development of the Chou aristocracy. For the Shang period we have little certain evidence concerning the social situation. As we have seen, there are those who argue that the Shang had a fully developed feudal system; but while this is possible, it is uncertain. It seems highly probable, however, that there was a Shang aristocracy. Hu Hou-hsüan identifies in the oracle bones a number of names that he believes to be the surnames of aristocratic families with which the Shang Kings intermarried.[72] But whether enough Shang aristocrats were able to maintain their status after the Chou conquest, so that we may speak of the persistence of a Shang aristocratic class, is open to question. We know that a few years after the conquest, immediately after the great Shang revolt, the Chou transported a large number of the principal men among the Shang to the new Chou capital that they built in the east, where they could be kept under surveillance.

Such catastrophic events as conquests very commonly bring funda-

---

72. Hu, *Chia-ku Hsüeh, Ch'u-chi*, "Yin-tai Hun-yin Chia-tsu Tsung-fa Sheng-yü Chih-tu K'ao." Ch'en ("Hsi-Chou Yin-jen," 90) considers the term *shih* to have denoted an aristocratic class in Shang times, but I do not find his argument convincing.

mental changes to a society.[73] And where a new aristocracy must be formed from the beginning, the process is necessarily a somewhat slow one. This was the case in Europe, after the collapse of the previous political and social order eventuated in medieval feudalism. Bloch writes:

> For the writers who first gave feudalism its name . . . the idea of nobility seemed inseparably linked with it. It would scarcely be possible, however, to find an association of ideas more palpably false—at least if we set any store by the exact use of historical terms. Certainly there was nothing egalitarian about the societies of the feudal era; but not every dominant class is a nobility . . . nobility made its appearance relatively late in Western Europe. The first lineaments of the institution did not begin to emerge before the twelfth century . . .[74]

After the Chou conquered the Shang, some descendants of men of consequence in Shang continued to enjoy wealth and position. Some rulers of small states, who submitted to the Chou and became their vassals, were allowed to hold some degree of power. Yet it is quite clear that the standards came increasingly to be Chou standards, and the basis of pride came to be affiliation with the Chou. Under these circumstances, it would have been difficult for previous patterns of aristocratic behavior and affiliation to remain viable.

When the Chou took over the eastern regions as conquerors, there is little indication that the Chou people themselves were divided into clearly demarcated classes of aristocrats and plebeians.[75] We have seen

73. Concerning social changes produced in England by the Norman conquest, see Bloch, *Feudal Society*, 270–271, and *Cambridge Medieval History*, V, 505–506.

74. Bloch, *Feudal Society*, 283.

75. The only evidence that might be alleged as a definite indication of this, of which I am aware, is in the opening passage of the section of the *Documents* called "Tzu Ts'ai," in which the speaker is probably King Wu, addressing his brother. The passage (*Shu*, 46) reads: "The King said: 'Feng! Through his common people and his retainers to establish good relations with the great families, and through his retainers to establish good relations with the King—that is the task of the ruler of a state!' This is a curious statement, not easy to understand. It can be argued, of course, that these "great families" were the aristocracy, but if they were a Chou aristocracy brought into the state with its ruler, it would seem that the ruler, as a Chou appointee, would have had better relations with them than with the common people. It seems most probable that these "great families" were influential persons among the conquered population. Even so, it is hard to understand why the ruler was urged to cultivate good relations with them "through the common people." This passage is a puzzle. In any case, I do not think that it demonstrates the existence of an aristocratic class among the Chou conquerors.

that King Wu repeatedly expressed concern because of unrest among the common people, and that the Duke of Chou warned King Ch'eng that he should "fear the danger of the common people."[76] Nothing of the kind is said about aristocrats. In the Spring and Autumn period, on the other hand, it is the aristocrats that are almost exclusively the cause of concern to kings and other rulers.[77]

This is by no means to say that there was not a group of powerful and privileged men early in the Western Chou period. Of course there was. After the conquest the Chou gave fiefs to their principal relatives and to other leaders among those who had assisted them; at the same time their more humble followers were undoubtedly given offices and other rewards. The *Poetry* depicts the situation:

The road of Chou is smooth like a whetstone,
It is straight like an arrow.
That is where the gentlemen [literally, "rulers' sons"] tread
While the small people look on.
With longing I look upon it,
Flowingly I shed tears.

In the Lesser East and the Greater East[78]
The shuttles and warp-cylinders are empty . . .
Alas for our exhausted people,
They also should have rest.

The sons of the men of the east,
They only toil and are not encouraged;
The sons of the men of the west,
They have beautiful clothes.
The sons of the men of Chou,

76. *Shu*, 42, 49.

77. Concern for the welfare and the opinions of the common people does appear late in the Spring and Autumn period, precisely when the aristocracy has begun to lose its importance. Demagogues then court the favor of the people, as a tool with which to undermine the rulers, paving the way for the centralized regimes of the Warring States period.

78. "Lesser East" and "Greater East" were the names of two eastern regions held by the Chou. Fu Ssu-nien ("Ta-tung Hsiao-tung Shuo") locates the Lesser East approximately in the west portion of the modern Shantung province, and the Greater East in its central portion.

They have the skins of black bears and brown-and-white
    bears for furs.
The sons of their petty henchmen
Hold all of the offices.[79]

This is the lament of a man of the conquered east, who says that the
conquerors have not only impoverished the region but also put their
very hangers-on into all of the places of authority. This does not,
however, give the impression that plebeians are being oppressed by
aristocrats, but rather that the conquered are being exploited by their
conquerors. The rulers and those associated with them were undoubtedly a dominant group, but as Bloch well says "not every dominant
class is a nobility"—nor is it necessarily an aristocracy.

An aristocrat can exist, no doubt, in isolation. But an aristocratic
class implies not only the existence of a number of aristocrats, but
something more: a network of ties between them, a system of customs and usages, a code of aristocratic conduct to which conformity
is expected. Although unusual individuals may rise from humble birth
to membership in an aristocracy—there are often such cases—an
aristocratic class cannot be produced in one generation. There must
develop between its members a network of kinship by blood and by
marriage, and of ties of friendship and alliance. Standards of conduct
must not merely be promulgated but become second nature, and age
like good wine. These things take time; they require generations if not
centuries.

Certainly centuries did elapse, in medieval Europe, between the beginnings of feudalism and the emergence of a genuine feudal aristocracy. And all of the phenomena of the Western Chou period seem
to indicate that it was a time in which the aristocratic class that would
emerge into full flower in Spring and Autumn times was still in the
process of becoming.

Authorities on European feudalism commonly speak of two periods, an earlier and a later. In many respects the Western Chou appears to correspond to the earlier feudal age in Europe, and the Spring
and Autumn time to the later. Strayer has said that "as to chivalry,
there were two periods: in that of high feudalism, there was really no
cult of chivalry; that came only later in the 'age of pretension.' "[80]
Concerning the question of social classes, Bloch writes:

79. *Shih*, 154–155.
80. "A Comparative Discussion of Feudalism," 57.

The most striking feature of the history of the dominant families in the first feudal age is the shortness of their pedigrees—at least if we agree to reject not only the fables invented by the Middle Ages themselves, but also the ingenious though improbable conjectures which in our own day various scholars have founded on very hypothetical principles for the transmission of proper names.

Quite comparable fables and hypotheses are found in the literature, both early and recent, on ancient China. Bloch further says:

Now, it is not enough in this case to lay the blame on the poverty of our sources. . . . In the days of their greatness the Ludolfings, the Attoni, the lords of Amboise, among others, all had their historians. How did it happen that those learned men were unable or unwilling to tell us anything about the ancestors of their masters? It is a fact that the genealogies of Icelandic peasants, transmitted for centuries by a purely oral tradition, are much better known to us than those of our medieval barons. So far as the latter were concerned, it seems evident that no interest was taken in their ancestry until the moment —relatively recent, as a rule—when for the first time one of them attained a really exalted rank. . . . The chief reason for what appears to be so strange a silence was that these powerful individuals did not constitute a noble class, in the full sense of the word. To speak of no-bility is to speak of pedigrees: in the case in point, pedigrees did not matter because there was no nobility.[81]

Since we are treating feudalism as a functional institution, we must ask: how, specifically, did it function? Why were fiefs created; what functions were vassals expected to perform? Who was enfeoffed? How were fiefs created, and vassals set up? What functions did vassals, in fact, perform? These questions are easy to ask; some of them are very difficult to answer.

The Chou conquerors created fiefs for the same reasons that have impelled, and even compelled, many conquerors to some similar action. First of all, they had to reward those who had helped them. No

81. Bloch, *Feudal Society*, 284–285.

one man can win broad territories without help, and once the conquests have been consolidated, his most able generals are the conqueror's most dangerous potential rivals. William John Corbett says that after his conquest of England, "William was faced with a dilemma; for he could not safely allow his new dominions to remain without a Norman garrison, or risk offending the soldiery to whom he owed his triumph by disappointing them of their promised rewards. To feel secure he had to allot extensive estates to his chief followers, which they, in their turn, could deal out to their retainers."[82] In China a somewhat similar situation obtained when the Former Han dynasty was established at the beginning of the second century B.C. The founder was able to maintain his position only by giving fiefs, often very unwillingly, to generals who would have rebelled from him if he had not done so.[83]

Naturally, overlords do not commonly advertise the fact that they have created vassals because they could not do otherwise, and it is only by conjecture that we can suppose that this motivation must have played some role in enfeoffments after the Chou conquest. The great state of Ch'i may have originated as a reward to a general who played a major part in the Chou conquest. This state, which came to occupy much of the territory of the modern Shantung province, was one of the most important of all fiefs awarded to vassals not of the Chou surname.

There is little in the Western Chou sources that can certainly be linked with Duke T'ai, the first ruler of Ch'i.[84] In the Tso-chuan, however, we read that his services to the Chou house were so great that without them it might have been destroyed.[85] In the Historical Records Ssu-Ma Ch'ien summarizes a considerable body of legend about Duke T'ai, and concludes that in later generations he has been venerated as the source of the military power of the Chou. Fu Ssu-nien cites evidence to show that he was a great general who played an important role in the Chou conquest of the Shang.[86] One poem is interpreted to mean

82. *Cambridge Medieval History*, V, 502.
83. Dubs, *Han-shu*, I, 9–11.
84. He is said to be referred to in *Shih*, 188, where he is identified with Commander Shang-fu, but this is uncertain. The significance of the name *T'ai Kung* 太公 is uncertain. It may mean simply "Grand Duke"; see *Shih-chi*, 32.2–3, commentary.
85. *Tso*, 462::467 (Hsiang 14); see also 139::140 (Hsi 4) and 197::198 (Hsi 26).
86. *Shih-chi*, 32.1–6; *Mémoires historiques*, IV, 34–37. Fu ("Ta-tung Hsiao-tung Shuo," 103–106) argues that Duke T'ai was not at first enfeoffed with what was later the territory of Ch'i, but with a place called Lü 呂 to the south of the

that he was the principal commander under King Wu in the decisive defeat of the Shang armies.[87]

Although the evidence is less than might be wished, it seems very likely that Duke T'ai was in fact a formidable warrior, who played a considerable role in the Chou conquest. If so, he had to be rewarded. And King Wu may well have had two reasons for sending him to Ch'i, in the far northeast. This removed this potent military leader, who was not a blood kinsman, from too dangerous proximity to the ruling power. Furthermore, it placed him in an area where there were serious threats both from the unpacified and from barbarians, and the Chou needed a powerful champion to keep the peace. The *Tso-chuan* quotes a minister of Ch'i as saying, in the seventh century B.C., that Duke T'ai had been charged by the Chou with policing the eastern portion of the Empire, from the Yellow River to the sea. There may have been some basis for this claim.[88]

If these were the motivations for enfeoffing Duke T'ai with Ch'i, the policy was evidently quite successful. There is little evidence of any difficulty between the royal house and Ch'i until late in Western Chou. The ruler of Ch'i is mentioned as taking a prominent place in the ceremonies attending the death of King Ch'eng.[89] A tradition found only in the genuine *Bamboo Books* and other relatively late works says that King Í (894–879 B.C.) "caused the feudal lords to boil Duke Ai of Ch'i in a cauldron." The *Historical Records* explains this as an intervention by the King, who set up a younger brother of the executed Duke in his place.[90] A bronze inscription dated to the

---

eastern capital in what is modern Honan province. He thinks the state was moved east subsequently. But *Tso*, 139::140 (Hsi 4), distinctly says that the fief given to Duke T'ai was in the east, and implies that it was near the seacoast. Ch'en Meng-chia ("Hsi-Chou T'ung-ch'i," [1].157) includes Ch'i among the eastern states set up by King Wu.

87. *Shih*, 188. See *Mao-Shih*, 16(2).10a–11b.

88. *Tso*, 139::140 (Hsi 4). It has been pointed out that this speech by Kuan Chung was certainly politically motivated and includes some points that are more than doubtful. Certainly he was trying to make Ch'i look as important as possible. This does not negate the possibility, however, that there may have been some basis in fact for a part of his statements.

89. *Shu*, 70.

90. Wang, *Ku Chu-shu*, 8a. *Kung-Yang Chuan*, 6.11a. *Shih-chi*, 32.11a; *Mémoires historiques*, IV, 41. There is a chronological difficulty in connection with this tradition. The *Bamboo Books* says that this happened in the third year of King Í, 892 B.C. But Tchang (*Synchronismes chinois*) gives the dates of Duke Ai as 934–894 B.C. In *Kung-Yang Chuan*, 6.11a, the commentary quotes a statement to the effect that Duke Ai was killed not by King Í but by King I, who reigned from 934 to 910 B.C.

reign of King Li (878–828 B.C.) tells of a military expedition dispatched by the King to Ch'i, but whether or not this was an attack on Ch'i seems impossible to determine.[91]

In any case it appears that through most of Western Chou the state of Ch'i functioned as an effective bastion of Chou power in the northeast. A poem that is dated to the last century of the period says that the reigning King sent his chief minister "to fortify that eastern region," and that he "marched to Ch'i and quickly returned home." Arthur Waley suggests that this expedition may have been made "to help the people of Ch'i fortify their new capital at Lin-tzŭ, 859 B.C."[92] After the end of Western Chou, when the controlling power of the Chou was at an end, Ch'i was initially the most powerful of the Chinese states, and stepped into the breach to support the royal house and exercise some of the functions that the King could no longer perform. Ch'i continued to be a major power until 221 B.C., when it was swallowed up in the general conquest that created the Ch'in dynasty.

THE Chou rulers also had to share the conquered lands with their relatives. The *Tso-chuan* quotes a scion of the Chou house as saying that the early Kings declared, "We will not monopolize the enjoyment of the fruits of the achievements of King Wen and King Wu."[93] Two of the uncles of King Ch'eng revolted against him even though they had been given fiefs. If the rulers had not shared the spoils with their relatives, they might well have been unable to hold the conquered territory together.

It is entirely probable, however, that the Chou Kings wished to enfeoff their relatives. This is a widely used formula for bringing solidarity to feudal domains. It is well known that the Normans established, in Normandy, a feudal state of very unusual stability. And Corbett points out that "in no instance . . . had a *comté* ever been set up in Normandy in favor of a baron who was unrelated to the ducal house."[94] Once the founder of the Former Han dynasty felt himself to be secure, he set about the task of eliminating those vassals he had been compelled by circumstances to enfeoff. He got rid of all of them,

---

91. Kuo, "Ch'ang-an Ming-wen," 6. See p. 298, note 187.
92. *Shih*, 228–230. Waley, *Shih*, 141–143. Concerning the date of this poem, see ibid., 141, n. 2, and *Mao-shih*, 18(2).11a.
93. *Tso*, 714::717 (Chao 26).
94. *Cambridge Medieval History*, V, 485–486.

except one whose fief was so small it was of no consequence. In their place, he set up his own sons and relatives.[95]

The *Tso-chuan* seems to be our earliest source that discusses the motivation underlying the Chou policy of enfeoffment. It quotes a royal officer as saying, in 636 B.C., that the Duke of Chou enfeoffed relatives of the royal house "in order that they might constitute a fence and a protecting wall for Chou." (Whether in fact the Duke of Chou was the originator of this policy is uncertain; we have already seen that in Spring and Autumn times there was a growing tendency to attribute a preponderant share of the early Chou achievements to him.) We are repeatedly told in the *Tso-chuan* that the motivation for the enfeoffment of members of the royal family was to furnish protection to the royal house. One passage says that fiefs were given to sixteen sons of King Wen, four sons of King Wu, and six descendants of the Duke of Chou. Another says that "formerly, when King Wu vanquished Shang ... [he enfeoffed] fifteen of his brothers with states, and forty [states were held by his relatives] bearing the Chi surname."[96] The book of *Hsün-tzu*, dating from the third century B.C., repeatedly says that at the beginning of Chou seventy-one states were established, of which fifty-three were given to men having the Chi surname, that of the royal family.[97] These persistent traditions seem to make it clear that the Chou gave a major share of the fiefs to their relatives.

The *Poetry* also speaks of the enfeoffed members of the royal family as a protection to the throne. "The great states are a screen, the great [royal] family is a buttress. . . . The sons of the [royal] family form an encircling wall; may that wall not be ruined, may [the King] not have to fear being left solitary!"[98] In two bronze inscriptions we

95. Dubs, *Han-shu*, I, 9–11.

96. *Tso*, 189::192 (Hsi 24), 624::625 (Chao 9), 714::717 (Chao 26), 725::727 (Chao, 28), 750::754 (Ting 4).

97. *Hsün-tzu*, 4.1a, 4.7b, 8.7a; Dubs, *Hsüntze*, 92, 106. Gennosuke Amano, in "Chūgoku Kodai Nōgyō no Tenkai," 114, citing the emendation of Hao I-hsing (1757–1825), argues that the latter figure ought to read "thirty-three" rather than "fifty-three," on the basis that "five" and "three" in Chinese are similar and might easily be confused by scribal error. In one case this might be quite possible, but that the same error would be repeated in three widely separated passages does not seem very probable. Amano also says that in the *Ch'un-ch'iu* some one hundred seventy and more states are mentioned, of which fifty-one belonged to rulers of the Chi surname. He does not state the basis on which he determined the surnames; whether they could be certainly known in every case seems problematical.

98. *Shih*, 213–214.

find two Kings exhorting their vassal kinsmen: "be a protecting fence to the royal throne," and "act as a fence to my throne."[99]

THIS matter of protection naturally causes us to think of the military service which, it is commonly supposed, feudal vassals always—or at least normally—owe to their overlords. In medieval Europe, as is well known, elaborate feudal contracts were drawn up that prescribed minutely the military service that was due from the vassal to the lord. Strayer cites a document that lists by name twenty-one knights, holding thirteen and three-eighths fees. "Only one owes the service of two knights, 6 owe half a knight, and three a quarter of a knight, i.e., 20 days or ten days service when a knight does 40 days' service."[100] Such contracts, normally sealed by oaths, have sometimes been held to be the essence of feudalism, so that in their absence feudalism cannot be said to exist.[101] But such detailed contracts seem, like many other factors that are sometimes held to be most typical of "true" feudalism, to be in reality phenomena of the decline of that institution. Bloch says:

> "To serve" or (as it was sometimes put) "to aid" and "to protect"—it was in these very simple terms that the oldest texts summed up the mutual obligations of the armed retainer and his lord. Never was the bond felt to be stronger than in the period when its effects were stated in the vaguest and, consequently, the most comprehensive fashion. When we define something, do we not always impose limitations on it?

In medieval Europe the detailed and specific contracts developed, as Strayer points out, in the period when vassals were seeking to reduce the burden of their obligations.[102]

99. *Chin-wen*, 20b, 134b. Ch'en, "Hsi-Chou T'ung-ch'i," (2).71.
100. Strayer, *Feudalism*, 130.
101. "A Comparative Discussion of Feudalism," 42–43. Strayer (*Feudalism*, 13) says under the heading "Definition of Feudalism": "Third, a key element in the armed forces—heavy-armed cavalry—is secured through individual and private agreements. Knights render military service not because they are citizens of a state or subjects of a king, but because they or their ancestors have promised to give this service to a lord in return for certain benefits. . . . The essential point is that military service is provided through a series of private contracts between the lord and his men."
102. Bloch, *Feudal Society*, 219. Strayer, *Feudalism*, 37, 51–52, 113. Stephenson, *Medieval Feudalism*, 27–28.

Some students of feudalism in Chou China have supposed an oath of loyalty with the promise of service to be an essential part of the creation of a vassal.[103] Since our sources are so meager, we can hardly prove that it was not; but there seems to be little evidence of this in the Western Chou materials.[104] They contain, on the whole, remarkably little reference to the taking of oaths.[105] In the Spring and Autumn period, by contrast, the swearing of oaths and sealing of treaties with invocation of the spirits as guarantors became very common phenomena.[106] But this was not a symptom of greater feudal loyalty, but of less. It was like the situation in medieval Europe that Strayer describes: "when the kings realized that they were losing control of their great officials" they tried, in order to retrieve the situation, "to bind them more closely by personal oaths."[107] Even in the Spring and Autumn period, however, it is not clear that an oath by the vassal was a feature of all enfeoffments.[108]

One passage in the Poetry, traditionally attributed to the very end of Western Chou but possibly written a little later,[109] indicates that

---

103. Yamada, "Shūdai Hōken Seido," 161. Amano, "Chūgoku Kodai Nōgyō no Tenkai," 114. For a discussion of this problem, quoting differing views, see Kurihara, "Hōshaku no Sei ni tsuite."

104. See p. 369, note 192.

105. Kuo (Chin-wen Ts'ung-k'ao, 10ab) cites only a few cases in the bronze inscriptions. In the Poetry there are two cases of what appear to be lovers' oaths: (Shih, 49, 150). But only one poem (Shih, 147) seems to refer to oaths sworn for political purposes. Maspero, in "Le serment dans la procédure judiciaire de la Chine antique," cites very few instances of oaths in Western Chou source materials.

106. This is evident to anyone who reads the Tso-chuan. Some objective evidence of this may be gained from comparison of the number of occurrences, in Western Chou literature and in the Tso-chuan, of the character meng 盟 , commonly used to mean "to swear a covenant" and "a sworn covenant." In the Book of Changes this character does not occur at all, nor is it found in the twelve sections of the Book of Documents that I accept as of Western Chou date. In the Poetry it occurs only once (Shih, 147). But in the Tso-chuan it occurs no less than 475 times, according to the Ch'un-ch'iu Ching-chuan Yin-te, 1545–1553.

107. Strayer, Feudalism, 36.

108. In fact there seems to be very little evidence for anything of the kind. Maspero ("Le régime féodal," 144) cites a passage in the Tso-chuan (Tso, 184:: 186 [Hsi 23]) which he interprets to mean that new officials bound themselves to their lord with an oath. But there are variant interpretations of this passage; see Couvreur, Tso, I, 339, and Tso-chuan, 15.7b. Whether an oath was involved here at all is unclear, and in any case this does not seem clearly to refer to investiture with a fief.

109. This passage is traditionally attributed to the reign of King Yu (781–771 B.C.); see Mao-shih, 12(3).10a. Waley ("The Eclipse Poem and Its Group") includes this among poems he believes to date from "the beginning of the Eastern Chou period," that is, early Spring and Autumn time.

the making of sworn covenants for political purposes had then become common. But this same passage expresses the deepest doubt of their effectiveness. It says: "The lord frequently makes covenants; the disorder thereby grows."[110] In the Spring and Autumn period, when the swearing of covenants had become very frequent indeed, there seems to have been little confidence in them. A passage in the *Tso-chuan* comments: "If there is no good faith, covenants are useless."[111]

It would be difficult to prove what role, if any, sworn compacts normally played in Western Chou feudalism. There does not even seem to be any concrete proof to which we can point indicating that feudal lords were necessarily obligated to give military assistance to the King. And yet there is little doubt that the obligation, however tacit, did exist. We have seen that one bronze inscription tells us that a group of underlings of Commander Ch'i were punished because they "did not follow the King" on a military expedition.[112] If these humble men had this duty, it is improbable that the rulers of states were free of it. But it is entirely likely that—as Bloch tells us was the case in the earliest period of European feudalism—this was understood to be implied as a part of the simple obligation of mutual assistance on the part of lord and vassal. In the early days, when the Chou were still struggling to establish themselves, and the barbarians were a perennial threat, an attack on one was a menace to all, and help to the King was self-help on the part of the vassal.

In a feudal regime the military role of the chief vassals is of crucial importance. If the preponderant military force lies in the armies of the various feudal lords, and each lord leads his own troops to fight for the King when commanded to do so, the authority of the King depends upon the continued willingness of the feudal lords to obey his orders. This was the situation in the Spring and Autumn period, and it had a great deal to do with the fact that during much of that time the Kings were virtually impotent.

For Western Chou our evidence on this point is not entirely clear. In the *Poetry*, rather surprisingly, there seems to be only one clear case that can be ascribed to Western Chou date in which a man holding a feudal title is named as taking part in war. One poem relates

110. *Shih*, 147. "The lord" is Karlgren's translation of *chün-tzu* 君子 . That clearly seems to be its meaning in this context. Legge (*Shih*, 341) translates it as "our sovereign."
111. *Tso*, 58::59 (Huan 12).
112. *Chin-wen*, 26a.

that "the Duke of Chou marched to the east" and brought order to the realm.[113] This, of course, refers to his command of the royal troops when he was acting as a royal officer; his army was certainly not limited to soldiers drawn from his own fief.

Yet the feudal lords did have their own troops, and at least in some cases led them in fighting for the King. A bronze inscription from the early reign of King Ch'eng records a command by the King to the Duke of Mao to lead the troops of "great lords of states" to attack certain Jung in the east. The King then commands the Earl of Wu "with your army" to assist the Duke in this undertaking, and gives this same command to the Earl of Lü.[114]

In general, however, the bronze inscriptions give an impression similar to that derived from the *Poetry*, in that they provide little evidence that feudal lords, leading their own troops, commonly played a decisive role in the greater conflicts during the Western Chou period. While thirty-four of the inscriptions of my corpus refer to warfare, only seven of them (including the one just mentioned) depict men holding the titles of feudal lords as playing a role in war. In two of these the feudatories are definitely royal officials.[115] In each of the other five cases the feudal lords are fighting under the orders of the King, and we cannot always be sure whether they are leading troops drawn from their own fiefs or simply acting as military officers for the King.[116] It is rarely if ever possible to identify these feudal lords as rulers of large and important fiefs.[117]

One inscription tells us of a Marquis who commands a military guard post for the King, and whose soldiers evidently do not consist —exclusively at least—of his own troops.[118] In another we meet—

113. *Shih*, 103.
114. *Chin-wen*, 20b. Ch'en, "Hsi-Chou T'ung-ch'i," (2).70–73.
115. *Chin-wen*, 27a. Ch'en, "Hsi-Chou T'ung-ch'i," (1).168.
116. The Earl mentioned in *Chin-wen, 54a*, who "followed the King" on a military expedition, may of course have been leading troops from his own fief. And it appears rather likely that Duke Wu, named in *Ch'ing-t'ung-ch'i T'u-shih*, 24, was leading his own troops. But in *Chin-wen*, 10b, it is likely that a royal army is in question, and in 147a it may have been. In *Chin-wen*, 20b, as we have seen, the Earl of Wu and the Earl of Lü were leading their own troops, while the Duke of Mao was commanding a royal army which included them.
117. It has been argued with some plausibility that Duke Wu, who appears in *Ch'ing-t'ung-ch'i T'u-shih*, 24, was ruler of the large and important state of Wèi, but Hsü Chung-shu denies this; see Hsü, "Yü Ting," 57–59. For further discussion of this identification, see below, p. 431, n. 36.
118. *Chin-wen*, 65b. Here the King orders an official to assist the Marquis in his guard duty. This seems to make it improbable that the command consisted exclusively of troops drawn from the fief of the Marquis. Furthermore, guard posts of this type appear, wherever we have evidence, to have been manned by troops of the King.

according to the interpretation of Kuo Mo-jo, which is probably correct—with the redoubtable Marquis of E, probably before he led the barbarians in rebellion, and possibly before he had succeeded to the rule of E, which was located in the south.[119] The inscription relates that the Hsien-yün barbarians have made an incursion, and the King has ordered one of his officers to push them back to the west. This officer in turn orders the Marquis (present or future) to take charge of the officer's chariots and use them to attack the barbarians, which he does with great success.

There seems to be only one instance, described in our Western Chou materials, in which the military forces of the King proved inadequate and the troops of a feudal lord had to be called upon for assistance. This occurred at the time when the Marquis of E revolted and led the southern Huai I and the eastern I in a great uprising. The King threw all of his fourteen armies into the effort to stem the invasion, but apparently they were so occupied that they could not move on the seat of the culprit and attack the Marquis himself. This was done by the troops of Duke Wu (whose identity is disputed), who captured the Marquis and presumably ended the rebellion.[120] This event is dated to the last century of Western Chou; it may have been an omen of the collapse of the royal power.

While the military forces of the feudal states appear to have had limited importance in crises of wide scope, their role within each state was undoubtedly great. They were needed to act as guards and police, and also to defend the state against enemies, especially barbarians. We have seen that some states were specifically said to have the function of keeping barbarians under control. Vigilance against barbarians was of course especially necessary for those states located near powerful groups of them; and while barbarians were interspersed throughout the country, the danger was particularly great for border states. They were in effect marches.

In the early days of Chou, the establishment of each capital of a fief was to some degree the implanting of a garrison in hostile territory. We have no description of the process by which this was done at that time, but it must have had some resemblance to the way in

119. In *Chin-wen*, 106a, he is not called "Marquis of E," but only by his personal name; but this name appears as that of the Marquis in *Chin-wen*, 107b, and in *Ch'ing-t'ung-ch'i T'u-shih*, 24, and there are other coincidences also that seem to affirm the correctness of Kuo's identification. We have already observed that men holding feudal titles are not always called by them. It may be, however, that this inscription dates from a time when the future Marquis had not yet succeeded, when he was perhaps serving a sort of apprenticeship in the royal service.

120. *Ch'ing-t'ung-ch'i T'u-shih*, 24.

which the state of Shen was created, around the end of the ninth
century B.C., near the southern border of the modern Honan province.
The *Poetry* tells us that it was established to be a "protecting wall"
to all the Chinese states. In sending off the Earl of Shen to his new fief,
the King charged him to "protect the southern territories." The King
sent the Earl of Shao with him, to organize the work and levy taxes so
as to provide the necessary grain. The Earl of Shen took a large army
to his new state. Whether the Earl of Shao also took a force of troops,
we are not told, but it seems probable; the period of the construction
of a fortified capital was a time of special danger, for which extra protection was necessary. Local labor was used to build the wall. Finally,
with the construction of the ancestral temple of its ruling house—the
religious and ideological center of the state—the new fief was
complete.[121]

THE Chou Kings needed vassals to perform for them another very
essential function. They derived revenue from their territories and
provided a part of it to the royal house. Regrettably, we know very
little about the way this was done; what is known has been set down
earlier.[122]

It is commonly held that the Chou Kings also had the right to exact
labor service from their vassals. As instances of this there are cited
the building of the eastern capital near the present site of Loyang,
and the construction of the walls of the capital of the northern state
of Hán by the army of the state of Yen. The evidence is not wholly
clear in either of these cases.[123] It would be difficult to prove either

121. *Shih*, 226–228.
122. See above, pp. 151–155.
123. Ch'i Ssu-ho, in "Hsi-Chou Cheng-chih Ssu-hsiang," 21–22, cites *Tso*,
739::740 (Chao 32), concerning the walling of the eastern capital. The *Tso-chuan*
here reads: "Formerly King Ch'eng assembled the feudal lords to wall Ch'eng-
Chou, that it might be the eastern capital." But this speech is made by the reigning Chou ruler, King Ching (519–476 B.C.), who has experienced many vicissitudes
and is seeking to persuade the state of Chin to lead other states in building walls
for his capital; thus he has a reason for alleging that the original walling of the
eastern capital was done by labor provided by various vassal states. This early
event is discussed in many passages in the *Documents*; see *Shu*, 39, 48–59. From
these passages it does appear that a number of feudal lords were present when the
new city was built, but it also appears that at least a large share of the actual labor
was performed by the Yin people, many of whom had been transported to this
spot after their great rebellion was crushed. It is not clear whether or not labor
was also provided by workers from other states.

The building of walls for the state of Hán by the army of Yen is related, as Ch'i
points out, in the *Poetry* (*Shih*, 232). The text does not specifically state, however,
that this was done by royal command, though it may well have been.

that the King had an unlimited right to demand labor service from the feudal lords, or that such a right was specified or limited by any definite contract. It seems probable that, like other matters of the sort, this was rather a question of mutual assistance in case of need. We have seen that the King sent a royal official to supervise the fortification of the capital of Shen, and another to build walls in the east, probably for the state of Ch'i.

IMPORTANT though all their other functions were, the greatest single contribution that the feudal lords made to the Chou state lay in the fact that they provided the stabilizing presence of governmental authority in every part of the Empire. The King's armies could repel invaders, and his officials could deal with crises, but it was essential that in every area there was the continuing presence of his resident representative, able to settle disputes and deal with local problems promptly, without the need to communicate with the capital. The military role of the local armies of the feudal lords, awing those who must be overawed, was certainly important. But a populace kept in order only by fear does not, over the long term, constitute a truly orderly and prosperous state. For this, there must be provided government which, in return for what it takes from the people in freedom and wealth, gives them some reasonable degree of security and stability.

We have seen that there are many indications that, although the Chou came as invaders and were at first regarded as barbarous intruders, the people as a whole soon became reconciled to their rule. The tradition that Western Chou was a period of relative tranquillity and even goodwill is so general and so persistent, and agrees with so much of the evidence, that it cannot be wholly false. This implies, among other things, that the individual feudal states must on the whole have been reasonably well governed.

This function of the government of local areas is seldom listed among the reasons for which vassals were enfeoffed. It was probably just taken for granted. It can be inferred from such an exhortation as that of King Wu to one of his vassals, to conduct himself so as "to tranquilize and govern the people."[124] But concerning the details of the governments of the states of the feudal lords we have very little information.

The *Tso-chuan* quotes a statement, attributed to an officer of Wèi in 506 B.C., describing the establishment of the state of Lu. It says

124. *Shu*, 43.

that the first ruler was given six groups of the Yin people, lands, priests, diviners, secretaries, records, and officials.[125] In a passage in the *Documents*, King Wu appears to refer to various officers of the government of his younger brother and vassal, K'ang Shu. It is difficult to interpret and may be in part corrupt.[126] Two of the titles, Grand Secretary and Interior Secretary, also occur as those of royal officials.[127] Another—also that of a royal officer—is generally interpreted as meaning "Minister of War," but whether that is in fact the function of this officer, or whether he is charged with dealing with criminals, is uncertain.[128] Another of these officials is clearly concerned with agriculture; his office is said to correspond to that of the royal Director of the Multitude. The meaning of the title of another of these officers seems quite uncertain, but he is said—on what seems dubious ground—to perform the function of the royal Director of Works.[129] Another passage in the *Documents* lists, as officers of a feudal state, the Director of the Multitude, Director of Horses, and Director of Works.[130]

The bronze inscriptions also mention various officials in the service of the feudal lords; their titles are usually essentially the same as those of royal officials.[131] Such indications as we have seem to justify

125. *Tso*, 750::754 (Ting 4). Legge translates the latter portion of this passage as "priests, superintendents of the ancestral temple, diviners, historiographers, all the appendages of State, the tablets of historical records, the various officers and the ordinary instruments of their offices."

126. For the emendation of Karlgren, following Chang Ping-lin, see Karlgren, "Glosses on the Book of Documents," (1).306.

127. On "Grand Secretary," see above, pp. 109–111. The "Interior Secretary," *Nei-shih* 內 史, as a royal official, is mentioned in a number of bronze inscriptions; see *Chin-wen*, 39a, 57a, etc.

128. On the title *Ch'i-fu* 圻 父 see p. 303, n. 204.

129. *Shu*, 46. For the grounds on which these various officers are identified, see Karlgren, "Glosses on the Book of Documents," (1).305–306, and Legge, *Shu*, 411, notes. *Nung-fu* 農 父 may reasonably be supposed to have something to do with agriculture, but the identification of *Hung-fu* 宏 父 as Director of Works seems quite conjectural. Neither of these titles seems to appear anywhere else in the Western Chou sources.

130. *Shu*, 46.

131. The extremely difficult inscription found in *Chin-wen*, 129ab, contains a number of titles that are common as those of royal officers, but which here appear to be those of the functionaries of feudal lords; see Ch'en, "Hsi-Chou T'ung-ch'i," (6).94. *Chin-wen*, 45a, mentions a Secretary who is apparently the subordinate of a Duke. The inscription in *Chin-wen*, 230b, is made by a Director of the Multitude of the state of Chin. In *Chin-wen*, 77a, we find the King ordering an officer to carry on the office of his father and his grandfather, acting as *Pang-chün Ssu-ma* 邦 君 司 馬, literally "State Ruler's Director of Horses," of a state that is not certainly identified; see Ch'en, "Hsi-Chou T'ung-ch'i," (6).93–94. In *Chin-wen*, 57a,

the natural supposition that the feudal lords sought in a general way to duplicate the royal government, on a smaller scale, in their fiefs.

ANOTHER essential function that was performed by the fief—in Europe as well as in China—was that of providing emolument for officials.[132] Although we have numerous cases in which men holding feudal titles are named as royal officers, it might be difficult to prove, from the Western Chou sources alone, that this was a motive for enfeoffment. We have seen that in the bronze inscriptions there are indications that there may have been some use of salaries for officials, even as early as Western Chou.[133] But these are almost impossible to interpret with certainty, and in any case it seems very unlikely that salary was widely employed, or constituted the basic recompense for officers of the King.

More direct evidence is provided by the *Tso-chuan*. That work repeatedly indicates that in the Spring and Autumn period there were fiefs, within states, that were given as emolument to men holding particular offices, and taken away from them when they no longer held the office.[134] And it includes, in connection with a dispute over lands in 580 B.C., some statements highly pertinent to our inquiry. A certain Ch'i Chih of the state of Chin was disputing, with the Chou King, possession of the district called Wen, alleging that it had long ago been given to his family and was therefore his by hereditary right. The King appointed two of his officials to state the case for the royal house. They said:

> Formerly, when Chou conquered Shang, it caused the feudal lords to tranquilize the various fiefs. Su Fen Sheng was given Wen to be Director of Crime. . . .[135] If

we even find the King appointing a *Chia Ssu-ma* 家司馬, literally, "Family Director of Horses." In Spring and Autumn times *chia* in such a context referred to the estate of a subordinate of a feudal lord, such as a *ch'ing* 卿 or *tai-fu* 大夫, but whether that is what is involved here seems uncertain.

132. Concerning the European situation, see: Bloch, *Feudal Society*, 168. Stephenson, *Medieval Feudalism*, 11. Strayer, *Feudalism*, 36–37. In Europe there was some tendency to regard "true" fiefs as including only those given for military service, but Bloch points out that this is a late distinction.

133. See above, p. 150.

134. *Tso*, 401::404 (Ch'eng 17), 677::681 (Chao 20).

135. The text says that Su Fen Sheng 以溫為司寇, literally, "used Wen to be *Ssu-k'ou*," or "by means of Wen was *Ssu-k'ou*." Legge (*Tso*, 376) translates this as "Soo Fun-sang received Wan, and was Minister of Crime," and Couvreur (*Tso-chuan*, II, 90) says "Sou Fen cheng eut Ouen et fut ministre de la justice." But

you examine its history, it is clear that Wen was the fief of a royal officer.[136]

It must have been difficult for the rulers of important fiefs distant from the capital to serve as royal officers, and in fact we do not often find such feudal lords mentioned as being in the royal service. Nevertheless we have an inscription, apparently of early Western Chou date,[137] that begins: "[When] the Marquis of Yen first saw service in Tsung-Chou . . ." Here we have a feudal lord who has journeyed all the way from the northeastern corner of the empire, in the region of modern Peking and Tientsin, to serve at the capital.[138]

We cannot tell, of course, how extensive or prolonged the "service" that this Marquis of Yen performed at the capital may have been; it could have been no more than a court visit, as a symbol of loyalty. But if vassals whose responsibilities included the rule of large and distant fiefs were also charged with major offices in the royal government, the burden must have been considerable.

THE most famous of all royal officers, during the Chou dynasty, was the Duke of Chou. Yet we do not certainly know the name of the office he held, if in fact he had an official post. He was a younger brother of King Wu. The title "Duke of Chou" is said to derive from the fact that he was enfeoffed with the ancient Chou territory in the Wei valley, in the modern west central Shensi. This is uncertain, but in any case it is probable that his fief was not very distant from the Chou capital.[139]

---

both of these translations omit the close relationship between the fief and the office. The point of the argument is precisely that Wen was given to him as recompense for performing the office.

136. *Tso*, 375::376 (Ch'eng 11). The character that I have translated as "fief" in the final sentence is *i* 邑 . Whether this is ever used to mean "fief" has been debated; Henri Maspero insists that it designates rather a *domaine*, and that it is not a fief. See Maspero, "La société chinoise," 366. In my opinion this distinction is not valid. In this very passage we have *i* used as the equivalent of the term *feng* 封 , which certainly does not mean "fief."

137. Ch'en, "Hsi-Chou T'ung-ch'i," (2).102–103.

138. On the location of the state of Yen, see Ch'en, "Hsi-Chou T'ung-ch'i," (2).103, 122–133. Ch'en (ibid., 139–141) argues that Tsung-Chou was the ancient seat of the Chou in the Wei valley, rather than the capital; here, he says, ancestral temples were located and vassals came to make their ceremonial visits to the court.

139. The earliest evidence we have for the enfeoffment of the Duke of Chou with territory in the Wei valley seems to consist in the statements of commentators of Chin and T'ang times; see *Tso-chuan*, 4.3b, and *Shih-chi*, 33.2. They may have merely deduced that he was enfeoffed with the ancestral Chou territories,

The Duke's family was entrusted with the very important state of Lu, with territory lying in the western portion of the modern Shantung province. The fief of Lu was given to his eldest son, who became the first Duke of Lu, while the Duke of Chou remained at the court to assist in the royal government.[140] We are told, on rather late authority, that the Duke's second son inherited the title "Duke of Chou," and remained at the court to assist the royal house.[141] This title presumably continued to be transmitted to his descendants. At the beginning of the Spring and Autumn period, in 717 B.C., we find a Duke of Chou acting as close adviser to the reigning Chou King. In the *Tso-chuan* a holder of this title is mentioned as contending (unsuccessfully) for a principal voice in the royal government as late as 580 B.C.[142]

A very similiar arrangement is said to have been made in connection with the outstanding colleague of the Duke of Chou, the Duke of Shao. He too is said to have been kept at the Chou court, while his eldest son went to the remote northeast to become ruler of the state of Yen. But this has been strongly contested. The issues are so important for our whole understanding of the Chou achievement that we must investigate this matter in some detail.

The Duke of Shao was clearly an extremely important figure in the early days of Western Chou. He held the title of Grand Protector. In one of the *Documents*, an address directed to him by the Duke of Chou, the latter—who was by no means a humble man—speaks to

---

from his title. But "Duke of Chou" could have been merely an honorific title, not derived from his fief. Fu Ssu-nien ("Ta-tung Hsiao-tung Shuo," 102–103) makes a good argument for the association of the Duke of Chou with a territory in what is modern south central Honan, but he considers this the original site of the state of Lu. This whole question is a very tangled one. It seems not impossible that this site could have been that of a fief of the Duke of Chou. It is entirely possible, and perhaps even probable, that he held lands in more than one location.

140. This is a difficult and confused business. The *Historical Records* says that the Duke of Chou was enfeoffed with Lu; see: *Shih-chi*, 33.3; *Mémoires historiques*, IV, 89. Fu Ssu-nien ("Ta-tung Hsiao-tung Shuo," 102–103) says that the fief called Lu was first located in what is modern south central Honan, and later moved eastward to the Shantung area. But both the *Poetry* (*Shih*, 259–260) and the *Tso-chuan* (*Tso*, 750::754 [Ting 4]) say that Lu was originally established in the east, and that the son of the Duke of Chou was its first ruler. These, as the earliest sources we have, seem to deserve the most serious consideration.

141. The earliest authority for this that we have seems to be a commentary of the Latter Han period; see Ch'en, "Hsi-Chou T'ung-ch'i," (2).94.

142. *Tso*, 20::21 (Yin 6), 375::376 (Ch'eng 11). In 694 B.C. the current Duke of Chou was killed in connection with an intrigue in which he is alleged to have had the intention of killing the reigning King and putting another contender on the throne; see *Tso*, 70::71 (Huan 18).

the Duke of Shao as an equal, whose cooperation is essential.[143] He was probably, though on this point we cannot be certain, a member of the royal family.[144]

We have seen that the contributions of the Duke of Chou, which were certainly very great, were embellished and exaggerated in later times. The Duke of Shao, on the other hand, has probably been given less credit in the tradition than he deserves. The information about him that we find in the early literature is confirmed and supplemented by bronze inscriptions. A tradition recorded in the Han dynasty says that during the time of King Ch'eng the eastern portion of the empire was supervised by the Duke of Chou, while the Duke of Shao had charge of the western part.[145] On the basis of what we know from the literature and the bronze inscriptions, this is not implausible.[146] The inscriptions appear to give some indication that the Duke of Shao, like the Duke of Chou, led military expeditions adding to the conquered territory, and the *Poetry* says: "How great was the richness of the former time! . . . When the former kings received the Mandate there were those like the Duke of Shao, who in one day enlarged the realm by a hundred *li*."[147]

The *Historical Records* says: "When King Wu of Chou had annihilated Chòu [the last Shang King], he enfeoffed the Duke of Shao at Northern Yen."[148] The reason for which the state is called "Northern Yen" is debated.[149] In any case this state is supposed to have been

---

143. *Shu*, 59–62.

144. There seems to be no direct early evidence on this point, but it seems rather likely in view of his position that he was a member of the royal family. Karlgren emends the text of *Shu*, 62 (section 19), so that the Duke of Chou calls the Duke of Shao *hsiung* 兄 , "elder brother." He justifies this on the basis of the Wei stone classics; see Karlgren, "Glosses on the Book of Documents," (2).130. But even if this is correct, it does not necessarily give us certainty, since while *hsiung* means "elder brother" it may also apply to cousins. Various sources— but most of them not earlier than Han—tell us that the Duke of Shao was a son of King Wen, or a member of a branch of the Chou house, or merely that he had the Chi surname. For quotation of these sources, see Ch'en, "Hsi-Chou T'ung-ch'i," (2).122. Considering his eminence, the ancestry of the Duke of Shao is remarkably difficult to determine.

145. *Shih-chi*, 34.2; *Mémoires historiques*, IV, 133–134. A part of this statement occurs in *Kung-Yang Chuan*, 3.4a; the history of this work, before Han times, is not clear. The precise dividing point between the eastern and western regions is debated; see *Shih-chi*, 34.2–3, commentary.

146. See Ch'en, "Hsi-Chou T'ung-ch'i," (2).94–98.

147. Ibid., (1).170, (2).94–98. *Shih*, 238–239.

148. *Shih-chi*, 34.2; *Mémoires historiques*, IV, 133.

149. It may be that Ssu-Ma Ch'ien called the area by this name to indicate that it lay to the north of, or in the northern part of, the area that later came to be the

situated, like the state of Yen of Spring and Autumn and Warring States times, in the far northeast. Ch'en Meng-chia concludes that its capital was probably located in a spot roughly sixty miles north of the city of Tientsin, and approximately the same distance east of Peking.[150]

This is more than four hundred miles from even the eastern capital of the Chou, and it would obviously have been difficult for the Duke of Shao to spend much time there and still function as a principal officer of the royal government. Two commentators—of whom the earliest lived in the second century A.D.—tell us that in this situation the same measure that was used in the case of the Duke of Chou was employed. The eldest son of the Duke of Shao was sent to act as ruler of Yen, while the Duke himself remained at the court to assist the royal house. And his second son inherited the title Duke of Shao.[151] His fief is said to have been located, like that of the Duke of Chou, near the ancestral home of the Chou in the Wei valley.[152]

Ch'i Ssu-ho, in a long article, rejected this whole story. He pointed out that the history of the state of Yen is very obscure, so that after the Duke of Shao the *Historical Records* does not even give the names of its rulers until the middle of the ninth century B.C., merely saying that there were nine generations. As for the Duke of Shao being enfeoffed with Yen, no ancient source can be cited to this effect. The remote northeastern territory of Yen was "beyond the reach of the power of the Western Chou." The *Stratagems of the Warring States*, Ch'i noted, quotes a ruler of Yen as saying, in the middle of the fourth century B.C., "I am a barbarian living in a rustic land." Thus, Ch'i concluded, "even as late as Warring States times the men of Yen still spoke of themselves as barbarians in a rustic land; at the beginning of Western Chou, how could the Duke of Shao have been enfeoffed there?"[153]

Ch'i treated the story of Yen together with that of the state of Wu, located in the southeast along the lower course of the Yangtze River.

---

state of Yen; see Ch'en, "Hsi-Chou T'ung-ch'i," (2).122–133. It is also argued that it is so called to distinguish it from another state called Yen, located in the area of the modern Honan province. A T'ang dynasty commentary on the *Historical Records* locates this other Yen in the northern projection of Honan (*Shih-chi*, 5.19; see also *Mémoires historiques*, II, 24, note 2).

150. Ch'en, "Hsi-Chou T'ung-ch'i," (2).119.

151. *Shih-chi*, 34.2. Ch'en, "Hsi-Chou T'ung-ch'i," (2).94.

152. *Shih-chi*, 34.2, commentary.

153. Ch'i, "Yen Wu Fei Chou Feng-kuo Shuo," 175–188. The quotation is from *Chan-kuo Ts'e*, 29.4b. Ch'i dates this passage to the reign of Duke Wen of Yen (361–333 B.C.).

The first ruler of Wu, it will be recalled, was supposed to have been a certain T'ai-po who was the son of the early Chou ancestor, the Ancient Duke Tan-fu. According to the tradition T'ai-po, an uncle of King Wen, renounced his title to become ruler of the Chou and went to live among barbarians. One group of them revered him so highly that he became their ruler, thus founding the state of Wu. Just as in the case of Yen, the history of Wu is little known until a late date; the *Historical Records* says little that is specific about it until 584 B.C., when the *Tso-chuan* indicates that it first came into contact with the Chinese states.[154] In the case of Wu as of Yen, its barbarian culture was explained as the result of the fact that its rulers, although descendants of the Chou house, had long lived surrounded by barbarians and had therefore been corrupted. Ch'i concluded that in fact both Wu and Yen were barbarian states, and that their rulers falsely pretended to belong to the ruling family of Chou.[155]

Ch'i's arguments are entirely logical. On the basis of the evidence that was available when he published them, in 1940, they were convincing. It is certainly true that, as he said, it seems very unlikely that the Chou could have planted a fief in the remote northeast, in territory virtually surrounded by fierce barbarians, at the beginning of Western Chou.[156]

Unlikely or not, however, it seems to have been done. In recent years a very considerable number of bronzes, apparently of early Western Chou date, have been unearthed in the very northeastern region in which the state of Yen has been supposed to be located. A number of them bear its name, and some of them were evidently made by its ruler. Ch'en Meng-chia has made an extensive study of these inscriptions, and concludes that at the beginning of Western Chou the fief of Yen was established in this area precisely because of the necessity of setting up a bulwark against the barbarian danger.[157] A number of inscriptions found in eastern locations also refer to the Duke of Shao, which would seem to increase the possibility that he did have some connection with a fief in that area. Ch'en has published

---

154. *Shih-chi*, 31.1–7; *Mémoires historiques*, IV, 1–5. *Tso*, 362::364 (Ch'eng 7).
155. Ch'i,"Yen Wu Fei Chou Feng-kuo Shuo."
156. Fu Ssu-nien, in "Ta-tung Hsiao-tung Shuo," 101–102, argues that the state of Yen could not have been established in the northeast as early as the time of King Wu. He believes that the Duke of Shao was enfeoffed with a territory located in what is the east central portion of the modern Honan province, and that the state of Yen in the northeast was established somewhat later.
157. Ch'en, "Hsi-Chou T'ung-ch'i," (2).94–104, 122–133. See also Cheng, *Chou China*, 141–142.

an inscription, which is unfortunately not completely clear, that appears to associate the Duke of Shao with the state of Yen.[158]

The situation with regard to Yen is not wholly the same as that with regard to Wu. In these times of rapid change in our information, caution is certainly necessary. In the light of our present evidence, however, the tradition concerning the founding of the state of Wu seems dubious,[159] while it is not impossible that the state of Yen was indeed entrusted to the keeping of a son of the Duke of Shao.

The *Records on Ceremonial* quotes Confucius as explaining the movements of the dancers in certain ritual dances representing the events of the beginning of Chou.

> They grasp their shields and stand firm as mountains, in the manner of King Wu. They move their arms and stamp their feet, representing the determination of Duke T'ai. At the conclusion they all kneel, symbolizing the orderly government brought about by [the Duke of] Chou and [the Duke of] Shao.[160]

These three men figure, in the tradition, as primary helpers of King Wu in the founding of the dynasty.

It is not impossible that, as tradition holds, their families were depended upon to guard the northeastern corner of the empire. We

158. Ch'en, "Hsi-Chou T'ung-ch'i," (2).96–99.

159. The enfeoffment with Yen could have taken place, not under King Wu, but later under King Ch'eng, when the eastern areas had been pacified by the Duke of Chou and others. Such a planting of a fief, under the protection of the Chou armies, is by no means incredible. On the other hand, it does seem a little dubious that, long before the end of Shang, T'ai-po should have crossed the Shang realm and been received, in the far southeast, with such acclaim that he was set up as ruler. As was pointed out earlier, it is not certain that in his time the Chou were any more advanced in culture than the people of Wu. Furthermore, there does not seem to be, as yet, the specific archeological evidence for this story that has been discovered to support the existence of Yen as an early Chou fief. Kwang-chih Chang, in *Archaeology of Ancient China*, 389, says concerning the story of the establishment of Wu by T'ai-po that "to what extent the details of this story are valid is debatable." Cheng Te-k'un in *Chou China*, xxvii, includes Yen, at the beginning of the Spring and Autumn period, in "the confederation of the Chou states. . . . This connection appeared to rest basically on genealogical ties, implying identity of surname, and on the practice of intermarriage of different surnames among the states." He includes Wu in a group of "states which were not necessarily of Chou origin and tradition, but which . . . were finally regarded as a part of the central group." In this same work, however (ibid., 147–149), Cheng says that the discovery of certain inscribed bronzes "testifies to the ancient records that the ruling house of the southern state [Wu] was a member of the royal Chou." I find his argument on this latter point somewhat dubious.

160. *Li-chi*, 39.9b; Legge, *Li-chi*, II, 122.

know that a son of the Duke of Chou was enfeoffed with Lu, and Duke T'ai was the first ruler of Ch'i.[161] If the eldest son of the Duke of Shao was established at Yen, he was in the most exposed position, the outmost northeastern bastion of Chou rule. Although, as we have seen, a very early Western Chou inscription relates that a Marquis of Yen attended at the Chou court, communications must have been difficult. The earliest mention of the state in the *Tso-chuan* tells of its suffering from the attacks of certain "Mountain Jung" barbarians, and it is clear that Yen must have been subject to more or less constant pressure from every side. It was located, furthermore, in terrain more like that of some of the barbarian tribes than of China, and it clearly would have had to adopt some of their methods in order to survive (as Chinese states on the northern border were later forced to imitate their barbarian neighbors in developing cavalry, in the fourth century B.C.).[162]

In these circumstances it is not surprising if the keeping of historical records, in the state of Yen, was less than meticulous, or if its people came to seem rustic and barbarian in comparison with those of the more central states. It might be argued that here Chou policy had overreached itself, attempting to extend Chinese culture into an area in which it could hardly take root. And yet the state of Yen did maintain itself, having some relations with the other Chinese states throughout the Spring and Autumn and Warring States periods, until 222 B.C. when it vanished like the rest. That it played an important role in neutralizing or at least softening barbarian attacks from its quarter cannot be doubted. And Chinese culture did ultimately triumph in this area; it eventually spread, in fact, to the north of Yen, and deeply influenced Korea to the east. The maintenance of this bastion was undoubtedly a struggle for the hardy Chinese who manned it, but for China as a whole it was clearly a gain.

Whether the Duke of Shao had, in fact, any connection with Yen may perhaps be debated. But in any case it seems very clear that he, like the Duke of Chou, handed his own title down to descendants. We have already seen something—and will see more—of the career of an Earl of Shao, his descendant, who played a great role as one of the principal officers of the King late in the Western Chou period.[163]

---

161. *Tso*, 139::140 (Hsi 4).

162. *Tso*, 117::118 (Chuang 30). Ch'en, "Hsi-Chou T'ung-ch'i," (2).123. Creel, "The Horse in Chinese History."

163. That he is called "Earl" in the *Poetry* (*Shih*, 180, 227) does not represent a demotion from the title of "Duke" held by his ancestor. We have seen that the titles are sometimes used interchangeably. And while the original Duke of Shao is so called in *Shih*, 234, a poem also supposed to refer to him (*Mao-shih*, 1[4].8a,

Men holding this title continued to be prominent in the royal government as late as the end of the sixth century B.C.[164]

THE dual enfeoffment of the family of the Duke of Chou—and possibly of that of the Duke of Shao—shows that it was realized that important royal officers could not easily control, or live on the income from, fiefs that were distant from the capital. It seems fairly evident that men who had to govern large and important fiefs far removed from the capital were recognized to have their hands full with that duty. If such vassals were appointed to high royal office, experience no doubt demonstrated that this was impractical. As a result, the Kings probably appointed as their high officials men who held fiefs within reasonable reach of the capital, or gave such fiefs to those they appointed. We know almost nothing about the actual situation, but it is easy to suppose that the Empire must thus have consisted, in a very rough and unsystematic sort of way, of two "zones." Near the capital —or rather capitals, since there were two—there were no doubt many fiefs held by royal officials. Farther away there were fiefs held by feudal lords who could not readily, for reasons of convenience, be taken into service by the royal government.

This situation gave the opportunity for, if it did not give rise to, a curious misconception that has become almost universal among both Chinese and Western scholars. It is supposed that Western Chou China was divided into two distinct areas. One was the "royal domain," within which the King gave out fiefs to his officers. Beyond this domain there was, according to this theory, the area of the other fiefs, in which the King could not bestow lands upon his officers, and the royal authority was minimal.

A passage in the *Tso-chuan*, which is not very clear, may refer to such a strictly demarcated royal domain; if it does, it appears to be the only reference, from a time as early as the Spring and Autumn period, to a royal domain as having existed in Western Chou times.[165] In the

---

commentary) calls him "Earl of Shao." *Shih*, 234, seems clearly to indicate that the Earl of Shao it names was a descendant of the Duke of Shao who aided in the founding of the dynasty. Ting Shan has written a biography of the later man; see Ting, "Shao Mu Kung Chuan."

164. Ting, "Shao Mu Kung Chuan," 100.

165. *Tso*, 512::516 (Hsiang 25). The text says: "Anciently the Son of Heaven's territory was one *ch'i* 圻 , that of the various states [of the feudal lords] was one *t'ung* 同 , and from this on down." Legge, basing himself upon commentary, translates: "the domain of the Son of Heaven was fixed at 1000 *le [li]* square, and that of the States at 100 *le*, and less according to a scale." But this is scarcely warranted by the text.

Warring States period and later the theory of the royal domain was greatly elaborated. It became standard doctrine that during Western Chou times the royal domain had consisted of a territory of exactly one thousand *li* square, while feudal states were—properly at least— also of a standard size, often said to be 100 *li* square. Highly fanciful maps were produced,' showing the empire as a schematized series of concentric squares, with the royal domain in the center, various feudal states farther out, and various kinds of barbarians on the periphery.[166]

Modern scholars reject these absurdities of schematization, but it is still widely believed that in Western Chou there was a definitely de-marcated "royal domain."[167] Maspero wrote that "the Royal Domain comprised the ancient familial domains of the Wei valley, with the ancient seignorial capital Hao 鎬 , where the kings continued to re-side during the initial centuries (near to the present Sian-fu), and the territory of the valley of the Le and of the middle Yellow River, with the new capital Le-i 洛邑 . . . (near the present Honan-fu [i.e., Lo-yang])."[168]Ch'i Ssu-ho writes that "the territory that the King con-trolled directly was only the royal domain, that is Tsung-Chou and Ch'eng-Chou,"[169] which he describes as a belt of territory extending from west of modern Sian to Loyang on the east, and presumably in-cluding their environs.[170]

This problem of the supposed "royal domain" bears very directly upon the history of government. A recent work on China's military history says: "The Hsia, Shang, and Chou dynasties all belonged to the most flourishing period of feudal society. In the feudal period, while the royal house was sovereign over the whole realm, the terri-tory that it controlled directly amounted only to a thousand *li;* the re-mainder was all under the control of feudal lords. The prosperity or decline of the royal house depended upon whether the feudal lords re-volted from or adhered to it . . . For this reason the gaining or losing of the empire by the three dynasties was entirely determined on the

166. Many of the most important references are listed in Kuo, *Chin-wen Ts'ung-k'ao*, 36a–39a. See also: Legge, *Shu*, 142–149. Karlgren, "Glosses on the Book of Documents," (1).159–165.

167. It must be understood that when it is argued that there was no royal do-main in Western Chou, this does not mean that the Kings did not have lands that were their own property, from which they received revenue. No doubt they did. But this is not the sense in which the conventional term "royal domain" is used.

168. Maspero, *La Chine antique*, 68.

169. By Tsung-Chou 宗周 and Ch'eng-Chou 成周 , Ch'i here presumably re-fers to the western and the eastern capital of Western Chou, and their environs. The meaning of these terms is debated; see Ch'en, "Hsi-Chou T'ung-ch'i," (2).133–142.

170. Ch'i, "Hsi-Chou Cheng-chih Ssu-hsiang," 20.

basis of their success or failure in securing the adherence of the feudal lords."[171] The degree to which the King did or did not exercise control over the various feudal lords will be examined in some detail in the next chapter. Here we are concerned with the question of the royal domain.

Kuo Mo-jo was the first, to my knowledge, to point out that there is no support in the Western Chou sources for the opinion that the institution of a "royal domain" existed at that time. In fact, he says, it was mistakenly attributed to that period by later men.[172] There is much evidence for this view. The term ch'i 畿 , which is the one most commonly employed to mean "royal domain," does not seem to occur in the bronze inscriptions.[173] As denoting territory it occurs only once in the Western Chou sources, in the *Poetry*. But there it refers not to the Chou but to the Shang state, and even so it is by no means clear that its sense is that of a royal domain.[174] And nothing else in the sources seems to suggest that there was such a "royal domain" in Western Chou times.

How, then, did this opinion obtain currency? In Spring and Autumn times the power of the Chou King was much restricted, and for much of the time was in effect limited to an area that is commonly called the "royal domain." Within this domain the King parceled out small fiefs to men who held the titles of feudal lords and functioned as his officers, but who in fact had little if any authority beyond the limits of this restricted territory.[175] This situation became very familiar to scholars because of the relatively full records that we have for the Spring and Autumn period, and they evidently assumed that conditions had been essentially similar in Western Chou.

There is some analogy between the theory of a limited royal domain in Western Chou and that of the division of the early Roman Empire into "imperial provinces" and "senatorial provinces." This distinction does correspond to some of the facts, if not pressed too far.

171. Chang, *Chung-kuo Chan-shih Lun-chi*, "Yin-Chou Chan-shih," 2.

172. Kuo, *Chin-wen Ts'ung-k'ao*, 36a–39a.

173. In ibid., 39a, Kuo says that it does not occur on the bronzes, and I have not found it in the inscriptions.

174. *Shih*, 263. Karlgren, and Legge (*Shih*, 637), both translate this as "royal domain," but it is somewhat doubtful that they would have done so without the tradition embodied in various late works. Waley (*Shih*, 276) renders it as "inner domain." The "thousand *li*" here is so coincidental that it suggests that this passage may underly the later tradition.

175. Such an official, apparently, was the Earl of Shan who is named in the text of the *Ch'un-ch'iu; Tso-chuan*, 8.1ab (see especially the commentary). See also *Tso*, 72::72 (Chuang 1), and Legge's discussion on the following page.

But the *Cambridge Ancient History* points out that in the circumstances of the Roman Empire "it was impossible to apply to administration a rigid system of dyarchy." Heichelheim and Yeo assert that "the 'clear-cut' distinction between imperial and senatorial provinces is a modern myth."[176]

All this does not mean that the Chou King exercised the same degree of control over fiefs remote from his capital that he did over those near at hand. That is unlikely. But the differences were probably the result of more subtle causes than the drawing of a sharp boundary around a "royal domain." Even in our own day, governments that employ all the resources of modern technology can still not control remote territories under strong leadership so completely as they do areas adjacent to the capital.

How, exactly, were fiefs created? How were men made vassals? What was the ceremony of enfeoffment? On these points we have far less information for Western Chou than is available for feudal Europe. This is not in itself remarkable, in view of the vast disparity between the preserved historical records. Yet even when allowance is made for this, our precise data on the procedure and the nature of enfeoffment in the Western Chou period is surprisingly sparse.

It seems reasonably clear, however, that the procedure was essentially similar to that of other presentation ceremonies that we have already seen, in which the individual to receive a charge appeared before the King in a temple or other hall.[177] Such ceremonies were conducted according to a definite ritual and, we may deduce, with considerable pomp. Since enfeoffments were certainly very important, it is reasonable to suppose that they were solemnized with more than ordinary ceremony. And since the enfeoffment of a feudal lord was perhaps the most important event of his life, we might expect to find many splendid bronze vessels that describe the ceremony in detail. But in fact we do not. We seem to have very few Western Chou bronzes that can certainly be said to recount the circumstances of enfeoffment at all, and most of those that do are almost curt in reporting them.

This is rather a mystery. Ch'i Ssu-ho observes that inscriptions "recording the investiture of feudal lords are relatively few, probably be-

---

176. *Cambridge Ancient History*, X, 212. Heichelheim and Yeo, *The Roman People*, 299.

177. Ch'en Meng-chia says ("Hsi-Chou T'ung-ch'i," [3].103–104) that it is a mistake to suppose, as is sometimes done, that the bestowal of royal charges always took place in a temple. He lists other places, including the abodes of subjects, in which this ceremony was also performed.

cause most of the vessels that have been preserved come from the middle of Western Chou and later, a time when the great bulk of enfeoffments were already past."[178] But this scarcely seems a sufficient explanation, for we do after all have a good many early Western Chou bronzes.

There is some difference of opinion as to what constituted enfeoffment. Ch'i argues that "anciently one who had noble rank had to have an official position, for which he had to have emolument, and to have emolument he had to have land; therefore enfeoffment and appointment to office were in fact the same thing."[179] Thus Ch'i considers all appointments to office enfeoffments, and it might seem reasonable to deduce that every gift of land by the King was in fact an enfeoffment. But Maspero would distinguish sharply between land given as a fief and land given as a nonfeudal domain.[180] To what extent this distinction may be valid we shall consider later. In my opinion we can only be *certain* that enfeoffment is involved if a feudal title is specifically conferred, or if land is conferred that is specifically said to constitute a fief.

Among the inscriptions of my corpus the one most clearly reporting an enfeoffment ceremony occurs on a bronze recently unearthed in Kiangsu province. It has been studied by a number of scholars; unfortunately some of its characters are obscure or missing, so that there are considerable variations in interpretation.[181] Thus we cannot even be certain of the place in which the ceremony was held. In any case it is clear that the inscription does not give some of the details concerning the circumstances that are commonly furnished, even in connection with far less momentous presentations. The language of the enfeoffment reads: "The King charged Marquis Nieh of Ch'ien saying, '[Be?] Marquis[182] in I.'" The King then lists a very long roster of gifts presented as part of the ceremony. These include a bronze vessel, bows, and various kinds of arrows, as well as various lands and a

178. Ch'i, "Chou-tai Hsi-ming-li K'ao," 215.
179. Ibid., 197, 212.
180. Maspero, "Le régime féodal."
181. To name only four of these studies, they include: Ch'en, "Hsi-Chou T'ung-ch'i," (1).165–167. Kuo, *Wen-shih Lun-chi*, 308–311. T'ang, "I Hou Nieh Kuei K'ao-shih." Barnard, "A Bronze of Western Chou Date." Ch'en, Kuo, and Barnard date this inscription to the reign of King Ch'eng, which I believe to be correct; T'ang, however, places it in the following reign, that of King K'ang.
182. Where I have supplied "[Be?]" there is an indistinguishable character. From comparable contexts it appears likely that this character, whatever it is, has the sense of "act as." I am not at all sure that Hou 侯 ought here to be translated as "Marquis"; the King may simply be telling Nieh to "be ruler in I." But since Nieh does refer to himself later as Marquis of I, the translation "Marquis" is perhaps justified.

number of people of different categories. The inscription concludes: "Marquis Nieh of I celebrates the King's favor [by] making [for his] Father Ting,[183] Duke of Ch'ien, [this] sacrificial vessel." Here, then, we see the Marquis of Ch'ien charged by the King to be Marquis in I, after which the recipient of the charge calls himself "Marquis of I." This is clearly an enfeoffment.

This vessel is somewhat unusual in embodying the name of the King who granted the fief, King Ch'eng (1115–1079 B.C.). Ch'en Meng-chia would date another inscription, which he believes to report an enfeoffment, still earlier, to the time of King Wu. Kuo Mo-jo, however dates this latter inscription also to the time of King Ch'eng, and interprets it as not referring to an enfeoffment at all. That it does report an enfeoffment seems dubious. If it does, the language is extremely terse. As Ch'en reads it, it merely says, "The King charged Pao," not even giving the name of the fief.[184]

We find enfeoffment mentioned only very briefly, not unnaturally, when it is merely referred to in an inscription that deals principally with other matters. Thus one inscription begins: "The King charged [my] lord the Marquis of Hsing . . . to be Marquis in Hsing."[185] Another begins: "The King attacked the Shang capital, and charged Marquis T'u of K'ang [to rule] in Wèi."[186]

An inscription dated to the reign of King Li (878–828 B.C.) recounts the confirmation of a Marquis in possession of a fief held by his ancestors. It begins merely with the date, and continues: "The King charged the Marquis of Keng,[187] Po Ch'en, saying, 'Succeed[188] your

183. *Fu Ting* 父 丁 is a kind of designation of an ancestor that is common in the Shang bone inscriptions and occurs on some Chou bronzes. It consists of the name of the relationship plus one of the ten *kan* 干 or so-called "stems," which were used to designate the cycle of ten days that was somwhat comparable to our week.

184. Ch'en, "Hsi-Chou T'ung-ch'i," (1).157–160. Kuo, *Wen-shih Lun-chi,* 320–322.

185. *Chin-wen,* 40a. The character denoting the place is *ching* 井 , but Kuo Mo-jo (ibid., 39a) and Ch'en, "Hsi-Chou T'ung-ch'i," (3).74, agree in reading it as Hsing 邢 .

186. Various problems in connection with this inscription have been debated at great length; see; Ch'en, "Hsi-Chou T'ung-ch'i," (1).161–165. Chou, *Chin-wen Ling-shih,* 1–37. The attack on the Shang capital mentioned here is probably that made by King Ch'eng after the great Shang revolt against the Chou.

187. The character standing for the name of this fief seems to be unidentified. I am arbitrarily giving it the sound of its right-hand element, as suggested by Kuo Mo-jo in *Chin-wen,* 116a.

188. The identification of this character given by Kuo (*Chin-wen,* 115b) seems uncertain on the basis of the original, but in the context the sense seems almost certainly correct.

grandfather and your father [in being] Marquis in Keng.'" A long list of gifts follows, and the King concludes: "Use [these gifts] early and late to serve. Do not disregard my commands."

Although references to enfeoffment in the inscriptions are surprisingly few,[189] there are a certain number of passages in the *Poetry* that mention it, in language reminiscent of the inscriptions; in none of these, however, is there a full description of the ceremony.[190] In the *Tso-chuan* we find a number of cases of investiture—not with new fiefs, but in confirmation of those inherited—by the King. In at least two of these the charge appears to be given in full, and its language is very similar to what we find on Western Chou bronzes.[191]

It is worth noting that in connection with the Western Chou enfeoffments we rarely if ever find an oath of allegiance, or even so much as a pledge of loyalty.[192] This is more impressive than any num-

189. Some scholars have supposed them to be abundant, on the basis of what seems to be a misconception derived from the article of Ch'i Ssu-ho, "Chou-tai Hsi-ming-li K'ao." It must be said that the article provides scope for misconception. The English translation of the title, accompanying the English summary published in the same journal, is: "Investiture Ceremony of the Chou Period." Here *hsi-ming* 錫命 is clearly translated as "investiture." On page 202 the article says that out of 162 inscriptions dated as Western Chou in Kuo Mo-jo's *Liang-Chou Chin-wen-tz'u Ta-hsi K'ao-shih*, 55 include "relatively clear instances of *hsi-ming* by a Chou King." It is not surprising that some have interpreted this as 55 cases of feudal investiture. But if we examine the inscriptions that Ch'i lists, it is clear that what he means here by *hsi-ming* is simply "conferring a charge," and in fact many of these inscriptions have to do with nothing more than the bestowal of gifts, in some cases merely so many cowries. Ch'i himself says, on page 215, that "in the inscriptions on ritual vessels . . . those recording the conferring of charges (*hsi-ming*) enfeoffing feudal lords are relatively few."

190. *Shih*, 227, 230, 234, 259–260.

191. *Tso*, 205::210–211 (Hsi 28), 462::467 (Hsiang 14). In the first of these instances the ceremony is described as being somewhat more elaborate than that depicted on the bronzes. It is not certain whether this means that the accounts in the inscriptions are abbreviated, or that by this time (632 B.C.) the ceremony had been embellished. It should be noted, also, that in this case the King was "investing" the Duke of Chin with the title of "Leader of the Feudal Lords," recognizing a status which in fact he already had—and that the Duke was considerably more powerful than the King.

192. One inscription does, in fact, seem to embody an oath of allegiance, *not* as a part of the presentation ceremony but as a part of the addendum closing the inscription; see: *Chin-wen*, 39a. Ch'en, "Hsi-Chou T'ung-ch'i," (3).73–77. But while opinions differ as to the precise subject matter of this inscription, no one seems to have supposed that it concerns an enfeoffment. In the *Tso-chuan*, at the end of the charge to Duke Wen of Chin (*Tso*, 205::210–211) the Duke makes elaborate affirmation (but with no oath) of his obedience to the King, but this, in the circumstances of the Spring and Autumn period, is almost ironic, for the King is now almost powerless.

ber of sworn covenants could be. The oaths binding feudal contracts in medieval Europe were notoriously ineffective in preventing disloyalty; the Chou King, to judge from our evidence, had power and did not need them.

Few if any of the cases of enfeoffment that have been mentioned would qualify to be considered such according to a criterion stated by Henri Maspero, which has met with wide acceptance. He supposed that all genuine enfeoffments—as distinguished from gifts of lands as simple "domains"—consisted of a series of ceremonies, including that of "taking, from the altar of the great god of the Soil which is in the royal capital, a piece of earth of the color corresponding to the region of the Empire in which the territory [to be given as a fief] is located, and giving it to the seigneur for his own altar of the god of the Soil."[193]

This so-called "god of the soil," the *she* 社 , was essentially a mound of earth; apparently it was thought of sometimes as representing the agricultural potential of the soil, and sometimes as representing the land as territory. Such a mound has existed in the palace grounds in Peking to our own day, a small flat-topped pyramid composed of earth of five colors: green on the east, red on the south, white on the west, black on the north, and yellow on top.[194] Just how early such mounds consisting of five colors existed is not clear; Maspero quotes a description of one from a work that he attributes to the fourth century B.C.[195] It is unlikely that they existed much earlier, for the whole complex of numerology in China, with five colors keyed to five directions, can hardly be traced to a time much before the fifth century B.C.

The early history of the *she* is obscure.[196] Certainly it existed in

193. Maspero, "Le régime féodal," 134.

194. Presumably it is still there; I last saw it, I believe, in 1940.

195. Maspero, "Le régime féodal," 134–135. Concerning the work in question, commonly called the *I Chou-shu*, see pp. 480–482.

196. What is still referred to as "the classical" study of the *she* is "Le dieu du sol dans la Chine antique," by Édouard Chavannes. Chavannes was a very great scholar, but he wrote in 1910, before the beginning of what was undoubtedly the most fruitful half century, in terms of excavation and research, in all of the history of the study of ancient China. Chavannes' study is based largely on documents, such as the *Records on Ceremonial*, that critical scholars do not use today as sources for very early China. Karlgren ("Some Sacrifices in Chou China," 19–25) cites a great many passages concerning the *she* in the literature, which underline the complexity of the problem.

The character *she* 社 is quite rare in the early sources. It does not seem to occur in the Shang bone inscriptions, or in the original text of the *Book of Changes*. In the *Poetry* we find it only twice (*Shih*, 165, 225), in both cases apparently as a

Western Chou times, but whether enfeoffments were performed at it is a question. While inscriptions describing enfeoffments may mention the general locale in which the ceremony is performed, they seldom if ever state the specific place in which it takes place. We have one inscription that may do so, but unfortunately its characters are almost completely illegible at the critical point. Some scholars read this inscription as including an abbreviated form of the character *she,* while others interpret it altogether differently; it is impossible to be certain that it does refer to the *she.*[197]

Even in the *Tso-chuan,* where the ceremony by which the King bestowed a title on Duke Wen of Chin in 632 B.C. is described in considerable detail, the exact place in which the ceremony was performed is not specified. There is no mention of a *she,* and no mention of the bestowal of a clod of earth.[198] It is my impression that this ceremony involving the *she* and the clod of earth is not mentioned anywhere in the *Tso-chuan* in connection with enfeoffment.[199] It is most unlikely that the ceremony Maspero describes, involving a *she* constructed with earth of five colors, was practiced in Western Chou times.

Since Maspero thought that a genuine feudal relationship could be established only by this ceremony at the *she,* and that it was not used by feudal lords in conferring lands upon their vassals, he supposed that in ancient China, unlike the situation in medieval Europe, there

---

very local object of agricultural sacrifices. In the *Documents* it occurs only once (*Shu,* 48), but here the *she* is located at the eastern capital of the Chou. The problem is complicated, however, by the fact that we have a number of occurrences of *t'u* 土 , "earth," which is in some cases supposed to be an abbreviated form of *she.* It probably is in some cases. But there seems also to have been another earth deity called *T'u* or, sometimes, *Hou T'u* 后土 , "Sovereign Earth"; see, for instance, *Tso,* 729::731 (Chao 29). How these are to be distinguished is not wholly clear. Karlgren ("Some Sacrifices in Chou China," 11–12) says that *T'u* is identical with *Ti* 地 , which I very much doubt; see p. 447, n. 10.

197. The character that some scholars read as occurring here is *t'u* 土 . It is so read by T'ang Lan ("I Hou Nieh Kuei K'ao-shih," 79), Kuo Mo-jo (*Wen-shih Lun-chi,* 308), and Noel Barnard ("A Bronze of Western Chou Date," 20). T'ang and Barnard interpret the character as being, in fact, *t'u,* but Kuo supposes it to be the abridged form of *she.* Ch'en Meng-chia ("Hsi-Chou T'ung-ch'i," [1].165) reads it altogether differently, as *hou* 侯 , "Marquis."

198. *Tso,* 205::210–211 (Hsi 28). Bloch (*Feudal Society,* 173) says that in medieval Europe in the enfeoffment ceremony the vassal was sometimes given "a clod of earth, representing the soil conceded."

199. I feel quite sure that it is not; I have gone through the entire text of the *Tso-chuan* several times, and I believe that I would have noted it if I had encountered it. But with a text so long and complex as that of the *Tso-chuan,* I do not wish to make a definite statement unless I have made a specific search on the point; I have not done so on this one.

was no "subinfeudation"—no creation of vassals of vassals. This argument has received a good deal of attention in the literature, but there seems to be little basis for it.[200] Ch'i Ssu-ho says that there was a definite system of subinfeudation, and that the relation of a subvassal to his overlord was quite like that of a feudal lord to the King.[201]

Ch'en Meng-chia has concluded, from his extensive study of the bronze inscriptions, that the feudal lords had "their own small courts" patterned on the royal model, in which they gave charges to their retainers using the same ritual employed by the King.[202] It is very difficult, however, to find inscriptions that record, beyond all question, the enfeoffment of subordinates by feudal lords.[203] But this is not really very surprising, since even enfeoffments of feudal lords are so rarely mentioned.

A very interesting inscription, apparently from the time of King Ch'eng, opens by giving the date and saying that the King was at a certain place, and continues:

> The King conferred upon the Grand Secretary Hsiung the territory of Li. The King said, "Chung . . . now Hsiung gives to you the territory of Li, to be your ts'ai 汆 ."[204]

Here we see the King first giving a piece of territory to the Grand Secretary and then, at his request, conferring it upon Chung. It seems clear that Chung is a subordinate of the Grand Secretary.[205] This would appear then to be a case of subinfeudation—if a ts'ai is a fief.

200. Maspero, "Le régime féodal," 133, 143–144. Bodde, "Feudalism in China," 57–58. Hsu ("Western Chou Government," 515–516) cites Maspero but says that he has found "explicit evidence . . . that subinfeudation was practiced."

201. Ch'i, "Chinese and European Feudal Institutions," 11–12. Ch'i, "Hsi-Chou Cheng-chih Ssu-hsiang," 22.

202. Ch'en, "Hsi-Chou T'ung-ch'i," (3).105.

203. Hsu ("Western Chou Government," 516) finds Chin-wen, 85b, to be such an inscription. It may be. Certainly it records the bestowal by an Earl, upon a subordinate, of functions and of lands at four different places. If every bestowal of land is an enfeoffment, this certainly is one. But I am not sure that it is quite unmistakably so.

204. Chin-wen, 16a. Ch'en, "Hsi-Chou T'ung-ch'i," (2).116. Kuo Mo-jo and Ch'en Meng-chia read certain characters in this inscription differently, but this does not alter the sense. Kuo interprets the passage I have omitted in Chin-wen, 16b, but I am not certain what it means; for the present purpose it is unimportant. Maspero ("La société chinoise," 370) give a translation of this inscription, but it seems to me that he omits the translation of a part of the text; he interprets it as involving only a single gift from the King to Chung.

205. A series of inscriptions seems to indicate this; see Chin-wen, 16a–19a.

The character *ts'ai* is evidently a pictograph of a hand plucking fruit from a tree.[206] Thus it is well suited to stand for an "appanage," a territory given to an officer so that its production may serve as his emolument. This is the way in which it is commonly understood. Maspero considers *ts'ai* to be one of the terms designating a "private domain," not at all a fief. But there seems to be no way to be certain that this distinction existed in fact, and even Maspero says that there was a tendency for the holder of a *ts'ai* to increase his power and become a feudal vassal."[207]

It seems quite likely that *ts'ai* was merely another name for "fief."[208] Another inscription dated to the reign of King Ch'eng relates that the King "gave to Ch'ien a *ts'ai* called . . ." The name of the place is given, but it seems to be impossible to identify it as any known character.[209] Judging from references to him in two other inscriptions, Ch'ien was a very high royal official; it seems probable that this *ts'ai* was a fief.[210]

We have other inscriptions that record the gift of lands by the King, and a few by lesser persons, with no clear indication as to whether they were fiefs or not. Furthermore, we find lands in various places given to the same individual; in one inscription the King gives to a single officer lands in seven different places.[211] Were they all fiefs?

FOR well over two thousand years, and continuing into our own day, scholars have been trying to discover elaborate rules by which feudalism functioned in ancient China. Mencius, who dealt with the prob-

---

206. What appear to be forms of this character in the Shang inscriptions clearly show the fruit; see *Yin-ch'i Ch'ien-pien*, 5.36.1, 7.40.1. Later forms show only the hand and the tree.

207. Maspero, "Le régime féodal," 114–115, 143. Maspero, "La société chinoise," 366.

208. See: Ch'i, "Hsi-Chou Cheng-chih Ssu-hsiang," 22. Ch'en, "Hsi-Chou T'ung-ch'i," (2).116. A work compiled in the second century B.C., the *Han-shih Wai-chuan*, says (8.10a): 古者天子為諸侯受封謂之采地 By itself, I think that this passage would have to be translated: "Anciently the Son of Heaven caused fiefs to be conferred upon the feudal lords, calling them *ts'ai* lands." In itself, this passage seems to equate *ts'ai* with *feng*, "fiefs." Yet the context that follows is very strange, so that James Hightower, in *Han Shih Wai Chuan*, 270, translates even this introductory passage differently to make it harmonize with what follows. This section of the text as a whole is very curious, and while I am not sure that Hightower's interpretation of it is correct, I do not pretend to be certain of its meaning.

209. *Chin-wen*, 15b. Ch'en, "Hsi-Chou T'ung-ch'i," (2).115–116.

210. *Chin-wen*, 20a, 20b. Ch'en, "Hsi-Chou T'ung-ch'i," (1).173, (2).70–73.

211. *Chin-wen*, 121ab.

lem around 300 B.C., may not have had all of the bronze inscriptions available to us today, but he certainly had access to a great deal of evidence that we can never know. Yet Mencius said that it was impossible for him to learn the details of the early feudal regulations. He blamed this on certain feudal lords who had, he said, destroyed the records embodying these rules.[212] But perhaps we should consider another possibility: that the rules, in the sense of meticulous distinctions between "fiefs" and "domains," and elaborate prescriptions that enfeoffment could be performed in one way and no other, and precise regulations that were always and everywhere the same, simply did not exist.

The Chou rulers found themselves with an immense amount of territory that had to be brought under control. They also had relatives, retainers, and officials who had to be provided for. By giving the land into the keeping of their followers, they achieved a number of results that we have considered. But it seems rather unlikely that, when they bestowed a piece of territory of considerable size on a retainer, they specified whether he was or was not to have the right to govern it. They needed to have their territories governed. Certainly they cared something about the way they were governed; we have seen that King Wu, in particular, dwelt at great length in a communication to his brother on the necessity of treating the people justly and well.[213] It does not seem to be true that the King, and his officials, did not have the *right* to concern themselves with the government of local areas. But it would have been physically impossible for them to do so to any considerable extent. Almost necessarily those who held large areas of territory from the King must have administered them as well, and thus have been feudatories in fact—whether there were any rules that designated them as such or not.

There must, also, have been a whole multitude of persons who had some kind of control over small parcels of land, or at least enjoyed the produce from them, who had no political power considerable enough to entitle them to be called feudal vassals. But our sources almost never tell us anything about people that far down in the scale.

A happy exception is provided by an inscription of very early Chou date. It was cast by a certain Hsien, who was evidently a retainer of K'ang Shu, the first ruler of the state of Wèi. K'ang Shu was set up as ruler of this state over a portion of the conquered Shang people, after they had revolted against the Chou and been crushed. This inscription relates that when K'ang Shu first visited his new fief, Hsien accom-

212. *Mencius*, 5(2).2.
213. *Shu*, 39–43.

panied him. The ruler charged Hsien to perform certain functions, which are not specified. Then, the inscription relates, "the Duke 'acred' Hsien [with] one hundred 'acres' of grain." Hsien celebrated the gift by casting the bronze.[214]

What I have translated as "acre" is the character *mou* 畝 , which is conventionally called a "Chinese acre." As is common with Chinese measurements, it has varied greatly in extent at various times. It is said that the *mou* of Chou times was very small, so small that a hundred *mou* would have amounted to slightly less than four and three-quarters English acres (the acre in common use today).[215] But whether this was the actual extent of the *mou* in use in the state of Wèi around 1100 B.C. seems impossible to determine. Certainly a gift of grain produced by an area of less than five of our acres seems rather small to occasion the casting of a bronze.

In this inscription the character *mou* is used as a verb; literally it says that the ruler "'acred' Hsien." Kuo Mo-jo supposes *mou* to be used as a loan for another character which means "to present (something of value)."[216] It seems to me, however, that this text may indicate to us that there was already, at the very beginning of Western Chou, a practice whereby feudal lords "endowed with 'acres' " their functionaries. But was Hsien merely given the grain produced by this land, or was he endowed with an actual piece of grain-producing acreage? We cannot tell. In any case it seems unlikely that any considerable political authority was involved, over so small an area. It would appear that here we have a man charged with certain specified functions, for the performance of which he is recompensed either with land, or with the grain produced by a stated amount of land. Insofar as we may judge from this inscription, it appears that Hsien was not a feudal vassal; if he was not a bureaucrat, he was something very close to one.[217] As much as two thousand years later Chinese officials were still being paid allowances in grain as part of their salaries, although money was in extensive use as early as the Warring States period.[218]

THE family as an institution was already very important at the beginning of Western Chou. We have seen that King Wu said that those

---

214. *Chin-wen*, 225a.

215. Swann, *Food and Money*, 360–361.

216. Chin-wen, 225a.

217. As I define bureaucrats, they are professional functionaries; our data is scarcely sufficient to determine whether Hsien might properly be called a professional functionary or not.

218. Kracke, *Sung Civil Service*, 83.

who failed in love and respect toward the members of their families
were worse than murderers. And the *Poetry* says of his father, King
Wen:

> He was obedient to his noble ancestors,
> So that the spirits were never resentful,
> The spirits were never dissatisfied.
> He was an example to his royal wife;
> It extended to his brothers,
> And so he governed his family and state.[219]

This conception of the family as a microcosm of the state is so fundamental in Chinese thinking that we find this poem quoted in admonitions to rulers in the *Tso-chuan* and again in the *Mencius.*[220]

King Hsiang (651–619 B.C.) is quoted as saying: "There can be no
litigation between ruler and subject. . . . If there could be, this would
lead to litigation between father and son, so that there would no longer
be any distinction between superior and inferior."[221] It is quite clear
that the family was believed to provide the pattern for government.

The family was clearly important in Chou feudalism, from the beginning. We have seen that a large proportion of the major fiefs appear to have been given to members of the royal family. Many of the
most important officials in the royal government were close relatives
of the King. Since marriage with persons of the same surname was
normally avoided,[222] states that had ruling families of different surnames provided the most appropriate opportunities for intermarriage
with the royal house, and with ruling families having its surname. We
know from bronze inscriptions that the wife of the second Chou King,
Ch'eng, had the surname of the ruling house of the state of Ch'i; Ch'en
Meng-chia suggests that she was the daughter of Duke T'ai, the first
Duke of Ch'i.[223] The inscriptions, the *Poetry*, and the *Tso-chuan* contain many references to such intermarriage.[224] One inscription that

219. *Shu*, 42. *Shih*, 192. Some of the terms in this poem are variously interpreted, but the sense is clear and it is not worth while to go into these fine points.
220. *Tso*, 176::177 (Hsi 19). *Mencius*, 1(1).7.12.
221. *Kuo-yü*, 2.6a.
222. It is generally said to have been forbidden, but there are so many cases
of violation of this tabu as to raise some question about it. It appears that there
was a strong feeling that persons of the same surname should not marry, yet
they sometimes did. Duke Wen of the state of Chin is supposed to have been born
of parents both of whom had the royal Chou surname, Chi, but this was apparently
considered exceptional; see *Tso*, 185::187 (Hsi 23).
223. Ch'en, "Hsi-Chou T'ung-ch'i," (2).117.
224. *Shih*, 14, 38, 231. *Tso*, 855::855 (Ai 24). Fu, "Ta-tung Hsiao-tung Shuo,"
104–105.

Kuo Mo-jo dates to late Western Chou indicates that a woman of the royal family married an official of the state of Chin.[225]

Beyond question the network of ties by blood or marriage that came to link the Chou Kings with their chief vassals was a factor of strength that helped to hold the feudal structure together. We have seen that in Normandy the principal vassals were all related to the ruler. But in medieval European feudalism generally, the role of kinship was less important than in that of China. Yet in Europe, too, the desirability that vassals should be kindred was recognized. Bloch says:

> The best-served hero was he whose warriors were all joined to him either by the new, feudal relationship of vassalage, or by the ancient tie of kinship . . . Devotion reached its highest fervour when the two solidarities were mingled, as happened, according to the *geste*, to Duke Bègue whose thousand vassals were *trestous d'une parenté*—"everyone of the same kin." Whence did a feudal noble, whether of Normandy or Flanders, derive his power according to the chroniclers? From his castles, no doubt, from his handsome revenues in silver coin, and from the number of his vassals; but also from the number of his kinsmen.[226]

There is another side to this, however. If we regard feudalism strictly as a method of attaining certain political objectives, regard for family ties was in a sense incompatible with it. Bloch observes that "the ties based on blood relationship . . . were by their very nature foreign to the human relations characteristic of feudalism."[227] A ruler seeking the best man to whom to delegate authority over a portion of his realm ought, in order to secure the best results, to appoint the most qualified individual regardless of relationship. And if the appointee fails, he should be replaced, again without regard to kinship.

Situations involving people, however, are never simple. A brother of the King might be the best man to appoint as a vassal, not only because his loyalty could be depended upon but also because the very fact of his relationship to the King endowed him with prestige that another would lack. And to dismiss a close relative of the ruler from his post might, in a society that placed high value on family solidarity, injure the ruler's standing more than it would to leave an inferior man

225. *Chin-wen*, 230b.
226. Bloch, *Feudal Society*, 124.
227. Ibid., 123.

in his place. There was in fact a kind of spiral effect in the relations of the Chou Kings with their vassal relatives. Initially the King was so powerful that it was difficult for his relatives to oppose him. Relatives as vassals had definite advantages. And the code of family loyalty made it at least embarrassing to oust a relative and his heirs from a fief. Thus they were, usually at least, left in possession. But the longer they were in possession, and the more the feudal lords developed into an entrenched aristocracy with a multitude of mutual ties between themselves, the more his enfeoffed relatives became a potential danger to the King. The same factors enhanced the code of family solidarity, under which it was felt that the King's vassal kinsmen held their fiefs by inherent right. All this made them a much greater potential threat to the King, and at the same time created a situation in which it would have been difficult and perhaps perilous for him to attempt to deprive an important relative of his fief.

It is universally recognized that for at least three thousand years the family has been one of the most important institutions—perhaps even *the* most important single institution—in Chinese civilization. Confucius and Confucians have laid great stress on the importance of family relationships and familial duty. But what is not always recognized is that, if the situation is to be understood, we must realize that the meaning of the word "family" in this proposition has not always been entirely the same.

Confucius and his disciples, as their sayings are reported in the *Analects*, treat kinship as the archetype of the social and political order. But it is highly significant that the only specific kinship ties mentioned in the *Analects* are those between parents and children and those between brothers.[228] These are relationships within the immediate family composed of a man and a woman and their children—regardless of whether the children are or are not married. This is what is sometimes called the "nuclear family."

In Spring and Autumn times what is commonly known as "the aristocratic family" was the kinship group called the *shih* 氏 . It consisted of not one but a number of "nuclear" families; it was an "extended family," living under the headship of its chief. The *shih* had some resemblance to the Roman *familia*, which has been described as a

228. *Analects*, 1.2, 6–7, 11; 2.5–8, 20–21; 4.18–21; 9.15; 11.4, 21, 23; 12.5, 11; 13.7, 18, 20, 28; 17.9, 21; 19.18. *Analects*, 1.13 and 8.2, may refer to relationships with *ch'in* 親 in the sense of "kindred," but neither passage is wholly unambiguous.

"largely self-sufficing household which included slaves and other servants as well as members connected by common descent or marriage."[229] But the *shih* was commonly a feudal estate—a small state, in fact, within the feudal state, with considerable lands and its own political identity. We find it said in the *Tso-chuan* that for a retainer of a *shih* to act in the interest of the ruler of the state, rather than of the *shih*, is "the greatest of crimes."[230]

Cho-yun Hsu writes:

> A Ch'un Ch'iu [Spring and Autumn] state was not a purely political institution. The state resembled an enlarged household; the ruler reigned but did not rule. Ministers were not important because they held their offices; they were important and received offices because they were kin to the ruler or because they were heads of prominent families. In the state of Lu for example, each of the three most important houses, Chi-sun, Shu-sun, and Meng-sun, was entitled to fill one of three ministerial offices. The *Tso Chuan* mentions their official titles only once.[231]

That a man was chief minister of the state of Lu was less impressive than the fact that he was the head of the Chi-sun *shih*.

The *Tso-chuan* gives us a superbly detailed panorama of life—especially the life of the aristocrats—in Spring and Autumn times. Kinship between aristocrats, and especially relationship to the royal house, is a dominant theme. The order of precedence among states was determined in terms of the relationship of their rulers to the royal family. Questions of diplomacy and war were debated in terms of the relationship of the founders of states to each other. Lack of such relationship was considered to place a state "beyond the pale." At the end of the period, Confucius said that "the governments of Lu and Wèi are elder and younger brother," because they had been founded (some six centuries previously) by brothers.[232]

Since such emphasis was placed on kinship, and especially on relationship to the Chou house, great pride was naturally taken in possession of the royal surname, Chi. Thus in the *Tso-chuan* we find re-

229. Carl Brinkmann, "Family, Social Aspects," in *Encyclopedia of the Social Sciences*, VI, 67.

230. *Tso*, 654::655 (Chao 14).

231. Hsu, *Ancient China*, 78.

232. *Tso*, 30–31::32 (Yin 11), 197::198–199 (Hsi 26), 354::354–355 (Ch'eng 4), 637–638::640–641 (Chao 12). *Analects*, 13.7.

peated reference to "the various Chi," that is, the states ruled by lords possessing the Chi surname.[233]

When we turn from the Spring and Autumn documents to those of Western Chou, it is almost, in this respect, as if we entered another country. We do indeed find much reference to parents and brothers, in keeping with the Chinese emphasis on the family. But reference to relationship beyond the "nuclear family" is rare indeed. Larger kinship groups, as factors of political power, are almost never mentioned.

It is in the *Poetry* especially that, if the Western Chou situation resembled that of the Spring and Autumn time, we should expect to meet with emphasis on the large group of kindred. But even when major feasts and sacrifices are described, it is rarely that relatives are mentioned beyond the immediate family. Although there is much mention of warfare, there is no indication that groups of related warriors fought together. The *Poetry* has many detailed laments about deplorable conditions (most of these seem to come from late in Western Chou), which bitterly criticize the government and the rapacity of officials; here we should expect to find complaint that members of kinship groups favor each other. Yet in fact the only case of the kind is a condemnation of favor to relatives by marriage; this is quite different from the ties of the aristocratic kinship group of Spring and Autumn times—the *shih*—which emphasized blood relationship in the male line of descent from a common ancestor.[234] We have already seen that, in sharp contrast to the Spring and Autumn situation, where the *shih* is ubiquitous, the Western Chou sources seem to show no single case where *shih* is clearly the name of a kinship group.

The surname of the royal house, Chi, flaunted so proudly as an emblem of relationship to the Chou rulers in the Spring and Autumn period, occurs with surprising rarity in the Western Chou sources. In the *Book of Changes* and the *Documents* it is wholly absent. And in the bronze inscriptions of my corpus, and in the *Poetry*, it is not only rare, but is used exclusively in connection with women, like any other surname.[235] There is never any mention of "Chi" states as constituting a special, privileged group.

In Spring and Autumn times the King, in addressing or speaking of feudal lords, and feudal lords speaking to each other, commonly

233. *Tso*, 189::192 (Hsi 24), 204::209 (Hsi 28), 454::455 (Hsiang 12), 545::549 (Hsiang 29), 624::625 (Chao 9).

234. *Shih*, 133–134.

235. *Chin-wen*, 89a, 106a, 126a, 134a, 230b. *Shih*, 14, 25, 89. The *hsing* was commonly used only as part of the names of women; men were known by the names of their fiefs.

used relationship terms. (This is familiar to us from the practice of European sovereigns, who customarily address each other, and noblemen of their own countries, as "cousin.") Thus we find the Chou King speaking of feudal lords as "uncles," "nephews," or even "brothers."[236] While such usage can be found in the Western Chou sources, it is rare. In the bronze inscriptions the King, in addressing his vassals and officers, commonly does so in the simplest possible manner, calling them only by the personal name.[237]

In short, while the family motif was certainly important in Western Chou, and was considered to provide the pattern for conduct and government, it was usually the nuclear family, not an "extended family," that was in question. When King Wu denounced those who failed in their familial duty as worse than murderers, he specifically referred to "sons," "fathers," "younger brothers," and "elder brothers." And we have seen that the *Poetry* says that King Wen ruled by giving the proper example to his wife and his brothers.[238]

What role did kinship actually play in Western Chou feudalism? It was certainly considerable, but it seems probable that it has been exaggerated; here as elsewhere the tendency has been to transfer the patterns of the well-known Spring and Autumn period back to the relatively unknown Western Chou situation. Certainly many of the principal feudatories and many of the most important officers of the Chou Kings were their relatives, but we have reason to believe that they were expected, nonetheless, to justify their posts by their performance. Ichisada Miyazaki is undoubtedly correct in pointing out that familial ties must have tended to lessen the strict control that the King could exercise over his vassals, and that in time relatives of the royal house holding fiefs came to consider themselves privileged persons.[239] But at the beginning of Western Chou, at least, these factors were probably less operative.

236. The terms used commonly distinguish between lords of the Chi surname, sometimes called "paternal uncles," and those of other surnames, sometimes called "maternal uncles." In the latter case this usage was commonly justified by intermarriage, but was probably used as a convention even where there was no intermarriage. For some examples see *Tso*, 159::159 (Hsi 12), 194::196 (Hsi 25), 343::349 (Ch'eng 2), 624::625 (Chao 9), 739::740 (Chao 32).

237. Hsu ("Western Chou Government," 518–519) writes: "The Western Chou traditionally was attributed to have maintained its political excellence by means of incorporating the kinship lineage into the feudal system. Though in the Ch'un Ch'iu [Spring and Autumn] period such kinship consciousness was very dominant, the bronze inscriptions do not contain very explicit manifestations of the kinship lineage." This must, I think, strike anyone who studies them.

238. *Shu*, 42. *Shih*, 192.

239. Miyazaki, "Chūgoku Jōdai wa Hōkensei ka Toshi Kokka ka," 151.

One of the *Documents* is a proclamation addressed by King Wu to one of his younger brothers, probably made at the time when he was invested with an office or a fief, or both. Wu warns him: "The charge [that I have given you] is not irrevocable.[240] Think of it! May I not have to cut off your enjoyment [of your charge]." In another somewhat similar proclamation to this same brother, Wu spoke in even stronger terms: "If you do not follow my instructions then I, the One Man, will have no pity. If your service is not pure you shall share in the death penalty."[241]

Immediately after the conquest of the Shang, King Wu established two of his brothers as "Inspectors" to watch over two groups of conquered people. After Wu died, the Shang people rose in revolt, and these Inspectors, uncles of King Ch'eng, joined them. When the revolt was crushed, they were not treated with the clemency that might have been expected, in view of their relationship to the King. Accounts vary as to whether punishment was meted out by their nephew, the King, or their brother, the Duke of Chou, but they agree that one was banished and the other executed.[242]

Although kinship ties were certainly important in Western Chou feudalism, there is reason to doubt that they were permitted to interfere with efficiency to an unreasonable degree. The empire functioned —insofar as we can judge—with a smoothness remarkable in the circumstances. The fact that we have so little evidence of dissidence, until late in the period, would seem to indicate that the Kings and the royal government did not allow vassals to presume upon their relationship to the royal house to such a degree as to encourage rebellion.

240. The text reads 惟命不于常, "the mandate is not constant." Karlgren (*Shu*, 43) translates it as "the mandate is not (in a constant place =) invariable," and Legge (*Shu*, 397) renders it "*Heaven's* appointments are not constant." This is also the interpretation of commentators in *Shang-shu*, 14.13b–14a. It is quite true that *ming* 命 commonly means "the Mandate of Heaven," and that its precarious nature is a common theme. But *ming* is also the common term used for the charge of the King to a feudal lord, and it is so used repeatedly in this immediate context. I believe that King Wu is here drawing a deliberate parallel between the Mandate that Heaven gives to the King, which can be retained only on condition of good behavior, and the similar charge that the King gives to a feudal lord.

After having arrived at the above translation, I checked that in Couvreur, *Shu*, 244, and was pleased to find that it reads: "Mais le mandat qui vous est confié n'est pas irrévocable."

241. *Shu*, 43, 46.

242. The voluminous and often conflicting reports on these events are collected and discussed in Ch'en, "Hsi-Chou T'ung-ch'i," (1).142–144. According to some accounts three brothers were Inspectors.

Certainly kinship was not the only qualification that brought royal favor. The bronze inscriptions give the impression that rather more attention was paid to merit, to achievements aiding the royal house. Frequently we find the King acknowledging the past benefits conferred by the ancestors of a vassal upon the King's own forebears: "When greatly illustrious [King] Wen and [King] Wu grandly received Heaven's Mandate . . ."[243] your sage ancestors ably assisted the former Kings, acting as their arms and legs, assisting their ruler to establish the great Mandate."[244] "Your ancestors labored for the Chou state, assisting in opening up the four quarters, according with and enlarging Heaven's Mandate. Your diligence [like theirs] has been unfailing. I give you . . ." (here follows a long list of prized and costly gifts).[245]

RELIGION has generally been believed to have played an important role in early Chinese feudalism. Maspero, as we have seen, supposed that all enfeoffments took place at the mound called the *she* or "god of the soil." Many Chinese scholars, from Han times to the present, have held that the act of investiture was always performed in an ancestral temple.

Religion was certainly an important factor in the political situation as a whole, of which feudalism was an integral part. The King was the Son of Heaven. Some, at least, of the feudal lords traced their ancestry to divine or quasi-divine ancestors, as did the Chou.[246] We find officers of the King saying such things as: "[My] greatly illustrious ancestors were able grandly to establish their virtue; their majesty is above; they broadly open the way for their grandsons and sons below."[247] But when we look for *specific* links between feudalism and religion, they are elusive.

We have seen that there seems to be no adequate evidence that enfeoffment was carried out, in Western Chou times, at the *she*. Ch'i

243. Four characters are left untranslated here. The latter two of them are very uncertain, so that the meaning of the passage is unclear. The reading proposed by Kuo Mo-jo in *Chin-wen*, 139ab, may be correct, but is certainly conjectural.

244. *Chin-wen*, 139a.

245. Ibid., 62ab. For other inscriptions having comparable passages, see: Ibid., 114a. Ch'en, "Hsi-Chou T'ung ch'i," (5).119. *Ch'ing-t'ung-ch'i T'u-shih*, 27.

246. See *Shih*, 226. We find relatively little mention of divine founders of the ruling houses of states in the Western Chou sources, while there is much more when we come to later times. This may be because the Western Chou sources are relatively scanty. It may also be because it became the fashion to have such ancestors in later times. No doubt both factors were operative.

247. *Chin-wen*, 133a.

Ssu-ho quotes three Han works that say that enfeoffment was always performed in an ancestral temple, and concludes: "Generally speaking, in an age of 'divine right,' all great affairs must be carried on under pretence of being in accord with the divine will. The Chou people considered their ancestors to be deities, and therefore performed the ritual of the bestowal of charges in the ancestral temple." But Ch'en Meng-chia says that study of the bronze inscriptions shows that the Kings did not always deliver charges to their vassals in temples, but in halls of other kinds as well—and even in offices and residences.[248]

The culture and the society within which Western Chou feudalism operated was permeated with religion. But feudalism itself seems to have had little of specifically religious overtones. Why should it? It was a technique of government.

We tend to associate feudalism with religion on the basis of European practice, where the candidate for knighthood maintained a vigil, fasting and praying, and attending mass, and might take his sword from an altar, or be given his arms by a priest. But in fact the whole ceremony of "dubbing" a knight was relatively late, and the introduction of Christian elements into it was later still. "Chivalry," as Carl Stephenson has said, "was originally non-Christian."[249] In Europe as in China feudalism was a means for the attainment of certain ends, and its association with religion was incidental.

WERE fiefs hereditary in Western Chou?

There is a strong tendency to think of feudalism as a system of the hereditary transmission of privilege, and even scholars sometimes write as if "feudal" were a synonym for "hereditary."[250] One Chinese scholar has described feudalism as consisting in the division of the state into territories under hereditary rulers.[251]

The most careful students of feudalism seem to be agreed, however, that the hereditary transmission of fiefs was not a part of the essential

248. Ch'i, "Chou-tai Hsi-ming-li K'ao," 201. Ch'en, "Hsi-Chou T'ung-ch'i," (3).103–104, 110. As we have seen, there is almost never any specification in the inscriptions as to the place in which an enfeoffment took place.

249. Stephenson, Medieval Feudalism, 47–55. Strayer, Feudalism, 58–59, 155–156. Bloch, Feudal Society, 312–319.

250. Max Weber evidently equated the hereditary tenure of office with feudalism. Writing of the period around A.D. 1387 he said: "The officers and officials . . . demanded the right to designate their successors, which meant a demand for re-feudalization." Weber, Gesammelte Aufsätze, I, 407; Weber, Religion of China, 117–118.

251. Chang, "Feng-chien She-hui," 803.

nature of feudalism. F. L. Ganshof says that "the relations of vassal and seigneur were not in themselves hereditary" and might in fact be terminated by the death of either party.[252] Strayer points out that in the first stage of European feudalism lands granted to vassals not only might be, but often were, taken back by the lord at the vassal's death, if not even before.[253] Logically feudalism, as a system of administration, would seem to leave no place for the inheritance of fiefs. Its *raison d'être* was to provide loyal and capable administrators to manage local areas for the overlord. But how could one be sure that each vassal's heir would be both loyal and capable?

Maspero says that in Chou China both fiefs and what he calls "private domains"—what some would call the fiefs of subvassals—were hereditary from the beginning.[254] Others, however, believe that the fief was not, strictly speaking, hereditary, since each heir must be confirmed by his overlord in order to succeed to its rule.[255]

In the Western Chou inscriptions there seems to be only one clear case in which a vassal is "confirmed" in his enjoyment of an inherited fief. In this inscription the King says to a certain Marquis (the name of whose fief is unidentifiable), "Succeed your grandfather and your father in being Marquis at . . ."[256] In the *Poetry* there is a passage that is very like the charges found in bronze inscriptions, which may well record the confirmation of a Marquis of Hán in his inheritance. It reads: "The Marquis of Hán received the charge, the King personally charged him, 'Continue [the service of] your ancestors, do not disregard my charge, early and late do not slacken.' " Another poem, using similar language, evidently records the confirmation of Earl Hu as ruler of Shao.[257]

For the Spring and Autumn period a number of cases are recorded in which the King "enfeoffed" or confirmed the heirs to states that had, in actual fact, been handed down as hereditary possessions for many generations. Since the King had little real power in this later time, such "investiture" had little real meaning; in 693 B.C. a royal envoy journeyed to Lu to confer investiture on Duke Huan, who had

252. Ganshof, *La féodalité*, 22, 121.

253. Strayer, *Feudalism*, 21–25, 97–99.

254. Maspero, "Le régime féodal," 117, 135. The evidence that Maspero cites in the first of these passages seems to me somewhat tenuous.

255. Hsu, "Western Chou Government," 516–517. Ch'i, in "Hsi-Chou Cheng-chih Ssu-hsiang," 21, says that fiefs were hereditary, but that heirs had to be invested by the King before they could assume the place of rule.

256. *Chin-wen*, 115b. "Your grandfather and your father" in such a context may in fact simply mean "your ancestors."

257. *Shih*, 230, 234.

been dead for more than a year![258] Farcical though these late ceremonies sometimes were, it is probably correct to see in them a survival of a custom that had had real force in Western Chou times: the royal investiture of an heir to a fief, as a ceremony to legitimize his tenure.

It seems clear that in theory the King had the power to take back a fief that he had bestowed. We have seen that King Wu warned one of his younger brothers, who was also his vassal, that the charge with which he had been entrusted was not irrevocable, and that if he did not give satisfaction he would not only be cut off from his enjoyment (presumably of his fief) but even put to death.[259] It seems difficult however to find actual Western Chou cases in which vassals were ousted from their fiefs. In one inscription we find the Earl of Mao ordered by the King to take over the duties of a Duke, but this appears to be the transfer of official functions rather than of a fief.[260] Another inscription tells of the transfer of land by the King from one subject to another; this may have involved the revocation of a fief, but it seems impossible to be sure.[261]

On the other side of the argument, a case may be made for the proposition that fiefs were regarded from the beginning as hereditary. First of all, we cannot disregard the hard fact that, in virtually every case concerning which we have information, fiefs seem to have been transmitted hereditarily. And in the same one of the *Documents* in which King Wu warns his younger brother and vassal that if his conduct is not upright he will be killed, the King also tells him that if he is diligent and virtuous the people of his fief "will hereditarily be your arms and legs"—that is, they will serve him and his posterity.[262] We find a similar statement in a passage in the *Poetry*, ascribed to the later years of Western Chou, which tells of the establishment of the state of Shen. It says that the King ordained that its ruler was to hold it "hereditarily."[263]

258. *Tso*, 72::73–74 (Chuang 1) (text of the *Ch'un-ch'iu*). Ch'i ("Chou-tai Hsi-ming-li K'ao," 223–226) lists and discusses these enfeoffments in Spring and Autumn times.

259. *Shu*, 43, 46.

260. *Chin-wen*, 20b–23a. Ch'en, "Hsi-Chou T'ung-ch'i," (2).70–73. In my opinion, little significance is to be attached to the fact that we here find an Earl taking over the duties of a Duke. Ch'en Meng-chia points out, however, that in this inscription the Earl of Mao is ordered to take over the duties of a Duke, and is afterward addressed as Duke of Mao; he apparently thinks that a new title was conferred with the charge.

261. *Chin-wen*, 87b.

262. *Shu*, 43.

263. *Shih*, 227.

In seeking to understand the degree to which fiefs were or were not hereditary in Western Chou, a look at medieval Europe is again useful. Bloch points out that although, strictly speaking, fiefs could not be inherited, in most circumstances "the lord had no power to refuse investiture to the natural heir, provided the latter did homage beforehand. The triumph of heritability in this sense was the triumph of social forces over an obsolescent right." In any case, he says, "the bond of fealty tended to unite not so much two individuals as two families, one of them pledged to exercise authority, the other to submit to it. Could it have been otherwise in a society in which the ties of kinship were so strong?" The interest of the lord, Bloch points out, "led him to insist strongly on the principle of revocability. On the other hand he was not necessarily opposed to hereditary succession. For above everything he needed men, and where better could he recruit them than among the descendants of those who had already served him?"[264]

All of these factors must have operated as strongly in ancient China as in medieval Europe. Because of the special importance of the family in Chinese culture, that of kinship may have exerted even greater force. It probably created a powerful presumption that, once the head of a family had been entrusted with a fief, his descendants might enjoy it during good behavior. Yet just as Heaven might and sometimes did revoke the Mandate of an erring King and replace his house with a new dynasty, so the King had the right to remove an untrustworthy or incompetent vassal from his fief and turn it over to another. Yet our sources from Western Chou seem to indicate that this seldom happened. In fact fiefs were inherited. It seems very likely, although we have little evidence on this point, that during most of the Western Chou period at least, the Kings were careful to see that each new vassal acknowledged the royal authority. Yet when fiefs were inherited for generation after generation in fact, it was almost inevitable that it should come to be believed that they were inherited by right. And in such matters, whatever is believed by enough people for a long enough time becomes the truth.

264. Bloch, *Feudal Society*, 190–191.

CHAPTER

12

Royal Techniques of Control

THE Western Chou Kings maintained control over their territories by a number of means. We have already considered some of them. The most obvious was military force. Less conspicuously, the royal officials, because of their activities in connection with such matters as finance and legal problems, had a wide network of contacts with the great and some of the less great. Through this avenue the Kings were undoubtedly kept informed about many problems, so that they could deal with them before they became serious. But the Kings also used techniques that were less obvious, and it is these that will be discussed in this chapter.

It has been pointed out that in some ways Western Chou government had more resemblance to the pattern of imperial government as it existed during the Christian Era than to the administrations of the Spring and Autumn period. But in one respect government in Western Chou—especially in the early reigns—differed very sharply from the later pattern of imperial government. This difference lay in the personal involvement of the King in a wide range of activities.

As early as the Ch'in dynasty (221–207 B.C.) the Emperor was conceived as an august personage so far above ordinary mortals that he could hardly be imagined as having social intercourse with them. The second Ch'in Emperor seldom saw anyone except the eunuchs who attended him inside the palace; one of them was given virtually complete control of the government, and acted as the Emperor's spokesman to the outside world.[1]

The founder of the next dynasty, the Han, remained essentially an uncouth peasant to his death. After he had first gained the Empire, his palace was the scene of drunken carousals in which the Emperor took

---

1. *Shih-chi*, 87.34–35. This is translated in Bodde, *China's First Unifier*, 44.

part. But even he came to see that this would not do, and he authorized the establishment of a court ritual that elevated the Emperor to a position of majesty.[2] There was wide variety, of course, in later practice, but in general the Emperor was a remote figure seldom if ever seen by ordinary men and women. In extreme cases there were Emperors who were not often seen even by some of those who were nominally their highest ministers.

This made it possible for those in constant attendance upon the Emperor, such as specially trusted ministers or eunuchs, sometimes to usurp power and make the Emperor a virtual puppet. But some Emperors, even though they did not see many of their subjects, were able to maintain firm and sometimes despotic control of affairs. They did this by means of tightly organized mechanisms of government, and systems whereby various officials kept watch on each other and reported directly to the Emperor. We have seen, however, that the evidence gives little indication that Western Chou government was tightly organized. The Kings did, in fact, use techniques of control that are not immediately apparent. But above all they seem to have held the reins of the Empire in their own hands, maintaining personal touch with various parts of the realm and a great many of their subjects, in a manner that was not characteristic of imperial government in later times.

MENCIUS, our great—if sometimes very unreliable—reporter of early practices, describes the personal inspection of the entire realm as a regular institution. It consisted, he relates, of a progress through all of the feudal states, made twice every year, in the spring and in the autumn. Mencius attributes this practice not only to the Chou Kings, but also to the rulers of the Hsia and Shang dynasties.

> When the son of Heaven visited the feudal lords, this was called "touring the fiefs." . . . In the spring he inspected the plowing and supplied any deficiency [of seed]. In the autumn he examined the harvest, and made up any insufficiency.

The ruler also, Mencius says, examined the condition of each state and its government and rewarded or reprimanded the vassal in charge of it accordingly.[3]

2. *Shih-chi*, 99.13–18; Watson, *Records*, I, 293–295. Dubs, *Han-shu*, I, 21.
3. *Mencius*, 6(2).7.2; see also ibid., 1(2).4.5.

It appears likely that here, as in some other cases, Mencius has based what he says upon some valid information as to what actually happened in Wesern Chou times. He has then elaborated this, formalized it, and erected it into an institution supposed to have existed throughout antiquity. Certainly there was some basis for his assertion. In the *Poetry* we have a description of a triumphal progress through the states, which some critics plausibly suppose to have been made by King Wu,[4] and a bronze inscription tells us of an inspection trip by King Ch'eng that extended far to the southeast, almost to the sea.[5]

It seems unlikely, however, that any King made a regular practice of visiting all of the vassal states twice a year. Indeed, we seem to have no evidence in the sources that such all-inclusive tours were ever undertaken. Such visits that could be regularly foreseen would have been less effective, for purposes of inspection, than less frequent trips that were unexpected. Although the sources only rarely tell us that the King made a trip for the express purpose of inspection, we have seen that there was a great deal of travel to various parts of the Empire, and it may be assumed that the ruler was not unaware of the opportunity this gave for informing himself of conditions.

The King personally commanded a great many military expeditions. The stated objective of these trips (and no doubt a real one) was military action, sometimes at a remote border of the Chou territories. But such expeditions were also parades through the states they traversed, which at once gave the King an opportunity to observe the state of affairs and meet the local rulers, and to display the royal pomp and might to all. The poem mentioned above, telling of the progress of the King through the states, says that he "overawes them, there are none who do not shake and fear."[6] Another poem gives us the impression made by the sight of the passing of the royal armies:

> Stately is our ruler, the King;
> On his left and right they hold insignia.
> They hold the insignia high
> As befits the fine officers. . . .
> The Chou King marches
> And the six armies follow him. . . .

---

4. *Shih*, 242. Karlgren begins his translation: "He makes his seasonal tour of the state," but it seems unlikely that this really refers to a "seasonal" tour. It is not so rendered by Waley, Legge, or Couvreur. See: Waley, *Shih*, 230. Legge, *Shih*, 577. Couvreur, *Shih*, 424. *Mao-shih*, 19(2).5a–7a.

5. Ch'en, "Hsi-Chou T'ung-ch'i," (1).165–167.

6. *Shih*, 242.

Long life to the King of Chou,
Is he not a man indeed![7]

Such trips were probably made, at times, for complex objectives. We have seen that late in Western Chou the barbarians of the south and east were a serious problem, and that it has been suggesed that the Chou depended upon the Marquis of E to keep some of them in order. A bronze inscription relates that "the King made a military expedition to the south" and on his return met with the Marquis of E, who served the King with liquor; the King in turn gave a banquet for the Marquis. The King and the Marquis then took part in an archery contest, and the King in person (as a special mark of favor) presented the Marquis with jade, four horses, and arrows.[8] Since the Marquis later led the barbarians in rebellion, it would appear that this rather elaborate gesture by the King was a failure.[9] It is not necessarily true, however, that the King was naïve. He undoubtedly knew that trouble with the barbarians of this quarter was a possibility, and he may even have had some doubt about the loyalty of the Marquis. If so, he made the military expedition to demonstrate his preparedness and tried, by showing unusual favor to the Marquis, to secure his adherence. If that was his purpose, he did not succeed in this instance.

In any case, this incident involves one of the means that the Kings used to cement their hold upon their Empire: extensive social activity. They did not fraternize; there was never any question of the immense superiority of the King. He was the Son of Heaven, endowed with quasi-divine attributes. But precisely because of his superiority, any gift that he presented, or any association to which he condescended, conferred immense prestige upon the beneficiary. We find bronzes cast to celebrate the bestowal by the King of three deer, or even of a single fish.[10]

The *Poetry* tells of a group of lords who have come to the royal court, making a brave show in their splendidly colored clothing. The Son of Heaven rewards them with horses and carriages and fine

7. *Shih*, 191.

8. *Chin-wen*, 107b. Hsü, "Yü Ting," 61.

9. I am assuming that this inscription dates from before the rebellion. We have no clear evidence of the sequence of events, so that one must proceed on the basis of probability. Hsü Chung-shu ("Yü-ting," 61) makes the assumption that I do. T'ang Lan, however (*Ch'ing-t'ung-ch'i T'u-shih*, 3) supposes that the Marquis was pardoned after the rebellion and that this inscription records a later event. I find this implausible.

10. Ch'en, "Hsi-Chou T'ung-ch'i," (5).115, 120. Lo, *Chen-sung T'ang*, 3.23b. The latter inscription is not a part of my basic corpus.

clothes, and at the same time he uses this opportunity to "take their measure."[11]

An inscription cast by an officer of the Marquis of Ching, Maker of Books Mai, tells how the Marquis was received when he went to the capital after his enfeoffment. The Marquis first attended, with other guests of the King, at a sacrifice. Later he went with the King to the Circular Moat, where the King rode in a boat and shot arrows at birds.[12] The Marquis rode in a boat adorned with a red banner. The King later gave the Marquis many fine gifts, and the Marquis in turn presented Maker of Books Mai with a gift of metal. Mai cast the bronze to record these events and dated it "in the year in which the Son of Heaven favored Mai's lord, the Marquis."[13]

The *Poetry* tells us that when the Earl of Shen set off for his new fief in the south, "the King gave him a parting feast in Mei."[14] A number of bronze inscriptions record banquets given by the King, and one tells of a banquet given for him. One of these royal entertainments is known to us only from the account of a certain Ta, who commanded the guards outside the hall where the banquet was held. The King directed Steward K'e to invite Ta and his men inside, and then told another officer to give Ta thirty-two piebald horses. In the inscription that he cast to commemorate this event, Ta is understandably enthusiastic in his appreciation of the King's generosity.[15] Actions of this kind must have done much to strengthen the hold of the Chou on the hearts of their subjects.

We have almost no details about the royal banquets. It is reasonable to deduce, however, that they were accompanied by music.[16] And the *Poetry* has a description of a concert by what was evidently an orchestra of some size:

> There are blind [musicians] at the court of Chou.
> We have arranged the horizontal boards and the vertical posts [forming the bell frames],

11. *Shih*, 175–176.

12. The *Pi-yung* 辟雍, mentioned in the *Poetry*, is equated by Kuo Mo-jo with the characters that occur here (*Chin-wen*, 40a). Concerning this pool in the form of a ring, see below, pp. 407–408.

13. *Chin-wen*, 40ab.

14. *Shih*, 227.

15. *Chin-wen*, 55a, 84a, 88a, 107b. Ch'en, "Hsi-Chou T'ung-ch'i," (5).113, 121, (6).85, 101a.

16. That the Kings esteemed music may be judged from the honor paid to musicians of two generations, recorded in *Chin-wen*, 149a, and Kuo, *Wen-shih Lun-chi*, 328. In the *Poetry* we find music mentioned in connection with banquets (*Shih*, 104–105, 119, 162–163, 202).

The toothed ornaments and the upright plumes,
The [small] responding drums and introducing drums,
The [big] suspended drums, the hand drums and the
    musical stones,
The resounding boxes and the musical clappers.
All being complete, the music is struck up.
The flutes all start; ringing is their sound;
Solemn and harmonious they blend their notes.
The ancestors listen; our guests come;
Long they watch the complete performance.[17]

The glimpses of the royal hospitality that we can glean from the
sources show clearly that it was varied and princely. The *Poetry* includes a stirrring description of a great hunt on "the grounds of the
Son of Heaven," and we have a bronze made by a feudal lord who
took part in a royal hunt and was presented, by order of the King, with
part of the game.[18] The King also fished with his guests, and we have
seen that he took the Marquis of Ching for a boat ride during which
they shot at birds.[19] In connection with almost all of these entertainments it is recorded that the King presents gifts, sometimes small, but
more often very consequential, to his guests.

Archery appears to have been the favorite sport—if that is the
proper term for it—of the ruling group. Archery contests are mentioned in connection with feasts and even, in the *Poetry*, with sacrifices, and with other occasions as well. The King frequently joined in
the shooting, and sometimes rewarded skillful performance.[20] There
is some evidence that already in Western Chou times, as later, the
shooting in these contests was a matter of highly stylized motion,
probably done in time with music, and that elegance of form was quite
as important as hitting the mark.[21]

The Kings went among their subjects on a variety of occasions. One
inscription begins by saying that the King turned the soil at a certain

17. *Shih*, 245–246. I have followed the translation of Bernhard Karlgren almost
completely, except that he translates "in the courtyard of Chou" where I translate
"at the court of Chou." Karlgren's translation is in accord with those of Waley,
Legge, and Couvreur. It may be correct. But *t'ing* 庭 , which they translate here
as "courtyard," clearly is used to stand for the Chou court in *Shih*, 142, 230, 236.
In the context, I find my translation preferable.

18. *Shih*, 124. Ch'en, "Hsi-Chou T'ung-ch'i," (5).115–116.

19. *Chin-wen*, 40ab, 55a. Ch'en, "Hsi-Chou T'ung-ch'i," (6).85.

20. *Shih*, 69, 173–174, 202. *Chin-wen*, 30b, 40b, 55b, 69a, 107b. Ch'en, "Hsi-
Chou T'ung-ch'i," (5).121, (6).97–98, 105.

21. See especially *Shih*, 69, and Karlgren's notes.

field. This appears to be an early instance of the practice whereby the King inaugurated the planting season by breaking the ground with his own hand.[22] This inscription has been attributed to the reign of King Ch'eng, and in the *Poetry* we read:

> Oh! King Ch'eng,
> Brightly he came and drew near,
> Leading the husbandmen
> In sowing the various grains.[23]

The occasion described in this inscription was clearly a festive one. After the turning of the soil, there was archery, in which the King participated with a number of others. On the return trip, the King personally drove. Two men of rank preceded his chariot. The King rewarded them richly, and one of them cast this bronze, which has preserved the record for us.[24]

Not only the Kings but also the Queens carried on social activities of importance. We have already seen evidence that their lives did not conform to the pattern of sequestration that we sometimes think of as typical for royal consorts in China. In fact, women of position appear to have enjoyed a good deal of freedom in Western Chou times. The *Poetry* might lead us to suspect this, and the inscriptions seem to show it very clearly. Two bronzes, cast by a woman who was evidently the wife of a feudal lord, commemorate the fact that she was given cowries, jades, and other gifts by the King. In one of these she relates that the gifts were bestowed during a royal visit to her residence. This has been regarded by some scholars as scandalous.[25]

22. *Chin-wen*, 30b. The character *chi* 耤 is usually regarded as a noun, but here it seems clearly to function as a verb. The form in the inscription is a very graphic representation of a man holding an agricultural implement, with turned soil under his feet; see Kuo, *Chin-wen Lu-pien*, 14b (the second page of this number).

I have found no other early evidence for this ritual breaking of the soil by the ruler. But the Chou traced their descent from an agricultural deity, and the *Poetry* seems to indicate that King Ch'eng personally took part in some ceremony exhorting the farmers to till and sow; see below. The *Discourses of the States* includes a long account of this ceremony, in a conversation that is supposed to have taken place in Western Chou times (Kuo-yü, 1.6b–8b); the account was clearly written much later, so that its value as evidence is problematical. The *Records on Ceremonial* repeatedly refers to ritual plowing by the ruler, and one passage says that it was done by King Wu. See *Li-chi*, 14.20a, 39.14a, 48.1a, 11b–12a; Legge, *Li-chi*, I, 254–255, II, 124, 222, 231.

23. *Shih*, 244. This translation varies only slightly from that of Karlgren, but a good deal from those of Waley, Legge, and Couvreur. I believe that the rendering I have given is justified by the text.

24. *Chin-wen*, 30b–31a.

25. Ch'en, "Hsi-Chou T'ung-ch'i," (3).91–93.

We have a number of inscriptions that refer to the activities of Queens.[26] Queens had their own officers, who were persons of high status.[27] We have seen that the Queen of King Ch'eng, who was probably the daughter of Duke T'ai of Ch'i, issued orders on some governmental matters, quite like those issued by the King. We see her traveling about the country with the King, and even accompanying him on a military expedition. A number of inscriptions acknowledge her gifts to various persons.[28] One records an entertainment given to her by Maker of Books Nieh Ling.[29]

One inscription, on a bronze cast by a Duchess Chi, relates that her husband, Duke Mu (of what state we do not know), built for the Duchess a temple in the Yu grove. The Queen, not forgetting the distinguished services of Duke Mu to the former King, went to the temple of the Duchess and there performed a ceremony in which she gave the Duchess a number of pieces of jade and four horses. The Duchess cast the bronze to commemorate this generosity.[30] Another bronze records that the Queen entertained Duchess Chi at a fishing party and caused her to be presented with three hundred fish.[31] The ladies were evidently rather intimate.

Not only the members of the royal family but also the King's officers must have maintained social relationships throughout the Empire that helped to hold it together. The commanders of royal garrisons and guard posts, and officers in charge of patrolling roads, must have come in contact with the local dignitaries. No doubt they were considered in some sense intelligence officers of the King, and no doubt they were; and there may well have been friction between them and local officials. The sources do not seem to record this, but perhaps we could not expect them to. There is some indication, however, that relations were not always hostile.

We have a number of inscriptions that concern Commander Yung Fu. He was evidently a very important man, in charge of a royal gar-

26. Ibid., (2).117–118.
27. *Chin-wen*, 102b. Ch'en, "Hsi-Chou T'ung-ch'i," (2).104.
28. *Chin-wen*, 3b, 14a. Ch'en, "Hsi-Chou T'ung-ch'i," (2).65, 76–77, 117–118, (3).65.
29. *Chin-wen*, 3b. Ch'en, "Hsi-Chou T'ung-ch'i," (2).76. The text reads 矢 令 偅俎于王姜. In the context, I interpret this to mean that Nieh Ling gave a feast, with both liquor and meat, to the Queen, Lady Chiang.
30. Ch'en, "Hsi-Chou T'ung-ch'i," (5).119–120). Ch'en Meng-chia deduces that the Queen here was in fact the Queen Dowager; this is quite possible, but the inscription does not seem to make it certain. Duke Mu had evidently been an officer of the former King.
31. Ibid., (5).120.

rison in the south guarding against incursions by the Huai I. He also had the responsibility of patrolling the road up to the state of Fu, which we know that he visited. And one inscription reports that one of the officers of Commander Yung Fu served the Marquis of Fu, who rewarded him with metal.[32]

It is quite generally held that offices in Western Chou were inherited. Ch'en Meng-chia says that many offices were hereditary both in the royal government and in the feudal states.[33] If this had been true, it would seem that it would have been difficult for the Kings to maintain their control of the Empire. In the Spring and Autumn period hereditary office was quite common, and this is certainly one of the factors that made for decentralization.

The evidence for hereditary office that is usually cited is the fact that a number of inscriptions recording appointment quote the King as saying such things as "continue"—or "carry on"—"the office of your father and your grandfather," or even "the former Kings ordered your father and your grandfather for successive generations to supervise . . . "[34] This seems rather convincing, and I formerly considered it definite evidence that offices were inherited. But after further study I believe that we have little indication that genuinely hereditary office played any major role in the Western Chou period.

It was evidently, and understandably, a matter of pride to occupy an office that had been held by one's ancestors for generations. It appears likely, therefore, that where this factor was present it would have been mentioned. Of the 184 inscriptions of my corpus, some eleven record appointments to office with the statement that the same function had been performed by one or more of the appointee's ancestors. But there are some thirty-four appointments, more than three times as many,

---

32. See: Ch'en, "Hsi-Chou T'ung-ch'i," (5).107–111. *Chin-wen*, 59b–62a. Hsü, "Yü Ting," 59–60. There are many problems involved in the explanation of these inscriptions; I have principally followed the interpretation of Ch'en Meng-chia.

33. Ch'en, "Hsi-Chou T'ung-ch'i," (6).92, 94. Cho-yun Hsu, "Western Chou Government," 520, suggests that perhaps "at one time the heredity of office was a standing rule," but that late in the dynasty it was not always followed.

34. *Chin-wen*, 73b, 88b, 96b. For discussion of these formulas, see Ch'en, "Hsi-Chou T'ung-ch'i," (6).93. Ch'en interprets *shih* 世 , occurring in *Chin-wen*, 88b, as equivalent to *shih* 襲 and as having the sense of "inherited," but I believe that at most we are justified only in understanding it in the sense of "for successive generations." In the same inscription he reads *ssu* 司 , which normally means "to take charge of," as a loan for *ssu* 嗣 , "to inherit," but I see no reason why it cannot have its normal sense in this and other similar contexts.

with no mention that the office had ever been held by an ancestor.[35]

We could not, it is true, expect hereditary officers at the beginning of the dynasty; no one could succeed his grandfather as an official of the Chou Kings until they had reigned for some time. And in fact all eleven appointees who were named to succeed ancestors were appointed in the second half of Western Chou. But over against these we have, in the same period, twenty-six appointments that do not mention ancestors. Furthermore, of the eleven appointees who carried on the office of ancestors, eight are named in inscriptions dated to a period of only fifty-one years, from 946 to 895 B.C. This brief period occurs just after the middle of Western Chou. Appointment to offices held by ancestors was not (insofar as this evidence indicates) characteristic of its first half, nor was it very prevalent in its latter years.

Neither is it the case that offices held by several generations of the same family were distinctly more important, or less important, than others. In this respect there seems to be no definite pattern.

Furthermore, it is by no means certain that men who were appointed to offices that had been held by their ancestors must have inherited them. Even today, men of two or more generations of the same family may hold the same office, where there is no question of inheritance. If offices were hereditary in Western Chou, the heir should have come into the office almost automatically at the death of his father, or should at least have been recognized to hold a compelling right to the office. But we have some evidence that this was not the case.

In some cases we find the same man appointed at different times to various offices, only one of which is said to have been held by one or more of his ancestors. And this one was not always the first office he held.

We have already encountered Steward K'e. K'e held many offices. In a recently published inscription the King says to him:

> Formerly I appointed you [to office]. Now I continue
> and extend your charge, ordering you to take the place

---

35. I do not say "some" as a mere excuse for carelessness. It is not always easy to be sure of what is an appointment to office in the inscriptions, and it is best to leave some margin for possible error. I have not included among these appointments to office *Chin-wen*, 115b, in which a Marquis is ordered, "succeed your father and your grandfather in being Marquis"; that fiefs were commonly hereditary was stated earlier. Neither have I included ibid., 86b, in which the King in making an appointment tells the appointee that "for generations your sons and grandsons" are to carry on the function; this is a case of prospective heredity, which will be discussed below.

of your grandfather and father, in charge of [the office of] Assistant Tiger Retainer.[36]

It is evident that it was only after being in the King's service for some time that K'e was appointed to this office that had been held by his ancestors. That it was inherited appears dubious. Among the various offices that K'e held (which will be considered later), this one was relatively unimportant, so that if inherited office played any role in his career at all, it was clearly minor.

That appointment to office that had been held by ancestors definitely did not always involve inheritance is demonstrated by two very interesting inscriptions cast by an official named Li. He appears to have served successively under King Li (878–828 B.C.) and King Hsüan (827–782 B.C.). From the language in which he is addressed and the gifts he receives, it is evident that he was a person of consequence. The precise meaning of the titles bestowed upon him is uncertain; he was, certainly, a musician, and he was probably one of those in general charge of music at the court. A bronze vessel unearthed by a farmer in 1957 bears an inscription that says:

> The King ordered . . . to command Li saying, "Take the place of your grandfather and father in charge of [the office of Master of] Bells."[37]

This newly discovered inscription provides the background for another one that has long been known, which comes from the following reign. In it, the King is quoted as saying to Li:

> Previously, the former King . . . ordered you to take the place of your grandfather and father in charge of [the office of] Lesser [Master of] Bells.[38] Now I continue and extend your charge, and order you to take charge of your grandfather's old office, [as both] Lesser [Master of] Bells and Striker of Bells.[39]

36. *Ch'ing-t'ung-ch'i T'u-shih*, 27.
37. Kuo, *Wen-shih Lun-chi*, 328–332. Kuo suggests, quite plausibly, that the office in question here is one that is named in the *Ritual of Chou*. See *Chou-li*, 24.5ab; Biot, *Tcheou-li*, II, 62–63.
38. There seems to be no discernible reason for the introduction of the qualification of this office as "Lesser," which did not occur in the earlier inscription. The discrepancy is simply a fact. I do not think, however, that this casts doubt on the genuineness of either inscription. Such things are more likely to be encountered in genuine inscriptions, which reflect the irregularities of life, than in the work of forgers, who tend to avoid them.
39. *Chin-wen*, 149a. Kuo Mo-jo, in *Wen-shih Lun-chi*, 328–332, has greatly revised his earlier interpretation of this inscription.

It seems quite clear that these inscriptions do not involve hereditary office. It appears that Li's grandfather held two offices: Master of Bells and Striker of Bells. His father was appointed to the former, and Li was later appointed by King Li to this same office. The succeeding King, Hsüan, appointed Li to hold both offices. Thus Li's father never did hold the office of Striker of Bells, and it was only in the eleventh year of King Hsüan, as the inscription tells us, that Li finally was appointed to hold both of the offices that his grandfather had filled.

All this does not mean that there was no hereditary office in the Western Chou period. Apparently there was. In one inscription the King orders an officer to act as assistant to another, and then says that his "sons and grandsons, for generations," are to perform the same function.[40]

It is rather surprising, in fact, that we find so little definite evidence of hereditary office in Western Chou. Fiefs seem to have been, for the most part, hereditary in fact if not in theory; and in a culture in which the family was so important, there was undoubtedly strong pressure on the King to appoint each official's heir to the same office. At the end of Western Chou its last King was killed, and his son was installed, as King P'ing, in the eastern capital under the tutelage of a group of feudal lords. The *Tso-chuan* quotes an officer as saying:

> When King P'ing removed to the east, seven families of us followed him, and he was dependent on them to supply victims for his sacrifices. He granted them a sworn covenant, sacrificing a red bull, saying: "From generation to generation you shall not lose your offices."[41]

If inherited office had been the regular practice in the Western Chou period, there would seem to have been no need for this sworn covenant just after its conclusion. It was probably given in response to importunities that the King, now powerless, could not resist.

There must have been similar pressure throughout Western Chou, but most of the time the Kings appear to have been strong enough to withstand it. In the bronze inscriptions of my corpus, almost all of the appointments to office succeeding ancestors occur, as has been said, in a period of fifty-one years just after the middle of Western Chou. Although this data is certainly far from conclusive, it may be that the Kings then came to feel that this practice tended to concentrate too

---

40. *Chin-wen*, 86b. Ch'en Meng-chia ("Hsi-Chou T'ung-ch'i," (6).97) deduces from this inscription that offices of this category were regularly hereditary, for which I see no ground.

41. *Tso*, 445::449 (Hsiang 10).

much power in particular families, and therefore virtually discontinued it.[42] Certainly it was the case that in the Spring and Autumn period inheritance of office was an important factor in sometimes rendering not only Kings but also rulers of states powerless to exercise effective control.

In an effective administration the ruler must have reasonable freedom to select, appoint, and promote his officials on the basis of ability and performance. There are many indications that the Western Chou Kings were able to do this.

It was noted earlier that the Kings, in assigning tasks to their officers, appear in many cases to have paid little attention to the question of whether the title held was—insofar as we can judge—appropriate to the particular function to be performed. It is reasonable to suppose that what they did pay attention to, in making such assignments, was past performance. We also find in the inscriptions a number of individuals who are appointed, at various times, to a number of different offices. It is logical to assume that the ruler, in making a second appointment, took into account the manner in which the appointee had discharged his previous functions. Unfortunately, however, since it is not easy to date bronze inscriptions within a narrow range of years, it is commonly very difficult if not impossible to determine with any precision the sequence in which offices were held.

We can, however, see with some clarity the development of a career in one type of situation: that in which a man is appointed as an assistant to another holding a particular office, and then appointed to the office itself. Even if we cannot date the bronzes, it is unlikely that the appointment as assistant is the later. One case is especially clear. An inscription quotes the King as ordering Commander Tui to act as Assistant Runner of Horses; this was cast in the first year of the King. An inscription of the third year quotes the King as saying to Tui: "I have already ordered you to . . . have charge of [the office of] Assistant Runner of Horses. Now I . . . order you to have charge of [the office of] Runner of Horses."[43]

---

42. As was pointed out earlier, among the inscriptions of my corpus only eleven record appointments of men whose ancestors are said to have held the same office, and eight of these fall in this fifty-one–year period. Of the remaining three inscriptions, two concern the same officer, the musician Li, so that only two individuals figure as receiving such appointments after this period.

43. *Chin-wen*, 154a, 155b. For other cases of apparent promotion of assistants, see Ch'en, "Hsi-Chou T'ung-ch'i," (6).96–97.

A number of men named as high royal officials, including some of the highest, are also found in various lower offices. It is reasonable to suppose that they worked their way up, though this is usually difficult to prove.[44]

We have already met the officer K'e, who held various titles. He is mentioned on a number of bronzes, including some long known and others only recently unearthed or published. These inscriptions present the usual problems, insofar as chronological sequence and other questions are concerned, but they give us nonetheless some very interesting glimpses of a career. Kuo Mo-jo believes that K'e served both King Í (894–879 B.C.) and King Li (878–828 B.C.); T'ang Lan calls him "a man of the time of King Li."[45]

In a lengthy inscription that has long been known, K'e holds forth concerning the virtues, and the great services to the royal house, of his grandfather. This looks rather like boasting. But in another, only recently published, the King addresses him as follows:

> Commander K'e! When the greatly illustrious Kings Wen and Wu received the great Decree and grandly came into possession of the four quarters your ancestors exerted themselves for the Chou realm. They protected the Kings' persons from harm and acted as their claws and teeth.

This makes K'e's remarks concerning his grandfather seem rather modest, compared with the claims that he might have made.[46]

In the inscription in which he lauds his grandfather, K'e relates that the King, remembering the illustrious services of his grandfather, "selected K'e for the King's service, to take out, and to bring in [reports about], the King's orders."[47]

It seems impossible to be completely certain of the sequence in

44. The difficulty is not only one of proving which inscriptions are chronologically earlier, but also the possibility that where men are denoted only by a name of a single character, such as K'e or Yao, they are not always the same individual. Those who have worked closely with these materials do not doubt that numerous offices were held by these men, but they often differ concerning details. For some discussion of official careers, see: Ch'ing-tung-ch'i T'u-shih, 6. Kuo, "Ch'ang-an Ming-wen," 4. Ch'en, "Hsi-Chou T'ung-ch'i," (1).165–167, (6).116.

45. The career of K'e is discussed by T'ang Lan in Ch'ing-t'ung-ch'i T'u-shih, 6, and by Kuo Mo-jo both in Chin-wen, 110b–111b, and in "Ch'ang-an Ming-wen," 4. Kuo Mo-jo interprets the inscription that he publishes in Chin-wen, 110b, as being made by the same K'e; this may well be true, but I have left it out of account.

46. Chin-wen, 121a. Ch'ing-t'ung-ch'i T'u-shih, 27.

47. Chin-wen, 121a.

which K'e held his various offices. It appears that his ancestors were
—among other things, no doubt—military men; and T'ang Lan suggests, with a good deal of plausibility, that early in his career he held
the title of Commander.[48] One inscription reads: "The King personally
ordered K'e to patrol the area from Chīng east up to the Ching garrison."[49] In another the King addresses him as Commander K'e, and
says: "Formerly I appointed you [to office]. Now I continue and extend your charge, ordering you to take the place of your grandfather
and father in charge of [the office of] Assistant Tiger Retainer."[50] This
was a fairly important military office.

A bronze vessel unearthed in 1961 bears an inscription relating
that, in a court ceremony, the King commanded K'e, as Supervisor of
Makers of Books, to deliver the King's orders to a Commander who is
entrusted with a certain office.[51] Kuo Mo-jo says that the Supervisor
of Makers of Books was the chief of all of the officers of the secretarial
category.[52]

It seems probable that K'e reached the highest point of his power as
Steward. As Steward we see him receiving many rich gifts, including
people and lands in various places, and performing various functions
in the royal government. For instance: "The King ordered Steward
K'e to promulgate orders in Ch'eng-Chou to rectify the eight armies."[53]
It was probably as Steward that K'e had the important duty of "taking
out, and carrying in [reports about], the King's orders."[54]

These inscriptions tell us a good deal. K'e was descended from ancestors who had served the Chou house with distinction from the time
of the conquest, and this undoubtedly had something to do, as he tells

48. *Ch'ing-t'ung-ch'i T'u-shih,* 6.
49. *Chin-wen,* 112a.
50. *Ch'ing-t'ung-ch'i T'u-shih,* 27.
51. Kuo, "Ch'ang-an Ming-wen." Kuo indentifies this K'e as the individual
named in the other inscriptions under discussion.
52. Ibid., 2–4. Presumably Kuo means that the Supervisor of Makers of Books
had this inclusive responsibility at this particular time. As we have seen, the names
of offices and the functions and power attaching to them tended to change considerably over time. Concerning the title *Tso-ts'e Yin* 作 冊 尹, see also: *Chin-
wen,* 152b. Ch'en, "Hsi-Chou T'ung-ch'i," (6).106. Ssu, "Liang-Chou Chih-kuan
K'ao," 15–16.
53. *Chin-wen,* 121ab, 123a, 123b, 124b.
54. The inscription in *Chin-wen,* 121ab, consists of two quite distinct parts.
The first is a general one in which K'e lauds his grandfather and tells us of his own
selection for the royal service, to promulgate the King's orders. The second part
reports a specific charge and refers to K'e as Steward. The inscription seems to
imply that the transmission of orders was a part of his service as Steward, but this
is not completely certain.

us, with winning him preferment. But it is hardly likely that he would have been appointed successively to such a variety of important posts if he had not proved his own mettle. Only one of the specific offices he occupied is said to have been held by his ancestors, and he was not appointed to that at the beginning of his career.

As we have seen, it appears probable that all high royal officials were feudal lords. They were not always designated by feudal titles, though we do encounter reference to the "Duke Grand Secretary," "Duke Grand Protector," "Director of Horses Earl of Ching," and so forth.[55] We have also considered the probability—which seems to be indicated by such data as we have—that in most cases such royal officials had their fiefs, as a matter of necessity, fairly close to one of the two seats of the royal government. But feudal lords holding the more distant fiefs would have had much less occasion for contact with the royal court—a condition very disadvantageous from the royal point of view.

Medieval European rulers had the same problem, and they tried to overcome it by having the sons of vassals reared as pages in the household of the lord. This served the dual purpose of educating the future vassal in the arts of war and the etiquette of the court, and of—it was hoped—forging ties of loyalty.[56] There seems to be no indication that the heirs of vassals were reared by the Western Chou Kings, but it is not unlikely that some of them spent some time in the royal service, and at the royal court, before succeeding to the rule of states.

We saw earlier that Maker of Books Nieh Ling reported, in an inscription, that he had given an entertainment—probably a banquet—to the Queen of King Ch'eng. This was done at a place in the east, while the Queen was accompanying her husband on a military expedition against the Earl of Ch'u. The Queen responded with gifts for Nieh Ling: ten double strings of cowries, ten families of retainers, and one hundred men of servile status. The royal party was no doubt on the move, and the Queen had these presents bestowed on Nieh Ling at the place where he was on guard duty. Thus we see that, although his title was Maker of Books, he was apparently on military service.[57]

In a second inscription we see Maker of Books Nieh Ling assisting the son of the Duke of Chou, Ming Pao. Ming Pao here figures as a

---

55. Ch'en, "Hsi-Chou T'ung-ch'i," (1).170, (2).111, (6).95. *Chin-wen*, 27a, 78b.
56. Bloch, *Feudal Soicety*, 225–226.
57. *Chin-wen*, 3b. Ch'en, "Hsi-Chou T'ung-ch'i," (2).76–79.

principal officer of the King, and Nieh Ling is entrusted by him with important commissions, and given gifts.[58] It is not difficult to visualize Nieh Ling as a scion of a prominent family, serving about the court in capacities that are by no means inconsiderable, moving easily among the great, even including the Queen, serving his turn at military duty, becoming fitted and seasoned for more onerous responsibilities. Both of these bronzes were reportedly dug up, in 1929, not far from the site of the eastern capital.[59]

In 1954 a boy digging in a field in Kiangsu province, not a great distance from the east coast of China, found a bronze vessel bearing an important inscription that, many signs indicate, was probably cast by Nieh Ling.[60] But here he is not called Maker of Books, but "Nieh, Marquis of Ch'ien."[61]

The Marquis was accompanying the King on an inspection of his eastern territories. When the royal party arrived at I, the King enfeoffed Nieh with the state of I, at the same time presenting him with many gifts including various lands and people of different categories. Thus whereas the newly enfeoffed vassal refers to himself at the beginning of the inscription as "Nieh, Marquis of Ch'ien," at its close he calls himself "Nieh, Marquis of I." The state of I has not been certainly identified. It is plausibly believed, however, to have been located in the general area in which the bronze vessel was found.[62]

There is a very logical progression in these events. We see Nieh

58. *Chin-wen*, 5b. Ch'en, "Hsi-Chou T'ung-ch'i," (2).86. He is not called "Nieh Ling" here, but "Nieh" and "Ling" by turns.

59. Ch'en, "Hsi-Chou T'ung-ch'i," (2).77–78.

60. "Chiang-su Tan-t'u Hsien T'ung-ch'i." Ch'en, "Hsi-Chou T'ung-ch'i," (1).165–167. This vessel twice refers to its maker as Nieh, and calls his father Fu Ting 父丁, as does *Chin-wen*, 5b–6a. This vessel is evidently from the time of King Ch'eng or his successor, and in one of the previous vessels we saw Nieh Ling entertaining, and being rewarded by, the Queen of King Ch'eng. Ch'en Meng-chia (loc. cit.) and Kuo Mo-jo (*Wen-shih Lun-chi*, 311) both think that these three vessels were probably cast by the same man. Barnard ("A Bronze of Western Chou Date," 39–40) recognizes the points that link these bronzes, but considers the identification "highly improbable." For further evidence in support of this identification, see pp. 472–473.

61. The location of Ch'ien 虔 is not known, nor is it even certain that this is the character that occurs in the inscription; see T'ang, "I Hou Nieh Kuei K'ao-shih," 81–82.

62. For some of the many studies of this inscription, see: Ch'en, "Hsi-Chou T'ung-ch'i," (1). 165–167. Kuo, *Wen-shih Lun-chi*, 308–311. T'ang, "I Hou Nieh Kuei K'ao-shih." Barnard, "A Bronze of Western Chou Date." All of these scholars except T'ang Lan date this bronze to the time of King Ch'eng, which I believe to be correct; T'ang, however (op. cit., 81), places it in the following reign, that of King K'ang.

Ling at the court, holding the office of Maker of Books and carrying out commissions for the son of the Duke of Chou. We see him accompanying the King on a military expedition, assigned to duty at a guard post, and on such terms of acceptance in court circles that he can entertain the Queen at a banquet. At some point—just when is not clear—he succeeded to his father's fief. The King then takes him along on an inspection tour of his territories, to an area not far from the ocean and the Yangtze River. This must have been very near the southeastern corner of the territories that the Chou could pretend to control—an area constantly menaced by very fierce barbarians. It is not surprising that the King chose this vassal, trained and seasoned by service at the court, and on terms of intimacy with the royal family, to hold it for him.[63]

The case of Nieh Ling is perhaps the one of this kind that is best evidenced in our sources, but it is unlikely that it was unique. Various royal officers refer to their fathers as holding the titles of feudal lords; some of them were no doubt younger sons, but others were surely destined to succeed to fiefs. Even the Marquis of E, apparently before he succeeded to the title, performed military service in an army under the orders of the King and was rewarded for outstanding achievement in fighting barbarians.[64]

We have seen that K'e says proudly that he was "chosen for the King's service." There was a definite concept of the King's service, and a good deal of *esprit de corps* among those who belonged to it. The *Poetry* says:

> All the officers,
> Early and late, are engaged in service.
> In the service to the King there must be no flaw,
> But I grieve for my father and mother.

Time after time in the poems we read that "in the service to the King there must be no flaw," usually followed by a lament at the heavy

63. The fact that the state of I 宜 does not seem to be mentioned in later times may indicate an unfortunate outcome; the Marquis, or his heirs, may have been unable to hold the area. It must also be noted that there seems to be no certain evidence that the inscription in which Nieh is called Marquis is later than the other two. It seems very improbable, however, that a vassal charged with so distant and dangerous a fief would thereafter be found in prolonged service at the court. Ch'en Meng-chia ("Hsi-Chou T'ung-ch'i," [1].167) supposes the inscription in which he is called Marquis to be the latest of the three.

64. *Chin-wen*, 106a–107a.

burden. But there is never any suggestion of any inclination not to follow the path of duty, and sometimes it looks as if the one who complains is using this as a subtle method of making it clear that he is a very important person who carries heavy responsibility.[65] Another poem says, "In the service to the King there are many difficulties, but it is urgent."[66]

Were men educated for the King's service? It is tempting to think so. In the *Documents* there is an official title that Karlgren translates as "tutors of the noble youths,"[67] and several titles of officers that occur in the bronze inscriptions are explained as being those of teachers.[68] This may be correct, but unfortunately the contexts never seem to make it certain.

One long inscription comes to us from Yü, an officer who had been the tutor of King K'ang. It quotes the King as acknowledging his indebtedness to Yü for his great services in giving the King his elementary education, and stimulating him to exert himself. The King then entrusts Yü with great responsibilities in the government and urges him not to hesitate to criticize his ruler.[69] This inscription is quite in harmony with the "Confucian" attitude toward the teacher—an attitude that was often exemplified in later history in the treatment that Emperors accorded their former tutors.

We saw earlier that the musician Li was the son and grandson of men who held office as musicians at the royal court, and that he was first given an office that both of these ancestors had held, and later another that had been held by his grandfather, though not by his father. But even before he was given his first office, he was taught and apparently tested. The second King under whom he served said to him:

> Previously the former King gave you elementary education. You were diligent [and showed yourself] fit [to be employed in the King's] service. He then ordered you to take the place of your grandfather and your father in charge of [the office of] Lesser [Master of] Bells.[70]

65. *Shih*, 78–79, 105, 111, 114, 157–158.
66. *Shih*, 112.
67. *Shu*, 42. Karlgren, "Glosses on the Book of Documents," (1).293.
68. *Chin-wen*, 138b (note in upper margin). Ssu, "Liang-Chou Chih-kuan K'ao," 11–12, 21.
69. *Chin-wen*, 33b–34b. Ch'en, "Hsi-Chou T'ung-ch'i," (3).93–97. That Yü was indeed an important officer under King K'ang can be seen from another inscription: *Chin-wen*, 35a–36a. Ch'en, "Hsi-Chou T'ung-ch'i," (4).85–90.
70. *Chin-wen*, 149a. Kuo Mo-jo revises his interpretation of this inscription in *Wen-shih Lun-chi*, 328–329.

The only actual school of which we seem to have any record was for the teaching of archery. An inscription records that "the King ordered Ching to supervise the archery school." It lists four classes of functionaries who studied archery there, and then goes on to say that on a certain day the King, with four other men, "practiced archery at the Great Pool. Ching taught untiringly," and the King rewarded him. Evidently the archery master not only taught his regular pupils, but also coached the King and other dignitaries when they shot.[71]

There are some strange echoes of these things in the later literature. Mencius says that schools having three different names were established by the Hsia, Shang, and Chou dynasties, and that the name of the one established under the Shang had the sense of "archery." The object of each of these schools, he says, was "to make clear human relations."[72] The *Records on Ceremonial* says that rulers in antiquity had schools for "elementary education" and for "higher education." The higher institution of the Son of Heaven was called the "Circular Moat," and that of a feudal lord was called the "[Hall of] the Semicircular Pool."[73]

In the Latter Han period there was built an institution called the "Circular Moat," which was connected with the Imperial University. Concerning Emperor Ming (A.D. 58–75), we read that he personally took part in the ceremonies at the Circular Moat, which included a feast and archery. Then the Emperor took part in a discussion, and scholars brought the classics and asked difficult questions, while a vast throng of people looked on.[74]

There was another association between archery and education in Han times. Students in the Imperial University were examined in a very curious manner. Various questions were written on tablets, which

71. *Chin-wen*, 55b–56a. What I have translated as "archery school" is *she hsüeh kung* 射學宮 , literally "archery study building." The *Book of Etiquette and Ceremonial*, in its description of the "great archery meeting," says that the archery master gives a demonstration of the correct manner of shooting, and stands behind the ruler and corrects his aim. See *I-li*, 16–18; Biot, *Tcheou-li*, I, 150–188.

72. *Mencius*, 3(1).3.10.

73. *Li-chi*, 12.3a; Legge, *Li-chi*, I, 219. In making these translations I have in part followed Karlgren, "Glosses on the Ta Ya and Sung Odes," 55–56. It is difficult to know how *Pi-yung* 辟廱 should be translated. Karlgren (*Shih*, 197 and 199) renders it as "(Hall of the) Circular Moat." Waley (*Shih*, 260) translates it as "Moated Mound." Legge (*Shih*, 463) has "hall with its circlet of water." William Edward Soothill (*The Hall of Light*, 124–131) translates it as "the Jade-Ring Moat." I have seen no certain evidence that it necessarily included a building, although it may have surrounded one.

74. *Hou-Han-shu*, 79A.1ab.

407

were then set up as targets. The examinees shot arrows at the targets, and each was required to answer the question on the tablet he hit. It is said that this method was used to make it impossible for the student to know in advance what his question would be.[75]

Is there any possible connection between the Imperial University of Han times and the royal archery school of Western Chou? It is very hard to say.

There can be little doubt that the Circular Moat associated with the Han University derived its name from Western Chou sources, since we find it mentioned in two famous poems in the *Poetry*.[76] And we have seen that an inscription tells us that when the Marquis of Ching visited the capital, the King took him to the Circular Moat, where they road in boats and shot arrows at birds.[77] In the inscription that mentions the archery school, we find the King shooting with others, and apparently being instructed by the archery master, at "the Great Pool."[78]

It is clear that already in Western Chou the shooting in archery contests was governed by ritual; one poem suggests, as Bernhard Karlgren points out, that there was a "kind of ritual dance connected with the contests in shooting." Certainly the demeanor of the contestants was considered of the first importance, in Western Chou as it was in later times.[79] It is entirely possible, therefore, that the training in the archery school was conceived as teaching decorum as well as skill.

We have seen that the *Records on Ritual* says that in antiquity there were schools of "elementary education"—*hsiao hsüeh* 小學, literally "small studies"—and of "higher education"—*ta hsüeh* 大學, literally "great studies." It is an interesting fact that in two Western Chou bronze inscriptions we find the first of these terms, "elementary education."[80] Certainly this does not necessarily imply the existence

75. *Han-shu*, 78.2a, commentary. *Hou-Han-shu*, 6.5b, commentary. Biot, *Essai sur l'histoire de l'instruction publique en Chine*, 115–116. Shryock, *The Origin and Development of the State Cult of Confucius*, 71.

76. *Shih*, 197, 199. The passage mentioned above (n. 74) in the *History of the Latter Han* dynasty, which describes the visit of Emperor Ming to the Circular Moat, also refers to the *Ling T'ai* (which Karlgren translates as "Divine Tower"), which is also mentioned in *Shih*, 197; see *Hou-Han-shu*, 79A.1b. There can be no doubt, I think, that the model was drawn from Western Chou.

77. *Chin-wen*, 40ab.

78. Ibid., 55b. Karlgren ("Glosses on the Ta Ya and Sung Odes," 55–56) discusses this inscription together with the traditions concerning the archery school.

79. *Shih*, 69, 173–174, 202.

80. In *Chin-wen*, 34a, the King refers to "my elementary education." The second occurs in *Chin-wen*, 149a; Kuo Mo-jo revises his interpretation of this inscription in *Wen-shih Lun-chi*, 328–329. Here *hsüeh* occurs as a verb meaning "to teach," a sense that it sometimes has in early texts. Thus we might translate the

of an elementary school. But since the inscriptions speak of "elementary education," there would seem to have been a definite concept of education, and at more than one level. Was there then a higher curriculum, of which archery was a part?

Certainly Chinese tradition has regarded the Circular Moat of Western Chou as a forerunner of the Imperial University of later times.[81] Karlgren says that it was the site of "the archery school hall." Arthur Waley says that it was "a holy place surrounded by water, where the sons of the Chou royal house were trained in the accomplishments of manhood." James Legge says that it was the site of "a building attached to the royal court, called a school or gymnasium . . . where archery and other arts were taught to the cadets of the royal House."[82]

What we can definitely say on the basis of the Western Chou sources is that there was a concept of the royal service and a concept of education at more than one level, and that in at least one case one officer was educated by the King to prepare him for the royal service. There was also a royal school of archery, at which various officers studied. They may have studied other subjects, there or elsewhere. As to that, we can only speculate.

In any feudal realm, the great problem of the overlord is that of control of his vassals. By the nature of feudalism, vassals must be allowed a large measure of self-government, but how is it possible to prevent their limited sovereignty from being transformed into complete sovereignty? In the long run it is commonly not possible, for which reason feudalism is often, as has been observed, a transitory phenomenon.

The Western Chou Kings succeeded in maintaining their feudal realm for a relatively long period. Many of the means by which they did it have already been considered, but some others remain to be discussed.

Mencius, speaking in his usual grand manner concerning antiquity in general, says:

> When the feudal lords appeared at the court of the Son
> of Heaven, this was called "giving a report of [their dis-

---

passage in question as "the former King elementarily educated you," or, more freely, "gave you elementary education."

81. See for instance the commentaries in *Mao-shih*, 16.1a–4b. See also Soothill, *The Hall of Light*, 124–131.

82. *Shih*, 197. Waley, *Shih*, 259. Legge, *Shih*, 458.

charge of their] functions." . . . [If a feudal lord] once failed to appear at court, he was reduced in rank. If he failed to appear a second time, he was deprived of some of his territory. If he did so a third time, the six armies removed him.[83]

This does not specify the frequency with which vassals were expected to visit the court, and in fact there seems to be no evidence in the sources of any such regulation.

There was clearly, however, the idea that vassals were supposed to make their appearance at the royal court. A bronze inscription from late in Western Chou says that Kings Wen and Wu "led and gathered together regions that had not come to court," and in one of the poems the King tells the Marquis of Hán to "keep in order those regions that do not come to court."[84] Another poem says that after the Hsü region had been conquered, it "came to court," evidently meaning that its ruler appeared at the Chou court in sign of submission. And an inscription states that after a great attack, twenty-six states of the southern I and eastern I "appeared"—presumably at the court, to pledge their future obedience.[85]

We have a record, as was mentioned earlier, of a visit to the court, early in Western Chou, by the Marquis of Yen, from the remote northeastern corner of the Empire.[86] How frequently the rulers of such distant territories could, or did, attend at the court is uncertain. But we have seen a number of cases of visits by various vassals to the court, sometimes in considerable groups.

These court visits must have accomplished several purposes. The entertainment and the gifts that were presented undoubtedly fostered good will toward the King. This social intercourse among the feudal lords, and between them and the King's ministers, promoted a sense of solidarity and common purpose and must have facilitated joint action in times of crisis—such as threats from the barbarians. These gatherings also, as the *Poetry* tells us, gave the King an excellent opportunity to appraise his vassals.[87]

The King kept watch over his feudatories in other ways. His own travels, sometimes called tours of inspection but probably more often not proclaimed as such, were one means. He also used emissaries.

83. *Mencius*, 6(2).7.1–2.
84. *Chin-wen*, 134b. *Shih*, 230.
85. *Shih*, 236. *Chin-wen*, 51a.
86. Ch'en, "Hsi-Chou T'ung-ch'i," (2).102.
87. *Shih*, 176.

One inscription reports that two officials were "dispatched to the feudal lords and the various Inspectors." From the context it seems fairly clear that this was a mission of inspection.[88] Another inscription says that the King sent Chung to "inspect" a certain state in the south, and in still another, Secretary Sung is sent by the King on a similar mission to the state of Su.[89]

The Queen of King Ch'eng sent Maker of Books Huan to "tranquilize" the Earl of I, and the King sent Yü to "tranquilize" the Earl of Teng.[90] In these two inscriptions I have translated two different characters as "tranquilize," because this seems in each case to be the most suitable English word.[91] One can only speculate as to their precise meaning. It is unlikely that these feudatories were in rebellion so that they had to be "pacified"; it may be that they were given help to put their states in order and strengthen their positions. It is generally agreed that these, too, were probably terms that denoted inspection.[92] Both of these Earls presented gifts to the royal inspectors. In fact, with only a single exception, all of the royal inspectors named in this paragraph and the preceding one report that they received gifts from those they inspected—usually handsome ones.

There were also officials resident in—or near—the feudal states they were charged with overseeing, who held the title of Inspector (*Chien* 監) and represented the King. But how many of them there were, and for how long this institution persisted, is a difficult question.

It will be recalled that after the conquest King Wu appointed his brothers—whether two of them or three is a much debated question—to be Inspectors over the Shang people.[93] When the Shang rebelled, these Inspectors joined with them and were eliminated when the rebel-

---

88. Kuo, "Pao Yu Ming Shih-wen," 2a. Ch'en, "Hsi-Chou T'ung-ch'i," (1).144, 158. Their reports that they received gifts are in exactly the same language as that used by others making trips of inspection. The identity of the "Inspectors" mentioned here will be discussed below.

89. *Chin-wen*, 17a, 71a. Ch'en, "Hsi-Chou T'ung-ch'i," (1).158, 166. The character I have translated as "inspect" in these two inscriptions is *hsing* 省 , which might more strictly be rendered as "examine." The forms in which the character occurs in these inscriptions are unusual. but Ch'en Meng-chia reads both of them as *hsing*, and I believe this is correct.

90. *Chin-wen*, 14a, 49b. Ch'en, "Hsi-Chou T'ung-ch'i," (2).117, 119.

91. The characters are an 安 and 寧 *ning*.

92. Ch'en, "Hsi-Chou T'ung-ch'i," (2).117-119.

93. Concerning the problem of whether there were two or three Inspectors, see: *Shih-chi*, 4.29–30, commentary; *Mémoires historiques*, I, 237, and n. 3. Ch'en, "Hsi-Chou T'ung-ch'i," (1).143–144. Ch'en gives the location of three fiefs, belonging to three brothers, from which they are supposed to have supervised the Shang people.

lion was crushed. But it would appear that new Inspectors were appointed in their places. For the Duke of Chou, in one of the *Documents* that dates from after the rebellion, says to the Shang people: "Now you have hastened about and served our Inspectors for five years."⁹⁴

There are a few scattered bits of evidence that there may have been a considerable number of Inspectors. In another of the *Documents*, which probably comes to us from King Wu, the King says:

> The King instructs his Inspectors about their governing and managing the people. . . . When the King gives injunctions to the rulers of states and the managers of affairs, what are his orders? He leads them on to nourish and to tranquilize the people. From of old the Kings have acted thus, and the Inspectors [therefore] have none to punish.⁹⁵

This sounds as if the Inspectors were empowered to punish rulers of states who did not rule as they should.

In 1958, while an athletic field was being leveled off, a bronze vessel of early Western Chou type was unearthed. Its inscription includes two characters that Kuo Mo-jo suggests probably mean "Inspector [of the state of] Ying."⁹⁶ And we saw above that one inscription appears to indicate that two officials were ordered to make a visitation of "the feudal lords and the various Inspectors." Apparently even the Inspectors were inspected.

Almost all of the references to Inspectors in the sources come from rather early in Western Chou. It may be that this was an institution that was used only in the early period, when the Kings were consolidating the Empire. The *Tso-chuan*, however, in an entry for the year 660 B.C., quotes an officer of the state of Ch'i as saying that two other Ch'i officers were "the Son of Heaven's two Guardians."⁹⁷ This has been interpreted as meaning that even as late as the Spring and Autumn period the King had resident officials to protect his interests in at least one feudal state, and that this may indicate a practice that

94. *Shu*, 65.
95. *Shu*, 46. Karlgren here translates "inspectors (i.e. feudal lords)," but I see no necessity for this interpretation.
96. Kuo, "Shih Ying Chien Hsien." Kuo points out that *chien* 監 could also be a man's name rather than meaning "Inspector," but he considers the latter more probable.
97. *Tso*, 159::159 (Hsi 12).

had been general in Western Chou. But this situation is so obscure that it is difficult to draw any definite conclusion from it.[98]

MONARCHIES enjoy a peculiar advantage in the special luster that attaches to the individual who is at once the permanent head and the symbol of the state. This luster cements loyalty among those who are privileged to associate with the monarch, even in humble capacities. It lends a particular desirability to anything that the ruler bestows, and especially to regalia that may be worn or used as a visible symbol of royal favor.[99]

This tendency to desire association with the head of the state is commonly deprecated as snobbery. Yet it is undoubtedly one of the most important factors that give cohesion and viability to any monarchy—and perhaps to any state. That the Western Chou Chinese had their full share of this human tendency is made clear in the *Poetry:*

> They appear before their lord, the King,
> Seeking their emblems of distinction.
> The dragon banners blaze,
> The carriage bells and the banner bells chime,
> The metal-ornamented reins tinkle.
> The gifts shine with splendor.[100]

The role of trappings for horses and chariots was discussed earlier. The Kings also presented their retainers with articles of clothing of various sorts, and there appears to have been some correspondence between the status of the individual and the color and other characteristics of the clothing he was given.[101] Flags and banners of various kinds were often bestowed by the King and were evidently prized highly.

The esteem in which flags have been held is, if viewed with com-

98. See Hsu, "Western Chou Government," 517–518, and Ku, *Ch'un-ch'iu Ta-shih Piao*, 10(Preface).1ab, 11.9b–11a. The character I have translated as "Guardians" is *shou* 守 , and in another passage in the *Tso-chuan* (and in another connection), *shou* is said to be equivalent to *chien* 監 , "inspector." But whether these officials in Ch'i, in the Spring and Autumn period, really had any connection with the Western Chou Inspectors, seems impossible to determine on the basis of our slender data.

99. It is interesting that the word "regalia," much used even in republics, derives from the Latin word for "king."

100. *Shih*, 246.

101. Ch'en, "Hsi-Chou T'ung-ch'i," (6).97, 112.

plete objectivity, astonishing. They are, after all, no more than pieces of cloth sewed together in various patterns. Yet among a great variety of peoples, from very ancient times to the present, they have functioned as almost—and sometimes quite—sacred symbols. The ancient Chinese had as much emotional involvement with flags as anyone else. In the *Tso-chuan*, which is full of romantic military episodes, many of them center about flags or banners. When Ti barbarians invaded the state of Wèi, the Marquis refused to abandon his flag in battle, which made the defeat of the Wèi army more disastrous.[102] The Western Chou sources give us no such detailed stories, but we have seen that in the *Poetry* descriptions of armies setting forth, and even of hunting parties, dwell in detail on the waving flags and banners with their various devices. And in the great triumphal ceremony celebrating victory over the Demon Territory, described in an inscription, banners have a prominent role in the pageantry.[103]

It must have been a matter of great pride to flaunt a banner that had belonged to one's father or one's grandfather. And in two inscriptions we find the King saying, "I give you your grandfather's banner." In two others the King presents articles of clothing that had belonged in one case to the recipient's father and in another to his grandfather.[104]

These cases present something of a problem. Since the King bestows them, these flags and clothing are evidently in some sense under his control; he or one of his predecessors had undoubtedly given them to the ancestor in question in the first place. Did the physical objects then revert to the King's possession at the death of the recipient? Or were they in the possession of his heirs who could not, however, use them until the right to do so was given by the King? It seems impossible to say, but one or the other of these situations must have obtained.

The idea, which has been widely held from an early time to our own day, that the Western Chou Kings did not and perhaps could not concern themselves with affairs within the fiefs of their vassals, is clearly fallacious. We have seen, for instance, that when the Grand Secretary Hsiung wished to give lands—which he had received from the King—to his subordinate Chung, he did not do so himself. Instead, the King made the presentation, telling Chung that Hsiung was giving him the land as his fief. And in the inscription in which he commemorated the

102. *Tso*, 126::129 (Min 2).
103. Ch'en, "Hsi-Chou T'ung-ch'i," (4).86–87.
104. *Chin-wen*, 34a, 65b, 141a, 154a.

event, Chung acknowledged the gift, not as from his direct overlord, but as from the King.[105]

A bronze unearthed in 1959 bears an inscription, dated to late in Western Chou, in which the King commands one of his subordinates to assist the Earl of Mi. In another inscription the King orders its author to act as assistant to a Marquis. In both cases the King gives presents to these assistants to feudal lords, for which they acknowledge the King's generosity.[106]

The King also appoints a Director of Horses to serve one of his vassals, whose feudal title is not stated.[107] In another inscription the King orders a man to succeed his grandfather and his father as State Ruler's Director of Horses, in a state of which the name is illegible.[108] In this case it is clear that the King not only appointed the holder of this office within the state, but had been doing so for generations. Both of these inscriptions are dated to the middle portion of Western Chou.

We have seen other indications, in previous chapters, that Kings and their officers concerned themselves in various ways with what went on inside feudal states. They must, in fact, have interfered a good deal. Traditions, recorded at a relatively early date, relate that on two occasions late in Western Chou Kings intervened decisively, dictating the succession to the rule of two important states. Neither of these episodes is mentioned in the Western Chou sources, but the sources give us very little light on any aspect of the late history of the period.

The genuine *Bamboo Books* says (as was mentioned earlier) that King Í (894–879 B.C.) "caused the feudal lords to boil Duke Ai of Ch'i in a cauldron." The *Historical Records* say that the King had the Duke disposed of in this unpleasant fashion so that he might replace him, as Duke, with his younger brother.[109]

The second case is more complicated. It is reported in the *Discourses of the States*, and the account is enlarged upon in the *Historical Records*. It appears that King Hsüan (827–782 B.C.) designated the second son of the reigning Duke of Lu to be his successor, although his elder

105. Ibid., 16a.

106. Kuo, *Wen-shih Lun-chi*, 347–348. *Chin-wen*, 65b.

107. *Chin-wen*, 57a. The title conferred here is *Chia Ssu-ma* 家司馬. This might be translated literally as "Family Director of Horses," but this would not make much sense. It seems quite clear that this is an office within the government of a state. In Spring and Autumn times *chia* often has virtually the sense of a "feudal estate," in fact a small state; whether that is its sense here is difficult to say.

108. *Chin-wen*, 77a. Ch'en, "Hsi-Chou T'ung-ch'i," (6).93–94.

109. For the sources concerning this event, and the problems of its chronology, see p. 344, n. 90.

son, Po-yü, was alive. On the Duke's death this younger son was installed as Duke I (815–807 B.C.). After he had reigned for nine years, the people of Lu killed him and set up the elder brother, Po-yü, as ruler. After this brother had reigned for eleven years, King Hsüan attacked Lu, killed Po-yü, and established Duke Hsiao in his place. Duke Hsiao then reigned for twenty-seven years.[110]

For what they are worth, these accounts indicate that even late in Western Chou the Kings were able to intervene decisively in the internal affairs of important vassal states, even on the eastern border of the Empire.

110. *Kuo-yü*, 1.8b–9a. *Shih-chi*, 33.22–25; *Mémoires historiques*, IV, 104–106.

13

The Dilemma of Western Chou

THERE is reason for the widely held conviction that the Western Chou Kings could not, with the resources and the techniques available to them, organize and maintain a centralized administration adequate to control the broad territories to which they laid claim. It was, indeed, virtually impossible. But the Chou rulers had one great advantage: they did not know this.

Francesco Guicciardini, reflecting on events in Renaissance Italy, makes a comment that is very pertinent.

> The pious say that faith can do great things ... The reason is that faith breeds obstinacy. To have faith means simply to believe firmly—to deem almost a certainty—things that are not reasonable; or, if they are reasonable, to believe them more firmly than reason warrants. A man of faith is stubborn in his beliefs; he goes his way, undaunted and resolute, disdaining hardship and danger, ready to suffer any extremity. Now, since the affairs of the world are subject to chance and to a thousand and one different accidents, there are many ways in which the passage of time may bring unexpected help to those who persist in their obstinacy.[1]

There must have been many reasonable men in China just after the Chou conquest who were fully aware of the dimensions of the task that these relatively inexperienced invaders from the west had undertaken, and of the odds against their success. This consideration probably encouraged the Shang to make their attempt to regain their freedom after the death of King Wu. A realistic evaluation of the probabilities

---

1. Guicciardini, *Maxims and Reflections*, 39.

may well have been a factor in causing his brothers, who had been appointed as Inspectors over the Shang people, to join in the rebellion. The response of the Chou court was not merely to crush the rebels, but to proceed to conquer a territory larger than that which the Shang had ruled. The Duke of Chou stated the objective clearly:

> We must go on, never flagging, to complete the work of
> King Wen, until it is so grandly all-encompassing that
> from the corners of the sea and the sunrising there are
> none who do not follow and obey.[2]

Faith and self-confidence could go no further.

The early Romans and the Chou were very different in some respects, but rather similar in others. It has been said that the Romans never made an equal treaty; they always insisted on being recognized as the superior party. So did the Chou. Their ruler was the Son of Heaven, which made the definition of the boundaries of his territory a very easy matter. The *Poetry* says:

> Under the vast heaven
> There is no land that is not the King's
> To the very borders of the earth
> There are none who are not the King's servants.[3]

Of course there were territories and people that were outside the Empire, but that status was *de facto* and not *de jure*. They represented— in theory at least—unfinished business. This theory that the Empire rightfully included "all under heaven" was one of the legacies that the Chou left to later China. It is for this reason that flags inscribed "Ambassador bearing tribute from the country of England" were affixed to the boats and carts bearing the embassy from Great Britain, headed by Earl Macartney, to Peking in 1793.

Much of the strength of the Chou position derived from its very extravagance. It is possible to argue and perhaps compromise with one who claims a particular piece of territory, but how can one deal with a King who claims the whole world? One can only deny and resist, or agree and submit. Hitler publicized the advantages of "the big lie"; but regardless of truth or falsity, the large claim has much to recommend it. It gets attention, even if that attention consists only of sneers. But if grandiosely stated intentions begin to be realized, the sneers change to wonder. And in time the scoffers decide that they had better join the winning side before it is too late.

2. *Shu*, 62.
3. *Shih*, 157–158.

The early Western Chou Kings must obviously have been men of boundless energy, as unsparing of themselves as of others. They were also earnest, to the utmost degree. The more sophisticated of those around such men often find them amusing—until they one day realize that, both for good and for ill, a historical phenomenon is seldom really amusing. King Wen and King Wu became legends, and it is fairly evident that they must have been regarded as almost legendary even by their contemporaries.

It has often been said that in fact the Chou Kings were merely suzerains—overlords of their vassals but without power to interfere in the vassals' states—rather than sovereigns. The extent to which this may have been true may be debated. But what is beyond question is that it was no part of the intention of the early Kings to establish a realm of which they were not in full control. They had not conquered "all under heaven" merely for the sake of giving it away.

The Kings could not do everything themselves—though some of the early ones seem to have made a considerable effort in this direction. To perform various functions, they appointed officials. They also set up feudal lords over various portions of their territory. But the status of these vassals appears to have been definitely subordinate to that of the King's officials, and it seems to be implied in the *Documents* that the royal Inspectors were empowered to punish feudal lords whom they judged to be remiss.[4]

Perhaps the greatest contribution that the feudal lords made to the Chou realm lay in the fact that they provided government, on the local level, within their states, but this is almost never mentioned in the sources. It may be that the Kings did not wish to admit that it was beyond their power to oversee, always and everywhere, every one of their subjects; and in fact we constantly see stressed the concern of the Kings for the common people, even the humblest. But the function of the feudal lords that is mentioned most frequently is that of protecting the royal house.

King Wu, the founder of the dynasty and of its government, regarded the feudatories as his instruments. He gave them explicit orders and made it clear that the orders were to be followed. He threatened one of them not only with the loss of his fief but also with death as the penalty for disobedience.[5]

There is little doubt that King Wu and others would have liked to

4. In *Shu*, 70–71, we twice find royal ministers named before feudal lords. Concerning the authority of royal Inspectors, see *Shu*, 46.
5. *Shu*, 39–48.

set up something like a bureaucracy: a government in which every official was charged with precise functions, and obliged to discharge them as directed. We have seen that Wu said that when officials depart from the course prescribed for them, and "promulgate innovations," they should be put to death.[6]

It has often been remarked that tightly centralized control over a very large territory can scarcely be achieved without the use of bureaucratic techniques. Feudalism has seldom proved successful for a long period of time as a means of governing a great area; Carl Stephenson says that we may "conclude that the feudal state . . . had to be small."[7] From this point of view the Chou tendency toward tight controls would seem to have been soundly motivated.

The difficulty was, of course, that the Western Chou rulers had no real concept of bureaucracy, or of how to make it work. The somewhat sophisticated techniques that would have been necessary to achieve tightly centralized control over the large realm they had conquered, for a long period of time, were in that day unknown—in China and perhaps everywhere. And even those techniques that they did know and use were applied so sporadically as to be ineffective. On the whole the Chou Kings seem to have spurned technique in favor of the personal approach.

This appears most clearly in connection with official titles. Although we cannot really construct a table of organization for the Western Chou government, we can get some idea of it, for there are a number of titles that appear to relate to various functions. But they are not used consistently. A Secretary leads armies. A Maker of Books is sent to inspect a feudal state, and another serves at a guard post. A military officer is made Steward, and then as Steward is commanded to rectify the royal armies. From the point of view of strict bureaucratic procedure, this is a Mad Hatter's Tea Party.

This procedure can be explained on the ground that the King was concerned to appoint the best man, regardless of title, for each particular task. Even though the disregard of title must have introduced some confusion, this is at least a defensible principle. But it seems clear that it was not always followed consistently, for in one period we find a number of cases in which men of three generations were appointed to the same post. It seems unlikely that these descendants were in each case the best qualified of all available appointees.

6. *Shu*, 42.

7. Stephenson, *Medieval Feudalism*, 76. Concerning the need for bureaucracy in a state of large size see Von Mises, *Bureaucracy*, 15, and Blau, *Bureaucracy in Modern Society*, 20.

Beginnings were made, in some respects, toward systematic supervision of the administration. Royal officers were sent to inspect the states of vassals, and resident Inspectors were installed to supervise some—possibly all—states. This could have developed into something like the Censorate, which checked on the entire official structure for the Emperors of later times, but there is no indication that it did. On the contrary, almost all of our information concerning such activity comes from early Western Chou, and we have little indication that it persisted beyond the early reigns.

BUREAUCRACY tends, it is generally recognized, to minimize if not to suppress the individual characteristics of the functionary. The professional bureaucrat is typically, as Max Weber has said, "a single cog in an ever-moving mechanism which prescribes to him an essentially fixed route of march."[8] It has often been observed that such qualities as independence, imagination, and originality do not commonly make for success in a tightly controlled bureaucracy; they may even make their possessors unfit to function within it. Bureaucratic functionaries should be highly trained for their particular duties and perform them as directed. The individual, as a person, is de-emphasized within the typical bureaucratic organization.[9]

In feudalism, on the contrary, personality is emphasized—at least among the ruling group. The ruler delegates limited sovereignty to his vassals and leaves them free to govern their fiefs as they will, within certain guidelines. A feudal lord, to be effective, must be intelligent and resourceful. In retainers, skills are certainly desirable—especially the ability to fight—but the greatest stress is laid on such personal qualities as courage and, above all, loyalty.

In Western Chou the great emphasis was undoubtedly personal. Above all, the focus was on the King. After death, Kings became in effect divinities. The *Poetry* says:

> The Chou march on in succession,
> Generation after generation producing wise Kings.
> Three rulers are in Heaven,
> And the King is their counterpart in the capital.[10]

By a kind of anticipation, the living King was quasi-divine.

8. Weber, *Essays in Sociology*, 228.
9. Blau, *Bureaucracy in Modern Society*, 14–19.
10. *Shih*, 197.

The King was not only the great overlord, but also the great model. He was of course the model for his vassals. But beyond that, the Duke of Chou asserted, he was the model for "imitation by the small people everywhere under heaven."[11] That there was genuine reverence for the royal person is evident throughout the sources. "In the service to the King there must be no flaw" is a constant refrain. Soldiers toiling on a distant expedition long to return home, but they are deterred, the poem says, not by fear of their officers, but because "we are in awe of the writing on those bamboo slips"—meaning, beyond doubt, the orders of the King.[12] All those who could allege any kind of association with the royal person, even at second hand, were eager to proclaim it. Thus when Maker of Books Mai was given some metal by his ruler, he used the occasion to cast an inscription that described in detail the entertainment given to his ruler by the King, and dated it "in the year in which the Son of Heaven favored Mai's lord, the Marquis."[13]

The Kings themselves, in their employment of their officials, appear to have given far more attention to personal factors than to the rational allocation of functions characteristic of an ordered bureaucracy. Several offices of quite different character were often given to the same man. Civilian officials were given military command, and the same individual was shifted from military office to civil, and back again.

This personal emphasis is what we should expect in a feudal regime. And undoubtedly the Western Chou administration was to some degree feudal from the beginning. But here again it was not wholly or consistently so, at least if it is judged by the standard of an ideal or "pure" feudalism. For the Kings injected themselves into affairs within fiefs to a very considerable extent. They gave presents, and even lands, to subordinates of their vassals. They appointed some of their vassals' officials. And even late in Western Chou we find the King ordering one of his officers:

> Open up the regions of the four quarters,
> Tax my territories and soil . . .
> Go through all the royal states,
> Go and draw boundaries, go and make divisions,
> All the way to the southern sea.[14]

11. *Shu*, 51, 80.
12. *Shih*, 112.
13. *Chin-wen*, 40ab.
14. *Shih*, 234. Some evidence that something like this may actually have been done is found in *Shih*, 227, and in *Chin-wen*, 142a and 143b.

Although we know little of the circumstances, this would seem to call for action that feudal lords might well have considered infringement on their autonomy.

THE Chou rulers were faced with a dilemma. They had to administer the broad territories they had conquered, if they were to hold them; and in the broadest terms they had two choices. They could install a completely feudal regime, partitioning their territories among vassals to whom they would give virtual autonomy within their fiefs, while demanding their loyalty to the King and their help, when it was needed, in war. Or they could attempt to set up a centralized government that would control the country through functionaries directly accountable in detail to the royal court. Neither alternative was wholly acceptable to them, and indeed neither was completely feasible.

Feudalism was to some extent forced upon the Chou, as it has been upon some other conquerors, by the necessity to reward, with lands, those who had assisted them. The early Kings were glad, also, to put much of their territory in the keeping of their relatives, upon whose loyalty they could hope to depend. But a feudal system that gave too much autonomy to vassals spread over such a vast area would quickly have dissolved into a group of independent states. It is clear that King Wu, and no doubt his successors, desired to keep the vassals under as tight a rein as possible. They kept watch over them by means of inspections by royal officials. They evidently established a machinery for taxation, though we know nothing of its early history. Above all they kept the preponderance of military power in their own hands, with many standing armies, and garrisons and guard posts in various localities. And they rather constantly interfered in the affairs of their vassals, in various ways. Thus while they had a feudal system, it was not without severe limitations. At the same time it should be noted that, except for the maintenance of the royal military strength, most of the techniques for the control of the feudal lords do not appear to have been systematically planned or firmly and constantly applied.

A royal government intended to exercise centralized control over the whole Empire was set up. But its organization is so elusive, and subject to such rapid change, that it appears unlikely that it was the product of profound thought. In fact the sources, whether the *Documents*, the *Poetry*, or the bronze inscriptions, while they indicate a great deal of interest in government, show almost no concern with the technique of administration. They have a great deal to say about good rulers and officials, and wicked ones, but almost nothing about methods by which a government can be made to work.

If we look at the way in which the rulers seem to have paid little regard even to such organization as their administrations did have—their apparent carelessness, for instance, in matching official titles with assigned tasks—it seems evident that they not only knew very little about the construction and maintenance of a carefully ordered official hierarchy, but cared less. Their approach was personal; their flair was for improvisation. Their style was that of the inspired feudal leader, not of the head of a bureaucracy.

Faced with the choice between presiding over quasi-independent feudal states or over a carefully organized official hierarchy, the Chou Kings found neither acceptable, and they accepted neither. Their state was a hybrid, which perhaps even they did not wholly understand. From the point of view of theory this is abhorrent, and may seem to have assured disaster. But the realities of politics and history often mock theory.[15]

It may well be that this kind of administration, with all of its inconsistencies, was the only one that could have achieved the all but impossible task of holding their subjects and their territories together in some degree of unity. If we may judge from the degree of change, this government had great flexibility; and in a situation like that of Western Chou, flexibility can be a great virtue. There were those, as there are in the case of every government, who were eager to attack it both from within and from without. But a regime that undergoes constant change does not suffer from the same weaknesses long enough to make it easy to attack them.

There were, nonetheless, points of great potential weakness and

15. An example of this may be found in the theory and the practice of bureaucracy. In theory a bureaucracy should function in the manner of a machine, with all of the individuals who compose it responding to the orders of their superiors and to no other stimuli. But in fact, of course, bureaucracies are composed not of cogs but of people, who respond to many different stimuli. They are not only motivated by personal friendships and enmities, but also form cliques that are devoted to furthering the personal interests of the members of the group. Such informal organizations, outside of and sometimes inimical to the formal administrative structure, may certainly interfere with efficiency, and this phenomenon has commonly been regarded as incompatible with the proper functioning of a bureaucracy. But Chester I. Barnard (*The Functions of the Executive*, 120) says that "formal organizations . . . create and require informal organizations." And Peter M. Blau (*Bureaucracy in Modern Society*, 56), while recognizing that the action of cliques often does militate against efficiency, says that "many studies have found that the existence of cohesive bonds between coworkers is a prerequisite for high morale and optimum performance of duties."

difficulty. Feudal lords must have chafed against the royal interference. Rivalries and enmities certainly developed between the King's officials and his vassals. Differences arose not only between various officials of the court, but even on occasion between the King and his officials. The scope for such troubles was especially great because of the lack of settled procedures consistently adhered to. Everything depended upon the personal capacity and impartiality of the King and his officers.

It has been observed that a principal weakness of benevolent despotism is the difficulty of ensuring an unending succession of benevolent despots. The Western Chou political system demanded that it be headed by a King of great energy, industry, and perspicacity, seconded by a body of loyal, trustworthy officials similarly endowed. Together they must be able to meet political, military, and economic problems with solutions that had to be, in large degree, improvised, since there was but a small body of carefully established technique and procedure. It was hardly to be expected that China could be so fortunate as to find such men in every generation.

THE history of the Western Chou period is almost unknown. We are fortunate in having ten important documents from the first half century of the period,[16] but for later times there is little that can be certainly dated that is highly informative. When Ssu-Ma Ch'ien compiled the *Historical Records*, around 100 B.C., he read widely in the extant sources and quoted extensively from them. But his history of Western Chou, after the earliest decades, leaves much to be desired. It consists largely of anecdotes; these may reflect attitudes and trends correctly, but their details, which are sometimes trivial and sometimes preposterous, do not always inspire confidence. And at some points even anecdotes fail, leaving only a skeleton. Three reigns, covering the years 934–879 B.C., are dismissed with a total of forty-nine characters, which tell us very little more than that the three Kings came to the throne and died.[17]

16. That is to say, all of the twelve sections of the *Documents* that I regard as of Western Chou date, except for the "Pi Shih" and "Wen Hou chih Ming"; see pp. 449–454.

17. *Shih-chi*, 4.51–52; *Mémoires historiques*, I, 268. It is true that these "basic annals" are intended to be only an outline, leaving more detailed information to be given elsewhere in the work. And there are a few bits of information elsewhere about each of these Kings; but in no case do they, added together, approximate a history of the reign.

The *Tso-chuan* contains a thumbnail sketch of the history of Western Chou, which seems to be the earliest thing of the sort that we have. The credentials of its supposed author are good, since he was the son of King Ching (544–520 B.C.). At the death of Ching, this son, Chao, contended unsuccessfully for the succession, and later succeeded in gaining the throne briefly before being driven into exile. After being expelled from the capital, he circulated a proclamation to the feudal lords, which began with a recapitulation of the history of the Chou house. The portion on Western Chou says:

> Anciently King Wu conquered Yin, King Ch'eng tranquilized all the lands of the four quarters, and King K'ang gave rest to all the people. They all gave fiefs to their brothers, in order that they might constitute a fence and a protecting wall for Chou, and they also said, "We will not monopolize the enjoyment [of the fruits] of the achievements of King Wen and King Wu." Furthermore, [they had another reason for establishing vassals:]in order that, if any of their descendants should go astray and be defeated or overthrown, and plunged into calamity, [the feudal lords] might help and rescue them.
>
> When [the throne] came to King Í, he suffered from disease, and all the feudal lords hurried to sacrifice, praying for his recovery. Coming to King Li, he was tyrannical and cruel. The myriad people found him intolerable, [so that he was forced to go into exile and] live in Chih. The feudal lords removed him from the throne, so that there was an interregnum [during which there was no] royal government. When [his son,] King Hsüan, [showed himself] possessed of character, [the feudal lords] handed over the government to him. When [the rule] came to King Yu, Heaven had no mercy on Chou. The King was benighted and perverse, so that he lost his throne.[18]

He also lost his life, and Western Chou ended with him.

There are a number of interesting points in this synopsis by Prince

18. *Tso-chuan*, 52.7a–8a. *Tso*, 714::717 (Chao 26). Couvreur, *Tso-chuan*, 411–412. My translation differs substantially from those of Legge and Couvreur, and with the interpretations of the standard commentaries, especially with regard to the events of the time of King Li. I believe that my translation does less violence to the evident sense of the text than do these standard versions, which seem to me to have been forced in order to make them conform with the orthodox tradition.

Chao.[19] One of the most striking is the fact that he mentions the achievements of Kings Wen, Wu, Ch'eng, and K'ang, and then omits any mention of the next five rulers, whose reigns covered more than a century and a half. He then names the last four rulers, but of them he praises only Hsüan.

This focus of attention on Wen, Wu, Ch'eng, and K'ang is a common pattern. We have seen that King Wen was celebrated above all others, and one of the Chou sacrificial odes says:

> Terrifying and strong was King Wu;
> How mighty his ardor!
> Grandly illustrious were Ch'eng and K'ang,
> Shang Ti gave them majesty.
> From the time of Ch'eng and K'ang
> We have possessed all the broad lands of the four quarters.
> How penetrating was their brilliance![20]

In the *Historical Records*, similarly, all of the Kings are depicted as able and energetic through K'ang. But in the time of his successor, King Chao, we are told that "the royal way became diminished and defective."[21] And thereafter the *Historical Records* has praise only for King Hsüan, and even this is rather overbalanced by lengthy criticisms.

This points to a rather surprising conclusion. Whatever the facts may have been, the tremendous prestige that Western Chou enjoyed in later times was based primarily on tradition relating to the achievements of only four Kings, of whom one—King Wen—died before the conquest. The other three reigned (according to the traditional chronology) only for the first seventy years of the dynasty. This is a brief period in which to establish a legend of such historic consequence as that of Chou.

Circumstances as well as personalities certainly had much to do with the events of these early reigns. Undoubtedly the achievements and the character of these four Kings have been exaggerated by tradition. But it is also perfectly certain that their feat was made possible, in very large measure, by the fact that during this brief time the Chou cause was served by a whole series of very remarkable men—not only Kings but also ministers, generals, and a host of more humble men

---

19. I translate *Wang-tzu* 王 子 , literally "King's son," as Prince. Some writers on early China translate all feudal titles indiscriminately as Prince, which seems to me confusing and undesirable.

20. *Shih*, 243.

21. *Shih-chi*, 4.42; *Mémoires historiques*, I, 250.

whose capacities may not have been more than normal but who became caught up in the sense that they were making history—as indeed they were.

It may seem improbable that a concentration of particularly able men should occur in one time and place, but it is not impossible. The most remarkable example of this is, no doubt, Greece in the "age of Pericles." The persons of note who spent all or part of their lives in the single city of Athens during the fifth century B.C. included among many others: Aeschylus, Alcibiades, Anaxagoras, Aristophanes, Aspasia, Euripides, Gorgias, Herodotus, Hippocrates, Pericles, Phidias, Pindar, Plato, Protagoras, Socrates, Sophocles, Thucydides, and Xenophon. Such things can happen.

THE same tendency that causes certain Kings to be singled out as heroes and given exaggerated praise causes others to receive less than their due. Western Chou Kings could not possibly have been so lacking in capacity, after the early period, as tradition indicates, or their realm would not have continued to flourish. Yet there was undoubtedly some slackening after the ebullience of the beginning years; this would have been almost inevitable.

The successor of King K'ang, King Chao (1052–1002 B.C.), reigned over an Empire that suffered little, insofar as our evidence indicates, from internal troubles, even though the *Historical Records* says that "the royal way became diminished and defective." But this was a time when the barbarians of the south were a frequent worry; no doubt the rising power of Ch'u was making itself felt. King Chao led a number of military expeditions in that direction, from the last of which he mysteriously failed to return.[22]

The reign of King Mu (1001–947 B.C.) became the subject of a number of legends, which attribute to him many military expeditions and other trips that, according to some interpreters, may have taken him even as far as Central Asia.[23] The *Tso-chuan* reports a conversation in which it is said: "Formerly, King Mu wished to give free rein to his desires and travel so extensively that the ruts of his chariot wheels and the marks of his horses' hoofs should be imprinted everywhere under heaven."[24] It appears that King Mu must, indeed, have

22. See pp. 233–235.
23. See p. 235. See also *Shih-chi*, 5.6, 43.3–4; *Mémoires historiques*, II, 5–6, V, 9–10. For an extensive discussion of traditions concerning King Mu's travels to the west, see Chavannes' note in ibid., II, 6–8.
24. *Tso*, 638::641 (Chao 12).

been a formidable traveler, but to separate fact from fiction in these stories is difficult if not impossible. The *Historical Records* says that in the time of King Mu "the royal way declined and diminished."[25]

Concerning the next King, Kung (946–935 B.C.), we seem to have virtually no information.[26]

The *Historical Records* says that in the time of his successor, King I (934–910 B.C.), "the royal house continued to decline, and poets wrote satires." Upon his death there may have been some kind of intrigue, although we have no record of it, for King I was not succeeded by his son but by his uncle, a younger brother of King Kung; this involved setting aside the son and heir of King I.[27] Concerning the reign of this uncle, as King Hsiao (909–895 B.C.), nothing of note is recorded.[28]

The next King, Í (894–879 B.C.), was neither the son nor the brother of Hsiao, but rather the son and heir of King I, who had previously been passed over. It will be recalled that Prince Chao is quoted in the *Tso-chuan* as saying that he "suffered from disease"; it could be for this reason that he had not initially inherited the throne.[29] But it is quite clear that some unusual maneuvering went on, for the *Historical Records* says that "the feudal lords again set up the heir of King I . . . this was King Í."[30] This is the first recorded instance in which the succession in the Chou house was determined, not by its members, but by its vassals.

Whether King Í conspired with those who placed him on the throne we do not know, but the *Records on Ritual* says that he was the first King to mingle in undue familiarity with the feudal lords in the court.[31] According to the *Historical Records*, the ruler of the state of Wèi gave

---

25. *Shih-chi*, 4.42; *Mémoires historiques*, I,.250.

26. There is one anecdote in which he is involved, in the *Discourses of the States*, which is repeated in the *Historical Records*, but it has very little to do with King Kung. See: *Kuo-yü*, 1.4ab. *Shih-chi*, 4.50–51; *Mémoires historiques*, I, 265–266.

27. *Shih-chi*, 4.51; *Mémoires historiques*, I, 268. Although the *Historical Records* here says that King Hsiao was a younger brother of King Kung, it says elsewhere (*Shih-chi*, 13.26) that Hsiao was a younger brother of King I. But Takigawa Kametaro, in his commentary on this latter passage, says that it is in error.

28. The *Historical Records* relates an anecdote which says that King Hsiao had the intention of naming an heir to a small state, but was dissuaded. But this has the appearance of legend, and refers to the activities of the supposedly early Emperor Shun, whose name does not occur in Western Chou material. See *Shih-chi*, 5.9–10; *Mémoires historiques*, II, 10–11.

29. *Tso*, 714::717 (Chao 26). Physical weakness was a ground on which an heir might be barred from succession; see ibid., 614–615::619 (Chao 7).

30. *Shih-chi*, 4.51; *Mémoires historiques*, I, 268.

31. *Li-chi*, 25.14a; Legge, *Li-chi*, I, 421.

many presents to King Í, and Í made him a Marquis instead of—as rulers of that state had previously been styled—an Earl. Whether this is true or not, it may reflect a climate of intrigue within the court.[32] In fact, we are told, "in the time of King Í the royal house was so weak that the feudal lords sometimes did not come to court, and fought among themselves."[33]

It is King Í of whom the genuine *Bamboo Books* says that he "caused the feudal lords to boil Duke Ai of Ch'i in a cauldron." The *Historical Records* gives more details, saying that the King did this because of an accusation brought against Duke Ai by another feudal lord. The King then established Ai's young brother as Duke Hu. Later another brother of Duke Ai attacked and killed Duke Hu, setting himself up as Duke Hsien.[34] Although it is difficult to be certain of the facts of these tangled affairs, there seems to be no doubt that, as T'ang Lan has said, the fortunes of the Chou house were at a low point.[35]

For a very long period the Chinese had been bothered very little by the barbarians. It may well be that the internal dissension within the Empire encouraged attacks against it from without. Bronze inscriptions and other evidence indicate that there were a number of barbarian invasions in the time of King Li (878–828 B.C.). The great invasion by a trusted vassal of the Chou, the Marquis of E, leading the southern Huai I and the eastern I, is dated to this reign. It will be recalled that although the King sent his fourteen armies against the invaders, they were not able to capture the Marquis. According to one opinion they were afraid to move against him, but it seems more likely that the invasion was mounted at so many points that they were fully occupied in meeting it. In any case, the capture of the Marquis of E was accomplished by troops under the command of a Duke Wu, whose

32. *Shih-chi*, 37.4; *Mémoires historiques*, IV, 192. Commentaries quoted in *Shih-chi*, 37.4–5, indicate skepticism concerning this story, and it seems justified. As has been pointed out previously, it is not clear that in Western Chou times the titles of Marquis and Earl had definite hierarchical meaning.

33. *Shih-chi*, 40.6; *Mémoires historiques*, IV, 340.

34. Wang, *Ku Chu-shu*, 8a. *Shih-chi*, 32.11; *Mémoires historiques*, IV, 41. *Kung-Yang Chuan*, 6.11a; 6(*Chiao-k'an Chi*).3a. The chronology is difficult. As it is given in Tchang, *Synchronismes chinois*, 36–37, the third year of King Í, in which the *Bamboo Books* places the execution of Duke Ai, was 892 B.C., while Duke Ai died in 894 B.C. A comment quoted in *Kung-Yang Chuan*, 6.11a, ascribes this deed to King I, but this does not help much because he is supposed to have died in 910 B.C. The account in the *Historical Records* does not say explicitly under what King Duke Ai was killed, but may imply that this was done before the time of King Í.

35. *Ch'ing-t'ung-ch'i T'u-shih*, 2–3.

identity is uncertain.[36] This inability of the King's armies to deal decisively with his enemies must have been a severe blow to his prestige and his power.

King Li is unanimously condemned as a wicked ruler. The *Discourses of the States* reports that he appointed as a high officer the Duke of Jung, who was extremely avaricious. When his councilors and others criticized the King for this, and for his cruelty, Li responded by employing a magician to point out the critics; everyone he indicated was put to death. The King was pleased when this silenced his detractors, but he was warned that he had not eliminated resentment, but only dammed it up.[37]

The inscription that reports the revolt of the Marquis of E at the head of barbarian tribes prefaces its announcement of this event with the words: "Alas! Woe! Heaven has sent down destruction upon all the states." The same sentiment, sometimes in the same words, is expressed in other bronze inscriptions and in numerous poems that are dated to the reign of King Li and to the next two—and final—reigns of Western Chou. The accuracy of this dating is not always certain; there is a tendency to date statements about bad conditions to times that are generally deprecated as evil. Yet there can be no doubt that there was, in the final century of the period, a sense of impending doom. The early reigns had been buoyed by the sense that Heaven was with Chou—a counterpart to the conviction in our own day that "God (or destiny) is on our side." This was now replaced by its reverse. Eclipses of the sun and other natural phenomena were interpreted as the results of bad government. The King and all those in authority were accused of incompetence or malevolence or both. One poem warns that "Heaven's Mandate is not conferred twice." Another says that "the people desire disorder."[38]

We saw that Prince Chao said:

> Coming to King Li, he was tyrannical and cruel. The myriad people found him intolerable, [so that he was forced to go into exile and] live in Chih. The feudal

36. See pp. 237–238. Hsü Chung-shu ("Yü Ting," 57–59) discusses at great length the hypotheses that Duke Wu was a ruler of Wèi, and that he was the Earl He of Kung who took over the royal prerogatives after King Li had been driven out. He concludes that Duke Wu was an important royal official, but that his identity is otherwise impossible to discover on the basis of our present evidence.

37. *Kuo-yü*, 1.4b–6a. *Shih-chi*, 4.51–55; *Mémoires historiques*, I, 268–274.

38. *Ch'ing-t'ung-ch'i T'u-shih*, 24. *Chin-wen*, 134b–135b, 139ab. *Shih*, 133–134, 135–137, 138–140, 140–141, 142–143, 144–145, 147–148, 210–212, 212–214, 217–219, 220–223, 224–226, 236–238, 238–239.

lords removed him from the throne, so that there was an interregnum [during which there was no] royal government.[39]

That there was such an interregnum is certain, but about the details there is much difference of opinion.

The *Historical Records* says that certain unnamed persons "joined in revolt and made a surprise attack on King Li. The King fled to Chih." (Chih was in what is now south central Shansi province.) The rebellion was evidently savage, for it is said that when the son of King Li (the future King Hsüan) took refuge in the residence of the Duke of Shao, the rebels surrounded it and demanded his death. The Duke saved him only by turning over his own son in his stead. Thereupon, the *Historical Records* says, "the Duke of Shao and the Duke of Chou together carried on the government. The name [of this period] was *Kung He* 共 和 ."[40] Ssu-Ma Ch'ien probably understood this expression as meaning something like "Shared Harmony."

This idea of a joint regency was formerly generally accepted. But the genuine *Bamboo Books* says that Earl He of Kung (共 伯 和) "usurped the King's place." This version is supported by a number of other sources and is now commonly favored, though often with various modifications. The question of exactly what happened at this time is extremely complex, and it may be impossible to determine this with certainty.[41] But in any case there was an interregnum, from 841 to 828 B.C.

WHAT had brought the Chou to this, after their great beginnings?

In the first place there is the fact that no hereditary line is likely to go on producing remarkable men forever; four generations, from Wen to K'ang, was already a long time. And there is a certain debilitating effect in being born to security, wealth, and power. The later Kings must have known that they could scarcely hope to duplicate the feats of their ancestors, and that to attempt to do so would only project them into suicidal adventures. In such circumstances, men turn to other interests. Cupidity is a vice to which many Kings, in China and elsewhere, have been prone, and we have it on the best authority

---

39. *Tso*, 714::717 (Chao 26).

40. *Shih-chi*, 4.55–56; *Mémoires historiques*, I, 274–275. *Kuo-yü*, 1.6ab.

41. Concerning this tangled problem see the following: Wang, *Ku Chu-shu*, 8a. *Shih-chi*, 4.56–57 (commentaries). Ch'en, *Hsi-Chou Nien-tai K'ao*, 31–33. Hsü, "Yü Ting," 57–59. Kuo, *Shih P'i-p'an Shu*, 45. Ting, "Shao Mu Kung Chuan," 90–93.

that even King K'ang was not free of it. His father, King Ch'eng, on his deathbed, giving his last instructions to his ministers, told them that they should not, because his heir was "covetous, make him presents in improper quantities."[42]

In the matter of succession the Roman Empire had a system that, in some respects, was clearly superior. Heredity played a very minor role. Edward Gibbon says that in the early Empire there was "no example of three successive generations on the throne," and "only three instances of sons who succeeded their fathers."[43] The imperial purple was commonly won in rather fierce competition. This did not always produce Emperors who were morally good, but they were often energetic. If the rule went to one who was notably weak, he was likely to be soon replaced by a more aggressive rival.

Where the throne is transmitted hereditarily over a long period of time, the continued vigor of government can be assured only by a machinery of administration that will carry on, by its own momentum, when the current ruler is unable or unwilling to provide firm guidance. For this purpose the machinery of government was inadequately developed in Western Chou. Some of the Kings were certainly more able than the semi-legendary history that remains to us would indicate. King Li was undoubtedly, as T'ang Lan has pointed out, a more capable ruler than he is represented by tradition to have been.[44] The fact that Western Chou Kings sometimes led their own armies, even near the end of the period, is very significant. Yet there are indications that as time went on the Kings held less and less of the reins of government in their own hands. This may have been inevitable; the affairs of their broad Empire undoubtedly became more and more complex, increasingly beyond the grasp of—as the King was called—"the One Man."

Ch'en Meng-chia points out some significant differences, in the court ceremonies recorded in bronze inscriptions, between the early time of Kings Ch'eng and K'ang and the later days of Western Chou. In the early period the King commonly gives his orders in person, but later through the intermediation of an official. The titles of different kinds of officials taking part in such ceremonies also became more numerous after the beginning of the dynasty. And certain elaborations of these ceremonies do not appear before the middle of Western

---

42. *Shu*, 70. This is Karlgren's translation, which is supported by a passage in the *Historical Records*. See *Shih-chi*, 4.41; *Mémoires historiques*, I, 249.

43. Gibbon, *Roman Empire*, I, 132, note.

44. *Ch'ing-t'ung-ch'i T'u-shih*, 3.

Chou.[45] All this would seem to indicate less and less direct, relatively informal contact between the King and those who served him.

In later China eunuchs, who managed the living quarters of the Emperor, sometimes rose to commanding power; and it seems reasonable to suppose that when close attendants of the ruler become important officers of the realm, this signifies a tendency for the monarch to diminish his personal contact with affairs. The title of Intendant, which may at first have been that of a virtual servant, does not appear as that of an official until after the first century of Western Chou, and that of Steward appears still later. We find a Steward charged to "take out and bring in [reports about]" the King's commands. Both the Steward and the Intendant came to be listed among the highest royal officers, and the Intendant was at times, in late Western Chou, the commanding figure at the court.[46]

Among the founders of the Chou power there was certainly respect for the services of ministers, but (except for the Duke of Chou) none of them assigned to ministers a place comparable in importance to that of the ruler. But the role of the ministers is increasingly magnified, and in each of two late inscriptions the King appears to confide the entire direction of the government to a single minister. In one of these the King says that his orders are not to be promulgated by anyone but this single officer; Ssu Wei-chih says that this meant that the King's orders lacked authority until they had been countersigned by this minister.[47] Two poems dated to the late reigns also tell of single ministers who appear to have wielded complete power over the administration.[48]

The minister named in one of these poems is extolled as a paragon of virtue; the other is damned as a tyrant. Undoubtedly there were both good and bad officials. But power does tend to corrupt, and a government that had no adequate mechanisms to control its officials subjected them, when they were endowed with great power, to temptations that would be irresistible to a large proportion of mortals. Many undoubtedly succumbed; we have seen that a great many poems from late in Western Chou complain, often in the bitterest tones, of the iniquities of ministers. These same poems also tell of rivalries and

45. Ch'en, "Hsi-Chou T'ung-ch'i," (3).98–99.
46. See pp. 118–121.
47. *Chin-wen*, 134b–135b, 139ab. Ssu, "Liang-Chou Chih-kuan K'ao," 23. Kuo Mo-jo dates both of these inscriptions to the reign of King Hsüan; T'ang Lan, in *Ch'ing-t'ung-ch'i T'u-shih*, 2, dates the former to the previous reign, that of King Li.
48. *Shih*, 133–134, 228–230.

enmities between individuals and groups. And in bronze inscriptions two Kings complain of wrong-doing by officials, including the taking of bribes. In one the King warns the very officer to whom he is confiding power over his government not to be oppressive, and not to misappropriate money collected as taxes.[49]

There were causes enough for dissension. Early in Western Chou, when royal officers were sent to inspect the domains of feudal lords, they regularly received handsome presents from those they inspected. And when they expressed thanks for these presents in the inscription cast to celebrate the event, the thanks were not directed to the donor, but to the King (or in one case the Queen) who had made it possible for them to be so rewarded.[50] Nothing suggests that there was anything improper about these transactions, or that the gifts were bribes for making a good report. But the situation was obviously one that could lend itself to abuse, and it is unlikely that the inspected vassals were as delighted as the royal officers whom they enriched.

It seems clear that officers of the Chou court, like a great many officials in other times and places, made the most of their opportunities. Kuo Mo-jo argues from the bronzes that it was regular practice for officials who had officiated at court ceremonies, in which the King had conferred a benefit, to be given valuable jades by the beneficiary.[51] No doubt there was such a custom. But we have some evidence that the making of such presentations was not always voluntary.

We have seen that Earl Hu of Shao was a very important man, clearly one of the King's most honored vassals and officials. Nevertheless, he had his problems with the Intendant Tiao Sheng, who appears to have had charge of the royal government.[52] In one inscription Hu relates that he reported a success, possibly a victory, to the King, who apparently assigned him certain lands as a reward. But he still had to get the document attesting his title to the lands from the officials, and this process was delayed. It was then suggested to him that the matter might be expedited if he would present a valuable carved jade to Tiao Sheng.[53]

A second inscription describes the incident that was related in an

49. *Chin-wen*, 75b–76a, 134b–135b.
50. See p. 411.
51. *Chin-wen*, 73ab.
52. See p. 158. Although Earl Hu is commonly identified with Duke Mu of Shao, who rescued the future King Hsüan at the time of the revolt, I doubt this. As the virtual foster father of the King, he would not, I think, have been given such trouble by Tiao Sheng. For details, see p. 156, n. 100.
53. *Chin-wen*, 144b–145a.

earlier chapter, in which Earl Hu was called to the capital by Tiao Sheng in connection with the auditing of his accounts. Hu was apparently in charge of the collection of taxes over a wide area, and was accused of a shortage in his payments. The solution of this affair also involved the presentation of a valuable gift to Tiao Sheng.[54]

The recently unearthed inscription that tells of the honoring of the musician Li by King Li may indicate that the King was not even in firm control of the officers of his own court. It relates that "the King ordered the Supervisor of Makers of Books to 'documentarily' charge Li, saying . . . " There follows the text of the document that had been drawn up by the secretariat, conferring upon Li the office that had been held by his grandfather and his father, and enumerating gifts presented to him. After this has apparently come to an end, there is a very curious addition, which begins: "Furthermore, now I increase your gifts,[55] giving you . . . "

Kuo Mo-jo says that this second charge was spoken by the King, who on the spot decided that the gifts named in the prepared document were not sufficient, and added to them orally. And these second gifts, he says, were of a much finer sort, befitting a higher rank than those of the document. Kuo thinks that this shows King Li's mercurial temperament, in that he gave one set of orders to his secretaries who were to draw up the charge and then, during the ceremony, changed his mind.[56]

This is certainly one possibility, but there may be another. It is not inconceivable that the Supervisor of Makers of Books, jealous of the high favor that Li enjoyed with the King, chose deliberately to misunderstand the King's orders and substituted less valuable gifts, expecting that the King would accept the document as an accomplished fact once it was read out in the ceremony. Whatever the explanation, this inscription would seem to indicate that the court of King Li, even during its ceremonies, was not always characterized by the utmost decorum.

Upon the death of King Li in exile, his son, who had been reared in the home of the Duke of Shao, was established as King Hsüan (827–782

---

54. Ibid., 142a. See pp. 158–159.

55. The inscription here reads *ling* 令, which commonly has the sense of "to command, to charge." But in the inscriptions this character often has the sense of "to give," and since what follows is a series of presents, "gifts" seems to be the best translation here.

56. Kuo, *Wen-shih Lun-chi*, 328–332.

B.C.). It will be recalled that Prince Chao said that after the interregnum, "when King Hsüan [showed himself] possessed of character, [the feudal lords] handed over the government to him." The *Historical Records* says that after he assumed the rule he "took for his pattern the principles bequeathed by [Kings] Wen, Wu, Ch'eng, and K'ang. The feudal lords again looked up to Chou."[57]

There was indeed, in this later time, a nostalgic looking backward to the glorious early days of the founders. In the early literature and inscriptions there was a great deal of mention of King Wen and King Wu, but usually they were mentioned singly. In the placid and prosperous middle years we do not find them named often. But in the latter reigns we find frequent reference to "Wen Wu," almost like an incantation that, it was hoped, might help to bring back the glory of their time. We find it, as T'ang Lan points out, in sources dated to the time of King Li, as well as to later times.[58]

"All sources agree," Ch'en Meng-chia writes, "that Hsüan Wang [King Hsüan] was an exceptionally able ruler throughout the forty-six years of his reign."[59] Undoubtedly he was a good King. But reputations—whether for evil or for good—once established, tend to grow of themselves, and it is not certain that Hsüan was a complete paragon. It is under his reign that the Intendant Tiao Sheng is believed, for some of the time, to have controlled the government. King Hsüan is criticized in two stories in the *Discourses of the States*, although these do not inspire much confidence in their historicity.[60] That work and the *Historical Records* also report his intervention, in a manner that was perhaps unwise, in the succession to the rule of the state of Lu; in the course of this intervention he killed one of Lu's rulers.[61]

In any case, Hsüan could not escape the troubles that increasingly beset the Chou, though he did try. He made strenuous efforts to keep the precariously subject barbarians under control, and established his relative, the Earl of Shen, in a state intended to serve as a buffer against the tribes of the south. As a result, the *Poetry* says, "All of the Chou states rejoice, for warfare they have an excellent support; the greatly illustrious Earl of Shen, eldest uncle of the King, is a model in

---

57. *Tso*, 714::717 (Chao 26). *Shih-chi*, 4.57–58; *Mémoires historiques*, 1, 275–276.

58. *Chin-wen*, 134b, 139a, 147a. Kuo, *Wen-shih Lun-chi*, 348. *Ch'ing-t'ung-ch'i T'u-shih*, 27. *Shih*, 234. *Shu*, 78–80.

59. Ch'en, "The Greatness of Chou," 58.

60. *Kuo-yü*, 1.6b–8b, 9b–10a. These are greatly condensed in *Shih-chi*, 4.59–60; *Mémoires historiques*, I, 276–278.

61. See pp. 415–416.

peace and war." Nevertheless, Hsüan's military campaigns against the barbarians were by no means uniformly successful.[62] The glorious days of Wen and Wu were not to return.

Under Hsüan's son, King Yu (781–771 B.C.), Western Chou came to its end. Few losers become heroes, and Yu has become a proverbial example of a bad King. Anecdotes about him abound in natural calamities—presaging the fall of the royal house—and in strange and even supernatural events.[63] Prince Chao said that "when [the rule] came to King Yu, Heaven had no mercy on Chou. The King was benighted and perverse, so that he lost his throne." We have few facts on which to judge him. One of the few specific charges laid against him is that he named as a high minister the ruler of Kuo, who was "eloquent, cunning, skilled in flattery, and avaricious," which made all the people resentful.[64]

No doubt King Yu had follies of his own, but it seems probable that the debacle would have come in any case as the result of the accumulated problems of the Chou house, which had ceased to be equal to the responsibilities it had undertaken. Among these problems, one of the greatest, certainly, was that of the barbarians. The *Tso-chuan* says that King Yu made a covenant, concerning which we have no further details. In the context it appears to have been a covenant with his vassals, looking to action against the barbarians. The result was, however, to cause the Jung and the Ti to revolt from him.[65]

Tradition places the chief burden for the fall of Western Chou on a woman, named Pao Ssu. She is named in the *Poetry*, in a passage that says that Chou has been destroyed by Pao Ssu.[66] The developed legend is certainly much later, but there is no doubt some substratum of truth to parts of it. It is related that in the time of the Hsia dynasty two dragons appeared in the palace and deposited some spittle, which was sealed in a coffer and handed down. In the time of the Chou King Li the box was opened, and the spittle impregnated a young girl in the harem. The result of this strange pregnancy was the lady, Pao Ssu, who eventually ended up in the harem of King Yu. Yu became smitten with her, and she bore him a son.

Pao Ssu did not smile easily. The King tried many expedients to

---

62. See pp. 238–240.

63. *Kuo-yü*, 1.10ab, 16.1a–6b. *Shih-chi*, 4.60–65, 42.3–5; *Mémoires historiques*, I, 278–285, IV, 449–452.

64. *Tso*, 714::717 (Chao 26). *Kuo-yü*, 16.5a. *Shih-chi*, 4.65; *Mémoires historiques*, I, 284.

65. See p. 240, n. 181.

66. *Shih*, 136. This poem is quoted in *Tso*, 570::577 (Chao 1).

amuse her, and finally succeeded. He had beacons that were to be lighted in case of invasion, to summon the feudal lords. But the King lighted them when there was no invasion so that the feudal lords rushed to do battle but found no enemy, which made Pao Ssu laugh and laugh. This delighted the King, who lighted the beacons repeatedly. And fewer and fewer of his vassals answered the summons. Pao Ssu is said to have intrigued with the King's minister, the ruler of Kuo, to have her son made the heir. In any case the King did make Pao Ssu his Queen, and her son his heir. But to do this he had to set aside the rightful Queen and her son, who had been designated heir. It happened that the rightful Queen was the daughter of the Marquis of Shen, who was understandably irritated. Together with the state of Tseng, the western Jung, and the Dog Jung, he attacked the King. King Yu lighted his beacons, but no help came. The King was killed, Pao Ssu was taken prisoner, and all of the Chou treasure was carried off. The feudal lords then set up Yu's son by the rightful Queen as King P'ing. In order to escape the danger from the Jung, P'ing then removed from the western capital to the eastern capital, near the modern Loyang, thus beginning Eastern Chou.[67]

THE remarkable point about all this it not that Western Chou came to an end, but that the Chou, however diminished in power, continued to be Kings. Innumerable papers and numerous books have been written to explain the fall of the Roman Empire; this event seems to be regarded as so extraordinary as to require elaborate explanation. But to fall is the most normal and inevitable thing that empires do. The problem for the historian, and it is a very real one, is to account for the fact that Rome's empire lasted so amazingly long. The fact that Chou Kings continued on the throne until 256 B.C. is perhaps even more astonishing.

Our conceptions of feudalism are almost all based on medieval Europe, and we tend to think of a feudal state as highly centrifugal. We imagine feudal lords as being held together by a kind of tension, and eager to assert their independence at the first possibility. Marc Bloch writes:

> The very epics which set such great store by the 'virtue'
> of the vassal are nothing but one long recital of the wars
> launched by vassals against their lords. . . . Of all the

67. *Kuo-yü*, 7.2b, 16.1a–6b. *Shih-chi*, 4.62–66, 42.3–5; *Mémoires historiques*, I, 280–285, V, 449–452.

occasions for going to war, the first that came to mind
was to take up arms against one's lord.[68]

Certainly there were centrifugal tendencies in Chou China, too, but
the centripetal force must have been very strong.

If it had not been, the realm should have dissolved into its component states at the time of the interregnum that lasted for fourteen
years beginning in 841 B.C., or failing that, another line should have
taken the throne. Neither happened; the Chou were restored. At that
time the organization of the royal government no doubt persisted in
a sense, under other direction, but that organization must have been
shattered when Western Chou came to an end, in 771. Even then,
however, the feudal lords placed a Chou scion on the throne and
helped him to move to a more secure capital in the east. And it was the
rulers of states who made it possible for the Chou to continue to reign,
if seldom to rule, for an additional five centuries. Why?

The *Historical Records* says that the heir of King Yu was set up by
the feudal lords "in order that he might continue to offer the Chou
sacrifices."[69] This implies that they were motivated by respect for the
Chou ancestors, who continued as spirits to have great power to intervene in human affairs. No doubt this was a part of the reason, but it
could hardly be the whole. If the Chou ancestors had been so potent,
why had they not protected their descendants? And if they had been
so feared, it is hard to explain the disrespect with which their descendants were often treated, even late in Western Chou, and still more in
later times. Certainly this religious motivation must have become very
weak in the latter centuries of the Chou dynasty, when belief, both in
religion and in tradition, reached a low ebb that has perhaps never
been duplicated, in later Chinese history, before the twentieth century. There were more compelling and more practical reasons.

The Chou had joined together more people than had ever been
brought into political and cultural unity before—perhaps anywhere.
This unity is no illusion. There is solid evidence for it of many kinds,
not least in the bronzes that have come, and are still continuing to
come, out of the earth. Those who have studied them agree that their
shapes and decoration show that, as Cheng Te-k'un writes:

> In Western Chou, the uniformity of the art extended to
> every corner of Chou China and the tradition was up-

68. Bloch, *Feudal Society*, 235.
69. *Shih-chi*, 4.66; *Mémoires historiques*, I, 285.

held even after the decline of the Chou house. The rise
and expansion of the feudal lords did dissect the country
into a number of independent states but the cultural
development remained to link the country together.[70]

This unity had solid value, both in war and in peace.

Beyond that, the Chou had given China much more, a vision: a vision of a world, "all under heaven," united in peace and harmony and
cooperation, under "the Son of Heaven." The vision, of course, was of
China as it had existed under the first Chou rulers, and it rapidly became exaggerated into a dream of a Utopia. Kings were never so great,
their vassals were never such heroes, there was never such uniform justice, the people were never so prosperous and happy, as they were believed to have been under Wen and Wu and Ch'eng and K'ang. But
the dream grew. Eventually, when the philosophers took it over, they
needed more scope than was afforded by an actual historical past;
after all, there was some limiting knowledge of what had actually existed in early Chou. So the philosophers projected this golden age back
to the glorious days of remotely early legendary Emperors, where
fancy was free to invent as it would. But this did not begin until late
in Spring and Autumn times. The original golden age, and the proto-
type for later invention, was early Western Chou. The Chou had given
the Chinese people a goal and a vision which they would never, perhaps, completely lose.

To be a part of this dramatic union of all men was a splendid thing.
To be a trusted associate of the Son of Heaven, to wear robes and to
drive a chariot adorned with insignia that were marks of his special
favor, to feel one's self a part of the vast historical process by which
China had come into being and grown great—how much more satis-
fying than to be a mere lord of a state, however independent. But none
of this was possible, of course, unless there were a Son of Heaven. If
there were not, it would be necessary to invent him. And in fact the
Chinese did this, in later history, again and again.

It was inherent, of course, in the very doctrine of the Mandate of
Heaven that a dynasty that had lost its virtue might be replaced by
another. And it has been suggested, as we have seen, that Earl He of
Kung sought to usurp the throne at the time of the revolution against
King Li. But if there was the intention to set up a new dynasty then, it
did not succeed. And the prestige of the Chou was so great that this

70. Cheng, *Chou China*, 233. See also Ch'en, "Hsi-Chou T'ung-ch'i," (2).103.

idea seems to have seldom been mentioned until near the end of the Spring and Autumn period.

THE Chou failed in their attempt to set up, as a permanent institution, a government that could maintain firm centralized control, by the Son of Heaven and officials under his direction, over all under Heaven They failed chiefly, if the analysis that has been attempted here is correct, because they gave little attention to the development and application of the administrative techniques that might have made their ambitious program possible. But their goal remained a legacy that was never forgotten, even in the days of virtually complete disunion in Warring States times, when every ambitious ruler of a state hoped that he might become Son of Heaven, and the chief stock in trade of philosophers was a series of formulas designed to make this possible.

The most interesting of these philosophers, insofar as the theory of administration is concerned, was Shen Pu-hai. He was a very practical philosopher, and indeed a practicing statesman, who had a highly successful career as Chancellor of the state of Hán,[71] up to the time when he died in office in 337 B.C. In the surviving fragments of his writings or sayings there seems to be no mention of the Western Chou experience, but some of his aphorisms point directly at weaknesses that were present in the Western Chou administration.

The emphasis that Shen placed on administrative technique was mentioned earlier.[72] He was a steadfast opponent of improvisation. The problems of government, he felt, are too complex and too difficult to be dealt with on the basis of impromptu decisions. He said:

> The wise ruler depends upon methods, not sagacity.
> He employs technique, not theory.[73]

Shen laid great stress upon the orderly hierarchical organization of all the officials, and on the careful allocation of titles, and of duties in conformity with them. He would certainly have deplored the carelessness, in this respect, that prevailed in Western Chou. He also said:

71. This state, which came into existence in 403 B.C., is of course not the same as the state of Hán that we have seen mentioned in Western Chou sources, though their names are identical. How and when the earlier state of Hán came to an end is uncertain.

72. See pp. 4–5.

73. *I-wen Lei-chü*, 54.1b–2a.

> When a single minister monopolizes the confidence of
> the ruler, the whole body of ministers is overshadowed
> and demoralized. . . . For this reason the intelligent ruler
> causes all of his ministers to advance together, like the
> spokes of a wheel that converge in the hub, so that no
> one minister can gain the ascendancy.[74]

Shen warned that it was folly for a ruler to attempt to do too much personally, but he would have strongly approved of King Wu's insistence upon holding the control of the administration in his own hands and treating his officials as his instruments.

> The intelligent ruler is like the trunk, the minister is like
> an arm. . . . The ruler controls the principles, the minister carries them out in detail. The ruler holds the controls, the minister carries on routine functions.[75]

This authoritarian emphasis, subordinating the role of the minister, is of course one that would not have been approved by either the Duke of Chou or Confucius; they stressed the role of the minister as a framer as well as an instrument of policy. Throughout later Chinese history, the interplay between these two points of view would help to prevent rigidity, and give viability to the governmental system.

GOVERNMENT in China, in later times, would develop into a system having little in common, in its details, with that of Western Chou. Yet its goal would still be that of bringing all under heaven into union under a centrally controlled regime guided by the Son of Heaven. To make this practicable many techniques would have to be developed over many centuries, correcting the mistakes of Western Chou, and making and correcting others, in a long process of trial and error. But that is another story.

---

74. *Ch'ün-shu*, 36.25b.
75. Ibid., 36.26a.

Appendix A

The Sources

Since Western Chou has been a subject of perennial interest, works that discuss it have been produced in almost every period of Chinese history. Works actually written in Western Chou times are of course most important for our study, and our first task must be to attempt to determine what materials are genuinely contemporary and what have mistakenly been believed to be so.

We cannot, however, confine our attention merely to works that date from Western Chou times. These are relatively few, and in many respects the information they yield is very meager. That information can often be very usefully supplemented and illumined by traditions concerning Western Chou that are contained in works of later date. Of course, the utilization of traditions involves very difficult problems. A completely genuine work of the Spring and Autumn period may contain statements about Western Chou that are demonstrably false—made, perhaps, for purposes of political propaganda. All traditions, no matter where they are recorded, must be evaluated on their merits. Nevertheless, a tradition recorded in a very early work has a greater claim on our attention than one found only in a late compilation.

It would be desirable, therefore, to subject every work embodying traditions concerning Western Chou to critical scrutiny, but this is, unfortunately, impossible. Here we cannot even consider all of the works that are drawn upon in the body of this volume. We shall, however, examine those with serious claims to be regarded as contemporary sources, and some other works that have been cited frequently.

The order in which these works are listed is very roughly chronological, but it has no significance and may be considered arbitrary.

Book of Changes

This work is commonly known in Chinese simply as the *I* 易 ,

"Changes." The meaning of this name is uncertain; one explanation is that it refers to the continual metamorphosis of all things.[1] Other names for the book are *I-ching* 易經 , "Classic of Changes," and *Chou I* 周易 . There are varying explanations for the character Chou here; one is that the work was produced during the Chou dynasty.

It is necessary to distinguish clearly between the original text of this work and its appendices, commonly called the "Ten Wings." The latter were produced long after the Western Chou period and need not concern us.[2]

The authorship of the original text has traditionally been attributed to various individuals, either singly or in collaboration; early sages, King Wen, and the Duke of Chou. There appears to be no clear evidence as to its origin. It seems most probable, however, since this work is a diviner's manual, that it was produced by diviners. We have seen that diviners played an important role at the Shang court, and the Chou Kings also had such officials. In one bronze inscription the King says: "I order you to continue [the office of] your grandfather and father, in charge of the business of divination."[3]

The composition of the original text of the *Book of Changes* is generally attributed to the Western Chou period, and usually to the beginning of Western Chou.[4] There is some positive evidence for this. References in it to persons, places, events, and activities almost all

---

1. Fung Yu-lan, in *A History of Chinese Philosophy*, I, 380, states a quite different view. One of the meanings of the character *i* is "easy." According to this explanation, the method of divination used with this book was less difficult than that involving the tortoise shell, and the book was so named "because its method of divination was an easy one."

2. The content of the "Ten Wings" was undoubtedly composed by various persons and at different times, but to assign specific dates to its various portions is difficult. Modern critical scholars are rather generally agreed that this composition took place over a period beginning not earlier than the Warring States period and ending not later than some time in the Former Han dynasty. For discussions of this problem see the following: *Ku-shih Pien*, III, 1–308. *Wei-shu T'ung-k'ao*, 41–80. Waley, "The Book of Changes," 141. Fung, *A History of Chinese Philosophy*, I, 379–395. The usual arrangement of the Chinese text intersperses some of the appendices with the original text, so that it is very difficult to discriminate them. The most practical guide for doing so is the translation of James Legge (Legge, *I-ching*). In that work the original text is translated on pages 57–210; the appendices follow.

3. *Chin-wen*, 96b.

4. *Ku-shih Pien*, III, 1–308. *Wei-shu T'ung-k'ao*, I, 24–41. Maspero, *La Chine antique*, 370. Wang, *Kuan-t'ang Chi-lin*, 13.1b. Waley, "The Book of Changes," 121, 140. Waley says that "the work has always been known as the *Chou I*, 'Changes of the Chou dynasty,' and we shall be quite safe in saying that it reached something like its present form during the first half of the Chou period, say between 1000 and 600 B.C."

seem to be associated with or suggest the Shang period—usually late Shang—or early Western Chou. Since there are clear references to the early Chou period, this material could not have been put into its present form earlier than that time.[5]

Evidence that it probably comes from a time not much later than Western Chou is chiefly negative, but not unimpressive. The character *li* 禮 does not occur at all in the original text of the *Book of Changes*, but is frequent in the appendices, where it has the sense of aristocratic or (in the Confucian sense) moral conduct.[6] It was pointed out earlier that *li* in this sense rarely if ever occurs in Western Chou texts, while it is extremely common throughout Spring and Autumn times and in later periods.[7]

If the original text had been produced in late Spring and Autumn or in Warring States times, it would almost certainly include reference to certain mythological Emperors and religious and philosophical conceptions that were current in these later periods. But while these are mentioned in the "Ten Wings," they are not in the original text.[8] Similarly all but two of the appendices include references to *yin* and *yang*, the "negative" and "positive" principles that are not found in the literature until long after Western Chou times, but these are never mentioned in the original text.[9] The metaphysical concept of *ti* 地 , Earth, as the counterpart of Heaven in the Heaven-Earth dualism, is lacking in Western Chou material, but in the appendices it occurs with

5. *I-ching*, 1.28a, 2.10b, 4.11a, 15b, 5.10b, 34a, 6.22a, 25a; Legge, *I-ching*, 62, 72, 131, 135, 160, 182, 205, 208. It should be noted that the reference to the Marquis of K'ang was missed in *I-ching*, 4.11a, and in Legge, *I-ching*, 131; it also passed unrecognized in Wilhelm, *I-ching*, 137. For discussion of this reference by Ku Chieh-kang see *Ku-shih Pien*, III, 17–19. See also Waley, "The Book of Changes," 137–138. Ku Chieh-kang discusses a number of these references in *Ku-shih Pien*, III, 1–25.

6. *I-ching*, 1.10a, 4.9b, 7.15b, 16b, 19a, 32b, 8.18a, 9.11b, 13a; Legge, *I-ching*, 309, 359, 360, 363, 378, 398, 408, 434, 436.

7. See pp. 336–338.

8. This point is discussed at length by Ku Chieh-kang in *Ku-shih Pien*, III, 25–43.

9. It is necessary to distinguish clearly between the characters *yin* 陰 and *yang* 陽 used in other senses, and cases where they refer to this philosophical concept. There is one occurrence of *yin*, but not as the concept, in the original text: *I-ching*, 6.16a; Legge, *I-ching*, 200. In the appendices the concept occurs as follows: *I-ching*, 1.9b, 17a, 27ab, 2.20b, 24a, 7.11a, 13b, 15a, 8.8b, 9a, 15ab, 9.2b, 3b, 5b.

The concept of *yin* and *yang* is also absent from other Western Chou literature; it does not occur either in the *Documents* or the *Poetry*. I believe that it does not occur in any Western Chou bronze inscription. And it is not found even in a text as late as the *Analects*.

great frequency. In the original text, however, it is never mentioned.[10]

There appears to be sound basis for the opinion that has been generally held, from antiquity to our own day, that the original text of the *Book of Changes* was produced during the Western Chou period.

Documents

THIS work has often been called the *Book of History*, but that is misleading. It is in no sense a connected history, but consists of a series of documents. Such of these as are genuine appear in most cases to be writings that were preserved in the royal archives. It is sometimes called the *Shu-ching* 書經 , "Document Classic," or *Shang-shu* 尚書 , which in my opinion probably means "Preserved Writings," that is, archives.[11] The most common term for it in Chinese is simply *Shu* 書 , "Writings," for which *Documents* seems the best translation.

The problems of criticism concerned with this text are probably as complex and difficult as those of any text in any language. It exists in two versions, called the "modern text" (chin-wen 今文) and the "ancient text" (ku-wen 古文). But the so-called "ancient text" is

---

10. In the early literature, "earth" is usually denoted by *t'u* 土 ; even the character *ti* is rare. It does not seem to occur on the Shang oracle bones. It is not listed either in Sun, *Chia-ku Wen Pien,* or in Chin, *Hsü Chia-ku Wen Pien.* Tung Tso-pin told me that he had never encountered it in his long work with the Shang inscriptions (verbal communication of 21 October 1947). Neither does *ti* seem to appear in Western Chou bronze inscriptions. It is not listed in Jung, *Chin-wen Pien,* and Kuo Mo-jo wrote (*Chin-wen Ts'ung-k'ao,* 32b–33a) that despite attempts to identify other characters with it, "the character *ti* is not present in the bronze inscriptions." It does not occur in any of the *Documents* that I consider to date from Western Chou. In the *Poetry, ti* is found twice (*Shih,* 131, 136), but only with the physical sense of "earth." Even its three occurrences in the *Analects* (9.18, 14.39, 19.22) have no metaphysical sense. Bernhard Karlgren, however, in "Some Sacrifices in Chou China," 11–12, appears to think that Ti as a metaphysical concept was present in Western Chou. He says that a certain character appearing in the *Poetry* "is a technical term for a sacrifice by burial to Ti Earth," but the texts he cites as evidence for this are much later than Western Chou. Again he says that "the documentation for the divine character of Earth will, however, be fuller if we realize that this deity is alternatively called T'u Earth," but here again his cited evidence is all from relatively late documents. This does not, in my opinion, constitute solid proof concerning the Western Chou situation.

In the original text of the *Book of Changes* the character *ti* appears once: *I-ching,* 4.15b; Legge, *I-ching,* 135. In that instance, however, it is definitely not a metaphysical concept. In the appendices, on the other hand, it is so used constantly. For a few examples, see: *I-ching,* 1.20a, 23a, 24a; Legge, *I-ching,* 268, 269, 417.

11. See Creel, *Confucius,* 308, n. 18::109, n. 1.

universally agreed to be a late forgery, of perhaps the third or fourth century A.D. while the "modern text" was certainly in existence as early as the second century B.C.

The *Documents* as it is found in Chinese editions of the canonical "Thirteen Classics," and in the translations of James Legge and Seraphin Couvreur, is the "ancient text" version. This includes—with some small differences that cannot always be certainly defined—the twenty-eight documents of the "modern text" along with others, so that it has a total of fifty sections.[12]

Chinese scholars showed decisively, centuries ago, that the so-called "ancient text" of the *Documents* was a late forgery, and more recent investigations by both Chinese and Western scholars have confirmed this.[13] It need not, therefore, concern us. But it is not by any means the case that all of the "modern text" can be regarded as reliable source material for research, either.

Nine of the twenty-eight documents of the "modern text" are traditionally supposed to have been written before the beginning of the Chou dynasty. I have stated elsewhere the reasons for which I believe that in fact none of them were.[14]

Nineteen documents remain. Of these, two have traditionally been dated to early Spring and Autumn times. In my opinion one of the two is correctly so dated, while the other is probably of late Western Chou

12. This does not mean, however, that the "ancient text" version has twenty-two more documents than the "modern text," for two of those in the latter are divided into two parts in the former. The problem of how many sections this work has had, particularly at various times through history, is one of its complexities. The documents belonging to the two texts may conveniently be identified by bearing in mind that Karlgren's translation includes only the "modern text."

13. For an extensive review of this problem, see Pelliot, "Le *Chou King*," 124–158. Also see: Karlgren, "On the Tso Chuan," 49–53. Ch'ü, *Shang-shu Shih-i*, 12–14. Ch'en, *Shang-shu T'ung-lun*, 114–135.

14. Creel, *Studies*, 55–93, 97–99 (n. 2). Much has been published on these supposedly pre-Chou documents since I recorded these opinions in 1937, but nothing that has caused me to believe that my conclusions were not essentially sound. Ch'en Meng-chia, in *Shang-shu T'ung-lun*, 112, suggests that all nine may date from as late as the Warring States period. If as seems possible, some of these documents were written in Western Chou times, it might be argued that they should be used as source documents for that period. In theory that is true. But in practice it is often more difficult to date a forgery than a genuine work. In his analysis of the "ancient text" and the "modern text" of the *Documents*, Karlgren concluded that the forger of the former had studied the grammatical system of the "modern text" so meticulously that there are less grammatical irregularities in the forgery than in the genuine work. He says ("On the Tso Chuan," 53) that "the faker in the 3d century A.D. was so anxious to be *true to the style* of the Shu king [*Documents*], the normal grammatical system of the genuine chapters, that *he overdid it.*" The dating of forgeries is such a doubtful business that I prefer not to use any of these supposedly pre-Chou documents as source materials.

date.[15] Of the remaining seventeen, I believe that eleven may be accepted as reliable source materials dating from the Western Chou period. Six remain; these I consider in some cases very doubtful, and in others quite certainly productions of a later time.

There are, then, twelve writings in the *Documents* that are in my opinion usable as reliable source materials for Western Chou. A number of criteria form the basis of this judgment. These documents are plausible as writings that might have been preserved, in most cases in the Western Chou royal archives. They harmonize, within acceptable limits, with other material that appears to emanate from the time. They do not include anachronisms: characters, or expressions, or ideas that belong to a context other than that of Western Chou. And while there has been much difference of opinion about the authorship and the precise date of some of these documents, their authenticity as Western Chou writings has seldom been questioned.

The reasons for which I do not accept the six supposedly Western Chou documents that seem to me questionable will be set forth below. First, it will be useful to discuss the date, authorship, and nature of the twelve documents that have been used as source materials. They will be considered in the order in which they appear in the *Documents*, which is not necessarily chronological.

The "Ta Kao" ("Great Announcement," *Shu*, 36–39) seems clearly to refer to the conditions that obtained after the death of King Wu, when King Ch'eng and the Duke of Chou were faced by a great revolt on the part of the conquered Shang people and others allied with them. This document is evidently an appeal to the supporters of the Chou to rally and crush the rebels. It may have been issued by King Ch'eng himself, or possibly by the Duke of Chou in his name. The traditional view, and that of some modern scholars, ascribes it to the Duke of Chou, while others suppose it to be the words of King Ch'eng himself.[16] Fu Ssu-nien held that the "Ta Kao" was an announcement

---

15. The "Ch'in Shih" (*Shu*, 81) appears, in style and in content, to be a document of fairly early Spring and Autumn date, as tradition has supposed. "Wen Hou chih Ming" (*Shu*, 78–80) is ascribed by tradition to the beginning of Spring and Autumn times, but I think it more likely that it is late Western Chou; see p. 454.

16. Karlgren says, in "Glosses on the Book of Documents," (1).262, that "all the commentators" have supposed that this announcement was made by the Duke of Chou on behalf of the King. Homer H. Dubs ("Royal Jou Religion," 227, n. 2) also attributes it to the Duke of Chou. But Karlgren (loc. cit.) says that "there is, in fact, not the slightest support for the traditional opinion that the discourse was made by Chou Kung . . . The discourse throughout has a tenor of a king himself speaking." Karlgren appears to suppose that the author is King Ch'eng.

made by King Wu upon his accession to the throne, but I find his argument unconvincing.[17] It seems reasonably clear that we have here the words either of King Ch'eng, or of the Duke of Chou speaking in the King's name, but it is difficult to choose between these alternatives with certainty.[18]

The "K'ang Kao" ("Announcement to K'ang," *Shu*, 39–43) is said by the *Tso-chuan* to have been a charge given to K'ang Shu, a son of King Wen, when he was enfeoffed with the state of Wèi by King Ch'eng.[19] This is awkward, however, for in this document the King speaks of K'ang Shu as his "younger brother," and of himself as "elder brother," although King Ch'eng was in fact a nephew of K'ang Shu. This difficulty was eliminated by the supposition that the document actually emanated from the Duke of Chou, speaking for the King, and it was attributed to the Duke of Chou by early commentators.[20] But commentators of Sung times, and almost all modern scholars, recognize that the text is much more comprehensible if the speaker is understood to be King Wu. The difficulty apparently arose because K'ang Shu was enfeoffed twice: first with a state called K'ang, and only later with Wèi. This fact, which all but dropped out of history, has now been made quite clear by bronze inscriptions.[21]

That King Wu was the author of the "K'ang Kao" seems to be beyond question, but two small problems remain. The first forty-eight characters of the document seem to have nothing to do with the remainder. It was pointed out as early as Sung times that these characters were undoubtedly placed here by mistake, through confusion in the archives. It has been suggested that they belong at the head of various other documents, but there would seem to be little doubt that they constitute in fact the opening of the "Le Kao."[22]

A second problem concerns the nature of this text. It is almost universally regarded as being a charge given to a newly enfeoffed feuda-

---

17. Fu, "Ta-tung Hsiao-tung Shuo," 107, note.

18. Ch'ü Wan-li (*Shang-shu Shih-i*, 70) cites the tradition attributing this work to the Duke of Chou speaking on behalf of King Ch'eng, and concludes that while it is impossible to be certain whether this document was or was not the work of the Duke of Chou, "there is no doubt that it was produced in the opening years of Western Chou." Ch'en Meng-chia (*Shang-shu T'ung-lun*, 112, 207–220) finds a few problems in the "Ta Kao" but concludes that it is an early Chou document.

19. *Tso*, 750.:754 (Ting 4).

20. *Shu*, 39. Karlgren, "Glosses on the Book of Documents," (1).278–279.

21. Ch'ü, *Shang-shu Shih-i*, 76. Chou, *Chin-wen Ling-shih*, 22–28. Karlgren, "Glosses on the Book of Documents," (1).278–279, 296. Dubs, "Royal Jou Religion," 227, n. 2. Fu, "Ta-tung Hsiao-tung Shuo," 107, note.

22. Karlgren, "Glosses on the Book of Documents," (1).278–279. Ch'ü, *Shang-shu Shih-i*, 76–77.

tory, yet in fact it is devoted almost entirely to matters concerned with crime and its punishment. The *Tso-chuan* says that K'ang Shu was appointed Director of Crime by King Wu.[23] If this is true, it may well be that the "K'ang Kao" is a charge that Wu gave to K'ang Shu when he appointed him as Director of Crime and, simultaneously, gave him the fief of K'ang in lieu of emolument.

The "Chiu Kao" ("Announcement Concerning Liquor," *Shu*, 43–46) is also a charge given by a King to K'ang Shu.[24] This King appears to have had almost a phobia concerning the use of intoxicating liquor, except in connection with sacrifices. He attributes the decay and fall of the Yin house to improper indulgence in liquor, and he instructs K'ang Shu, whose fief was peopled by conquered Yin people, to take stern measures to repress it.

Thus far there is no difference of opinion. But one tradition attributes this charge to King Ch'eng, or to the Duke of Chou speaking for the King. It has been pointed out, however, that there are serious difficulties with this view. Like a number of other scholars, I believe that the language of the "Chiu Kao" points to the authorship of King Wu, and that it is more in harmony with his time and his character. While certainty on such a point is almost impossible, I believe that the overwhelming probability points to King Wu as its author.[25]

The "Tzu Ts'ai" ("Catalpa Wood," *Shu*, 46–48) is a brief and rather baffling document.[26] Its opening and longest section is again a statement made by a King to K'ang Shu. The speaker later changes, and there are various interpretations as to the number of different sections (by different speakers) into which the text should be divided, and as to the identity of the speakers. The meaning of some portions of the "Tzu Ts'ai" is unusually difficult to determine, even for the *Documents*. One explanation that has been proposed is that pieces of more than one document in the archives were mistakenly put together to form this one.[27]

23. *Tso*, 750::754 (Ting 4).

24. In this document, as in the "K'ang Kao" and the "Tzu Ts'ai," he is not called K'ang Shu 康叔, but Feng 封. But a number of bronze inscriptions, in addition to the literature, show that the name of K'ang Shu was Feng. See Ch'en, "Hsi-Chou T'ung-ch'i," (1).163.

25. For evidence in favor of the authorship of King Wu, see: Karlgren, "Glosses on the Book of Documents," (1).296. Ch'en, "Hsi-Chou T'ung-ch'i," (1).163-164. Dubs, "Royal Jou Religion," 227–228, n. 2. Ch'ü Wan-li, however, in *Shang-shu Shih-i*, 83, appears to accept the authorship of the Duke of Chou.

26. Its name is derived from the fact that, in the body of the text, the working of catalpa wood is used as a simile.

27. Karlgren, "Glosses on the Book of Documents," (1).296, 307–315. Ch'ü, *Shang-shu Shih-i*, 88.

There seems to be no basis on which to resolve these problems definitely. I agree with those who hold that the first part of this document probably records the words of King Wu. Who the other speaker or speakers may be appears impossible to determine. At the same time, there seems to be no good reason to deny that the "Tzu Ts'ai" is a genuine document of early Western Chou date, if a somewhat puzzling one.

The "Shao Kao" ("Announcement of Shao," *Shu*, 48–51) consists, after a rather lengthy introduction, of a long pronouncement made on the occasion of the initiation of work on the eastern capital at Le. It is said to be addressed to the Yin people (who were apparently to do the bulk of the work), and some of it apparently is, but it also includes many admonitions advising the Chou King how to rule.

The controversy over this document concerns its authorship. On the basis of its title, one would suppose it to have emanated from someone called Shao. And there are four references in the prefatory section to the Grand Protector, who at this time was apparently the Duke of Shao. Commentators, and some scholars at the present time, have supposed the body of the document to be by the Duke of Shao.[28]

Ssu-Ma Ch'ien, however, appears to have attributed the "Shao Kao" along with the "Le Kao" to the Duke of Chou.[29] Yü Sheng-wu argues convincingly that in fact the body of this document does consist of the words of the Duke of Chou; others agree with him.[30] The problems are sufficiently complex to leave room for varying opinion. But when we consider, in addition to other indications, the remarkable similarities between this document and others that all agree come from the Duke of Chou, the probability that he is in fact the author seems very great indeed.[31]

The "Le Kao ("Announcement Concerning Le," *Shu*, 51–55) consists of a series of statements by the Duke of Chou and King Ch'eng

28. Karlgren, in "Glosses on the Book of Documents," (2).63, says that "from Han down to our own days" the body of the document "has always been taken to be a harangue made by Shao Kung." Ch'ü (*Shang-shu Shih-i*, 91) ascribes it to the Duke of Shao.

29. *Shih-chi*, 4.39–40; *Mémoires historiques*, I, 247. The attribution seems fairly clear in the text, but Chavannes avoids the problem by translating that *on composa* the two documents.

30. Yü, *Shang-shu Hsin-cheng*, 3.1a–4a. Karlgren, "Glosses on the Book of Documents," (2).63–64. Ch'en, "Hsi-Chou T'ung-ch'i," (3).111.

31. Not only are the style and content of this document like those of others from the Duke of Chou, but so is the almost dictatorial attitude toward the King. We cannot prove that the Duke of Shao also did not speak in this way, since we seem to have no documents from him, but it seems rather unlikely.

to each other; they concern the new capital at Le, and also the manner in which the government should be carried on. There is also a brief introductory and a brief closing section, presumably written by a secretary when the document was placed in the archives. While there are many differences of opinion concerning specific portions of this document, it is generally agreed that the speakers are the Duke of Chou and King Ch'eng.[32]

"To Shih" ("Many Officers," *Shu*, 55–56) is a proclamation made by the Duke of Chou, speaking in the name of King Ch'eng, to the conquered Shang officers who have been moved to the new city at Le after their rebellion has been crushed.[33]

"Chün Shih" ("Lord Shih," *Shu*, 59–62) is a speech made by the Duke of Chou to the Duke of Shao, whose name was Shih. These two Dukes were the most important officers in the government early in the reign of King Ch'eng, and the Duke of Chou here urges his colleague to help him carry on the task of establishing the dynasty firmly.[34]

"To Fang" ("Numerous Territories," *Shu*, 62–65)[35] is a proclamation very similar to the "To Shih." The Duke of Chou, in the name of the King, makes a further address to the officials of the conquered Shang who have been settled at Le, promising them a bright future if they cooperate, but threatening punishment if they continue to be recalcitrant. It appears to date from a time several years later than that of the "To Shih." There are differences of opinion as to its date and other details, but all seem to agree that it is such a proclamation by the Duke of Chou.[36]

32. Karlgren, "Glosses on the Book of Documents," (2).74. Ch'en, "Hsi-Chou T'ung-ch'i," (3).111. Ch'ü, *Shang-shu Shih-i*, 95. Dubs, "Royal Jou Religion," 228, n. 2.

33. Ch'en Meng-chia ("Hsi-Chou Yin-jen," 88) says that both the "To Shih" and the "To Fang" are the words of King Ch'eng. In my opinion, however, while the Duke of Chou says that he is speaking for the King, it is very unlikely that a man of such positive character would have merely transmitted a speech written for him by the King. Ch'en also, in "Hsi-Chou T'ung-ch'i," (3).113, suggests that half of each of these documents belongs with half of the other; to me this rearrangement seems unnecessary. "To Shih" is interpreted as I understand it in: Ch'ü, *Shang-shu Shih-i*, 102. Dubs, "Royal Jou Religion," 228, n. 2.

34. There seems to be no difference of opinion as to the genuineness of this document, or the identity of those involved; see: Karlgren, "Glosses on the Book of Documents," (2).115. Ch'ü, *Shang-shu Shih-i*, 110. Dubs, "Royal Jou Religion," 228, n. 2.

35. The character *fang* 方 , which I translate as "territory," often has the sense of "state" in early literature. This proclamation is addressed to the men of the "numerous territories" that had been under the rule of the Shang.

36. Except that Ch'en Meng-chia thinks that the Duke of Chou is merely repeating the words of King Ch'eng—which I find implausible. Concerning Ch'en's

The "Ku Ming" ("Retrospective Charge," *Shu*, 70–74)[37] is an account of the last meeting of King Ch'eng with his ministers, his death, the arrangements for his funeral, and finally the accession of his son, King K'ang. It was apparently written by some officer, no doubt a secretary, for inclusion in the archives.[38]

"Wen Hou chih Ming" ("The Charge to Marquis Wen," *Shu*, 78–80) is a charge by a King to a feudal lord, quite similar to such charges found on Western Chou bronzes. On the basis of its style and content, both Ch'en Meng-chia and Kuo Mo-jo date it as having been written quite late in Western Chou.[39]

The "Pi Shih" ("Harangue at Pi," *Shu*, 80)[40] is a speech made by a Duke, evidently of the state of Lu, to his army that is setting forth to attack the Huai I and the Jung of Hsü. It has traditionally been ascribed to the time of the first Duke of Lu, the son of the Duke of Chou. Some contemporary scholars would date it to the Spring and Autumn period, but their arguments are not convincing.[41] The style of this docu-

---

argument that this document and the "To Shih" have become confused together, see n. 33 above. In favor of the view that the "To Fang" is a unit, and later than the "To Shih," see: Ch'ü, *Shang-shu Shih-i*, 116. Dubs, "Royal Jou Religion," 228–229, n. 2.

37. The meaning of the characters *ku ming* 顧命 in this title is something of a problem. Legge translates it as "The Testamentary Charge." I agree with Legge (Legge, *Shu*, 544, note) that the explanation commonly given for *ku* here is not very satisfactory. My own understanding of it is different. As the text makes clear, this is a charge that was left by the King, which was delivered to his heir after his death. At that time it was a "retrospective charge" that looked back to the wishes of the dead King.

In the "ancient text" version of the *Documents*, this one is divided to become two.

38. The "Ku Ming" seems to be generally accepted as a Western Chou document; Kuo Mo-jo, for instance, cites it in *Chin-wen Ts'ung-k'ao*, 56a–57a. Its style and content are such as to establish a strong probability, in my opinion, that it is a Western Chou document. Ch'en Meng-chia (*Shang-shu T'ung-lun*, 112) dates it as probably Western Chou.

39. Ch'en, "Hsi-Chou T'ung-chi," (3).113. Kuo, *Chin-wen Ts'ung-k'ao*, 299b–301a.

40. The name of this book is written variously; see Ch'ü, *Shang-shu Shih-i*, 134.

41. Yü Yung-liang, in *Ku-shih Pien*, II, 75–81, dates the "Pi Shih" to the reign of Duke Hsi of Lu (659–627 B.C.). Ch'ü Wan-li, in *Shang-shu Shih-i*, 134–135, not only accepts this argument but suggests that it was produced either in the thirteenth or the sixteenth year of his reign.

Yü says, as his first point, that the Huai I 淮夷 and Hsü Jung 徐戎 of this text are names for barbarians of a kind that is found in the Spring and Autumn period, but not in Western Chou. But in fact I and "eastern I" are mentioned in bronze inscriptions dated to the reign of King Ch'eng (*Chin-wen*, 20a, 23a, 27a, 28a), and war with the Huai I is mentioned in an inscription that Ch'en Meng-chia,

ment is similar to that of Western Chou inscriptions, and Kuo Mo-jo dates it as early Western Chou.[42] In my opinion it is not possible to date this document precisely, but it appears to come from Western Chou times, and very possibly from early in the period.

There remain to be considered six documents of the "modern text" that have been supposed to come to us from Western Chou times, but which I do not feel justified in using as source materials for that period. Some of these are so obviously productions of later times that critical scholars are almost unanimous in denying that they can be Western Chou. In the case of others the evidence is less certain, but leaves them at least in the very doubtful category.

The "Mu Shih" ("Harangue at Mu," *Shu*, 29) is a speech supposed to have been delivered by King Wu, exhorting his army before the battle in which it overcame the Shang. The King begins his harangue by denouncing the last Shang King for following the advice of a woman, and comparing a dominating woman to a crowing hen. He says:

> The men of antiquity had a saying: "The hen does not
> announce the morning . . ." Now the Shang King, Shou,
> follows only the words of his wife.

Elsewhere in Western Chou documents we have numerous catalogues of the crimes of the last Shang King, yet nowhere else does there seem to be mention of his having been under female influence. If King Wu considered this important enough to use to begin his harangue to his troops, on this crucial day, it is curious that we do not find it elsewhere.

There is also rather general agreement that, as early Western Chou

in "Hsi-Chou T'ung-ch'i," (5).108, dates to the following reign, that of King K'ang. And while there seems to be no early occurrence of the term Hsü Jung, an inscription dated by both Kuo Mo-jo and Ch'en Meng-chia to the reign of King Ch'eng speaks of war with the Yüan Jung 猜 戎 ; see *Chin-wen*, 20b, and Ch'en, "Hsi-Chou T'ung-ch'i," (2).70. The argument that such names could not occur in Western Chou is therefore without force.

Neither is it persuasive to argue, as Yü does, that this speech could not have been made in Western Chou times because the Duke does not specifically avow that this military expedition is made by order of the King. Nor is it possible to argue, as both Yü and Ch'ü do, that such a document can be dated by finding a time when the *Tso-chuan* says that Lu was fighting with the Huai I and the people of Hsü. Such struggles went on over many centuries, both in Western Chou and later.

42. Kuo, *Chin-wen Ts'ung-k'ao*, 330ab. Ch'en Meng-chia, in "Hsi-Chou T'ung-ch'i," (1).149, cites it among documents relating to the time of King Ch'eng, but in *Shang-shu T'ung-lun*, 112, dates it as merely probably Western Chou.

prose, the "Mu Shih" simply does not ring true.[43] The criterion of "style" tends to be an elusive one, which can be so subjective as to be unreliable.[44] Yet when several scholars who have made long study of the literature of a particular period agree that a document clearly does not conform to its style, their opinions merit close attention. When possible, however, it is desirable to cite specific, objective characteristics of style in support of such a contention. In the case of the "Mu Shih" it is possible to cite the rather anomalous use of the character *shih* 是 .[45] To date this text accurately appears difficult, but it is almost certainly not what it purports to be, a speech by King Wu. Ch'en Meng-chia suggests that it may date from as late as Warring States times.[46]

The "Hung Fan" ("Great Plan," *Shu*, 29–35) has been supposed to consist chiefly of the words of a relative and vassal of the last Shang King, addressed to King Wu after the conquest. This is one of the most celebrated and frequently quoted writings in the *Documents*. It is also one of the most unmistakably false of those attributed to Western Chou time.

43. Yü, *Shang-shu Hsin-cheng*, 3.1a. Ch'ü, *Shang-shu Shih-i*, 57. Ch'en, "Hsi-Chou T'ung-ch'i," (6).121. Ch'ü, "Lun Yü-kung Chu-ch'eng ti Shih-tai," 64.

44. One criterion that was formerly much used by Chinese scholars is, I think, dubious. There has been a tendency to suppose that texts difficult to read are earlier, while those easy to read are later. But this clearly depends very much on the background of the reader. Most persons would probably feel, for instance, that the *Mencius* is easy to read, while the *Han-fei-tzu* is difficult, but this obviously does not prove the *Han-fei-tzu* to be earlier. What it does indicate, I think, is that the *Mencius* is in the main stream of the Chinese literary tradition, and therefore is more comprehensible to those familiar with that main stream. This suggests that such a criterion can only be used with great caution.

45. In all of the sections of the "modern text" of the *Documents*, traditionally dated to the Western Chou period, this character *shih* occurs only twenty-one times. It is most frequent (six occurrences) in the "Mu Shih." It also occurs with some frequency in the "Hung Fan" (five times), the "Li Cheng" (four times), and the "Chin T'eng" (three times); all of these, as will be shown below, are indicated by other criteria to be later than Western Chou. In the twelve documents that I accept as of Western Chou date there are only two occurrences of the character: one in the "Le Kao" and one in the "Chün Shih." In five of its six occurrences in the "Mu Shih" this character is inserted between the subject and the verb. For example, in the first case, there is 婦言是用 , which might perhaps be translated literally as "wife's speech, this [he] uses." The case in the "Le Kao" (*Shu*, 52, paragraph 13) has some similarity, but is not exactly the same. It is true that the character *shih* is frequent in the *Poetry*, so that high frequency of the character can hardly be declared proof, by itself, of late date. But the high frequency of this uncharacteristic pattern is, at any rate, a piece of objective evidence that can be cited for what many, including myself, have observed—that the style of the "Mu Shih" is not that of early Western Chou.

46. Ch'en, *Shang-shu T'ung-lun*, 112.

An outstanding characteristic of the "Hung Fan" is its ubiquitous use of numbers: "three virtues," "five elements" (*wu hsing* 五 行), "six extremities," "eight [factors in] government," and so on and so on. Such categorization into numbered groups is decidedly uncharacteristic for Western Chou, but became a prominent feature of some of the literature of Warring States times. In the first fifteen chapters of the *Analects* it is not present at all; these are believed to compose the earliest version of the text, while the last five chapters appear to have been added later. In the last five chapters there are nine sections in which Confucius is quoted as speaking of the "three errors," "four bad qualities," "nine cares," and so forth.[47] This would seem to indicate that in Confucian circles, at least, this manner of speaking did not become widely prevalent until the Warring States period.

The "Hung Fan" contains other evidences of a date much later than Western Chou: references to the "five elements," *yin* and *yang*, and much more.[48] Its style is also quite clearly not that of Western Chou. There is rather general agreement that this can not be a Western Chou document. In a long and careful study of this text, Liu Chieh concluded that it was written after the end of the Warring States period but before the state of Ch'in had completed the unification of China.[49] Ch'ü Wan-li would put it at the beginning of Warring States times.[50]

The "Chin T'eng" ("Metal-bound [Coffer]," *Shu*, 35–36) discusses a series of events supposed to have begun in the second year after the Chou conquest of the Shang. King Wu became ill. The Duke of Chou thereupon made a sacrifice and addressed the spirits of the three previous Chou rulers, asking them to spare the life of King Wu and take his instead. The oracles were favorable, and King Wu recovered. The Duke of Chou then placed the documents concerning this affair in a metal-bound coffer. After King Wu had died, some of the uncles of the young King Ch'eng (who were also, of course, brothers of the Duke of Chou) spread reports that the Duke intended harm to King Ch'eng. The Duke of Chou spent two years in the east and captured the criminals. King Ch'eng did not dare to blame the Duke. In the autumn, Heaven sent a great storm which flattened the unharvested grain, uprooted great trees, and frightened the people. The King then

47. *Analects*, 16.4–8, 10, 17.6, 8, 20.2. Also see Creel, *Confucius*, 291, 293::313, 315.

48. On the date of the concepts of *yin* and *yang*, and of the "five elements," see pp. 164, 446.

49. *Ku-shih Pien*, V, 388–403. Presumably this means between 256 and 221 B.C.

50. Ch'ü, *Shang-shu Shih-i*, 59–60. Ch'en Meng-chia, in "Hsi-Chou T'ung-ch'i," (6).121, dates the "Hung Fan" to the Warring States period.

opened the metal-bound coffer and learned from its documents that the Duke had offered his life in place of that of King Wu. King Ch'eng wept and said that he had formerly not appreciated the Duke, so that "now Heaven has set in motion its terrible majesty to signalize the virtue of the Duke of Chou." Heaven then sent a wind in the opposite direction, which raised up the grain so that there was a bountiful harvest.

This is clearly fiction; it seems possible that it may be the first Chinese short story. But even so it might be a valuable source document if we could be sure that it had been written in Western Chou times. This, however, seems improbable. It treats history carelessly, giving the impression that the expedition of the Duke of Chou to the east was undertaken solely to punish slanderous statements made concerning himself; there is no mention of the fact that his brothers had joined with the Shang and others in revolt against the Chou rule. And its style, as more than one critic has observed, is definitely not that of early Western Chou prose. Ch'ü Wan-li considers it to date from late Western Chou or Spring and Autumn time; Ku Chieh-kang suggests that it was written after the Western Chou period.[51]

It was pointed out earlier that in Western Chou literature as it is preserved to us there is remarkably little praise of the Duke of Chou, while in Spring and Autumn times and later he was increasingly esteemed and celebrated.[52] It seems probable that the "Chin T'eng" was written at a time difficult to determine but probably later than Western Chou, by one of his admirers.

"Wu I" ("Without Idleness," Shu, 56–59) opens with the words, "The Duke of Chou said," and is in the form of a series of admonitions by the Duke of Chou to a King. There are reasons for grave doubt that this is, in fact, a Western Chou document, but it is regarded

---

51. Ch'ü, Shang-shu Shih-i, 67. Ku-shih Pien, II, 64. Kuo Mo-jo (Chin-wen Ts'ung-k'ao, 33b) calls the "Chin T'eng" a work subject to doubt, and says that the occurrence in it of the character ti 地 proves that it is not a genuinely Western Chou production. Ch'ü Wan-li also says (loc. cit.) that ti is not characteristic of early Western Chou. But one should, I think, distinguish between the mere occurrence of the character ti, and its use as a metaphysical counterpart to Heaven. The latter seems definitely to be later than Western Chou. But it was pointed out earlier (page 447, n. 10) that the character ti occurs twice in the Poetry and once in the original text of the I-ching— but in none of these cases as a metaphysical concept. The occurrence of ti in the "Chin T'eng" (Shu, 35) does not, I think, denote the metaphysical concept. I do not think that the "Chin T'eng" is a Western Chou document, but I doubt that it can be condemned on the basis of this single character.

52. See pp. 72–79.

as genuine by eminent and critical scholars. It has even been used as a principal source for Western Chou ideas.[53] It is necessary, therefore, to examine it with special care.

This document has traditionally been supposed to contain words addressed by the Duke of Chou to King Ch'eng. But as Ch'ü Wan-li points out, it names Chou rulers up through King Wen and then says: "The Duke of Chou said, 'Oh, the succeeding King, who will continue [the line] from now on, should . . .'"[54] The King who succeeded Wen was Wu, and it seems entirely clear that the document, as written, was supposed to consist of statements addressed by the Duke of Chou to King Wu. But if that is the case, it is very strange indeed—and this may well be why it has almost always been supposed that these remarks were directed to King Ch'eng.

The "Wu I" says:

> The Duke of Chou said: Oh, the succeeding King, who will continue [the line] from now on, should not indulge excessively in liquor, nor be licentious in excursions and hunting. . . . Do not moreover say, "Today I will indulge in pleasure." . . . Do not be like Shou, the [last] Yin King, in his errors and disorders, and his disposition to become maddened by liquor. . . . Now if you are not wise, people may impose on you and deceive you, saying, "The small people bear resentment against you and revile you," and you will believe it. When it is like this you will not forever bear in mind the rules, and make your heart generous, but will confusedly punish the guiltless and kill the innocent. The resentment will become unanimous, and it will be heaped upon your person.[55]

This would be strong language to use to any King. It is true that the Duke of Chou does use admonitory language in addressing his nephew, King Ch'eng, in some sections of the *Documents*, but even toward him the Duke's language is never so unrestrained. That he

---

53. In his study of Western Chou political thought, Ch'i Ssu-ho repeatedly cites the "Wu I" and at one point quotes four-fifths of its text verbatim; see Ch'i, "Hsi-Chou Cheng-chih Ssu-hsiang," 28, 29, 31. Ch'en Meng-chia, Yü Sheng-wu, and Ch'ü Wan-li have all indicated that they believe this document to be by the Duke of Chou; see: Ch'en, "Hsi-Chou Yin-jen," 92. Yü, *Shang-shu Hsin-cheng*, 3.1ab. Ch'ü, *Shang-shu Shih-i*, 106.

54. *Shu*, 58. Ch'ü, *Shang-shu Shih-i*, 106.

55. *Shu*, 58–59.

would have dared to speak in this way to his elder brother, the formidable King Wu, to whom the excessive use of liquor was anathema,[56] is incredible.

Statements concerning the Shang Kings, attributed to the Duke of Chou in the "Wu I," contrast sharply with what he says elsewhere. In the "Wu I" the Duke is quoted as saying:

> Tsu Chia enjoyed the realm for thirty-three years.
> Those who became King after this enjoyed ease during
> their whole lives, and thus did not know the hardships
> of husbandry, nor hear of the toil of the people. They
> gave themselves up to being steeped in pleasure.[57]

The Shang King Tsu Chia reigned, according to the traditional chronology, from 1258 to 1226 B.C. After him there were six more Shang Kings, all of whom were, according to the above statement, "steeped in pleasure." But in the "To Shih" and the "To Fang"—both documents that seem to be universally accepted as containing authentic utterances of the Duke of Chou—he speaks very differently.

In the "To Shih" the Duke of Chou says:

> From Ch'eng T'ang [the first Shang King] down to Ti I
> [the next to the last Shang King] there were none who
> did not make bright their virtue and carefully attend to
> the sacrifices. . . . There were none who did not corre-
> spond to Heaven in benefiting [the people].[58]

And in the "To Fang" the Duke says of the Shang Kings that from the beginning of the dynasty:

> Right up to Ti I there were none who did not make
> bright their virtue and exercise care about punishments,
> and thus they were able to stimulate [the people].[59]

Thus in these documents the Duke says that the five Kings between Tsu Chia and the last Shang King were exemplary, while in the "Wu I" he is quoted as branding them as "steeped in pleasure."

Much more is wrong with the "Wu I."[60] In my opinion this document is a forgery, written at a time when the legend of the Duke of

56. See p. 95.
57. *Shu*, 58.
58. *Shu*, 55.
59. *Shu*, 64.
60. It says that no Shang King after Tsu Chia reigned for more than ten years, which does not agree with any reckoning; see: *Shu*, 58. Tung, "Tuan-tai Yen-chiu," 390. Ch'en, *Yin Tz'u Tsung-shu*, 214–216.

Chou had developed to such a point that it was considered a matter of course that he should preach sermons without restraint, from the eminence of his lofty virtue, to King Wu or anyone else. It appears likely that it was written after the end of Western Chou, but before the time of Confucius.[61]

The "Li Cheng" ("Establishment of Government," *Shu*, 67–70) purports to be a treatise written by the Duke of Chou, dealing—in part at least—with the organization of the government. If genuine, this would be a most important document for our investigation. And a number of excellent scholars do accept it as coming to us from the beginning of Western Chou.[62] But there are grave difficulties with this text.

Its opening words are translated by Karlgren as follows:

> Chou Kung [the Duke of Chou] spoke thus: Saluting and bowing down the head I report to the succeeding Son of Heaven and king. Now he admonished the king about all and said: (Those in the left and right of =) the nearest assistants of the king are the permanent leader

---

At the beginning of the "Wu I" the term *chün-tzu* 君子 is used in what I suspect is its Confucian sense, as denoting a man of noble character rather than of high hereditary status. Commentators explain it differently, and the point is not worth laboring; but I consider this another suspicious factor.

The "Wu I" says (*Shu*, 58) that when the Shang King called Kao Tsung first came to the throne, it is said that he went into seclusion and "for three years did not speak. His speaking without words was harmonious." Eight characters of this passage are quoted in *Analects*, 14.43 (on textual variations see Karlgren, "Glosses on the Book of Documents," [2].107–108). Confucius there explains it as referring to the three years of mourning, and says that in antiquity it was the general practice for new rulers to remain inactive for three years, leaving the government in the hands of their ministers. This passage in the "Wu I" has generally, though not universally, been considered to relate to the three years of mourning; see Ch'ü, *Shang-shu Shih-i*, 108, and Yü, *Shang-shu Hsin-cheng*, 3.27b–29a. Kao Tsung is understood to be King Wu Ting (1324–1266 B.C.). He is shown by the Shang inscriptions to have been an extremely energetic ruler, and this three years of inactivity seems unlikely. Futhermore, there seems to be no definite evidence that the practice of three years of mourning—at least to anything like this extent—was in fact this early, although the Confucians tried to represent it as having been. Even as late as the time of Mencius it seems to have been by no means universal; see Creel, *Confucius*, 309, n. 3::124, n. 3. Kuo Mo-jo says ("Ch'ang-an Ming-wen," 14): "That the custom of mourning for three years was never practised in Early Chou is here confirmed by one of these inscriptions. Very probably this custom was first advocated by Confucius himself."

61. Since it is quoted from and discussed in *Analects*, 14.43.

62. Ch'i, "Hsi-Chou Cheng-chih Ssu-hsiang," 32. Yü, *Shang-shu Hsin-cheng*, 3.1ab. Ch'ü, *Shang-shu Shih-i*, 3, 121.

[常伯], the permanent (man in charge =) manager [常任], the man of law [準人], the stitcher of garments [綴衣] and the (chief of the) tiger braves [虎賁].

Here we have five titles of what were supposedly the chief officials in the government. It would be reasonable to expect, then, that we might find these titles in other Western Chou literature: the bronze inscriptions, the original text of the *Book of Changes*, the *Documents*, and the *Poetry*. In fact, in the whole of this source material, only one of these titles seems to occur—and it occurs only once, and then not as the title of a high officer. The term that Karlgren translates as "tiger braves" is found once in the *Documents*, but in that case there are a hundred of them.[63] It is true that among the many official titles given later in this document there are some that occur in the Western Chou sources, but this completely anomalous list of the chief offices, with which it opens, is reason enough to question its authenticity.

There is more. This work contains many occurrences of numbered categories. Using Karlgren's translations, there are the "nine virtues," the "three (high) positions" (twice), the "three holders of (high) positions" (three times), the "three holders of talents" (twice), the "three (men of) talents," the "three executives," and the "three Po."[64] Such categorization is foreign to Western Chou documents. As was pointed out earlier, it does not appear to have become prevalent much before the Warring States period.[65]

The "Li Cheng" is a rambling document, but insofar as it has a point, it would seem to be to urge the King to select his officers with care and let them, once installed, govern without interference. It may have been written at the time when officials were making their campaign for a freer hand in the government; if so, its attribution to the Duke of Chou was natural, since they regarded him as their champion. Ch'en Meng-chia has stated that the "Li Cheng" is not a genuine document from the beginning of Western Chou.[66] In my opinion it can not be used as a source for Western Chou.

63. *Shu*, 70. Earlier in this document there is the term *hu ch'en* 虎臣 ; this apparently is the title of a fairly high officer, and is found elsewhere in the literature. The characters *cho i* 綴衣 occur twice in the *Documents* (*Shu*, 70, 71), not, however, as an official title, but only with the sense of "stitched garments."

64. *Shu*, 67–68. Karlgren discusses the meaning of "the three Po" in "Glosses on the Book of Documents," (2).150.

65. See p. 457.

66. Ch'en, "Hsi-Chou T'ung-ch'i," (6).121. This appears to conflict, however, with his statement in Ch'en, *Shang-shu T'ung-lun*, 112, although the two were published within a few months of each other.

The "Lü Hsing" ("Punishments of Lü," *Shu*, 74–78) was discussed earlier.[67] It has traditionally been dated to the tenth century B.C., but its whole pattern of thought is that of the Warring States period. It treats "Earth" as a metaphysical concept, the counterpart of Heaven, which was unknown in Western Chou times.[68] It refers to categories of threes, and especially and almost innumerably of fives. It is constructed around the concept of the "five punishments." This concept does not appear in any Western Chou text, nor even in works as late as the *Analects* and the *Tso-chuan*.[69] The late date of the "Lü Hsing" is now rather generally recognized.[70] It cannot possibly be used as a source for the Western Chou period.

Poetry

FAR fewer problems of authenticity beset the *Poetry* than the *Documents*.[71] The poems in this anthology range from light-hearted songs to solemn sacrificial odes used in the royal temples. The dating of individual poems is often difficult and sometimes impossible, but they are generally believed to have been composed between the approximate dates of 1122 and 600 B.C.[72] Thus they are all either of Western Chou date, or from a time not much later.

---

67. See p. 161.

68. *Shu*, 74. See pp. 446–447.

69. I have found no reference to the "five punishments" in any bronze inscription, nor in the original text of the *Book of Changes* or in the *Poetry*. In the "modern text" of the *Documents* it occurs, aside from the "Lü Hsing," only in the "Yao Tien" and the "Kao Yao Mo" (*Shu*, 5, 7, 9). The late date of the latter two documents is clear and recognized; see Creel, *Studies*, 97–98, n. 2, and *Wei-shu T'ung-k'ao*, I, 120–125.

70. Ch'i Ssu-ho ("Hsi-Chou Cheng-chih Ssu-hsiang," 32) says that the "Lü Hsing" was probably written at the beginning of the Warring States period. See also *Hsien-Ch'in Ching-chi K'ao*, I, 87–95. Derk Bodde, in Bodde and Morris, *Law in Imperial China*, places its composition "several centuries later" than 950 B.C., but not later than the fourth century B.C.

71. The *Shih* or *Shih-ching* 詩經 is sometimes called the *Mao-shih* 毛詩, supposedly because a scholar named Mao edited the recension of the text that has come down to us.

72. A few scholars would, however, place the final compilation of the *Poetry* after the time of Confucius. For various opinions concerning its dating, see: Maspero, *La Chine antique*, xix, 354–356. Waley, *Shih*, 11. *Wei-shu T'ung-k'ao*, I, 211–223. Dobson, "Linguistic Evidence and the Dating of the Book of Songs." One section of the *Poetry* was formerly believed to have been written in Shang times, but it is now generally recognized that in fact these poems were written in the state of Sung in the Chou period; see Creel, *Studies*, 49–54, and *Ku-shih Pien*, III, 504–510.

Bronze Inscriptions

INSCRIPTIONS on bronze objects—chiefly vessels—are in some respects the most important documents we have from early Chou times. Some of them are quite long, and some incorporate the texts of documents written for various purposes. These are, then, our only *physical documents* remaining from that remote time.[73] They not only provide us much information on many subjects, but give us unaltered examples of the writing of the time which can be used to test the authenticity of documents that have been handed down. They are invaluable—*if* they are genuine and we can read them. These are very large reservations.

Chinese bronze vessels were valuable even in antiquity; a single piece was enough to bribe a Duke, or to occasion enmity between a feudal lord and the King.[74] And wherever there is profit to be made, there will be those who try to make it. The *Han-fei-tzu* relates that the state of Ch'i attacked Lu and demanded a certain bronze vessel. Lu sent them a forgery, at which Ch'i immediately protested, but the ruler of Lu maintained that it was genuine. Those of Ch'i said, "Let Yo-Cheng Tzu-ch'un come; we will listen to him." The Lu ruler summoned Yo-Cheng, who asked him, "Why did you not send the real one?" "Because I love it," the ruler replied. "And I," said Yo-Cheng, "love my reputation for honesty."[75] This probably occurred, if the story is true, in the fifth century B.C.[76] Whether it is true or not, it shows that the Chinese were long ago familiar with the problem of the faking of bronzes and the need for expertise in the detection of forgeries. Yet the forgery of both bronzes and inscriptions has continued to be a problem at all periods, including our own. As in all such fields, the forgers and those who seek to unmask them are engaged in a constant race to improve their methods.

The reading of inscriptions is no less a problem. Chinese scholars have been doing serious work in this field for at least a thousand

73. Unfortunately, however, not all of our Western Chou inscriptions do remain to us as physical objects. The attrition of antiquities in China has been very great, and many vessels bearing important inscriptions have disappeared. In many cases, however, squeezes of the inscriptions are preserved, while in others we have only hand copies; the former are of course much more valuable. Such squeezes or copies of inscriptions must, of course, be examined with great care, bearing in mind the possibility of forgery.

74. *Tso*, 37::39 (Huan 2), 100::101 (Chuang 21).

75. *Han-fei-tzu*, 8.5b; Liao, *Han Fei Tzŭ*, I, 255.

76. Yo-Cheng Tzu-ch'un is named together with Confucius' disciple Tseng-tzu in the *Records on Ceremonial*. *Li-chi*, 6.18a; Legge, *Li-chi*, I, 128.

years,[77] and the greatest strides have undoubtedly been made in the twentieth century. Yet it is improbable that any really competent scholar would claim that he could read every character of any very long inscription, without any possibility of error. It is necessary to make allowance for the fact that there are some points of which we cannot be sure, even though others seem quite clear. The dictum laid down by Wang Kuo-wei a half century ago is still valid: it is a mistake to insist upon explaining every character in an inscription, so that one forces meanings into what one cannot understand—and it is equally wrong to say that, since we cannot explain everything, we cannot use these materials at all.[78]

The study of bronze inscriptions is necessarily a highly specialized field. In the entire world only a small number of scholars are really expert in it. They have necessarily developed a rather complex apparatus and jargon. There is a large literature on the subject, but even to read this effectively requires a good deal of study, for which only a few have the time and the inclination. It is difficult to present one's arguments concerning bronze inscriptions fully, in a manner that will be wholly convincing to others who have not made such study. Thus the credentials of those who undertake to write in this field are important.

I had better state my own credentials. I am not an expert on bronze inscriptions, but I have studied them. I was initiated into the field by Liu Chieh; in 1933 and 1934 I spent some hours each week with him, learning about inscriptions and discussing their problems. Professor Liu gave his invaluable time to an unknown American student purely out of the goodness of his heart, and I could never repay the obligation I owe him. I have also discussed bronze inscriptions, on numerous occasions, with Jung Keng, Shang Ch'eng-tso, and T'ang Lan. For many years I had the privilege of close friendship with Tung Tso-pin, who worked on bronze inscriptions as well as oracle bones; in 1948 Professor Tung and I gave a joint seminar on bronze inscriptions at the University of Chicago. I know Ch'en Meng-chia, but have not discussed inscriptions with him as much as with the other scholars I have named.

Because the bronze inscriptions require a good deal of preparation before one can hope to deal with them competently, it is not surprising that many scholars dealing with early Chinese history have omitted them from consideration. Some have expressed regret that they had to do so. Some, not surprisingly, have been frankly suspicious of the reliability of the bronze inscriptions altogether.

---

77. Rudolph, "Preliminary Notes on Sung Archaeology."
78. Wang, *Kuan-t'ang Chi-lin*, 6.13b.

Such doubts have usually been voiced by scholars who had made little study of the inscriptions. An exception, however, is Noel Barnard, who for a decade has been expressing thoroughgoing skepticism concerning the authenticity of a large proportion of the inscriptions that most scholars in the field consider genuine. He has written:

> Scientifically excavated inscriptions are slowly growing in numbers with the result that systematic research based on dependable documents will soon lead to a better understanding of ancient China while the sometimes fanciful accounts of forgers concealed among unattested materials will soon no longer be able to distort the picture. Hitherto, scholars have had to work with inscribed vessels the majority of which lack any record of provenance; the few with some sort of testimony are vaguely and insubstantially authenticated. With material of this kind reliable research has not been possible, while those who have studied the inscriptions have seldom considered the possibility that a serious proportion of the bronze texts they have consulted are merely the products of unscrupulous craftsmen of recent centuries.[79]

If the latter statement is intended to mean that scholars working with bronze inscriptions have not commonly been aware of the possibility, or even the likelihood, of forged vessels and inscriptions, it is incorrect. In a footnote to the above statement, Barnard lists some studies of forgeries published by Chinese scholars. Techniques for the discovery of forged bronzes were discussed in books published as much as a thousand years ago.[80] And in many discussions in which I have taken part with eminent Chinese scholars in this field—to some of whose works Barnard refers—the possibility of forgery has been a very frequent topic; some of them have seemed to me to carry skepticism quite far. This is not to say that they may not have accepted, as genuine, inscriptions that were not; that possibility always exists. But as a group they are by no means so naïve as Barnard would sometimes seem, here and elsewhere, to suggest.

The proposition that the highest degree of credence should be given to "scientifically excavated inscriptions" is irreproachable. It is my impression, however, that the number of such inscriptions that are very long and revealing is limited. Elsewhere in this same article Barnard refers to "the several thousands of fully attested inscriptions I have

79. Barnard, "A Bronze of Western Chou Date," 12.
80. Rudolph, "Preliminary Notes on Sung Archaeology," 175–176.

studied."[81] Are we to understand that all of these were "scientifically excavated"? He frequently speaks of "unattested" as contrasted with "fully attested" inscriptions. The former apparently refers to virtually the entire body of bronze inscriptions that were published before very recent decades. What he means by "fully attested inscriptions" may perhaps be discerned from his reference (in 1965) to "unquestionably authentic materials obtained under the controlled conditions of archaeological discovery over the last two or three decades."[82]

That some of the inscriptions that Barnard calls "fully attested" were obtained under "controlled conditions of archaeological discovery" is certainly true, but in the case of others this is doubtful. One of his papers is called "A Recently Excavated Inscribed Bronze of Western Chou Date." Its second sentence speaks of "scientifically excavated inscriptions"; one might therefore suppose that the bronze of which he is writing was scientifically excavated. Of it he writes:

> In June 1954, an inscribed *Kuei*-vessel with four handles —one of a dozen bronze artifacts excavated—was unearthed in Tan-t'u Hsien 丹徒縣 , Kiangsu; details of the find are recorded in the *Wen-wu ts'an-k'ao tzu-liao* 文物參考資料, 1955 (5/58). The inscription contains 121 characters describing events datable in early Western Chou times; as an historical document the *Yi Hou Nieh Yi* 宜庚矢彝 (or, ins. *121.3*, according to my system of serial numbers) ranks foremost among the most important inscriptions definitely datable in this period—as to its authenticity there is not the slightest doubt.[83]

The *Wen-wu Ts'an-k'ao Tzu-liao*, on the page to which Barnard refers, says that "during June of 1954" a farmer, while digging in a field, "unexpectedly dug up a *ting* [bronze tripod vessel] at a depth of one-third of a meter below the surface. He then carefully enlarged the scope of his digging, and at a depth of two-thirds of a meter unearthed a total of twelve bronzes." These bronzes were handed over to the local authorities and were forwarded up through channels, reaching the Kiangsu Provincial Committee in Charge of Cultural Objects in October 1954. In that same month the Committee sent an inspection party to the site of the discovery. Digging further, they found some

81. Barnard, "A Bronze of Western Chou Date," 37.
82. Barnard, "Chou China," 398.
83. Barnard, "A Bronze of Western Chou Date," 13.

fragments of bronze in the hole from which they were told the twelve had come, and excavated some other objects, made of bronze and other materials, nearby.[84]

All of this is, of course, admirable. After the bronzes were found by the farmer, they were turned over to the authorities to be examined and cared for by qualified persons. As soon as they reached the hands of archeologists, they were recognized as important, and a team of excavators was sent to learn everything possible about the circumstances of discovery. This is the manner in which a large number of bronzes have become known in recent years, adding very greatly to our knowledge. Nevertheless, the fact that the site at which the farmer found the bronzes was examined by archeologists, four months later, does not make these "materials obtained under the controlled conditions of archaeological discovery." They were certainly not "scientifically excavated," and it is a question whether even the word "excavated" can be employed here in the sense in which it is used by archeologists. That an article has been "excavated," archeologically, means that it has been removed from the earth by a person trained to observe and record the circumstances, and to determine whether the ground has been disturbed in recent times. These twelve bronzes were not.

In fact, the circumstances under which the I Hou Nieh Kuei—the vessel that Barnard calls the *Yi Hou Nieh Yi*—was found are relatively satisfactory, from an archeological point of view. It is regrettable that the vessel was not excavated by a trained archeologist, and that four months elapsed before the site came under expert scrutiny. But the fact that trained excavators did find other objects near the point at which the twelve vessels were unearthed, and the circumstances as they reported them, tend to indicate that in fact the bronzes in question had lain in the ground since ancient times. In some other cases, however, finds have been isolated, and there has been much less of corroborative evidence.

This certainly does not mean that objects found in this manner are not genuine; I know of no such find that has been challenged. But *in any individual case* a bronze so unearthed *could* be a forgery, without any bad faith being involved. Forged bronzes have been made for a long time, and one could easily have been buried. Forgers sometimes bury bronzes to "age" them, and such a piece could easily have been forgotten. Only an archeologist well trained—and alert—can hope to judge whether the soil has remained undisturbed since ancient times.

84. "Chiang-su Tan-t'u Hsien T'ung-ch'i," 58.

Thus the fact that a bronze has been unearthed in this way does not provide such unquestionable evidence of provenance as might be supposed.

Even the sincere testimony of eminent scientists that an object has been scientifically excavated does not prove it genuine. In 1912 the discovery of "Piltdown man" was announced with great fanfare by Arthur Smith Woodward, Keeper of the Department of Geology at the British Museum. Woodward himself took part in some of the excavation and contributed toward its expense. It was later announced that Teilhard de Chardin—who would later be one of the world's most famous paleontologists—had excavated another tooth of "Piltdown man," and had found, *in situ,* one of the numerous stone utensils associated with the find. There was some skepticism, but great authorities, including Sir Arthur Keith and G. Elliot Smith, championed "Piltdown man," which "passed into the general histories and encyclopaedias as easily the best-known of the primal ancestors of the human species."[85]

The Piltdown materials, deposited in the British Museum, were newly subjected to various and exhaustive tests in 1953. These showed that while the cranial fragments were old, and human, the jawbone was that of a fossil orangutang. The bones had been altered and the teeth had been filed to produce the desired configurations. These, and stone and bone utensils found with them, had been artificially discolored. It it now generally recognized that "Piltdown man" was a hoax.[86]

Careful investigation has shown, however, that none of the eminent scientists who have been named was implicated in the fraud; they were imposed upon. Teilhard de Chardin undoubtedly believed that he had found *in situ*—that is, in strata that had lain undisturbed for thousands of years—objects that had in fact been placed there after being forged very recently. It is easier than one might suppose to be deceived in this way.[87]

What all this means is that provenance—an account of the circum-

85. Weiner, *The Piltdown Forgery,* 14.
86. This account is based on Weiner, *The Piltdown Forgery.*
87. Such deception is easy if it is practiced by one of those taking part in an excavation. I learned this as a student of archeology. Digging in an Indian mound in Illinois, I was excavating a flexed burial. While I was away at lunch my colleagues "planted" an Aztec statuette between the knees and elbows of the skeleton. Since the site was guarded at all times, I had no reason to be suspicious, and dug out this rare find with great elation—until they told me of the joke. I planted on them some unusual flint objects of my own manufacture—rather good ones, I thought—which they accepted until I enlightened them.

stances under which an object is reported to have been found—does not provide unquestionable proof of either the antiquity or the nature of the object. Yet provenance is extremely important, and always highly desirable. In the case of fossil bones, accurate knowledge that they were found in a particular undisturbed stratum may be the best, if not the only, definite evidence of their age. But Chinese bronzes have often been buried long after they were made, so that the date at which they were buried is not conclusive evidence as to their date of manufacture.[88] Fortunately, however, bronzes, unlike bones, have many characteristics that, if properly interpreted, can be used to date them, especially if they are inscribed. These include mode of manufacture, shape, decor, and in inscriptions, the forms of characters, syntax, vocabulary, and proper names and references to historical events.

It is unfortunate, certainly, that we have so little record of the provenance of the great bulk of the inscriptions with which scholars work. Barnard finds this very suspicious. Concerning the Ta Yü Ting he notes that one scholar "records a Mr. Sung as its first possessor who hid the vessel and allowed no one to see it."[89] Concerning the famous Mao Kung Ting, which he has repeatedly denounced as a forgery, Barnard says that in the facsimile publications of the correspondence of its first owner, "nowhere amongst his letters, around 1840, is the Mao Kung Ting mentioned. It was about this time he pretended to purchase the vessel . . ."[90]

In fact, however, such reticence is not wholly surprising. Bronze vessels have always been extremely valuable, and even in the West, collectors sometimes do not advertise their collections, for fear of robbery. In China there has been another danger. Officials, and even

88. For instance, in October 1954 a farmer unearthed seventeen bronzes near Ch'ang-an, and archeological excavation at the site found further pieces. Ch'en Meng-chia dated the various bronzes found at this site as ranging in age from the beginning of Western Chou to the reign of King Mu (1001–947 B.C.); see Ch'en, "Hsi-Chou T'ung-ch'i," (5).121–123. In 1961 a group of fifty-three bronzes was unearthed, also in the region of Ch'ang-an. Kuo Mo-jo dated these pieces as including some from as early as the time of King Ch'eng (1115–1079 B.C.) and others from as late as the middle of Western Chou or somewhat later. Kuo stated that he was inclined to believe that these bronzes were buried at the time of King Yu, the last Western Chou King, to protect them from invading barbarians. Kuo also states that a number of other hoards of bronzes have been found that were probably buried at the time of disorders in late Western Chou; see Kuo, "Ch'ang-an Ming-wen." If Western Chou bronzes could have thus been buried at that time, it is clear that this could also have happened later.

89. Barnard, "Some Remarks on the Authenticity of a Western Chou Style Inscribed Bronze," 240, n. 19.

90. Barnard, "Chou China," 399.

the Emperor, have sometimes found it possible to secure articles of value without bothering to pay for them. An especially notorious episode occurred in the twelfth century, when confiscations were made on a grand scale to enrich the Emperor's collections. It is said that one particularly zealous collector of tribute, whenever he "discovered that a family owned some valuable object . . . would dispatch soldiers, who would place on the coveted goods the yellow seal, which marked imperial tribute to be confiscated."[91] According to one report, the bronze collection of the Emperor Hui-tsung (1101–1126) increased from 500 to 10,000 items. To what extent this increase was effected by confiscations is uncertain, but at least one magistrate around this time hit upon another effective means of acquiring bronzes. Richard Rudolph writes:

> One official, undoubtedly one of the more serious collectors, when serving as magistrate . . . ordered people brought before him for criminal offenses to pay their fines in early bronzes. In this way he created a collection of fifty or sixty objects.[92]

The danger of the official confiscation of books has been more or less perennial in China, beginning with the famous book burning by the First Emperor of Ch'in in 213 B.C.[93] In the Ch'ing dynasty (1644–1912) the suppression of literature reached a high point, especially during the reign of Ch'ien-lung (1736–1795). Books that were suppressed included not only those considered to be anti-dynastic or rebellious, or insulting to the Manchus or to other non-Chinese dynasties, but also books that contained opinions concerning the classics that were not officially approved, or some that were merely considered "unliterary" in style. Luther Carrington Goodrich says that this literary inquisition caused "irritation to the Chinese through constant invasion of their homes and seizure of their property, the books in some instances and the woodblocks in nearly all being heirlooms, bearing the authorship of a distinguished ancestor."[94] It is not unreasonable to suppose that this also may have contributed toward a Chinese tendency not always to proclaim valuable possessions.

Whatever the reason, it is a well-known fact that Chinese owning

91. McKnight, "The Rebellion of Fang La," 20.

92. Rudolph, "Preliminary Notes on Sung Archaeology," 173–175.

93. Bodde, *China's First Unifier*, 80–85, 162–166. For other confiscations and destruction of books at various times, see Goodrich, *The Literary Inquisition of Ch'ien-lung*, 3–65.

94. Goodrich, *The Literary Inquisition of Ch'ien-lung*, 19–65.

valuable bronzes have in many cases kept their possession of them secret. T'ang Lan writes that in the nineteenth century and in the first half of the twentieth important bronzes often disappeared immediately after they were unearthed, so that in effect "the day they came out of the ground was the moment at which they ceased to exist."[95] And even in Communist China bronzes that are found are sometimes secreted.[96] Lack of available information concerning the discovery of a bronze is regrettable, but it is not always proof that the bronze is a forgery.

In any case, provenance is not the only thing that is necessary to make an object usable in research. It must also fit, harmoniously, into its proper place in the body of knowledge. It may be that the body of knowledge must itself be modified to accommodate it, but in some manner the harmony must be achieved. It was not dubious provenance that caused "Piltdown man" to be exhaustively reinvestigated— though a few had lingering doubts. It was, rather, the fact that it simply did not fit with the rest of what was known about human evolution. But much of our present knowledge of human evolution was achieved *after* "Piltdown man" had become accepted—which helps to explain the forty years that elapsed before it was exposed.[97]

Similarly, bronzes supposed to be Western Chou must be tested, regardless of their provenance or lack of it, by the way in which they fit into our whole body of knowledge concerning the period. As touchstones we must of course give primacy to bronzes that have been scientifically excavated, and to others like the I Hou Nieh Kuei concerning the provenance of which we have relatively good information. The crucial question then becomes: do recently unearthed bronzes tend to verify, or to discredit, the great body of those that critical scholars have long believed to be genuine? It is my impression that almost all scholars working in the field would agree overwhelmingly—however much they might differ about an occasional piece—that they tend to verify them.

In case after case that has been mentioned in the text of this volume, recently unearthed inscriptions refer to persons and events known to us from inscriptions that have long been current. Sometimes they fill in a missing piece in a picture that has been all but complete. And the bronzes and their inscriptions do not seem to differ beyond a normal range of variation. It was pointed out in chapter 12 that the I Hou Nieh Kuei—to which Barnard rightly attaches great importance—ap-

---

95. *Ch'ing-t'ung-ch'i T'u-shih*, 1.
96. Kuo, *Wen-shih Lun-chi*, 347, 350.
97. Weiner, *The Piltdown Forgery*, 18–35.

pears to show us the culmination of the career of Nieh Ling, concerning which two previously known inscriptions also inform us.[98] The I Hou Nieh Kuei does differ somewhat, both in the craftsmanship of the vessel and in the fact that its characters are rather less elegant, from the other two, but in fact this is what we might expect. It appears probable that the other two vessels were produced at or near the eastern capital, where fine craftsmanship would surely have been available.[99] The I Hou Nieh Kuei, on the other hand, was unearthed near the southwestern corner of the Western Chou territories. It may well have been made in that area and therefore represent "provincial" craftsmanship.[100] The differences are not incompatible with this interpretation.[101]

Barnard has denounced as forgeries a number of bronzes and inscriptions, including some that have been considered very important.[102] Some of his points are not without weight, and I have considered them. In most cases, however, his denunciations have on balance seemed to me to be unconvincing; it is my impression that scholars in the field generally find them so. I have, however, eliminated from my corpus one inscription that Barnard has called in question—not solely for the reasons he gives, but partly.[103]

Barnard is an intelligent, learned, and extremely industrious

---

98. See pp. 403–405.

99. When these bronzes were cast, Nieh Ling was in the royal service, and they are reported to have been unearthed not far from the site of the eastern capital; see Ch'en, "Hsi-Chou T'ung-ch'i," (2).77–78.

100. While the location of the state of I is not certainly known, Barnard, in "A Bronze of Western Chou Date," 18, says that "the location of the find indicates the area of ancient Yi." I believe that this is the general opinion.

101. Barnard "A Bronze of Western Chou Date," 39–40) denies the relationship between these three inscriptions, contrary to the opinions of the Ch'en Meng-chia and Kuo Mo-jo. He points to differences both in the script and in "the whole atmosphere of the record"; the latter is scarcely surprising, since the circumstances were quite different. He also finds it incongruous that Nieh Ling, who "appears with the lowly rank of a scribal official, Tso-ch'e 乍 冊 " could be identical with the Marquis of Ch'ien. But the rank of a royal Maker of Books was by no means lowly, and the inscriptions indicate that while holding this rank Nieh Ling was quite an important person at the royal court.

102. See especially his criticism of the Mao Kung Ting in Barnard, "Chou China," 395–403.

103. This is the inscription on the vessel that Kuo Mo-jo calls the Kuo Chi Tzu Po P'an (Chin-wen, 103b–104a). Barnard, who numbers it in his system as "T. 104.4," discusses it in "Some Remarks on the Authenticity of a Western Chou Style Inscribed Bronze," 227. I have long felt uneasy both about some of the language and about some of the content of this inscription—more uneasy, I think, than about any other generally accepted inscription. I may have been wrong to exclude it, but I prefer to use as basic materials only those concerning which I feel basic assurance.

scholar. He has performed a service by causing even more attention to be paid to problems of authenticity. His specific criticisms of bronzes and inscriptions do not seem to have won a following. To what extent they may in time be proved correct, only the future can tell. One point, however, needs to be borne in mind. An inscription recently carved into an old bronze, or even an inscription carved or cast into a modern forgery, *may* still be a historical document of value.[104]

The bronze inscriptions bristle with problems. Yet as research on them progresses, it becomes increasingly clear that the great body of the inscriptions that are accepted by the best scholars in the field offer a coherent and extremely important complex of information. They fit —with the transmitted literature, with what seems to be the most reliable tradition, and with the small number of inscriptions concerning which we have reliable evidence of provenance. With all of the risks that they involve, it seems impossible not to use them.

I have tried to use a number large enough—one hundred eighty-four, to be exact—so that even if a few of them should ultimately be found to be unreliable, the results would not be wholly invalidated. These are in large part relatively long inscriptions. All of them have been studied, and accepted as genuine, by at least one scholar—and in a number of cases by many scholars—in whose competence I have confidence.

The basis of this corpus is formed by the inscriptions in the first section of Kuo Mo-jo's *Liang-Chou Chin-wen Tz'u Ta-hsi K'ao-shih*.[105] This compendium was first published in 1932. A greatly enlarged and revised edition was issued in 1935, and minor revisions were made in the edition of 1958. I have omitted one inscription included in this section in my corpus, leaving a total of 161.[106] In addition I include two further inscriptions, dated to Western Chou times, from the second section of this work.[107]

104. Fakers of inscriptions often copy inscriptions, rather than composing their own. And it may happen that such a copy of a genuine inscription may remain to us, while the genuine inscription has become lost. In this case the copy in bronze becomes like the copies of inscriptions handed down in books. Some of the latter are false, but the problem with all of these materials then becomes one of studying the text to determine whether in fact it is ancient—just as we study the transmitted texts of the *Documents*, even though no physical copy remains to us from Chou times. Such copied inscriptions are not, of course, in any sense as valuable as inscriptions that have come to us, physically, from Chou times. But they may have a certain value.

105. *Chin-wen*, 1a–156b.

106. The omitted inscription is *Chin-wen*, 103b–104a. My reasons for omitting it were just discussed above; see p. 473.

107. *Chin-wen*, 225a, 230b.

Many of the inscriptions in this work have been discussed by other scholars, and I have taken into account their interpretations, and sometimes their better versions of the texts, as well as those of Kuo Mo-jo. In particular I have departed from the dating made by Kuo in the case of many of the inscriptions. It would be impracticable to discuss the basis on which I have dated each inscription, but where Ch'en Meng-chia, in his "Hsi-Chou T'ung-ch'i Tuan-tai," differs significantly from the dating of Kuo, I have usually followed Ch'en—but not always. I have discussed the dating of a number of individual inscriptions in footnotes.

In addition to the 163 inscriptions in the *Liang-Chou Chin-wen Tz'u Ta-hsi K'ao-shih*, I have used twenty-one other inscriptions, which are published in the following works:

> Ch'en, "Hsi-Chou T'ung-ch'i," (1).157, 161, 165, 168; (2).99, 102 (no. 4), 111, 117 (second inscription), 120 (no. 34); (3).66, 83 (no. 48); (5).115, 119; (6).103–104 (no. 84), 118–119 (no. 96).
> Kuo, *Wen-shih Lun-chi*, 313–314, 328, 347.
> *Ch'ing-t'ung-ch'i T'u-shih*, 27 (plate 102).
> Kuo, "Ch'ang-an Ming'wen," 2–4, 6.

Many of these inscriptions are also discussed in other publications, which I have taken into account.

The added inscriptions have been selected because, in one way or another, they were considered especially important for the study of Western Chou government. This corpus of 184 inscriptions includes only a fraction of the many thousands of inscriptions, supposedly of Western Chou date, that have been published. Many of those that are omitted are brief and unenlightening. I believe that this corpus does include the great majority of relatively long inscriptions that have been carefully studied and that throw a great deal of light on government.

Tso-chuan

THE nature of this important work was briefly described in chapter 3.[108] Its entries are dated from 722 through 464 B.C., but as we have seen, it also contains many references to events and persons of the Western Chou period. So many critical studies have been written on the *Tso-chuan* that it would require a volume even to adequately summarize their content.

The traditional view was that the *Tso-chuan* was a commentary on

108. See p. 48.

the *Spring and Autumn Annals*, and that the latter work was edited by Confucius. But it is now rather generally agreed that there is no real evidence that Confucius edited the *Annals*, which is an extremely bare chronicle of events, kept in the state of Lu. And while the *Tso-chuan* does at some points comment on entries in the *Annals*, it remains silent concerning others and has long entries about matters of which the *Annals* says nothing.

It is generally agreed that the *Tso-chuan* is a work that must have been composed on the basis of a variety of documents, chiefly historical in nature. Bernhard Karlgren found, however, that the entire work has a homogeneous grammar, indicating that it was not compiled merely by joining together earlier materials without any alteration. On the basis of a wide variety of criteria it is generally believed that this text was put into the form in which we now have it in the Warring States period, possibly in the neighborhood of 300 B.C.[109] William Hung has suggested, however, that it may have been compiled in the second century B.C., but few others seem disposed to place it so late.[110]

Since this text did not reach its present form until relatively late, it must always be used with care. Wherever it becomes especially wordy and moralizing, the possibility of late interpolation is considerable. Yet this text seems to bear within itself evidence that it is, in large measure, a faithful history of the times of which it treats, based upon records, and not just a fanciful account written by men of later times.[111] In working intensively with the *Tso-chuan* over several decades I have come increasingly to feel respect for the essential soundness of its historical base. Yet this does not mean, of course, that all statements that it makes about the Western Chou period are necessarily true; some of them are, in fact, demonstrably false. But in many cases, at least, the *Tso-chuan* does give us an accurate report of what was believed about

109. For some of the discussions of the nature and date of the *Tso-chuan*, see: Karlgren, "On the Tso Chuan." Maspero, "La composition et la date du Tso tchouan." Hsu, *Ancient China*, 184–186. *Ku-shih Pien*, V, 1–22, 263–313, 538–554. Yang, "Lun Tso-chuan yü Kuo-yü." *Wei-shu T'ung-k'ao*, I, 350–411. *Ch'un-ch'iu Ching-chuan Yin-te* (Preface by William Hung), I, i–cvi. The latter work is summarized in Ch'i, "Professor Hung on the Ch'un-Chi'iu."
110. *Ch'un-ch'iu Ching-chuan Yin-te*, I, xcii–xcv.
111. For instance, we know that the state of Ch'u became gradually transformed in its social organization to be more like the northern states, during the Spring and Autumn period, but it is rather unlikely that the compilers of the *Tso-chuan* were aware of this. Yet in that text we find that kinship groups (*shih*) like those of the north are mentioned as existing in Ch'u only in the latter third of the Spring and Autumn period. I have given detailed evidence for this in Creel, "Beginnings of Bureaucracy in China," 178–179, and notes 118–119.

Western Chou, by some persons, in Spring and Autumn times. And
in many cases there is reason to believe that its traditions concerning
Western Chou may well be valid.

Discourses of the States

THIS work deals with much the same period, and treats many of the
same incidents, as does the *Tso-chuan*. It is by no means, however, a
historical source of equal importance. Where the *Tso-chuan* consists,
in a general way, of a running historical account, the *Discourses of the
States* is a series of narratives, anecdotal in character and often lacking
any connection with each other. And where an incident related in the
Tso-chuan is also described in the *Discourses of the States*, the latter
work commonly devotes much more space to it.[112] But since the *Discourses* is only about one-third the length of the *Tso-chuan*, it follows
that it must treat of far fewer incidents.[113]

Much more important is the fact that the treatment of incidents in
the *Discourses of the States* not infrequently taxes credulity, and suggests that whoever wrote it took as his basis what was, no doubt, a
historic event, but then embroidered it into a good story.[114] Quantities
of ink have been used in the effort to demonstrate that the *Discourses*
was based upon the *Tso-chuan*, or vice versa. Neither proposition is
necessary, nor perhaps even probable. Both used historical materials
that were current at the time—in some cases the same materials, since
some of their wording is identical. But the arrangement and manner
of the two works is quite different.

Karlgren found the grammar of the *Discourses of the States* to be
similar to, though not identical with, that of the *Tso-chuan*, which
would tend to indicate that they were written at around the same time.
Hung concludes that the *Discourses* may have been finally edited in

112. A few examples are given in Yang, "Lun Tso-chuan yü Kuo-yü," 75–77;
they could be multiplied indefinitely.

113. Ch'i Ssu-ho writes that the *Discourses of the States* consists of about
60,000 words, as compared with about 180,000 for the *Tso-chuan*; see Ch'i, "Professor Hung on the *Ch'un-Ch'iu*," 52, 61, 65.

114. Compare, for instance, the account of the return of Kuan Chung to the
state of Ch'i in the *Discourses of the States* (*Kuo-yü*, 6.1a–2a) with that in the *Tso-
chuan* (*Tso*, 83::84 [Chuang 9]). The account in the *Tso-chuan* is brief and believable. That in the *Discourses* is a great deal longer and, in such details as representing the Duke of Ch'i as going to the border to welcome his erstwhile enemy, hardly
credible. The latter account is rather clearly a piece of fiction based upon the actual
event, but embroidered in keeping with the legend of Kuan Chung that developed
in later times.

the third century B.C.[115] It appears probable that this work comes to us from late Warring States times. Such information as it offers about the Western Chou period should be evaluated, like all other traditions. But my personal inclination is to look with a somewhat more critical eye on the statements of the *Discourses of the States* than on those of the *Tso-chuan*.

Ritual of Chou

FOR two thousand years, many—though not all—scholars have believed that this work is a detailed description of the Western Chou government, written by the Duke of Chou. Its influence has been incalculable. For all of that time, Hu Shih has written, it "has always been a source of inspiration for all political reformers."[116] Even in the twentieth century it has still been cited, not only by Chinese conservatives, but even in the polemical literature of Chinese communism.[117]

In a paper based on voluminous research, published in 1961, Sven Broman concluded that:

> The Chou Li *[Ritual of Chou]* depicts a governing system which, in all essentials, prevailed in middle and late feudal Chou in the various states and had its roots in the system pertaining to late Yin and early Chou. This governing system continued to exist in a more or less modified form up to 221 B.C.[118]

It is doubtful that many scholars would agree with this conclusion. Broman has performed a service by showing the occurrence, in relatively early works, of many of the titles found in the *Ritual of Chou*.[119]

---

115. Karlgren, "On the Tso Chuan," 58–59, 64. *Ch'un-ch'iu Ching-chuan Yin-te*, I, lxxxii–lxxxvi.

116. Hu, "Wang Mang," 222–223.

117. Levenson, *Confucian China*, III, 11, 37, 42–43.

118. Broman, "Studies on the Chou Li," 73–74.

119. Broman's results are not, however, so convincing as he seems to suppose. The works he has used for comparison are, as he says (ibid., 2), chiefly pre-Han, but a number of them are not certainly any older than the *Ritual of Chou* itself; they may therefore merely reflect essentially the same view, held in the Warring States period, of Western Chou government. And he has omitted the best of all sources from his study; he says ("Studies on the Chou Li," 2): "Nor are references made to the bronze inscriptions, as that would go beyond the scope of this article." When there is added to this the fact that in some cases he has been able to find correspondences to the offices mentioned in the *Ritual of Chou* only by assuming very dubious equivalences between titles, the total argument is weak.

But it is precisely the "governing system," so highly organized and elaborately set forth in that work, that does not correspond with the facts of Western Chou government as we know them—as has often been pointed out.[120]

It is not merely the circumstance that we find no evidence of such an elaborate scheme that causes doubt. Even more telling is the fact that this scheme is organized in patterns of a kind that do not appear in other works much before the Warring States period. Six principal ministers are called, respectively, those of heaven, earth, spring, summer, autumn, and winter. Each of these has sixty subordinates, making a total of three hundred sixty. Kuo Mo-jo suggests that this symmetrical number was chosen for reasons connected with astronomical calculations.[121] Not only this preoccupation with numbers, but also the numerous references to *yin* and *yang*, show that this text could not have been written until long after Western Chou time.[122]

A number of Chinese scholars have questioned the *Ritual of Chou* for a very long time. The imperial librarian Liu Hsin, who died in A.D. 23, found it in the archives, edited it, and brought it to public attention. It was attacked immediately. A little later He Hsiu (129–182), in a remarkable anticipation of the conclusion of modern scholarship, asserted that it was not written by the Duke of Chou, but was produced during the Warring States period. There have also been many, even down to our own day, who have believed that the book was forged by Liu Hsin.[123] But studies by a number of recent scholars have shown that it is unlikely that the *Ritual of Chou* was produced much before or much after the Warring States period, and preponderant opinion attributes it to that time.[124] Yet this does not mean that it must necessarily be called a forgery. It should probably be considered an attempt, by one or more scholars, to describe the Western Chou government on the basis of the information available to them. At the same time—perhaps without any conscious distortion—they depicted it as being what they conceived to be an ideal government.

Their description, heavily influenced by the preoccupations of the

120. Ssu, "Liang-Chou Chih-kuan K'ao," 1, 22–23. Kuo, *Chin-wen Ts'ung-k'ao*, 79b–82b. Karlgren, "Legends and Cults in Ancient China," 202, n. 1.

121. *Chou-li*, 3.2ab; Biot, *Tcheou-li*, I, 44–46. Kuo, *Chin-wen Ts'ung-k'ao*, 80a.

122. *Chou-li*, 10.11b, 23.10b, 20a, 24.18b, 25.1a, 39.13b, 41.10b.

123. *Chou-li*, Preface. *Wei-shu T'ung-k'ao*, I, 282-327. The early history of this text is summarized in Karlgren, "Chou Li and Tso Chuan," 1–8.

124. Kuo, *Chin-wen Ts'ung-k'ao*, 49a–81b. Maspero, "La société chinoise," 335. Ch'i, "Hsi-Chou Cheng-chih Ssu-hsiang," 19. *Ch-ing-t'ung-ch'i T'u-shih* (Preface by T'ang Lan), 6, n. 14. Shih, "Chou-li Ch'eng-shu Nien-tai K'ao." Ssu, "Liang-Chou Chih-kuan K'ao," 23. Karlgren, "Some Sacrifices in Chou China," 7.

Warring States period, was fallacious. It may not properly be used—as too many scholars still do use it, even after proclaiming its late date—as in any sense depicting the general nature or organization of Western Chou government. Yet in some matters of detail it is evident that this work does, here and there, preserve surprisingly accurate information. Where the Western Chou sources give us fully adequate assurance of the existence and the nature of an institution, the *Ritual of Chou* can sometimes fill out the picture most usefully.[125]

I Chou-shu

THE name— 逸周書 —by which this work is most commonly known should perhaps be translated as "Lost Chou Documents." It is also sometimes called simply *Chou-shu*, "Chou Documents," or *Chi-chung Chou-shu* 汲家周書, "Chi Tomb Chou Documents." The latter name comes from the fact that this work is said to have been among those found in the district of Chi, in the modern Honan province, in A.D. 281 when the tomb of King Hsiang of the state of Wei (who died in 296 B.C.) was opened. There is much doubt, however, that in fact this was among the books recovered from that tomb.[126]

The *I Chou-shu*, considered in general, is full of the preoccupation with numbers, Heaven-Earth dualism, *yin* and *yang*, and numerous other characteristics of works produced in the Warring States period. It is generally agreed that this work as we have it could not have been compiled before that time.[127] But it consists of a series of documents that concern episodes, often without connection. Many of these episodes relate to Western Chou time. Ssu-Ma Ch'ien, in recounting the conquest of the Shang by the Chou, has a number of passages that are similar and at some points identical with the section of the *I Chou-shu* that describes these events.[128] This does not necessarily prove, as

125. Instances of this have repeatedly been cited in this volume; see for example pp. 126–127 and 184–185. See also: Kuo, *Chin-wen Ts'ung-k'ao*, 79b–81b. *Chin-wen*, 118ab. Kuo, "Ch'ang-an Ming-wen," 4. Maspero, "La société chinoise," 335. Ssu, "Liang-Chou Chih-kuan K'ao," 1, 22–25. Ch'en, "Hsi-Chou T'ung-ch'i," (3).109–110.

126. Édouard Chavannes says definitely that it was not, in *Mémoires historiques*, I, 233, n. 1. Also see *Wei-shu T'ung-k'ao*, I, 505–511.

127. *Wei-shu T'ung-k'ao*, I, 504–511. Li, *Yin-yang Wu-hsing Hsüeh-shuo*, 38–42.

128. *Chi-chung Chou-shu*, 4.2a–3b. *Shih-chi*, 4.25–30; *Mémoires historiques*, I, 233–238. The account in the *Historical Records* is in no sense, however, a copy of that of the *I Chou-shu*. It not only differs in language, but also is much longer and differently arranged. Some of the differences are interesting. For instance, the *Historical Records* says that at the final battle "the assembled troops of the feudal

is sometimes supposed, that the *I Chou-shu* was used by Ssu-Ma Ch'ien as a source, but it does indicate at least that a document incorporated in (or drawn upon by) that work was available to him.

The various sections of the *I Chou-shu* must be evaluated individually. And many scholars who do not consider the book as a whole early or reliable nevertheless quote sections of it concerning events of Western Chou time, and apparently consider them valid source materials. Sections that are sometimes used in this way include those called "K'e Yin Chieh 克殷解," "Shih Fu Chieh 世俘解," "Shang Shih Chieh 商誓解," and "Tso Le Chieh 作雒解."[129] But all of these give ground for doubt.

The "K'e Yin Chieh" says that King Wu gave commands concerning the moving of the "nine *ting*." These "nine *ting*," bronze vessels regarded as symbols of the royal power and virtue, are not mentioned in any Western Chou source, and the conception seems more in place in the context of Warring States times.[130] The statement that, immediately after the conquest, a large number of people were released from prison by King Wu appears to relate to the tradition that the wicked last Shang King had imprisoned many of his subjects who had protested against his evil ways, but the Western Chou sources do not seem to attest this.[131] The "Shih Fu Chieh" tells us that King Wu took "heads [or ears? of the slain?] to the number of 177,779, captured 310,230 men, and in all conquered 652 states."[132] These are large figures. Fu Ssu-nien called them "mere illusory conjectures by men of the Warring States period."[133] Yet one can hardly say that this section could not have been written in Western Chou times; nevertheless, I

---

lords numbered four thousand chariots" fighting for Chou, while the *I Chou-shu* speaks of "three hundred fifty Chou chariots." The latter figure seems more believable, since we do not see large numbers of chariots mentioned in the sources for the beginning of Chou.

129. These are not, of course, the only sections of the *I Chou-shu* that are cited. For some references to these four, see: Ch'en, "Hsi-Chou T'ung-ch'i," (1).142, 143, 147. Ch'en, "Hsi-Chou Yin-jen," 103. In the latter paper Ch'en Meng-chia says: "The so-called *I Chou-shu* contains a good deal of relatively late material. But some of its chapters, such as 'Shih Fu,' 'Tso Le,' 'Shang Shih,' and others nevertheless contain a certain amount of genuine material; they often agree with what is related in the bronze inscriptions, and can not be mentioned in the same breath with other chapters of this book."

130. *Chi-chung Chou-shu*, 4.3b. There is, it is true, one mention of the "nine *ting*" in the *Tso-chuan*, in an entry dated to 710 B.C. (*Tso*, 38::40 [Huan 2]). But this is in a long moralizing speech, including mention of the "five colors," which may well be a late interpolation.

131. *Chi-chung Chou-shu*, 4.3ab.

132. Ibid., 4.11a.

133. Fu, "Chou Tung Feng yü Yin I-min," 285.

find it less than certain that it was.[134] The "Shang Shih Chieh" seems to provide less basis for suspicion than the other three sections, yet it is doubtful as a Western Chou document.[135] The "Tso Le Chieh" was definitely written later than that time—probably as late as the Warring States period.[136]

To catalogue all of the characteristics of the *I Chou-shu* that stamp it as a relatively late work would be an almost endless task, and of little usefulness. For a few examples: In various of its sections we find the Duke of Chou speaking in terms of long series of numbered categories, of the "five elements," of *yin* and *yang*, and of Earth as a metaphysical concept.[137] King Wu, as heir apparent, is even quoted as referring to the institution of the *Pa* 霸 —an institution that did not arise until well into Spring and Autumn times, when one of the feudal lords, as *Pa*, exercised some of the functions of the—by that time —almost powerless Chou King.[138]

Not all sections of the *I Chou-shu* contain such glaring anachronisms. They must be evaluated individually, as has been said. Traditions concerning Western Chou that are found in this work must be considered, certainly. But I find it impossible to be assured that any portion of it is, beyond question, a document from Western Chou times that has come to us without alteration.

---

134. The mention of "nine *chung* 終 " and three references to "three *chung*" seem strange. And this document as a whole does not seem, to me, quite right for Western Chou.

135. *Chi-chung Chou-shu*, 5.2b, quotes King Wu as speaking of "the Way of the former Kings," 先王之道 . This is of course a common Confucian cliché. I believe that there is no place in the Western Chou sources in which *tao* 道 is used in this way; see Creel, *Confucius*, 122–123, 310 n. 12::132–133. This section also speaks (*Chi-chung Chou-shu*, 5.2b) of the "three virtues," which is anachronistic for Western Chou. Furthermore the language of this section as a whole seems to me to be a good attempt to write in the style of Western Chou, rather than a piece of actual Western Chou prose.

136. *Chi-chung Chou-shu*, 5.7b–9a. This section speaks of dividing territory into "100 *hsien* 縣 ," but the *hsien* as an administrative district seems to have been unknown in Western Chou times, and the manner in which it is spoken of here strongly suggests the usage of the Warring States period; see Creel, "Beginnings of Bureaucracy in China." This section also speaks of the enfeoffment of vassals at a *she* consisting of earth of five colors, which was discussed earlier; see pp. 370–371. These are only two among many points that could be cited to indicate that this section represents the thought of the Warring States period. Henri Maspero, in "Le régime féodal," 134, dates this document to the fourth century B.C. See also Li, *Yin-yang Wu-hsing Hsüeh-shuo*, 42.

137. *Chi-chung Chou-shu*, 3.1b–3a, 8a–10a, 10a–11a, 4.6b–9a, 5.5a–6a, 6a–7b, 6.5a–10b.

138. Ibid., 3.7a.

Bamboo Books

THE work known as the *Chu-shu Chi-nien* 竹書紀年 , literally "Bamboo Book Annals," is commonly called simply the *Bamboo Books*. It was among books that were found in A.D. 281 when the tomb of a ruler who had died in 296 B.C. was opened, and consisted of annals written on strips of bamboo. It is generally agreed that this work has long been lost, and that the work that has been current under that name in recent centuries is a forgery.[139] Wang Kuo-wei collected many quotations that he believed were derived from the original work, and thus reconstituted a considerable portion of it.[140] It is this reconstituted text to which I have referred as "the genuine *Bamboo Books*."

Certain reservations must be made, however, even with regard to this work. Wang was a very great scholar, and in most cases there seems to be no doubt that the passages he has used were quoted from the original *Bamboo Books*. In some instances, however, there is room for difference of opinion. For this reason it is necessary, when dealing with a passage of critical importance, to make careful examination as to Wang's source and his basis for selection.

Furthermore, it is by no means certain that the original *Bamboo Books* consisted, as one might expect annals to do, of entries that were in all cases set down at the time to which they refer. It includes statements concerning early Emperors whose names do not appear in other literature until late, and who are regarded by critical scholars as legendary. Three passages in Wang's reconstruction of the *Bamboo Books* mention the Yellow Emperor, who has traditionally been supposed to be very ancient, but who seems not to be named in other works or in bronze inscriptions until the fourth century B.C.[141] Since it is fairly evident that he could not have been mentioned in a genuine entry written at an early date, it has been argued that these entries have been falsely attributed, by the works that quote them, to the *Bamboo Books*.[142] That is certainly possible, but this approach leaves

139. Creel, *Studies*, xix–xxi, 25. Wang, *Chin Chu-shu*, Preface. *Wei-shu T'ung-k'ao*, I, 490–500.

140. Wang, *Ku Chu-shu*.

141. Ibid., 1ab. Kuo, *Shih P'i-p'an Shu*, 152. *Ku-shih Pien*, VII (*shang*), 189–209.

142. *Ku-shih Pien*, VII (*shang*), 189–190. In this paper Yang K'uan argues that the original *Bamboo Books* did not include entries for any period earlier than the Hsia dynasty. But this presumably means acceptance of the references in the genuine *Bamboo Books* to the founder of Hsia, Yü 禹 (Wang, *Ku Chu-shu*, 1b). But

us in a somewhat embarrassing position. For in this case in order to decide whether a particular entry was really a part of the original *Bamboo Books* we must first decide whether it is historically accurate —which is not always possible.

Certainly we do not by any means possess, in quotations from it, all of the text of the original *Bamboo Books*, and legitimate question can be raised concerning the authenticity of some of the supposed quotations. But we do have enough to give us some idea of the nature of the original work, and this makes it evident that even if we did possess the text that was placed in the tomb at the end of the third century B.C. we would still not have a chronicle of unimpeachable veracity, as some have seemed to suppose.

Entries that concern very early time appear rather clearly to have been fabricated, in some cases, at least, as late as the Warring States period. Some passages tax credulity; we read that "the heavens rained blood, there was ice in summer . . . the sun came forth in the night and did not come forth in the day," and again that "ten suns came out together."[143] There are generalizations that are by no means certainly correct, such as the statement that: "In the time of [Kings] Ch'eng and and K'ang the whole world was tranquil; punishments were set aside, and for forty years were not used."[144] Some of those who write on chronology attach great value to the general statements in the *Bamboo Books* concerning long spans of time, but at least one of these is most doubtful. The text says: "From Yü to Chieh there were seventeen generations. Including the time when there were Kings and when there was none, there were four hundred seventy-one years." But since Yü does not appear to have been mentioned in other works as a ruler until Spring and Autumn times, this entry must have been written so late as to make it valueless.[145]

The original *Bamboo Books* was evidently compiled in the Warring States period. Numerous ingredients went into this compilation. Many of its statements, as they are preserved to us in qotations, appear quite factual and may well have been handed down in much earlier records.

---

although Yü is mentioned several times in the *Poetry* as a culture hero, there seems to be no reference to him as a ruler until the Spring and Autumn period; see *Ku-shih Pien*, I, 106–134. Thus it is unlikely that references to Yü in the original *Bamboo Books* were written before Spring and Autumn times, and the reputation of that work as a series of contemporary records would not be saved even if passages mentioning the Yellow Emperor were eliminated.

143. Wang, *Ku Chu-shu*, 1ab, 3a.

144. Ibid., 7a.

145. Ibid., 3b. See n. 142, above.

The information that they give us may often be very valuable, but it must be weighed on the basis of its inherent credibility along with everything else that we know.

❧ ❧

Other Sources

SOME other works that have been cited frequently may be discussed briefly.

The *Analects* (*Lun-yü* 論語) consists chiefly of purported sayings of Confucius and his disciples, and their conversations between themselves and with others. Most of these are probably essentially authentic, but they were collected at different times and certainly in some cases underwent alteration. There is also some material in this text that has nothing to do with Confucius or his disciples, and there are some interpolations. I have published a detailed critique of the *Analects* elsewhere.[146]

The *Mencius* (*Meng-tzu* 孟子) is generally agreed to be a genuine work, probably compiled by his students shortly after the death of Mencius (c.372–c.289 B.C.). It appears to be a reasonably factual account of his actions and sayings, though no doubt as in all such books the accounts were sometimes retouched to make an impression more favorable to Mencius. If there are interpolations in this work, they are probably minor.[147]

The *Book of Etiquette and Ceremonial* (*I-li* 儀禮) gives minute descriptions of the way in which a variety of ceremonies—at marriages, banquets, archery contests, funerals, sacrifices, and so forth—should be carried out by aristocrats. It has been attributed to the authorship of the Duke of Chou, but no critical scholars credit this. It has been pointed out elsewhere that there is no indication that *li* 禮 as an aristocratic code had yet been developed in Western Chou times; if it had not, this extensive and detailed treatise on *li* could hardly have been written that early.[148] It seems probable that this work is a depiction —regularized, stylized, and no doubt idealized—of the ceremonies that were carried on in the Spring and Autumn period, the high time of the development of the aristocracy. But such works, giving precise rules for the functioning of institutions that in practice were undoubtedly as various as the exigencies of life, are commonly set down

---

146. Creel, *Confucius*, 291–294::313–315.

147. Ch'ien, *Hsien-Ch'in Chu-tzu Hsi-nien*, I, 374. Creel, *Confucius*, 194, 316 n. 15::208–209.

148. See pp. 336–338.

after the institutions they describe have declined, if not ceased to exist. And it is likely, as is commonly supposed, that the *Book of Etiquette and Ceremonial* was written down in the Warring States period.[149] Nevertheless this book has characteristics that make it appear possible that much of it, at least, may have been written with relatively little influence from the thought of the Warring States period.[150]

The *Records on Ceremonial* (*Li-chi* 禮記) is a very miscellaneous collection of documents, brought together in the first century B.C.[151] It is a mine of information on many subjects, and undoubtedly incorporates many valid traditions handed down from early times. But the documents of which it is composed very often show unmistakable evidence that they were written, or at least edited, not earlier than the Warring States period. Its content must, therefore, be used with great care.

149. *Wei-shu T'ung-k'ao*, I, 269–280. Ch'i, "Chou-tai Hsi-ming-li K'ao," 223. Yang, *Ku-shih Hsin-t'an*, 2.

150. It seems to have not been influenced by the *yin* and *yang* and "five elements" ideas, and to contain little of numerology. See Li, *Yin-yang Wu-hsing Hsüeh-shuo*, 23–24. Fung Yu-lan, in *A History of Chinese Philosophy*, I, 65, calls it "an early work transmitted by the Confucianists."

151. *Wei-shu T'ung-k'ao*, I, 327–342.

Appendix B

Problems of Chronology

Problems of chronology hamper the study of almost every aspect of ancient China. They are difficult enough when one deals with periods after 841 B.C., when at least the various systems of chronology are in essential harmony. But before that date these problems are almost insoluble.

Ssu-Ma Ch'ien, who wrote around 100 B.C., no doubt knew more about ancient China than any other man of his age, and had at his command a great deal of information that is forever lost to us. But he frankly confessed that the records relating to the period before 841 B.C. involved so many contradictions and divergences that he found it impossible to assign dates to events of that time; instead, he simply related them in chronological order. Édouard Chavannes praised this scholarly caution, and in his translation of the *Historical Records* did not attempt to provide dates before 841 B.C.[1] The practice is attractive, but unfortunately it is impossible to follow in a book like this one. To give no dates would be totally confusing. One is compelled to use dates as a framework to keep the various events in some kind of order, however hypothetical the dates themselves may be.

If one must use dates, one would of course like them to be correct, or as nearly correct as possible. It is necessary then to examine the various chronological systems and try to choose between them. For a volume like this one it is especially desirable to determine, if possible, the date of the beginning of the Chou dynasty. But this is, as it happens, one of the most debated problems in the whole field of the study of ancient China.

Two basic documents have most commonly been appealed to as

---

1. *Shih-chi*, 13.3–4. *Mémoires historiques*, I, CLXXXVI–CLXXXVII, 275 n. 2; III, 1–2.

sources for early chronology. One of these is a chapter on chronology in the *History of the Former Han Dynasty*.[2] From this there is derived the date of 1122 B.C. as that of the first year of the Chou dynasty; it has been widely used and is commonly known as the "orthodox" or traditional date.

The second source used as a chronological basis is the annals known as the *Bamboo Books*, which was discussed in Appendix A.[3] As was indicated there, the history of that work is complex, and as might be expected, more dates than one—and even more than two—have been alleged to be derived from it.

The current *Bamboo Books* appears to indicate that the Chou dynasty began in 1050 B.C., and that date has been adopted by a number of scholars.[4] In 1932 C. W. Bishop published a paper espousing this date and seeking to establish its accuracy by means of various other data. One of the principles that he used was that "we may accept the figure of twenty years as in round numbers the average length of a reign in ancient China."[5]

In an article published in 1933, W. Perceval Yetts discarded both of these sources and sought to fix the date of the beginning of Chou by calculating backward from 841 B.C. He assigned "an average of fifteen years to each reign," multiplied this by ten Kings ruling before 841 B.C., and arrived at 991 B.C. for the beginning of Chou.[6]

In 1937 I dealt with the problem of whether to use the traditional date of 1122 B.C. or one derived from the *Bamboo Books*. I pointed out that the current *Bamboo Books*, from which the date of 1050 is derived, is rather generally agreed by critical scholars to be a late forgery. And the genuine *Bamboo Books*, as partially reconstituted by Wang Kuo-wei, appears to support a quite different date for the beginning of Chou: 1027 B.C. But even the genuine *Bamboo Books* was compiled only in the Warring States period, and it is by no means certain that its data on early chronology is reliable.[7]

I pointed out that since no system of chronology appeared to be certain, the traditional one had some definite advantages.

---

2. *Han-shu*, 21.

3. See pp. 483–485.

4. Chavannes believed that various dates given in the *Historical Records* indicate that Ssu-Ma Ch'ien followed a chronology that agreed with this; see *Mémoires historiques*, I, CXCI–CXCVI.

5. Bishop, "The Chronology of Ancient China."

6. Yetts, "The Shang-Yin Dynasty and the An-yang Finds," 683–684.

7. Creel, *Studies*, xvi–xxii. For additional data on the dubious character of even the genuine *Bamboo Books* as a source for chronology, see above, pp. 483–484.

A Chinese Jesuit, Père Mathias Tchang, made an exhaustive study of various Chinese works on chronology and published his results in 1905 under the title *Synchronismes chinois*. Based on the traditional chronology, this volume has the great advantage that it not only gives a system of dates for the kings but also includes, in relation to this and to the Christian era, chronologies for a number of the most important of the feudal states during the Chou period. This work is eminently convenient for the Occidental and even for the Chinese scholar, and among the former at least it has come to be used very widely as a standard.[8]

These tables could be duplicated for another system only by means of an amount of labor that the result would scarcely justify—especially since one has no assurance that another system is accurate. I concluded that the best course was to use the traditional chronology as a convention, recognizing that it may well involve a factor of error and should only be supposed to date events relatively to each other, rather than absolutely.

As new materials and new research have advanced our knowledge of early China, a number of Chinese scholars have addressed themselves to the problem of dating the beginning of Chou, with varying results. One of the most important and perhaps the most influential of the new chronologies they have produced is that of Tung Tso-pin. Its authority derives both from his enormous expertise on the Shang inscriptions and his long and careful study of the Chou inscriptions and other sources; he also appealed to a variety of astronomical data in support of his conclusions. In a series of publications, beginning in 1945, he espoused 1111 B.C. as the date of the conquest of the Shang and the beginning of the Chou dynasty.[9] When Tung and I were colleagues at the University of Chicago, in 1947 and 1948, we had many conversations about his chronology. I cannot pretend to be qualified to judge it but, while having the greatest respect for his scholarship, I never became convinced that its accuracy was certain beyond any possible doubt.[10]

8. Creel, *Studies*, xvi–xvii.

9. Tung, *Yin-li P'u, shang pien*, 4. 13a–18a. Tung, "Chung-kuo Ku-li yü Shih-chieh Ku-li." Tung, "Hsi-Chou Nien-li P'u."

10. This is of no importance, since I have no flair for the kind of calculations involved in chronology. But my wife, Dr. Lorraine Creel, does, and she and Tung used to carry on long discussions of Shang chronology that I could not pretend to

Bernhard Karlgren, in 1945, espoused the date of 1027 B.C. that has been derived from the genuine *Bamboo Books*. He found Yetts' practice of assigning "an average of fifteen years to each reign" to be "quite unallowable," and sought to verify the 1027 date by means of various other data, He concluded:

> In three ways quite independent of each other: data about the kings of Chou, the pronouncements of Mencius, and the genealogical list of the princes of Lu reproduced by Sï-ma [Ssu-Ma Ch'ien] with allied pre-Han sources, we have arrived at results that tally exceedingly well with the Chu shu [i.e. the genuine *Bamboo Books*] statement that the start of the Chou dynasty took place in 1027 B.C. . . . The date . . . may be slightly inaccurate, but the margin of error cannot be greater than a decade in either direction. We may safely operate with the year 1027 as the best figure that we can ever arrive at for the victory of Chou over Yin. It is not an imaginary figure but a comparatively very well documented date.[11]

This firm pronouncement by an eminent scholar has had great influence, and there has been a tendency among many Western scholars to consider the matter closed.

Noel Barnard, in 1960, published an extensive review of the problem, drawing on a wide range of materials and challenging the validity of a number of Karlgren's arguments. By various calculations, Barnard concluded that the genuine *Bamboo Books* in fact indicates, for the beginning of Chou, not 1027 but 1137 B.C. Barnard did not, however, propose that this date be adopted, but he did conclude that "a really comprehensive investigation amongst traditional sources cannot possibly result in a date for the commencement of Chou later than 1100 B.C."[12]

All of this tends, to say the least, to be confusing. The variation in the proposed dates is almost dizzying: 1122, 1050, 991, 1111,

---

understand. But she too was unable to feel that his chronological system had eliminated the possibility of a margin of error. Tung's astronomical calculations led to a great deal of controversy, entered into by both Chinese and Western scholars. A resume of some of this controversy was given by Chou Fa-kao in "On the Dating of a Lunar Eclipse in the Shang Period," published in 1965.

11. Karlgren, "Some Weapons and Tools of the Yin Dynasty," 114–120.

12. Barnard published this extensive study of chronology as part of a book review, in *Monumenta Serica*, XIX (1960), 488–515.

1027, 1137—not to mention at least six other dates that have been proposed.

For students of chronology, such debates and such differences of opinion are natural and present no great problem. But for those who attempt to write history, they create an almost impossible situation. The period from the beginning of Chou to 841 B.C. occupied, according to the traditional chronology, 281 years. The other dates listed in the preceding paragraph would lengthen this time to 296 years, or shorten it to as little as 150 years. Since the reigns and events within this period remain the same, if a new date for the beginning of Chou is adopted, every intervening date must be changed. And if one makes these changes today, and if in the next year or the next decade still another new date is adopted, they must all be changed again.

Practice today is various. Among archeologists, Cheng Te-k'un uses 1111, while Kwang-chih Chang uses "1100 as an approximation."[13] Some historians use 1050, others 1027; one volume offers its readers a choice of either 1122 or 1027.

In the course of his extensive review of this problem, Barnard wrote: "I am of the opinion that attempts to compile an acceptable pre-Ch'in chronology will remain merely academic exercises and hopes of precision illusory. . . . I am sure that the best solution is to accept the 'orthodox' chronology until such time as archaeological evidence allows modifications."[14]

If there were any single date for the beginning of Chou upon which even a majority of qualified scholars who have studied the problem were agreed, it might be argued that it should be adopted—but there is not. As matters stand, and as they appear likely to continue unless important new evidence becomes available, the only practicable solution is to use the traditional date, 1122 B.C., as a convention, recognizing that it may well involve a factor of error.

THE years of the reigns of Chinese rulers are dated in a manner different from that to which we are accustomed, which it is necessary to understand. It can be observed in the *Spring and Autumn Annals*. That work says that Duke Yin of Lu died in the eleventh month of 712 B.C., and the *Tso-chuan* adds that he was murdered and was succeeded by Duke Huan. The *Spring and Autumn Annals* also says that, in the first month of the following year, Duke Huan "took his

13. Cheng, *Chou China*, xxiv. Chang, *Archaeology of Ancient China*, 257.
14. *Monumenta Serica*, XIX (1950), 497–499.

place" as Duke, that is, succeeded as ruler.[15] Thus Duke Huan began to reign in the eleventh month of 712, but in accounts of the reigns of the Dukes of Lu that entire year is ascribed to Duke Yin. The reign of Huan is officially reckoned to begin at the beginning of 711, and not to end until the end of 694, even though he died in the fourth month of that year.

It is clear that the successor of a ruler normally assumed power very soon after his death, but the remainder of the year was officially considered a part of the reign of the deceased. This can be confusing, for one may sometimes find that a King or other ruler performed important acts of his reign before the official span of his reign had begun.

15. *Tso*, 30::32, 32::34 (Yin 11); 35::35 (Huan 1).

Appendix C

The Origin of the Deity T'ien

For three thousand years it has been believed that from time imme-
morial all Chinese revered T'ien 天 , "Heaven," as the highest deity,
and that this same deity was also known as Ti 帝 or Shang Ti
上 帝 . But the new materials that have become available in the present century, and especially the Shang inscriptions, make it evident
that this was not the case. It appears rather that T'ien is not named
at all in the Shang inscriptions, which instead refer with great frequency to Ti or Shang Ti. T'ien appears only with the Chou, and was
apparently a Chou deity. After the conquest the Chou considered
T'ien to be identical with the Shang deity Ti (or Shang Ti), much as
the Romans identified the Greek Zeus with their Jupiter.[1]

The Chou doctrine of the Mandate of Heaven held that the destiny
of "all under heaven" was controlled, at least as far back as the Hsia
dynasty, by T'ien, and this implied that T'ien was not merely a deity
of the Chou, but had been acknowledged by all Chinese from an early
time. We have seen that the Chou advocated the acceptance of the
doctrine of the Mandate of Heaven with vigor and with great success;
the acceptance of T'ien as an ancient and universal deity was presumably one aspect of this success. And this acceptance appears to
have been rapid and complete; there seems to be no statement in the
surviving literature that T'ien was not a deity of all Chinese before
Chou times.

Nonetheless there are surviving indications of this, and bits of

---

1. This same theme was treated in an article in Chinese published in 1935:
Ku Li-ya 顧立雅 (H. G. Creel), "Shih T'ien" 釋天 , in *Yen-ching Hsueh-pao*
燕京學報, XVIII (1935), 59–71. This appendix differs greatly, however, from
that article. It is differently arranged, and includes much new material. I have
also ommitted some data, and corrected some errors, that were present in that
earlier treatment of the subject.

evidence that throw some light upon the original nature of T'ien. But the clues are obscure and difficult to follow; they must be unraveled one by one, and with great care.

FIRST of all let us examine the literature. It was formerly believed that a considerable body of Shang literature (as distinguished from the inscriptions) remained to us. One section of the *Poetry* was dated to the Shang period, but it has long since been agreed that in fact it was written in Chou times.[2] Five sections of the "modern text" of the *Documents* purport to be Shang productions, but I have elsewhere given detailed evidence for the proposition that none of them dates from a time earlier than the beginning of Chou, and a number of other scholars agree with this judgment.[3] Our written sources for the Shang period are restricted, therefore, to the inscriptions, which will be examined in detail below.

For Western Chou, however, our literary sources are considerable. If T'ien was a Chou deity, while Ti was not, we might expect that early Chou literature would show more occurrences of the former than of the latter. And it does indeed. The testimony of the original text of the *Book of Changes* is inconclusive, since T'ien as certainly referring to the deity occurs only twice as against once for Ti.[4] But in the *Poetry* there are 140 references to the deity T'ien, as opposed to only 43 to Ti or Shang Ti. Twenty-two of these occurrences are in the royal title, "Son of Heaven." These are certainly references to the deity, but even if they are eliminated, there remain 118 occurrences of T'ien, almost three times as many as of Ti or Shang Ti.

2. Wang, *Kuan-t'ang Chi-lin*, 2.16a–18b. *Ku-shih Pien*, II, 504–510. Creel, *Studies*, 49–54.

3. Creel, *Studies*, 55–95; I there cited the opinions of other scholars in addition to my own. Ch'ü Wan-li, in *Shang-shu Shih-i*, 40, 42, 52–53, 54, and 55, suggests that the first of these sections was written later than the time of Confucius, and casts doubt on the date of composition of each of the others. Ch'en Meng-chia, in *Shang-shu T'ung-lun*, 112, suggests that all five may date from the Warring States period.

4. For Ti see *I-ching*, 4.31a; Legge, *I-ching*, 150. For instances in which T'ien clearly refers to the deity, see *I-ching*, 2.30a, 2.31a; Legge, *I-ching*, 88. There are two further occurrences of Ti, as the title of a Shang ruler. The character T'ien occurs seven times in the original text of the *Book of Changes*, which stands in striking contrast to its absence from the Shang inscriptions, which will be demonstrated below. In current texts of the *Book of Changes* there is one further instance of the character T'ien, which is interpreted as meaning a punishment, either shaving or branding the head; see *I-ching*, 4.11b, Legge, *I-ching*, 139. But one commentator has suggested that this may be a copyist's error for another character, and this seems not impossible; see *Chung-hua Ta Tzu-tien*, Yin-chi, 21.

In our twelve Western Chou sections of the *Documents*, the deity
T'ien is named 116 times, as compared with only 25 mentions of Ti
or Shang Ti.[5] In Western Chou bronze inscriptions of my corpus, the
deity T'ien is mentioned 91 times, Ti or Shang Ti only 4.[6] Of the occurrences of T'ien on the bronzes, 71 are in the royal title "Son of
Heaven," and 3 in what may be other royal titles.[7] But even if these
are eliminated, the deity T'ien is mentioned 17 times, more than four
times as often as Ti is named.

In all of our Western Chou sources, if the meaning of the character
is disregarded, T'ien occurs 383 times.[8] This stands in sharp contrast
to the fact that in all of the known Shang inscriptions this character
seems never to occur at all.

ALTHOUGH in 1935 I published evidence for the proposition that the
deity T'ien was not mentioned in the oracle bone inscriptions, and
that the character T'ien did not appear in them, some scholars still
believe that T'ien was a Shang deity. The index to these inscriptions
published by Sun Hai-po in 1934 listed twelve occurrences of T'ien.[9]
A supplement to this work, published by Chin Hsiang-heng in 1959,
listed nine more.[10] Li Hsiao-ting, in his sixteen-volume compendium
on the explication of characters in the Shang inscriptions, published
in 1965, quoted the opinions of a number of scholars who found the

5. It is a somewhat curious fact that the title "Son of Heaven," which is common in the *Poetry* and extremely common in the bronze inscriptions beginning as
early as the reign of King Ch'eng, occurs only once in these Western Chou sections
of the *Documents*. That one occurrence, however, is in a fairly early document,
datable to the end of the reign of King Ch'eng (*Shu*, 73). This distribution probably indicates merely that the title was more commonly used in some kinds of
contexts than in others.

6. There are in fact three more occurrences of what is read as being the character T'ien, but interpreted as being a surname; see *Chin-wen*, 1a, 31b. I have left
these completely out of account as occurrences of the character T'ien, in order
to avoid any possibility of error; they might (though there are reasons for doubt-
ing this) be variant forms of the character *ta* 大 .

7. There is one occurrence of *Huang T'ien Wang* 皇天王 (*Chin-wen*, 51a);
the exact meaning of this is debatable. In Ch'en, "Hsi-Chou T'ung-ch'i," (5).119,
the title *T'ien Chün* 天君 is used twice. This is a title by which Queens were designated; see ibid., (2).117.

8. This includes, for instance, cases in which T'ien appears to refer merely to
the sky, but it does not include instances in which it is interpreted as being a surname. The numbers of occurrences are as follows: *Book of Changes*, 8. *Poetry*,
162. *Documents*, 122. Bronze inscriptions, 91.

9. Sun, *Chia-ku Wen Pien*, 1.1ab.

10. Chin, *Hsü Chia-ku Wen Pien*, 1.1ab.

character T'ien in them.[11] Others, however, disagree. Tung Tso-pin told me in 1948 that in all of his intensive study of the Shang inscriptions he had never encountered what he believed to be a single occurrence of the character T'ien.[12]

This is a question of far more than lexicographical importance. It has crucial bearing on both intellectual and political history. We must therefore inquire in detail whether, in fact, the deity T'ien is or is not mentioned in the Shang inscriptions.

Since the characters in inscriptions are the result of handwork, each is to some degree unique. The character T'ien occurs, in Western Chou bronze inscriptions, in a wide range of variations such as 夨 , 夨 , 夨 , and—at the very end of the period— 夨 .[13] As was mentioned above, Sun Hai-po listed twelve characters in the Shang bone inscriptions as forms of T'ien, but in the originals I can find only eleven of these.[14] And while Chin Hsiang-heng listed nine more, his references appear in fact to add only seven.[15] There are eight further occurrences in the Shang inscriptions of characters that sufficiently resemble those cited so that they should be included in our examination.[16] There are then, in the Shang bone inscriptions, at least twenty-

11. Li, *Chia-ku Wen-tzu Chi-shih*, I, 0013–0021.

12. Ch'i Ssu-ho, in "Hsi-Chou Cheng-chih Ssu-hsiang," 23, accepted my conclusion that the deity T'ien appeared only with the Chou. Ch'en Meng-chia, in "Hsi-Chou Yin-jen," 93, appears to indicate that he does not believe T'ien to occur in the Shang inscriptions.

13. Kuo, *Chin-wen Lu-pien*, 17b, 55a, 56b, 256a. Kuo Mo-jo (*Chin-wen*, 213a) dates the last inscription to the reign of Duke Chuang of Ch'i (794–731 B.C.). This form with two lines at the top also occurs in Kuo, *Chin-wen Lu-pien*, 277b–278a; Kuo dates this inscription to 380 B.C. (*Chin-wen*, 234b).

14. In his *Chia-ku Wen Pien*, 1.1b, Sun says that there are two occurrences of T'ien in *Yin Ch'i Ch'ien-pien*, 8.9.2, but I can find only one.

15. In his *Hsü Chia-ku Wen Pien*, 1.1a, Chin writes that the character T'ien occurs in Shang, *Yin-ch'i I-ts'un*, No. 640. But in that inscription I can find no character like the one Chin shows, nor does Shang Ch'eng-tso give one in his transcription of this inscription; see Shang, *Yin-ch'i I-ts'un K'ao-shih*, 80b. Chin also says that this inscription occurs in "Fan-chiang Chai So-ts'ang Chia-ku Wen-tzu" 凡將齋所藏甲骨文字, 20.1. Thanks to Mr. Chao Lin, I have been able to consult a microfilm copy of this unpublished work; it shows a character having some resemblance to forms that have been held to be T'ien, but it looks more like forms that Chin lists as *fu* 夫 in *Hsü Chia-ku Wen Pien*, 10.23a. In any case, the character appears to function here as a place name. Chin also lists T'ien as occurring in *Yin Ch'i Hsü-pien*, 5.13.6, but that is in fact another squeeze of the same piece that was published in *Yin Ch'i Ch'ien-pien*, 4.15.2, and included in Sun's work to which Chin's is a supplement.

16. One of these occurs in *Yin Ch'i Hsü-pien*, 6.21.4, as I pointed out in "Shih T'ien," 60. Its form, given below as (G), does not differ from the others beyond the possible range of variation in such characters. Three others are found in *Yin-hsü*

six instances that have been held to be, or to resemble, the character T'ien. Neglecting minor variations, these may be classified as having seven forms, as follows:

(A)   (B)   (C)   (D)   (E)   (F)   (G)

All of these forms are sufficiently like forms of T'ien found on Chou bronzes so that they could be the same character. Since the Shang inscriptions were cut on bone, they often have straight lines where curves might appear in bronze inscriptions, and a square like that at the top of (A) is quite a normal equivalent, on the Shang bones, of the disk that appears at the top of most Chou bronze forms of T'ien.

There is no great problem, then, of form. But the identification of a character, or even of an English word, depends not only on its form but also on the context in which it appears. For instance, the English "saw" represents at least three wholly different words, which can be differentiated only by the contexts in which they are used. We must therefore examine the contexts in which these characters are found.

The bones and tortoise shells on which the Shang inscriptions appear are often broken into fragments, destroying the context of the inscriptions. It is not surprising, then, that eight of these twenty-six characters occur in contexts that do not provide enough clues to make it possible to determine, or even to conjecture with some reasonable probability of accuracy, the meaning of the character.[17]

This leaves eighteen cases to be discussed. Since these have been supposed by some scholars to be instances of T'ien, but I do not believe that in fact they are, they will be called (T'ien?).

In eleven of these cases, (T'ien?) seems rather clearly to be a variant form of the character *ta* 大 , meaning "large" or "great." This is not in the least surprising. *Ta* appears in the bone inscriptions in forms such as 大 and 大 .[18] This is clearly, as everyone agrees, a line

---

Wen-tzu I-pien, Nos. 5384, 9067, and Kuo, *Yin-hsü Wen-tzu Cho-he*, No. 87; these were kindly called to my attention by Mr. Chao Lin. And six more characters, of the form called (A) below, occur in Tseng, *Chia-ku Cho-he Pien*, No. 183; two of these, however, had already been listed by Sun Hai-po in his *Chia-ku Wen Pien*.

17. The references to these inscriptions will be followed by the letter, in parentheses, that was used above to denote the form of the character. These inscriptions that do not provide sufficient context are: Yeh, *T'ieh-yün Ts'ang-kuei Shih-i*, 10.18 (B). *Yin Ch'i Ch'ien-pien*, 8.9.2 (D). *Yin Ch'i Hsü-pien*, 6.21.4 (G). *Yin-hsü Wen-tzu I-pien*, No. 1538 (C), No. 4505 (C), No. 6390 (D), No. 9067 (F). T'ang, *T'ien-jang Ke Chia-ku Wen*, No. 50 (D).

18. *Yin Ch'i Ch'ien-pien*, 1.5.5, 1.48.1.

drawing of a man. Originally it probably denoted a "great" man, standing erect and seen from the front, as distinguished from ordinary men who appear on the bones in forms like 〉 , seen from the side. But *ta* became specialized in the sense of "great" or "large," no longer referring to men.

In depicting men and women in the inscriptions, Shang scribes might occasionally depict the head, but this seems often to have been optional. There is, for instance, a character closely resembling *ta* that we find written as 大 . But on the same bone the same character is also written as 大 , and forms that depict the head and those that do not seem to be about equally common.[19] Another convention used to represent the head was a horizontal line, and we find variant forms of many characters that show it.[20]

The most conspicuous case of the addition of such a horizontal line representing the head is in the case of the character *wang* 王 , "king." In the earliest inscriptions we know it has the form 大 , which appears to be the same "great" man found in *ta*, who is standing on a line representing the territory that he possesses.[21] Later a line was added at the top, so that we have 王 . In this case, however, the addition or omission of the line did not depend on the whim of the diviner; this was coordinated with other cultural changes, so that at some times the line was regularly added, and at others regularly omitted.[22] But with or without the line, it was still the same character.

It seems quite clear, then, that the character that is interpreted as (T'ien?) could be a variant form of *ta*. And there is very good evidence that in these eleven cases it is. One of the Shang Kings is regularly referred to in the inscriptions as Ta Wu, but in two of these cases is called "(T'ien?) Wu."[23] Again a Shang city is repeatedly called Ta I Shang 大邑商 , which presumably means "the Great City Shang."[24] In nine of our cases we find reference to "(T'ien?) I Shang."[25] Such

19. *Yin Ch'i Ch'ien-pien*, 1.45.3. Sun, *Chia-ku Wen-Pien*, 10.14a. In 鄉 the two men are normally depicted without any representations of heads, but occasionally heads are depicted; compare *Yin Ch'i Ch'ien-pien*, 4.22.1–8.

20. For instance: 奴 , *Yin Ch'i Ch'ien-pien*, 4.26.5, *Yin Ch'i Hou-pien, hsia*, 34.4. 鄉 , *Yin Ch'i Pu-tz'u*, No. 588.

21. Some Chinese scholars give other explanations for this character, which I find unconvincing.

22. Tung, *Yin-li P'u, shang pien*, 1.3b–4a.

23. *Yin Ch'i Ch'ien-pien*, 4.16.4 (D); (T'ien?) appears twice on this one piece.

24. Ch'en Meng-chia (*Yin Tz'u Tsung-shu*, 255–257) cites a number of occurrences of Ta I Shang. Ch'en says that this is not necessarily the same place as (T'ien?) I Shang, but I believe that most scholars suppose them to be identical.

25. All of these have form (A). *Yin Ch'i Ch'ien-pien*, 2.3.7, 4.15.2 (these are two fragments of the same bone). *Yin-hsü Wen-tzu Chia-pien*, No. 3690. Tseng, *Chia-ku Cho-he Pien*, No. 183 (six occurrences).

confusion of Ta and T'ien persisted even in references to Shang time in Chou literature.[26]

In three further cases (T'ien?) is evidently a place name. One inscription speaks of someone—although part of the inscription is missing, this is almost certainly the King—going "to (T'ien?)."[27] In the second we read of "the King hunting [at] (T'ien?)." In both of these inscriptions (T'ien?) is probably a variant form of Ta, for there was a place of that name, and we read of the King hunting at Ta.[28] The third inscription inquires concerning the possibility of an attack by "(T'ien?) *fang* 方 ," the "(T'ien?) territory."[29] The character *fang* appears frequently with the sense of "territory" or even "state," referring to groups with which the Shang had relations that were often warlike. (T'ien?) here is the name of such a territory, and seems clearly to be a place name.

In all of the contexts we have considered so far, if the character (T'ien?) were in fact the character T'ien, this would still not indicate that T'ien were a Shang deity. For in none of these contexts is there anything to indicate that it is a deity that is in question. But there remain four more cases to be considered; and at least three of these do —upon first examination—seem to refer to a deity, for all have to do with sacrifice.

In these three inscriptions we find three different terms meaning "to sacrifice," in each case followed or preceded by "yü 于 (T'ien?)."[30] These certainly could be interpreted as referring to sacrifices "to Heaven." But there is another possibility. Another inscription has one of these same terms for sacrifice followed by "at this [place]."[31] It is clear, therefore, that it is equally possible to interpret these inscriptions as referring to sacrifices at a place called (T'ien?).

There is one other inscription that might be argued to refer to a sacrifice to (T'ien?), but that is by no means certain.[32]

26. In the *Documents* there is a reference to "(T'ien?) I Shang;" *Shu*, 56. And in the *Hsün-tzu* the ruler who is called Ta I in the Shang inscriptions is twice called "(T'ien?) I;" see *Hsün-tzu*, 18.4a.

27. *Yin Ch'i Ch'ien-pien*, 2.20.4 (E). This does not refer to the King "going to heaven" at death; this is a well-known type of inscription, asking about "going and return," referring to travel.

28. *Yin Ch'i Ch'ien-pien*, 2.27.8 (E); 2.28.1.

29. Kuo, *Yin-hsü Wen-tzu Cho-ho*, No. 87 (A).

30. Yeh, *T'ieh-yün Ts'ang-kuei Shih-i*, 5.14 (C). *Yin-hsü Wen-tzu I-pien*, 5384 (C). *Chan-hou Ching-Ching Hsin-huo Chia-ku Wen Chi*, No. 2963 (D).

31. 叀在玆. *Yin Ch'i Ch'ien-pien*, 4.27.5.

32. *Yin-hsü Wen-tzu I-pien*, No. 9067 (F). Mr. Chao Lin brought this inscription to my attention. It ends with the characters *chen* (T'ien?) 朕 (天 ?). Although *chen* is not usually so interpreted, Mr. Chao believes that by analogy with some other inscriptions *chen* is, in contexts like this one, a verb denoting the per-

If these four inscriptions are assumed in fact to refer to sacrifices to T'ien, it is then very strange indeed that the four seem to be the only inscriptions that could reasonably be interpreted as referring to a deity of such importance. The indexes to the Shang inscriptions published by Sun Hai-po and Chin Hsiang-heng are very far from being complete, but they alone list 175 occurrences of Ti.[33] It seems abundantly clear that whereas Ti—sometimes called Shang Ti—was a very important deity of the Shang people, T'ien was not.

WE saw earlier that in the Western Chou literature references to the deity T'ien were far more frequent than to Ti or Shang Ti. In the twelve Western Chou sections of the *Documents*, Ti is named only twenty-five times. The distribution of these occurrences is particularly interesting.

In the two sections that can be ascribed with some confidence to the conqueror, King Wu, there is only one mention of Ti and one of Shang Ti, while he speaks of T'ien fifteen times.[34] It is reasonable to suppose that this represents the normal usage of the Chou people, before there had been extensive mingling of their culture with that of the Shang. So we might imagine a Roman speaking normally of Jupiter but occasionally mentioning "Zeus" to evidence his cosmopolitan sophistication.

Of all twenty-five references to Ti or Shang Ti in the Western Chou *Documents*, eighteen occur in the words of the Duke of Chou.[35] And in all but four of these cases the Duke is addressing the conquered Shang people. This is clearly a part of the deliberate attempt by the Duke of Chou to assimilate the Shang people to Chou culture and make the two peoples one. This is obviously his purpose in the document called the "Many Officers," in which the Duke is addressing the conquered Shang officials who have been moved to the new city at Le after their rebellion against the Chou has been crushed. And here Ti is named nine times, more than twice as frequently as in any other Western Chou section of the *Documents*.[36]

---

formance of a kind of sacrifice. Thus, he believes, it could be argued that this means "sacrifice to T'ien." But alternatively (T'ien?) might be regarded as a place name, so that this would refer to a sacrifice at a certain place. Mr. Chao does not think that this inscription does, in fact, refer to the deity T'ien. (Verbal communication of March 7, 1969.)

33. Sun, *Chia-ku Wen Pien*, 1.1b–2a. Chin, *Hsü Chia-ku Wen Pien*, 1.1b–2a.
34. *Shu*, 39–46.
35. *Shu*, 48, 49, 55, 56, 59, 61, 62, 64.
36. *Shu*, 55–56.

The concern of the Duke of Chou to identify T'ien with Ti is evident. He repeatedly uses the two names as synonyms, and once uses a combined name, Huang T'ien Shang Ti 皇天上帝 , "August Heaven Shang Ti."[37] He repeatedly tells the Shang people that T'ien gave the Mandate to the founder of their own Shang dynasty.[38] And without ever being so clumsy as to say so overtly, the Duke makes it very clear that it is useless for the Shang to hope for help, in regaining their independence from the Chou, from their deity, Ti. For he says repeatedly that not merely T'ien, but Ti, rejected the last Shang King and commanded the Chou to overthrow him and take over the Mandate to rule.[39]

THAT T'ien was not a deity of the Shang people may be considered, I think, to be established. But a further question remains. What was the origin of the Chou deity, T'ien? This cannot be easy to answer. By Western Chou times the character T'ien had already acquired a whole series of meanings that indicate that it had undergone a good deal of development. It denoted the very definite deity, T'ien, who could decree the transfer of the Mandate and to whom the King could be understood to stand in relationship as "Son of Heaven." In the *Poetry* we also see T'ien as a more vaguely conceived overruling providence, sometimes comparable to "fate." T'ien was also the place in which the former Kings lived, and sometimes denoted the literal heavens, the sky.[40]

It would be difficult to account for this range of significance if we simply looked at the earliest Chou forms of the character and supposed—as has sometimes been done—that T'ien was strictly anthropomorphic, a "man in the sky." The ancient dictionary, the *Shuo-wen Chieh-tzu*, defined T'ien 天 as meaning "the highest," and analyzed it as being composed of 一 one and 大 great.[41] But its author, living in the Han dynasty, probably did not know that the earliest forms of T'ien that we have, on early Chou bronzes, did not have a line at the top, but a disk. Other theories, including some very recent ones, do not come a great deal closer to solving all of the problems.[42]

37. *Shu*, 48, 49, 55.
38. *Shu*, 55, 64.
39. *Shu*, 48, 55, 56.
40. For a few examples, see: *Shu*, 49, 51, 71. *Shih*, 84, 118, 134, 140, 151–152, 164.
41. *Shuo-wen*, 12b.
42. For a review of a number of theories concerning the character T'ien, see Li, *Chia-ku Wen-tzu Chi-shih*, I, 0013–0021.

It may never be possible, with the evidence that remains to us, to construct an explanation of the origin of T'ien that can be proved correct beyond all doubt. What will be presented here can only be called a theory, but one for which there is a good deal of evidence.

This theory holds that the character T'ien is a variant form of the character *ta*. *Ta* is a pictograph of a large or great man, and it no doubt had that sense originally among the Chou people as well as the Shang. But among the Chou a particular form of *ta* became specialized to refer only to the greatest men, the Kings, and especially the dead Kings, who were even more powerful and therefore greater than the living King. *Ta* in this sense came to be differentiated by the depiction of a head on the man, and came to have its own pronunciation, "T'ien." Thus T'ien came to mean the group of ancestral Kings. They controlled the destinies of men on earth, and thus T'ien came to have the sense of providence or fate. Since Chinese does not distinguish singular and plural, T'ien as the group of ancestral Kings came gradually to be the single powerful deity, T'ien, "Heaven." T'ien was also used as the name of the place where the ancestral Kings lived, in the heavens. And T'ien was also used to mean the literal, visible sky. All this may seem farfetched, but let us examine the evidence.

One early Chou inscription has *ta* in the form 𢀳 , and T'ien in the form 𠀡 .[43] These are both clearly pictographs of men, and they differ only in that the head of the latter is larger. It is not surprising that these two characters were sometimes confused. And it is clear that they could have had a common origin.

A number of characters include the basic pictograph of a standing man seen from the front, which is the character *ta*. One places a line under his feet, thus 𡗲 , making a character meaning "to stand" and pronounced *li*. This can refer to any standing person, but the element *ta* seems to have given a kind of special significance to many of the characters of which it became part. Thus we find a character meaning "place, position, rank," and pronounced *wei*; it appears in the same inscription that contains the above form of *li*, as 𡗲 . The two are of course identical, and can be distinguished only by the context.[44] *Wei* came to be used as we use the word "throne"; for a ruler to come to power, as we say to "be enthroned," was literally to "go to the *wei*."

It will have been noticed that these characters meaning "to stand"

---

43. Kuo, *Chin-wen Lu-pien*, 17b.

44. Ibid., 45a. Because of this identity, in later Chinese the character *wei* was written 位 , with the addition of the "man" determinative to distinguish it.

and "position" are rather similar to some Shang forms of the character *wang* 王 , King. But by Western Chou times the addition of the horizontal line at the top of *wang*, done only at certain periods during the Shang dynasty, had become a fixed convention.

It is not, perhaps, wholly surprising that there was at times some confusion between these characters based on *ta*. There are various instances of the use of *wang*, "King," evidently as a substitute for *ta*, "great."[45] Instances of the use of T'ien for *ta* were mentioned earlier.

According to my theory the character *ta* became specialized, among the Chou people, to designate particularly important men, especially the rulers. Such a man, standing on a line representing the territory he held, came to mean "King." A form only slightly different had the sense of "position," "rank," and "throne." *Ta* with an enlarged head became T'ien, which, it is suggested, originally denoted the greatest of all persons, Kings whose power was enhanced by the fact that, being deceased, they were almost omnipotent spirits. Direct testimony to this is almost impossible to find in the sources, but there is a good deal that suggests that the character had such a history.[46]

The relationship between the Chou King and Heaven was conceived to be peculiarly intimate. There seems to be no evidence that the Shang King was ever called the "son of Ti,"[47] but the Chou King was the "son of Heaven." And this was not merely a formal title. A poem says of the King, literally, "may T'ien son him," that is, treat him as its son.[48] If T'ien were in fact the former Kings as a body, this could explain the relationship perfectly.

There are passages in the literature that are difficult to interpret according to the usual understanding of T'ien, which seem easier to

45. In relationship terms, we find *wang fu* 王父 and *wang mu* 王母 meaning "grandfather" and "grandmother," even with regard to quite ordinary persons. But *ta fu* 大父 and *ta mu* 大母 were also used in the same sense; see Feng, *Chinese Kinship System*, 67–78. It seems reasonable to suppose that these terms were in some manner considered equivalent. In *Chin-wen*, 111b–112a, Kuo Mo-jo interprets *wang* in an inscription as being used for *ta*.

46. Here we shall leave out of account a large body of what might be considered evidence for this view, because it lacks certainty. Thus Kings are repeatedly called "T'ien *Wang* 天王 ," and Queens "T'ien *chün* 天君 ," and the throne is called "T'ien *wei* 天位 ." These could indicate that rulers were considered to belong to the body of those who make up T'ien, but other explanations are possible. Thus "T'ien *Wang*" could be interpreted as meaning something like "the King by Heaven's grace."

47. Ch'en Meng-chia states flatly in *Yin Tz'u Tsung-shu*, 581, that in the Shang period "the King and Ti did not have the relationship of father and son."

48. *Shih*, 242. Of course the founder of a new dynasty was not the descendant of the former Kings, but such a ruler might be considered an adopted son.

understand if we take T'ien as meaning the royal ancestors. In a passage in the *Documents*, the Duke of Chou is quoted as exhorting a fellow officer in words that Karlgren translates as:

> May you be able together with me to scrutinize Yin's
> ruin and great wickedness, and so consider our Heaven
> (-given) majesty.

The last three characters of this passage are 我天威, for which Karlgren's rendering is not very convincing in the context. James Legge renders them literally in a footnote as "our Heavenly terrors," which does not seem a great deal better.[49] The point of this passage is that the Chou must be diligent and careful, that they must look upon the terrible fate that overtook Yin and draw a lesson from it. The three characters in question are hard to translate unless we take T'ien to have, here, the sense of the ancestral Kings. If we do, the sense of the closing words of this passage is that "we must bear in mind the awful power of our ancestral Kings," who will punish any dereliction.

In some passages T'ien appears to have the sense of ancestors who are not necessarily royal. James Legge translates some lines in the *Poetry* as follows:

> But mysteriously Great Heaven
> Is able to strengthen anything;
> Do not disgrace your great ancestors,
> And it will save your posterity.[50]

But in fact the word "it" in the last line does not correspond to anything in the Chinese. On the basis of the text, it should be the ancestors, just mentioned, who do the saving. But in this case, of course, there would have been no point in mentioning T'ien above—which is undoubtedly why Legge supplied "it."[51] The problem is resolved, however, if we suppose T'ien and the ancestors to be identical.

A similar point is involved in a passage in the *Book of Etiquette and Ceremonial*. It gives a detailed description of a sacrificial ceremony in which the personator—playing the role of the ancestor—gives some grain to the one who sacrifices. The liturgist says: "The great

49. *Shu,* 62. Legge, *Shu,* 484 note.
50. Legge, *Shih,* 564.
51. Karlgren (*Shih,* 238) translates the last line as "then you will save your person." The difference between "posterity" and "person" need not concern us in the present connection. But the "you" that Karlgren supplies is as gratuitous as Legge's "it," and seems even less apposite to the context.

personator has commanded me, the official liturgist, to pass on this abounding and limitless blessing to you, the filial descendant. Come near, you filial descendant, that you may be caused to receive riches bestowed by Heaven."[52] In this passage what is bestowed by the personator of the ancestor is said to be given by T'ien.

One of the Chou sacrificial poems is translated by Karlgren as follows:

We present our offerings,
There are sheep, there are oxen;
May Heaven esteem them.

We should make Wen Wang's (statutes=) rites our pattern;
We daily secure the tranquillity of the (states of) the four quarters;
The great Wen Wang has esteemed and enjoyed them (the offerings).

May we night and day fear the majesty of Heaven,
And thereby preserve it.

Karlgren explains the final "it" as meaning "what Heaven has conferred."[53]

In this poem the interplay between T'ien and King Wen is very clear. The first stanza says "may T'ien esteem," that is, find acceptable, the offerings. The second says that "King Wen has esteemed and enjoyed them." And the third again speaks of T'ien. The superficial appearance is that T'ien and King Wen are identical, but that is of course impossible. But the difficulty disappears if T'ien is the group of ancestral Kings as a body, among whom King Wen is an outstanding individual.

NONE of these passages, or others that could be cited, is conclusive.[54] Taken together, however, they suggest that T'ien had a sense somewhat different from that in which it is commonly understood. I do not mean to say that, even at the beginning of Chou, those who spoke of

52. *I-li*, 48.9; Steele, *I-li*, II, 172. The text reads *shou lu yü* T'ien 受祿于天, which John Steele translates "receive riches from heaven." But "*yü* T'ien" can hardly mean "from the place, T'ien." It must rather have some such sense as "by the agency of T'ien."

53. *Shih*, 241.

54. See, for example, the curious use of T'ien in *Chin-wen*, 51a.

Works Cited

Abi Usayi 'a, Ibn. *'Uyūn al-anbā' fī ṭabaqāt al-aṭibbā'*. Edited by August Müller. Cairo and Königsberg, 1882–1884.

"Advice to a Prince." In W. G. Lambert, *Babylonian Wisdom Literature*, 110–115. Oxford, 1960.

al-Idrīsī. *Nuzhat al-mushtāq fī ikhtirāq al-āfāq*. French translation by P. Amédée Jaubert published as *Géographie d'Edrisi*. 2 vols. Paris, 1836–1840.

Allee, W. G. "Dominance and Hierarchy in Societies of Vertebrates." *Colloques Internationaux du Centre National de la Recherche Scientifique*, XXXIV (Paris, 1952), 157–181.

al-Nadīm, Ibn. *Kitāb al-Fihrist*. Edited by Gustav Flügel. Leipzig, 1871.

al-Qifṭi, Ibn. *Tarikh al-ḥukamā*. Edited by Juilius Lippert. Leipzig, 1903.

Altmann, "Sociobiology of Rhesus Monkeys."
Stuart A. Altmann. "A Field Study of the Sociobiology of Rhesus Monkeys, *Macaca mulatta*." *Annals of the New York Academy of Sciences*, CII (1962), 338–435.

Amano Gennosuke 天野元之助 ."Chūgoku Kodai Nōgyō no Tenkai" 中國古代農業の展開. *Tōhō Gakuhō* 東方學報, No. 30 (December 1959), 67–166.

Analects.
Lun-yü 論語. In English commonly called *Confucian Analects*. References are given according to the numbering system used in the translations of Legge and Waley.

Ancient India as Described by Megasthenes and Arrian. Translated by J. W. McCrindle. London, 1877.

Andersson, J. Gunnar. *Children of the Yellow Earth*. London, 1934.

Aristotle. *Politics*. Translated by Benjamin Jowett. In *The Basic Works of Aristotle*. Edited and with an introduction by Richard McKeon. (Pagination as in Bekker.) New York, 1941.

Das Arthaçāstra des Kautilya.
Das altindische Buch vom Welt-und Staatseleben, das Arthaçāstra des Kautilya. Translated by Johann Jakob Meyer. Leipzig, 1926.

Ashton, Leigh, "China and Egypt, A Paper Read by Leigh Ashton on April 4th, 1934." *Transactions of the Oriental Ceramic Society*, No. 11 (1933–1934), 62–72.

Baas, J. H. *Grundriss der Geschichte der Medecin und des Heilenden Standes*. Stuttgart, 1876.

Baerends, G. P. "Les sociétés et les familles de poissons." *Colloques internationaux du Centre National de la Recherche Scientifique*, XXXIV (Paris, 1952), 207–219.

Bahgat, Aly Bey, and Massoul, Félix. *La céramique musulmane de l'Égypt*. Cairo, 1930.

Balazs, Etienne. *Chinese Civilization and Bureaucracy*. Translated by H. M. Wright; edited by Arthur F. Wright. New Haven and London, 1964.

Ball, W. W. Rouse. *A History of the Study of Mathematics at Cambridge*. Cambridge, 1889.

Banerjea, Pramanath. *Public Administration in Ancient India*. London, 1916.

Barnard, Chester I. *The Functions of the Executive*. Cambridge, Mass., 1938; reprinted 1962.

Barnard, "A Bronze of Western Chou Date."
Noel Barnard. "A Recently Excavated Inscribed Bronze of Western Chou Date." *MS*, XVII (1958), 12–46.

Barnard, Noel. "Chou China: A Review of the Third Volume of Cheng Te-k'un's Archaeology in China." *MS*, XXIV (1965), 307–459.

Barnard, "The Ch'u Silk Manuscript."
Noel Barnard. "A Preliminary Study of the Ch'u Silk Manuscript." *MS*, XVII (1958), 1–11.

Barnard, "New Approaches in Chin-Shih-Hsüeh."
Noel Barnard. "New Approaches and Research Methods in Chin-Shih-Hsüeh." *Tōyō Bunka Kenkyūjo Kiyō* 東洋文化研究所紀要, XIX (1959), 1–31.

Barnard, Noel. "Some Remarks on the Authenticity of a Western Chou Style Inscribed Bronze." *MS*, XVIII (1959), 213–244.

Beasley, W. G., and Pulleyblank, E. G., eds. *Historians of China and Japan*. London, 1961; reprinted 1962.

BEFEO. Bulletin de l'École Française de l'Extrême-Orient.

Bendix, Reinhard. "Bureaucracy and the Problem of Power." *Public Administration Review*, V (1945), 194–209.

Bielenstein, Hans. "The Census of China During the Period 2–742 A.D." *BMFEA*, XIX (1947), 125–163.

Bielenstein, Hans. "The Restoration of the Han Dynasty." *BMFEA*, XXVI (1954), 1–209.

BIHP. Bulletin of the Institute of History and Philology, Academia Sinica.

Biot, Édouard. *Essai sur l'histoire de l'instruction publique en Chine.* Paris, 1847.

Biot, *Tcheou-li.*
Édouard Biot, trans. *Le Tcheou-li ou Rites des Tcheou.* 3 vols. Paris, 1851.

Bishop, C. W. "The Chronology of Ancient China." *JAOS*, LII (1932), 232–247.

The Black Pottery Site at Lung-shan-chên.
Li Chi, Liang Ssu-young, Tung Tso-pin, et al. *Ch'êng-tzŭ-yai: The Black Pottery Culture Site at Lung-shan-chên in Li-ch'êng-hsien, Shantung Province.* Translated by Kenneth Starr. New Haven, 1956.

Blau, Peter M. *Bureaucracy in Modern Society*. New York, 1956; reprinted 1961.

Blau, Peter M. *The Dynamics of Bureaucracy*. Chicago, 1955.

Bloch, Marc. *Feudal Society*. Translated by L. A. Manyon. Chicago, 1961; reprinted 1962.

BMFEA. *Bulletin of the Museum of Far Eastern Antiquities (Östasiatiska Samlingarna)*, Stockholm.

Boak, E. R., and Sinnigen, William G. *A History of Rome to A.D. 565*. 5th ed. New York and London, 1965.

Bodde, Derk. "Basic Concepts of Chinese Law: The Genesis and Evolution of Legal Thought in Traditional China." *Proceedings of the American Philosophical Society*, CVII (1963), 375–398.

Bodde, Derk. *China's First Unifier*. Leiden, 1938.

Bodde, Derk. "Feudalism in China." In *Feudalism in History*, edited by Rushton Coulborn, 49–92. Princeton, 1956.

Bodde, Derk. "Henry A. Wallace and the Ever-Normal Granary." *Far Eastern Quarterly*, V (1946), 411–426.

Bodde, Derk, and Morris, Clarence. *Law in Imperial China*. Cambridge, Mass., 1967.

Bowra, C. M. *The Greek Experience*. Cleveland and New York, 1957.

Brecht, Arnold. "How Bureaucracies Develop and Function." *Annals of the American Academy of Political and Social Science*, CCXCII (1954), 1–17.

Broman, Sven. "Studies on the Chou Li." *BMFEA*, XXXIII (1961), 1–89.

Browne, Edward G. *Arabian Medicine*. Cambridge, 1921.

Bryce, James. *The Holy Roman Empire*. 8th ed., rev. London and New York, 1897.

Bünger, Karl. "Die Rechtsidee in der chinesischen Geschichte." *Saeculum*, III (1952), 192–217.

Buote, Edward L. "Chu-ko Liang and the Kingdom of Shu-Han." Ph.D. dissertation, University of Chicago, 1968.

Burckhardt, *Renaissance in Italy.*
Jacob Burckhardt. *The Civilization of the Renaissance in Italy.* Translated by S. G. C. Middlemore. 4th ed., rev. New York, 1951.

Cahen, "L'usage du mot de 'féodalité.'"
Claude Cahen. "Au seuil de la troisième année: Reflexions sur l'usage du mot de 'féodalité.'" *Journal of the Economic and Social History of the Orient*, III (1960), 2–20.

The Cambridge Ancient History.

The Cambridge Medieval History.

Campbell, Donald. *Arabian Medicine.* 2 vols. London, 1926.

Carpenter, "Behavior and Social Relations of Howling Monkeys."
C. R. Carpenter. "A Field Study of the Behavior and Social Relations of Howling Monkeys." *Comparative Psychology Monographs*, X (1934), No. 48.

Carpenter, C. R. "Characteristics of Social Behavior in Non-Human Primates." *Transactions of the New York Academy of Sciences*, Ser. II, IV (1941–1942), 248–258.

Carpenter, C. R. "Social Behavior of Non-human Primates." *Colloques internationaux du Centre National de la Recherche Scientifique*, XXXIV (Paris, 1952), 227–245.

Carpenter, C. R. "Societies of Monkeys and Apes." *Biological Symposia*, VIII (Lancaster, Pa., 1942), 177–204.

Carter, T. F. *The Invention of Printing in China and Its Spread Westward.* 2d. ed., revised by L. Carrington Goodrich. New York, 1955.

Caspar, Erich. *Roger II (1101–1154) und die Gründung der normannisch-sicilischen Monarchie.* Innsbruck, 1904.

Chan-hou Ching-Ching Hsin-huo Chia-ku Wen Chi 戰後京津新穫甲骨文集 , compiled by Hu Hou-hsüan 胡厚宣 . 1954.

Chan-kuo Ts'e 戰國策. *Ssu-pu Pei-yao* edition.

Chang Ch'i-yün 張其昀 et al. *Chung-kuo Chan-shih Lun-chi* 中 國 戰史論集. Taipei, 1954.

Chang, Kwang-chih. *The Archaeology of Ancient China*. Rev. ed., New Haven and London, 1968.

Chang. "Feng-chien She-hui."
Chang Yin-lin 張蔭麟. "Chou-tai ti Feng-chien She-hui" 周 代 的封建社會. *CHHP*, X (1935), 803–836.

Chang, Y. Z. "China and English Civil Service Reform." *American Historical Review*, XLVII (1942), 539–544.

Ch'ang-tuan Ching 長短經. *Ts'ung-shu Chi-ch'eng* edition.

Chavannes, Édouard. "Le Dieu du Sol dans la Chine Antique." Appendix to Chavannes, *Le T'ai Chan*, 437–525.

Chavannes, Édouard. *Le T'ai Chan*. Paris, 1910.

Ch'en Chin-i 陳進宜. "Yü Ting K'ao-shih" 禹鼎考釋. *Kuang-ming Jih-pao Hsüeh-shu* 光明日報學術. No. 40, 7 July 1951.

Ch'en Meng-chia. "The Greatness of Chou." In *China*, edited by Harley Farnsworth MacNair, 54–71. Berkeley and Los Angeles, 1946.

Ch'en Meng-chia 陳夢家. *Hsi-Chou Nien-tai K'ao* 西周年代考 Chungking, 1945.

Ch'en Meng-chia 陳夢家. "Hsi-Chou T'ung-ch'i Tuan-tai" 西周銅器斷代. In *KKHP*. Six parts: (1) IX(1955), 137–175; (2) X(1955), 69–142; (3) 1956, No. 1, 65–114; (4) 1956, No. 2, 85–94; (5) 1956, No. 3, 105–127; (6) 1956, No. 4, 85–122.

Ch'en, "Hsi-Chou Yin-jen."
Ch'en Meng-chia 陳夢家. "Hsi-Chou Wen Chung ti Yin-jen Shen-fen" 西周文中的殷人身分. *Li-shih Yen-chiu* 歷史研究, 1954, No. 6, 85–106.

Ch'en Meng-chia 陳夢家. *Shang-shu T'ung-lun* 尚書通論. Shanghai, 1957.

Ch'en Meng-chia 陳夢家. "Wu-hsing chih Ch'i-yüan" 五行之起源. *YCHP*, XXIV (1938), 35–53.

Ch'en, *Yin Tz'u Tsung-shu.*
Ch'en Meng-chia 陳夢家 . *Yin-hsü Pu-tz'u Tsung-shu* 殷虛卜辭
綜述. Peking, 1956.

Cheng Te-k'un. *Chou China. Archaeology in China*, Vol. III. Toronto,
1963.

Cheng Te-k'un. *New Light on Prehistoric China. Archaeology in
China*, Supplement to Vol. I. Cambridge and Toronto, 1966.

Cheng Te-k'un. *Prehistoric China. Archaeology in China*, Vol. I. Toronto, 1959.

Cheng Te-k'un. *Shang China. Archaeology in China*, Vol. II. Toronto,
1960.

CHHP. Ch'ing-hua Hsüeh-pao 清華學報 [*The Tsing Hua Journal*].

Chi-chung Chou-shu 汲冢周書 [also called *I Chou-shu* 逸周書].
Ssu-pu Ts'ung-k'an edition.

Ch'i, "Chinese and European Feudal Institutions."
Ch'i Ssu-ho. "A Comparison between Chinese and European Feudal
Institutions." *Yenching Journal of Social Studies*, IV (1948), 1–13.

Ch'i Ssu-ho 齊思和 . "Chou-tai Hsi-ming-li K'ao" 周代錫命禮考 .
YCHP, XXXII (1947), 197–226.

Ch'i, "Hsi-Chou Cheng-chih Ssu-hsiang."
Ch'i Ssu-ho 齊思和 . "Hsi-Chou Shih-tai chih Cheng-chih Ssu-
hsiang" 西周時代之政治思想 . *Yen-ching She-hui K'e-hsüeh*
燕京社會科學 , I (1948), 19–40.

Ch'i Ssu-ho 齊思和 . "Hsi-Chou Ti-li K'ao" 西周地理考 . *YCHP*,
XXX (1946), 63–106.

Ch'i Ssu-ho. "Professor Hung on the *Ch'un-Ch'iu*." *Yenching Journal
of Social Studies*, I (1938), 49–71.

Ch'i Ssu-ho 齊思和 . "Yen Wu Fei Chou Feng-kuo Shuo" 燕吳非周
封國說 . *YCHP*, XXVIII (1940), 175–196.

"Chiang-su Tan-t'u Hsien T'ung-ch'i."
"Chiang-su Tan-t'u Hsien Yen-t'un-shan Ch'u-tu ti Ku-tai

Ch'ing-t'ung-ch'i"江蘇丹徒縣煙墩山出土的古代青銅器, by the Chiang-su Sheng Wen-wu Kuan-li Wei-yüan-hui 江蘇省文物管理委員會, Wen-wu Ts'an-K'ao Tzu-liao 文物參考資料, 1955, No. 3, 58–62.

Ch'ien Mu 錢穆. Hsien-Ch'in Chu-tzu Hsi-nien 先秦諸子繫年. 2 vols. Rev. ed. Hong Kong, 1956.

Ch'ien Mu 錢穆. Kuo-shih Ta-kang 國史大綱. Shanghai, 1947.

Childe, V. Gordon. "The First Waggons and Carts—from the Tigris to the Severn." Proceedings of the Prehistoric Society, XVII (1951), 177–194.

Chin Hsiang-heng 金祥恆. Hsü Chia-ku Wen Pien 續甲骨文編. Taipei, 1959.

Chin-wen.
    Kuo Mo-jo 郭沫若. Liang-Chou Chin-wen Tz'u Ta-hsi K'ao-shih 兩周金文辭大系考釋. Peking, 1958.

Ch'ing-t'ung-ch'i T'u-shih 青銅器圖釋. Compiled by the Shensi Provincial Museum, with a preface by T'ang Lan 唐蘭. 1960.

Chou Fa-kao 周法高. Chin-wen Ling-shih 金文零釋. Taiwan, 1951.

Chou Fa-kao. "On the Dating of a Lunar Eclipse in the Shang Period." HJAS, XXV (1965), 243–247.

Chou-li.
    Chou-li Chu-su 周禮注疏. In Shih-san Ching Chu-su.

Chou Yü-t'ung 周予同. Ching Chin-ku-wen Hsüeh 經今古文學. Shanghai, 1926.

Chu, Chung-kuo Ssu-hsiang chih Ying-hsiang.
    Chu Ch'ien-chih 朱謙之. Chung-kuo Ssu-hsiang Tui-yü Ou-chou Wen-hua chih Ying-hsiang 中國思想對於歐洲文化之影響. Changsha, 1940.

Ch'un-ch'iu Ching-chuan Yin-te 春秋經傳引得. Edited by William Hung et al. 4 vols. Peiping, 1937.

Chung-hua Ta Tzu-tien 中華大字典. Edited by Hsü Yüan-kao 徐元

語 , Ou-Yang P'u-ts'un 歐陽溥存 , and Wang Ch'ang-lu 汪長祿 . 2nd ed. Shanghai, 1920.

Ch'ü, T'ung-tsu. *Law and Society in Traditional China*. Paris and The Hague, 1961.

Ch'ü Wan-li 屈萬里 . "Lun Yü-kung Chu-ch'eng ti Shih-tai" 論禹貢 著成的時代 . *BIHP*, XXXV (1964), 53–86.

Ch'ü Wan-li 屈萬里 . *Shang-shu Shih-i* 尚書釋義 . Taipei, 1956.

Ch'ün-shu Chih-yao 羣書治要 . *Ssu-pu Ts'ung-k'an* edition.

Ciasca, Raffaele. *L'Arte dei Medici e Speziali nella Storia e nel Comercio Fiorentino dal Secolo XII al XV*. Florence, 1927.

Cicero, *De Re Publica, De Legibus, with an English Translation by Clinton Walker Keyes*. Cambridge and London, 1928; reprinted 1943.

"A Comparative Discussion of Feudalism." Edited by Rushton Coulborn. Report of a conference held by the American Council of Learned Societies at Princeton University, October 31–November 1, 1950. Mimeographed.

Constantine Porphyrogenitus. *De Administrando Imperio*. Greek text edited by Gy. Moravcsik, English translation by R. J. H. Jenkins. Budapest, 1949.

Coulborn, Rushton, ed. *Feudalism in History*. Princeton, 1956.

Course of the Exchequer.
   The Course of the Exchequer by Richard, Son of Nigel. Translated from the Latin with Introduction and Notes by Charles Johnson. London, etc., 1950.

Couvreur, *Li-chi.*
   Li Ki [Li-chi]. Translated by Séraphin Couvreur. 2 vols. 2d ed. Ho Kien Fu, 1913.

Couvreur, *Shih.*
   Cheu King [Shih-ching]. Translated by Séraphin Couvreur. 3d ed. Sien Sien, 1934.

Couvreur, *Shu.*
    Chou King [Shu-ching]. Translated by Séraphin Couvreur. Sien Hsien, 1927.

Couvreur, *Tso-chuan.*
    Tch'ouen Ts'iou [Ch'un-ch'iu] et Tso Tchouan [Tso-chuan], La Chronique de la Principauté de Lòu. Translated by Séraphin Couvreur. 3 vols. Paris, 1951.

Creel, H. G. "The Beginnings of Bureaucracy in China: The Origin of the *Hsien.*" In *Journal of Asian Studies,* XXIII (1964), 155–184.

Creel, H. G. *The Birth of China.* London, 1936; New York, 1937.

Creel, H. G. "Bronze Inscriptions of the Western Chou Dynasty as Historical Documents." *JAOS,* LVI (1936), 335–349.

Creel, H. G. *Confucius, the Man and the Myth.* New York, 1949. London, 1951. Also published as *Confucius and the Chinese Way.* Harper Torchbook. New York, 1960. [Pagination is identical in the New York editions. Page references are given first to the New York editions, followed by a double colon (::), followed by the page numbers of the London edition.]

Creel, H. G. "The *Fa-chia* 法家 'Legalists' or 'Administrators'?" In *Studies Presented to Tung Tso Pin on His Sixty-Fifth Birthday, BIHP,* Extra Vol. No. 4 (1961), 607–636.

Creel, "The Horse in Chinese History."
    H. G. Creel. "The Role of the Horse in Chinese History." *American Historical Review,* LXX (1965), 647–672.

Creel, H. G. "The Meaning of *Hsing-ming* 刑名 ." In *Studia Serica, Bernhard Karlgren Dedicata,* 199–211. Copenhagen, 1959.

Creel, H. G. "On the Origin of Wu-wei 無為 ," In *Symposium in Honor of Dr. Li Chi on His Seventieth Birthday,* I, 105–107. Taipei, 1965.

Creel, H. G. "Shih T'ien" 釋天 . *YCHP,* XVIII (1935), 59–71.

Creel, H. G. *Studies in Early Chinese Culture.* Baltimore, 1937.

Cronisti e Scrittori Sincroni della Dominazione Normanna nel Regno di Puglia e Sicilia. Edited by Giuseppe Del Re. 2 vols. Naples, 1845 and 1868.

Curtis, Edmund. *Roger of Sicily and the Normans in Lower Italy, 1016–1154.* New York, 1912.

Davis, Arthur K. "Bureaucratic Patterns in the Navy Officer Corps." In *Reader in Bureaucracy*, 380–395.

Description de l'Afrique et de l'Espagne par Edrîsî. Edited and translated by R. Dozy and M. J. de Goeje. Leyden, 1866.

Des Rotours, Robert. "Les insignes en deux parties (fou 符) sous la dynastie des T'ang (618–907)." *TP*, XLI (1952), 1–148.

Des Rotours, Robert. *Le Traité des examens, traduit de la Nouvelle Histoire des T'ang.* Paris, 1932.

Des Rotours, Robert. *Traité des fonctionnaires et Traité de l'armé, traduit de la Nouvelle Histoire des T'ang.* 2 vols. Leiden, 1947 and 1948.

De Stefano, Antonino. *La cultura in Sicilia nel periodo Normanno.* New ed. Bologna, 1954.

Dewall, Magdalene von. "New Data on Early Chou Finds." In *Symposium in Honor of Dr. Li Chi on His Seventieth Birthday* II, 503–570. Taipei, 1967.

Dewall, Magdalene von. *Pferd und Wagen im frühen China.* Bonn, 1964.

Dimock, Marshall E. "Bureaucracy Self-examined." In *Reader in Bureaucracy*, 397–406.

Dobson, W. A. C. H. "Linguistic Evidence and the Dating of the *Book of Songs*." *TP*, LI (1964), 322–334.

Drake, F. S. "Mohammedanism in the T'ang Dynasty." *MS*, VIII (1943), 1–40.

Dubs, Homer H. "The Great Fire in the State of Lu3TU in 492 B.C." *JAOS*, LXXXIV (1964), 14–18.

Dubs, *Han-shu.*
Pan Ku, *The History of the Former Han Dynasty [Ch'ien-Han-shu].* Translated by Homer H. Dubs, with the collaboration of P'an Lo-chi and Jen T'ai. 3 vols. Baltimore, 1938–1955.

Dubs, *Hsüntze.*
The Works of Hsüntze [Hsün-tzu]. Translated by Homer H. Dubs. London, 1928.

Dubs, "Royal Jou Religion."
Homer H. Dubs. "The Archaic Royal Jou [Chou] Religion." *TP,* XLVI (1958), 217–259.

Duyvendak, *Lord Shang.*
The Book of Lord Shang [Shang-chün Shu]. Translated with an introduction by J. J. L. Duyvendak. London, 1928.

Eberhard, Wolfram. "Early Chinese Cultures and Their Development: A new Working-Hypothesis." In *Annual Report of the Board of Regents of the Smithsonian Institution,* 1937, 513–530. Washington, 1938.

Eberhard, Wolfram. *Kultur und Siedlung der Randvölker Chinas.* Leiden, 1942.

Eberhard, Wolfram. *Lokalkulturen im alten China, I.* Supplement to *TP,* Vol. XXXVII. Leiden, 1942.

Eberhard, Wolfram. *Lokal-kulturen im alten China, II.* Peking, 1942.

"Egyptian Instructions." Translated by John A. Wilson. In *Ancient Near Eastern Texts Relating to the Old Testament,* edited by James B. Pritchard, 412–424. Princeton, 1950.

Einaudi, "Imaginary Money."
Luigi Einaudi. "The Theory of Imaginary Money from Charlemagne to the French Revolution." Translated by Giorgio Tagliacozzo. In *Enterprise and Secular Change,* edited by Frederic C. Lane and Jelle C. Riersma, 229–261. Homewood, Ill., 1953.

Eisenstadt, S. N. *The Political Systems of Empires.* London, 1963.

Emlen, John T., Jr., and George B. Schaller. "In the Home of the Mountain Gorilla." *Animal Kingdom,* LXIII (1960), 98–108.

Encyclopaedia of the Social Sciences. Edited by Edwin R. A. Seligman. 15 vols. New York, 1930; reissue of 1937.

Erkes, Eduard. "Das Pferd im alten China." *TP,* XXXVI (1942), 26–63.

Erkes, Eduard. "Ist die Hsia-Dynastie geschichtlich?" *TP,* XXXIII (1937), 134–149.

Erman, *Aegypten im Altertum.*
Adolf Erman. *Aegypten und Aegyptisches Leben im Altertum,* revised by Hermann Ranke. Tübingen, 1923.

Escarra, Jean. *Le droit chinois.* Peking and Paris, 1936.

Essays on Examinations. Published by the International Institute Examinations Enquiry Committee. London, 1935.

Essays on the Scientific Study of Politics. Edited by Herbert J. Storing. New York, 1962.

Fairbank, John King. *The United States and China.* Rev. ed. Cambridge, Mass., 1958.

Fairclough, *Virgil.*
Virgil, with an English Translation by H. Rushton Fairclough. Loeb Classical Library edition. 2 vols. London and Cambridge, Mass. 1960.

Feng, Han-yi. *The Chinese Kinship System.* Cambridge, Mass., 1948.

Fesler, James W. "French Field Administration: The Beginnings." *Comparative Studies in Society and History,* V (1962–1963), 76–111.

Fesler, James W. "The Political Role of Field Administration." In *Papers in Comparative Public Administration,* edited by Ferrel Heady and Sybil L. Stokes, 117–143. Ann Arbor, Mich., 1962.

Finer, *Modern Government.*
Herman Finer, *Theory and Practice of Modern Government.* Rev. ed. New York, 1949; reprinted 1957.

Fitzgerald, C. P. *The Empress Wu.* Melbourne, 1955.

Forke, *Alten chinesischen Philosophie.*
Alfred Forke. *Geschichte der alten chinesischen Philosophie.* Hamburg, 1927.

Forke, Alfred, trans. *Lun-Hêng. Philosophical Essays of Wang Ch'ung.* 2 vols. 2d ed. New York, 1962.

Friedrich, Carl Joachim. *The Philosophy of Law in Historical Perspective.* 2d ed. Chicago, 1963.

Fu Ssu-nien 傅斯年. "Chiang Yüan" 姜原 . *BIHP*, II (1930), 130–135.

Fu Ssu-nien 傅斯年. "Chou Tung Feng yü Yin I-min" 周東封與殷遺民. *BIHP*, IV (1934), 285–290.

Fu Ssu-nien 傅斯年. "Hsin-huo Pu-tz'u Hsieh-pen Hou-chi Pa" 新獲卜辭寫本後記跋. *An-yang Fa-chüeh Pao-kao* 安陽發掘報告, II (Peiping, 1930), 349–386.

Fu Ssu-nien 傅斯年. "I Hsia Tung Hsi Shuo" 夷夏東西説. In *Academia Sinica, Studies Presented to Ts'ai Yuan P'ei on His Sixty-fifth Birthday*, II (Peiping, 1935), 1093–1134.

Fu Ssu-nien 傅斯年, "Lun So-wei Wu-teng Chüeh" 論所謂五等爵 , *BIHP*, II (1930), 110–129.

Fu Ssu-nien 傅斯年. "Ta-tung Hsiao-tung Shuo" 大東小東説. *BIHP*, II (1930), 101–109.

Fung Yu-lan. *A History of Chinese Philosophy.* Translated by Derk Bodde. Vol. I, 2d ed, Princeton, 1952. Vol. II, Princeton, 1953.

Gale, *Salt and Iron.*
Discourses on Salt and Iron [*Yen-t'ieh Lun*, by Huan K'uan], *Chapters I–XIX.* Translated and annotated by Esson M. Gale. Leyden, 1931.

Ganshof, *La féodalité.*
F. L. Ganshof. *Qu'est-ce que la féodalité?* 2d ed. Brussels, 1947.

Gibb, H. A. R. "Chinese Records of the Arabs in Central Asia." *Bulletin of the School of Oriental Studies, London Institution* II (1921–1923), 613–622.

Gibbon, *Roman Empire.*
Edward Gibbon. *The History of the Decline and Fall of the Roman Empire.* Edited by J. B. Bury. 3 vols. New York, 1946.

Giunta, Francesco. *Bizantini e Bizantinismo nella Sicilia Normanna.* Palermo, 1950.

Gladden, *Public Administration.*
E. N. Gladden. *An Introduction to Public Administration.* 2d ed. London and New York, 1952.

Goldschmidt, L. *Rechtsstudium und Prüfungsordnung.* Stuttgart, 1887.

Goodrich, Chauncey. *A Pocket Dictionary (Chinese-English) and Pekingese Syllabary.* Rev. ed. Hong Kong, 1965.

Goodrich, Luther Carrington. *The Literary Inquisition of Ch'ien-lung.* Baltimore, 1935.

Gotō Kinpei 後藤均平 . "Seishū to Ōjō." 成周と王城, In Oriental Studies Presented to Sei (Kiyoshi) Wada, (Tokyo, 1960), 399–410.

Granet, Marcel. *Chinese Civilization.* Translated by Kathleen E. Innes and Mabel B. Brailsford. New York, 1960.

Granet, Marcel. *Danses et légendes de la Chine ancienne.* Paris, 1926.

Granet, Marcel. *La pensée chinoise.* Paris, 1934.

Griffith, Samuel B., trans. *Sun Tzu, The Art of War.* Oxford, 1963.

Guicciardini, Francesco. *Maxims and Reflections of a Renaissance Statesman (Ricordi).* Translated by Mario Domandi. New York, 1965.

Gwynn, Aubrey. *Roman Education from Cicero to Quintilian.* Oxford, 1926.

Haenisch, Erich. *Politische Systeme und Kämpfe im alten China.* Berlin, 1951.

Hall, John Whitney. "Feudalism in Japan—A Reassessment." *Comparative Studies in Society and History,* V (1962), 15–51.

Han-fei-tzu 韓非子. *Ssu-pu Pei-yao* edition.

Hansard's Parliamentary Debates, Third Series. London. CXXVIII, 1853. CXXIX, 1853. CXXXI, 1854.

Han-shih Wai-chuan 韓詩外傳. *Ssu-pu Ts'ung-k'an* edition.

Han-shu.
Wang Hsien-ch'ien 王先謙. *Ch'ien-Han-shu Pu-chu* 前漢書補注. Changsha, 1900.

Hartwell, Robert M. "Iron and Early Industrialism in Eleventh-century China." Ph.D. dissertation, University of Chicago, 1963.

Hawkes, David. *Ch'u Tz'u, The Songs of the South.* Boston, 1962.

Heichelheim and Yeo. *The Roman People.*
Fritz M. Heichelheim and Cedric A. Yeo. *A History of the Roman People.* Englewood Cliffs, N.J., 1962.

Herodotus.
The History of Herodotus. Translated by George Rawlinson. New York, Tudor Publishing Co., 1932.

Herson, Lawrence J. R. "China's Imperial Bureaucracy: Its Direction and Control." *Public Administration Review*, XVII (1957), 44–53.

Hightower, James Robert, trans. *Han Shih Wai Chuan.* Cambridge, Mass., 1952.

HJAS. Harvard Journal of Asiatic Studies.

Hobbes, Thomas. *Leviathan.* Everyman's Library, 1934.

Hofmann, Max. *Die Stellung des Königs von Sizilien nach den Assisen von Ariano (1140).* Münster i.W., 1915.

Holtze, Friedrich. *Geschichte des Kammergerichts in Brandenburg-Preussen.* Berlin, 1901.

Hou-Han Shu 後漢書. Ching-ling Shu-chü, 1869.

Hsiao-ching Chu-su 孝經注疏. In *Shih-san Ching Chu-su.*

Hsieh Shang-Kung　薛尚功. *Li-tai Chung-ting I-ch'i K'uan-shih Fa-t'ieh* 歷代鐘鼎彝器款識法帖. Liu Shih edition. Wuchang, 1903.

Hsieh Ch'eng-chia 謝成俠. *Chung-kuo Yang-ma Shih* 中國養馬史. Peking, 1959.

Hsien-Ch'in Ching-chi K'ao 先秦經籍考. Edited and translated by Chiang Chia-an 江俠菴. 3 vols. Shanghai, 1933.

Hsi-Han Hui-yao 西漢會要. Compiled by Hsü T'ien-lin 徐天麟. *Kuo-hsüeh Chi-pen Ts'ung-shu.* Shanghai, 1935.

Hsu, Cho-yun. *Ancient China in Transition.* Stanford, Calif., 1965.

Hsu, "Western Chou Government."
Cho-yun Hsu. "Some Working Notes on the Western Chou Government." *BIHP*, XXXVI (1966), 513–524.

Hsü Chung-shu　徐中舒. "Pin-feng Shuo" 豳風說. *BIHP*, VI (1936), 431–452.

Hsü Chung-shu　徐中舒. "Yin Chou Wen-hua chih Li-ts'e" 殷周文化之蠡測, *BIHP*, II (1931), 275–280.

Hsü Chung-shu　徐中舒. "Yü Ting ti Nien-tai chi Ch'i Hsiang-kuan Wen-t'i" 禹鼎的年代及其相關問題. *KKHP*, 1959, No. 3, 53–66.

Hsüan-tsang. *Buddhist Records of the Western World.* Translated from the Chinese of Hiuen Tsiang by Samuel Beal. London, *Popular edition,* n.d.

Hsün-tzu 荀子. *Ssu-yu Pei-yao* edition.

Hu, *Chia-ku Hsüeh, Ch'u-chi and Er-chi.*
Hu Hou-hsüan 胡厚宣. *Chia-ku Hsüeh Shang-shih Lun Ts'ung* 甲骨學商史論叢. *Ch'u-chi* 初集, 4 vols., Chengtu, 1944. *Er-chi* 二集, 2 vols., 1945.

Hu, *Chia-ku Hsüeh Chu-mu.*
Hu Hou-hsüan 胡厚宣, *Wu-shih Nien Chia-ku Hsüeh Lun Chu-mu* 五十年甲骨學論著目. Shanghai, 1952.

Hu Hou-hsüan 胡厚宣 . "Ch'u Min-tsu Yüan yü Tung-fang K'ao" 楚民族源於東方考. *Shih-hsüeh Lun-ts'ung* 史學論叢, I (1934), 2–42.

Hu Shih. "Wang Mang, the Socialist Emperor of Nineteen Centuries Ago." *Journal of the North China Branch of the Royal Asiatic Society*, LIX (1928), 218–230.

Hu, "Yin Feng-chien K'ao."
Hu Hou-hsüan 胡厚宣 . "Yin-tai Feng-chien Chih-tu K'ao" 殷代封建制度考. In Hu, *Chia-ku Hsüeh, Ch'u-chi.*

Hu, "Yin Hun-yin Chia-tsu Tsung-fa K'ao."
Hu Hou-hsüan 胡厚宣. "Yin-tai Hun-yin Chia-tsu Tsung-fa Sheng-yü Chih-tu K'ao" 殷代婚姻家族宗法生育制度考. In Hu, *Chia-ku Hsüeh, Ch'u Chi.*

Huai-nan-tzu 淮南子 . *Ssu-pu Pei-yao* edition.

Hucker, Charles O. "Confucianism and the Chinese Censorial System." In *Confucianism in Action.* Edited by David S. Nivison and Arthur F. Wright. Stanford, Calif., 1959.

Hudson, G. F. *Europe and China.* London, 1931, reprinted Boston, 1961.

Hughes, Thomas. *Loyola and the Educational System of the Jesuits.* New York, 1899.

Huillard-Bréholles, J. L. A. *Historia Diplomatici Frederici Secundi.* 12 vols. Paris, 1852–1861.

Hulsewé, *Han Law.*
A. F. P. Hulsewé. *Remnants of Han Law.* Vol. I, Leiden, 1955.

Hung Liang-chi 洪亮吉 . *Keng-sheng-chai Wen Chia-chi* 更生齋文甲集 . 1802.

Ibn Khorradādhbeh. *Kitāb al-masālik wa'l-mamālik.* Published with French translation and notes by M. J. de Goeje. Lugduni-Batavorum, 1889.

I-ching. Chou-i Chu-su 周易注疏. In *Shih-san Ching Chu-su.*

I-li Chu-su 儀禮注疏. In *Shih-san Ching Chu-su.*

I-lin 意林 . *Ssu-pu Pei-yao* edition.

Irsay, Stephen d'. *Histoire des universités*. 2 vols. Paris, 1933–1934.

I-wen Lei-chü 藝文類聚. Edited by Ou-yang Hsün 歐陽詢. 1879.

Jacob, Georg. "Oriental Elements of Culture in the Occident." In *Annual Report of the Board of Regents of the Smithsonian Institution for the year ending June 30, 1902* (Washington, 1903), 509–529.

JAOS. Journal of the American Oriental Society.

Jenkinson, Hilary. "Exchequer Tallies." *Archaeologia*, LXII (1911), 367–380.

Jenkinson, Hilary. "Medieval Tallies, Public and Private." *Archaeologia*, LXXIV (1925), 289–351.

Jones, A. H. M. *The Later Roman Empire 284–602*. 2 vols. Norman, Oklahoma, 1964.

Jung Keng 容庚 . *Chin-wen Pien* 金文編. 1939.

Kantorowicz, Ernst. *Kaiser Friedrich der Zweite*. Berlin, 1936.

Karlgren, "Chou Li and Tso Chuan."
Bernhard Karlgren. "The Early History of the Chou Li and Tso Chuan Texts." *BMFEA*, III (1931), 1–59.

Karlgren, Bernhard. "Glosses on the Book of Documents." (1), *BMFEA*, XX (1948), 39–315; (2), *BMFEA*, XXI (1949), 63–206.

Karlgren, Bernhard. "Glosses on the Kuo Feng Odes." *BMFEA*, XIV (1942), 71–247.

Karlgren, Bernhard. "Glosses on the Siao Ya Odes." *BMFEA*, XVI (1944), 25–169.

Karlgren, Bernhard. "Glosses on the Ta Ya and Sung Odes." *BMFEA*, XVIII (1946), 1–198.

Karlgren, Bernhard. "Grammata Serica Recensa." *BMFEA*, XXIX (1957), 1–332.

Karlgren, Bernhard. "Legends and Cults in Early China." *BMFEA*, XVIII (1946), 199–365.

Karlgren, Bernhard. "Some Sacrifices in Chou China." *BMFEA*, XL (1968), 1–31.

Karlgren, Bernhard. "Some Weapons and Tools of the Yin Dynasty." *BMFEA*, XVII (1945), 101–144.

Karlgren, "On the Tso Chuan."
Bernhard Karlgren, "On the Authenticity and Nature of the Tso Chuan." *Göteborgs Högskolas Arsskrift*, XXXII (1926), 3–65.

Kautilya's Arthaśastra. Translated by R. Shamasastry. 5th ed. Mysore, 1956.

Keay, F. E. *Indian Education in Ancient and Later Times*. London, 1938.

KK. K'ao-ku 考古 .

KKHP. K'ao-ku Hsüeh-pao 考古學報.

Khairallah, Amin A. *Outline of Arabic Contributions to Medicine*. Beirut, 1946.

Kracke, "Chinese Government."
Edward A. Kracke, Jr. "The Chinese and the Art of Government." In *The Legacy of China*. Edited by Raymond Dawson (Oxford, 1964), 309–339.

Kracke, *Sung Civil Service*.
Edward A. Kracke, Jr. *Civil Service in Early Sung China—960–1067*. Cambridge, Mass., 1953.

Ku Chieh-kang 顧頡剛. "Chou E Ch'i-shih Shih ti Fa-sheng Tz'u-ti" 紂惡七十事的發生次第. In *Ku-shih Pien*, II, 82–91.

Ku Chieh-kang 顧頡剛. "Lun Chin-wen Shang-shu Chu-tso Shih-tai Shu" 論今文尚書著作時代書 . In *Ku-shih Pien*, I, 200–206.

Ku Chieh-kang 顧頡剛. *Shang-shu T'ung-chien* 尚書通檢 Harvard-Yenching Institute, 1936.

Ku-hsiang-chai Chien-shang Hsiu-chen Ch'u-hsüeh-chi 古香齋鑒賞袖珍初學記. 1883.

Ku Tung-kao 顧棟高 .*Ch'un-ch'iu Ta-shih Piao* 春秋大事表. In *Huang-Ch'ing Ching-chieh Hsü-pien* 皇清經解續編 (1886–1888), 67–133.

Kung-Yang Chuan.
Ch'un-ch'iu Kung-Yang [Chuan] Chu-su 春秋公羊[傳]注疏. In *Shih-san Ching Chu-su.*

Küntzel, Georg. *Die drei grossen Hohenzollern und der Aufstieg Preussens im 17. und 18. Jahrhundert.* Stuttgart, 1922.

Ku-shih Pien 古史辨. Edited by Ku Chieh-kang and others. 7 vols. I–V, Peiping, 1926–1935. VI–VII, Shanghai, 1938–1941.

Kuo Jo-yü 郭若愚 . *Yin-hsü Wen-tzu Cho-he* 殷虛文字綴合. Peking, 1955.

Kuo, "Ch'ang-an Ming-wen."
Kuo Mo-jo 郭沫若 ."Ch'ang-an Hsien Chang-chia P'o T'ung-ch'i Ch'ün Ming-wen Hui-shih" 長安縣張家坡銅器群銘文彙釋 *KKHP*, 1962, No. 1, 1–14.

Kuo Mo-jo 郭沫若 . *Chin-wen Hsü-k'ao* 金文續考. In *Ku-tai Ming-k'e Hui-k'ao.*

Kuo, *Chin-wen Lu-pien.*
Kuo Mo-jo 郭沫若 . *Liang-Chou Chin-wen Tz'u Ta-hsi Lu-pien* 兩周金文辭大系錄編. Tokyo, 1935.

Kuo Mo-jo 郭沫若 . *Chin-wen Ts'ung-k'ao* 金文叢考. Peking, 1954.

Kuo Mo-jo 郭沫若 . *Chung-kuo Ku-tai She-hui Yen-chiu* 中國古代社會研究. 5th ed. Shanghai, 1932.

Kuo Mo-jo 郭沫若 , "Hsin-yang Mu ti Nien-tai yü Kuo-pieh" 信陽墓的年代與國別. In *Wen-wu Ts'an-k'ao Tzu-liao* 文物參考資料 1958, No. 1, 5.

Kuo Mo-jo 郭沫若 . *Ku-tai Ming-k'e Hui-k'ao* 古代銘刻彙考. Tokyo, 1933.

Kuo Mo-jo 郭沫若 . "Pao Yu Ming Shih-wen" 保卣銘釋文 . KKHP, 1958, No. 1, 1–2.

Kuo Mo-jo 郭沫若 . Pu-tz'u T'ung-tsuan 卜辭通纂. Tokyo, 1933.

Kuo Mo-jo 郭沫若 , Shih P'i-p'an Shu 十批判書 . Peking, 1954.

Kuo Mo-jo. 郭沫若 . "Shih Ying Chien Hsien" 釋應監甗. KKHP, 1960, No. 1, 7–8.

Kuo Mo-jo 郭沫若 . Wen-shih Lun-chi 文史論集. Peking, 1961.

Kuo Mo-jo 郭沫若 . Yin Ch'i Ts'ui-pien 殷契粹篇. Tokyo, 1937.

Kuo Mo-jo 郭沫若 . Yin-Chou Ch'ing-t'ung-ch'i Ming-wen Yen-chiu 殷周青銅器銘文研究. 2 vols. Shanghai, 1931.

Kuo Mo-jo 郭沫若 . "Yü Ting Po" 禹鼎跋 . In Kuang-ming Jih-pao Hsüeh-shu 光明日報學術 . No. 40, 7 July 1951.

Kuo-yü 國 語 . Ssu-pu Pei-yao edition.

Kurihara Tomonobu 栗原朋信 . "Hōshaku no Sei ni tsuite" 封爵之誓 について . In Shakai Keizai Shigaku 社會經濟史學 . XVII (1951), 503–516.

Kuwubara, Jitsuzô. "On P'u Shou-keng, A Man of the Western Regions, Who Was Superintendent of the Trading Ships' Office in Ch'üan-chou Towards the End of the Sung Dynasty, Together with a General Sketch of the Trade of the Arabs in China During the T'ang and Sung Eras." MRDTB, I: No. 2 (1928), 1–79. II: No. 7 (1935), 1–104.

Lach, Donald F. "The Chinese Studies of Andreas Müller." JAOS, LX (1940), 564–575.

Lach, Donald F. The Preface to Liebniz' Novissima Sinica: Commentary, Translation, Text. Honolulu, 1957.

Lane, Arthur. Early Islamic Pottery. London, 1947.

Lao, Chü-yen Han-chien K'ao-shih.
    Lao Kan 勞榦 , Chü-yen Han-chien, K'ao-shih chih Pu 居延 漢簡，考釋之部 . (Academia Sinica Special Publications, No. 40.

Documents of the Han Dynasty on Wooden Slips from Edsin Gol. Part 2: Translations and Commentaries.) Taipei, 1960.

Lattimore, Owen. *Inner Asian Frontiers of China.* New York, 1940.

Leclerc, Lucien. *Histoire de la médecine arabe.* Paris, 1876.

Legge, *I-ching.*
James Legge, trans. *The Yî King. The Sacred Books of the East,* Vol. XVI. 2d. ed. Oxford, 1899.

Legge, *Li-chi.*
The Lî Kî. Translated by James Legge. *The Sacred Books of the East,* XXVII–XXVIII. 2 vols. London, 1885; second impression, 1926.

Legge, *Shih.*
The Chinese Classics. Translated by James Legge. *Vol. IV. The She-King [Shih-ching].* 2 pts. London, 1871.

Legge, *Shu.*
The Chinese Classics. Translated by James Legge. Vol. III. *The Shoo King [Shu-ching].* 2 pts. London, 1865.

Levenson, Joseph R. *Confucian China and Its Modern Fate.* 3 vols. Berkeley and Los Angeles, 1958–1965.

Li Hsiao-ting 李孝定 . *Chia-ku Wen-tzu Chi-shih* 甲骨文字集釋. 16 vols. 1965.

Li-chi.
Li-chi Chu-su 禮記注疏. In *Shih-san Ching Chu-su.*

Li, *Yin-yang Wu-hsing Hsüeh-shuo.*
Li Han-San 李漢三 . *Hsien-Ch'in Liang-Han chih Yin-yang Wu-hsing Hsüeh-shuo* 先秦兩漢之陰陽五行學說. Taipei, 1967.

Liang Ch'i-hsiung 梁啟雄 . *Hsün-tzu Chien-shih* 荀子柬釋 . Shanghai, 1936.

Liao, *Han Fei Tzŭ.*
The Complete Works of Han Fei Tzŭ. Translated by W. K. Liao. 2 vols. London, 1939 and 1959.

Lin Hui-hsiang 林惠祥. *Chung-kuo Min-tsu Shih* 中國民族史. 2 vols. Shanghai, 1937.

Liu-ch'en-chu Wen-hsüan 六臣註文選. *Ssu-pu Ts'ung-k'an* edition.

Liu Tsung-yüan 柳宗元. *Liu He-tung Chi* 柳河東集. *Kuo-hsüeh Chi-pen Ts'ung-shu* edition.

Lo Chen-yü 羅振玉. *Chen-sung T'ang Chi Ku I-wen* 貞松堂集古遺文. 1931.

Loewe, Michael. *Records of Han Administration*. 2 vols. Cambridge, 1967.

Lovejoy, Arthur O.
"The Chinese Origin of a Romanticism." In Lovejoy, *Essays in the History of Ideas* (Baltimore, 1948), 99–135.

Lun-yü Chi-shih 論語集釋. Compiled by Ch'eng Shu-te 程樹德. 2 vols. Peking, 1943.

Lü-shih Ch'un-ch'iu 呂氏春秋. *Ssu-pu Pei-yao* edition.

Machiavelli, Niccoló. *The Prince and the Discourses*. Translated by Luigi Ricci and Christian E. Detmold. Modern Library edition, New York, 1940.

Malden, Henry. *On the Origin of Universities and Academical Degrees*. London, 1835.

Mao-shih.
Mao-shih Chu-su 毛詩注疏. In *Shih-san Ching Chu-su.*

Maspero, Henri. *La Chine antique*. New edition. Paris, 1955.

Maspero, Henri. "La composition et la date du Tso tchouan." In *Mélanges chinois et bouddhiques*, I (1932), 139–215.

Maspero, Henri. *Mélanges Posthumes sur les Religions et l'Histoire de la Chine*. 3 vols. Paris, 1950.

Maspero, Henri. "Le régime féodal et la propriété foncière dans la Chine antique." In Maspero, *Mélanges Posthumes*, III, 111–146.

Maspero, Henri. "Le serment dans la procédure judiciare de la Chine antique." In *Mélanges chinois et bouddhiques*, III (1934–1935), 257–317.

Maspero, "La société chinoise."
Henri Maspero. "Contribution a l'Étude de la société chinoise à la fin des Chang et au début des Tcheou." *BEFEO*, XLVI (1954), 335–402.

McGovern, *Central Asia.*
William Montgomery McGovern. *The Early Empires of Central Asia.* Chapel Hill, 1939.

McKnight, Brian E. "The Rebellion of Fang La." Ph.D. dissertation, University of Chicago, 1964.

Mei, "Ch'un-ch'iu Cheng-chih."
Mei Ssu-p'ing 梅思平 , "Ch'un-ch'iu Shih-tai ti Cheng-chih he K'ung-tzu ti Cheng-chih Ssu-hsiang"春秋時代的政治和孔子的政治思想. In *Ku-shih Pien*, II, 161–194.

Mei, *Motse.*
The Ethical and Political Works of Motse. Translated by Yi-pao Mei. London, 1929.

Meissner, Bruno. *Babylonien und Assyrien.* 2 vols. Heidelberg, 1920–1925.

Mémoires historiques.
Se-ma Ts'ien, *Les Mémoires historiques.* Translated by Édouard Chavannes. 5 vols. Paris, 1895–1905.

Mencius.
Meng-tzu 孟子 . References are given according to the numbering system used in the translation of James Legge.

Meng-tzu Hui-chien 孟子會箋 . Compiled and edited by Wen Chin-ch'eng 温晉城 . Shanghai, 1946.

Michels, "Assimilation into the Bureaucracy."
Robert Michels. "Assimilation of the Discontented into the State Bureaucracy." In *Reader in Bureaucracy*, 140–143.

Mills, C. Wright. *The Power Elite.* New York, 1957.

Minns, Ellis H. *Scythians and Greeks. A Survey of Ancient History and Archaeology on the North Coast of the Euxine from the Danube to the Caucasus.* Cambridge, 1913.

Miyazaki, Ichisada 宮崎市定 . "Chūgoku Jōdai wa Hōkensei ka Toshi Kokka ka" 中國上代は封建制か都市國家か'. *Shirin* 史林 , XXXIII (1950), 144–163.

Miyazaki, Ichisada. "Kodai Shina Fuzei Seido" 古代支那賦税制度. *Shirin* 史林 , XVIII (1933). Three parts: (1), 187–204. (2), 481–505. (3), 681–714.

Momigliano, Arnaldo. "The Place of Herodotus in the History of Historiography." *History*, XLIII (1958), 1–13.

Montesquieu, *Grandeur des Romains*.
Montesquieu. *Grandeur et décadence des Romains, Politique des Romains, Dialogue de Sylla et d'Eucrate, Lysimaque, et Pensées. Lettres persanes et Temple de Gnide*. Paris, 1846.

Mo-tzu 墨子 . *Ssu-pu Pei-yao* edition.

MRDTB. Memoirs of the Research Department of the Toyo Bunko (The Oriental Library, Tokyo).

MS. Monumenta Serica.

Needham, Joseph. *Science and Civilization in China*. Vols. I–IV:2. Cambridge, 1954–1965.

Nizām al-Mulk. *The Book of Government or Rules for Kings*. Translated by Hubert Darke. London, 1960.

Olrik, Axel. *Viking Civilization*. Translated by Jacob Wittmer Hartmann and Hanna Astrup Larsen. New York, 1930.

Ordinances of Manu.
The Ordinances of Manu. Translated by Arthur Coke Burnell. London, 1891.

Papyrus Erzherzog Rainer. Führer durch die Ausstellung. Vienna, 1894.

Parsons, Talcott. *Structure and Process in Modern Societies*. Glencoe, Ill., 1960.

Parsons, Talcott. *The Structure of Social Action*. New York and London, 1937.

Pei-t'ang Shu-ch'ao 北堂書鈔 . 1888.

Pelliot, Paul. "Le *Chou King* en Caractères Anciens et le *Chang Chou Che Wen.*" In *Mémoires concernant l'Asie orientale*, II (1916), 123–177.

P'eng Hsin-wei 彭信威 . *Chung-kuo Huo-pi Shih* 中國貨幣史 . Shanghai, 1958.

Pinot, Virgile. *La Chine et la formation de l'esprit philosophique en France (1640–1740).* Paris, 1932.

Plato, *Dialogues.*
The *Dialogues of Plato.* Translated by B. Jowett. Eighth printing. 2 vols. New York, 1937. (Pagination given is that of Stephens.)

Plato, *Laws.* In Plato, *Dialogues*, II, 407–703.

Plato, *The Republic.* In Plato, *Dialogues*, I, 591–879.

Pufendorf, Samuel. *De Jure Naturae et Gentium Libri Octo*, Vol. II. *The Translation of the Edition of 1688*, by C. H. Oldfather and W. A. Oldfather. Oxford and London, 1934.

Pulleyblank, Edwin G. "Neo-Confucianism and Neo-Legalism in T'ang Intellectual Life, 755–805." In *The Confucian Persuasion.* Edited by Arthur F. Wright. Stanford, Calif., 1960.

Pulleyblank, Edwin G. "The Origins and Nature of Chattel Slavery in China." *Journal of the Economic and Social History of the Orient*, I (1958), 185–220.

Rashdall, Hastings. *The Universities of Europe in the Middle Ages.* New edition. Edited by F. M. Powicke and A. B. Emden. 3 vols. Oxford, 1936.

Reader in Bureaucracy. Edited by Robert K. Merton, Ailsa P. Gray, Barbara Hockey, and Hanan C. Selvin. Glencoe, Ill., 1952, reprinted 1960.

Reichwein, Adolf. *China and Europe; Intellectual and Artistic Contacts in the Eighteenth Century.* London, 1925.

Reischauer, Edwin O. "Notes on T'ang Dynasty Sea Routes." *HJAS*, V (1940), 142–164.

Relation de la Chine et de l'Inde rédigée en 851. Translated and annotated by Jean Sauvaget. Paris, 1948.

Rhoades, *Virgil*.
   The Poems of Virgil. Translated by James Rhoades. *Great Books* edition. Chicago, 1952.

Ricci, *Journals*.
   China in the Sixteenth Century: The Journals of Matthew Ricci: 1583–1610. Translated by Louis J. Gallagher. New York, 1953.

Rosenberg, Hans. *Bureaucracy, Aristocracy, and Autocracy: The Prussian Experience 1660–1815*. Cambridge, Mass., 1958.

Rostovtzeff, *Roman Empire*.
   M. Rostovtzeff. *The Social and Economic History of the Roman Empire*. 2d edition, revised by P. M. Fraser. 2 vols. Oxford, 1957.

Rotours, Robert des. "Les insignes en deux parties (fou 符) sous la dynastie des T'ang (618–907)." *TP*, XLI (1952), 1–148.

Rotours, Robert des. *Le Traité des examens, traduit de la Nouvelle Histoire des T'ang*. Paris, 1932.

Rotours, Robert des. *Traité des fonctionnaires et Traité de l'armée, traduits de la Nouvelle Histoire des T'ang*. 2 vols. Leyden, 1947–1948.

Rowe, John Howland. "Inca Culture at the Time of the Spanish Conquest." In *Handbook of the South American Indians*, Vol. II. Edited by Julian H. Steward (Washington, 1946), 183–330.

Rubin, V. A. "Tzu-ch'an and the City-State of Ancient China." *TP*, LII (1965), 8–34.

Rudolph, R. C. "Preliminary Notes on Sung Archaeology." *Journal of Asian Studies*, XXII (1963), 169–177.

Sankalia, Hasmukh D. *The University of Nālandā*. Madras, 1934.

San-tai Chin-wen.
   San-tai Chi Chin-wen Ts'un 三代吉金文存 . Compiled by Lo Chen-yü 羅振玉 , 1936.

Sarton, George. "Chinese Glass at the Beginning of the Confucian Age." *ISIS*, XXV (1936), 73–79.

Sarton, *History of Science*.
George Sarton. *Introduction to the History of Science*. 3 vols. Carnegie Institution of Washington, Publication No. 376. Baltimore, 1927–1948.

Schafer, Edward H. *The Golden Peaches of Samarkand*. Berkeley and Los Angeles, 1963.

Schachner, Nathan. *The Medieval Universities*. New York, 1938.

Schaller and Emlen. "Social Behavior of the Mountain Gorilla."
George B. Schaller and John T. Emlen, Jr. "Observations on the Ecology and Social Behavior of the Mountain Gorilla." In *African Ecology and Human Evolution*. Edited by F. Clark Howell and Francois Bourlière. Viking Fund Publications in Anthropology, No. 36. New York, 1963.

Schmoller, Gustav. "Der preussische Beamtenstand unter Friedrich Wilhelm I." *Preussische Jahrbücher*, Vol. 26 (Berlin, 1870), 148–172.

Schoff, *The Periplus*.
The Periplus of the Erythraean Sea. Translated and annotated by Wilfred H. Schoff. New York, 1912.

Schurmann, H. F. "Traditional Property Concepts in China." *Far Eastern Quarterly*, XV (1956), 507–516.

Seligman, C. G., and Beck, H. C. "Far Eastern Glass: Some Western Origins." *BMFEA*, 10 (1938), 1–64.

Shang Ch'eng-tso 商承祚. *Yin-ch'i I-ts'un* 殷契佚存. Nanking, 1933.

Shang Ch'eng-tso 商承祚. *Yin-chi' I-ts'un K'ao-shih* 殷契佚存考釋. Nanking, 1933.

Shang-chün Shu 商君書. *Ssu-pu Pei-yao* edition.

Shang-shu Chu-su 尚書注疏. In *Shih-san Ching Chu-su*.

Shih.
The Book of Odes [Shih-ching]. Translated by Bernhard Karlgren. Stockholm, 1950.

Shih, "Yin-hsü Fa-chüeh ti Kung-hsien."
Shih Chang-ju 石璋如, "Yin-hsü Fa-chüeh Tui-yü Chung-kuo Ku-tai Wen-hua ti Kung hsien" 殷虛發掘對於中國古代文化的貢獻. In Hsüeh-shu Chi-k'an 學術季刊, II (1954), No. 4, 8–23.

Shih Chang-ju 石璋如. "Yin-tai ti Kung yü Ma" 殷代的弓與馬. BIHP, XXXV (1964), 321–342.

Shih Ching-ch'eng 史景成. "Chou-li Ch'eng-shu Nien-tai K'ao" 周禮成書年代考. TLTC, XXXII (1966), 135–142, 171–178, 216–223.

Shih-chi.
Takigawa Kametaro 瀧川龜太郎, Shih-chi Hui-chu K'ao-cheng 史記會注考證. 10 vols. Tokyo, 1932–1934.

Shih-san Ching Chu-su 十三經注疏. Nanchang, 1815.

Shryock, John K. The Origin and Development of the State Cult of Confucius. New York and London, 1932.

Shu.
Bernhard Karlgren, trans. "The Book of Documents" [Shu-ching]. BMFEA, XXII (1950), 1–81.

Shuo-wen.
Ting Fu-pao 丁福保, ed. Shuo-wen Chieh-tzu Ku-lin 說文解字詁林. 1928.

Sickman, Lawrence, and Soper, Alexander. The Art and Architecture of China. Penguin Books, 1956.

Simon, Herbert A. Administrative Behavior. 2d ed. New York, 1961.

Singer et al., History of Technology.
A History of Technology. Vol. I. Edited by Charles Singer, E. J. Holmyard, and A. R. Hall. Oxford, 1954, republished 1958. Vol. II. Edited by Singer, Holmyard, Hall, and Trevor I. Williams. Oxford, 1956, reprinted 1957.

Smith, David Eugene, and Karpinski, Louis Charles. *The Hindu-Arabic Numerals*. Boston and London, 1911.

Smith, Vincent A. *The Oxford History of India*. 2d ed. Oxford, 1923, reprinted 1928.

Soothill, William Edward. *The Hall of Light*. London, 1951.

Southwick, "Intergroup Behavior in Primates."
Charles Southwick. "Patterns of Intergroup Behavior in Primates, with Special Reference to Rhesus and Howling Monkeys." In *Annals of the New York Academy of Sciences*, CII (1962), 436–454.

Ssu, "Liang-Chou Chih-kuan K'ao."
Ssu Wei-chih 斯維至 , "Liang-Chou Chin-wen So-chien Chih-kuan K'ao"兩周金文所見職官考. *Chung-kuo Wen-hua Yen-chiu Hui-k'an* 中國文化研究彙刊 , VII (1947), 1–25.

Ssu-Ma Kuang 司馬光. *Tzu-chih T'ung-chien* 資治通鑑. *Ssu-pu Ts'ung-k'an* edition.

Steele, John, trans. *The I-li or Book of Etiquette and Ceremonial*. 2 vols. London, 1917.

Stein, *Central-Asian Tracks*.
Aurel Stein. *On Ancient Central-Asian Tracks*. London, 1933.

Stein, "China's Silk Trade."
Stein, Aurel. "Central-Asian Relics of China's Ancient Silk Trade." *TP*, XX (1921), 130–141.

Stephenson, Carl. *Medieval Feudalism*. Ithaca, New York, 1942.

Stevenson, G. H. *Roman Provincial Administration*. Oxford, 1939, reprinted 1949.

Strayer, Joseph R. *Feudalism*. Princeton, N.J., 1965.

Strayer, Joseph R. "Feudalism in Western Europe." In Coulborn, *Feudalism in History*, 15–25.

Strayer, Joseph R. "Medieval Bureaucracy and the Modern State." Prepared for delivery at the 1965 Annual Meeting of the American Political Science Association. Mimeographed.

Strayer and Coulborn, "The Idea of Feudalism."
Joseph R. Strayer and Rushton Coulborn. "The Idea of Feudalism."
In Coulborn, *Feudalism in History*, 3–11.

Sun Hai-po 孫海波. *Chia-ku Wen Pien* 甲骨文編. Peiping, 1934.

Sun K'ai 孫楷. *Ch'in Hui-yao* 秦會要. Supplemented and revised
by Shih Chih-mien 施之勉 and Hsü Fu 徐復. Taipei, 1956.

Sun-tzu 孫子. *Ssu-pu Pei-yao* edition.

Swann, Nancy Lee. *Food and Money in Ancient China*. Princeton,
1950.

Sylwan, Vivi. *Investigation of Silk from Edsen-gol and Lop-nor*. Reports from the Scientific Expedition to the North-western Provinces of China under the Leadership of Dr. Sven Hedin, The Sino-
Swedish Expedition, Publication 32, VII. Archaeology 6. Stockholm,
1949.

Sylwan, Vivi. "Silk from the Yin Dynasty." *BMFEA*, IX (1937), 119–
126.

Syme, Ronald. *The Roman Revolution*. London, 1960.

T'ai-p'ing Yü-lan 太平御覽. 1892.

Takezoe Kōkō 竹添光鴻, *Tso-shih Hui-chien* 左氏會箋. 1903.

T'ang Lan 唐蘭. "I Hou Nieh Kuei K'ao-shih" 宜侯矢𣪘考釋.
KKHP, 1956, No. 2, 79–83.

T'ang Lan 唐蘭. *T'ien-jang Ke Chia-ku Wen Ts'un ping K'ao-shih*
天壤閣甲骨文存並考釋. Peiping, 1939.

T'ang Lan. See also *Ch'ing-t'ung-ch'i T'u-shih*.

T'ang-Sung Pai-K'ung Liu-t'ieh 唐宋白孔六帖. Ming Chia-ching
edition.

Tchang, Mathias. *Synchronismes chinois, chronologie complète et
concordance avec l'ère chrétienne* (*Variétiés sinologiques* No. 24)
Shanghai, 1905.

Teng, Ssu-yü. "Chinese Influence on the Western Examination System." *HJAS*, VII (1943), 267–312.

Teng Ssu-yü 鄧嗣禹 . *Chung-kuo K'ao-shih Chih-tu Shih* 中國考試制度史. Nanking, 1936; reprinted, Taipei, 1966.

Teng, S. Y. "Herodotus and Ssu-ma Ch'ien: Two Fathers of History." In *East and West*, New Series, XII (1961), 233–240.

Ting Shan 丁山 . "Shao Mu Kung Chuan" 召穆公傳. *BIHP*, II (1930), 89–100.

Ting, V. K. Review of *La Civilisation Chinoise*, by M. Granet. *Chinese Social and Political Science Review*, XV (1931), 265–290.

TLTC. Ta-lu Tsa-chih 大陸雜誌.

TP. T'oung Pao, Archives concernant l'histoire, les langues, la géographie, l'ethnographie et les arts de l'Asie orientale.

"Trois généraux chinois de la dynastie des Han Orientaux." Translated by Édouard Chavannes. *TP*, VII (1906), 210–269.

Tseng I-kung 曾毅公 . *Chia-ku Cho-he Pien* 甲骨綴合編. 1950.

Tsien, Tsuen-hsuin. *Written on Bamboo and Silk: The Beginnings of of Chinese Books and Inscriptions.* Chicago, 1962.

Tso.
  The Chinese Classics, translated by James Legge. *Vol. V. The Ch'un Ts'ew [Ch'un-ch'iu], with the Tso Chuen [Tso-chuan].* 2 pts. London, 1872. Page numbers are first given for the Chinese text, followed by a double colon [::], followed by the page number of the translated passage. This is followed by the name and year of the Duke, in parentheses.

Tso-chuan.
  Ch'un-ch'iu Tso-chuan Chu-su 春秋左傳注疏 . In *Shih-san Ching Chu-su.*

Tsou Pao-chün 鄒豹君 . "Chung-kuo Wen-hua Ch'i-yüan Ti" 中國文化起源地. *CHHP*, VI (1967), 22–34.

Ts'ui Shu 崔述. "Feng Hao K'ao-hsin Lu" 豐鎬考信錄. In *Ts'ui Tung-pi I-shu* 崔東壁遺書. Edited by Ku Chieh-kang 顧頡剛. Shanghai, 1936.

Tung, "Chia-ku Wen Ku-chi."
Tung Tso-pin 董作賓, "Chia-ku Wen Ts'ai-liao ti Tsung Ku-chi" 甲骨文材料的總估計. *TLTC*, VI (1953), 375–381.

Tung Tso-pin 董作賓. "Chung-kuo Ku-li yü Shih-chieh Ku-li" 中國古曆與世界古曆. *TLTC*, II, No. 10 (1951), 28–35.

Tung Tso-pin 董作賓. "Hsi-Chou Nien-li P'u" 西周年曆譜. *BIHP*, XXIII, Part 2 (1952), 681–760.

Tung, "Tuan-tai Yen-chiu."
Tung Tso-pin 董作賓, "Chia-ku Wen Tuan-tai Yen-chiu Li" 甲骨文斷代研究例. In *Academia Sinica, Studies Presented to Ts'ai Yuan P'ei on His Sixty-fifth Birthday* I (Peiping, 1933), 323–424.

Tung Tso-pin 董作賓. "Wu-teng Chüeh Tsai Yin-Shang" 五等爵在殷商. *BIHP*, VI (1936), 413–430.

Tung Tso pin 董作賓. *Yin-li P'u* 殷曆譜. Li-chuang, 1945.

T'ung-tien.
Tu Yu 杜佑, *T'ung-tien* 通典. *Shih-t'ung* 十通 edition. Shanghai, 1935.

Van der Sprenkel, Otto B. "Max Weber on China." In *History and Theory*, III (1964), 348–370.

Vishnu Purana.
The Vishnu Purana. Translated by H. H. Wilson. 5 vols. London, 1864–1877.

"The Vizier of Egypt." Translated by John A. Wilson. In *Ancient Near Eastern Texts Relating to the Old Testament*, edited by James B. Pritchard (Princeton, 1950), 212–214.

Voltaire.
Oeuvres complètes de Voltaire. 92 vols. Impr. de la Société Littéraire-typographique, 1785–1789.

Von Mises, Ludwig. *Bureaucracy*. Yale Paperbound edition. New Haven and London, 1962.

Wainwright, G. A. "Early Foreign Trade in East Africa." *Man*, XLVII (1947), 143–148.

Waldo, Dwight. *Perspectives on Administration*. University, Ala., 1956.

Waley, *Analects*.
The Analects of Confucius. Translated by Arthur Waley. London, 1938, reprinted 1945.

Waley, Arthur. "The Book of Changes." *BMFEA*, V (1933), 121–142.

Waley, *Shih*.
The Book of Songs [Shih-ching]. Translated by Arthur Waley. Boston and New York, 1937.

Waley, Arthur. "The Eclipse Poem and Its Group." *T'ien Hsia Monthly*, III (1936), 245–248.

Waley, Arthur. *An Introduction to the Study of Chinese Painting*. New York, 1923.

Waley, *Po Chü-i*.
Arthur Waley. The Life and Times of Po Chü-i. London, 1949.

Waley, Arthur. *The Way and Its Power, A Study of the Tao Tê Ching*. London, 1934, reprinted 1949.

Wang Ch'ung 王充 . *Lun-heng* 論衡 . *Ssu-pu Pei-yao* edition.

Wang Hsien-ch'ien王先謙. *Hsün-tzu Chi-chieh* 荀子集解. 1891.

Wang, *Chin Chu-shu*.
Wang Kuo-wei王國維 *Chin-pen Chu-shu Chi-nien Su-cheng* 今本竹書紀年疏證. In Wang, *I-shu*, *San-chi* 三集 .

Wang Kuo-wei 王國維. *Kuan-t'ang Chi-lin* 觀堂集林. In Wang, *I-shu*.

Wang Kuo-wei 王國維. *Kuan-t'ang Pieh-chi Pu-i* 觀堂別集補遺. In Wang, *I-shu*.

Wang, *Ku Chu-shu.*
Wang Kuo-wei 王國維 . *Ku-pen Chu-shu Chi-nien Chi-chiao* 古本竹書紀年輯校. In Wang, *I-shu, San-chi* 三集 .

Wang Kuo-wei 王國維 . *Ku-shih Hsin-cheng* 古史新證. Peiping, 1935.

Wang, *I-shu.*
Wang Kuo-wei 王國維 . *Wang Chung-ch'io Kung I-shu* 王忠慤公遺書 . 1927–1928.

Wang Li 王力 . "Chung-kuo Yü-yen-hsüeh Shih" 中國語言學史 . In *Chung-kuo Yü-wen* 中國語文, 1963, No. 3, 232–245, 265.

Wang Ming-yüan 王名元 . *Hsien Ch'in Huo-pi Shih* 先秦貨幣史 . Canton, 1947.

Wang Yü-ch'üan. *Early Chinese Coinage.* The American Numismatic Society, Numismatic Notes and Monographs, No. 122. New York, 1951.

Wang, "Han Government."
Wang Yü-ch'üan, "An Outline of the Central Government of the Former Han Dynasty." *HJAS*, XII (1949), 134–187.

Wang, *Wo-kuo Huo-pi ti Ch'i-yüan.*
Wang Yü-ch'üan 王毓詮, *Wo-kuo Ku-tai Huo-pi ti Ch'i-yüan he Fa-chan* 我國古代貨幣的起源和發展. Peking, 1957.

Watson, Burton. *Records of the Grand Historian of China, Translated from the* Shih chi *of Ssu-ma Ch'ien.* 2 vols. New York and London, 1961.

Watson, Burton. *Ssu-ma Ch'ien, Grand Historian of China.* New York, 1958.

Weber, *Essays in Sociology.*
From Max Weber: Essays in Sociology. Translated, edited, and with an Introduction by H. H. Gerth and C. Wright Mills. New York, 1946.

Weber, Max. *Gesammelte Aufsätze zur Religionssoziologie.* 3 vols. Tübingen, 1922–1923.

Weber, Max. *The Religion of China: Confucianism and Taoism* Translated and edited by Hans H. Gerth. Glencoe, Ill., 1951.

Weber, *Theory of Organization.*
Max Weber: The Theory of Social and Economic Organization.
Translated by A. M. Henderson and Talcott Parsons. Edited with
an Introduction by Talcott Parsons. New York, 1947.

Weber, Max. *Wirtschaft und Gesellschaft. Grundriss der Sozialöko-
nomik,* Part III. 2 vols. Tübingen, 1925.

Webster's New International Dictionary of the English Language. 2d
ed., unabridged. Edited by William Allen Neilson. G. and C. Mer-
riam Co. Springfield, Mass., 1949.

Wei-shu T'ung-k'ao 偽書通考 . Compiled and edited by Chang Hsin-
ch'eng 張心澂. 2 vols. Changsha, 1939.

Weiner, J. S. *The Piltdown Forgery.* London, New York, Toronto,
1955.

Wheeler, Mortimer. "Archaeology in East Africa (The text of a public
lecture delivered on 19th August, 1955, and reproduced by courtesy of the Archaeological Society)." *Tanganyika Notes and Records,* No. 40 (1955), 43–47.

Wheeler, *Rome Beyond the Frontiers.*
Mortimer Wheeler. *Rome Beyond the Imperial Frontiers.* London,
1955.

White, *Public Administration.*
Leonard D. White. *Introduction to the Study of Public Administration.* New York, 1926; reprinted 1933.

White, William Charles. *Tombs of Old Loyang.* Shanghai, 1934.

Wilbur, *Slavery in Former Han.*
C. Martin Wilbur. *Slavery in China During the Former Han Dy-
nasty.* Anthropological Series, Field Museum of Natural History,
Vol. 34. Chicago, 1943.

Wilhelm, *I-ching.*
Richard Wilhelm, trans. *I Ging, Das Buch der Wandlungen.* Düssel-
dorf-Köln, 1960.

Wilson, John A. *The Culture of Ancient Egypt.* Chicago, 1957. [Pub-
lished as *The Burden of Egypt* in 1951.]

"The Words of Ahiquar." Translated by H. L. Ginsberg. In *Ancient Near Eastern Texts Relating to the Old Testament*, edited by James B. Pritchard (Princeton, 1950), 427–430.

Wu Ch'i-chang 吳其昌 . *Chin-wen I-nien Piao* 金文疑年表 . Pei-ping, 1933.

Wu Shih-fen 吳式芬 . *Chün Ku-lu Chin-wen* 攈古錄金文 1895.

Wu Tse 吳澤 . *Ku-tai Shih* 古代史 Shanghai, 1953.

Yamada Jun 山田統. "Shūdai Hōken Seido to Ketsuzoku Shūdan Sei" 周代封建制度と血族聚團制. *Shakai Keizai Shigaku* 社會經濟史學 , XVII (1951), 135–169.

Yang, "Lun Tso-chuan yü Kuo-yü."
Yang Hsiang-k'uei 楊向奎. "Lun Tso-chuan chih Hsing-chih chi Ch'i yü Kuo-yü chih Kuan-hsi" 論左傳之性質及其與國語之關係 . *Shih-hsüeh Chi-k'an* 史學集刊 , II (1936), 41–81.

Yang K'uan 楊寬 . "Chung-kuo Shang-ku-shih Tao-lun" 中國上古史導論. *Ku-shih Pien*, VII (A), 65–421.

Yang K'uan 楊寬 . *Ku-shih Hsin T'an* 古史新探. Peking, 1965.

Yang, Lien-sheng. *Money and Credit in China*. Cambridge, Mass., 1952.

Yang, *Chinese Institutional History*.
Lien-sheng Yang. *Studies in Chinese Institutional History*. Cambridge, Mass., 1961.

Yang-tzu Fa-yen 楊子法言 . *Ssu-pu Ts'ung-k'an* edition.

Yasuda Motohisa. "History of the Studies of the Formation of Japanese Hōken System (Feudalism)." *Acta Asiatica: Bulletin of the Institute of Eastern Culture*, VIII (1965), 74–100.

YCHP. *Yen-ching Hsüeh-pao* 燕京學報 [*Yenching Journal of Chinese Studies*].

Yeh Yü-shen 葉玉森 . *T'ieh-yün Ts'ang-kuei Shih-i fu K'ao-shih* 鐵雲藏龜拾遺附攷釋. 1925.

Yen-t'ieh Lun 鹽鐵論. *Ssu-pu Pei-yao* edition.

Yetts, W. Perceval. "The Shang-Yin Dynasty and the An-yang Finds." *Journal of the Royal Asiatic Society*, 1933, 657–685.

Yin Ch'i Ch'ien-pien.
　　Yin-hsü Shu-ch'i Ch'ien-pien 殷虛書契前編　Compiled by Lo Chen-yu 羅振玉 1912.

Yin Ch'i Hou-pien.
　　Yin-hsü Shu-ch'i Hou-pien 殷虛書契後編　Compiled by Lo Chen-yü 羅振玉 1916.

Yin Ch'i Hsü-pien.
　　Yin-hsü Shu-ch'i Hsü-pien 殷虛書契續編　Compiled by Lo Chen-yu 羅振玉 1933.

Yin Ch'i Pu-tz'u 殷契卜辭　Compiled by Jung Keng 容庚 Peiping, 1933.

Yin-hsü Wen-tzu Chia-pien 殷虛文字甲編. *Hsiao-t'un* 小屯, II. Compiled by Tung Tso-pin 董作賓　Academia Sinica, Nanking, 1948.

Yin-hsu Wen-tzu I-pien 殷虛文字乙編. *Hsiao-t'un* 小屯, II. Compiled by Tung Tso-pin 董作賓　Academia Sinica, 1948–1953.

Yü, "'Liu Shih' he 'Pa Shih'."
　　Yü Sheng-wu 于省吾 "Lüeh Lun Hsi-Chou Chin-wen Chung ti 'Liu Shih' he 'Pa Shih' chi Ch'i T'un-t'ien Chih" 略論西周金文中的 "六自"和 "八自 " 及其屯田制 *KK*, No. 3 (1964), 152–155.

Yü, *Shang-shu Hsin-cheng.*
　　Yü Sheng-wu 于省吾 *Shuang-chien-ch'ih Shang-shu Hsin-cheng* 雙劍誃尚書新證 Peiping, 1934.

Index

The end paper designs are squeezes of inscriptions appearing in a bronze vessel of the type known as fang-i, which is now in the Freer Gallery of Art; they are reproduced by permission. The squeeze appearing on the right is in the body of the vessel, that on the left in the cover; the two inscriptions are virtually identical. This handsome vessel was cast for Maker of Books Nieh Ling, who served at the royal court under King Ch'eng (1115–1079 B.C.). The inscription tells of services performed by Nieh Ling for the son of the famous Duke of Chou, and of gifts that he received from him. The vessel is dedicated to the deceased father of Nieh Ling.